Classical Literature and its Reception

This book is lovingly dedicated
to Alan and Jean Brown
and
to the memory of
Theodore and Grace Buzzeo

Classical Literature and its Reception

An Anthology

Edited by Robert DeMaria, Jr. and
Robert D. Brown

Blackwell
Publishing

Editorial material and organization © 2007 by Blackwell Publishing Ltd

BLACKWELL PUBLISHING
350 Main Street, Malden, MA 02148-5020, USA
9600 Garsington Road, Oxford OX4 2DQ, UK
550 Swanston Street, Carlton, Victoria 3053, Australia

The right of Robert DeMaria, Jr. and Robert D. Brown to be identified as the Authors of the Editorial Material in this Work has been asserted in accordance with the UK Copyright, Designs, and Patents Act 1988.

First published 2007 by Blackwell Publishing Ltd

1   2007

Library of Congress Cataloging-in-Publication Data

Classical literature and its reception : an anthology / edited by Robert DeMaria, Jr. and Robert D. Brown.
   p. cm.
   Includes bibliographical references and index.
   Contents: British, Irish, and Caribbean writers (a selection of the best British poems from Chaucer to Heaney, arranged in chronological order) – Classical writers (relevant classical works, presented in translation, and organized alphabetically)
   ISBN-13: 978-1-4051-1293-2 (hardcover : alk. paper)
   ISBN-10: 1-4051-1293-X (hardcover : alk. paper)
   ISBN-13: 978-1-4051-1294-9 (pbk. : alk. paper)
   ISBN-10: 1-4051-1294-8 (pbk. : alk. paper)
   1. English poetry. 2. English poetry–Appreciation. 3. English poetry–Classical influences. 4. Classical literature–Translations into English. 5. Classical literature–Appreciation–Great Britain. I. DeMaria, Robert. II. Brown, Robert D. (Robert Duncan), 1950–

   PR1175.C555 2007
   821.008'0142–dc22

2006012557

A catalogue record for this title is available from the British Library.

Set in 10 on 13 pt Galliard
by SNP Best-set Typesetter Ltd, Hong Kong
Printed and bound in Singapore
by COS Printers Pte Ltd

The publisher's policy is to use permanent paper from mills that operate a sustainable forestry policy, and which has been manufactured from pulp processed using acid-free and elementary chlorine-free practices. Furthermore, the publisher ensures that the text paper and cover board used have met acceptable environmental accreditation standards.

For further information on
Blackwell Publishing, visit our website:
www.blackwellpublishing.com

Contents

Acknowledgments

We wish to thank Rachel Kitzinger, our colleague in classics at Vassar, for advising us in the development of this book and in all our work as readers and teachers of classical literature. We also wish to thank our students, particularly those we taught in a class on Juvenal in 2002 when we first participated in teaching together and conceived the idea of compiling this anthology. Vassar College has supported us in every way for the past thirty years, supplying us with rewarding students, time for research, the opportunity to work together, and, not least of all, funding for the special demands of this project. Finally, we extend heartfelt gratitude to our families for their loving encouragement, especially to Joanne DeMaria and Diana Brown.

The editors and publisher gratefully acknowledge the permission granted to reproduce the copyright material in this book:

1   Asklepiades, "To His Mistress," p. 35 from *Poems from the Greek Anthology*, trans. Dudley Fitts. New York: New Directions, 1938, 1941, 1956. Copyright © 1938, 1941, 1956 by New Directions Publishing Corp. Reprinted by permission of New Directions Publishing Corp.

2   Meleagros, "Epitaph of a Pet Hare," p. 125 from *Poems from the Greek Anthology*, trans. Dudley Fitts. New York: New Directions, 1956. Copyright © 1938, 1941, 1956 by New Directions Publishing Corp. Reprinted by permission of New Directions Publishing Corp.

3   Robert Bridges, "Ibant Obscuri," pp. 444–6 (lines 268–316) *from Poetical Works of Robert Bridges*, 2nd edition, trans. Robert Bridges. London: Oxford University Press, 1936.

4   Lewis Campbell, "The Trachinian Maidens, lines 112–38," p. 180 ("For many as are billows . . . forsake his son") from *Sophocles: The Seven Plays in English Verse*, revised trans. Lewis Campbell. London: Oxford University Press, 1906, repr. 1911, 1921, 1924, 1925, 1928, 1930, 1933, 1936.

5   David Ferry, "i.11 – To Leuconoe," p. 33 from *The Odes of Horace*, trans. David Ferry. New York: Farrar, Straus and Giroux, 1997. Translation copyright © 1997 by David Ferry. Reprinted by permission of Farrar, Straus and Giroux, LLC.

6   David Ferry, "i.37 – Cleopatra," p. 97 from *The Odes of Horace*, trans. David Ferry. New York: Farrar, Straus and Giroux, 1997. Translation copyright © 1997 by David Ferry. Reprinted by permission of Farrar, Straus and Giroux, LLC.

7   William Ellery Leonard, "Book II, lines 646–60," pp. 68–9 ("For all the gods . . . Foul religion") from *Lucretius: Of the Nature of Things*, trans. William Ellery Leonard. London, Paris, Toronto, New York: J. M. Dent E. P. Dutton, 1916.

8   William Ellery Leonard, "Book III, lines 1–30," pp. 93–4 ("O thou . . . bare to man") from *Lucretius: Of the Nature of Things*, trans. William Ellery Leonard. London, Paris, Toronto, New York: J. M. Dent, E. P. Dutton, 1916.

9   William Ellery Leonard, "Book III, lines 894–911," p. 125 ("Thee now no more . . . sleep and rest") from *Lucretius: Of the Nature of Things*, trans. William Ellery Leonard. London, Paris, Toronto, New York: J. M. Dent, E. P. Dutton, 1916.

10   "Eclogue II," pp. 7–9 from *The Eclogues, Georgics, and Aeneid of Virgil*, trans. C. Day Lewis. Oxford: Oxford University Press, 1966. Copyright © The Estate of C. Day-Lewis 1966. Reproduced by permission of PFD (www.pfd.co.uk) on behalf of the Estate of C. Day Lewis.

11   "Eclogue V," pp. 21–4 from *The Eclogues, Georgics, and Aeneid of Virgil*, trans. C. Day Lewis. Oxford: Oxford University Press, 1966. Copyright © The Estate of C. Day-Lewis 1966. Reproduced by permission of PFD (www.pfd.co.uk) on behalf of the Estate of C. Day Lewis.

12   James Michie, "Book I, 3," p. 21 from *Martial: The Epigrams*, trans. James Michie. Harmondsworth: Penguin, 1976. Notes Copyright © 1972 by James Michie. Used by permission of Modern Library, a division of Random House, Inc.

13   James Michie, "Book III, 58," pp. 63–6 (English only) from *Martial: The Epigrams*, trans. James Michie. Harmondsworth: Penguin, 1977. Notes copyright © 1972 by James Michie. Used by permission of Modern Library, a division of Random House, Inc.

14   James Michie, "Book V, 78," pp. 94–7 (English only) from *Martial: The Epigrams*, trans. James Michie Harmondsworth: Penguin, 1978. Copyright © 1972 by James Michie. Notes copyright © 1972 by James Michie. Used by permission of Modern Library, a division of Random House, Inc.

15   J. A. Pott, "LII – To Julius Cerialis," p. 353 from *Martial, the Twelve Books of Epigrams*, trans. J. A. Pott. London, New York: G. Routledge, E. P. Dutton, 1924.

16   Ezra Pound, "This Monument Will Outlast," p. 407 from Hugh Kenner (ed.), *Ezra Pound: Translations*, trans. Ezra Pound. Norfolk, USA: New Directions, 1963. Copyright © 1963 by Ezra Pound. Reprinted by permission of New Directions Publishing Corp. and Faber and Faber.

17   W. G. Shepherd, "II.2 – Liber eram et vacuo meditabar vivere lecto," p. 60 from *The Poems of Propertius*, trans. W. G. Shepherd. Harmondsworth: Penguin, 1985. Translation and notes copyright © 1985 by W. G. Shepherd. Introduction copyright © 1985 by Betty Radice. Reprinted by permission of the Penguin Group (UK).

18   W. G. Shepherd, "II.15 – O me felicem! O nox mihi candida! Et o tu," pp. 73–4 from *The Poems of Propertius*, trans. W. G. Shepherd. Harmondsworth: Penguin, 1985. Translation and notes copyright © 1985 by W. G. Shepherd. Introduction copyright © 1985 by Betty Radice. Reprinted by permission of the Penguin Group (UK).

19   Arthur Symons, "Poem 8," from *From Catullus, Chiefly Concerning Lesbia*, trans. Arthur Symons. London: Martin Secker, 1924. Reprinted by permission of The Estate of Arthur Symons.

20   Arthur Symons, "Poem 101," from *From Catullus, Chiefly Concerning Lesbia*, trans. Arthur Symons. London: Martin Secker, 1924. Reprinted by permission of The Estate of Arthur Symons.

21   Robert Wells, "I – The Passion of Daphnis," pp. 55–9 from *The Idylls: Theocritus*, trans. Robert Wells. London: Penguin, 1989. Reprinted by permission of Carcanet Press.

22   Peter Whigham and J. P. Sullivan, "Martial Epigram 10.48," p. 377 from *Epigrams of Martial Englished by Divers Hands*, trans. Peter Whigham. Berkeley, Los Angeles, London: University of California Press, 1987. Reprinted by permission of University of California Press.

23   Wystan Hugh Auden, "The Shield of Achilles," pp. 596–8 from Edward Mendelson (ed.), *W. H. Auden: Collected Poems*, New York: Vintage, 1976, 1991. Copyright © 1952 by W. H. Auden. Reprinted by permission of Random House, Inc.

24   Seamus Heaney, "Bann Valley Eclogue," pp. 12–13 from *Electric Light*, New York: Farrar, Straus and Giroux, 2001. © 2001 by Seamus Heaney. Reprinted by permission of Farrar, Straus and Giroux, LLC, and Faber and Faber.

25   William Butler Yeats, "166 – A Thought from Propertius," p. 153 from Richard J. Finneran (ed.), *The Collected Works of W. B. Yeats, The Poems*, 2nd edition, Vol. I. New York: Scribner, 1997. Reprinted with the permission of Scribner, an imprint of Simon & Schuster Adult Publishing Group and A. P. Watt Ltd.

26   William Butler Yeats, "218 – Two Songs from a Play," pp. 216–17 from Richard J. Finneran (ed.), *The Collected Works of W. B. Yeats, The Poems*, 2nd edition, Vol. I. New York: Scribner, 1997. Reprinted with the permission of Scribner, an imprint of Simon & Schuster Adult Publishing Group and A. P.

Watt Ltd. © 1928 by The Macmillan Company; copyright renewed © 1956 by Georgie Yeats.

27 Derek Walcott, "Book One, Chapter I," pp. 3–9 from *Omeros*, New York: The Noonday Press, Farrar, Straus and Giroux, 1990. © 1990 by Derek Walcott. Reprinted by permission of Farrar, Straus and Giroux, LLC, and Faber and Faber.

Every effort has been made to trace copyright holders and to obtain their permission for the use of copyright material. The publisher apologizes for any errors or omissions in the above list and would be grateful if notified of any corrections that should be incorporated in future reprints or editions of this book.

Introduction

That the works of Roman and Greek authors are important to modern writers is a principle long accepted in the teaching of most courses in literature in English. For a variety of reasons, however, the principle has less and less been applied, and it has often been applied in unsatisfactory ways. The footnotes in school editions and scholarly editions of literary classics in English have since the eighteenth century chronicled the debts of their writers to the Greek and Latin classics. In an age when every schoolboy knew his Horace and Virgil, these citations frequently set off a chain of associations for the reader and brought the classical world into proximity with the world of the modern writers. In so doing they dignified the mere modern. Now, however, such citations are opaque for most students and for many teachers; they tend to show only the superficial fact that Virgil, for example, is important in the background of poetry written in English. That is an easy thing to say, and we all say it, but understanding how Virgil is important or in what way his verse has been used is more difficult. To begin with, in order to answer the more difficult questions, the reader needs some recent or vivid experience of Virgil, preferably in Latin but at least in translation. The purpose of this book is to make some experience of the classical background readily available to students and teachers working on literature written in English – to put the experience of reading the classics, rather than a mere reference to them, beside the experience of reading literature written in English.

There are two main parts to the book: one with British, Irish, and Caribbean texts and the other with classical texts. The English-language texts come first because we assume that most of our readers will be primarily students of literature in English. These texts form a brief anthology of poetry from Chaucer to Heaney, but the book is hardly a history of British, Irish, or Caribbean literature. (We excluded American literature from the start and concentrated on British literature in order to make the project manageable.) Our selection is limited to a few great works or works with aspirations to greatness, and it is heaviest on the period from about 1600 to 1900. At best, the poems suggest a core of study for students of

English, but we make no such claims. The poems are chosen for their excellence, for their usefulness to teachers of introductory courses, and for their relevance to classical models. By "relevance" we mean a whole host of relations which the English poems have to their classical forebears. Some poems are imitations or loose translations of classical originals, as is the case with Samuel Johnson's imitation of Juvenal's tenth satire, *The Vanity of Human Wishes*. Other poems adapt classical models or classical themes in less concentrated but equally unmistakable ways. Milton's *Lycidas*, for example, draws on a variety of classical poems and modes. In still other poems, such as Shakespeare's sonnets, the connection between the English poem and the classical background may be less direct, but it is still important. In a few cases we have selected poems that demonstrate respect for the classical tradition without drawing on it in a specific way. Gray's *Elegy* is such a poem. Deep in classical learning, Gray could not help but manifest a classical spirit, even when he sought to write something new and something pertaining specifically to rural England. Our introductions to the British, Irish, and Caribbean works try to explain some of the relations between each poem and the classical tradition, and they point readers to the relevant texts in the second part of the anthology.

After some hesitation we arranged the classical works in the second part of the anthology, like the works in English, in chronological order. We hesitated, and considered an alphabetical order, because we do not wish to suggest that these texts constitute a history of classical literature or even a balanced sampling of the field. The classical texts were chosen for their importance to the modern and early modern works in the first part. The result, however, is a group of texts well worth reading in themselves, and, since they also often display the influences of earlier classical texts, their best arrangement is chronological. It is important to remember that the "classical tradition," though naturally it was not called that at the time, had a history of a thousand years before it began influencing the "post-classical" world. In a way that resembles the awareness of modern and early modern European writers, Roman poets were aware of their predecessors and deeply aware of their Greek models. Although this assemblage of classical texts may not do justice to the classical tradition, it does demonstrate its existence, and a reader who completely peruses the second part of this anthology will have made some progress in understanding the greatness of Greek and Latin poetry.

It will come as no surprise to those with training in the subject that Horace, Ovid, and Virgil loom very large in the classical pages of our book, or that Latin works outweigh Greek. These proportions accurately reflect the knowledge of many major British, Irish, and Caribbean authors. Throughout the medieval and early modern period Latin was much better known in England and the rest of Western Europe than Greek. Going to school meant in large part studying Latin, as a virtue in itself and for the access it afforded to the literature of the classical world and the learned communities of the modern world. Greek was a secondary study, important for deep learning (as it had been for Romans), but not essential. The great Greek philosophers were usually read in translation and even the poets were often read in bilingual editions (Latin and Greek on facing pages). Greek, to be sure, was a biblical language, and students of theology had to know New Testament Greek as well as Hebrew, but these again were the accomplishments of specialists, whereas Latin was fundamental to everyone with an education and everyone with a profession in law, government, or medicine. Many modern and early modern writers seem to have the principal Latin authors in their memories as they write, but closer inspection sometimes reveals that they snatch graces from less conspicuous sources. We have tried to trace some of this fine intellectual history in our footnotes, but we have concentrated on the broader associations: these are indexed in the reference tables at the end of the book, where we list the principal sources for each work in English included, and, in another table, the works in English that each classical work influenced.

We wish, of course, that all of our readers could have the experience of reading the classical works in the original, but if that were possible, there might be little need for our book. We have compiled this volume mainly for those who do not read Latin or Greek, so, in addition to choosing English-language poets and classical poets, we had to choose a third class of writers called translators. Our goal at first was to find translations that presented no obstacles to the reader, translations that would be transparent, like good prose in a famous definition. We assumed that we could best achieve this by using the most recent translations, written in the most familiar and therefore the most transparent English. The possible flaws in this view apart, we soon found that such a plan was impossible because of the cost of copyright fees; we could only afford to print a few contemporary or even modern translations. (The law now protects works for 75 years after the death of the author or, in the case of corporate copyrights, for 90 years after the appearance of the work.) Of this necessity, however, we have made several virtues. We decided to choose translations from a broad chronological range and from a variety of translators. As a result, the group of translations as a whole represents something like a history of translation in English. (The translators have their own list at the back of the book along with those for the classical and the English-language authors.) We chose only verse renditions of the classics partly because we wanted the translations to be intensely literary and partly because that form of translation seemed always closer to the original than prose. Although these verse translations themselves often require notes and do present some obstacles to reading, they show the range of ways that the classical texts may be rendered in English; in showing that range, they suggest the reality of the original that is inevitably obscured by any single rendition. Moreover, the English-language writers in our anthology are in many cases likely to have read the translations that we include. Even if they read Latin and Greek, as most of our authors did, they knew many of the translations that we include and their own individual sense of the originals is closer to the historical translation than one written in the twenty-first century. For all of these reasons we are pleased, for example, to present Virgil's *Aeneid* as Dryden rendered it in his justly admired translation and to display his

Georgics in the earlier, less well-known, but brilliant translation of Thomas May. These are wonderful poems in themselves and they tell us how seventeenth- and eighteenth-century English-language poets heard the classics.

Although this is a book for students reading English (English majors, as they are called in America), it would be the highest justification of our work if some of those students were inspired to get still closer to the classical tradition by taking courses in Latin or Greek. We promise they will be rewarded with a deeper understanding of poetry in English, and, brilliant as the translations offered here are, the originals can, of course, only be truly understood in the original language. To those few readers who come at this anthology from the other side, as it were – those who study and teach the classics – we hope also to have something to offer. By suggesting the influence of some classical poems on later tradition and by providing modern responses to classical works we hope the book helps to prove the durability and relevance of the classical tradition. As our chronological arrangements suggest, we know that the classical poems existed fine on their own without reference to modern works. On the other hand, the presence of these English-language poems has arguably changed the way the originals are read by English speakers. Even if we wanted to, we could no longer read Juvenal's tenth satire without thinking of Johnson's *Vanity of Human Wishes*. We appreciate the importance of seeing Juvenal in his own rather than our literary tradition, but nothing prevents us from seeing him in both ways (or in any of a number of ways). To imagine that the past existed for the purpose of bringing the present into existence is foolish, but it can only expand our appreciation of the past to understand the ways in which it is still alive, ever finding new ways in which to exert its perpetual influence.

A Note on the Texts

As a rule, we base the texts presented here on first editions, except where an author subsequently revised the text in important ways. Such cases are noted, and earlier readings are sometimes compared with those introduced later (see, for example, Wordsworth's "Laodamia"; p. 167 below). We have retained the accidentals of the original texts (capitalization, italicization, and punctuation), but we have not hesitated to make small changes here and there for the sake of clarity. We have, for example, deleted where we encountered it the now antiquated comma before an open parenthesis and placed it after the close of the parenthesis according to modern usage. In addition, intervening more strongly, we have indicated direct speech by the use of quotation marks, even if the original texts lacked them or indicated speech in another way, as, for example, by italicization. In most texts, we have modernized spelling, but we have done so in a conservative way. We have used modern spelling where doing so did not seem to change the sound of the text or where the old spelling might mislead modern readers about the sound. For example, in most cases we have preferred the *-ed* spelling of past participles spelled '*d* in some sixteenth-, seventeenth-, and eighteenth-century texts. Where the *ed* is meant to constitute a separate syllable, contrary to normal pronunciation, we added an accent grave over the *e*. We have also added an accent acute over other vowels to indicate metrical stress or the presence of a surprising additional syllable, as, for example, over *i*, when it occurs in the sometimes disyllabic combination *sion* or *tion*. We have made a point of normalizing classical proper names for the sake of clarity in cross-referencing and indexing.

We have prepared the texts of our translations just as we prepared our primary British, Irish, and Caribbean texts, and we have numbered the lines of them as though they were independent poems, which of course they are. However, when we refer to the lines of a classical text, we give the line numbers as they appear in standard editions of those texts in the original languages. (Those line numbers do not correspond to the line numbers assigned to the translations used in this volume.) For the sake of clarity we have included the classical line numbers in the headers of the pages on which the translations appear. When we refer, for example, to *Aeneid* 2.1–56, we mean the Latin lines in that place; in reference to the English version of those lines included in our anthology, we provide merely the page number on which a complete selection begins (p. 371 below). When referring to a particular classical passage we provide a reference to the particular page or pages on which the translation of those lines appears.

Our footnotes to the British, Irish, and Caribbean poems contain, of course, many references to the classical poems, and vice versa. They also gloss proper names and words that are either antiquated or used in senses no longer familiar. In glossing the translations, we have sometimes suggested the translators' liberties with the texts by explaining that "literally," the original says "so and so." We have tried to restrain ourselves from offering interpretation or making explanations that a little work on the reader's part will easily uncover. We provide an index to our footnotes that should assist readers in locating information that it seemed more appropriate to insert in explanation of one place rather than another.

Also included in our index are references to our head notes. In addition to sketching the relationship between the text in English and its classical relatives, and vice versa, the head notes contain some biographical information. For this we are much indebted to the *Oxford Dictionary of National Biography* and the *Oxford Classical Dictionary*. We are also indebted to the editors of the standard editions and commentaries of the texts we include. We have made an effort to acknowledge information that seems to be the work of a single editor or commentator, but we have often benefited, we know, from editorial and glossarial traditions as venerable in many cases as the texts themselves. Other books which we have found particularly useful are: Stuart Gillespie, *The Poets on the Classics: An Anthology* (Routledge, 1988); Robin Sowerby, *The Classical Legacy in Renaissance Poetry* (Longman, 1994); and Hanne Carlsen, *A Bibliography to the Classical Tradition in English Literature* (University of Copenhagen, 1985).

British, Irish, and Caribbean Writers

Geoffrey Chaucer
(c. 1343–1400)

By the time he completed his second diplomatic mission to Italy in 1378, Chaucer had imbibed more Italian literary influence than any English poet ever had or ever would for at least another century and a half. If he did not meet Petrarch or Boccaccio, he certainly encountered their works and their admirers. In Florence, he became acquainted with the already monumental reputation of Dante. These great early humanists naturally impressed on Chaucer the importance and the pleasure of reading classical poetry of the Augustan age. However, his main sources among Latin texts remained those written in Christian times. He was deeply and directly influenced by Boethius' *Consolation of Philosophy*, for example, whereas Virgil seems to come to him mainly through Dante or through French romances.

Chaucer's two most important works are his epic poem *Troilus and Criseyde* and his late, unfinished *Canterbury Tales*. The former is based on Boccaccio's *Il Filostrato*, which itself borrows from Homer, Virgil, and many later writers who elaborated tales of the Trojan War. The earlier work is more ostentatiously learned, with obvious allusions, for example, to Ovid's *Heroides* and, at some length, Statius' *Thebaid*. The *Canterbury Tales* is one of the most delightful works in all of English literature, and, like any truly pleasurable work, wears its learning lightly. *The Knight's Tale*, for example, like *Troilus and Criseyde*, is influenced by Boccaccio's *Teseida*, but it is also an expression of the personality of the Knight. Chaucer lends his characters a dramatic presence that upstages the sources of their stories; we feel therefore that they are speaking from experience, and we forget that Chaucer is speaking from his reading.

Each of the pilgrims on the journey to Canterbury must tell a tale, according to the game that makes the pretext of the poem, but each is described in the general prologue, and each gets a further opportunity to develop dramatically in a personal prologue. The most famous of these prologues is the one spoken by the Wife of Bath. She is such a vivid character that it is easy to forget that Chaucer forged her only partly from his experience and partly from his reading in a work by Jerome (the fourth-century translator of the Bible into Latin) called *Adversus*

Jovinianum. In this work Jerome marshals all the arguments against marriage, sometimes drawing on biblical, sometimes on classical sources of misogyny such as Theophrastus' lost "golden book on marriage." Jerome was probably familiar too with Juvenal's *Satire* 6 (p. 472 below), which itself goes back to earlier writing on the theme by Greeks (such as Semonides and Hesiod – p. 279 below) and earlier Roman poems (such as Ovid's *Ars Amatoria* – p. 433 below). The Wife is on the side of Jovinian because she defends marriage, but her position is not only weak, because the authority of the ancients is against her, but it is also ironic, because her behavior exemplifies many of the female traits cited by classical writers as reasons to avoid marriage. Characteristic slurs against women that are common to Juvenal and Chaucer (especially in the section on Jankyn's book) include insatiable lust, unchastity, dominance, manipulativeness, deceit, scolding, greed, gadding about in public, inventing a husband's wrongdoings (e.g., a mistress) in order to criticize him, vanity, murder. The Wife gladly touts her participation in all of these except the last. Finally, her overall performance may also owe something to classical tradition. As William Matthews argued, the Wife is one of the medieval daughters of Dipsas, the old woman whose bawdy and cynical advice on handling men makes up Ovid's *Amores* 1.8.[1] Chaucer's nearer debt in this line of women is undoubtedly La Vieille in the medieval *Roman de la Rose*, as many commentators have shown, and it is characteristic of Chaucer to get his classics through modern sources, but the classical pattern persists even in his liveliest and most brilliantly imaginative work.

The text is based on F. N. Robinson's edition of 1930, which in turn is based on the Ellesmere manuscript at the Huntington Library. We have not modernized the spelling, as we have in most other texts, because the differences between Middle English and modern words are too often more than a matter of orthography. In addition, the spelling differences, such as the frequency of final *e*, often indicate important differences of pronunciation. We pick up the story near the end, when the wife recounts her marriage to her fifth husband, a "clerk" (what we would call a "scholar") named Jankyn.

from *The Wife of Bath's Prologue*

lines 627–822

What sholde I seye? but, at the monthes ende,
This joly clerk, Jankyn, that was so hende,[1]

GEOFFREY CHAUCER

1 "The Wife of Bath and All Her Sect," *Viator* V (1974), 413–43.

THE WIFE OF BATH'S PROLOGUE

1 *hende* clever; courteous; near at hand.

Hath wedded me with greet solempnytee;
And to hym yaf I al the lond and fee   630
That evere was me yeven therbifoore.
But afterward repented me ful soore;
He nolde suffre nothyng of my list.
By God! he smoot me ones on the lyst,[2]
For that I rente out of his book a leef,   635
That of the strook myn ere wax al deef.
Stibourn I was as is a leonesse,
And of my tonge verray jangleresse,[3]
And walke I wolde, as I had doon biforn,
From hous to hous, although he had it sworn;[4]   640
For which he often tymes wolde preche,
And me of olde Romayn geestes teche;[5]
How he Symplicius Gallus lefte his wyf,
And hire forsook for terme of al his lyf,
Noght but for open-heveded he hir say[6]   645
Lookynge out at his dore upon a day.
    Another Romayn tolde he me by name,
That, for his wyf was at a someres game
Withouten his wityng, he forsook hire eke.
And thanne wolde he upon his Bible seke   650
That ilke proverbe of Ecclesiaste
Where he comandeth, and forbedeth faste,[7]
Man shal nat suffre his wyf go roule aboute.[8]
Thanne wolde he seye right thus, withouten doute:
    "Whoso that buyldeth his hous al of salwes,[9]   655
And priketh his blynde hors over the falwes,[10]
And suffreth his wyf to go seken halwes,[11]
Is worthy to been hanged on the galwes!"
But al for noght, I sette noght an hawe[12]
Of his proverbes n' of his olde sawe,   660
Ne I wolde nat of hym correctèd be.
I hate hym that my vices telleth me,
And so doo mo, God woot, of us than I.
This made hym with me wood al outrely;[13]
I nolde noght forbere hym in no cas.[14]   665

2 *lyst* ear.
3 *jangleresse* chatterer; story-teller.
4 *sworn* forbidden.
5 *geestes* fables from Valerius Maximus' compilation of "memorable deeds and sayings."
6 *open-heveded* bare-headed; *say* saw.
7 *faste* sternly.
8 *roule* walk; wander.

9 *salwes* sallows; pale willow branches.
10 *falwes* fallows; open fields.
11 *go seken halwes* go on pilgrimage to shrines.
12 *hawe* hawthorn berry.
13 *wood* mad.
14 *nolde* would not; the double negative merely strengthens the assertion.

Now wol I seye yow sooth, by Seint Thomas,
Why that I rente out of his book a leef,
For which he smoot me so that I was deef.
    He hadde a book that gladly, nyght and day,
For his desport he wolde rede alway;   670
He cleped it Valerie and Theofraste,[15]
At which book he lough alwey ful faste.
And eek ther was somtyme a clerk at Rome,
A cardinal, that highte Seint Jerome,[16]
That made a book agayn Jovinian;   675
In which book eek ther was Tertulan,[17]
Crisippus, Trotula, and Helowys,[18]
That was abbesse nat fer fro Parys;
And eek the parables of Salomon,[19]
Ovides art, and bookes many on,[20]   680
And alle thise were bounden in o volume.
And every nyght and day was his custume,
Whan he hadde leyser and vacacioun
From oother worldly occupacioun,
To reden on this book of wikked wyves.   685
He knew of hem mo legendes and lyves
Than been of goode wyves in the Bible.
For trusteth wel, it is an impossible
That any clerk wol speke good of wyves,
But if it be of hooly seintes lyves,   690
Ne of noon oother womman never the mo.[21]
Who peyntede the leon, tel me who?[22]
By God! if wommen hadde writen stories,
As clerkes han withinne hire oratories,
They wolde han writen of men moore wikkednesse   695

---

15 *Valerie* short for Walter Map's *Dissuasio Valerii ad Ruffinum philosophum ne uxorem ducat* (Valerius' advice to the philosopher Ruffinus not to take a wife). *Theofraste* Greek philosopher of the fourth–third centuries BCE; Jerome quotes from what he calls his "golden book on marriage" (*liber aureolus de nuptiis*), a lost work that contained an attack on marriage.

16 *Jerome* Christian scholar and ascetic (347–420 CE) best known for his translation of the Bible into Latin (the Vulgate) and his vigorous engagement in theological controversies. His work *Adversus Jovinianum* (Against Jovinian) attacks the proposition that marriage is equal in worth to virginity.

17 *Tertulan* Tertullian, an early Christian theologian whose works contain misogynistic sentiments.

18 *Crisippus* mentioned in Jerome's *Adversus Jovinianum*; *Trotula* a female physician; *Helowys* Heloise, the penitent lover of Peter Abelard.

19 *parables of Salomon* Proverbs 10.1–22.16.

20 *Ovides art* the *Ars Amatoria* (Art of Love), a mock-didactic poem on the art of seduction and erotic intrigue (p. 433 below).

21 *never the mo* no way.

22 *Who peyntede the leon* refers to an Aesopian fable in which a lion and a man encounter a picture of a man standing over the body of a lion that he has killed; the lion points out that the picture would be different if it had been painted by a lion.

Than al the mark of Adam may redresse.[23]
The children of Mercurie and of Venus[24]
Been in hir wirkyng ful contrarius;
Mercurie loveth wysdam and science,
And Venus loveth ryot and dispence.[25]   700
And, for hire diverse disposicioun,
Ech falleth in otheres exaltacioun.[26]
And thus, God woot, Mercurie is desolat
In Pisces, wher Venus is exaltat;
And Venus falleth ther Mercurie is reysed.   705
Therfore no womman of no clerk is preysed.
The clerk, whan he is oold, and may noght do
Of Venus werkes worth his olde sho,
Thanne sit he doun, and writ in his dotage
That wommen kan nat kepe hir mariage!   710
    But now to purpos, why I tolde thee
That I was beten for a book, pardee!
Upon a nyght Jankyn, that was oure sire,
Redde on his book, as he sat by the fire,
Of Eva first, that for hir wikkednesse   715
Was al mankynde broght to wrecchednesse,
For which that Jhesu Crist hymself was slayn,
That boghte us with his herte blood agayn.
Lo, heere expres of womman may ye fynde,[27]
That womman was the los of al mankynde.   720
    Tho redde he me how Sampson loste his heres:[28]
Slepynge, his lemman kitte it with hir sheres;
Thurgh which treson loste he bothe his yen.[29]
    Tho redde he me, if that I shal nat lyen,
Of Hercules and of his Dianyre,[30]   725
That caused hym to sette hymself afyre.
    No thyng forgat he the care and the wo
That Socrates hadde with his wyves two;[31]

23   *al the mark of Adam* all members of the male sex.
24   *children of Mercurie and of Venus* those dominated astrologically by these planets; i.e. scholarly types and sensual types respectively.
25   *ryot and dispence* wanton living and extravagance.
26   *Ech falleth in otheres exaltacioun* when one planet is up, the other is down in astrological position and influence.
27   *expres* expressly stated.
28   *Tho* then.
29   *yen* eyes (two syllables).

30   *Dianyre* Deianira, wife of Hercules; to regain his affection she sent him a robe smeared with the poisoned blood of the centaur Nessus, who had told her it was an aphrodisiac; the pain of the poison caused Hercules to end his life by being burnt on a pyre.
31   *Socrates* Jerome says that Socrates had two wives who ganged up on him; when Xanthippe once followed up her abuse by pouring urine on his head, he said that he knew "a shower must follow such thunder as that" (*Adversus Jovinianum* 1.48).

How Xantippa caste pisse upon his heed.
This sely man sat stille as he were deed;   730
He wiped his heed, namoore dorste he seyn,
But "Er that thonder stynte, comth a reyn!"
    Of Phasipha, that was the queen of Crete,[32]
For shrewednesse, hym thoughte the tale swete;
Fy! spek namoore – it is a grisly thyng –   735
Of hire horrible lust and hir likyng.
    Of Clitermystra, for hire lecherye,[33]
That falsly made hire housbonde for to dye,
He redde it with ful good devocioun.
    He tolde me eek for what occasioun   740
Amphiorax at Thebes loste his lyf.[34]
Myn housbonde hadde a legende of his wyf,
Eriphilem, that for an ouche of gold
Hath prively unto the Grekes told
Wher that hir housbonde hidde hym in a place,   745
For which he hadde at Thebes sory grace.
    Of Lyvia tolde he me, and of Lucye:[35]
They bothe made hir housbondes for to dye;
That oon for love, that oother was for hate.
Lyvia hir housbonde, on an even late,   750
Empoysoned hath, for that she was his fo;
Lucia, likerous, loved hire housbonde so[36]
That, for he sholde alwey upon hire thynke,
She yaf hym swich a manere love-drynke
That he was deed er it were by the morwe;   755
And thus algates housbondes han sorwe.
    Thanne tolde he me how oon Latumyus[37]
Compleyned unto his felawe Arrius
That in his gardyn growèd swich a tree
On which he seyde how that his wyves thre   760

---

32 *Phasipha* Pasiphae, wife of Minos; she fell in love with the bull sent from the sea and copulated with it by means of a contraption built by Daedalus; their union produced the Minotaur (see Ovid, *Ars Amatoria* 1.289–326; p. 434 below). The examples of Pasiphae, Clytemnestra, and Eriphyle were probably taken from Jerome, though they also appear in Ovid's *Ars Amatoria*.

33 *Clitermystra* Clytemnestra; she murdered her husband, Agamemnon, on his return from Troy with the help of her lover Aegisthus.

34 *Amphiorax* Amphiaraus; his wife Eriphyle was bribed to make him participate in the expedition of the Seven Against Thebes, in which he knew he would be killed. Chaucer may have known the story from Statius' *Thebaid*.

35 *Lyvia* Livia, or Livilla; said to have murdered her husband Drusus to marry her lover Sejanus; *Lucye* Lucilla; said to have killed her husband, the poet Lucretius. Both stories come from Walter Map.

36 *likerous* lustful.

37 *Latumyus* the story comes from Walter Map; its ultimate source is Cicero, *De Oratore* 2.278.

Hanged hemself for herte despitus.
"O leeve brother," quod this Arrius,
"Yif me a plante of thilke blissèd tree,
And in my gardyn planted shal it bee."
    Of latter date, of wyves hath he red   765
That somme han slayn hir housbondes in hir bed,
And lete hir lecchour dighte hire al the nyght,
Whan that the corps lay in the floor upright.
And somme han dryve nayles in hir brayn,
Whil that they slepte, and thus they had hem slayn.   770
Somme han hem yeve poysoun in hire drynke.
He spak moore harm than herte may bithynke;
And therwithal he knew of mo proverbes
Than in this world ther growen gras or herbes.
"Bet is," quod he, "thyn habitacioun   775
Be with a leon or foul dragoun,
Than with a womman usynge for to chyde –
Bet is," quod he, "hye in the roof abyde,
Than with an angry wyf doun in the hous;
They been so wikked and contrarious,   780
They haten that hir housbondes loven ay." –
He seyde, "a womman cast hir shame away,
Whan she cast of hir smok"; – and forthermo,[38]
"A fair womman, but she be chaast also,
Is lyk a gold ryng in a sowes nose."[39]   785
Who wolde wene, or who wolde suppose,
The wo that in myn herte was, and pyne?
    And whan I saugh he wolde nevere fyne[40]
To reden on this cursèd book al nyght,
Al sodeynly thre leves have I plyght   790
Out of his book, right as he radde, and eke
I with my fest so took hym on the cheke
That in oure fyr he fil bakward adoun.
And he up stirte as dooth a wood leoun,
And with his fest he smoot me on the heed,   795
That in the floor I lay as I were deed.
And whan he saugh how stille that I lay,
He was agast, and wolde han fled his way,
Til atte laste out of my swogh I breyde.[41]
"O! hastow slayn me, false theef?" I seyde,   800
"And for my land thus hastow mordred me?
Er I be deed, yet wol I kisse thee."

38 *smok* slip; undergarment.
39 *A fair womman . . . nose* Proverbs 11.22.
40 *fyne* stop.
41 *breyde* started up.

And neer he cam and kneled faire adoun,
And seyde, "Deere suster Alisoun,
As help me God! I shal thee nevere smyte.   805
That I have doon, it is thyself to wyte.[42]
Foryeve it me, and that I thee biseke!"
And yet eftsoones I hitte hym on the cheke,
And seyde, "theef, thus muchel am I wreke;[43]
Now wol I dye, I may no lenger speke."   810
But atte laste, with muchel care and wo,
We fille acorded by us selven two.
He yaf me al the bridel in myn hond,
To han the governance of hous and lond,
And of his tonge, and of his hond also;   815
And made hym brenne his book anon right tho.
And whan that I hadde geten unto me,
By maistrie, al the soveraynetee,
And that he seyde, "Myn owene trewe wyf,
Do as thee lust the terme of al thy lyf;   820
Keep thyn honour, and keep eek myn estaat."
After that day we hadden never debaat.

---

42 *wyte* blame.   43 *wreke* avenged.

Edmund Spenser
(1552–1599)

Even before going to university, Spenser became learned and translated Petrarch and Du Bellay. At Pembroke College, Cambridge, he expanded his reading in Italian and French, as well as in Greek, Latin, and early English. At Cambridge too, Gabriel Harvey, a professional reader with an extraordinary library, became Spenser's friend, mentor, and supplier of books. His first major poem, *The Shepherd's Calendar*, uses the conventions of pastoral poetry (developed in Theocritus and Virgil) to treat a variety of subjects from love to religion and politics. The linguistic inventiveness of this popular work foreshadows the amazing versatility of *The Faerie Queene*, Spenser's most important work, the second most important British epic poem, and a crucial source for the greatest poem in English, *Paradise Lost*. Like other epic poems, *The Faerie Queene* employs characters, stories, and themes taken from Homer and Virgil. Spenser casts these classical features in an Arthurian mold reminiscent of Chaucer's *Troilus and Criseyde* and Thomas Malory's *Morte d'Arthur*. In addition, and most importantly, Spenser transfigures the classical materials and writes them as allegory. The practice of reading Homer as allegory began as early as the sixth century BCE, according to the *Oxford Classical Dictionary*, and there are certainly allegorical touches in Virgil's versions of the Homeric tales: Aeneas, for example, is sometimes an allegory for Augustus Caesar and sometimes a representative of the virtue of piety. However, Spenser's whole landscape is allegorical, and he confronts the reader with problems of interpretation so continuously that reading the poem itself resembles a quest for salvation. Such full allegory did not emerge in the classical world at least until Prudentius' *Psychomachia* (Battle of the Soul) in the fourth or fifth century CE, and Spenser blends that mode of writing more fully with classical epic than any earlier writer. For this reason David Kalstone, one of Spenser's best interpreters, used to refer to *The Faerie Queene* as the Elizabethan equivalent of James Joyce's *Ulysses*.

Spenser originally planned twelve books of twelve cantos each in his epic but only wrote six and some additional fragments called the "Two Cantos of Mutabilitie." Spenser's cantos contain on average about sixty stanzas of eight

pentameter lines capped off with an alexandrine (a line of six iambic feet – twelve
syllables). The Spenserian stanza (that is its name) comprises two quatrains with
a middle line that balances between the two in various ways. Thematically, each
book of *The Faerie Queene* focuses on a heroic knight who represents a particular
virtue, and each knight has a guide to help him in his quest. The hero of Book II
is Sir Guyon, who is aided by the Palmer. Guyon represents the virtue of temper-
ance. His last test in the book is the temptation of the Bowre of Bliss, a garden
of earthly delights recalling the garden of Alcinous in *Odyssey* 7 but ruled by
Acrasia, whose name means "lack of control." Spenser explicitly links her to Circe,
the sorceress who turns men into beasts in *Odyssey* 10. Whereas wily and worldly
Odysseus sleeps with Circe and receives guidance from her, Virgil's hero Aeneas
demonstrates his characteristic *piety* by steering clear of the magical isle. Spenser's
hero encounters the temptation and overcomes it by smashing it to bits. But he
is not a universal savior harrowing a sensual hell; he leaves behind those lost to
pleasure, as the Palmer bids him: he lets Gryll (literally, the hog) be Gryll and goes
forth into Book III where he meets his match in the female knight Britomart, the
representative of true chastity.

   The text presented here is based on the first edition (1590). Spenser intended
his language to look archaic, and he chose his spelling accordingly. Hence, we
mainly observe the original language of the text, although we make a few changes
in spelling and grammar for the sake of comprehension.

from *The Faerie Queene*

Book 2, Canto 12

1

Now ginnes this goodly frame of Temperaunce
Fayrely to rise, and her adornèd hed
To pricke of highest prayse forth to advaunce,[1]
Formerly grounded, and fast settlèd
On firme foundation of true bountyhed;[2]   5
And this brave knight, that for that vertue fights,
Now comes to point of that same perilous sted,[3]
Where Pleasure dwelles in sensuall delights,
Mongst thousand dangers, & ten thousand Magick mights.

2

Two dayes now in that sea he saylèd has,   10
Ne ever land beheld, ne living wight,[4]

THE *FAERIE QUEENE*

1 *To pricke of* in response to the desire for.
2 *bountyhed* the quality of being bounteous or
generously endowing.

3 *sted* place (the Bower of Bliss).
4 *Ne . . . ne* neither . . . nor.

Ne ought save perill, still as he did pas:
Tho when appeared the third *Morrow* bright,
Upon the waves to spred her trembling light,
An hideous roring far away they heard,   15
That all their senses fillèd with affright,
And streight they saw the raging surges reard
Up to the skyes, that them of drowning made affeard.

                3
Said then the Boteman, "Palmer stere aright,[5]
And keepe an even course; for yonder way   20
We needes must passe (God do us well acquight),[6]
That is the *Gulfe of Greedinesse*, they say,[7]
That deepe engorgeth all this worldès prey:
Which having swallowd up excessively,
He soone in vomit up againe doth lay,   25
And belcheth forth his superfluity,
That all the seas for feare do seeme away to fly.

                4
On th' other syde an hideous Rock is pight,[8]
Of mightie *Magnes* stone, whose craggie clift[9]
Depending from on high, dreadfull to sight,[10]   30
Over the waves his rugged armes doth lift,
And threatneth downe to throw his ragged rift
On whoso commeth nigh; yet nigh it drawes
All passengers, that none from it can shift:
For whiles they fly that Gulfes devouring jawes,   35
They on this Rock are rent, and sunck in helples wawes.[11]

                5
Forward they passe, and strongly he them rowes,
Untill they nigh unto that Gulfe arryve,
Where streame more violent and greedy growes:

5 *Palmer* a monk who travels perpetually on pilgrimage; here, a character acting as a guide to Sir Guyon, the hero of Book II.
6 *acquight* acquit; deliver or exonerate.
7 *Gulfe of Greedinesse* this and the *hideous Rock* (below) correspond to the hazards Charybdis and Scylla between which Odysseus must navigate in the *Odyssey* (12.73–110, 234–59; p. 274 below) and to which Aeneas gives a wide berth (*Aeneid* 3.420–32, 554–67). Charybdis was a whirlpool that sucked in water three times a day; Scylla, a cave-dwelling six-headed monster who devoured passing sailors.
8 *pight* placed.
9 *Magnes stone* loadstone or magnet.
10 *Depending* hanging; a Latinism.
11 *wawes* waves; the strangeness of the spelling is due to Spenser's playful archaism and does not represent an earlier pronunciation; "waves" never rhymed with "jaws."

Then he with all his puissance doth stryve   40
To strike his oares, and mightily doth dryve
The hollow vessell through the threatfull wave,
Which gaping wide, to swallow them alyve,
In th'huge abysse of his engulfing grave,
Doth rore at them in vaine, and with great terrour rave.   45

6

They passing by, that griesly mouth did see,
Sucking the seas into his entralles deepe,
That seemd more horrible then hell to bee,
Or that darke dreadfull hole of *Tartare* steepe,[12]
Through which the damnèd ghosts doen often creep   50
Backe to the world, bad livers to torment:
But nought that falles into this direfull deepe,
Ne that approcheth nigh the wide descent,
May backe retourne, but is condemned to be drent.[13]

7

On th'other side, they saw that perilous Rocke,   55
Threatning it selfe on them to ruinate,[14]
On whose sharp cliftes the ribs of vessels broke,
And shivered ships, which had beene weckèd late,
Yet stuck, with carcases exanimate[15]
Of such, as having all their substance spent   60
In wanton joyes, and lustes intemperate,
Did afterwards make shipwracke violent,
Both of their life, and fame for ever fowly blent.[16]

8

Forthy, this hight *The Rock of* vile *Reproch*,[17]
A daungerous and detestable place,   65
To which nor fish nor fowle did once approch,
But yelling Meawes, with Seagulles hoarse and bass,[18]
And Cormoyraunts, with birds of ravenous race,
Which still sat weiting on that wastfull clift,[19]
For spoile of wretches, whose unhappy case,   70

---

12 *Tartare* Tartarus; where sinners are punished in the underworld.
13 *drent* drowned.
14 *ruinate* fall; a Latinism, from *ruo*, to fall.
15 *exanimate* killed; a Latinism – literally, "deprived of soul."

16 *blent* cheated; deceived; turned aside.
17 *Forthy* therefore; *hight* is called.
18 *Meawes* gulls.
19 *weiting* making a shrill sound.

After lost credit and consumèd thrift,
At last them driven hath to this despairefull drift.

9

The Palmer seeing them in safetie past,
Thus said; "Behold th' ensamples in our sightes,
Of lustfull luxurie and thriftlesse wast: 75
What now is left of miserable wightes,
Which spent their looser daies in leud delightes,
But shame and sad reproch, here to be red,
By these rent reliques, speaking their ill plights?
Let all that live, hereby be counsellèd,   80
To shunne *Rock of Reproch*, and it as death to dread."

10

So forth they rowed, and that *Ferryman*[20]
With his stiffe oares did brush the sea so strong,
That the hoare waters from his frigot ran,[21]
And the light bubbles dauncèd all along,   85
Whiles the salt brine out of the billowes sprong.
At last far off they many Islandes spy,
On every side floting the floodes emong:
Then said the knight, "Lo I the land descry,
Therefore old Syre thy course doe thereunto apply."   90

11

"That may not bee," said then the *Ferryman*,
"Least we unweeting hap to be fordonne:
For those same Islands, seeming now and then,
Are not firme land, nor any certein wonne,[22]
But straggling plots, which to and fro do ronne   95
In the wide waters: therefore are they hight[23]
The *wandring Islands*. Therefore doe them shonne;[24]
For they have oft drawne many a wandring wight
Into most deadly daunger and distressèd plight.

12

"Yet well they seeme to him, that farre doth vew,   100
Both faire and fruitfull, and the grownd dispred

---

20 *Ferryman* corresponding to Charon, who ferries souls over the river Styx; Virgil describes him as old but hardy (*Aeneid* 6.304; p. 377 below).
21 *hoare* white.

22 *wonne* place.
23 *hight* named.
24 *wandring Islands* Homer's "Wandering Rocks" (*Odyssey* 12.61).

With grassy greene of delectable hew,
And the tall trees with leaves apparelèd,
Are deckt with blossomes dyde in white and red,
That mote the passengers thereto allure;[25]   105
But whosoever once hath fastenèd
His foot thereon, may never it recure,[26]
But wandreth ever more uncertein and unsure.

13

"As th' Isle of *Delos* whylome men report[27]
Amid th' *Aegaean* sea long time did stray,   110
Ne made for shipping any certeine port,
Till that *Latona* traveiling that way,
Flying from *Juno's* wrath and hard assay,[28]
Of her fayre twins was there deliverèd,
Which afterwards did rule the night and day;   115
Thenceforth it firmely was establishèd,
And for *Apollo's* temple highly herrièd."[29]

14

They to him hearken, as beseemeth meete,[30]
And passe on forward: so their way does ly,
That one of those same Islands, which doe fleet[31]   120
In the wide sea, they needes must passen by,
Which seemd so sweet and pleasaunt to the eye,
That it would tempt a man to touchen there:
Upon the banck they sitting did espy
A daintie damzell, dressing of her heare,   125
By whom a litle skippet floting did appeare.[32]

15

She them espying, loud to them can call,
Bidding them nigher draw unto the shore;
For she had cause to busie them withall;
And therewith lowdly laught: But nathemore   130

25   *mote* must or might.
26   *recure* move back.
27   *Delos* an island in the Cyclades which accord-
ing to myth floated on the surface of the sea until
Latona gave birth there to Apollo and Diana,
rulers of the sun and moon (Ovid, *Metamor-
phoses* 6.184–91, 332–4; Virgil, *Aeneid* 3.73–7);
whylome whilom, once upon a time.

28   *Juno's wrath* caused by Jupiter's impregna-
tion of Latona.
29   *herrièd* honored; praised (a common word
in Old English).
30   *meete* suitable; proper.
31   *fleet* float.
32   *skippet* a small boat.

Would they once turne, but kept on as afore:
Which when she saw, she left her lockes undight,[33]
And running to her boat withouten ore,
From the departing land it launchèd light,
And after them did drive with all her power and might.   135

16

Whom overtaking, she in merry sort
Them gan to bord, and purpose diversly,
Now faining dalliance and wanton sport,
Now throwing forth lewd words immodestly;
Till that the Palmer gan full bitterly   140
Her to rebuke, for being loose and light:
Which not abiding, but more scornfully
Scoffing at him, that did her justly wite,[34]
She turnd her bote about, and from them rowèd quite.[35]

17

That was the wanton *Phaedria*, which late[36]   145
Did ferry him over the *Idle lake*:
Whom nought regarding, they kept on their gait,
And all her vaine allurements did forsake,
When them the wary Boteman thus bespake;
"Here now behoveth us well to avyse,   150
And of our safety good heede to take;
For here before a perlous passage lyes,
Where many Mermayds haunt, making false melodies.

18

But by the way, there is a great Quicksand,
And a whirlepoole of hidden jeopardy,   155
Therefore, Sir Palmer, keepe an even hand;
For twixt them both the narrow way doth ly."
Scarse had he said, when hard at hand they spy
That quicksand nigh with water coverèd;
But by the checkèd wave they did descry   160
It plaine, and by the sea discolourèd:
It callèd was the quicksand of *Unthriftyhed*.

19

They passing by, a goodly Ship did see,
Laden from far with precious merchandize,

---

33 *undight* unrestrained.
34 *wite* blame.
35 *quite* thoroughly; away.

36 *Phaedria* the name evokes Phaedra, who
lusted after her stepson Hippolytus.

And bravely furnishèd, as ship might bee,   165
Which through great disaventure, or mesprize,
Her selfe had runne into that hazardize;
Whose mariners and merchants with much toyle,
Laboured in vaine, to have recured their prize,
And the rich wares to save from pitteous spoyle,   170
But neither toyle nor travell might her backe recoyle.

                                20
On th' other side they see that perilous Poole,
That callèd was the *Whirlepoole of decay*,
In which full many had with haplesse doole[37]
Beene suncke, of whom no memorie did stay: 175
Whose circled waters rapt with whirling sway,
Like to a restlesse wheele, still running round,
Did covet, as they passèd by that way,
To draw their bote within the utmost bound
Of his wide *Labyrinth*, and then to have them dround.   180

                                21
But th' earnest Boateman strongly forth did stretch
His brawnie armes, and all his bodie straine,
That th' utmost sandy breach they shortly fetch,
Whiles the dredd daunger does behind remaine.
Suddeine they see from midst of all the Maine,   185
The surging waters like a mountaine rise,
And the great sea puft up with proud disdaine,
To swell above the measure of his guise,
As threatning to devoure all, that his powre despise.

                                22
The waves come rolling, and the billowes rore   190
Outragiously, as they enragèd were,
Or wrathfull *Neptune* did them drive before
His whirling charet, for exceeding feare:
For not one puffe of wind there did appeare,
That all the three thereat woxe much afrayd,   195
Unweeting, what such horrour straunge did reare.
Eftsoones they saw an hideous hoast arrayd,
Of huge Sea monsters, such as living sence dismayd.

                                23
Most ugly shapes, and horrible aspects,
Such as Dame Nature selfe mote feare to see,   200

37   *doole* dole; fate.

Or shame, that ever should so fowle defects
From her most cunning hand escapèd bee;
All dreadfull pourtraicts of deformitee:
Spring-headed *Hydraes*, and sea-shouldring Whales,[38]
Great whirlpooles, which all fishes make to flee, 205
Bright Scolopendraes, armed with silver scales,[39]
Mighty *Monoceroses*, with immeasured tayles.[40]

24

The dreadfull Fish, that hath deserved the name
Of Death, and like him lookes in dreadfull hew,
The griesly Wasserman, that makes his game[41] 210
The flying ships with swiftnesse to pursew,
The horrible Sea-satyre, that doth shew
His fearefull face in time of greatest storme,
Huge *Ziffius*, whom Mariners eschew[42]
No lesse than rockes (as travellers informe) 215
And greedy *Rosmarines* with visages deforme.[43]

25

All these, and thousand thousands many more,
And more deformèd Monsters thousand fold,
With dreadfull noise, and hollow rombling rore,
Came rushing in the fomy waves enrold, 220
Which seemed to fly for feare, them to behold:
Ne wonder, if these did the knight appall;
For all that here on earth we dreadfull hold,
Be but as bugs to fearen babes withall,[44]
Compared to the creatures in the seas entrall. 225

26

"Feare nought," then said the Palmer well avized,[45]
"For these same Monsters are not these in deed,
But are into these fearefull shapes disguized
By that same wicked witch, to worke us dreed,
And draw from on this journey to proceed." 230
Tho lifting up his vertuous staffe on hye,[46]

---

38 *Hydraes* sea serpents whose name evokes the many-headed Lernaean hydra killed by Hercules.
39 *Scolopendraes* recalls a fish said by the ancients to be capable of vomiting its entrails in order to expel fish hooks (Aristotle, *Historia Animalium* 9, 621a).
40 *Monoceroses* fish, like the swordfish, resembling unicorns.

41 *Wasserman* a sea-monster with a half-human shape.
42 *Ziffius* the swordfish.
43 *Rosmarines* walruses or perhaps sea-horses.
44 *bugs* bugbears; hobgoblins; imaginary monsters.
45 *avized* counseled; taught
46 *Tho* then; thereupon.

He smote the sea, which calmèd was with speed,
And all that dreadfull Armie fast gan flye
Into great *Tethys'* bosome, where they hidden lye.[47]

27

Quit from that daunger, forth their course they kept,   235
And as they went, they heard a ruefull cry
Of one, that wayld and pittifully wept,
That through the sea the resounding plaints did fly:
At last they in an Island did espy
A seemely Maiden, sitting by the shore,   240
That with great sorrow and sad agony,
Seemèd some great misfortune to deplore,
And lowd to them for succour callèd evermore.

28

Which *Guyon* hearing, streight his Palmer bad,[48]
To stere the bote towards that dolefull Mayd,   245
That he might know, and ease her sorrow sad:
Who him avizing better, to him sayd;
"Faire Sir, be not displeasd, if disobayd:
For ill it were to hearken to her cry;
For she is inly nothing ill apayd,[49]   250
But onely womanish fine forgery,
Your stubborne hart t'affect with fraile infirmity.

29

"To which when she your courage hath inclind
Through foolish pitty, then her guilefull bayt
She will embosome deeper in your mind,   255
And for your ruine at the last awayt."
The knight was rulèd, and the Boteman strayt
Held on his course with stayèd stedfastnesse,
Ne ever shruncke, ne ever sought to bayt[50]
His tyred armes for toylesome wearinesse,   260
But with his oares did sweepe the watry wildernesse.

30

And now they nigh approchèd to the sted,
Whereas those Mermayds dwelt: it was a still[51]

---

47 *Tethys* wife of Oceanus and mother of sea-monsters; a metonymy for the sea itself.
48 *bad* ordered.
49 *apayd* satisfied; content.
50 *bayt* stop; hold back.
51 *Mermayds* corresponding to Homer's Sirens (*Odyssey* 12.39–54, 165–200; pp. 272–3 below), a pair of bird-women who lure sailors to their death with their enchanting songs. Odysseus had his sailors block their ears with wax and ordered himself bound to the mast, so that he could hear them with impunity. Guyon is tempted to listen but dissuaded by the Palmer.

And calmy bay, on th' one side shelterèd[52]
With the brode shadow of an hoarie hill,   265
On th' other side an high rocke tourèd still,[53]
That twixt them both a pleasaunt port they made,
And did like an halfe Theatre fulfill:
There those five sisters had continuall trade,
And usd to bathe themselves in that deceiptfull shade.   270

31

They were faire Ladies, till they fondly strived
With th' *Heliconian* maides for maystery;[54]
Of whom they over-comen were, deprived
Of their proud beautie, and th' one moyity[55]
Transformed to fish, for their bold surquedry,[56]   275
But th' upper halfe their hew retainèd still,[57]
And their sweet skill in wonted melody;
Which ever after they abusd to ill,
T' allure weake travellers, whom gotten they did kill.

32

So now to *Guyon*, as he passèd by,   280
Their pleasaunt tunes they sweetly thus applyde;
"O thou fayre sonne of gentle Faèry,
That art in mighty armes most magnifyde
Above all knights, that ever batteill tryde,
O turne thy rudder hither-ward a while: 285
Here may thy storme-bett vessell safely ride;[58]
This is the Port of rest from troublous toyle,
The world's sweet Inn, from paine & wearisome turmoyle."

33

With that the rolling sea resounding soft,
In his big bass them fitly answerèd,   290
And on the rocke the waves breaking aloft,
A solemne Meane unto them measurèd,[59]
The whiles sweet *Zephirus* lowd whistelèd[60]
His treble, a straunge kinde of harmony;
Which *Guyon's* senses softly tickelèd,   295
That he the boteman bad row easily,[61]
And let him heare some part of their rare melody.

---

52 *bay* reminiscent of the bay where Aeneas
lands in Africa prior to his encounter with Dido
(Virgil, *Aeneid* 1.157–69; p. 369 below).
53 *tourèd* towered.
54 *Heliconian maides* the Muses, who fre-
quented Mt. Helicon. They defeated the Sirens in
a song contest and plucked out their feathers.

55 *moyity* moiety; part; portion.
56 *surquedry* arrogance; presumption.
57 *hew* shape.
58 *ride* moor.
59 *meane* moan.
60 *Zephirus* personification of the west wind.
61 *that* so that; with the result that.

34

But him the Palmer from that vanity,
With temperate advice discounsellèd,
That they it past, and shortly gan descry   300
The land, to which their course they levelèd;
When suddeinly a grosse fog overspred
With his dull vapour all that desert has,
And heaven's chearefull face envelopèd,
That all things one, and one as nothing was,   305
And this great Universe seemd one confusèd mas.

35

Thereat they greatly were dismayd, ne wist[62]
How to direct their way in darkeness wide,
But feard to wander in that wastfull mist,[63]
For tombling into mischiefe unespide.   310
Worse is the daunger hidden, then descride.
Suddeinly an innumerable flight
Of harmefull fowles about them fluttering, cride,
And with their wicked wings them oft did smight,
And sore annoyed, groping in that griesly night.   315

36

Even all the nation of unfortunate
And fatall birds about them flockèd were,[64]
Such as by nature men abhorre and hate,
The ill-faste Owle, death's dreadfull messengere,
The hoars Night-raven, trump of dolefull drere,[65]   320
The lether-wingèd Bat, day's enimy,
The ruefull Strich, still waiting on the bere,[66]
The Whistler shrill, that whoso heares, doth dy,
The hellish Harpies, prophets of sad destiny.[67]

37

All those, and all that else does horrour breed,   325
About them flew, and fild their sayles with feare:
Yet stayd they not, but forward did proceed,
Whiles th' one did row, and th' other stifly steare;
Till that at last the weather gan to cleare,

---

62 *wist* knew.
63 *wastfull* desert-like; empty (of visual clues).
64 *unfortunate / And fatall birds* whose appearance presaged misfortune.
65 *trump* trumpet; herald

66 *Strich* screech-owl.
67 *Harpies* monstrous birds with women's faces; when Aeneas encountered them, the Harpy Celaeno predicted dire suffering for him and his men in Italy (*Aeneid* 3.210–67).

And the faire land it selfe did playnly show.   330
Said then the Palmer, "Lo where does appeare
The sacred soile, where all our perils grow;
Therefore, Sir knight, your ready armes about you throw."

38
He hearkned, and his armes about him tooke,
The whiles the nimble bote so well her sped,   335
That with her crooked keele the land she strooke,
Then forth the noble *Guyon* sallièd,
And his sage Palmer, that him governèd;
But th' other by his bote behind did stay.
They marchèd fayrly forth, of nought ydred,[68]   340
Both firmely armd for every hard assay,[69]
With constancy and care, gainst daunger and dismay.

39
Ere long they heard an hideous bellowing
Of many beasts, that roard outrageously,[70]
As if that hunger's poynt, or *Venus*' sting   345
Had them enragèd with fell surquedry;
Yet nought they feard, but past on hardily,
Untill they came in vew of those wild beasts:
Who all attonce, gaping full greedily,
And rearing fiercely their upstarting crests,   350
Ran towards, to devoure those unexpected guests.

40
But soone as they approcht with deadly threat,
The Palmer over them his staffe upheld,[71]
His mighty staffe, that could all charmes defeat:
Eftsoones their stubborne corages were queld,[72]   355
And high advauncèd crests downe meekely feld,
In stead of fraying, they them selves did feare,[73]
And trembled, as them passing they beheld:
Such wondrous powre did in that staffe appeare,
All monsters to subdew to him, that did it beare.   360

---

68 *ydred* afraid.
69 *assay* test.
70 *beasts* recalling the wild animals Circe had bewitched or transformed. Homer makes them fawn upon Odysseus' men (*Odyssey* 10.210–19, p. 267 below; cf. Ovid, *Metamorphoses* 14.254–9); Aeneas hears them roaring as he sails by (*Aeneid* 7.15–20).

71 *staffe* the Palmer's staff has the same effect as the magical herb moly that Hermes gives Odysseus to immunize him against Circe's spells (*Odyssey* 10.287–92; pp. 269–70 below).
72 *corages* hearts; spirits.
73 *fraying* scaring; making afraid.

41

Of that same wood it fram'd was cunningly,
Of which *Caduceus* whilome was made,[74]
Caduceus the rod of *Mercury*,
With which he wonts the *Stygian* realmes invade,[75]
Through ghastly horror, and eternall shade;   365
Th' infernall feends with it he can asswage,
And *Orcus* tame, whom nothing can persuade,[76]
And rule the *Furyes*, when they most do rage:[77]
Such vertue in his staffe had eke this Palmer sage.[78]

42

Thence passing forth, they shortly do arrive,   370
Whereas the Bowre of *Blisse* was situate;
A place pickt out by choice of best alyve,
That nature's worke by art can imitate:
In which what ever in this worldly state
Is sweet, and pleasing unto living sense,   375
Or that may dayntiest fantasie aggrate,[79]
Was pourèd forth with plentifull dispence,
And made there to abound with lavish affluence.

43

Goodly it was enclosèd rownd about,
As well their entred guestes to keepe within,   380
As those unruly beasts to hold without;
Yet was the fence thereof but weake and thin;
Nought feard theyr force, that fortilage to win,[80]
But wisedom's powre, and temperaunce's might,
By which the mightiest things efforcèd bin: 385
And eke the gate was wrought of substaunce light,
Rather for pleasure, then for battery or fight.

44

Yt framèd was of precious yvory,
That seemd a worke of admirable witt;[81]
And therein all the famous history   390

74 *Caduceus* a herald's staff with magic properties borne by Mercury (Hermes).
75 *wonts* is accustomed to; *Stygian realmes* the underworld, whither Mercury conducted the souls of the dead.
76 *Orcus* god of the underworld.
77 *Furyes* goddesses of vengeance, often shown carrying whips and wreathed with snakes.
78 *eke* also.
79 *aggrate* gratify.
80 *fortilage* fortress.
81 *witt* intelligence.

Of *Jason* and *Medea* was ywrit;[82]
Her mighty charmes, her furious loving fit,
His goodly conquest of the golden fleece,
His falsèd faith, and love too lightly flit,
The wondred *Argo*, which in venturous peece   395
First through the *Euxine* seas bore all the flowr of *Greece*.[83]

45

Ye might have seene the frothy billowes fry[84]
Under the ship, as thorough them she went,
That seemd the waves were into yvory,
Or yvory into the waves were sent;   400
And otherwhere the snowy substaunce sprent[85]
With vermell, like the boy's bloud therein shed,[86]
A piteous spectacle did represent,
And otherwhiles with gold besprinkelèd;
Yt seemd th' enchaunted flame, which did *Creüsa* wed.[87]   405

46

All this, and more might in that goodly gate
Be red; that ever open stood to all,
Which thither came: but in the Porch there sate
A comely personage of stature tall,
And semblaunce pleasing, more than naturall,   410
That travellers to him seemd to entize;
His looser garment to the ground did fall,
And flew about his heeles in wanton wize,
Not fit for speedy pace, or manly exercize.

47

They in that place him *Genius* did call:[88]   415
Not that celestiall powre, to whom the care

---

82 *Jason* leader of the Argonauts, a band of Greek heroes who sailed to Colchis in quest of Aeetes' golden fleece; *Medea* Aeetes' daughter, who fell in love with Jason, helped him to obtain the fleece, and fled with him to Greece, scattering pieces of her murdered brother in the sea to delay her father's pursuit; when Jason abandoned her in Corinth, she murdered their children and Jason's new bride.

83 *First* perhaps echoing Catullus 64.11, where the Argo is said to be the first ocean-going ship; *Euxine* the Black Sea; *all the flowr of Greece* the best Greek heroes.

84 *Ye might have seene* a conventional observation of the classical ekphrasis, or poetic description of a work of art; compare Virgil, *Aeneid* 8.676–7, "you might have seen all Leucate seethe with preparations for battle"; *fry* boil; foam.

85 *sprent* sprinkled.

86 *vermell* vermilion; red.

87 *Creüsa* Jason's new bride; Medea sent her a poisoned robe which burned her to death.

88 *Genius* defined as "The tutelary god or attendant spirit allotted to every person at his birth, to govern his fortunes and determine his character" (*OED*).

Of life, and generation of all
That lives, pertaines in charge particulare,
Who wondrous things concerning our welfare,
And straunge phantomes doth lett us oft forsee,   420
And oft of secret ill bids us beware:
That is our Selfe, whom though we doe not see,
Yet each doth in him selfe it well perceive to bee.

48

Therefore a God him sage Antiquity
Did wisely make, and good *Agdistes* call: 425
But this same was to that quite contrary,[89]
The foe of life, that good envyes to all,
That secretly doth us procure to fall,
Through guilefull semblants, which he makes us see.[90]
He of this Gardin had the governall,   430
And Pleasure's porter was devizd to bee,
Holding a staffe in hand for more formalitee.

49

With diverse flowres he daintily was deckt,
And strowèd rownd about, and by his side
A mighty Mazer bowle of wine was sett,[91]   435
As if it had to him bene sacrifide;
Wherewith all new-come guests he gratyfide:
So did he eke Sir *Guyon* passing by:
But he his idle curtesie defide,
And overthrew his bowle disdainfully;   440
And broke his staffe, with which he charmèd semblants sly.

50

Thus being entred, they behold arownd
A large and spacious plaine, on every side
Strowèd with pleasauns, whose fayre grassy ground[92]
Mantled with greene, and goodly beautifide   445
With all the ornaments of *Floraes* pride,[93]
Wherewith her mother Art, as halfe in scorne
Of niggard Nature, like a pompous bride
Did decke her, and too lavishly adorne,
When forth from virgin bowre she comes in th' early morne.   450

89 *contrary* the "evil genius."   92 *pleasauns* that which gives pleasure.
90 *semblants* shows; entertainments.   93 *Floraes* Flora was an Italian goddess of
91 *Mazer* maple or other hardwood.   flowers.

51

Therewith the Heavens alwayes Joviall,
Lookt on them lovely, still in stedfast state,
Ne suffred storme nor frost on them to fall,
Their tender buds or leaves to violate,
Nor scorching heat, nor cold intemperate   455
T' afflict the creatures, which therein did dwell,
But the milde ayre with season moderate
Gently attempred, and disposd so well,
That still it breathed forth sweet spirit & holesom smell.

52

More sweet and holesome, than the pleasaunt hill   460
Of *Rhodope*, on which the Nimphe, that bore[94]
A gyaunt babe, her selfe for griefe did kill;
Or the Thessalian *Tempe*, where of yore[95]
Fayre *Daphne Phoebus'* hart with love did gore;[96]
Or *Ida*, where the Gods loved to repayre,[97]   465
When ever they their heavenly bowres forlore;
Or sweet *Parnasse*, the haunt of Muses fayre;[98]
Or *Eden* selfe, if ought with *Eden* mote compayre.

53

Much wondred *Guyon* at the fayre aspect
Of that sweet place, yet suffred no delight   470
To sincke into his sence, nor mind affect,
But passèd forth, and lookt still forward right,
Bridling his will, and maystering his might:
Till that he came unto another gate,
No gate, but like one, being goodly dight   475
With boughes and braunches, which did broad dilate
Their clasping armes, in wanton wreathings intricate.

54

So fashioned a Porch with rare device,
Archt over head with an embracing vine,
Whose bounches hanging downe, seemed to entice   480
All passers by, to tast their lushious wine,

94   *Rhodope* mountain in Thrace; also the name
of a nymph who bore a son to Poseidon, the sea
god.
95   *Tempe* a beautiful valley in Thessaly.
96   *Daphne* Apollo's first love; his pursuit led to
her transformation into a laurel tree (Ovid, *Meta-
morphoses* 1.452–567; p. 439 below); *Phoebus*
Apollo.

97   *Ida* the mountain overlooking Troy; site of
the Judgment of Paris and of Hera's seduction of
Zeus in *Iliad* 14.
98   *Parnasse* Parnassus; a mountain near Delphi
associated with the worship of Apollo and the
Muses.

And did themselves into their hands incline,
As freely offering to be gatherèd:
Some deepe empurpled as the *Hyacint*,
Some as the Rubine, laughing sweetly red,[99]   485
Some like faire Emeraudes, not yet well ripenèd.[100]

55

And them amongst, some were of burnisht gold,
So made by art, to beautify the rest,
Which did themselves emongst the leaves enfold,
As lurking from the vew of covetous guest,   490
That the weake boughes, with so rich load opprest,
Did bow adowne, as over-burdenèd.
Under that Porch a comely dame did rest,
Clad in fayre weedes, but fowle disorderèd,
And garments loose, that seemd unmeet for womanhed.   495

56

In her left hand a Cup of gold she held,
And with her right the riper fruit did reach,
Whose sappy liquor, that with fulnesse sweld,
Into her cup she scruzd, with daintie breach[101]
Of her fine fingers, without fowle empeach,[102]   500
That so faire wine-presse made the wine more sweet:
Thereof she usd to give to drinke to each,
Whom passing by she happenèd to meet:
It was her guise, all Straungers goodly so to greet.

57

So she to *Guyon* offred it to tast;   505
Who taking it out of her tender hond,
The cup to ground did violently cast,
That all in peeces it was broken fond,[103]
And with the liquor stainèd all the lond:
Whereat *Excesse* exceedingly was wroth,   510
Yet no'te the same amend, ne yet withstond,[104]
But suffered him to passe, all were she loth;
Who nought regarding her displeasure forward goth.

58

There the most daintie Paradise on ground,
It selfe doth offer to his sober eye,   515

---

99 *Rubine* ruby.
100 *Emeraudes* emeralds, which are bright green in color.
101 *scruzd* squeezed; *breach* the action of breaking.
102 *empeach* damage; injury.
103 *fond* found.
104 *no'te* could not.

In which all pleasures plenteously abound,
And none does other's happinesse envye:
The painted flowres, the trees upshooting hye,
The dales for shade, the hilles for breathing space,
The trembling groves, the Christall running by;[105]   520
And that, which all faire workes doth most aggrace,
The art, which all that wrought, appearèd in no place.[106]

59

One would have thought (so cunningly, the rude,
And scornèd parts were mingled with the fine)
That nature had for wantonesse ensude[107]   525
Art, and that Art at nature did repine;
So striving each th' other to undermine,
Each did the other's worke more beautify;
So diff'ring both in willes, agreed in fine:[108]
So all agreed through sweete diversity,   530
This Gardin to adorne with all variety.

60

And in the midst of all, a fountaine stood,
Of richest substance, that on earth might bee,
So pure and shiny, that the silver flood
Through every channell running one might see;   535
Most goodly it with curious ymageree
Was over-wrought, and shapes of naked boyes,
Of which some seemd with lively jollitee,
To fly about, playing their wanton toyes,
Whilest others did them selves embay in liquid joyes.   540

61

And over all, of purest gold was spred,
A trayle of yvie in his native hew:
For the rich mettall was so colourèd,
That wight, who did not well avised it vew,
Would surely deeme it to be yvie trew: 545
Low his lascivious armes adown did creepe,
That themselves dipping in the silver dew,
Their fleecy flowres they tenderly did steepe,
Which drops of Christall seemd for wantones to weep.

105 *Christall* pure, clear water.
106 *art . . . appearèd in no place* an allusion to
the Latin tag *ars est celare artem* (the art is to hide
the art).

107 *ensude* followed; imitated; compare Ovid
Metamorphoses 3.158–9: "nature had imitated art
with its own genius."
108 *fine* end or goal.

62

Infinit streames continually did well   550
Out of this fountaine, sweet and faire to see,
The which into an ample laver fell,[109]
And shortly grew to so great quantitie,
That like a litle lake it seemd to bee;
Whose depth exceeded not three cubits hight,[110]   555
That through the waves one might the bottom see,
All paved beneath with Jaspar shining bright,[111]
That seemd the fountaine in that sea did sayle upright.

63

And all the margent round about was sett,
With shady Laurell trees, thence to defend   560
The sunny beames, which on the billowes bett,[112]
And those which therein bathèd, mote offend.
As *Guyon* hapned by the same to wend,
Two naked Damzelles he therein espyde,
Which therein bathing, seemèd to contend,   565
And wrestle wantonly, ne cared to hyde,
Their dainty parts from vew of any, which them eyd.

64

Sometimes the one would lift the other quight
Above the waters, and then downe againe
Her plong, as over maysterèd by might,   570
Where both awhile would coverèd remaine,
And each the other from to rise restraine;
The whiles their snowy limbes, as through a vele,
So through the christall waves appearèd plaine:
Then suddeinly both would themselves unhele,[113]   575
And th' amarous sweet spoiles to greedy eyes revele.

65

As that faire Starre, the messenger of morne,
His deawy face out of the sea doth reare:
Or as the *Cyprian* goddesse, newly borne[114]
Of th' Oceans fruitfull froth, did first appeare: 580
Such seemèd they, and so their yellow heare
Christalline humor dropped downe apace.[115]

---

109   *laver* water jug or basin.
110   *cubits* the length of a forearm; 18–22 inches.
111   *Jaspar* a precious stone; a kind of quartz.
112   *bett* beat.
113   *unhele* uncover.

114   *Cyprian goddesse* Venus, who landed on Cyprus having sprung from the foam produced by the genitals of Uranus when he was castrated by Cronus.
115   *humor* fluid.

Whom such when *Guyon* saw, he drew him neare,
And somewhat gan relent his earnest pace,
His stubborne brest gan secret pleasaunce to embrace.   585

66

The wanton Maidens him espying, stood
Gazing a while at his unwonted guise;[116]
Then th' one her selfe low duckèd in the flood,
Abasht, that her a straunger did avise:[117]
But th' other rather higher did arise,   590
And her two lilly paps aloft displayd,
And all, that might his melting hart entyse
To her delights, she unto him bewrayd:[118]
The rest hid underneath, him more desirous made.

67

With that, the other likewise up arose,   595
And her faire lockes, which formerly were bownd
Up in one knot, she low adowne did lose:
Which flowing long and thick, her cloth'd arownd,
And th' yvorie in golden mantle gownd:
So that faire spectacle from him was reft,   600
Yet that, which reft it, no lesse faire was fownd:
So hid in lockes and waves from looker's theft,
Nought but her lovely face she for his looking left.

68

Withall she laughed, and she blusht withall,
That blushing to her laughter gave more grace,   605
And laughter to her blushing, as did fall:
Now when they spyde the knight to slacke his pace,
Them to behold, and in his sparkling face
The secret signes of kindled lust appeare,
Their wanton meriments they did encreace,   610
And to him beckned, to approch more neare,
And shewd him many sights, that courage cold could reare.[119]

69

On which when gazing him the Palmer saw,
He much rebukt those wandring eyes of his,
And counseld well, him forward thence did draw.   615
Now are they come nigh to the *Bowre of blis*

---

116 *unwonted* unfamiliar.
117 *avise* view; observe.
118 *bewrayd* exposed.

119 *courage . . . reare* raise spirits; make the
spirit stand upright.

Of her fond favorites so named amis:
When thus the Palmer; "Now Sir, well avise;
For here the end of all our traveill is:
Here wonnes *Acrasia*, whom we must surprise,[120]   620
Else she will slip away, and all our drift despise."[121]

70

Etfsoones they heard a most melodious sound,
Of all that mote delight a daintie eare,
Such as attonce might not on living ground,
Save in this Paradise, be heard elswhere: 625
Right hard it was, for wight, which did it heare,[122]
To read, what manner musicke that mote bee:
For all that pleasing is to living eare,
Was there consorted in one harmonee,
Birdes, voices, instruments, windes, waters, all agree.   630

71

The joyous birdes shrouded in chearefull shade,
Their notes unto the voice attempred sweet;
Th' Angelicall soft trembling voyces made
To th' instruments divine respondence meet:
The silver sounding instruments did meet   635
With the bass murmure of the waters' fall:
The waters' fall with difference discreet,
Now soft, now loud, unto the wind did call:
The gentle warbling wind low answerèd to all.

72

There, whence that Musick seemèd heard to bee,   640
Was the faire Witch her selfe now solacing,
With a new Lover, whom through sorceree
And witchcraft, she from farre did thither bring:
There she had him now layd a slombering,
In secret shade, after long wanton joyes: 645
Whilst round about them pleasauntly did sing
Many faire Ladies, and lascivious boyes,
That ever mixt their song with light licentious toyes.

120   *wonnes* lives; *Acrasia* there are two Greek   121   *drift* progress.
words with this spelling, one meaning "lack of   122   *wight* person.
self-control," the other "bad mixture."

73

And all that while, right over him she hong,
With her false eyes fast fixèd in his sight, 650
As seeking medicine, whence she was stong,[123]
Or greedily depasturing delight:[124]
And oft inclining downe with kisses light,
For feare of waking him, his lips bedewd,
And through his humid eyes did sucke his spright, 655
Quite molten into lust and pleasure lewd;
Wherewith she sighèd soft, as if his case she rewd.

74

The whiles some one did chaunt this lovely lay;
"Ah see, who so fayre thing doest faine to see,
In springing flowre the image of thy day; 660
Ah see the Virgin Rose, how sweetly shee
Doth first peepe forth with bashfull modestee,
That fairer seemes, the lesse ye see her may;
Lo see soone after, how more bold and free
Her barèd bosome she doth broad display; 665
Loe see soone after, how she fades, and falles away.

75

"So passeth, in the passing of a day,
Of mortall life the leafe, the bud, the flowre,
Ne more doth flourish after first decay,
That earst was sought to decke both bed and bowre, 670
Of many a Ladie, and many a Paramowre:
Gather therefore the Rose, whilest yet is prime,
For soone comes age, that will her pride deflowre:
Gather the Rose of love, whilest yet is time,
Whilest loving thou mayst lovèd be with equall crime." 675

76

He ceast, and then gan all the quire of birdes
Their diverse notes t' attune unto his lay,
As in approvaunce of his pleasing wordes.
The constant payre heard all, that he did say,

---

123 *stong* pierced; mortally wounded.
124 *depasturing* consuming, like grazing cattle (a Latinism, from *depasco*); the description recalls Lucretius' picture of Mars "who often throws himself into [Venus'] lap, conquered by the eternal wound of love, and laying back his smooth neck looks up and, gazing upon you, goddess, feeds [*pascit*] his greedy eyes with love while as he reclines his breath hangs from your lips" (*De Rerum Natura* 1.33–7).

Yet swarvèd not, but kept their forward way,   680
Through many covert groves, and thickets close,
In which they creeping did at last display
That wanton Lady, with her lover lose,
Whose sleepie head she in her lap did soft dispose.

77

Upon a bed of Roses she was layd,   685
As faint through heat, or dight to pleasant sin,
And was arayd, or rather disarayd,
All in a vele of silke and silver thin,
That hid no whit her alabaster skin,
But rather shewd more white, if more might bee: 690
More subtile web *Arachne* can not spin,[125]
Nor the fine nets, which oft we woven see
Of scorchèd deaw, do not in th'ayre more lightly flee.

78

Her snowy brest was bare to readie spoyle
Of hungry eies, which no'te therewith be fild,   695
And yet through languour of her late sweet toyle,
Few drops, more cleare then Nectar, forth distild,
That like pure Orient perles adowne it trild,
And her faire eyes sweet smyling in delight,
Moystened their fierie beames, with which she thrild[126]   700
Fraile harts, yet quenchèd not; like starry light
Which sparckling on the silent waves, does seeme more bright.

79

The young man sleeping by her, seemd to bee
Some goodly swayne of honorable place,
That certes it great pitty was to see[127]   705
Him his nobility so fowle deface;
A sweet regard, and amiable grace,
Mixed with manly sternnesse did appeare
Yet sleeping, in his well proportiond face,
And on his tender lips the downy heare   710
Did now but freshly spring, and silken blossoms beare.

80

His warlike Armes, the idle instruments
Of sleeping praise, were hong upon a tree,

125 *Arachne* a woman who was turned into a   126 *thrild* penetrated.
spider (the meaning of her Greek name) for   127 *certes* surely.
angering Athena in a weaving contest.

And his brave shield, full of old moniments,[128]
Was fowly ra'st, that none the signes might see;[129]   715
Ne for them, ne for honour carèd hee,
Ne ought, that did to his advauncement tend,
But in lewd loves, and wastfull luxuree,
His dayes, his goods, his bodie he did spend:
O horrible enchantment, that him so did blend.[130]   720

81

The noble Elfe, and carefull Palmer drew
So nigh them, minding nought, but lustfull game,
That suddein forth they on them rusht, and threw
A subtile net, which onely for the same[131]
The skilfull Palmer formally did frame.   725
So held them under fast, the whiles the rest
Fled all away for feare of fowler shame.
The faire Enchauntresse, so unwares opprest,
Tryde all her arts, & all her sleights, thence out to wrest.

82

And eke her lover strove: but all in vaine;   730
For that same net so cunningly was wound,
That neither guile, nor force might it distraine.
They tooke them both, & both them strongly bound
In captive bandes, which there they readie found:
But her in chaines of adamant he tyde;   735
For nothing else might keepe her safe and sound;
But *Verdant* (so he hight) he soone untyde,[132]
And counsell sage in steed thereof to him applyde.

83

But all those pleasant bowres and Pallace brave,
Guyon broke downe, with rigour pittilesse;   740
Ne ought their goodly workmanship might save
Them from the tempest of his wrathfulnesse,
But that their blisse he turned to balefulnesse:
Their groves he feld, their gardins did deface,
Their arbers spoyle, their Cabinets supresse,[133]   745
Their banket houses burne, their buildings race,[134]
And of the fairest late, now made the fowlest place.

128 *moniments* marks of identification or commemoration.
129 *ra'st* razed; scraped to the metal.
130 *blend* blind.
131 *subtile net* like the net with which Hephaestus caught Ares in bed with his wife Aphrodite (*Odyssey* 8.272–84, pp. 261–2 below; *Metamorphoses* 4.176–84).
132 *hight* was named.
133 *Cabinets supresse* tear down their bowers.
134 *banket* banquet.

84

Then led they her away, and eke that knight
They with them led, both sorrowfull and sad:
The way they came, the same retourned they right,   750
Till they arrivèd, where they lately had
Charmed those wild-beasts, that raged with furie mad.
Which now awaking, fierce at them gan fly,
As in their mistresse reskew, whom they lad;[135]
But them the Palmer soone did pacify.   755
Then *Guyon* askt, what meant those beastes, which there did ly.

85

Sayd he, "These seeming beasts are men indeed,
Whom this Enchauntresse hath transformèd thus,
Whylome her lovers, which her lusts did feed,
Now turnèd into figures hideous,   760
According to their mindes like monstruous."
"Sad end," quoth he, "of life intemperate,
And mournefull meed of joyes delicious:
But, Palmer, if it mote thee so aggrate,
Let them returnèd be unto their former state."   765

86

Streight way he with his vertuous staffe them strooke,
And streight of beasts they comely men became;[136]
Yet being men they did unmanly looke,
And starèd ghastly, some for inward shame,
And some for wrath, to see their captive Dame: 770
But one above the rest in speciall,
That had an hog beene late, hight *Grille* by name,[137]
Repynèd greatly, and did him miscall,
That had from hoggish forme him brought to naturall.

87

Said *Guyon*, "See the mind of beastly man,   775
That hath so soone forgot the excellence
Of his creation, when he life began,
That now he chooseth, with vile difference,
To be a beast, and lacke intelligence."

135   *lad* led, in custody.
136   *streight . . . became* compare Circe's restoration of Odysseus' men, whom she had turned into pigs (*Odyssey* 10.388–96).

137   *Grille* Gryllus (Greek for *hog*), a companion of Odysseus who preferred to remain a pig; the story comes from a dialogue of Plutarch.

To whom the Palmer thus, "The donghill kind   780
Delights in filth and foule incontinence:
Let *Grill* be *Grill*, and have his hoggish minde,
But let us hence depart, whilest wether serves and wind."

Sir Philip Sidney (1554–1586)

On November 1, 1581, Lord Rich married Penelope Devereux, an 18-year-old woman whom Sidney's father had wished his son to marry. Sidney was by then a widely traveled diplomat and courtier. He knew many of the most powerful and many of the most learned men in Europe, and he had been writing poetry for some time. Along with Gabriel Harvey, Edmund Spenser's mentor, Sidney had been experimenting with writing English verse in classical meters, so he knew the classics well. He used the marriage of Rich and Devereux as the background for another poetic enterprise, a sequence of 108 sonnets from Astrophel (star lover) to Stella (star). Like all the many Elizabethan sonnet sequences, Sidney's work recalls the *Canzoniere* of Petrarch to his ideal beloved Laura, but it is also deeply indebted to classical poetry, such as Catullus' love lyrics and Ovid's *Amores* (pp. 329–36 and 416–28 below).

Like the *Amores*, Sidney's sonnet sequence begins with a poem about writing love poetry. Both poems contain jokes about metrical "feet" and other poetic devices, and both end up writing love poetry (allegedly) from the heart. Ovid overtly exposes the artificiality of this premise, whereas Sidney leaves it to the reader to draw that conclusion. Nevertheless, the sophisticated word-play and self-consciousness of Sidney's poem are quintessentially Ovidian. Both poets continue their focus on poetry for several poems, even withholding the names of their beloveds: Sidney breathes the name of Stella in number 3, and Ovid lets Corinna make her stately and sensual appearance in number 5 (p. 420 below). Throughout, Sidney is not as flippant as Ovid, and he invites readers to see his characters as real people – Astrophel as himself; Stella as Devereux; and anyone rich as Rich. However, he knew learned readers, like his friend Gabriel Harvey, would see shades of Ovid's Corinna in Stella, just as they would see Sidney as embodying the spirit of Ovid in an age perhaps more chaste but just as artful.

The text presented here is based on that found in *Sir P.S. His Astrophel and Stella. Wherein the excellence of sweete Poesie is concluded* (1591).

from *Astrophel and Stella*

1

Loving in truth, and fain my love in verse to show,[1]
That the dear *She*, might take some pleasure of my pain:
Pleasure might cause her read, reading might make her know,
Knowledge might pity win, and pity grace obtain.
   I sought fit words, to paint the blackest face of woe,   5
Studying inventions fine, her wits to entertain,[2]
Oft turning others' leaves, to see if thence would flow,[3]
Some fresh and fruitful shower, upon my Sun-burnt brain.
   But words came halting out, wanting invention's stay,
Invention, Nature's child, fled Stepdame study's blows: 10
And others' feet, still seemed but strangers in my way,[4]
Thus great with Child to speak, and helpless in my throws,
   Biting my tongue and pen, beating myself for spite:
"Fool," said my Muse to me, "look in thy heart and write."[5]

2

Not at first sight, nor with a dribbing shot,[1]   5
Love gave the wound, which while I breathe will bleed:[2]
But known, worth did in tract of time proceed,
Till by degrees it had full conquest got.
   I saw and liked, I liked but lovèd not,
I loved, but did not straight what Love decreed: 10
At length to Love's decrees, I first agreed.
Yet with repining at so partial lot.
   Now e'en that footstep of lost liberty
Is gone, and now like slave-born Muscovite:[3]
I call it praise to suffer tyranny,   15
And now employ the remnant of my wit
   To make myself believe that all is well,
While with a feeling skill I paint my hell.

ASTROPHEL AND STELLA 1

1 *fain* desiring.
2 *inventions* works of imagination such as poems.
3 *leaves* pages of books (Latin, *folia*).
4 *feet* metrical feet; syllables.
5 Compare Ovid's conversation with Cupid and his address to his Muse at the end of *Amores* 1.1 (p. 417 below).

ASTROPHEL AND STELLA 2

1 *dribbing shot* an arrow falling short of the mark.
2 *Love* Cupid, who is armed with a bow and arrows; compare Ovid, *Amores* 1.1 and 1.2 (pp. 416–19 below).
3 *slave-born Muscovite* Muscovy (Russia) was ruled at this time by Ivan the Terrible, an absolute monarch. In *Amores* 1.2, Ovid describes Cupid as an absolute emperor in whose triumphal train he must march.

3

Let Dainty wits cry on the Sisters nine,[1]
That bravely masked, their fancies may be told:[2]
Or Pindar's Apes flaunt in their phrases fine[3]
Enameling their pride with flowers of gold.[4]
   Or else let them in stately glory shine,   5
Ennobling newfound tropes, with problems old:
Or with strange similes, enrich each line,
Of herbs or beasts, which *Inde* or *Afric* hold.
   For me in sooth, no Muse but one I know,[5]
Phrases and Problems from my reach do grow,[6]   10
And strange things cost too dear for my poor sprites,
How then? even thus, in *Stella's* face I read,
   What love and beauty be, then all my deed
But copying is, what in her Nature writes.

47[1]

What, have I thus betrayed my liberty,
Can those black beams, such burning marks engrave[2]
In my free side, or am I born a slave,
Whose neck becomes such yoke of tyranny?[3]
   Or want I sense to feel my misery,   5
Or spirit, disdain of such disdain to have,
Who for long faith some gentle pity crave,
Yet get no alms, but scorn of beggary.
   Virtue awake; beauty but beauty is;[4]
I may, I must, I can, I will, I do   10
Leave following that which it is gain to miss,[5]
Let her go: soft, but there she comes; go to,[6]

ASTROPHEL AND STELLA 3

1 *Sisters nine* the Muses.

2 *bravely* splendidly; showily.

3 *Pindar* Greek lyric poet (518–after 446 BCE) famous for his elaborate odes in praise of victors in the pan-Hellenic games; *apes* imitators.

4 *flowers* a common metaphor for choice poems; *gold* may recall the classical phrase *carmina aurea* (golden verses), which was the title of verses ascribed to Pythagoras.

5 *no Muse but one I know* Likewise, Ovid in *Amores* 1.3 (p. 420 below) declares that he will always be faithful to his mistress and says, "Offer yourself to me as felicitous material for my poems."

6 *Phrases* set phrases or pithy expressions;

Problems "question[s] proposed for academic discussion" (*OED*).

ASTROPHEL AND STELLA 47

1 This poem recalls Catullus 8 (p. 333 below), in which the lover, out of favor with his beloved, exhorts himself to be detached and emotionally obdurate.

2 *beams* eyes.

3 *becomes* is suited to.

4 *Virtue* strength; spirit; manliness (Latin, *virtus*).

5 *Leave following* cf. Catullus 8, line 10, "Don't follow what flees. . . ."

6 *go to* an expression of remonstrance or protest.

Unkind, I love you not (O me) that I
Must make my heart thus give my tongue the lie.

83

Good brother *Phillip* I have forborne you long,[1]
I was content you should in favor creep,
While craftily you seemed your Cut to keep,[2]
As though that fair soft hand did you great wrong:
   I bear with envy, yet I hear your song,   5
When in her neck you did love ditties peep,
Nay (more fool I) oft suffered you to sleep,
In lily's nest where Love's self lies along,[3]
   What? doth high place ambitious thoughts augment?
Is sauciness reward of courtesy?[4]   10
Cannot such grace your silly self content,
But you must needs with those lips billing be?
   And through those lips drink Nectar from that tongue;
Leave that *Sir Phillip* lest your neck be wrung.

ASTROPHEL AND STELLA 83

1 *Phillip* the name of Stella's pet bird which balances on her finger, bills, and coos. This poem is clearly modeled on Catullus 2 (p. 330 below), which is addressed to Lesbia's pet sparrow. There are also some allusions to Catullus 3, on the death of the sparrow (p. 331 below). Numerous commentators and imitators of Catullus, from the poet Martial on, have read the sparrow as a double entendre for penis. Sidney has not exploited this tradition in an obvious way, but he must have been aware of it.

2 *Cut* lot in life; station.

3 *lily's nest* the beloved's bosom, which, of course, is lily white.

4 *sauciness* forwardness; impudence.

Sir Walter Ralegh (1554–1618)

Courtier, explorer, statesman, poet, and scholar, Ralegh was one of the most accomplished men of his age. How he managed to do so much is a mystery, but one of his biographers describes him as "an indefatigable Reader, whether by sea or Land."[1] "The Nymph's Reply to the Shepherd" is an answer to and a rebuttal of the charms of Christopher Marlowe's poem "The Passionate Shepherd to His Love" (p. 45 below). Ralegh's nymph says no to Marlowe's shepherd, rejecting his author's urbane call to country pleasures. Curiously, Ralegh employs *carpe diem* arguments (life is short) to argue against their conclusion (let us love). He deflates the buoyant urbanity of the pleasure-seeking Marlowe with references to the real state of things: time wastes flowers, luxurious clothes, love, and all other mortal things. Moreover, the alluring voice of the passionate shepherd thinly disguises the intemperate rapist in the allusion to Tereus, who in the terrible myth cut out the tongue of his victim Philomela. In the learned duel between Ralegh and Marlowe, the older man marshals the spirit of realistic satire to embarrass the poses struck by the younger's Theocritean and Virgilian personae. There is precedent for his anti-romantic procedure in Lucretius' diatribe against love (*De Rerum Natura* 4) and Ovid's witty *Remedia Amoris* (Remedies for Love). Similarly, Horace's *Odes* 1.33 addresses the poet Tibullus and chastises him for weeping over love and writing elegies when he ought to take a more realistic view of the world and himself.

The text is based on the one published anonymously in *England's Helicon* (1600).

Sir Walter Ralegh

1   Sir Robert Naunton; cited in *ODNB*.

The Nymph's Reply to the Shepherd

If all the world and love were young,
And truth in every Shepherd's tongue,
These pretty pleasures might me move
To live with thee, and be thy love.

But Time drives flocks from field to fold,   5
When rivers rage and rocks grow cold,
And *Philomel* becometh dumb,[1]
The rest complains of cares to come.

The flowers do fade and wanton fields
To wayward winter reckoning yields;   10
A honey tongue, a heart of gall,
Is fancy's spring, but sorrow's fall.

Thy gowns, thy shoes, thy beds of roses,
Thy cap, thy kirtle, and thy poesies,
Soon break, soon wither, soon forgotten;   15
In folly ripe, in reason rotten.

Thy belt of straw and ivy buds,
Thy coral clasps and amber studs,
All these to me no means can move
To come to thee, and be thy love.   20

But could youth last and love still breed,
Had joys no date nor age no need,
Then these delights my mind might move
To live with thee, and be thy love.

THE NYMPH'S REPLY TO THE SHEPHERD

1   *Philomel* the nightingale, into which Philomela was transformed after taking vengeance on Tereus for raping her and cutting out her tongue (Ovid, *Metamorphoses* 6.438–674). Ralegh imagines a second loss of voice for Philomel.

Christopher Marlowe (1564–1593)

John Greshop, the headmaster at King's School, Canterbury, was probably the first to introduce Marlowe to the classics. He is known to have copied books from Greshop's library as a young scholarship student on his way to Cambridge. He began his career as a writer at university, translating Ovid's *Amores* and Lucan's *Civil War*, or *Pharsalia*, before going to London and achieving great renown as a playwright. His murder at Deptford when he was 29 put an end to an immensely promising career, but his influence is widespread in the works of his exact contemporary William Shakespeare.

"The Passionate Shepherd to His Love" begins with an allusion to the first line of Catullus' *Carmen* 5, "Let us live, my Lesbia, and love" (p. 332 below). As a model for so much *carpe diem* poetry (lyric verse in which a lover beseeches his beloved to yield to passion, immediately), Catullus 5 may be the most frequently imitated poem in history. Marlowe's poem, however, is more fully and closely indebted to Theocritus 11 (p. 307 below). In this so-called "idyll" written by the founder of pastoral poetry, the Cyclops Polyphemus invites the sea nymph Galatea to marry him and entices her to leave the sea and join him in the paradise of his cave. Of course, Polyphemus is an ugly monster and the pleasures he offers are somewhat crude – cypresses, dark ivy, and cold water. His further temptations include a constant supply of sheep's milk, cute fawns, bear cubs, and flowers. The poem is a burlesque but charming imitation of a courtly lover's plea. Two hundred years later Virgil imitated it (in a more serious vein) in *Eclogue* 2 (p. 339 below), where the rustic Corydon yearns for the city-bred Alexis. Like the Cyclops, Corydon boasts (less convincingly) of his flocks and promises beautiful gifts of flowers and fruits: "Come hither, fair boy," he says, "look, the nymphs are bringing you lilies in full baskets . . ." (lines 45–8). Against the background of these classical models, however, Marlowe writes a poem fundamentally different in tone. His speaker is sophisticated and urbane; he displays his knowledge of the classics as he lightly assumes the role of the shepherd. He imagines himself beside his beloved among the rural folk, and he hears the birds sing courtly madrigals.

He promises elegant clothing with clasps and studs fashioned of natural materials, and he offers a fashionable seduction in a rustic retreat.

The text comes from *England's Helicon* (1600) where it appeared just before Ralegh's reply (p. 43 above).

The Passionate Shepherd to His Love

Come live with me, and be my love,
And we will all the pleasures prove,
That Valleys, groves, hills and fields,
Woods, or steepie mountain yields.

And we will sit upon the Rocks,   5
Seeing the Shepherds feed their flocks
By shallow Rivers, to whose falls
Melodious birds sing Madrigals.

And I will make thee beds of Roses,
And a thousand fragrant poesies,   10
A cap of flowers, and a kirtle,
Embroidered all with leaves of Myrtle.

A gown made of the finest wool,
Which from our pretty Lambs we pull,
Fair lined slippers for the cold,   15
With buckles of the purest gold.

A belt of straw and Ivy buds,
With Coral clasps and Amber studs,
And if these pleasures may thee move,
Come live with me, and be my love.   20

The Shepherds' Swains shall dance & sing
For thy delight each May morning.
If these delights thy mind may move,
Then live with me, and be my love.

William Shakespeare (1564–1616)

Shakespeare has for so long been England's most famous and most widely acclaimed author that it is difficult to believe he was not always so. However, despite immense success as a playwright in his lifetime, Shakespeare's reputation faltered in the next century because his works did not conform to neo-classical standards of decorum. He was seen as a natural genius "warbling his woodnotes wild," in Milton's phrase, but not as perfect and "artificial," in a good sense, as Ben Jonson. Part of what bolstered Shakespeare's reputation as a spontaneous "natural" was the belief that he was not learned in any academic sense. Ben Jonson described him as having "small Latin and less Greek," and succeeding generations took this to mean that he had no "book-learning." This is false, of course, and scholars have gradually made Shakespeare's admirers increasingly aware of his knowledge of the classics as well as plenty of other literature. His relationship to the classics is less academic than, say, Ben Jonson's, but it is equally strong in its way.

Like sonnet sequences from Petrarch's on, Shakespeare's has an uncertain relationship to the realities of his life, and it functions partly as a sketchbook for his other literary work. Love, passion, time, and, perhaps above all, poetry itself are the topics of his work. In addressing these problems in numerous ways across 154 poems, Shakespeare often draws on the classics, particularly Ovid and Horace. For example, Shakespeare's Sonnet 55 clearly recalls Horace, *Odes* 3.30. Horace's poem, an envoy for *Odes*, Books 1–3, makes bold claims for the immortality of both the body of poetry and its poet: "I have erected a monument more lasting than bronze . . ." (p. 401 below). Horace's claims were echoed a few years later by Ovid in his envoy to his *Metamorphoses*: "Now I have completed a work which neither the anger of Jupiter nor fire nor iron nor gnawing age can destroy. . . ." (p. 456 below). Parallels in the imagery and tone abound among all three poems, but Shakespeare's sonnet is a love poem, and his speaker, largely unlike classical lovers, conflates the immortality of his verse with that of his subject, his beloved. Between the first century CE and 1600, of course, other traditions of love poetry intervened to make Shakespeare's conflation possible, just as religious developments make possible, if not necessary, his substitution of the Christian idea of Judgment Day for Horace's pagan priest. However, though we see them through the prism of Christianity, the renaissance art of courtly love, and Shakespeare's own genius, Horace and Ovid are still clearly present in Shakespeare's sonnet.

The texts of the four sonnets presented here are based on the quarto edition of the sonnets published in 1609.

Sonnet 55

Not marble, nor the gilded monuments
Of Princes shall outlive this powerful rhyme,
But you shall shine more bright in these contents
Than unswept stone, besmeared with sluttish time.[1]
When wasteful war shall *Statues* overturn,   5
And broils root out the work of masonry,[2]
Nor *Mars* his sword, nor war's quick fire shall burn
The living record of your memory.
'Gainst death, and all oblivious enmity[3]
Shall you pace forth; your praise shall still find room,   10
Even in the eyes of all posterity
That wear this world out to the ending doom.[4]
So till the judgment that yourself arise,[5]
You live in this, and dwell in lovers' eyes.

Sonnet 60

Like as the waves make towards the pebbled shore,
So do our minutes hasten to their end,
Each changing place with that which goes before,
In sequent toil all forwards do contend.[1]
Nativity once in the main of light,   5
Crawls to maturity, wherewith being crowned,
Crooked eclipses 'gainst his glory fight,
And time that gave, doth now his gift confound.[2]

SONNET 55

1 *sluttish* dirty, unkempt.
2 *broils* tumults; turmoil.
3 *oblivious* causing or associated with oblivion, forgetfulness.
4 *doom* judgment or Judgment Day (Dooms-day), the day of final reckoning when, according to the Book of Revelation, God will judge all souls, the quick and the dead.

5 *arise* rise up from the grave for Judgment Day and thence to heaven.

SONNET 60

1 The first four lines derive from Ovid, *Metamorphoses* 15.181–5 (p. 454 below).
2 Lines 5–8 possibly echo the same speech, which in one memorable sequence runs through the seasons and the ages of man: *Metamorphoses* 15.199–227 (p. 455 below).

Time doth transfix the flourish set on youth,
And delves the parallels in beauty's brow,   10
Feeds on the rarities of nature's truth,
And nothing stands but for his scythe to mow.
And yet to times in hope, my verse shall stand
Praising thy worth, despite his cruel hand.

Sonnet 74[1]

But be contented when that fell arrest
Without all bail shall carry me away,
My life hath in this line some intèrest,
Which for memorial still with thee shall stay.
When thou reviewest this, thou doest review   5
The very part was consecrate to thee,
The earth can have but earth, which is his due,
My spirit is thine the better part of me,
So then thou hast but lost the dregs of life,
The prey of worms, my body being dead,   10
The coward conquest of a wretch's knife,
Too base of thee to be rememberèd;
The worth of that, is that which it contains,
And that is this, and this with thee remains.

Sonnet 77[1]

Thy glass will show thee how thy beauties were,[2]
Thy dial how thy precious minutes waste,[3]
The vacant leaves thy mind's imprint will bear,

SONNET 74

1   Like Sonnet 55, number 74 seems indebted to the end of Ovid's *Metamorphoses*. Shakespeare's speaker addresses his beloved, whereas the author of Ovid's poem is talking to himself; but the passages share a fatalistic acceptance of death, a sense that earth can only claim the body, while the spirit lives on, and a belief that enduring poetry immortalizes the poet.

SONNET 77

1   Like Horace's ode to Ligurinus (4.10; p. 402 below), Sonnet 77 is addressed to a young man with whom the speaker is in love. Both poems warn the youth that his beauty will soon fade, and both urge him to witness his demise in a mirror. Both poems also look forward to the youth's moment of recognition and his painful acquisition of self-knowledge. The tone of both poems is somewhat resentful, and both speakers relish the prospect of the youth's shocking discovery. Shakespeare's poem adds to the mirror a second device of recognition – a notebook, whose blank leaves shall receive the youth's fearful thoughts and impress them further upon him.

2   *glass* mirror.
3   *dial* sundial.

And of this book, this learning may'st thou taste.
The wrinkles which thy glass will truly show,   5
Of mouthèd graves will give thee memory,
Thou by thy dial's shady stealth may'st know,
Time's thievish progress to eternity.
Look what thy memory cannot contain,[4]
Commit to these waste blacks, and thou shalt find[5]   10
Those children nursed, delivered from thy brain,
To take a new acquaintance of thy mind.
These offices, so oft as thou wilt look,[6]
Shall profit thee and much enrich thy book.

4   *Look what* whatever (*OED*, s.v. *look* I.4.b).

5   *blacks* many editors think this word should be *blanks*; it refers to the empty pages of the book given to the addressee by the speaker of the sonnet. It is possible that the blank book was ornamented with a mirror and a dial or clock face of some kind.

6   *offices* the duties of writing and contemplating what is written in the book.

Thomas Campion
(1567–1620)

In *Observations in the Art of English Poesie*, Campion made the case for writing English verse according to the rules of classical metrics – that is, by paying attention to the length of each syllable as well as its stress. As a musician, he was particularly sensitive to the rhythms of poetry, and he attempted, as he said, to "couple . . . Words and Notes lovingly together."[1] Many of his poems are songs. Campion also wrote Latin poetry, and he was deeply conversant with the tradition of Latin love poetry, though his writing is usually more modest than that of the poets whom he imitates.

The title and first stanza of the following poem mark it as an imitation of Catullus 5 (p. 332 below), but Campion omits the second half of Catullus' poem, which is all about kisses, and replaces it with poetry derived from Propertius and Tibullus. The second stanza seems directly indebted to Propertius 2.15.41–8 (p. 413 below), though Tibullus says similar things about the power of love to extinguish martial ambition and end war. The final stanza recalls the frequent occasions on which Propertius and Tibullus envision their own deaths and their girlfriends' behavior at the funeral. The closest parallel is Propertius 2.13, where the poet imagines being buried with three books of poetry while Cynthia presses final kisses on his lips. Normally, of course, those who survive their lover the poet are unhappy; Campion's mourners, however, are "lovers, rich in triumph"; they grace the poet's tomb with their amorous "pastimes," suggesting that his death, like the Lord's, is a triumph of love, though in this case the love is more erotic than religious.

The text is based on its publication in *A Booke of Ayres* (1601).

THOMAS CAMPION

1   *Two Bookes of Ayres*, cited in *ODNB*.

My Sweetest Lesbia

My sweetest Lesbia, let us live and love,[1]
And, though the sager sort our deeds reprove,
Let us not weigh them; heav'n's great lamps do dive
Into their west, and straight again revive,
But, soon as once set is our little light,   5
Then must we sleep one ever-during night.

If all would lead their lives in love like me,
Then bloody swords and armor should not be,
No drum nor trumpet peaceful sleeps should move,
Unless alarm came from the camp of love: 10
But fools do live, and waste their little light,
And seek with pain their ever-during night.

When timely death my life and fortune ends,
Let not my hearse be vexed with mourning friends,
But let all lovers, rich in triumph, come,   15
And with sweet pastimes grace my happy tomb;
And, Lesbia, close up thou my little light,
And crown with love my ever-during night.

MY SWEETEST LESBIA

1   *Lesbia* the addressee of Catullus 5.

John Donne (1572–1631)

Born a Catholic, Donne eventually became a Church of England priest and the author of numerous works of divinity including a large body of brilliant sermons. He spent some time at Hart Hall, Oxford, but he was more rigorously trained at Lincoln's Inn in law. He wrote many religious as well as secular poems, most of them probably dating from his rakish youth before his secret marriage to Ann More in 1601. He shows his knowledge of the classics in all of his writings. His so-called "Songs and Sonnets" (though there is only one formal 14-line sonnet among them) show the influence of Ovid, particularly his *Amores*, which had recently been translated by Christopher Marlowe (p. 416 below). Donne's "Elegies" and "Satires" also follow classical forms, referring not to mournful or mocking poems but to the shorter and longer verse forms indicated by those words among the ancients. The self-assured and challenging address implicit in Donne's tone is unmistakably his own but it is deeply indebted to the sophisticated burlesque of epic forms in Ovid.

The Sun Rising

The speaker in Ovid's *Amores* 1.13 (p. 421 below) begs Aurora not to rise so he can spend more time in bed with his lover. Donne rewrites his request as a bullying demand of the universe. He abuses the sun itself, not merely a demigod representing the sun, and in so doing he belittles all upon whom the sun shines. Ovid lists other people (schoolboys and farmers) as examples of the sun's victims, but Donne bids the sun go wake others while making an exception of him and his love. Ovid gives an attractive picture of a variety of occupations alongside that of the lover. Donne scornfully dismisses other callings and other lives: "Nothing else is."

Our text of "The Sun Rising" is based on the 1635 edition of Donne's poems.

Busy old fool, unruly Sun,
    Why dost thou thus,
Through windows, and through curtains call on us?[1]
Must to thy motions lovers' seasons run?
    Saucy pedantic wretch, go chide   5
    Late schoolboys, and sour prentices,[2]
  Go tell Court-huntsmen, that the King will ride,
  Call country ants to harvest offices;
Love, all alike, no season knows, nor clime,
Nor hours, days, months, which are the rags of time.   10

    Thy beams, so reverend, and strong
    Why shouldst thou think?
I could eclipse and cloud them with a wink,
But that I would not lose her sight so long:
    If her eyes have not blinded thine,   15
    Look, and to morrow late, tell me,
  Whether both th' Indias of spice and Mine
  Be where thou leftst them, or lie here with me.
Ask for those Kings whom thou saw'st yesterday,
And thou shalt hear, All here in one bed lay.   20

    She's all States, and all Princes, I,
    Nothing else is.
Princes do but play us; compared to this,
All honour's mimic; All wealth alchemy;
    Thou sun art half as happy'as we,   25
    In that the world's contracted thus.
  Thine age asks ease, and since thy duties be
  To warm the world, that's done in warming us.
Shine here to us, and thou art everywhere;
This bed thy centre is, these walls, thy sphere.[3]   30

Elegy 19: *To His Mistress Going to Bed*

In his elegies Donne employs rhyming couplets as an English equivalent of the unrhymed but symmetrical elegiac couplets of Latin poetry. He also imitates, in his own accents, the style of the classical elegy: concise, witty, clever, logically and

THE SUN RISING

1 *Busy . . . us?* compare Ovid *Amores* 1.13.3 (p. 422 below), "whither are you hurrying, Aurora?"

2 *schoolboys* compare Ovid *Amores* 1.13.17 (p. 422 below), "you deprive boys of sleep and hand them over to teachers."

3 *sphere* the spherical region in which the sun traveled in the Ptolemaic system of astronomy.

verbally playful, and even more dramatic and intellectual than the classical models. Ovid's elegies, or *Amores*, provide the patterns for Donne. Although some other classical poems have some of its elements,[1] the inspiration for *Elegy* 19 is clearly *Amores* 1.5 (p. 420 below), a highly erotic poem in which Ovid describes a sexual encounter with Corinna on a hot summer afternoon. Donne expresses the same frank interest in sex, although he is less direct than Ovid in describing the physical features of his lover. Whereas Ovid lists shoulders, arms, and breasts "fit to be squeezed," for example, Donne speaks of removing garments and uses double entendre to propose or demand sexual congress. Ovid's poem is a little narrative. It begins with atmospheric scene setting, proceeds to stripping, and concludes with sex. Donne's poem is more intellectual, and his speaker is as concerned to display himself (the erections of his imagination and his body) as his tempting beloved.

The text is based on that included in *Poems by J. D.* (1633), but we have benefitted from the work of later editors, including H. J. C. Grierson.

> Come, Madam, come, all rest my powers defy,
> Until I labour, I in labour lie.[2]
> The foe oft times, having the foe in sight,
> Is tir'd with standing, though he never fight. [3]
> Off with that girdle, like heaven's Zone glistering,[4]   5
> But a far fairer world encompassing.
> Unpin that spangled breastplate, which you wear,
> That th' eyes of busy fools might be stopt there;
> Unlace yourself, for that harmonious chime
> Tells me from you, that now 'tis your bedtime.   10
> Off with that happy busk, which I envy,[5]
> That still can be, and still can stand so nigh.
> Your gown going off such beauteous state reveals,
> As when from flowry meads th' hill's shadow steals.
> Off with your wiry Coronet, and show   15
> The hairy Diadem which on your head doth grow:
> Now off with those shoes, and then softly tread
> In this love's hallowed temple, this soft bed.
> In such white robes heaven's Angels used to be
> Revealed to men; thou Angel bring'st with thee   20

ELEGY 19

1 Propertius 2.15 (p. 412 below) celebrates nudity, and 1.2, like *Elegy* 19, compares natural beauty favorably with that of mere jewels.

2 *labour* sexual activity in one sense and pain in the other.

3 *The foe . . . fight* military analogies to love are common in Ovid (e.g., *Amores* 1.9).

4 *girdle* belt; *heaven's Zone* the belt of Orion, part of a constellation in the northern sky.

5 *busk* corset or the whale bone that keeps it rigid.

A heaven like Mahomet's Paradise; and though[6]
Ill spirits walk in white, we easily know
By this, these Angels from an evil sprite;
Those set our hairs, but these our flesh upright.
   License my roving hands, and let them go   25
Behind, before, between, above, below.
Oh my America! my new-found-land!
My Kingdom's safest when with one man manned.
My Mine of precious stones! my Emperie![7]
How am I blest in thus discovering thee!   30
To enter in those bonds is to be free;
Then where my hand is set, my seal shall be.[8]
   Full nakedness! all joys are due to thee;
As souls unbodied, bodies unclothed must be,
To taste whole joys. Gems, which you women use,   35
Are, as At'lanta's balls, cast in men's views;[9]
That when a fool's eye lighteth on a Gem,
His earthly soul might covet that, not them:
Like pictures or like books' gay coverings made
For laymen, are all women thus arrayed.   40
Themselves are only mystic books, which we[10]
(Whom their imputed grace will dignify)
Must see revealed. Then since that I may know,
As liberally as to thy Midwife show
Thyself; cast all, yea that white linen hence;   45
There is no penance due to innocence.
To teach thee, I'll be naked first; why, then
What needs thou have more covering than a man?

6 *Mahomet's Paradise* a heavenly garden of delights.
7 *Emperie* territory ruled by an emperor.
8 *seal* a wax seal indicating ownership, with a pun on sexual congress.
9 *At'lanta's balls* golden apples dropped by Hippomenes to distract Atalanta in a foot race to determine whether she would marry him; Donne takes the distracting baubles out of context and has them beguile men rather than the female Atalanta.
10 *we* initiates in love, opposed to *laymen*.

Ben Jonson (1572–1637)

Like John Dryden, George Herbert, and several other important poets of the seventeenth century, Ben Jonson learned Latin and Greek at the Westminster School in London. Instead of going to university after school, however, Jonson labored as a bricklayer in his stepfather's business and fought in the lowlands as a soldier. In 1592 he returned to London and took up work in the theater as an indifferent actor but a better director and a brilliant playwright. His earliest play imitated Plautus, and though his later comedies are more original, they all have a strong classical bent. *Epicoene, or the Silent Woman*, for example, makes much use of Juvenal's sixth satire. Jonson's tragedies – *Sejanus* and *Catiline his Conspiracy* – are even more explicitly Roman. In *Of Dramatic Poesy, An Essay* (1668), John Dryden discussed the dependence of English poets on classical writers and beautifully described the experience of reading Jonson, when one is aware of the classical background: "You track him everywhere in their snow."

In 1616 Jonson published his works in an impressive folio that, with the death of Shakespeare in that year, solidified his reputation as England's greatest poet. Unlike Shakespeare, Jonson was careful of the way he appeared in print and was transmitted to posterity. His folio presents him as a versatile poet, not only as a dramatist, and includes two collections of his verse: *Epigrams* and *The Forest*. Both titles are full of classical resonance, the first recalling the collections of Martial and the second the *Silvae* of Statius. *Silvae* means woods or forest but also raw material and, metaphorically, a miscellaneous collection.

To Penshurst, the longer of our two selections from Jonson, is part of *The Forest*, and it recalls Statius, *Silvae* 1.3 and 2.2. These are both long and laudatory villa descriptions, a poetic genre Statius may have invented, although there are prose equivalents (e.g., Pliny, *Epistles* 5.6).[1] Jonson is calmer and less hyperbolic than Statius. In fact, he is working against the grain of Statius, even as he imitates him,

BEN JONSON

1 See Carole Newlands, "Statius' Villa Poems and Ben Jonson's *To Penshurst*: The Shaping of a Tradition," *Classical and Modern Literature* 8 (1988), 291–300.

because many of the things that Statius praises in Roman villas are precisely those grand features that Penshurst lacks – lavish decorations, gold, marble, large halls, wonderful feats of engineering, and heated baths. What it lacks in grandeur, however, Penshurst supplies in the character of its inhabitants and its suitability to their refined tastes and interests. Statius also treats character; in 2.2, for example, a villa overlooking the sea is described as an appropriate bastion of philosophy ruled by a sage and his noble wife. Jonson's poem takes a moral tone, however, that brings it closer to the work of Horace than of Statius. In several of his *Odes*, Horace describes his Sabine farm as an embodiment of a philosophy of life based on contentment with what is sufficient, on friendship, hospitality, literature, love, even to the exclusion of wealth, position, and political power. This philosophy of place is implicit in *Odes* 2.18 (p. 398 below), an important source for Jonson's poem, though it is more explicitly stated in other poems, such as *Satires* 2.6 (which includes the town and country mouse fable; p. 388 below). The tone of Jonson's praise of county life is also found in *Epode* 2, which Jonson translated (p. 393 below), as well as in Virgil, *Georgics* 2 (p. 357 below). Like these classical poems, *Penshurst* idealizes agriculture (dwelling on the aesthetics of nature and its fruits rather than the labor of farming) and sees the homestead as a place of beauty, abundance, peace, and unblemished morality.

The ideal picture, however, may be slightly marred by the presence as a source of Martial, *Epigrams* 3.58 (p. 466 below). In this poem Martial contrasts Faustinus' country place and Bassus' suburban villa. The latter has pretensions to being a country place, but it is gaudy and unproductive. Faustinus' place is a model estate. No space is wasted. Everything is devoted to agricultural production. It is to Bassus' villa as Horace's Sabine farm is to the sterile mansions of the rich. As the notes below show, Jonson frequently followed Martial in the arrangement of details in *Penshurst*. He also alludes to another Martial epigram at the end of *Penshurst* (see n. 34 below). As always, Martial's tone is somewhat ironic. Faustinus' place is at Baiae – a rich resort – but he "delights in the true and unsophisticated countryside." There's a laughable boutique quality to the rural perfectionism of Faustinus' place, as though it were a theme park rather than a real farm. Such irony is not present in Jonson, but the allusions to Martial give it an opening in the informed reader's reception of the poem. It may be that Jonson is confident enough as a poet to incorporate Martial's poetic material into his work without sharing his tone. But Jonson is also subtle, and he has a certain urbanity of tone that seems at times to add a knowing wink to his performance and to make audible the keener notes of Martial's verse without departing from the dominant Horatian tone.

The text presented here is based on the first folio of Jonson's *Works* (1616).

To Penshurst

Thou art not, Penshurst, built to envious show,[1]
Of touch, or marble; nor canst boast a row[2]
Of polished pillars, or a roof of gold:
Thou hast no lantern, whereof tales are told;[3]
Or stair, or courts; but stand'st an ancient pile,[4]   5
And these grudged at, art reverenced the while.
Thou joy'st in better marks, of soil, of air,
Of wood, of water: therein thou art fair.
Thou hast thy walks for health, as well as sport:
Thy *Mount*, to which the *Dryads* do resort,[5]   10
Where Pan, and Bacchus their high feasts have made,[6]
Beneath the broad beech, and the chestnut shade;[7]
That taller tree, which of a nut was set,
At his great birth, where all the *Muses* met.[8]
There, in the writhèd bark, are cut the names   15
Of many a Sylvan, taken with his flames.[9]
And thence, the ruddy *Satyrs* oft provoke[10]
The lighter *Fauns*, to reach thy *Lady's oak*.[11]
Thy copse, too, named of Gamage, thou hast there,[12]
That never fails to serve thee seasoned deer,   20
When thou would'st feast, or exercise thy friends.
The lower land, that to the river bends,
Thy sheep, thy bullocks, kine, and calves do feed:[13]
The middle grounds thy mares, and horses breed.
Each bank doth yield thee conies; and the tops[14]   25
Fertile of wood, Ashour, and Sidney's copse,
To crown thy open table, doth provide

To Penshurst

1 *Penshurst* the estate in Kent of Robert Sidney, later earl of Leicester. Lines 1–8 are closely modeled on Horace, *Odes* 2.18.1–10 (p. 398 below), syntactically as well as in content.
2 *touch* touchstone, black marble or basalt.
3 *lantern* an architectural feature of various shapes at the top of some houses that admits light or serves for ventilation.
4 *stair* grand staircase; *pile* a small castle.
5 *Dryads* tree nymphs.
6 *Pan* the shepherds' god; *Bacchus* god of wine and revelry.
7 *broad beech* an allusion to Virgil, *Eclogues* 1.1, which depicts the shepherd Tityrus "reclining beneath the cover of a broad beech."

8 *his* refers to Sir Philip Sidney (1554–1586), courtier, poet, and elder brother of Robert.
9 *Sylvan* a forest deity or a courtier in love who, inspired by Sidney's love sonnets, inscribes the bark of a tree.
10 *Satyrs* goat-footed spirits of the wild.
11 *Fauns* the Roman equivalent of satyrs; *Lady's oak* a tree on the estate so named because a lady once went into labor beneath its branches.
12 *copse* a small wood; *Gamage* the maiden name of Robert Sidney's wife.
13 *kine* cows.
14 *conies* rabbits; *tops* hill tops.

The purpled pheasant, with the speckled side:
The painted partridge lies in every field,[15]
And, for thy mess, is willing to be killed.[16]   30
And if the high swoll'n *Medway* fail thy dish,[17]
Thou hast thy ponds, that pay thee tribute fish,
Fat, agèd carps, that run into thy net.
And pikes, now weary their own kind to eat,
As loath, the second draught, or cast to stay,[18]   35
Officiously, at first, themselves betray.[19]
Bright eels, that emulate them, and leap on land,
Before the fisher, or into his hand.
Then hath thy orchard fruit, thy garden flowers,
Fresh as the air, and new as are the hours.   40
The early cherry, with the later plum,
Fig, grape, and quince, each in his time doth come:
The blushing apricot, and woolly peach
Hang on thy walls, that every child may reach.
And though thy walls be of the country stone,   45
They're reared with no man's ruin, no man's groan,[20]
There's none, that dwell about them, wish them down;
But all come in, the farmer, and the clown:[21]
And no one empty-handed, to salute
Thy lord, and lady, though they have no suit.[22]   50
Some bring a capon, some a rural cake,
Some nuts, some apples; some that think they make
The better cheeses, bring 'hem; or else send
By their ripe daughters, whom they would commend
This way to husbands; and whose baskets bear   55
An emblem of themselves, in plum, or pear.
But what can this (more than express their love)
Add to thy free provisions, far above
The neede of such? whose liberal board doth flow,
With all, that hospitality doth know!   60
Where comes no guest, but is allowed to eat,
Without his fear, and of thy lord's own meat:
Where the same beer, and bread, and self-same wine,

---

15 *painted partridge* translating Martial's *picta perdix* (3.58.15).
16 *mess* meal; *willing* a piece of flattery perhaps taken from Juvenal 4.69, *ipse capi voluit,* "it wished to be caught" (speaking of a fish), though Martial also speaks of the power of his honorees to influence animals.
17 *Medway* the river Medway runs through the property.
18 *loath . . . to stay* unwilling to wait for the net to be thrown a second time.
19 *Officiously* dutifully.
20 *They're . . . groan* unlike houses in Horace *Odes* 2.18 (lines 23–8) that are built on land taken from poor tenants.
21 *clown* rustic; country laborer.
22 *suit* formal request.

That is his Lordship's, shall be also mine.[23]
And I not fain to sit (as some, this day,[24]   65
At great men's tables) and yet dine away.
Here no man tells my cups; nor, standing by,[25]
A waiter, doth my gluttony envy:
But gives me what I call, and lets me eat,
He knows, below, he shall find plenty of meat;   70
Thy tables hoard not up for the next day,
Nor, when I take my lodging, need I pray
For fire, or lights, or livery: all is there;[26]
As if thou, then, wert mine, or I reigned here:
There's nothing I can wish, for which I stay.[27]   75
That found King James, when hunting late, this way,
With his brave son, the Prince, they saw thy fires[28]
Shine bright on every hearth as the desires
Of thy *Penates* had been set on flame,[29]
To entertain them; or the country came,   80
With all their zeal, to warm their welcome here.
What (great, I will not say, but) sodayne cheer[30]
Did'st thou, then, make 'hem! and what praise was heaped
On thy good lady, then! who, therein, reaped
The just reward of her high huswifery;   85
To have her linen, plate, and all things nigh,
When she was far: and not a room, but dressed,
As if it had expected such a guest!
These, Penshurst, are thy praise, and yet not all.
Thy lady's noble, fruitful, chaste withal.   90
His children thy great lord may call his own:
A fortune, in this age, but rarely known.[31]
They are, and have been taught religion: Thence
Their gentler spirits have sucked innocence.
Each morn, and even, they are taught to pray,   95
With the whole household, and may, every day,
Read, in their virtuous parents' noble parts,[32]

23 *Without . . . mine* the idea is latent in Martial 3.58.42 (p. 467 below), but Jonson probably recalled Juvenal's elaborate contrast between a patron's and his clients' dinner servings (*Satire* 5).
24 *fain* glad or desirous.
25 *tells* counts.
26 *livery* dispensing of food and provisions.
27 *stay* wait.
28 *Prince* Henry who died in 1612, well before his father King James I (1566–1625).
29 *Penates* Roman household gods, often represented by small statues kept near the hearth.
30 *sodayne*   sudden,   instant,   spur-of-the-moment.
31 *but rarely known* a satirical touch reminiscent of Juvenal's condemnation of contemporary Roman women (*Satire* 6) (p. 472 below).
32 *parts* good qualities.

The mysteries of manners, arms, and arts.
Now, Penshurst, they that will proportion thee[33]
With other edifices, when they see 100
Those proud, ambitious heaps, and nothing else,
May say, their lords have built, but thy lord dwells.[34]

Inviting a Friend to Supper

The invitation poem was a minor genre of Greek epigram; the best is by Philodemus (*Greek Anthology* 11.44). Roman poets took it up, however, and worked it up into something more substantial. Important examples include Catullus 13 (p. 334 below), Horace, *Odes* 1.20, 3.29, 4.12, *Epistle* 1.5 (p. 403 below), and Martial 5.78, 10.48, and 11.52 (pp. 468, 469, and 470 below). The invitation is a vehicle for humor, friendship, and self-portraiture. Catullus 13, though not a direct influence on Jonson's poem, set the standard. As indicated in our notes, there are direct echoes of Martial in Jonson's contribution to the genre. As usual, however, Jonson's manner and tone are closer to Horace, even though specific correspondences in this case are lacking. The poem appears as number 101 among Jonson's "Epigrammes" in his collected *Workes* (1616), the source of our text.

Tonight, grave sir, both my poor house, and I
Do equally desire your company:
Not that we think us worthy such a guest,
But that your worth will dignify our feast,
With those that come; whose grace may make that seem 5
Something, which, else, could hope for no esteem.
It is the fair acceptance, Sir, creates
The entertainment perfect: not the cates.[1]
Yet shall you have, to rectify your palate,[2]
An olive, capers, or some better salad 10
Ush'ring the mutton; with a short-leg'd hen,
If we can get her, full of eggs, and then,
Lemons, and wine for sauce: to these, a coney[3]
Is not to be despaired of, for our money;

33 *proportion* compare favorably.
34 *their ... dwells* compare Martial 12.50.8, *quam bene non habitas*, "how well you don't dwell there!" – words spoken to a man who has built a luxury villa with "no place for dining or sleep."

INVITING A FRIEND TO SUPPER

1 *It ... cates* compare Martial 5.78.16, "you will make the wine good by drinking it"; *cates* cakes.
2 *rectify* purify.
3 *coney* rabbit.

And, though fowl, now, be scarce, yet there are clerks,[4]   15
The sky not falling, think we may have larks.
I'll tell you of more, and lie, so you will come:[5]
Of partridge, pheasant, woodcock, of which some
May yet be there; and godwit, if we can:[6]
Knat, raile, and ruffe too. How so ere, my man[7]   20
Shall read a piece of VIRGIL, TACITUS,[8]
LIVY, or of some better book to us,[9]
Of which we'll speak our minds, amidst our meat;
And I'll profess no verses to repeat:[10]
To this, if ought appear, which I know not of,   25
That will the pastry, not my paper, show of.[11]
Digestive cheese, and fruit there sure will be;
But that, which most doth take my *Muse*, and me,
Is a pure cup of rich *Canary*-wine,[12]
Which is the *Mermaids*, now, but shall be mine: 30
Of which had HORACE, or ANACREON tasted,[13]
Their lives, as do their lines, till now had lasted.
Tobacco, Nectar, or the *Thespian* spring,[14]
Are all but LUTHER's beer, to this I sing.[15]
Of this we will sup free, but moderately,   35
And we will have no *Pooly,* or *Parrot* by;[16]
Nor shall our cups make any guilty men:[17]
But, at our parting, we will be, as when
We innocently met. No simple word,
That shall be uttered at our mirthful board,   40
Shall make us sad next morning: or affright
The liberty, that we'll enjoy to night.

---

4   *clerks* scholars or bookish men, engaged here in foolish prognostication.

5   *lie* compare Martial 11.52.13, "I'll lie so that you'll come."

6   *godwit* a marsh bird.

7   *Knat, rail, and ruffe* various species of birds; *man* servant.

8   *Tacitus* historian of the early Roman empire. Compare Juvenal 11.180–1, "The author of the *Iliad* will be recited [at a dinner party] and the poems of sublime Virgil which make the palm of victory doubtful."

9   *Livy* author of a history of Rome from its foundation to the time of Augustus.

10   *profess* vow.

11   *To this . . . show of* the only writing of his own displayed at dinner will be what is written in icing on the pastry. In his invitations Martial promises that "the host will not read a thick book" (5.78.25) and "I'll recite nothing to you" (11.52.16).

12   *Canary-wine* a light sweet wine from the Canary Islands.

13   *Anacreon* Greek lyric poet famous for his drinking poems.

14   *Thespian spring* Thespiae was a city near Mt. Helicon, site of the springs Hippocrene and Aganippe which were sacred to the Muses.

15   *Luther's* Martin Luther's, i.e. German.

16   *Pooly, or Parrot* Polly, a name for a Parrot; a fool or dimwit, or perhaps a stool pigeon or spy.

17   *cups* drinking or drunkenness. Compare Martial 10.48.21–4 (p. 469 below), which Jonson also echoes in the last five lines of the poem.

Robert Herrick
(1591–1674)

In 1647 Herrick was driven from his post as curate of Dean Priory in Devonshire by the success of the Parliamentary side. He returned with some joy to his native London and the next year published *Hesperides, or, The Works both Humane & Divine of Robert Herrick Esq.* This carefully collected and arranged book of 1,130 poems was an early attempt by a writer to present his whole body of work to the public. Herrick's avowed poetic masters were Ben Jonson, who had also taken care in the presentation of his collected works, and Horace. Herrick's poetry delights in country things and in the sensual pleasures of life. He draws on his experiences in Devon, of course, but the way he writes about them is deeply indebted to classical writers of pastoral and love poetry.

"To the Virgins, to Make Much of Time" may be the most famous and influential *carpe diem* poem in English. It draws on Asclepiades (*Greek Anthology* 5.85; p. 299 below), Catullus 5 (p. 332 below), Horace, *Odes* 4.10 (p. 402 below) and 1.11 (p. 396 below), where the phrase *carpe diem* first appears. However, though there are hints of seduction in *Odes* 1.11 and especially in 4.10, *carpe diem* is in Horace more an exhortation to drink than an invitation to sex. Herrick's comparison between the sun's course and human life, which seems deeply traditional, echoes Catullus 5, although Catullus emphasizes the ability of the sun to rise again after setting. The image from the most famous line of Herrick's poem may come from a more obscure source, a poem doubtfully ascribed to Ausonius called *De Rosis Nascentibus*, "On Blooming Roses." The poem ends with the sage advice:

> Young ladies, gather rosebuds while both the rose
> And you are young, for life too soon ends.[1]

ROBERT HERRICK

1 Compare also Spenser, *Faerie Queene* 2.12.75

(p. 33 above): "Gather therefore the Rose, whilest yet is prime."

Unlike the speaker of the Latin poem, Herrick does not tell his listeners that maidens may share in the regenerative abilities of roses.

"To His Muse" is part of the rich vein of verse in *Hesperides* that is concerned introspectively with the poet and his book. Herrick worries about his position in the country and his immersion in country things; he thinks of what he is missing at court; but he usually decides he is better off where he is. In this poem, Herrick uses Martial 1.3 (p. 465 below) as his pattern, echoing the Roman's address to his book and the idea of being "safer at home." However, Herrick expresses a tension in this poem that runs throughout the *Hesperides* when he alludes to the contrast between the sometimes serious and momentous *Eclogues* of Virgil and the lighter *Bucolics* of Theocritus. Herrick needs, it appears, to rein in his muse and keep her close, suggesting that part of his discipline as a poet and a man is to teach himself a contented modesty against the temptations of the court, fame, and politics.

To the Virgins, to Make Much of Time

Gather ye Rosebuds while ye may,
    Old Time is still a flying:[1]
And this same flower that smiles to day
    Tomorrow will be dying.

The glorious Lamp of Heaven, the Sun,   5
    The higher he's a getting;
The sooner will his Race be run,[2]
    And nearer he's to Setting.

That Age is best, which is the first,
    When Youth and Blood are warmer;   10
But being spent, the worse, and worst
    Times, still succeed the former.

Then be not coy, but use your time;
    And while ye may, go marry:
For having lost but once your prime,   15
    You may forever tarry.

TO THE VIRGINS, TO MAKE MUCH OF TIME

1 *Time is still a flying* a translation of the phrase *tempus fugit*, which is first found in Virgil (*Georgics* 3.284); Horace includes a variation of it in the original *carpe diem* poem, *Odes* 1.11 (p. 396 below).

2 *Race* alluding to the classical conception of the sun as a chariot driven by the sun god.

To His Muse

Whither *Mad maiden* wilt thou roam?
Far safer 'twere to stay at home:
Where thou mayst sit, and piping please
The poor and private *Cottages*.
Since *Cots*, and *Hamlets*, best agree   5
With this thy meaner Minstrelsy.
There with the Reed, thou mayst express[1]
The Shepherd's Fleecy happiness:
And with thy *Eclogues* intermix[2]
Some smooth, and harmless *Bucolics*.[3]   10
There on a Hillock thou mayst sing
Unto a handsome Shepherdling;
Or to a Girl (that keeps the Neat)[4]
With breath more sweet than Violet.
There, there (perhaps) such Lines as these   15
May take the simple *Villages*.
But for the Court, the Country wit
Is despicable unto it.
Stay then at home, and do not go
Or fly abroad to seek for woe.[5]   20
Contempts in Courts and Cities dwell;
No *Critic* haunts the Poor man's Cell:[6]
Where thou mayst hear thine own Lines read
By no one tongue, there, censurèd.
That man's unwise will search for Ill,   25
And may prevent it, sitting still.

To His Muse

1   *Reed* shepherd's pipe.
2   *Eclogues* the traditional title of Virgil's pastoral poems (though he himself called them *Bucolica*). Virgil introduced political, religious, and literary themes into pastoral that expanded the definition of the genre.
3   *Bucolics* from Greek βουκόλος (herdsman); a name first used to describe the pastoral poems of Theocritus, which are on the whole more lighthearted than Virgil's often melancholy *Eclogues*.
4   *Neat* cattle.
5   *Stay . . . woe* recalling Martial 1.3.12 (p. 466 below), *i, fuge: sed poteras tutior esse domi*, "go on then, fly off; but you could have been safer at home."
6   *Cell* humble abode.

John Milton (1608–1674)

Milton was a profound scholar, proficient not only in Latin and Greek, but also in Hebrew and in other biblical languages, such as Syriac and Aramaic. He was also fluent in French and Italian. His studies began early and were continued at St. Paul's under the linguistic projector Alexander Gil. His learning, like that of the spelling reformers, who tended also to be political reformers, ran more to Greek and Hebrew than the largely Latin learning of more orthodox scholars of the seventeenth century. But early in life Milton was orthodox enough to sign allegiance to the English articles of faith and to earn a BA at Christ's College, Cambridge. There he wrote poetry and prose in several languages and was called, after the young Virgil, "the Lady." Milton traveled to Italy in 1638–1639 and met many of the great scholars of his day, including Galileo, Buonmattei, and Cardinal Barberini. He returned to an England that was on the verge of civil war, and he quickly took up rhetorical arms on the Parliamentary side. He wrote several polemical tracts against the Church of England under Charles; in the *Tenure of Kings and Magistrates* (1649) he provided an intellectual justification for the execution of the monarch. Milton worked for the Parliamentary regime for the next ten years, and in *A Ready and Easy Way* (1660) he made a last-ditch attempt to save it from annihilation. Upon the restoration of the monarchy Milton was obliged to go into hiding. He was briefly imprisoned in the Tower and heavily fined, but he escaped the death sentence imposed on several of his fellow apologists for the execution of Charles I. Milton had gradually gone blind from about 1648 to 1652, and he lived his last years in darkness and obscurity. However, in 1667 he published *Paradise Lost*, the greatest poem ever written in English, a work he had begun around 1640. This work, revised in 1674, is made to stand up to the great epics of the classical world – the *Iliad* and, especially, the *Aeneid*. Milton's poem incorporates many features of classical epics, and it adds a thorough understanding of the Judeo-Christian tradition as well, stretching from the Bible through the whole period of Christian humanism in renaissance Europe. Milton seeks to outdo his forerunners and to leave a work, "so written to aftertimes as they should not willingly let it die." Similar ambitions may be perceived in his lesser works.

Lycidas

Milton was asked to contribute *Lycidas* to a memorial volume for Edward King, a poet and a fellow of Christ's College who drowned in a shipwreck off the coast of Anglesey in 1637. Many of the poems in the volume are metaphysical works full of witty conceits in the manner of John Donne, but Milton chose to write in the classical form of the pastoral elegy. The main precedents for classical pastoral elegy are the song of Thyrsis about Daphnis in Theocritus *Idyll* 1 (p. 302 below); Bion's *Lament for Adonis* (p. 312 below); the *Lament for Bion* attributed to Moschus (p. 319 below); and Virgil's *Eclogues* 5 and 10 (pp. 345 and 349 below). Milton shows his mastery of these generic antecedents throughout the poem, as our notes below indicate. In fact, many readers have felt that a display of his literary mastery was Milton's primary intention in the poem and far more important to him than any expression of grief for Edward King. Whether or not this is true, Milton consciously chose to follow or, some would say, challenge Virgil in this form rather than other writers, although he frequently acknowledges the precedence of Theocritus. In so doing, Milton is declaring his intention to seek the highest possible literary station.

Milton's use of allegory, his introjection of a personal element, and his application of portentous themes are all Virgilian. His adoption of a noble tone – "somewhat loudly sweep the string" – specifically echoes the beginning of the fourth *Eclogue*. Yet it is *Eclogues* 5 and 10 that come most to mind. *Eclogue* 5 is a song competition, in which the first singer mourns the death of Daphnis and the second celebrates his apotheosis. The optimistic second song is Virgil's innovation and provides an exalted model for the ending of *Lycidas*. However, Milton is not a passive imitator: he christianizes the Virgilian ending, but he also, in a sense, enters into the song competition himself. *Eclogue* 10, in which Virgil describes the poet Gallus dying of love in an Arcadian landscape, may be even more squarely in Milton's sights. We have indicated important points of contact in notes 5, 9, 20, 34, 37, 41, and 68. As in Virgil's *Eclogue* 10, Milton's shepherd-poet (the uncouth swain) does not appear until the end, in an eight-line coda. Virgil's poem is a culmination of the previous nine eclogues, his "last task" (line 1), and an expression of his own place in poetic tradition. When Milton's poet "twitches his mantle blue" and walks off at the end of *Lycidas* he is not only recalling Virgil's farewell to his pastoral muse in *Eclogue* 10, he is also reinscribing with his own signature the history of this poetic genre.

The text presented here is based on the one that appeared in *Poems of John Milton* (1645).

In this Monody the Author bewails a learned Friend, unfortunately drowned in his Passage from *Chester* on the *Irish* Seas, 1637. And by occasion foretells the ruin of our corrupted Clergy then in their height.[1]

Yet once more, O ye Laurels, and once more
Ye Myrtles brown, with Ivy never-sere,[2]
I come to pluck your Berries harsh and crude,[3]
And with forced fingers rude,
Shatter your leaves before the mellowing year.   5
Bitter constraint, and sad occasion dear,
Compels me to disturb your season due:
For *Lycidas* is dead, dead ere his prime[4]
Young *Lycidas*, and hath not left his peer:
Who would not sing for *Lycidas*? he knew[5]   10
Himself to sing, and build the lofty rhyme.
He must not float upon his watry bier
Unwept, and welter to the parching wind,[6]
Without the mead of some melodious tear.
   Begin then, Sisters of the sacred well,[7]   15
That from beneath the seat of *Jove* doth spring,
Begin, and somewhat loudly sweep the string.[8]
Hence with denial vain, and coy excuse,
So may some gentle Muse[9]
With lucky words favor my destined Urn,   20
And as he passes turn,

LYCIDAS

1   This head note was added in 1645. A monody is a mournful song.

2   *Laurels . . . never-sere* The plants addressed by Milton evoke a trio of deities: the laurel was sacred to Apollo, the myrtle to Venus, and the ivy to Bacchus. Compare Virgil, *Eclogues* 2.54, *et vos, o lauri, carpam et te, proxima myrte*, "I will pluck you, o laurels, and you, neighboring myrtle." The "never-sere" (ever-green) leaves represent the permanent sources of poetry or poetic inspiration.

3   *crude* unripe; a Latinism (*crudus*).

4   *Lycidas* a pastoral figure in Theocritus and Virgil, notably in *Eclogue* 9 where he laments the powerlessness of poetry to thwart injustice.

5   *Who . . . Lycidas?* an echo of Virgil, *Eclogues* 10.3 (p. 349 below), *neget quis carmina Gallo?*, "who would deny songs to Gallus?"

6   *welter* "roll to and fro (on the waves)" (*OED*).

7   *Begin . . . well* compare Theocritus, *Idylls* 1.64 (p. 304 below)," Begin, dear Muses, begin the bucolic song"; pseudo-Moschus, *Lament for Bion* 8 (p. 319 below). The cult of the Muses was linked to sacred springs that poets imagined as sources of inspiration. The allusion is either to the Pierian spring on Mt. Olympus, the Muses' birthplace, or to Aganippe or Hippocrene on Mt. Helicon, where there was a sanctuary of Zeus (see Hesiod, *Theogony* 1–80; p. 275 below).

8   *somewhat . . . string* recalls Virgil, *Eclogues* 4.1 (p. 342 below), *Sicelides Musae, paulo maiora canamus*, "Sicilian Muses, let us sing of somewhat greater things," i.e. "things transcending the pastoral genre."

9   *So may* a formal imitation of Virgil *Eclogues* 10.4–5 (p. 349 below).

And bid fair peace be to my sable shroud,
For we were nursed upon the self-same hill,
Fed the same flock, by fountain, shade, and rill.
   Together both, where the high Lawns appeared   25
Under the opening eyelids of the morn,
We drove afield, and both together heard
What time the Grey fly winds her sultry horn,[10]
Batt'ning our flocks with the fresh dews of night,[11]
Oft till the Star that rose, at Ev'ning, bright[12]   30
Toward Heav'n's descent had sloped his west'ring wheel.
Meanwhile the Rural ditties were not mute,
Tempered to th' Oaten Flute,[13]
Rough *Satyrs* danced, and *Fauns* with clov'n heel,[14]
From the glad sound would not be absent long,   35
And old Damoetas loved to hear our song.[15]
   But O the heavy change, now thou art gone,
Now thou art gone, and never must return!
Thee Shepherd, thee the Woods, and desert Caves,
With wild Thyme and the gadding Vine o'ergrown,   40
And all their echoes mourn.
The Willows, and the Hazel Copses green,[16]
Shall no more be seen,
Fanning their joyous Leaves to thy soft lays.[17]
As killing as the Canker to the Rose,[18]   45
Or Taint-worm to the weanling Herds that graze,
Or Frost to Flowers, that their gay wardrobe wear,
When first the White thorn blows;[19]
Such, *Lycidas*, thy loss to Shepherd's ear.

---

10   *What time* a Latinism (*quo tempore*); *Grey fly*
a bee or beetle that makes a loud humming
noise.

11   *dews* the dewy grass of dawn, which Virgil
says the flocks prefer (*Eclogues* 8.14–15).

12   *Star* the evening star Hesperus.

13   *Oaten Flute* a convention deriving from
Virgil, *Eclogues* 1.2, *silvestrem tenui Musam medi-
taris avena*, "you compose the woodland Muse
on a slender oat." Virgil, with little concern for
realism, probably means the panpipes, an instru-
ment made of reeds not oat-straws; the ultimate
source is the Theocritean taunt "pipe of straw"
(*Idylls* 5.7, imitated by Virgil in *Eclogues* 3.27 and
in turn by Milton in lines 123–4 below).

14   *Satyrs . . . Fauns* mythical creatures of the
wild with human and horse- or goat-like
features.

15   *Damoetas* a name taken directly from Virgil's
Eclogues.

16   *Copses* small wooded areas.

17   *lays* songs.

18   *As . . . Rose* rustic analogies are traditional
in pastoral poetry from Theocritus onwards;
compare, e.g., Virgil, *Eclogues* 2.63–65 (p. 341
below), 5.16–18 (p. 346 below).

19   *White thorn* hawthorn; *blows* blossoms.

Where were ye Nymphs when the remorseless deep[20]   50
Closed o'er the head of your loved *Lycidas?*
For neither were ye playing on the steep,
Where you old *Bards*, the famous *Druids* lie,
Nor on the shaggy top of *Mona* high,[21]
Nor yet where *Deva* spreads her wizard stream:[22]   55
Ay me, I fondly dream!
Had ye been there – for what could that have done?
What could the Muse herself that Orpheus bore,[23]
The Muse herself, for her enchanting son
Whom Universal nature did lament.   60
When by the rout that made the hideous roar,[24]
His gory visage down the stream was sent,
Down the swift *Hebrus* to the *Lesbian* shore.[25]
    Alas! What boots it with uncessant care
To tend the homely slighted Shepherd's trade,   65
And strictly meditate the thankless Muse?[26]
Were it not better done as others use,
To sport with *Amaryllis* in the shade,[27]
Or with the tangles of *Neaera's* hair?[28]
Fame is the spur that the clear spirit doth raise   70
(That last infirmity of Noble mind)
To scorn delights, and live laborious days;
But the fair Guerdon when we hope to find,[29]
And think to burst out into sudden blaze,

20 *Where were ye Nymphs* an imitation, in content and form, of Virgil, *Eclogues* 10.9–12: *quae nemora aut qui vos saltus habuere, puellae / Naides, indigno cum Gallus amore peribat? / nam neque Parnasi vobis iuga, nam neque Pindi / ulla moram fecere* . . . (p. 349 below). The description of drowning possibly echoes Theocritus, *Idylls* 1.140–1 (p. 306 below).
21 *Mona* the old name of Anglesey, an island off the northern coast of Wales.
22 *Deva* a stream in western England.
23 *Orpheus* son of Apollo and a Muse; a mythical poet of Thrace whose songs had the power to charm beasts, trees, and rocks. When his bride Eurydice was killed by a snakebite, Orpheus so enchanted the rulers of the underworld with his songs that Eurydice was permitted to return to life on condition that Orpheus not look back at her as he left the underworld. He looked back and lost her forever. Consumed by grief, he was murdered and decapitated by a band of Thracian women or maenads enraged by his aloofness (Virgil, *Georgics* 4.453–527; Ovid, *Metamorphoses* 11.1–66). The question is reminiscent of Ovid, *Amores* 3.9.21: "What use were his mother and father to Ismarian Orpheus?"
24 *rout* mob (here of maenads).
25 *Hebrus* river of Thrace; *Lesbian shore* the island of Lesbos in the eastern Aegean Sea, home of the poet Sappho.
26 *meditate* compose; a Latinism based on *meditaris* in Virgil, *Eclogues* 1.2 (see n. 13 above).
27 *sport* disport; idle the time away in amorous dalliance; *Amaryllis* compare Virgil, *Eclogues* 2.14–15 (p. 340 below).
28 *Neaera* a name found in Virgil's *Eclogues* (3.3), but Milton was thinking of Horace, *Odes* 3.14.21: "Tell tuneful Neaera to hurry up and bind her brown hair in a knot."
29 *Guerdon* reward.

Comes the blind *Fury* with th' abhorrèd shears,[30]   75
And slits the thin-spun life. "But not the praise,"
Phoebus replied, and touched my trembling ears;[31]
"Fame is no plant that grows on mortal soil,
Nor in the glistering foil[32]
Set off to th' world, nor in broad rumour lies,   80
But lives and spreads aloft by those pure eyes,
And perfect witness of all-judging *Jove*;
As he pronounces lastly on each deed,
Of so much fame in Heav'n expect thy meed."[33]
　　O Fountain *Arethuse*, and thou honoured flood,[34]   85
Smooth-sliding *Mincius*, crowned with vocal reeds,[35]
That strain I heard was of a higher mood:
But now my Oat proceeds,[36]
And listens to the Herald of the Sea[37]
That came in *Neptune*'s plea,   90
He asked the Waves, and asked the Felon winds,
What hard mishap hath doomed this gentle swain?
And questioned every gust of rugged wings
That blows from off each beakèd Promontory;
They knew not of his story,   95
And sage *Hippotades* their answer brings,[38]
That not a blast was from his dungeon strayed,
The Air was calm, and on the level brine,
Sleek *Panope* with all her sisters played.[39]
It was that fatal and perfidious Bark[40]   100
Built in th' eclipse, and rigged with curses dark,
That sunk so low that sacred head of thine.

30　*Fury* Atropos, the Fate who cuts the thread
of life; Milton assimilates the Fates to the Furies
– powers of the underworld associated with
death.

31　*Phoebus* Apollo, the god of poetry. Virgil
relates that Apollo stopped him from writing epic
by plucking his ear and admonishing him that a
shepherd should feed his flock fat but sing a fine-
spun song (*Eclogues* 6.1–5).

32　*foil* the metal put underneath a jewel to set
off its brightness.

33　*meed* reward.

34　*Arethuse* Arethusa, a famous Sicilian spring
invoked by Virgil (*Eclogues* 10.1); by metonymy,
the poetic inspiration of Theocritus.

35　*Mincius* the river of Mantua, Virgil's home-
town; its reedy banks are mentioned in *Eclogues*
7.12–13.

36　*Oat* the *Oaten Flute* of line 33; metaphori-
cally, his poetic voice, which is returning to pas-
toral utterance after being briefly distracted by a
higher calling.

37　*Herald* the sea god Triton. He is first in
a list of gods which imitates the pastoral conven-
tion of the dead or dying person being visited
by a procession of deities and/or rustic
characters: compare, e.g., Theocritus, *Idylls* 1.77
ff. (p. 305 below), Virgil, *Eclogues* 10.19 ff.
(p. 350 below).

38　*Hippotades* Aeolus, son of Hippotes, god of
the winds, which he keeps imprisoned in a cave
(see Virgil, *Aeneid* 1.50–63; p. 365 below).

39　*Panope* a Nereid or sea nymph.

40　*Bark* boat.

Next *Camus*, reverend Sire, went footing slow,[41]
His Mantle hairy, and his Bonnet sedge,
Inwrought with figures dim, and on the edge   105
Like to that sanguine flower inscribed with woe.[42]
"Ah! Who hath reft," quoth he, "my dearest pledge?"
Last came, and last did go,
The Pilot of the Galilean lake,[43]
Two massy Keys he bore of metals twain   110
(The Golden opes, the Iron shuts amain).
He shook his Mitred locks, and stern bespake,[44]
"How well could I have spared for thee, young swain
Enow of such as for their bellies' sake,[45]
Creep and intrude, and climb into the fold?[46]   115
Of other care they little reck'ning make,
Than how to scramble at the shearers' feast,
And shove away the worthy bidden guest.
Blind mouths! That scarce themselves know how to hold
A Sheep-hook, or have learned aught else the least   120
That to the faithful herdsman's art belongs!
What recks it them? What need they? They are sped;[47]
And when they list, their lean and flashy songs
Grate on their scrannel Pipes of wretched straw,[48]
The hungry Sheep look up, and are not fed,   125
But swoll'n with wind, and the rank mist they draw,
Rot inwardly, and foul contagion spread:
Besides what the grim Wolf with privy paw[49]
Daily devours apace, and nothing said,
But that two-handed engine at the door,[50]   130
Stands ready to smite once, and smite no more."

41   *Camus* god of the river Cam; allegorically, Cambridge University. Compare Virgil, *Eclogues* 10.24–5 (p. 350 below): "Silvanus came too, with rustic decoration on his head, waving flowering fennels and large lilies"; and his description of the Tiber god in *Aeneid* 8.31–4.

42   *flower . . . woe* a flower inscribed with the sounds "ai, ai" that grew from the blood of handsome young Hyacinthus when he was killed by Apollo (Ovid, *Metamorphoses* 10.215 and 13. 396). The hyacinth is mentioned at the beginning of the *Lament for Bion* 6–7 (p. 319 below).

43   *Pilot* St. Peter, who holds the "massy Keys" to heaven (Matthew 16.19).

44   *Mitred locks* hair covered by the mitre (a tall ceremonial hat) of a bishop.

45   *Enow* enough.

46   *such . . . fold*   metaphorically,   corrupt clergymen.

47   *sped* confirmed, usually, in a beneficial situation, but sometimes in a harmful one (such as a disease); nicely ambiguous here. Milton's use of pastoral imagery as a trope for clerical corruption is based on biblical metaphors, but also on details concerning shepherds who neglect their sheep that he found in Virgil, *Eclogues* 3.3–6.

48   *Grate . . . straw* inspired by Virgil, *Eclogues* 3.27, *stridenti miserum stipula disperdere carmen*, "to ruin a wretched song on a squeaking straw."

49   *Wolf* the Church of England.

50   *two-handed engine* a broad sword and an instrument of divine justice; a slighting reference to the threat of impending apocalypse used by the established church to frighten its communicants and potential converts.

Return, *Alpheus*, the dread voice is past,[51]
That shrunk thy streams; return *Sicilian* Muse,
And call the Vales, and bid them hither cast
Their Bells, and Flow'rets of a thousand hues.   135
Ye valleys low where the mild whispers use,[52]
Of shades and wanton winds, and gushing brooks,
On whose fresh lap the swart Star sparely looks,[53]
Throw hither all your quaint enameled eyes,
That on the green turf suck the honied showers,   140
And purple all the ground with vernal flowers.
Bring the rathe Primrose that forsaken dies.[54]
The tufted Crow-toe, and pale Jessamine,[55]
The white Pink, and the Pansy freaked with jet,[56]
The glowing Violet.   145
The Muskrose, and the well-attired Woodbine,
With Cowslips wan that hang the pensive head,
And every flower that sad embroidery wears:
Bid *Amaranthus* all his beauty shed,[57]
And Daffadillies fill their cups with tears,   150
To strew the Laureate Hearse where *Lycid* lies.[58]
For so to interpose a little ease,
Let our frail thoughts dally with false surmise.
Ay me! Whilst thee the shores, and sounding Seas
Wash far away, where'er thy bones are hurled,   155
Whether beyond the stormy *Hebrides*,
Where thou perhaps under the whelming tide
Visit'st the bottom of the monstrous world;[59]
Or whether thou to our moist vows denied,
Sleep'st by the fable of *Bellerus* old.[60]   160
Where the great vision of the guarded Mount[61]
Looks toward Namancos and Bayona's hold[62]
Look homeward Angel now, and melt with ruth.

51 *Alpheus* river of Arcadia, which in myth pursued the nymph Arethusa under the sea to Sicily.
52 *use* spend their time.
53 *swart Star* Sirius, the Dog Star, which rises in the hottest part of summer.
54 *rathe* early blooming. The list of flowers is a pastoral convention; compare, for example, the *Lament for Bion* 4–7 (p. 319 below); Virgil, *Eclogues* 2.45 ff., 4.18 ff., and 5.36 ff. (pp. 341, 343, and 347 below).
55 *Crow-toe* a name for hyacinth; *Jessamine* jasmine, a climbing plant with white flowers.

56 *freaked with jet* splashed with black.
57 *Amaranthus* an immortal flower found in Eden (*Paradise Lost* 3.353–7); the word is Greek for "unfading."
58 *Laureate* bedecked with laurel.
59 *monstrous world* the underwater world was sometimes so imagined.
60 *Bellerus* a giant inhabiting Bellerium, the Latin name for Land's End.
61 *Mount* St. Michael's Mount, off the coast of Cornwall on the southwestern coast of England.
62 *Namancos and Bayona's hold* a fortification on the coast of Spain.

And, O ye *Dolphins*, waft the hapless youth.[63]
    Weep no more, woeful Shepherds, weep no more,[64]   165
For *Lycidas* your sorrow is not dead,
Sunk though he be beneath the watry floor,
So sinks the day star in the Ocean bed,
And yet anon repairs his drooping head,
And tricks his beams, and with new-spangled Ore,   170
Flames in the forehead of the morning sky:
So *Lycidas* sunk low, but mounted high,
Through the dear might of him that walked the waves[65]
Where other groves, and other streams along,
With *Nectar* pure his oozy Locks he laves,   175
And hears the unexpressive nuptial Song,
In the blest Kingdoms meek of joy and love.
There entertain him all the Saints above,
In solemn troops, and sweet Societies
That sing, and singing in their glory move,   180
And wipe the tears forever from his eyes.
Now *Lycidas* the Shepherds weep no more;
Henceforth thou art the Genius of the shore,[66]
In thy large recompense, and shalt be good
To all that wander in that perilous flood.   185
    Thus sang the uncouth Swain to th' Oaks and rills,
While the still morn went out with Sandals grey,
He touched the tender stops of various Quills,
With eager thought warbling his *Doric* lay:[67]
And now the Sun had stretched out all the hills,[68]   190
And now was dropt into the Western bay;
At last he rose, and twitched his Mantle blue:[69]
Tomorrow to fresh Woods, and Pastures new.

---

63 *And ... youth* probably a mixed allusion both to Melicertes, who after drowning was carried to shore by a dolphin and made a sea deity, and to the legendary rescue of the poet Arion (Herodotus, *Histories* 1.23–4).

64 *Weep no more* similar to the Theocritean refrain, "Muses, cease your bucolic song," which signals the end of the dirge for Daphnis (*Idylls* 1.127). However, the optimism of Milton's passage is modeled on Virgil's description of the apotheosis of Daphnis (*Eclogues* 5.56 ff.).

65 *him that walked the waves* Christ (Matthew 14:25–31).

66 *Genius* presiding spirit or deity; similarly, Daphnis is hailed as a new god in Virgil, *Eclogues* 5.64 ff. (p. 348 below).

67 *Doric* the Greek dialect used by Theocritus, Bion, and Moschus.

68 *And ... hills* the lengthening of the hills' shadows echoes the last line of Virgil, *Eclogue* 1; *Eclogues* 6 and 10 also end with the onset of dusk. Milton's eight-line coda (lines 186–93) matches the coda of *Eclogue* 10 (lines 70–7), which rounds off the collection of *Eclogues*.

69 *twitched* tugged at; plucked.

from *Paradise Lost*

Book 1, lines 1–74

In its beginning Milton's poem engages with ancient epic and didactic proems in complex ways. Although the *Iliad* and *Odyssey* are always in the background, the relationship between *Paradise Lost* and the *Aeneid* is especially close in shape, syntax (e.g., the long opening period), and detail. Both works open with a statement of theme (*Aen.* 1.1–7/*PL* 1–5); an invocation of the Muse (*Aen.* 1.8/*PL* 6–16); a question of divine justice (*Aen.* 1.8–11/*PL* 25–6); and a foundational account of the anger of a heavenly being which runs counter to the will of the supreme deity (*Aen.* 1.12–32/*PL* 27–74). Milton's announced object in the whole poem to follow is to "justify the ways of God to men." In a sense, this is an answer to Virgil's question at *Aeneid* 1.11: "do divine minds hold such great anger?" Virgil wants to know why a pious man like Aeneas was made to suffer, and his question is not fully answered by the epic. Milton, on the other hand, takes divine providence for granted and is confident in his ability to reveal it (with divine assistance). He completes the work begun by Virgil and perhaps takes his place in the pantheon of poets.

Having incorporated the three major epics, replacing their heroic themes with that of man's fall, Milton draws on Hesiod and Ovid in lines 8 and following in order to express the novelty of his project. In the prologue to the *Theogony* Hesiod describes how, as he tended his flocks on Helicon, he was met by the Muses, who gave him a laurel staff and breathed into him the gift of song, telling him to sing first and last of the gods. Later he calls on them to "tell how at the first gods and earth came to be" and so on (p. 277 below). The *Theogony* narrative then begins, and *Paradise Lost* corresponds rather closely to it. To Hesiod, Milton juxtaposes Moses (the Shepherd); to Helicon, Oreb or Sinai; to the Muses, the Heavenly Muse (Urania) or the word of God; to the generation of the gods beginning with Chaos, the creation of earth and heaven out of Chaos.

Hesiod's encounter with the Muses was the classic expression of the poet's divine inspiration. Ancient poets used it as a touchstone for defining their own inspiration and originality. For example, Lucretius in the proem to Book 4 says he walks untrodden paths on Helicon and picks flowers where no one has before. Milton is also positioning himself in the realm of divine inspiration, and, unsurprisingly, he finds he stands on the highest peak. Hesiod sang of the gods, but Milton proposes to sing of God. Hesiod was inspired by the Muses, but Milton by the Holy Spirit. Milton sees himself soaring above Helicon, thereby transcending Hesiod and his pagan epic sources with their false, earthbound theology.

There are also connections between Ovid's *Metamorphoses* and *Paradise Lost*. Ovid too tells a creation myth and charts the decline of man from an Edenic Golden Age to a corrupt state. Ovid aimed for a comprehensiveness lacking in earlier poems; he wants to tell the story of creation from beginning to end. But

Milton seeks still greater comprehensiveness. His story goes from creation to decline to final redemption, incorporating the classical myths into the transcendental biblical framework, concluding with the redemption of the New Testament and the story of the Last Judgment in the Book of Revelation. In general terms, such incorporation was the work of renaissance humanism throughout Europe for several centuries. However, Milton's achievement is very much individual, and his claims for success in reshaping the classical tradition to his purposes are very much personal.

The text presented here is based on the second edition of *Paradise Lost* (1674).

Of Man's First Disobedience, and the Fruit
Of that Forbidden Tree whose mortal taste
Brought Death into the World, and all our woe,
With loss of *Eden*, till one greater Man
Restore us, and regain the blissful Seat,   5
Sing, Heav'nly Muse, that on the secret top[1]
Of *Oreb*, or of *Sinai*, didst inspire[2]
That Shepherd, who first taught the chosen Seed,
In the Beginning how the Heav'ns and Earth
Rose out of *Chaos*: or, if *Sion* hill[3]   10
Delight thee more, and *Siloa*'s Brook that flowed[4]
Fast by the Oracle of God; I thence
Invoke thy aid to my adventrous Song,
That with no middle flight intends to soar [5]
Above th' *Aonian* Mount, while it pursues[6]   15

BOOK 1, LINES 1–74

1 *Sing, Heav'nly Muse* compare Homer *Iliad*, 1.1 (p. 241 below), "sing, goddess, of the wrath . . ."; *Odyssey* 1.1 (p. 255 below), "Muse, tell me of the man . . ."; Virgil *Aeneid* 1.8 (p. 363 below), "Muse, tell me the reasons. . . ." The *Heav'nly Muse* is Urania, Muse of astronomy (see *Paradise Lost* 7.1), who is identified with the word of God.

2 *Oreb . . . Sinai* mounts where Moses (*That Shepherd*) may have received the word of God. The word *Shepherd* also invokes Hesiod, who met the Muses while tending his sheep on Mt. Helicon (*Theogony*, p. 277 below).

3 *Chaos* probably in the Hesiodic sense of "chasm, void" rather than confused matter, which would imply that something existed before the Creation; *Sion* or Zion, one of the hills of

Jerusalem, where David brought the ark of the covenant.

4 *Siloa*'s *Brook* a pool in Jerusalem, used by Jesus for healing (John 9.7), but perhaps Shiloh is meant, a town where there was an annual feast of Jehovah and where the ark resided for some time.

5 *soar* compare *Paradise Lost* 7.3, "above th' Olympian hill I soar"; Milton imagines himself riding to Heaven ("*no middle flight*") on a "flying steed," as Bellerophon tried unsuccessfully to do on Pegasus (*Paradise Lost* 7.1–20). To represent poetic composition as a journey is a classical trope.

6 *Aonian* Boeotian; the mountain is Helicon, the site of Hesiod's meeting with the Muses (*Theogony*, p. 276 below) and of the Muses' spring Hippocrene, which was said to have been created by the hoof of Pegasus.

Things unattempted yet in Prose or Rhyme.
And chiefly Thou, O Spirit, that dost prefer
Before all Temples th' upright heart and pure,
Instruct me, for Thou know'st; Thou from the first
Wast present, and with mighty wings outspread   20
Dove-like sat'st brooding on the vast Abyss,
And mad'st it pregnant: What in me is dark
Illumine, what is low raise and support;
That to the heighth of this great Argument,
I may assert Eternal Providence,   25
And justify the ways of God to men.
   Say first, for Heav'n hides nothing from thy view,
Nor the deep tract of Hell, say first what cause[7]
Moved our Grand Parents, in that happy State,
Favoured of Heav'n so highly, to fall off   35
From their Creator, and transgress his Will
For one restraint, Lords of the World besides?
Who first seduced them to that foul revolt?[8]
Th' infernal Serpent; he it was, whose guile,
Stirred up with Envy and Revenge, deceived   40
The Mother of Mankind, what time his Pride[9]
Had cast him out from Heav'n, with all his Host
Of Rebel Angels, by whose aid aspiring
To set himself in Glory above his Peers,
He trusted to have equaled the Most High,   45
If he opposed; and with ambitious aim
Against the Throne and Monarchy of God
Raised impious War in Heav'n and Battle proud
With vain attempt. Him the Almighty Power
Hurled headlong flaming from th' Ethereal Sky,   50
With hideous ruin and combustion down
To bottomless perdition, there to dwell
In Adamantine Chains and penal Fire,
Who durst defy th' Omnipotent to Arms.
Nine times the Space that measures Day and Night[10]   55
To mortal men, he with his horrid crew
Lay vanquisht, rolling in the fiery Gulf,
Confounded though immortal: But his doom

---

7 *say first what cause* compare Virgil, *Aeneid* 1.8
(n. 1 above).
8 *Who ... revolt?* The pattern of question and
immediate answer, as well as the verbal structure,
imitates Homer, *Iliad* 1.8–9 (p. 242 below),
"Which of the gods brought these two into con-
flict? / The son of Leto and Zeus." Satan corre-
sponds to Apollo in the *Iliad* and Juno in the
Aeneid and shares with both a sense of outrage.
  9 *what time* a Latinism (*quo tempore*).
10 *Nine times ... Night* the fall of nine days and
nights is based on Hesiod's description of the
Titans' fall into Tartarus having been defeated by
Zeus (*Theogony* 722–5).

Reserved him to more wrath; for now the thought
Both of lost happiness and lasting pain   60
Torments him; round he throws his baleful eyes,
That witnessed huge affliction and dismay,
Mixt with obdúrate pride and steadfast hate:
At once as far as Angels ken he views
The dismal Situation waste and wild,   65
A Dungeon horrible, on all sides round
As one great Furnace flamed; yet from those flames
No light, but rather darkness visible
Served only to discover sights of woe,
Regions of sorrow, doleful shades, where peace   70
And rest can never dwell, hope never comes
That comes to all; but torture without end
Still urges, and a fiery Deluge, fed
With ever-burning Sulphur unconsumed.
Such place Eternal Justice had prepared   75
For those rebellious, here their Prison ordained
In utter darkness, and their portion set
As far removed from God and light of Heav'n
As from the Centre thrice to th' utmost Pole.[11]

Book 4, lines 411–91

At the opening of Book 4 the narrator cries, "O for that warning voice," and goes on to describe Satan in Paradise full of envy and hate. He crouches down in the shape of a tiger and listens to the conversation of Adam and Eve. Adam reviews their blessed situation and the one prohibition under which they live – not to eat of the tree of good and evil. Eve replies that her situation is doubly blessed because she has Adam as well as God's blessings, and she recalls the moment of her creation. The first creature she sees is actually the image of herself in a pool of water. Then she is led by an angel to the side of Adam, whom she finds not as beautiful as herself but full of admirable "manly grace / And wisdom, which alone is truly fair." The first couple are completely happy, but there are signs of trouble apparent to the savvy reader. Eve's story recalls the myth of Narcissus (Ovid, *Metamorphoses* 3; p. 446 below), who lies by a pool enraptured by his reflection, not knowing – at first – that it is himself he loves. Milton imitates the description of the *locus amoenus* (charming place) and Ovid's verbal mirror effects (e.g., *Metamorphoses* 3.425–6 and 458–60). Narcissus, of course, dies because of his vanity, and so will Eve. However, Milton complicates the Ovidian narrative by having Eve relate her

11 *As ... Pole* based on Virgil's description of
Tartarus as being twice as far below the earth as
heaven is above it (*Aeneid* 6.577–9).

own story and by making Eve the "image" of Adam ("he whose image thou art"). In a sense Milton's Eve is torn between two images – the insubstantial and the fleshly, the self-enclosed and the complementary. She is Adam's "other half," the equivalent of what Echo would have been to Narcissus had he responded to her love, and she resembles the "other half" in the myth invented by Aristophanes in Plato's *Symposium* – that people were once round, but being cut in half by Zeus as a punishment, they had in love to seek their other half. The classical allusions in this passage amount to the "warning voice" for which the narrator asked in the proem of the book.

Another note of warning can be heard in Adam's words "whom fli'st thou?" because they recall Aeneas' words to Dido in the underworld and Apollo's to Daphne (see n. 5 below). Both of these women run away from their seducers, but Eve stays. Her union with Adam is a marriage sanctioned by God, unlike those in the classical situations, which involve adultery, suicide, attempted rape, and metamorphosis. Still, the connection is ominous because another suitor is looking on. Eve is, like her classical forerunners, headed for destruction. This is presaged earlier in Book 4 (lines 268–75), where the description of Eden alludes to the *locus amoenus* where Proserpina is carried off by Pluto in Ovid's version (*Metamorphoses* 5.385–408). Proleptically and metaphorically, Eve is Proserpina, just as she is, in this figuratively allusive way, Narcissus, Dido, and Daphne.

> "Sole partner and sole part of all these joys,
> Dearer thy self than all; needs must the Power
> That made us, and for us this ample World
> Be infinitely good, and of his good
> As liberal and free as infinite,   415
> That raised us from the dust and placed us here
> In all this happiness, who at his hand
> Have nothing merited, nor can perform
> Aught whereof he hath need, he who requires
> From us no other service than to keep   420
> This one, this easy charge, of all the Trees
> In Paradise that bear delicious fruit
> So various, not to taste that only Tree
> Of knowledge, planted by the Tree of Life,
> So near grows Death to Life, what e'er Death is,   425
> Some dreadful thing no doubt; for well thou knowst
> God hath pronounced it death to taste that Tree,
> The only sign of our obedience left
> Among so many signs of power and rule
> Conferred upon us, and Dominion giv'n   430
> Over all other Creatures that possess
> Earth, Air, and Sea. Then let us not think hard
> One easy prohibition, who enjoy

Free leave so large to all things else, and choice
Unlimited of manifold delights: 435
But let us ever praise him, and extol
His bounty, following our delightful task
To prune these growing Plants, and tend these Flow'rs,
Which were it toilsome, yet with thee were sweet."
    To whom thus *Eve* replied. "O thou for whom   440
And from whom I was formed flesh of thy flesh,
And without whom am to no end, my Guide
And Head, what thou hast said is just and right.
For we to him indeed all praises owe,
And daily thanks, I chiefly, who enjoy   445
So far the happier Lot, enjoying thee
Preeminent by so much odds, while thou
Like consort to thyself canst nowhere find.
That day I oft remember, when from sleep
I first awaked, and found myself reposed   450
Under a shade of flow'rs, much wond'ring where
And what I was, whence thither brought, and how.
Not distant far from thence a murmuring sound
Of waters issued from a Cave and spread
Into a liquid Plain, then stood unmoved   455
Pure as th' expanse of Heav'n; I thither went
With unexperienced thought, and laid me down
On the green bank, to look into the clear
Smooth Lake, that to me seemed another Sky.
As I bent down to look, just opposite,   460
A Shape within the watry gleam appeared
Bending to look on me, I started back,
It started back, but pleased I soon returned,
Pleased it returned as soon with answering looks
Of sympathy and love; there I had fixed   465
Mine eyes till now, and pined with vain desire,[1]
Had not a voice thus warned me, 'What thou seest,
What there thou seest fair Creature is thyself,
With thee it came and goes: but follow me,[2]
And I will bring thee where no shadow stays[3]   470
Thy coming, and thy soft embraces, he
Whose image thou art, him thou shalt enjoy
Inseparably thine, to him shalt bear
Multitudes like thyself, and thence be called

BOOK 4, LINES 411–91

1 *pined* just as Narcissus wasted away to nothing.

2 *What...goes* based on Ovid, *Metamorphoses* 3.433–6 (p. 450 below).

3 *stays* awaits.

Mother of human race': what could I do,   475
But follow straight, invisibly thus led?
Till I espied thee, fair indeed and tall,
Under a Platan; yet methought less fair,[4]
Less winning soft, less amiably mild,
Than that smooth watry image; back I turned,   480
Thou following cryd'st aloud, 'Return fair *Eve*,
Whom fli'st thou? whom thou fli'st, of him thou art,[5]
His flesh, his bone; to give thee being I lent
Out of my side to thee, nearest my heart
Substantial Life, to have thee by my side   485
Henceforth an individual solace dear;[6]
Part of my Soul I seek thee, and thee claim
My other half': with that thy gentle hand
Seized mine, I yielded, and from that time see
How beauty is excelled by manly grace,   490
And wisdom, which alone is truly fair."

---

4   *Platan* plane tree.
5   *Whom fli'st thou* thus Corydon addresses the boy who rejects him (Virgil, *Eclogues* 2.60, "whom do you flee, madman?") and Aeneas Dido in the underworld (*Aeneid* 6.466, "Whom do you flee? This is the last time I am fated to address

you"); compare too Apollo's words to the fleeing Daphne: Ovid, *Metamorphoses* 1.514–15 (p. 441 below), "You don't know, rash one, whom you flee and that's why you flee."
6   *individual* "Undivided; not to be parted or disjoined" (Johnson's *Dictionary*).

Richard Lovelace (1618–1658)

When Lovelace entered college in Oxford he was "accounted the most amiable and beautiful person that ever eye beheld," according to his near contemporary, the historian Anthony à Wood. A courtier loyal to the crown, Lovelace was imprisoned by Cromwell's government for the second time in 1648. While in prison he wrote a volume of poetry called *Lucasta* (1649) and exhausted his patrimony supporting the lost cause of Charles I, who was beheaded in the year that *Lucasta* was published.

The Golden Age is a classical myth developed in Hesiod and, later, in Virgil's *Eclogues* and Ovid's *Metamorphoses*.[1] Tibullus in *Elegy* 2.3 (p. 406 below) used the myth to imagine a time of free love, mixing in some of Lucretius' account of early man in *De Rerum Natura* 5. In *Amores* 3.8 Ovid deplores the power of gold to influence girls and thinks longingly of the age of Saturn (the Golden Age) when there was no gold; but he does not depict the Golden Age as one of promiscuity. Like Tibullus and Ovid, Lovelace uses the myth of the Golden Age to complain about his romantic situation. However, instead of coming to the obvious conclusion that he and his lover should indulge their natural passion for each other, he tells Chloris that his Golden Age erotic fantasy is so satisfying that he no longer needs her. The surprise and wit of the ending, of course, are much sharper in light of the classical background of the poem.

The text comes from *Lucasta: Posthume Poems of Richard Lovelace, Esq.* (1659).

RICHARD LOVELACE

1   See our introduction to Aphra Behn's poem "The Golden Age," p. 95 below.

Love Made in the First Age: To Chloris

1

In the Nativity of time,
Chloris! it was not thought a Crime
In direct *Hebrew* for to woo.
Now we make Love, as all on fire,
Ring Retrograde our loud Desire,[1]   5
And Court in *English* Backward too.

2

Thrice happy was that golden Age,
When Compliment was construed Rage,
And fine words in the Center hid;
When cursèd *No* stained no Maid; Bliss,   10
And all discourse was summed in *Yes,*
And Nought forbad, but to forbid.

3

Love then unstinted, Love did sip,
And Cherries plucked fresh from the Lip,
On Cheeks and Roses free he fed;   15
Lasses like *Autumn* Plums did drop,
And Lads, indifferently did crop
A Flower, and a Maidenhead.

4

Then unconfinèd each did Tipple
Wine from the Bunch, Milk from the Nipple,   20
Paps tractable as Udders were.
Then equally the wholesome Jellies,
Were squeezed from Olive Trees, and Bellies,
Nor Suits of Trespass did they fear.

5

A fragrant Bank of Strawberries,   25
Diapered with Violets' Eyes,[2]
Was Table, Tablecloth, and Fare;
No Palace to the Clouds did swell,

LOVE MADE IN THE FIRST AGE   2 *Diapered* variegated.

1 *Retrograde* backward.

Each humble Princess then did dwell
In the *Piazza* of her Hair.[3]   30

6

Both brokèn Faith, and the cause of it,
All damning Gold was damned to the Pit;
Their Troth sealed with a Clap and Kiss,
Lasted until that extreme day,[4]
In which they smiled their Souls away,   35
And in each other breathed new bliss.

7

Because no fault, there was no tear;
No groan did grate the granting Ear;
No false foul breath their Del'cate smell:
No Serpent kiss poisoned the Taste,   40
Each touch was naturally Chaste,
And their mere Sense a Miracle.

8

Naked as their own innocence,
And unembroidered from Offence
They went, above poor Riches, gay;   45
On softer than the Signet's Down,[5]
In beds they tumbled off their own;
For each within the other lay.

9

Thus did they live: Thus did they love,
Repeating only joys Above;   50
And Angels were, but with Clothes on,
Which they would put off cheerfully,
To bathe them in the *Galaxy*,
Then gird them with the Heavenly Zone.[6]

10

Now, *CHLORIS!* miserably crave,   55
The offered bliss you would not have;
Which evermore I must deny,
Whilst ravished with these Noble Dreams,
And crownèd with mine own soft Beams,
Enjoying of myself I lie.   60

3 *Piazza* colonnade or covered gallery (errone-
ously used; see *OED*).
4 *extreme* final, last.

5 *Signet's Down* baby swan feathers.
6 *Zone* belt or girdle; perhaps the constellation
of Orion's belt.

Andrew Marvell (1621–1678)

Unlike John Milton, Marvell made a smooth transition from his role as Cromwell's Latin secretary during the interregnum to government service under King Charles II. However, he soon lost faith in the monarchy and ridiculed supporters such as John Dryden in sensational anti-government pamphlets. His literary fame depends entirely on his unusually intellectual pastoral poetry, most of which was published posthumously. There is latent political meaning in much of this poetry, but Marvell's most explicitly political verse was suppressed. In every known copy but two of *Miscellaneous Poems* (1681), for example, "An Horatian Ode upon Cromwell's Return from Ireland" was cancelled. The poem in praise of the then long dead Protector did not appear widely in print until 1776. The censor, given his objectives, may have known what he was doing, because the poem is a dangerously brilliant endorsement of revolutionary violence.

By linking his voice with that of Horace's in the Roman's grand political odes,[1] Marvell implicitly links Cromwell with Augustus Caesar. He thereby activates a strain of Protestant rhetoric (also employed by Milton) that described the "rebels" as the legitimate rulers whose reign had been interrupted by the so-called establishment in religion and in politics. Marvell's meter (the four-line pattern of two longer and two shorter couplets) is an imitation of Horace's preferred meter for the political odes, alcaics. This imitation is an audible signal of the subtle way that Marvell hits a tone that is both Horatian and, of course, his own: civic yet individual; partisan but detached; politically motivated but finely artistic. Marvell's translation of Horace's tone depends very little on specific allusions to particular Horatian odes, but learned readers will recall *Odes* 3.14 and 4.5, on the return of Augustus, and there is a specific reference to the "Cleopatra Ode," 1.37 (p. 397 below), which celebrates the victory over a flawed but noble adversary.

ANDREW MARVELL

1 See *Odes* 1.2, 12, 35, 37; 3.1–6; 4.4, 5, 14, 15.

To his other main classical source in this poem Marvell alluded more directly. The first 16 lines of the poem refer to passages from Lucan's *Civil War*, or *Pharsalia* (pp. 461–3 below), a poem about the contest in Rome between Julius Caesar and Pompey. Lucan's poem, available in the recent translation by Thomas May, was on the minds of many writers during the British Civil War. Marvell's debt to Lucan extends to the use of specific images, but his overall evocation of the earlier writer is complex. Lucan was sympathetic to the republican Pompey, and Marvell was supporting the republican Cromwell against the monarch Charles; he specifically casts Charles as Caesar at line 23. However, Marvell's initial portrait of Cromwell recalls Lucan's description of Caesar, as does his image of Cromwell as lightning "burning through the air." Characteristically, in his "Horatian Ode" Marvell appropriates, rather than merely borrows, material from the classics and uses what he finds to make his own poetic world.[2]

Appropriation is also at work in Marvell's delightful *carpe diem* poem "To His Coy Mistress." Here Marvell had an ample store of classical commonplaces on which to draw. Horace's *Ode* 1.11 and Catullus 5 are the most obvious sources of the general theme (pp. 396 and 332 below). A tighter connection appears between a section of Marvell's poem and a relatively obscure poem in the *Greek Anthology* attributed to Asclepiades (p. 299 below). Like the earlier poet, Marvell develops the notion that there is no love after death. He may have written lines 25–32 with Asclepiades in mind, but Marvell drew many parts of his appeal from other classical poems: his itemization of the beloved's parts, for example, from Ovid's *Amores* 1.5 (p. 42. below), his *Ars Amatoria* (1.619–30), and from another poem in the *Greek Anthology* (5.132). Earlier English poets had also used these commonplaces, and Marvell expresses a sophistication tinged with weariness in his use of them. His speaker's rejection of the grave as a place of erotic satisfaction, for example, is a sophisticated rejection of an outlandish image in a love poem by Propertius (4.7). There is so much mastery of the genre in "To His Coy Mistress" that a close reader may feel the poet is displaying his plumes for learned readers rather than the object of his amorous desires. Marvell's own art, at least, suggests a detachment from its apparent aims, which secures the poet a kind of sexual independence here, just as it gives him a measure of political independence in the Cromwell Ode.

The texts are based on those collected in *Miscellaneous Poems* (1681).

2 The classical background to Marvell's *Ode* is discussed by R. H. Syfret (*RES* 12, 1961, 160–72); John Coolidge (*MP* 63, 1965, 111–20), and A. J. N. Wilson (*Critical Quarterly*, Winter 1969, 325–41), among others. We are also indebted to the long standard edition of Marvell's poetry, edited by H. M. Margoliouth (1927; rev. 1971), and to the recently published scholarly edition by Nigel Smith (2003).

An *Horatian* Ode upon *Cromwell's* Return from *Ireland*[1]

The forward Youth that would appear[2]
Must now forsake his *Muses* dear,
   Now in the Shadows sing
   His Numbers languishing.[3]
'Tis time to leave the Books in dust,   5
And oil th' unused Armor's rust:
   Removing from the Wall
   The Corslet of the Hall.[4]
So restless *Cromwell* could not cease[5]
In the inglorious Art of Peace,   10
   But through adventrous War
   Urged his active Star.[6]
And, like the three-forked Lightning, first[7]
Breaking the Clouds where it was nurst,
   Did thorough his own Side[8]   15
   His fiery way divide.
For 'tis all one to Courage high
The Emulous or Enemy;
   And with such to enclose[9]
   Is more than to oppose.   20
Then burning through the Air he went,
And Palaces and Temples rent:
   And *Caesar's* head at last[10]
   Did through his Laurels blast.[11]
'Tis Madness to resist or blame   25

AN HORATIAN ODE

1   Oliver Cromwell sailed to Ireland to put down a Royalist rebellion against Parliamentary rule in 1649; he returned in 1650 to launch a similar campaign against the Scots, becoming at that time commander-in-chief of the Parliamentary army.

2 *forward* "Warm; earnest" (Johnson's *Dictionary*); *appear* "to display oneself on the stage of action" (*OED*).

3 *Numbers* verses.

4 *Corslet* "A light armor for the forepart of the body" (Johnson's *Dictionary*).

5 *restless* compare the phrase "restless valour" in May's translation of Lucan (p. 462 below), where it applies to Julius Caesar; *cease* rest (a Latinism based on the verb *cessare*).

6 *Star* "Configuration of the planets supposed to influence fortune" (Johnson).

7 *Lightning* recalls Lucan's comparison of Caesar to lightning (p. 462 below).

8 *Side* "Party; interest; faction; sect" (Johnson).

9 *enclose* limit (the rise or career).

10 *Caesar* the monarch, Charles I.

11 *Laurels* laurel wreaths were a Roman emblem of victory worn by triumphing generals and emperors. Julius Caesar was granted the privilege of wearing laurel at all times (Suetonius, *Divus Julius* 45). According to Pliny (*Natural History* 2.146), laurel was also supposed to prevent lightning strikes.

The force of angry Heaven's flame:
    And, if we would speak true,
    Much to the Man is due.
Who, from his private Gardens, where
He lived reservèd and austere,   30
    As if his highest plot
    To plant the Bergamot,[12]
Could by industrious Valour climb
To ruin the great Work of Time,
    And cast the Kingdom old   35
    Into another Mould.
Though Justice against Fate complain,
And plead the ancient Rights in vain:
    But those do hold or break
    As Men are strong or weak.   40
Nature that hateth emptiness,[13]
Allows of penetration less:[14]
    And therefore must make room
    Where greater Spirits come.
What Field of all the Civil Wars,   45
Where his were not the deepest Scars?
    And *Hampton* shows what part[15]
    He had of wiser Art.
Where, twining subtle fears with hope,[16]
He wove a Net of such a scope,   50
    That *Charles* himself might chase
    To *Carisbrook's* narrow case.
That thence the *Royal Actor* born
The *Tragic Scaffold* might adorn:
    While round the armèd Bands   55
    Did clap their bloody hands.
He nothing common did or mean
Upon that memorable Scene:
    But with his keener Eye
    The Axe's edge did try:[17]   60
Nor called the *Gods* with vulgar spite
To vindicate his helpless Right,

12 *Bergamot* a kind of pear.

13 *Nature . . . hateth emptiness* nature abhors a vacuum, a proverbial axiom of classical physics.

14 *penetration* "a supposed or conceived occupation of the same space by two bodies at the same time" (*OED*).

15 *Hampton* the palace where Charles I was under arrest in 1647 until his escape to Caris-brook on the Isle of Wight, where he was recaptured. Marvell represents the events as part of Cromwell's plan to eliminate the king.

16 *subtle* "Nice; fine; delicate; not coarse" (Johnson).

17 *try* "To act on as a test" (Johnson) but also to experience.

But bowed his comely Head,
   Down as upon a Bed.
This was that memorable Hour   65
Which first assured the forcèd Pow'r.
   So when they did design
   The *Capitol's* first Line,[18]
A bleeding Head where they begun,
Did fright the Architects to run;   70
   And yet in that the *State*
   Foresaw its happy Fate.
And now the *Irish* are ashamed
To see themselves in one Year tamed:
   So much one Man can do,   75
   That does both act and know.
They can affirm his Praises best,
And have, though overcome, confessed
   How good he is, how just,
   And fit for highest Trust: 80
Nor yet grown stiffer with Command,
But still in the *Republic*'s hand:
   How fit he is to sway
   That can so well obey.
He to the *Commons' Feet* presents[19]   85
A *Kingdom,* for his first year's rents:
   And, what he may, forbears
   His Fame to make it theirs:
And has his Sword and Spoils ungirt,
To lay them at the *Public*'s skirt.   90
   So when the Falcon high[20]
   Falls heavy from the Sky,
She, having killed, no more does search,
But on the next green Bough to perch;
   Where, when he first does lure,[21]   95
   The Falc'ner has her sure.
What may not then our *Isle* presume
While Victory his Crest does plume!

18 *Capitol* the temple of Jupiter on the Capitoline Hill, which was begun by Rome's last king and dedicated in the first year of the Republic (509 BCE); a bloody head (*caput*) found during the excavation was interpreted by soothsayers to foretell that Rome would be head of the world (Livy 1.55.5–6; Pliny, *Natural History* 28.15).

19 *Commons' Feet* the House of Commons; this is a reading found in an annotated copy of the poem and adopted by Smith (p. 277n) because it is "more consistent with the politics of the republic" than "Common," the reading of the copy-text.

20 *Falcon* possibly recalls Horace's simile of the hawk and the dove to describe Octavian's pursuit of Cleopatra (*Odes* 1.37; p. 397 below).

21 *lure* "To call hawks" (Johnson).

What may not others fear
If thus he crown each year! 100
A *Caesar* he ere long to *Gaul*,[22]
To *Italy* an *Hannibal*,[23]
  And to all States not free
  Shall *Climacteric* be.[24]
The *Pict* no shelter now shall find[25] 105
Within his party-coloured Mind;
  But from this Valour sad
  Shrink underneath the Plaid:
Happy if in the tufted brake[26]
The *English Hunter* him mistake; 110
  Nor lay his Hounds in near
  The *Caledonian* Deer.[27]
But thou the War's and Fortune's Son
March indefatigably on;
  And for the last effect 115
  Still keep thy Sword erect:
Besides the force it has to fright[28]
The Spirits of the shady Night,
  The same *Arts* that did *gain*
  A *Pow'r* must it *maintain*. 120

To His Coy Mistress

Had we but World enough, and Time,
This coyness Lady were no crime.
We would sit down, and think which way
To walk, and pass our long Love's Day.
Thou by the *Indian Ganges'* side 5
Should'st Rubies find: I by the Tide
Of *Humber* would complain. I would[1]

22 *Gaul* France, conquered by Julius Caesar.
23 *Hannibal* the Carthaginian general who conquered much of the Italian peninsula (see Juvenal, *Satire* 10; p. 486 below).
24 *Climacteric* from *climacter*, "A certain space of time or progression of years, which is supposed to end in a critical or dangerous time" (Johnson)
25 *Pict* British ancestor of the Scots; the Roman name means "painted" or "parti-colored"; Marvell puns on "party."

26 *brake* "A thicket of brambles or of thorns" (Johnson).
27 *Caledonian* Scottish.
28 *the force it has to fright* it was once believed that shades fear the drawn sword; see *Odyssey* 11.48 and *Aeneid* 6.260.

TO HIS COY MISTRESS

1 *Humber* a river in northern England, in Yorkshire, Marvell's home county; from the Ganges to the Humber was about the extent of the classical world.

Love you ten years before the Flood
And you should if you please refuse
Till the Conversion of the *Jews*.[2]   10
My vegetable Love should grow
Vaster than Empires, and more slow.
An hundred years should go to praise
Thine Eyes, and on thy Forehead Gaze.
Two hundred to adore each Breast: 15
But thirty thousand to the rest.
An Age at least to every part,
And the last Age should show your Heart.
For Lady you deserve this State;
Nor would I love at lower rate.   20
    But at my back I always hear
Time's wingèd Chariot hurrying near:
And yonder all before us lie
Deserts of vast Eternity.
Thy Beauty shall no more be found;   25
Nor, in thy marble Vault, shall sound
My echoing Song: then Worms shall try
That long preserved Virginity:
And your quaint Honour turn to dust;
And into ashes all my Lust.   30
The Grave's a fine and private place,
But none I think do there embrace.
    Now therefore, while the youthful glew[3]
Sits on thy skin like morning dew,
And while thy willing Soul transpires[4]   35
At every pore with instant Fires,
Now let us sport us while we may;
And now, like am'rous birds of prey,
Rather at once our Time devour,
Than languish in his slow-chapt pow'r.[5]   40
Let us roll all our Strength, and all
Our sweetness, up into one Ball:
And tear our Pleasure with rough strife,
Thorough the Iron gates of Life.[6]
Thus, though we cannot make our Sun   45
Stand still, yet we will make him run.

---

2 *ten years before the Flood . . . Conversion of the*
Jews virtually all of biblical time, from Genesis to
Revelation.
3 *glew* perspiration; often emended to read
"hue" (see Smith, p. 83n).

4 *transpire* "To be emitted by insensible vapour"
(Johnson's *Dictionary*).
5 *slow-chapt* (eating) with slowly moving jaws.
6 *Thorough* through.

John Dryden (1631–1700)

Dryden was the most important playwright and critic and, with the exception of John Milton, the greatest poet of his age. He was also, and remains today, one of the best translators of classical poetry. Dryden is much more fully represented in this anthology as a translator (see the selections from Virgil and Juvenal, pp. 361–71 and 472–95 below) than as a creator of original works. He wrote his most ambitious translations toward the end of his career, after 1688, when he found himself on the wrong side of the Glorious Revolution, but his whole career as a writer depended upon his knowledge of the classics. His Westminster School Latin teacher, Richard Busby, was notorious as a disciplinarian and famous as a brilliant teacher; Dryden was certainly his most apt pupil, and everything he wrote is partly a translation of the classics, whether the subject was political or personal. When, for example, he set out to write an elegy for the satirist John Oldham, he thought first of a poem by Catullus (*Carmen* 101; p. 335 below) and embellished it with reference to episodes out of Virgil's *Aeneid* (pp. 375 and 381 below). Both allusions tighten the connection between Dryden and Oldham that the poem as a whole asserts, although the two were probably not that well acquainted in reality. Catullus wrote to his brother in the source poem, and one Virgilian passage describes the bond between two friends ready to sacrifice anything for each other. The other Virgilian passage to which Dryden alludes laments the death at age 20 of a wealthy and magnanimous member of the imperial family. Dryden may well have expected a learned reader of the time to see that there was a kind of hyperbole in his classical allusions and to appreciate that overstatement as an aspect of his admirable poetic performance.

The text presented here comes from *Remains of Mr. John Oldham in Verse and Prose* (1684).

To the Memory of Mr. *Oldham*[1]

Farewell, too little and too lately known,
Whom I began to think and call my own;
For sure our Souls were near allied; and thine
Cast in the same Poetic mould with mine.
One common Note on either Lyre did strike,   5
And Knaves and Fools were both abhorred alike:
To the same Goal did both our Studies drive,
The last set out the soonest did arrive.
Thus *Nisus* fell upon the slippery place,[2]
While his young Friend performed and won the Race.   10
O early ripe! to thy abundant store
What could advancing Age have added more?
It might (what Nature never gives the young)
Have taught the numbers of thy native Tongue.[3]
But Satire needs not those, and Wit will shine   15
Through the harsh cadence of a rugged line:[4]
A noble Error, and but seldom made,
When Poets are by too much force betrayed.
Thy generous fruits, though gathered ere their prime
Still showed a quickness; and maturing time[5]   20
But mellows what we write to the dull sweets of Rhyme.
Once more, hail and farewell; farewell thou young[6]
But ah too short, *Marcellus* of our Tongue;[7]
Thy Brows with Ivy, and with Laurels bound;
But Fate and gloomy Night encompass thee around.[8]   25

TO THE MEMORY OF MR. OLDHAM

1 John Oldham (1653–1683) was a poet best known for his *Satyrs upon the Jesuits* (1681); he probably met Dryden in London shortly after the publication of that work, but allusions in his earlier work show that he had admired Dryden for years.

2 *Nisus* having fallen near the finish line, Nisus tripped the next runner and gave the victory to his close friend Euryalus (*Aeneid* 5.315–39; p. 375 below).

3 *numbers* harmony, correct prosody.

4 The rugged harmony of this line exemplifies the kind of verse it praises.

5 *quickness* "Sharpness; pungency" (Johnson's *Dictionary*).

6 *hail and farewell* a translation of *ave atque vale* – Catullus' farewell to his dead brother (p. 336 below).

7 *Marcellus* son-in-law and adoptive son of Augustus Caesar, destined for empire; he died at the age of 20 and was memorialized in a famous passage of the *Aeneid* (6.860–86; p. 381 below). Specifically, Dryden recalls Anchises' apostrophe to Marcellus: "Alas, pitiable youth, if only you could break through harsh fate – you will be Marcellus" (p. 382 below).

8 *gloomy Night ... around* compare Virgil, *Aeneid* 6.866 (p. 382 below).

Aphra Behn (1640?–1689)

As a young woman Aphra Behn (born Johnson) was involved in government espionage on the continent and perhaps in Suriname where she lived for a time on a plantation. Her code name, which she later adopted in her poetry, was Astraea. Behn was a prolific author. She wrote at least 19 plays, much poetry, and numerous works of fiction, including the slave narrative *Oroonoko*, which has become a standard work in most surveys of Restoration and eighteenth-century literature. Behn's reputation suffered in the later eighteenth century and the nineteenth century, when her works were often regarded as shocking. Modern writers, including Virginia Woolf, however, recognized her importance to the development of a female tradition in literature, and her bold explorations of sex and power – in both the personal and political spheres – helped bring her back into prominence in the late twentieth century.

The poems selected here come from a period in which Behn was closely associated with Lord Rochester (p. 106 below) and his circle of libertines. "The Disappointment" was, in fact, originally thought to be by Rochester, who wrote a poem on the same theme, "The Imperfect Enjoyment." Rochester and his friends wrote mainly for each other rather than for the public, but Behn depended upon publication for her living (she may have been the first professional woman writer). Like private poetry, however, Behn's poems from this period – like much of her poetry – involve masking and the use of nicknames for the members of her circle.

As such poetic names as Astraea, Amyntas, Cloris, and Celladon suggest, Behn wished her works to recall classical poetry. Unlike the male libertines with whom she consorted, Behn may have read her classics in translation (French and English), but her verses in praise of Thomas Creech's Lucretius (1683) and Henry Higden's Juvenal (1687) show that she developed a critical appreciation of the tradition. Much of her other work, such as several Pindaric poems and "Ovid to Julia. A Poem," also demonstrates her interest in classical writing. In "The Disappointment" Behn evidently used a French source as well as, or perhaps instead of, Ovid's notorious Latin poem *Amores* 3.7 (p. 425 below). Unlike Ovid (and Rochester), Behn does not use a heroic verse form but rather the lower form of iambic tetrameter in stanzas; she makes the setting pastoral rather than urban or courtly; and she makes her heroine relatively innocent. Behn also writes a fuller narrative than Ovid (or Rochester), and she expresses an interest in the perspective of the woman in the story. Behn's woman is more visibly beautiful than Ovid's; her beauty contributes to the man's premature ejaculation; and her hasty departure from the scene of sexual failure is an important part of the story. Nevertheless, the story itself and the light, arch style, supported by mock-heroic language, are Ovidian. Behn's poem could not have existed without Ovid's, and the relationship of Behn's poem to Ovid's is a large part of its meaning.

"The Golden Age" takes its title from a concept that is widespread in classical poetry. Some of the main treatments of the theme are in Hesiod, *Works and Days* (p. 279 below), Virgil, *Eclogue* 4 (p. 342 below), and Ovid, *Metamorphoses* 1.89–112 (p. 436 below). The features of this perfect, pre-lapsarian world, which Milton and other Christian writers incorporated into their Edenic visions, include eternal spring, flowers, gentle breezes, clear skies, and harmony of all creatures, without excessive labor, war, greed, ambition, and private property. Like everyone else in her time, Behn got her classics partly through Milton and other humanists (including, in this poem, the Italian epic poet Torquato Tasso). Nevertheless, her evocation of classical originals is undeniable, partly because it is occasionally critical. Behn makes the appearance of the ambiguous and socially constructed concept of honor the chief villain in the death of the Golden Age. In her classical sources, the loss of some virtue usually signals the end. In many stories Justice leaves the world and the world lapses into its mortal state; in Juvenal, *Satire* 6 (p. 474 below), Chastity departs with Justice. But Behn reverses the action, seeing honor as a false standard (like Juvenal's chastity), imposed by men on women. Honor is the code that prevents women from enjoying the natural pleasures of paradise, especially sexual expression. Behn's ascription of sexual freedom to the Golden Age has a sort of precedent in Milton's *Paradise Lost* (angels have sex in heaven as do Adam and Eve in Eden), but is better exemplified in Tibullus' *Elegies* (2.3; p. 406 below). At the end of the poem, Behn glides from her condemnation of honor to the best-known theme of Latin love poetry, *carpe diem* (pluck the day), which is most famously exemplified in Catullus 5 (p. 332 below).

The texts presented here are based on those in *Poems upon Several Occasions* (1684).

The Disappointment[1]

1

One day the Amorous *Lysander*,[2]
By an impatient Passion swayed,
Surprised fair *Cloris*, that loved Maid,
Who could defend herself no longer.
All things did with his Love conspire;   5
That gilded Planet of the Day,
In his gay Chariot drawn by Fire,
Was now descending to the Sea,
And left no Light to guide the World,
But what from *Cloris'* Brighter Eyes was hurled.   10

2

In a lone Thicket made for Love,
Silent as yielding Maid's Consent,
She with a Charming Languishment,
Permits his Force, yet gently strove;
Her Hands his Bosom softly meet,   15
But not to put him back designed,
Rather to draw 'em on inclined:
Whilst he lay trembling at her Feet,
Resistance 'tis in vain to show;
She wants the power to say, "Ah! What d' ye do?"[3]   20

3

Her Bright Eyes sweet, and yet severe,
Where Love and Shame confus'dly strive,
Fresh Vigor to *Lysander* give;
And breathing faintly in his Ear,
She cried, "Cease, Cease–your vain Desire,   25
Or I'll call out–What would you do?
My Dearer Honour ev'n to You
I cannot, must not give–Retire,
Or take this Life, whose chiefest part
I gave you with the Conquest of my Heart."   30

THE DISAPPOINTMENT

1   This poem was long thought to be by John Wilmot (see pp. 106–8 below) and was first published, with many differences, in a poorly edited collection of his verse, *Poems on Several Occasions* (1680). It begins as a translation of a French poem called "Sur une Impuissance" by de Cantenac first published in 1661, which in turn is based on Ovid, *Amores* 3. 7 (p. 425 below).

2   *Lysander* like *Cloris*, a classical name used frequently in pastoral poetry in English.

3   *wants* lacks.

4

But he as much unused to Fear,
As he was capable of Love,
The blessèd minutes to improve,
Kisses her Mouth, her Neck, her Hair;
Each Touch her new Desire Alarms,   35
His burning trembling Hand he pressed
Upon her swelling Snowy Breast,
While she lay panting in his Arms.
All her Unguarded Beauties lie
The Spoils and Trophies of the Enemy.   40

5

And now without Respect or Fear,
He seeks the Object of his Vows,
(His Love no Modesty allows)
By swift degrees advancing–where
His daring Hand that Altar seized,   45
Where Gods of Love do sacrifice:
That Awful Throne, that Paradise
Where Rage is calmed, and Anger pleased;
That Fountain where Delight still flows,
And gives the Universal World Repose.   50

6

Her Balmy Lips encount'ring his,
Their Bodies, as their Souls, are joined;
Where both in Transports Unconfined
Extend themselves upon the Moss.
Cloris half dead and breathless lay;   55
Her soft Eyes cast a Humid Light,
Such as divides the Day and Night;
Or falling Stars, whose Fires decay:
And now no signs of Life she shows,
But what in short-breathed Sighs returns & goes.   60

7

He saw how at her Length she lay;
He saw her rising Bosom bare;
Her loose thin *Robes*, through which appear
A Shape designed for Love and Play;
Abandoned by her Pride and Shame.   65
She does her softest Joys dispense,
Off'ring her Virgin-Innocence
A Victim to Love's Sacred Flame;
While the o'er-Ravished Shepherd lies
Unable to perform the Sacrifice.   70

8

Ready to taste a thousand Joys,
The too transported hapless Swain
Found the vast Pleasure turned to Pain;
Pleasure which too much Love destroys:
The willing Garments by he laid,   75
And Heaven all opened to his view,
Mad to possess, himself he threw
On the Defenseless Lovely Maid.
But Oh what envying God conspires
To snatch his Power, yet leave him the Desire!   80

9

Nature's Support (without whose Aid
She can no Human Being give)
Itself now wants the Art to live;
Faintness its slackened Nerves invade:
In vain th' enragèd Youth essayed[4]   85
To call its fleeting Vigor back,
No motion 'twill from Motion take;
Excess of Love his Love betrayed:
In vain he Toils, in vain Commands;
The Insensible fell weeping in his Hand.   90

10

In this so Amorous Cruel Strife,
Where Love and Fate were too severe,
The poor *Lysander* in despair
Renounced his Reason with his Life:
Now all the brisk and active Fire   95
That should the Nobler Part inflame,
Served to increase his Rage and Shame,
And left no Spark for New Desire:
Not all her Naked Charms could move
Or calm that Rage that had debauched his Love.   100

11

Cloris returning from the Trance
Which Love and soft Desire had bred,
Her timorous Hand she gently laid
(Or guided by Design or Chance)
Upon that Fabulous *Priapus*,[5]   105

4   *essayed* tried.
5   *Priapus* Greek fertility god whose symbol is   the phallus; hence his name is synonymous with
                                                           phallus.

That Potent God, as Poets feign;
But never did young *Shepherdess*,
Gath'ring of Fern upon the Plain,
More nimbly draw her Fingers back,
Finding beneath the verdant Leaves a Snake: 110

12

Than *Cloris* her fair Hand withdrew,
Finding that God of her Desires
Disarmed of all his Awful Fires,
And Cold as Flow'rs bathed in the Morning-Dew.
Who can the *Nymph*'s Confusion guess?   115
The Blood forsook the hinder Place,
And strewed with Blushes all her Face,
Which both Disdain and Shame expressed:
And from *Lysander*'s Arms she fled,[6]
Leaving him fainting on the Gloomy Bed.   120

13

Like Lightning through the Grove she hies,
Or *Daphne* from the *Delphic God*,[7]
No Print upon the grassy Road
She leaves, t' instruct Pursuing Eyes.
The Wind that wantoned in her Hair,   125
And with her Ruffled Garments played,
Discovered in the Flying Maid
All that the Gods e'er made, if Fair.
So *Venus*, when her *Love* was slain,
With Fear and Haste flew o'er the Fatal Plain.[8]   130

14

The *Nymph*'s Resentments none but I
Can well Imagine or Condole:
But none can guess *Lysander*'s Soul,
But those who swayed his Destiny.
His silent Griefs swell up to Storms,   135
And not one God his Fury spares;

---

6 *fled* compare the departure in disgust of Ovid's more worldly mistress, who cleanses herself with water so her maids will think she has had intercourse (p. 428 below).

7 *Daphne ... Delphic God* the nymph's lengthy flight from Apollo ends with her transformation into a laurel tree (Ovid, *Metamorphoses* 1.452–567; pp. 439–43 below).

8 *Venus ... o'er the Fatal Plain* the goddess, seeing Adonis slain, turns her swan-borne chariot and jumps down from the sky (Ovid, *Metamorphoses* 10.720–2).

He cursed his Birth, his Fate, his Stars;[9]
But more the *Shepherdess*'s Charms,
Whose soft bewitching Influence
Had Damned him to the *Hell* of Impotence.   140

The Golden Age

A Paraphrase on a Translation out of French[1]

1

Blest Age! when every Purling Stream
Ran undisturbed and clear,
When no scorned Shepherds on your Banks were seen,
Tortured by Love, by Jealousy, or Fear;
When an Eternal Spring dressed every Bough,   5
And Blossoms fell, by new ones dispossessed;
These their kind Shade affording all below;
And those a Bed where all below might rest.
The Groves appeared all dressed with Wreaths of Flowers,
And from their Leaves dropped Aromatic Showers,   10
Whose fragrant Heads in Mystic Twines above,
Exchanged their Sweets, and mixed with thousand Kisses,
      As if the willing Branches strove
      To beautify and shade the Grove
      Where the young wanton Gods of Love   15
Offer their Noblest Sacrifice of Blisses.

2

Calm was the Air, no Winds blew fierce and loud,
The Sky was darkened with no sullen Cloud;
But all the Heav'ns laughed with continued Light,
And scattered round their Rays serenely bright.   20
      No other Murmurs filled the Ear
      But what the Streams and Rivers purled,
When Silver Waves o'er Shining Pebbles curled;

---

9 *He cursed . . . Stars* but not his penis, like Ovid (p. 428 below) and Rochester ("The Imperfect Enjoyment," ll. 46–72; p. 108 below).

THE GOLDEN AGE

1 *A Paraphrase on a Translation out of French*
As Janet Todd notes in her edition of Behn's *Works* (1992), Behn's poem derives from the opening chorus of Torquato Tasso's *Aminta* (1573); no intermediary French translation has been identified.

    Or when young *Zephyrs* fanned the Gentle Breeze,
      Gath'ring fresh Sweets from Balmy Flow'rs and Trees,   25
Then bore 'em on their Wings to perfume all the Air:
        While to their soft and tender Play,
        The Gray-Plumed Natives of the Shades
      Unwearied sing till Love invades,
Then Bill, then sing again, while Love and Music makes the Day.   30

              3
      The stubborn Plough had then,
    Made no rude Rapes upon the Virgin Earth;
Who yielded of her own accord her plenteous Birth,
      Without the Aids of men;
        As if within her Teeming Womb,   35
        All Nature, and all Sexes lay,
        Whence new Creations every day
        Into the happy World did come:
        The Roses filled with Morning Dew,
      Bent down their loaded heads,   40
    T'adorn the careless Shepherds' Grassy Beds
    While still young op'ning Buds each moment grew,
And as those withered, dressed his shaded Couch anew;
    Beneath whose boughs the Snakes securely dwelt,
    Not doing harm, nor harm from others felt;   45
    With whom the Nymphs did Innocently play,
    No spightful Venom in the wantons lay;
But to the touch were Soft, and to the sight were Gay.

              4
      Then no rough sound of Wars' Alarms,
    Had taught the World the needless use of Arms: 50
      Monarchs were uncreated then,
    Those Arbitrary Rulers over men;
    Kings that made Laws, first broke 'em, and the Gods
By teaching us Religion first, first set the World at Odds:
      Till then Ambition was not known,   55
    That Poison to Content, Bane to Repose;
    Each Swain was Lord o'er his own will alone,
    His Innocence Religion was, and Laws.
    Nor needed any troublesome defence
      Against his Neighbours' Insolence.   60
    Flocks, Herds, and every necessary good
    Which bounteous Nature had designed for Food,
    Whose kind increase o'er-spread the Meads and Plains,
Was then a common Sacrifice to all th'agreeing Swains.

5

Right and Property were words since made,   65
    When Power taught Mankind to invade:
When Pride and Avarice became a Trade;
    Carried on by discord, noise and wars,
    For which they bartered wounds and scars;
And to Enhance the Merchandise, miscalled it Fame,   70
    And Rapes, Invasions, Tyrannies,
    Was gaining of a Glorious Name:
    Styling their savage slaughters, Victories;
    Honour, the Error and the Cheat
    Of the Ill-natured Busy Great,   75
    Nonsense, invented by the Proud,
    Fond Idol of the slavish Crowd,
    Thou wert not known in those blessed days
Thy Poison was not mixed with our unbounded Joys;
    Then it was glory to pursue delight,   80
And that was lawful all, that Pleasure did invite,
    Then 'twas the Amorous world enjoyed its Reign;
And Tyrant Honour strove t'usurp in Vain.

6

The flow'ry Meads the Rivers and the Groves,
Were filled with little Gay-winged Loves: 85
That ever smiled and danced and Played,
And now the woods, and the streams invade,
And where they came all things were gay and glad:
When in the Myrtle Groves the Lovers sat
    Oppressed with a too fervent heat;   90
A Thousand Cupids fanned their wings aloft,
And through the Boughs the yielded Air would wait:
    Whose parting Leaves discovered all below,
And every God his own soft power admired,
And smiled and fanned, and sometimes bent his Bow;   95
Where'er he saw a Shepherd uninspired.
The Nymphs were free, no nice, no coy disdain,
Denied their Joys, or gave the Lover pain;
The yielding Maid but kind Resistance makes;
Trembling and blushing are not marks of shame,   100
    But the Effect of kindling Flame:
Which from the sighing burning Swain she takes,
While she with tears all soft, and downcast eyes,
Permits the Charming Conqueror to win the prize.

7

The Lovers thus, thus uncontrolled did meet,   105
Thus all their Joys and Vows of Love repeat:

Joys which were everlasting, ever new
   And every Vow inviolably true:
Not kept in fear of Gods, no fond Religious cause,
   Nor in Obedience to the duller Laws.   110
   Those Fopperies of the Gown were then not known,[2]
   Those vain those Politic Curbs to keep man in,[3]
Who by a fond mistake Created that a Sin;
Which freeborn we, by right of Nature claim our own.
   Who but the Learnèd and dull moral Fool   115
Could gravely have foreseen, man ought to live by Rule?

8

Oh cursèd Honour! thou who first didst damn,
   A Woman to the Sin of shame;
   Honour! that rob'st us of our Gust,[4]
   Honour! that hindered mankind first,   120
At Love's Eternal Spring to squench his amorous thirst.
   Honour! who first taught lovely Eyes the art,
   To wound, and not to cure the heart:
With Love t' invite, but to forbid with Awe,
And to themselves prescribe a Cruèl Law;   125
   To Veil 'em from the Lookers on,
   When they are sure the slave's undone,
And all the Charming'st part of Beauty hid;
Soft Looks, consenting Wishes, all denied.
   It gathers up the flowing Hair,   130
   That loosely played with wanton Air.
The Envious Net, and stinted order hold,
The lovely Curls of Jet and shining Gold,
No more neglected on the Shoulders hurled:
Now dressed to Tempt, not gratify the World,   135
Thou Miser Honour hord'st the sacred store,
And starv'st thyself to keep thy Votaries poor.

9

Honour! that put'st our words that should be free
   Into a set Formality.
Thou base Debaucher of the gen'rous heart,   140
That teachest all our Looks and Actions Art;
   What Love designed a sacred Gift,
   What Nature made to be possessed,
   Mistaken Honour, made a Theft,
   For Glorious Love should be confessed: 145

---

2 *Fopperies of the Gown* academic terms created by doctors of divinity or law.
3 *Politic* "Prudent" (Johnson's *Dictionary*, sense 2).
4 *Gust* "Height of perception; height of sensual enjoyment" (Johnson, sense 2).

For when confined, all the poor Lover gains,
Is broken Sighs, pale Looks, Complaints & Pains.
Thou Foe to Pleasure, Nature's worst Disease,
   Thou Tyrant over mighty Kings,
What mak'st thou here in Shepherds' Cottages;   150
Why troublest thou, the quiet Shades & Springs
    Be gone, and make thy Famed resort
       To Princes' Palaces;
Go Deal and Chaffer in the Trading Court,[5]
That busy Market for fantastic Things;   155
Be gone and interrupt the short Retreat,
   Of the Illustrious and the Great;
   Go break the Politician's sleep,
   Disturb the Gay Ambitious Fool,
   That longs for Scepters, Crowns, and Rule,   160
Which not his Title, nor his Wit can keep;
But let the humble honest *Swain* go on,
In the blessed Paths of the first rate of man;[6]
   That nearest were to Gods Allied,
And formed for love alone, disdained all other Pride.   165

          10
Be gone! and let the Golden age again,
    Assume its Glorious Reign;
   Let the young wishing Maid confess,
   What all your Arts would keep concealed:
   The Mystery will be revealed,   170
And she in vain denies, whilst we can guess,
She only shows the Jilt to teach man how,[7]
To turn the false Artillery on the Cunning Foe.
   Thou empty Vision hence, be gone,
      And let the peaceful *Swain* love on;   175
The swift paced hours of life soon steal away;
   Stint not ye Gods his short-lived Joy.
The Spring decays, but when the Winter's gone,
   The Trees and Flowers anew come on;
The Sun may set, but when the night is fled,   180
   And gloomy darkness does retire,
   He rises from his Wat'ry Bed:[8]

5 *Chaffer* To buy or barter.
6 *rate* "Degree; comparative height or valour" (Johnson, sense 3).
7 *shows the Jilt* plays the part of "A woman who gives her lover hopes, and deceives him" (Johnson).

8 *The Sun . . . Bed* the contrast between the sun's rebirth and the eternity of death recalls Catullus 5 (p. 332 below).

All Glorious, Gay, all dressed in Amorous Fire.
    But *Sylvia* when your Beauties fade,[9]
When the fresh Roses on your cheeks shall die,   185
    Like Flowers that wither in the Shade,
Eternally they will forgotten lie,
And no kind Spring their sweetness will supply.
When Snow shall on those lovely Tresses lie
And your fair Eyes no more shall give us pain,   190
    But shoot their pointless Darts in vain,
What will your duller honour signify?
Go boast it then! and see what numerous Store
Of Lovers, will your Ruined Shrine Adore.
    Then let us *Sylvia* yet be wise,   195
    And the Gay hasty minutes prize:
The Sun and Spring receive but our short Light,
Once set, a sleep brings an Eternal Night.[10]

9 *Sylvia* a Latin name meaning "girl of the woodlands."

10 *The Sun . . . Night* the couplet is indebted to Catullus 5 (p. 332 below).

John Wilmot, Second Earl of Rochester (1647–1680)

Rochester spent much of his short life as a profligate drunk at the court of King Charles II. He learned to drink and whore at Oxford, which he entered at age 12. He was already an accomplished student, wrote Latin poetry, and was given an MA at age 14. After touring the continent, Rochester returned to England to fight in the army, and to engage in vandalism, rape, and manslaughter with a pack of courtiers whose wit, family connections, and military valor usually excused them from the law. Late in life, when he became ill, Rochester repented and became serious about religion. He repudiated his former life and wished his writings to be destroyed. Fortunately, much has survived, despite the fact that the only contemporary edition of his poems (1680?) is poorly printed. Manuscripts passed around among his friends and friends of friends fill out the record.

Rochester's poetry so brazenly contemns standards of decorum that much of it remained largely unprinted for centuries. Despite his ethical transgressions, Rochester often observes classical models in his poetry. However, he chooses the bawdiest poems to imitate, poems that made it into print and general circulation only under the protection of the names of the great classical poets and because, being in Latin, they would be confined to the learned. Still, many of these poems were forbidden fruit. Rochester chooses one of the choicest of these, Ovid's *Amores* 3.7, as the model for his poem "The Imperfect Enjoyment." Although some writers on the classics apologized for such deviations into lewdness among the classical writers, and tried to bowdlerize them, Rochester outdoes Ovid for lewdness. He adds obscenity, additional sexual imagery, and the important event of premature ejaculation. He focuses his poem even more on the male's penis than Ovid had, making it practically a character in its own right. Nevertheless, Rochester is mainly embellishing (and exaggerating) Ovid, who used the same situation; engaged in similar boasting about previous conquests; wondered if he were under a magic spell; and likewise cursed his penis for failing him at the crucial moment. "The Imperfect Enjoyment" should be compared not only to Ovid's *Amores* 3.7 (p. 425 below) but also to Aphra Behn's "The Disappointment" (p. 96 above).

The text presented here comes from *Poems on Several Occasions* (1680?).

The Imperfect Enjoyment

Naked she lay, clasped in my longing Arms,
I filled with Love, and she all over Charms;
Both equally inspired with eager fire,
Melting through kindness, flaming in desire.
With *Arms*, *Legs*, *Lips* close clinging to embrace,   5
She clips me to her *Breast*, and sucks me to her *Face*.[1]
Her nimble *Tongue* (*Love*'s lesser Lightning) played
Within my *Mouth*, and to my thoughts conveyed
Swift Orders that I should prepare to throw
The *All-dissolving Thunderbolt* below.   10
My flutt'ring *Soul*, sprung with the pointed Kiss,
Hangs hov'ring o'er her *Balmy Lips* of Bliss.
But whilst her busy hand would guide that part,
Which should convey my *Soul* up to her *Heart*,
In Liquid *Raptures* I dissolve all o'er,   15
Melt into Sperm, and spend at every Pore.
A touch from any part of her had done 't:
Her Hand, her Foot, her very Look's a *Cunt*.
          Smiling, she Chides in a kind murm'ring *Noise*,
And from her Body wipes the Clammy Joys,   20
When, with a Thousand Kisses wand'ring o'er
My panting Bosom, "Is there then no more?"
She cries. "All this to Love and Rapture's due;
Must we not pay a Debt to Pleasure too?"
          But I, the most forlorn, lost Man alive,   25
To show my wished Obedience vainly strive:
I Sigh, alas! and Kiss, but cannot *Swive*.
Eager desires confound my first intent,
Succeeding shame does more success prevent,
And Rage at last confirms me Impotent.   30
Ev'n her fair Hand, which might bid heat return
To frozen Age, and make cold *Hermits* burn,
Applied to my dead *Cinder*, warms no more
Than Fire to Ashes could past Flames restore.
Trembling, confused, despairing, limber, dry,   35
A wishing, weak, unmoving Lump I lie.
This *Dart* of Love, whose piercing point, oft tried,

THE IMPERFECT ENJOYMENT

1   *clips* hugs.

With *Virgin blood Ten Thousand Maids* has dyed;
Which *Nature* still directed with such *Art*
That it through every *Cunt* reached every *Heart* –　　　　　40
Stiffly resolved, 'twould carelessly invade
Woman or *Boy*, nor aught its fury stayed:
Where e'er it pierced, a *Cunt* it found or made –
Now languid lies in this unhappy hour,
Shrunk up and Sapless like a withered Flower.　　　　　45
　　　　Thou treacherous, base deserter of my flame,
False to my Passion, fatal to my Fame,
Through what mistaken *Magic* dost thou prove
So true to Lewdness, so untrue to Love?
What *Oyster-Cinder-Beggar*-Common *Whore*[2]　　　　　50
Didst thou e'er fail in all thy Life before?
When *Vice, Disease*, and *Scandal* lead the way,
With what officious haste dost thou obey!
Like a Rude, roaring *Hector* in the Streets[3]
Who Scuffles, Cuffs, and Justles all he meets,　　　　　55
But if his King or Country claim his Aid,
The *Rascal Villain* shrinks and hides his Head;
Ev'n so thy Brutal Valour is displayed,
Breaks every *Stew*, does each small *Whore invade*,[4]
But if great *Love* the onset does command,　　　　　60
Base Recreant to thy *Prince*, thou dar'st not stand.
Worst part of me, and henceforth hated most,
Through all the *Town* a common *Fucking Post*,
On whom each *Whore* relieves her tingling *Cunt*
As *Hogs* on gates do rub themselves and grunt,　　　　　65
Mayst thou to rav'nous *Cankers* be a *Prey*,
Or in consuming *Weepings* waste away;
May *Stranguries* and *Stone* thy *Days* attend;[5]
May'st thou ne'er Piss, who didst refuse to spend
When all my Joys did on False thee depend.　　　　　70
　　　　And may *Ten Thousand* abler *Pricks* agree
To do the wronged *Corinna* right for thee.[6]

2　*oyster* oysterwench, "A woman whose business is to sell oysters. Proverbially. A low woman" (Johnson's *Dictionary*, compare Shakespeare, *Richard II*, 1.4.31).
3　*Hector* "A bully; a blustering, turbulent, pervicacious, noisy fellow" (Johnson).
4　*Stew* brothel.
5　*Strangury* "A difficulty of urine attended with pain" (Johnson); *Stone* a concretion in the kidneys or bladder that blocks urination.
6　*Corinna* Ovid's literary mistress.

Jonathan Swift (1667–1745)

Swift is best known for *Gulliver's Travels* (1726), a mock account of voyages into faraway places and a trenchant satire on both the politics of his day and human nature itself. Although it is not as frequently read as his prose, Swift's verse displays many of the same satirical qualities. A graduate of Trinity College, Dublin, Swift was a keen reader of the classics who was later ordained in the Church of Ireland, and eventually installed as the dean of St. Patrick's Cathedral in Dublin. The deanship was, however, a disappointment for him; he had hoped that his service to the Tory ministry under Queen Anne would get him a place as bishop in England. He wrote the following poem at the beginning of his longest stay in London (1710–1714), just after the Tory party gained control of the government from the Whigs. The heroic couplets of the poem are unusual for Swift, who favored the less heroic tetrameter, but the adaptation of a classical theme to the modern world is highly characteristic of his writings. Here Swift superimposes a modern urban scene on famous classical descriptions of country storms. Foremost in Swift's mind is Virgil, *Georgics* 1.311–423 (p. 353 below): he uses the passage as background not only for his description of the storm, but also for the prognostications of the storm's arrival. Swift reduces the shooting stars and soaring herons in Virgil's catalogue of storm signs to modern, urban sights: pensive cats, stinking sewers, and aching corns. In describing the storm itself, Swift must also have thought of *Aeneid* 1.50–156 (pp. 365–8 below), the most famous classical storm, and of Ovid's story of the great flood, *Metamorphoses* 1.274–312 (p. 437 below).

The text is based on the first appearance of the poem in *Tatler* 238 (October 17, 1710).

A Description of a City Shower

Careful Observers may foretell the Hour
By sure Prognostics when to dread a Show'r:

While Rain depends, the pensive Cat gives o'er
Her Frolics, and pursues her Tail no more.
Returning Home at Night, you find the Sink[1]   5
Strike your offended Sense with double Stink.
If you be wise, then go not far to dine:
You spend in Coach-hire more than save in Wine.
A coming Show'r your shooting Corns presage;
Old Aches throb, your hollow Tooth will rage:[2]   10
Saunt'ring in Coffee-house is *Dulman* seen;
He damns the Climate, and complains of Spleen.[3]
          Meanwhile the South, rising with dabbled Wings,[4]
A sable Cloud athwart the Welkin flings[5]
That swilled more Liquor than it could contain,   15
And, like a Drunkard, gives it up again.
Brisk *Susan* whips her Linen from the Rope,[6]
While the first drizzling Show'r is borne aslope:[7]
Such is that Sprinkling, which some careless Quean[8]
Flirts on you from her Mop; but not so clean:[9]   20
You fly, invoke the Gods; then turning, stop
To rail; she singing still whirls on her Mop.
Nor yet the Dust had shunned th' unequal Strife,
But, aided by the Wind, fought still for Life;
And wafted with its Foe by violent Gust,   25
'Twas doubtful which was Rain, and which was Dust.
Ah! where must needy Poet seek for Aid,
When Dust and Rain at once his Coat invade?
Sole Coat, where Dust cemented by the Rain,
Erects the Nap, and leaves a cloudy Stain.   30
          Now, in contiguous Drops the Flood comes down,
Threat'ning with Deluge this *devoted* Town.
To Shops in Crowds the daggled Females fly,[10]
Pretend to cheapen Goods, but nothing buy.[11]

A DESCRIPTION OF A CITY SHOWER

1 *Sink* "A drain; a jakes [outhouse]" (Johnson's *Dictionary*).
2 *Aches* a disyllable (as if "aitch-es").
3 *Spleen* "Melancholy; hypochondriacal vapours" (Johnson's *Dictionary*); the name of a variety of ills, like today's "depression."
4 *dabbled* muddy.
5 *Welkin* sky (consciously archaic and mock heroic).
6 *Susan* a typical maid's name.

7 *aslope* on a slant; obliquely (a word used to describe the way a lance or sword might strike a knight's shield).
8 *Quean* "A worthless woman; generally a strumpet" (Johnson); note the parody of an epic simile in lines 19–22 (see, e.g., Homer, *Odyssey* 12.251–5; p. 274 below).
9 *Flirt* "To throw anything with a quick, elastic motion" (Johnson).
10 *daggled* muddied.
11 *cheapen* "Attempt to purchase" (Johnson); shop for.

The Templer spruce, while every Spout's abroach,[12]   35
Stays till 'tis fair, yet *seems* to call a Coach.
The tucked-up Sempstress walks with hasty Strides,
While Streams run down her oil'd Umbrella's Sides.[13]
Here various Kinds, by various Fortunes led,
Commence Acquaintance underneath a Shed: 40
Triumphant Tories, and desponding Whigs,
Forget their Feuds, and join to save their Wigs.
Boxed in a Chair the Beau impatient sits,[14]
While Spouts run clatt'ring o'er the Roof by Fits,
And ever and anon with frightful Din   45
The Leather sounds; he trembles from within.
So when *Troy* Chairmen bore the wooden Steed,
Pregnant with *Greeks* impatient to be freed;
(Those Bully *Greeks*, who, as the Moderns do,
Instead of paying Chairmen, run them through)   50
Laocoon struck the Outside with his Spear,
And each imprisoned Hero quaked for Fear.[15]
      Now from all Parts the swelling Kennels flow,
And bear their Trophies with them, as they go:
Filths of all Hues and Odours seem to tell   55
What Street they sailed from, by the Sight and Smell.
They, as each Torrent drives with rapid Force,
From *Smithfield*, or *St. Pulchre*'s shape their course,[16]
And in huge Confluent joined at *Snow-hill* Ridge,
Fall from the *Conduit* prone to *Holborn-Bridge*.   60
Sweepings from Butchers' Stalls, Dung, Guts, and Blood,
Drowned Puppies, stinking Sprats, all drenched in Mud,
Dead Cats, and Turnip-Tops come tumbling down the Flood.

12 *Templer* law student; *abroach* overflowing.
13 *oil'd* so as to be waterproof.
14 *Chair* "A vehicle borne by men; a sedan" (Johnson); this one is covered.
15 *Troy Chairmen . . . quaked for Fear* tricked into believing the Greeks had given up the siege, the Trojans hauled a wooden horse (supposedly an offering to the gods) concealing lethal soldiers into their city; the priest Laocoon advised against this, struck the horse, and frightened the Greeks (Virgil, *Aeneid* 2.13–56; pp. 372–3 below).
16 *Smithfield* an open area just northwest of the City, used as a cattle market and sometimes for hangings; *St. Pulchre's* a suburban parish just west of the Newgate prison; the water would flow southeast past the other places mentioned on its way into the Fleet and through the City to the Thames.

Alexander Pope (1688–1744)

By 1706, before his seventeenth birthday, Pope completed a group of poems called *Pastorals* modeled on Virgil's *Georgics* and *Eclogues*. He received an offer of publication for them at that date from the most important bookseller in London. Six years later he wrote *Messiah, a Sacred Eclogue* in a more serious Virgilian vein. By then Pope had begun his translation of the *Iliad*, which was to make his name in the literary world, and he had also written the first version of his mock epic poem *The Rape of the Lock*. Two years later in 1714 he expanded the poem from two to five cantos; in this form it is one of the most frequently anthologized and best-loved works of the eighteenth century. In writing the poem, Pope responded to a request from a friend to heal a breach between two families that had evidently sprung from the celebrated incident. To the event Pope applies the full range of epic conventions, which he had been studying in his translations and imitations of classical poetry from his earliest years.

Pope's classical training and his translations are not meticulously scholarly. He was schooled at home by relatives and in certain Catholic schools; his status as a Catholic debarred him from the great public schools, such as Westminster, as well as from Oxford and Cambridge. Pope consciously and artfully adapts the classics to the manners of his age; he makes Homer prettier and less raw than he is in the original, but he does so without apology. Pope was a poet who channeled the works of his models into his own stream of refined and infinitely variable heroic couplets. He was a versifier without a peer who could write poetry on any subject. Later in his career, for example, he versified a fairly complete epistemology and metaphysics in *An Essay on Man*. This work of 1,300 lines was part of a planned *Opus Maximum*, which included an ethics in the form of several verse epistles. He also wrote another mock epic on an even grander scale than the *Rape of the Lock*. *The Dunciad* reached four books in its final revision and accumulated its own elaborate commentary, supplied by Pope and his friends. At various stages in his career Pope wrote brilliant direct imitations of Horace's *Odes* and *Epistles*, but nearly all of his poetry refers to the classics.

Although Pope's poetry transcends the boundaries of his learning and can be appreciated by those with no classical training, there is no doubt that he wrote for an audience that knew the classics and would appreciate the difference between his works and theirs. That difference, perpetually sounded in the versification, is a crucial aspect of Pope's meaning and of the pleasure in reading him. *The Rape of the Lock* should be read with heroic measures and the grand themes of Homer and Virgil in mind (see the selections on pp. 239–74 and pp. 361–85 below). However, as our notes point out, Pope also thought a good deal about Ovid as he composed his epic. In fact, he may have seen himself as occupying something like Ovid's position, for Ovid too was writing with Homer and Virgil in the background and using their epic themes as foils for his own tales. For the sake of space, we print here only Cantos 1 and 4. The whole poem is available in many anthologies and editions of Pope's works, including the standard Twickenham Edition, volume II, edited by Geoffrey Tillotson (1940).

The text is based on the first edition of the poem to present all five Cantos (1714).

The *RAPE* of the *LOCK*

AN

HEROI-COMICAL

POEM.

In Five Cantos

– A tonso est hoc nomen adepta capillo.

Ovid.[1]

TO

MRS. *ARABELLA FERMOR*[2]

MADAM,

It will be in vain to deny that I have some Value for this Piece, since I Dedicate it to You. Yet You may bear me Witness, it was intended only to divert a few young

---

CANTO 1

1   *A tonso . . . Ovid* "this name was taken from a shorn lock of hair" (*Metamorphoses* 8.151), from the story of Scylla, who is turned into a bird and renamed Ciris after she betrays her father by cutting off a special lock of his hair and presenting it to his handsome enemy. In later editions, Pope replaced the motto with a quotation from Martial: *Nolueram, [Belinda], tuos violare capillos / Sed juvat hoc precibus me tribuisse tuis* (*Epigrams* 12.84.1–2; "I did not wish, [Belinda], to violate

your locks, but I rejoice to have yielded this to your wishes").
2   *Arabella Fermor* (1690?–1738), Belinda in the poem, who really was the victim of the prank that Pope describes with such grandeur; "Mrs," as usual in the eighteenth century, is a title of respect rather than one that indicates marriage; Fermor married in 1714 or early 1715, shortly after this expanded version of the poem was first published.

Ladies, who have good Sense and good Humour enough, to laugh not only at their Sex's little unguarded Follies, but at their own. But as it was communicated with the Air of a Secret, it soon found its Way into the World. An imperfect Copy having been offered to a Bookseller, You had the Good-Nature for my Sake to consent to the Publication of one more correct:[3] This I was forced to before I had executed half my Design, for the *Machinery* was entirely wanting to complete it.

The *Machinery*, Madam, is a Term invented by the Critics, to signify that Part which the Deities, Angels, or Demons, are made to act in a Poem: For the ancient Poets are in one respect like many modern Ladies; Let an Action be never so trivial in itself, they always make it appear of the utmost Importance. These Machines I determined to raise on a very new and odd Foundation, the *Rosicrucian* Doctrine of Spirits.

I know how disagreeable it is to make use of hard Words before a Lady; but 'tis so much the Concern of a Poet to have his Works understood, and particularly by your Sex, that You must give me leave to explain two or three difficult Terms.

The *Rosicrucians* are a People I must bring You acquainted with. The best Account I know of them is in a French Book called *Le Comte de Gabalis*,[4] which both in its Title and Size is so like a *Novel*, that many of the Fair Sex have read it for one by Mistake. According to these Gentlemen, the four Elements are inhabited by Spirits, which they call *Sylphs, Gnomes, Nymphs*, and *Salamanders*. The *Gnomes*, or Dæmons of Earth, delight in Mischief; but the *Sylphs*, whose Habitation is in the Air, are the best-conditioned Creatures imaginable. For they say, any Mortals may enjoy the most intimate Familiarities with these gentle Spirits, upon a Condition very easy to all true *Adepts*, an inviolate Preservation of Chastity.

As to the following Cantos, all the Passages of them are as Fabulous, as the Vision at the Beginning, or the Transformation at the End (except the Loss of your Hair, which I always mention with Reverence). The Human Persons are as Fictitious as the Airy ones; and the Character of *Belinda*, as it is now managed, resembles You in nothing but in Beauty.

If this Poem had as many Graces as there are in Your Person, or in Your Mind, yet I could never hope it should pass through the World half so Uncensured as You have done. But let its Fortune be what it will, mine is happy enough, to have given me this Occasion of assuring You that I am, with the truest Esteem,

> *Madam,*
> *Your Most Obedient*
> *Humble Servant.*
> A. Pope

---

3   *Publication of one more correct* this was the version in two cantos, published in 1712.

4   *Le Comte de Gabalis* by Abbé de Montfaucon de Villars (1670).

Canto 1

What dire Offence from am'rous Causes springs,[5]
What mighty Quarrels rise from trivial Things,
I sing – This Verse to *C–l*, Muse! is due;[6]
This, ev'n *Belinda* may vouchsafe to view:
Slight is the Subject, but not so the Praise,   5
If She inspire, and He approve my Lays.
   Say what strange Motive, Goddess! could compel
A well-bred *Lord* t'assault a gentle *Belle*?[7]
Oh say what stranger Cause, yet unexplored
Could make a gentle *Belle* reject a *Lord*?   10
And dwells such Rage in softest Bosoms then?[8]
And lodge such daring Souls in Little Men?
Sol through white Curtains shot a tim'rous Ray,[9]
And op'd those Eyes that must eclipse the Day;
Now Lapdogs give themselves the rousing Shake,   15
And sleepless Lovers, just at Twelve, awake:
Thrice rung the Bell, the Slipper knocked the Ground,[10]
And the pressed Watch returned a silver Sound.[11]
Belinda still her downy Pillow prest,
Her Guardian *Sylph* prolonged the balmy Rest.   20
'Twas he had summoned to her silent Bed
The Morning Dream that hovered o'er her Head.
A Youth more glitt'ring than a *Birth-night Beau*,[12]
(That ev'n in Slumber caused her Cheek to glow)
Seemed to her Ear his winning Lips to lay,   25
And thus in Whispers said, or seemed to say,

---

5 Lines 1–12 imitate the ancient way of beginning an epic. Notice, for example, the announcement of the theme; the placement of the object before the verb; the phrase "I sing"; the invocation of the Muse; the emphasis on cause. Compare especially the opening of Homer's *Iliad* (p. 241 below) and Virgil's *Aeneid* (p. 362 below), both of which Pope draws upon for specific ideas. Also Virgilian in flavor is the dedication to John Caryll; compare *Eclogues* 10.1–8 (p. 349, below) and *Georgics* 4.1–7.

6 *C–l* John Caryll (1666?–1736), a wealthy landowner, friend, and correspondent of Pope; he was related both to Robert, Lord Petre (the Baron of the poem), and to Arabella Fermor (Belinda).

7 *Say what . . . Belle* compare Homer, *Iliad* 1.8 (p. 242 below).

8 *And . . . then* compare Virgil, *Aeneid* 1.11 (p. 363 below).

9 *Sol* Latin for "Sun."

10 *Thrice* triple repetition is common in epic poetry; *Slipper knocked* to call the maid from her station downstairs.

11 *pressed Watches* or "repeaters," sounded when pressed open.

12 *Birth-night Beau* a fashionable suitor, dressed up for the celebration of a royal birthday.

"Fairest of Mortals, thou distinguished Care[13]
Of thousand bright Inhabitants of Air!
If e'er one Vision touched thy infant Thought,
Of all the Nurse and all the Priest have taught,   30
Of airy Elves by Moonlight Shadows seen,
The silver Token, and the circled Green,[14]
Or Virgins visited by Angel-Powers,[15]
With Golden Crowns and Wreaths of heav'nly Flowers,
Hear and believe! thy own Importance know,   35
Nor bound thy narrow Views to Things below.
Some secret Truths from Learnèd Pride concealed,
To Maids alone and Children are revealed:
What though no Credit doubting Wits may give?
The Fair and Innocent shall still believe.   40
Know then, unnumbered Spirits round thee fly,
The light *Militia* of the lower Sky;
These, though unseen, are ever on the Wing,
Hang o'er the *Box*, and hover round the *Ring*.[16]
Think what an Equipage thou hast in Air,[17]   45
And view with scorn *Two Pages* and a *Chair*.[18]
As now your own, our Beings were of old,[19]
And once enclosed in Woman's beauteous Mold;
Thence, by a soft Transition, we repair
From earthly Vehicles to these of Air.   50
Think not, when Woman's transient Breath is fled,
That all her Vanities at once are dead:
Succeeding Vanities she still regards,
And though she plays no more, o'erlooks the Cards.
Her Joy in gilded Chariots, when alive,   55
And Love of *Ombre*, after Death survive.[20]

13 Lines 27–114 parody the convention of the epic dream or nocturnal apparition which warns, instructs, or cajoles the hero (for example, *Iliad* 2.1–34; 23.65–92; *Aeneid* 2.270–95; 3.147–71). The metaphysical content of the dream also recalls Anchises' speech in Virgil, *Aeneid* 6 (p. 378 below) and Pythagoras' speech in Ovid, *Metamorphoses* 15 (p. 452 below).

14 *circled Green* a fairy-ring, a circle of grass with a different color than the rest, supposed to be left, like silver coins, by fairies (but actually caused by fungus).

15 *Virgins* particularly, the Virgin Mary at the Annunciation, which is depicted with similar images.

16 *the Ring* a track cruised by fashionable coaches on the north side of Hyde Park.

17 *Equipáge* "Attendance; retinue" (Johnson's *Dictionary*).

18 *Chair* a sedan chair borne by two pages.

19 Lines 47–66 make fun of the Pythagorean doctrine of metempsychosis – the transmigration of souls – as expounded by Ovid (*Metamorphoses* 15.153 ff.; p. 453–4 below).

20 *Ombre* a card game in which one player (the ombre), depending on the deal, declares which cards are trumps and competes for tricks with the other two players.

For when the Fair in all their Pride expire,
To their first Elements their Souls retire:[21]
The Sprites of fiery Termagants in Flame[22]
Mount up, and take a *Salamander*'s Name.[23]   60
Soft yielding Minds to Water glide away,
And sip with *Nymphs*, their Elemental Tea.
The graver Prude sinks downward to a *Gnome*,
In search of Mischief still on Earth to roam.
The light Coquettes in *Sylphs* aloft repair,   65
And sport and flutter in the Fields of Air.
     "Know farther yet; Whoever fair and chaste
Rejects Mankind, is by some *Sylphs* embraced:
For Spirits, freed from mortal Laws, with ease
Assume what Sexes and what Shapes they please.   70
What guards the Purity of melting Maids,
In Courtly Balls, and Midnight Masquerades,
Safe from the treach'rous Friend, the daring Spark,[24]
The Glance by Day, the Whisper in the Dark;
When kind Occasion prompts their warm Desires,   75
When Music softens, and when Dancing fires?
'Tis but their *Sylph*, the wise Celestials know,
Though *Honour* is the Word with Men below.[25]
     "Some Nymphs there are, too conscious of their Face,
For Life predestined to the *Gnomes'* Embrace.   80
These swell their Prospects and exalt their Pride,
When Offers are disdained, and Love denied.
Then gay Ideas crowd the vacant Brain;
While Peers and Dukes, and all their sweeping Train,
And Garters, Stars and Coronets appear,[26]   85
And in soft Sounds, 'Your Grace' salutes their Ear.
'Tis these that early taint the Female Soul,
Instruct the Eyes of young *Coquettes* to roll,
Teach Infant Cheeks a bidden Blush to know,[27]
And little Hearts to flutter at a *Beau*.   90
     "Oft when the World imagine Women stray,
The *Sylphs* through mystic Mazes guide their Way,

21   *first Elements* the predominant of the four "elements" of fire, water, earth, and air, supposed to comprise all things and, by their proportions in the soul, to determine personality.

22   *Termagant* "A scold; a brawling, turbulent woman" (Johnson).

23   *Salamander's Name* because salamanders were popularly believed to live in fire (Sir Thomas Browne, *Pseudodoxia Epidemica*, chapter 14).

24   *Spark* dashing, bold man about town.

25   *'Tis . . . below* the idea that gods and humans name things differently derives from Homer.

26   *Garters, Stars and Coronets* badges of nobility.

27   In Ovid, *Amores* 1.8, Dipsas, an old dame, teaches her young protégée to dissemble in this way (lines 35–6).

Through all the giddy Circle they pursue,
And old Impertinence expel by new.
What tender Maid but must a Victim fall   95
To one Man's Treat, but for another's Ball?[28]
When *Florio* speaks, what Virgin could withstand,
If gentle *Damon* did not squeeze her Hand?
With varying Vanities, from every Part,
They shift the moving Toyshop of their Heart;   100
Where Wigs with Wigs, with Sword-knots Sword-knots strive,[29]
Beaus banish Beaus, and Coaches Coaches drive.[30]
This erring Mortals Levity may call,
Oh blind to Truth! the *Sylphs* contrive it all.
   "Of these am I, who thy Protection claim,   105
A watchful Sprite, and *Ariel* is my Name.
Late, as I ranged the Crystal Wilds of Air,[31]
In the clear Mirror of thy ruling *Star*
I saw, alas! some dread Event impend,
Ere to the Main this Morning's Sun descend.[32]   110
But Heav'n reveals not what, or how, or where:
Warned by thy *Sylph*, oh Pious Maid beware!
This to disclose is all thy Guardian can.
Beware of all, but most beware of Man!"
   He said; when *Shock*, who thought she slept too long,[33]   115
Leapt up, and waked his Mistress with his Tongue.
'Twas then *Belinda*! if Report say true,
Thy Eyes first opened on a *Billet-doux*;[34]
Wounds, Charms, and *Ardors*, were no sooner read,
But all the Vision vanished from thy Head.   120
   And now, unveiled, the *Toilet* stands displayed,[35]
Each Silver Vase in mystic Order laid.
First, robed in White, the Nymph intent adores
With Head uncovered, the *Cosmetic* Powers.
A heav'nly Image in the Glass appears,[36]   125

---

28   *Treat* "An entertainment given" (Johnson).
29   *Sword-knot* "Riband tied to the hilt of the sword" (Johnson), worn in fancy dress.
30   *Where . . . drive* in this couplet Pope imitates the epic figure of polyptoton, whereby a word is repeated and juxtaposed in different grammatical forms or functions.
31   Lines 107–14 allude again to the motif of nocturnal warnings in epic poetry; for examples, see n. 13 above.
32   *Main* ocean.
33   *Shock* stock name for a lap dog, as well as a breed from Iceland.

34   *Billet-doux* love letter.
35   Lines 121–48 parody epic descriptions of the arming of the hero (for example, Achilles in Homer, *Iliad* 19). In addition to this general allusion, Pope doubtless recalled Homer's application of the motif to Hera, when she adorns herself in order to seduce Zeus (*Iliad* 14). *Toilet* dressing table.
36   *Glass* mirror; Belinda's adoration of her "heavn'ly Image" recalls Narcissus (Ovid, *Metamorphoses* 3.316–510; p. 446 below).

To that she bends, to that her Eyes she rears;
Th' inferior Priestess, at her Altar's side,[37]
Trembling, begins the sacred Rites of Pride.
Unnumbered Treasures ope at once, and here
The various Off'rings of the World appear;   130
From each she nicely culls with curious Toil,
And decks the Goddess with the glitt'ring Spoil.
This Casket *India*'s glowing Gems unlocks,
And all *Arabia* breathes from yonder Box.
The Tortoise here and Elephant unite,   135
Transformed to *Combs*, the speckled and the white.[38]
Here Files of Pins extend their shining Rows,
Puffs, Powders, Patches, Bibles, Billet-doux.[39]
Now awful Beauty puts on all its Arms;
The Fair each moment rises in her Charms,   140
Repairs her Smiles, awakens every Grace,
And calls forth all the Wonders of her Face;
Sees by Degrees a purer Blush arise,
And keener Lightnings quicken in her Eyes.
The busy *Sylphs* surround their darling Care;   145
These set the Head, and those divide the Hair,
Some fold the Sleeve, whilst others plait the Gown;
And *Betty*'s praised for Labours not her own.

Canto 4

But anxious Cares the pensive Nymph oppressed,[1]
And secret Passions laboured in her Breast.
Not youthful Kings in Battle seized alive,
Not scornful Virgins who their Charms survive,
Not ardent Lovers robbed of all their Bliss,   5
Not ancient Ladies when refused a Kiss,
Not Tyrants fierce that unrepenting die,
Not *Cynthia* when her *Manteau*'s pinned awry,[2]

---

37 *Th' inferior Priestess* i.e. her maid. The
passage resembles Juvenal's description of a mis-
tress who punishes her maid for leaving a lock out
of place (*Satires* 6.486–95; p. 478 below).
38 *The Tortoise . . . white* an "Ovidian" meta-
morphosis; compare, for example, the transforma-
tion of Daphne into a utilitarian laurel tree
(*Metamorphoses* 1.548–67; pp. 442–3 below).
39 *Patch* "A small spot of black silk put on the
face" (Johnson).

CANTO 4

1 Lines 1–10 parody Virgil's description of
Dido's lovesickness at the beginning of Book 4 of
the *Aeneid* (4.1–30; p. 373 below). Pope echoes
Dryden's translation of that passage, which begins
"But anxious Cares . . . ."
2 *Manteau* or "mantua," a loose-fitting gown.

E'er felt such Rage, Resentment and Despair,
As Thou, sad Virgin! for thy ravished Hair.   10
    For, that sad moment, when the *Sylphs* withdrew,
And *Ariel* weeping from *Belinda* flew,
Umbriel, a dusky melancholy Sprite,[3]
As ever sullied the fair face of Light,
Down to the Central Earth, his proper Scene,   15
Repaired to search the gloomy Cave of *Spleen*.[4]
    Swift on his sooty Pinions flits the *Gnome*,
And in a Vapour reached the dismal Dome.
No cheerful Breeze this sullen Region knows,
The dreaded *East* is all the Wind that blows.[5]   20
Here, in a Grotto, sheltered close from Air,[6]
And screened in Shades from Day's detested Glare,
She sighs for ever on her pensive Bed,
Pain at her Side, and *Megrim* at her Head.[7]
    Two Handmaids wait the Throne: Alike in Place,   25
But diff'ring far in Figure and in Face.
Here stood *Ill-nature* like an *ancient Maid*,
Her wrinkled Form in *Black* and *White* arrayed;
With store of Prayers, for Mornings, Nights, and Noons,
Her Hand is filled; her Bosom with Lampoons.   30
    There *Affectation* with a sickly Mien
Shows in her Cheek the Roses of Eighteen,
Practiced to Lisp, and hang the Head aside,
Faints into Airs, and languishes with Pride;
On the rich Quilt sinks with becoming Woe,   35
Wrapped in a Gown, for Sickness, and for Show.

---

3 Lines 11–88: Umbriel's descent to the Cave of Spleen burlesques the heroic journey to the underworld. Homer installed it as an epic theme (*Odyssey* 11), but Virgil's magnificent description (*Aeneid* 6, p. 376 below) was the chief model for later poets such as Dante and Milton. Traditional features found in Pope include the descent, the gloomy terrain, allegorical inhabitants (from Virgil onwards), horrific punishments, and the talisman guaranteeing safe conduct to the hero – in Virgil, the golden bough; in Pope, "a Branch of healing *Spleenwort*." In its allegorical aspects the Cave of Spleen is also modeled upon Ovid's Cave of Envy, where Minerva goes to persuade the goddess to infect Aglauros with envy of her sister as a punishment for an act of disobedience (*Metamorphoses* 2.760–86; p. 443 below).

4 *Spleen* "The milt; one of the viscera, of which the use is scarcely known. It is supposed to be the seat of anger and melancholy [meaning all sorts of psychological ills]" (Johnson); also the name of an ill-defined constellation of ailments, like modern "depression" or eighteenth-century "vapours."

5 *East* the east wind was supposed to bring on spleen.

6 *Grotto* "A cavern or cave made for coolness. It is not used properly of a dark, horrid cavern" (Johnson); Pope had a grotto on his estate in Twickenham.

7 *Megrim* or "migraine," severe headache.

The Fair ones feel such Maladies as these,
When each new Night-Dress gives a new Disease.
   A constant *Vapour* o'er the Palace flies;
Strange Phantoms rising as the Mists arise;   40
Dreadful, as Hermit's Dreams in haunted Shades,
Or bright as Visions of expiring Maids.[8]
Now glaring Fiends, and Snakes on rolling Spires,
Pale Specters, gaping Tombs, and Purple Fires:
Now Lakes of liquid Gold, *Elysian* Scenes,[9]   45
And Crystal Domes, and Angels in Machines.
   Unnumbered Throngs on every side are seen[10]
Of Bodies changed to various Forms by *Spleen*.
Here living *Teapots* stand, one Arm held out,[11]
One bent; the Handle this, and that the Spout: 50
A Pipkin there like *Homer*'s *Tripod* walks;[12]
Here sighs a Jar, and there a Goose-pie talks;[13]
Men prove with Child, as powerful Fancy works,
And Maids turned Bottles, call aloud for Corks.
   Safe passed the *Gnome* through this fantastic Band,   55
A Branch of healing *Spleenwort* in his hand.[14]
Then thus addressed the Power – "Hail wayward Queen![15]
Who rule the Sex to Fifty from Fifteen,
Parent of Vapours and of Female Wit,
Who give th' *Hysteric* or *Poetic* Fit,   60
On various Tempers act by various ways,
Make some take Physic, others scribble Plays;[16]
Who cause the Proud their Visits to delay,
And send the Godly in a Pet, to pray.
A Nymph there is, that all thy Pow'r disdains,   65

---

8 *Hermit's Dreams . . . Visions of . . . Maids* these are religious hallucinations of hell and heaven.

9 *Elysian* the pleasantest place in the classical underworld.

10 Lines 47–54: "Pope intends a reference to the horrors of the epic Hades, and to the fantastic metamorphoses of Ovid's poem" (Twickenham Edition, p. 184n).

11 *living Teapots* Robert Burton records two instances of insane persons who think they are pitchers (*Anatomy of Melancholy* 1.3.1.3).

12 *Pipkin* "A small earthen boiler" (Johnson's *Dictionary*, 4th edn, 1773); *Tripod* See *Hom.* Iliad 18 [373–7], of *Vulcan*'s Walking tripods [Pope's note; they have wheels and move at his command].

13 *Goose-pie* Alludes to a real fact, a Lady of distinction imagined herself in this condition [Pope's note].

14 *Spleenwort* an herb said to be good for the spleen; this is a version of the golden bough that Aeneas used to pass safely through the underworld (*Aeneid* 6.136–48, 185–211, 405–10, 628–36).

15 Lines 57–79 follow the pattern of a Roman prayer: address to the divinity, identification of his or her attributes, reminder of former acts of piety, and request for help. Pope's classical model for the speech is Nisus' speech to Luna (Virgil, *Aeneid* 9.404–9).

16 *Physic* any medicine, but also, specifically, a purgative.

And thousands more in equal Mirth maintains.
But oh! if e'er thy *Gnome* could spoil a Grace,
Or raise a Pimple on a beauteous Face,
Like Citron-Waters Matrons' Cheeks inflame,[17]
Or change Complexions at a losing Game;   70
If e'er with airy Horns I planted Heads,[18]
Or rumpled Petticoats, or tumbled Beds,
Or caused Suspicion when no Soul was rude,
Or discomposed the Head-dress of a Prude,
Or e'er to costive Lap-Dog gave Disease,   75
Which not the Tears of brightest Eyes could ease:
Hear me, and touch *Belinda* with Chagrin;
That single Act gives half the World the Spleen."
    The Goddess with a discontented Air
Seems to reject him, though she grants his Prayer.   80
A wondrous Bag with both her Hands she binds,
Like that where once *Ulysses* held the Winds;[19]
There she collects the Force of Female Lungs,
Sighs, Sobs, and Passions, and the War of Tongues.
A Vial next she fills with fainting Fears,   85
Soft Sorrows, melting Griefs, and flowing Tears.
The *Gnome* rejoicing bears her Gifts away,
Spreads his black Wings, and slowly mounts to Day.
    Sunk in *Thalestris*' Arms the Nymph he found,[20]
Her Eyes dejected and her Hair unbound.   90
Full o'er their Heads the swelling Bag he rent,
And all the Furies issued at the Vent.
Belinda burns with more than mortal Ire,
And fierce *Thalestris* fans the rising Fire.
"O wretched Maid!" she spread her Hands, and cried,   95
(While *Hampton*'s Echoes, "wretched Maid!" replied),
"Was it for this you took such constant Care
The *Bodkin*, *Comb*, and *Essence* to prepare;
For this your Locks in Paper-Durance bound,
For this with tort'ring Irons wreathed around?   100
For this with Fillets strained your tender Head,[21]
And bravely bore the double Loads of Lead?[22]
Gods! shall the Ravisher display your Hair,

---

17 *Citron-Waters* a kind of liqueur.
18 *airy Horns* imagined signs that the wearer
has been cuckolded.
19 *Ulysses held the Winds* in the bag given him
by Aeolus at the beginning of *Odyssey* 10.

20 *Thalestris* name of a queen of the Amazons;
here, Mrs. Morley, Arabella's second cousin by
her marriage to Sir George Browne (Sir Plume).
21 *Fillet* "A band tied around the head"
(Johnson).
22 *Lead* soft wire ties.

While the Fops envy, and the Ladies stare!
Honour forbid! at whose unrivalled Shrine   105
Ease, Pleasure, Virtue, All, our Sex resign.
Methinks already I your Tears survey,
Already hear the horrid things they say,
Already see you a degraded Toast,
And all your Honour in a Whisper lost!   110
How shall I, then, your helpless Fame defend?
'Twill then be Infamy to seem your Friend!
And shall this Prize, th' inestimable Prize,
Exposed through Crystal to the gazing Eyes,
And heightened by the Diamond's circling Rays,   115
On that Rapacious Hand for ever blaze?
Sooner shall Grass in *Hyde*-Park *Circus* grow,[23]
And Wits take Lodgings in the Sound of *Bow*;[24]
Sooner let Earth, Air, Sea to *Chaos* fall,
Men, Monkies, Lap-dogs, Parrots, perish all!"   120
    She said; then raging to *Sir Plume* repairs,[25]
And bids her *Beau* demand the precious Hairs:
(*Sir Plume*, of *Amber Snuff-box* justly vain,
And the nice Conduct of a *clouded Cane*)[26]
With earnest Eyes, and round unthinking Face,   125
He first the Snuff-box opened, then the Case,
And thus broke out – "My Lord, why, what the Devil?
Z–ds! damn the Lock! 'fore Gad, you must be civil![27]
Plague on't! 'tis past a Jest – nay prithee, Pox!
Give her the Hair" – he spoke, and rapped his Box.   130
    "It grieves me much," replied the Peer again,
"Who speaks so well should ever speak in vain.
But by this Lock, this sacred Lock I swear.[28]
(Which never more shall join its parted Hair,
Which never more its Honours shall renew,   135
Clipped from the lovely Head where late it grew)
That while my Nostrils draw the vital Air,

---

23 Lines 117–20 parody the classical figure of the adynaton – an exaggerated declaration of impossibility; *Hyde-Park Circus* the Ring (Canto 1.106).
24 *Sound of Bow* the bells of the church of St. Mary-le-bow in Cheapside, which had become expensive and commercial.
25 *Sir Plume* Arabella's second cousin, Sir George Browne. Sir Plume's intervention resembles Nestor's, when he urges Agamemnon not to take Briseis from Achilles (*Iliad* 1.254–84; p. 249 below); Agamemnon remains as obdurate as the Baron.
26 *clouded Cane* one with a head of polished stone, variegated with dark veins.
27 *Z–ds!* "God's wounds," a mild curse.
28 Lines 133–8 allude to the oath that Achilles swears by the scepter he holds as he addresses the assembled Greeks (*Iliad* 1.233–44; p. 248 below).

This Hand, which won it, shall for ever wear."
He spoke, and speaking, in proud Triumph spread
The long-contended Honours of her Head.   140
    But *Umbriel*, hateful *Gnome*! forbears not so;
He breaks the Vial whence the Sorrows flow.
Then see! the *Nymph* in beauteous Grief appears,
Her Eyes half-languishing, half-drowned in Tears;
On her heaved Bosom hung her drooping Head,   145
Which, with a Sigh, she raised; and thus she said.
    "For ever cursed be this detested Day,[29]
Which snatched my best, my fav'rite Curl away!
Happy! ah ten times happy, had I been,
If *Hampton-Court* these Eyes had never seen!   150
Yet am not I the first mistaken Maid,
By Love of *Courts* to num'rous Ills betrayed.
Oh had I rather un-admired remained
In some lone Isle, or distant *Northern* Land;
Where the gilt *Chariot* never marked the way,   155
Where none learn *Ombre*, none e'er taste *Bohea*![30]
There kept my Charms concealed from mortal Eye,
Like Roses that in Deserts bloom and die.
What moved my Mind with youthful Lords to roam?
O had I stayed, and said my Prayers at home!   160
'Twas this, the Morning *Omens* did foretell;[31]
Thrice from my trembling hand the *Patch-box* fell;
The tott'ring *China* shook without a Wind,
Nay, *Poll* sate mute, and *Shock* was most Unkind!
A *Sylph* too warned me of the Threats of Fate,   165
In mystic Visions, now believed too late!
See the poor Remnants of these slighted Hairs!
My hands shall rend what ev'n thy rapine spares:[32]
These, in two sable Ringlets taught to break,
Once gave new Beauties to the snowy Neck.   170
The Sister-Lock now sits uncouth, alone,
And in its Fellow's Fate foresees its own;
Uncurled it hangs, the fatal Sheers demands;
And tempts once more thy sacrilegious Hands.
Oh hadst thou, Cruel! been content to sieze   175
Hairs less in sight, or any Hairs but these!"

29 Lines 147–76: Belinda's speech recalls the lament of Achilles for Patroclus (*Iliad* 18.79–126).
30 *Bohea* a fancy tea.

31 Lines 161–4: such lists of omens are commonplace in Roman epic.
32 Line 168: Belinda mimics the ritual tearing of hair by Greek women in mourning.

James Thomson (1700–1748)

Thomson grew up in the town of Southdean on the border of England and Scotland. He learned Latin at the grammar school in Jedburgh, which he entered in 1712, and he completed his classical education at Edinburgh College from 1715 to 1719. He studied divinity for another five years and began writing verse. Ambitious of literary fame, he went to London in 1725, and *Winter* was published in the next year. *Summer* followed in 1727, and soon *The Seasons* were offered by subscription. The suite of four poems was often republished, and the final revised edition (1746) was and is the mainstay of Thomson's reputation. His high-classical dramas *Agamemnon* and *Sophonisba* are all but forgotten, as are his more polemical plays, *Britannia*, *Edward and Eleonora*, and *Alfred*, although the latter contains the deathless ode "Rule Britannia." The late allegory, *The Castle of Indolence*, has recently been getting more attention, perhaps because of its Gothic associations, but the *Seasons* remain Thomson's most important poems, and the first edition of *Winter*, as Samuel Johnson suggested, best preserves the "race," or distinctive flavor, of Thomson's verse.

For all its attention to nature and for all its appeal to romantic sensibilities of the late eighteenth and early nineteenth centuries, *Winter* is still a poem steeped in the classics. In general, the parade of the seasons is a classical theme. Three good examples are Lucretius 5.737–47; Horace, *Odes* 4.7; and Ovid, *Metamorphoses* 15.199–213. The example from Ovid appears below (p. 455 below); Lucretius presents the seasons stepping through a kind of allegorical pageant in which winter, with chattering teeth, comes last. Thomson would surely have encountered these passages, and he probably also knew Hesiod's description of winter (*Works and Days* 504–35; p. 285 below) since his Edinburgh course of study included Greek.

Thomson's main debt in *Winter*, however, is to Virgil's *Georgics*, as Thomson himself acknowledged in the preface to the second edition of his poem (1726). Like the *Georgics*, *Winter* is a didactic poem about nature, and it incorporates many conventional features of Virgil's poem: the declaration of the theme; the invocation; apostrophes (e.g., to the shepherds at line 242); ordering of material with prosaic particles – "first, now, at last etc. . . . ."; the appeal to autopsy – "look!

behold! . . .."; and the statement of completion. Like the *Georgics*, *Winter* is written
in a high style that ennobles humble topics and rises to sublimity in extended
descriptive and panegyrical episodes. Both poems are ultimately concerned with
the relation of man to nature. Man in the *Georgics* lives in a challenging and dis-
orderly environment that he must labor to cope with, tame, and make productive,
and from his dedication to this goal (not only in agriculture but by extension in
other areas of life, such as politics) springs his dignity and moral worth. His task
is difficult – witness the wrecking of the crops by storms or floods, or of the state
by civil war – but nature offers the potential for a fulfilling existence that recalls
the peaceful, harmonious, and simple conditions of the Golden Age. Influenced
by Sir Isaac Newton and the "physicotheology" of his day, Thomson sees nature
more optimistically as a magnificent spectacle devised by God for our enjoyment,
contemplation, and instruction. Thomson's nature can be frightening, but that is
a feature of its aesthetically satisfying sublimity. Thomson's nature, unlike Virgil's,
is not arbitrary or cruel, for it is ruled by providence. The Christian conclusion of
Winter, with its assimilation of spring to resurrection and a blessed afterlife as a
reward for virtue, has no counterpart in Virgil and falls altogether outside the
scope of the classical ideas of nature that Thomson knew.

The text presented here is based on the first edition.

Winter: A Poem (1726)

See! Winter comes, to rule the varied Year,
Sullen, and sad; with all his rising Train,[1]
Vapours, and *Clouds*, and *Storms:* Be these my Theme,[2]
These, that exalt the Soul to solemn Thought,
And heavenly musing. Welcome kindred Glooms!   5
Wished, wint'ry, Horrors, hail! – With frequent Foot,
Pleased, have I, in my cheerful Morn of Life,
When, nursed by careless *Solitude*, I lived,
And sung of Nature with unceasing Joy,
Pleased, have I wandered through your rough Domains;   10
Trod the pure, virgin, Snows, myself as pure:
Heard the Winds roar, and the big Torrent burst:
Or seen the deep, fermenting, Tempest brewed,
In the red, evening, Sky. – Thus passed the Time,
Till, through the opening Chambers of the South,   15
Looked out the joyous *Spring*, looked out, and smiled.

WINTER: A POEM

1   *sad* serious.
2   *Be these my Theme* the prefatory declaration
and following invocation are typical of didactic

poetry; compare, e.g., Virgil, *Georgics* 2.2–3:
"Now I will sing of you, Bacchus, and with you
the woodland shrubs and offspring of the slow-
growing olive."

Thee too, Inspirer of the toiling Swain!
Fair AUTUMN, yellow robed! I'll sing of thee,[3]
Of thy last, tempered, Days, and sunny Calms;
When all the golden *Hours* are on the Wing,[4]   20
Attending thy Retreat, and round thy Wain,[5]
Slow-rolling, onward to the Southern Sky.
 Behold! the well-poised *Hornet*, hovering, hangs,
With quivering Pinions, in the genial Blaze;[6]
Flies off, in airy Circles: then returns,   25
And hums, and dances to the beating Ray.
Nor shall the Man, that, musing, walks alone,
And, heedless, strays within his radiant Lists,[7]
Go unchastised away. – Sometimes, a Fleece
Of Clouds, wide-scattering, with a lucid Veil,[8]   30
Soft, shadow o'er th' unruffled Face of Heaven;
And, through their dewy Sluices, shed the Sun,
With tempered Influence down. Then is the Time,
For those, whom *Wisdom*, and whom *Nature* charm,
To steal themselves from the degenerate Crowd,   35
And soar above this *little* Scene of Things:
To tread low-thoughted *Vice* beneath their Feet:
To lay their Passions in a gentle Calm,
And woo lone *Quiet*, in her silent *Walks*.
 Now, solitary, and in pensive Guise,   40
Oft, let me wander o'er the russet Mead,[9]
Or through the pining Grove; where scarce is heard
One dying Strain, to cheer the *Woodman*'s Toil:
Sad *Philomel*, perchance, pours forth her Plaint,[10]
Far, through the withering Copse. Meanwhile, the Leaves,   45
That, late, the Forest clad with lively Green,
Nipped by the drizzly Night, and Sallow hued,
Fall, wavering, through the Air; or shower amain,[11]

---

3 *Thee too ... thee* another invocation in the manner of *Georgics* 2.2–3.
4 *the golden Hours* the Horae, goddesses of the seasons.
5 *Wain* wagon; a name for Ursa Major or the Big Dipper, a northern constellation that rotates near the Pole Star and never goes below the horizon.
6 *genial* "That gives cheerfulness or supports life" (Johnson's *Dictionary*).
7 *Lists* borders, but also the enclosed ground on which knights jousted.

8 *lucid* made of light.
9 *Now ... Mead* loosely based on Virgil, *Georgics* 2.485–6 (p. 358 below), "Let the countryside please me and full-flowing valley streams; let me love the rivers and woods in obscurity"; *Mead* meadow.
10 *Philomel* the nightingale, the bird into which Philomela is transformed when she flees from Tereus, who raped her and cut out her tongue (see Ovid, *Metamorphoses* 6.412–674).
11 *amain* in full force.

Urged by the Breeze, that sobs amid the Boughs.
Then list'ning *Hares* forsake the rustling Woods,   50
And, starting at the frequent Noise, escape
To the rough Stubble, and the rushy Fen.
The *Woodcocks*, o'er the fluctuating Main,
That glimmers to the Glimpses of the Moon,
Stretch their long Voyage to the woodland Glade:[12]   55
Where, wheeling with uncertain Flight, they mock
The nimble *Fowler* 's Aim. – Now *Nature* droops;
Languish the living Herbs, with pale Decay:
And all the *various Family* of Flowers
Their sunny Robes resign. The falling Fruits,   60
Through the still Night, forsake the Parent-Bough,
That, in the first, grey, Glances of the Dawn,
Looks wild, and wonders at the wintry Waste.
   The *Year*, yet pleasing, but declining fast,
Soft, o'er the secret Soul, in gentle Gales,[13]   65
A philosophic Melancholy breathes,
And bears the swelling Thought aloft to Heaven.
The forming *Fancy* rouses to conceive,
What never mingled with the Vulgar's Dream:[14]
Then wake the tender *Pang*, the pitying *Tear*,   70
The *Sigh* for suffering Worth, the *Wish* preferred[15]
For Humankind, the *Joy* to see them blessed,
And all the *Social Off-spring* of the Heart!
   Oh! bear me then to high, embowering, Shades;
To twilight Groves, and visionary Vales;   75
To weeping Grottos, and to hoary Caves;[16]
Where Angel-Forms are seen, and Voices heard,
Sighed in low Whispers, that abstract the Soul,
From outward Sense, far into Worlds remote.
   Now, when the Western Sun withdraws the Day,   80
And humid *Evening*, gliding o'er the Sky,
In her chill Progress, checks the straggling Beams,
And robs them of their gathered, vapoury, Prey,
Where Marshes stagnate, and where Rivers wind,
Cluster the rolling *Fogs*, and swim along   85
The dusky-mantled Lawn: then slow descend,
Once more to mingle with their *Wat'ry Friends*.

12 *Stretch* direct, steer.
13 *Gale* "A wind not tempestuous, yet stronger
than a breeze" (Johnson's *Dictionary*).
14 *Vulgar* common, unlearned folk.

15 *prefer* "To offer solemnly" (Johnson's *Dictionary*), as a prayer.
16 *Oh! bear me . . . Caves* inspired by Virgil, *Georgics* 2.486–9 (p. 358 below).

The vivid Stars shine out, in radiant Files;
And boundless *Ether* glows, till the fair Moon[17]
Shows her broad Visage, in the crimsoned East;   90
Now, stooping, seems to kiss the passing Cloud:
Now, o'er the pure *Cerulean*, rides sublime.[18]
Wide the pale Deluge floats, with silver Waves,
O'er the sky'd Mountain, to the low-laid Vale;[19]
From the white Rocks, with dim Reflection, gleams,   95
And faintly glitters through the waving Shades.
    All Night, abundant Dews, unnoted, fall,
And, at Return of Morning, silver o'er
The Face of Mother-Earth; from every Branch
Depending, tremble the translucent Gems,[20]   100
And, quivering, seem to fall away, yet cling,
And sparkle in the Sun, whose rising Eye,
With Fogs bedimmed, portends a beauteous Day.
    Now, giddy Youth, whom headlong Passions fire,
Rouse the wild Game, and stain the guiltless Grove,[21]   105
With Violence, and Death; yet call it Sport,
To scatter Ruin through the Realms of *Love*,
And *Peace*, that thinks no Ill: But These, the *Muse*,
Whose Charity, unlimited, extends
As wide as *Nature* works, disdains to sing,   110
Returning to her nobler Theme in view –
    For, see! where *Winter* comes, himself, confessed,[22]
Striding the gloomy Blast. First Rains obscure[23]
Drive through the mingling Skies, with Tempest foul;
Beat on the Mountain's Brow, and shake the Woods,   115
That, sounding, wave below. The dreary Plain
Lies overwhelmed, and lost. The bellying Clouds
Combine, and deepening into Night, shut up
The Day's fair Face. The Wanderers of Heaven,[24]
Each to his Home, retire; save those that love   120
To take their Pastime in the troubled Air,

---

17 *Ether* "The matter of the highest regions above" (Johnson's *Dictionary*).
18 *Cerulean* the blue of the sky.
19 *sky'd* "Enveloped by the skies. This is unusual and unauthorized" (Johnson, citing this passage, in his *Dictionary*).
20 *Depending* hanging (a Latinism based on *pendere*, to hang).
21 *Rouse the wild Game* compare Virgil's

recommendation of hunting as a winter activity (*Georgics* 1.307–10; p. 353 below).
22 *confessed* openly appearing. The description of winter's arrival in lines 112–94 draws upon Virgil's storm description and list of weather signs in *Georgics* 1.311–423 (p. 353 below).
23 *obscure* dark and dismal.
24 *Wanderers of Heaven* birds.

And, skimming, flutter round the dimply Flood.
The Cattle, from th' untasted Fields, return,
And ask, with Meaning low, their wonted Stalls;[25]
Or ruminate in the contiguous Shade:[26]   125
Thither, the household, feathery, People crowd,[27]
The crested Cock, with all his female Train,
Pensive, and wet. Meanwhile, the Cottage-Swain
Hangs o'er th' enlivening Blaze, and, taleful, there,
Recounts his simple Frolic: Much he talks,   130
And much he laughs, nor recks the Storm that blows[28]
Without, and rattles on his humble Roof.
  At last, the muddy Deluge pours along,
Resistless, roaring; dreadful down it comes
From the chapped Mountain, and the mossy Wild,[29]   135
Tumbling through Rocks abrupt, and sounding far:[30]
Then o'er the sanded Valley, floating, spread,[31]
Calm, sluggish, silent; till again constrained,
Betwixt two meeting Hills, it bursts a Way,
Where Rocks, and Woods o'erhang the turbid Stream.   140
There gathering triple Force, rapid, and deep,
It boils, and wheels, and foams, and thunders through.
  Nature! great Parent! whose directing Hand
Rolls round the Seasons of the changeful Year,
How mighty! how majestic are thy Works!   145
With what a pleasing Dread they swell the Soul,
That sees, astonished! and, astonished sings!
You too, ye *Winds!* that now begin to blow,
With boisterous Sweep, I raise my Voice to you.
Where are your Stores, ye viewless *Beings!* say?   150
Where your aerial Magazines reserved,
Against the Day of Tempest perilous?
In what untraveled Country of the Air, –
Hushed in still Silence, sleep you, when 'tis calm?
  Late, in the louring Sky, red, fiery, Streaks[32]   155
Begin to flush about; the reeling Clouds[33]
Stagger with dizzy Aim, as doubting yet
Which Master to obey: while rising, slow,

25 *low* bellow of a cow.
26 *ruminate* chew the cud.
27 *People* "those who compose a community"
(Johnson's *Dictionary*).
28 *recks* minds.
29 *chapped* cleft.

30 *abrupt* "Broken; craggy" (Johnson's
Dictionary).
31 *sanded* covered with sand or silt.
32 *louring* "dark, stormy, and gloomy" (John-
son's *Dictionary*).
33 *flush* "To glow in the skin; to produce a
colour in the face" (Johnson's *Dictionary*).

Sad, in the Leaden-coloured East, the Moon
Wears a bleak Circle round her sullied Orb. 160
Then issues forth the Storm, with loud Control,[34]
And the thin Fabric of the pillared Air[35]
O'erturns, at once. Prone, on th' uncertain Main,
Descends th' Etherial Force, and plows its Waves,
With dreadful Rift: from the mid-Deep, appears, 165
Surge after Surge, the rising, wat'ry, War.
Whitening, the angry Billows roll immense,
And roar their Terrors, through the shuddering Soul
Of feeble Man, amidst their Fury caught,
And, dashed upon his Fate: Then, o'er the Cliff, 170
Where dwells the *Sea-Mew*, unconfined, they fly,[36]
And, hurrying, swallow up the sterile Shore.
   The Mountain growls; and all its sturdy *Sons*[37]
Stoop to the Bottom of the Rocks they shade:
Lone, on its Midnight-Side, and all aghast, 175
The dark, way-faring, *Stranger*, breathless, toils,
And climbs against the Blast –
Low, waves the rooted Forest, vexed, and sheds
What of its leafy Honours yet remains.
Thus, struggling through the dissipated Grove,[38] 180
The whirling Tempest raves along the Plain;
And, on the Cottage thatched, or lordly Dome,[39]
Keen-fastening, shakes 'em to the solid Base.
Sleep, frighted, flies; the hollow Chimney howls,
The Windows rattle, and the Hinges creak. 185
   Then, too, they say, through all the burthened Air,
Long Groans are heard, shrill Sounds, and distant Sighs
That, murmured by the *Demon* of the Night,
Warn the devoted *Wretch* of Woe, and Death![40]
Wild Uproar lords it wide: the Clouds commixed, 190
With Stars, swift-gliding, sweep along the Sky.
All Nature reels. – But hark! the *Almighty* speaks:
Instant, the chidden Storm begins to pant,
And dies, at once, into a noiseless Calm.
   As yet, 'tis Midnight's Reign; the weary Clouds 195
Slow-meeting, mingle into solid Gloom:

34 *Control* power.
35 *Fabric* building.
36 *Sea-Mew* "A fowl that frequents the sea" (Johnson's *Dictionary*).
37 *sturdy Sons* trees.
38 *dissipated* dispersed because its leaves are scattered.
39 *Dome* house (Latin, *domus*).
40 *devoted* cursed, doomed to destruction (a Latinism based on *vovere*, to promise something to a deity).

Now, while the drowsy World lies lost in Sleep,
Let me associate with the low-browed *Night*,[41]
And *Contemplation*, her sedate Compeer;
Let me shake off th' intrusive Cares of Day,   200
And lay the meddling Senses all aside.
   And now, ye lying *Vanities* of Life!
You ever-tempting, ever-cheating Train!
Where are you now? and what is your Amount?
Vexation, Disappointment, and Remorse.   205
Sad, sickening, Thought! and yet, deluded Man,
A Scene of wild, disjointed, Visions past,
And broken Slumbers, rises, still resolved,
With new-flushed Hopes, to run your giddy Round.
   Father of Light, and Life! Thou *Good Supreme!*[42]   210
O! teach me what is Good! teach me thyself!
Save me from Folly, Vanity and Vice,
From every low Pursuit! and feed my Soul,
With Knowledge, conscious Peace, and Virtue pure,
Sacred, substantial, never-fading Bliss![43]   215
   Lo! from the livid East, or piercing North,
Thick Clouds ascend, in whose capacious Womb,
A vapoury Deluge lies, to Snow congealed:
Heavy, they roll their fleecy World along;
And the Sky saddens with th' impending Storm.   220
Through the hushed Air, the whitening Shower descends,
At first, thin-wavering; till, at last, the Flakes
Fall broad, and wide, and fast, dimming the Day,
With a continual Flow. See! sudden, hoared,
The Woods beneath the stainless Burden bow,   225
Black'ning, along the mazy Stream it melts;
Earth's universal Face, deep-hid, and chill,
Is all one, dazzling, Waste. The Labourer-Ox
Stands covered o'er with Snow, and then demands
The Fruit of all his Toil. The Fowls of Heaven,   230
Tamed by the cruel Season, crowd around
The winnowing Store, and claim the little Boon,[44]
That *Providence* allows. The foodless Wilds
Pour forth their brown *Inhabitants*; the Hare,
Though timorous of Heart, and hard beset   235
By death, in various Forms, dark Snares, and Dogs,
And more unpitying Men, the Garden seeks,

---

41 *low-browed* louring, gloomy.
42 *Father of Light* Epistle of James 1.17.
43 *substantial* "Real; actually existing" (Johnson's *Dictionary*).

44 *winnowing Store* the stored grain being winnowed by the wind.

Urged on by *fearless* Want. The bleating Kind
Eye the bleak Heavens, and next, the glistening Earth,
With Looks of dumb Despair; then sad, dispersed,   240
Dig, for the withered Herb, through Heaps of Snow.
    Now, *Shepherds*, to your helpless Charge be kind;
Baffle the raging Year, and fill their Pens
With Food, at will: lodge them below the Blast,
And watch them strict; for from the bellowing East,   245
In this dire Season, oft the Whirlwind's Wing
Sweeps up the Burthen of whole wintry Plains,
In one fierce Blast, and o'er th' unhappy Flocks,
Lodged in the Hollow of two neighbouring Hills,
The billowy Tempest whelms; till, upwards urged,   250
The Valley to a shining Mountain swells,
That curls its Wreaths amid the freezing Sky.[45]
    Now, all amid the Rigours of the Year,[46]
In the wild Depth of Winter, while without
The ceaseless Winds blow keen, be my Retreat   255
A rural, sheltered, solitary, Scene;
Where ruddy Fire, and beaming Tapers join
To chase the cheerless Gloom: there let me sit,
And hold high Converse with the mighty Dead.[47]
Sages of ancient Time, as Gods revered,   260
As Gods beneficent, who blessed Mankind,
With Arts, and Arms, and humanized a World.
Roused at th' inspiring Thought – I throw aside
The long-lived Volume, and, deep-musing, hail[48]
The sacred *Shades*, that, slowly-rising, pass[49]   265
Before my wondering Eyes – First, *Socrates*,
Truth's early Champion, Martyr for his God:[50]
Solon, the next, who built his Commonweal,[51]
On Equity's firm Base: *Lycurgus*, then,[52]

45 *Wreaths* snowdrifts, Scottish.

46 The Virgilian inspiration for this passage (253–300) is *Georgics* 2.475 ff. (pp. 358–60 below), where Virgil asks the Muses first for knowledge of the universe (in homage to Lucretius), but, if that is not attainable, for a peaceful country existence far from the anxieties and ambitions of corrupt urban life.

47 *Converse with the mighty Dead* a conventional description of reading.

48 *long-lived Volume* Plutarch's *Parallel Lives* of Greeks and Romans; Plutarch wrote about all the heroes whom Thomson praises.

49 The list of Greek and Roman heroes from Plutarch is reminiscent of the roll-call of great Romans in *Aeneid* 6.

50 *Martyr for his God* Platonic dialogues such as *Parmenides* and the *Apology* were read by Christian humanists as showing that Socrates was a monotheist. Socrates is important in Plutarch's life of Alcibiades.

51 *Solon* (c. 639–559 BCE), great Athenian lawmaker.

52 *Lycurgus* legendary Spartan lawgiver.

Severely good, and him of rugged *Rome*,   270
Numa, who softened *her* rapacious *Sons*.[53]
Cimon sweet-souled, and *Aristides* just.[54]
Unconquered *Cato*, virtuous in Extreme;[55]
With that attempered Hero, mild, and firm,[56]
Who wept the Brother, while the Tyrant bled.   275
Scipio, the humane Warrior, gently brave,[57]
Fair Learning's Friend; who early sought the Shade,
To dwell, with *Innocence*, and *Truth*, retired.
And, equal to the best, the *Theban*, *He*[58]
Who, *single*, raised his Country into Fame.   280
Thousands behind, the Boast of *Greece* and *Rome*,
Whom *Virtue* owns, the Tribute of a Verse
Demand, but who can count the Stars of Heaven?
Who sing their Influence on this lower World?
But see who yonder comes! nor comes alone,   285
With *sober* State, and of *majestic* Mien,
The Sister-Muses in his Train – 'Tis He!
Maro! the best of Poets, and of Men![59]
Great *Homer* too appears, of *daring* Wing!
Parent of Song! and, *equal*, by his Side,   290
The *British Muse*, joined Hand in Hand, they walk,[60]
Darkling, nor miss their Way to Fame's Ascent.[61]
   Society divine! Immortal Minds!
Still visit thus my Nights, for *you* reserved,
And mount my soaring Soul to Deeds like yours.   295
Silence! thou lonely *Power!* the Door be thine:
See, on the hallowed Hour, that none intrude,

53 *Numa* Numa Pompilius, legendary second king of Rome who founded many of its religious institutions.
54 *Cimon* Athenian general and statesman of the fifth century BCE; *Aristides* Athenian politician and general of the early fifth century BCE, nicknamed "the just."
55 *Cato* Cato Uticensis, first-century BCE Roman general and statesman who killed himself rather than submit to the conquering Julius Caesar.
56 *that attempered Hero* Timoleon [d. 334 BCE] killed his brother when he tried to usurp the government of Corinth; expelled Roman tyrants from the Greek cities of Sicily and ruled well in their stead. [Thomson's note].

57 *Scipio* Scipio Africanus, Roman general of the third to second centuries BCE who defeated Hannibal; popular support defeated an attempt by political enemies to prosecute him 15 years later to the day; but after that he retired to his country estate.
58 *Theban* Pelopidas or Epaminondas, fourth-century BCE friends who expelled the Spartans from Thebes (Thomson changed "Theban" to "Theban pair" in later versions of the poem and indicated whom he meant in a footnote).
59 *Maro* Virgil's surname.
60 *British Muse* Milton.
61 *Darkling* because they were blind.

Save *Lycidas*, the Friend, with Sense refined,[62]
Learning digested well, exalted Faith,
Unstudied Wit, and Humour ever gay.   300
   Clear Frost succeeds, and through the blue Serene,
For Sight too fine, th' Etherial Nitre flies,[63]
To bake the Glebe, and bind the slipp'ry Flood.[64]
This of the wintry Season is the Prime;
Pure are the Days, and lustrous are the Nights,   305
Brightened with starry Worlds, till then unseen.
Meanwhile, the Orient, darkly red, breathes forth
An Icy Gale, that, in its mid Career,
Arrests the bickering Stream. The nightly Sky,
And all her glowing Constellations pour   310
Their rigid Influence down: It freezes on[65]
Till Morn, late-rising, o'er the drooping World,
Lifts her pale Eye, unjoyous: then appears
The various Labour of the silent Night,
The pendant Icicle, the Frost-Work fair,   315
Where thousand Figures rise, the crusted Snow,
Though white, made whiter, by the fining North.[66]
On blithesome Frolics bent, the youthful Swains,
While every Work of Man is laid at Rest,
Rush o'er the wat'ry Plains, and, shuddering, view   320
The fearful Deeps below: or with the Gun,
And faithful Spaniel, range the ravaged Fields,
And, adding to the Ruins of the Year,
Distress the Feathery, or the Footed *Game*.
   But hark! the nightly Winds, with hollow Voice,   325
Blow, blustering, from the South – the Frost subdued,
Gradual, resolves into a weeping Thaw.[67]
Spotted, the Mountains shine: loose Sleet descends,
And floods the Country round: the Rivers swell,
Impatient for the Day. – Those sullen Seas,   330
That wash th' ungenial Pole, will rest no more,[68]
Beneath the Shackles of the mighty North;
But, rousing all their Waves, resistless heave, –

---

62 *Lycidas* the title of Milton's famous elegy (see p. 67, above); the friend from whom the poet takes inspiration.

63 *Nitre* a salt thought to be borne by the north wind, impressing coldness on what it touched.

64 *Glebe* soil.

65 *Influence* "Power of celestial aspects operat-ing upon terrestrial bodies and affairs" (Johnson's *Dictionary*).

66 *fining* refining; *North* north wind.

67 *resolves* melts.

68 *ungenial* "Not kind or favourable to nature" (Johnson's *Dictionary*).

And hark! – the length'ning Roar, continuous, runs
Athwart the rifted Main; at once, it bursts,[69]   335
And piles a thousand Mountains to the Clouds!
Ill fares the Bark, the Wretches' last Resort,[70]
That, lost amid the floating Fragments, moors
Beneath the Shelter of an Icy Isle;
While Night o'erwhelms the Sea, and Horror looks   340
More horrible. Can human Hearts endure
Th' assembled *Mischiefs*, that besiege them round:
Unlist'ning *Hunger*, fainting *Weariness*,
The *Roar* of Winds, and Waves, the *Crush* of Ice,
Now, ceasing, now, renewed, with louder Rage,   345
And bellowing round the Main: Nations remote,
Shook from their Midnight-Slumbers, deem they hear
Portentous Thunder, in the troubled Sky.
More to embroil the Deep, Leviathan,[71]
And his unwieldy Train, in horrid Sport,   350
Tempest the loosened Brine; while, through the Gloom,
Far, from the dire, unhospitable Shore,
The Lion's Rage, the Wolf's sad Howl is heard,
And all the fell Society of Night.[72]
Yet, *Providence*, that ever-waking *Eye*   355
Looks down, with Pity, on the fruitless Toil
Of Mortals, lost to Hope, and *lights* them safe,
Through all this dreary Labyrinth of Fate.
    'Tis done! – Dread WINTER has subdued the Year,
And reigns, tremendous, o'er the desert Plains!   360
How dead the Vegetable Kingdom lies!
How dumb the Tuneful! *Horror* wide extends
His solitary Empire. – Now, fond *Man!*
Behold thy pictured Life: pass some few Years,[73]
Thy flow'ring SPRING, thy short-lived SUMMER's Strength,   365
Thy sober AUTUMN, fading into Age,
And pale, concluding, WINTER shuts thy Scene,
And shrouds *Thee* in the Grave – where now, are fled
Those Dreams of Greatness? those unsolid Hopes
Of Happiness? those Longings after Fame?   370
Those restless Cares? those busy, bustling Days?
Those Nights of secret Guilt? those veering Thoughts,
Flutt'ring 'twixt Good, and Ill, that shared thy Life?

---

69   *rifted* cleft, cloven.
70   *Bark* a poetic name for a boat; the passage
recalls *Paradise Lost* 1.203–8.
71   *Leviathan* biblical sea-monster, the whale.
72   *fell* cruel.

73   *Behold thy pictured Life* the allegory of human
life as a succession of seasons derives ultimately
from Ovid, *Metamorphoses* 15.199–213 (p. 455
below).

All, now, are vanished! *Virtue,* sole, survives,
Immortal, Mankind's never-failing Friend,   375
His Guide to Happiness on high – and see!
'Tis come, the Glorious *Morn!* the second Birth
Of Heaven, and Earth! – awakening *Nature* hears
Th' Almighty Trumpet's Voice, and starts to Life,
Renewed, unfading. Now, th' Eternal *Scheme,*   380
That Dark Perplexity, that Mystic Maze,
Which Sight could never trace, nor Heart conceive,
To *Reason* 's Eye, refined, clears up apace.
Angels, and Men, astonished, pause – and dread
To travel through the Depths of Providence,   385
Untried, unbounded. Ye vain *Learned!* see,
And, prostrate in the Dust, adore that *Power,*
And *Goodness,* oft arraigned. See now the Cause,
Why conscious *Worth,* oppressed, in secret long
Mourned, unregarded: Why the *Good Man*'s Share   390
In Life, was Gall, and Bitterness of Soul:
Why the lone *Widow,* and her *Orphans,* pined,
In starving Solitude; while *Luxury,*
In Palaces, lay prompting her low Thought,
To form unreal Wants: why Heaven-born *Faith,*   395
And *Charity,* prime Grace! wore the *red* Marks
Of *Persecution*'s Scourge: why licensed *Pain,*
That cruel *Spoiler,* that embosomed *Foe,*
Embittered all our Bliss. Ye Good *Distressed!*
Ye Noble *Few!* that, here, unbending, stand   400
Beneath Life's Pressures – yet a little while,
And all your Woes are past. *Time* swiftly fleets,
And wished *Eternity,* approaching, brings
Life undecaying, Love without Allay,[74]
Pure flowing Joy, and Happiness sincere.   405

---

74   *without Allay* undiminished; unstinting.

Samuel Johnson (1709–1784)

Samuel Johnson began his long conversation with classical literature in his father's bookshop in Lichfield, Staffordshire. His earliest verse includes translations of Horace and Virgil into English and Alexander Pope's *Messiah* into Latin. The first work for which he received acclaim was *London* (1738), an imitation of Juvenal's third satire. His most famous poem is *The Vanity of Human Wishes, the Tenth Satire of Juvenal Imitated* (1749). Johnson read and wrote Latin verse, and English translations of it, all his life: both his earliest and his latest poems include translations of Horace and autobiographical Latin verse. Johnson made his living as a writer and naturally he wrote his greatest works in English – the *Lives of the Poets*, the *Dictionary*, *Rasselas*, the *Rambler* – but when he wrote or read for pleasure, he often reverted to Latin.

The imitation was a popular form of poetry in the eighteenth century. In this form, the poet adapts a classical poem to the present times, changing the classical names and events to modern ones. Dryden says that John Denham and Abraham Cowley invented this very loose form of translation. In his preface to his translation of Ovid's *Epistles*, Dryden says, "I take Imitation of an Authour in their sense to be an Endeavour of a later Poet to write like one who has written before him on the same Subject: that is, not to Translate his words, or to be Confined to his Sense, but only to set him as a Pattern, and to write, as he supposes, that Authour would have done, had he lived in our Age, and in our Country."[1] Dryden's definition is precisely applicable to Johnson's imitation of Juvenal and it explains why Johnson's poem is not a translation (unlike Dryden's version of the poem, which appears on pp. 478–95 below).

SAMUEL JOHNSON
1 Preface to *Ovid's Epistles*, *Works of John*   *Dryden*, Vol. I (University of California Press, 1956), pp. 116–17.

The pleasure of imitations for eighteenth-century readers was partly a matter of appreciating the differences between the "pattern" and the performance, the original and the derivative but new poem. Early editions of the *Vanity* included references to the parts of Juvenal that are imitated. We restore those references here and point the reader to the sections of Dryden's translation of the poem that correspond to the lines referenced in Juvenal. Dryden's poem, of course, is not a strict and literal translation, but it is much closer to the original than Johnson's and, as Johnson deeply admired Dryden, it provides a plausible notion of what Johnson thought of when he read Juvenal.

The Vanity of Human Wishes sums up a great deal of the basic, satirical wisdom that Johnson transmitted in all of his writings. The themes of the poems were practically second nature to him not only because he knew Juvenal so well but also because he knew the proverbial wisdom underlying Juvenal. It was a poem of commonplaces for Johnson, and it is therefore somewhat less surprising, though no less astonishing, that he was able to compose most of it in his head as he walked around Hampstead, London, where he lived at the time. When he had as many as 50 lines ready, Johnson jotted down half of each line on scraps of notebook paper; only when he had finished composing the whole poem did he fill in the rest. (Johnson was sluggish about writing and he knew he could trust his capacious memory.) The themes of the *Vanity* recur in Johnson's most notable later works, especially the *Rambler* (1750–1752) and the *Lives of the Poets* (1779–1781), but they also fill the illustrative quotations of his greatest work, *A Dictionary of the English Language* (1755).

In his language Johnson tried to find an English equivalent for what he termed the "stateliness" and "declamatory grandeur" of Juvenal. He felt these qualities had been missed by many admirers and translators, although they had successfully captured Juvenal's "gaiety" (liveliness) and his "pointed sentences" (pithy wit). The work abounds in abstractions that seem to be growing into personifications without living long enough to get there. Observation, for example, is personified enough in the first two lines to have qualities of sight and to be the object of a hortatory clause, but it never becomes an allegorical figure. The same may be said of Hope and Fear and dozens of other abstract ideas in the poem. Yet the poem is close enough to allegory that one can speak about the features of its landscape. The scene of the *Vanity* is cloudy, misty, and perpetually overheated. It is a world in which ignorance is the rule and misdirection the law. The more one strives or hopes in this world, the more deeply lost one becomes. All hot desires lead to destruction, and no human way to be cool is presented until the very end of the poem. According to some critics, Johnson puts a Christian capstone on the pagan poem at the end, substituting faith in God for the impersonal stoicism of Juvenal. However, because so little in the rest of the poem suggests it is going that way, the ending may also be read as a concession to contemporary readers who expected a happy Christian ending and would have rejected a conclusion as cynical as the rest of the poem.

Our text is based on the first edition (1749), but we substitute some significant changes made by Johnson when he revised the poem in 1755.

The Vanity of Human Wishes

The Tenth Satire of *Juvenal,*

Imitated

Let Observation with extensive View,*
Survey Mankind, from *China* to *Peru*;
Remark each anxious Toil, each eager Strife,
And watch the busy Scenes of crowded Life;
Then say how Hope and Fear, Desire and Hate,   5
O'erspread with Snares the clouded Maze of Fate,
Where wav'ring Man, betrayed by vent'rous Pride,
To tread the dreary Paths without a Guide;
As treach'rous Phantoms in the Mist delude,
Shuns fancied Ills, or chases airy Good.   10
How rarely Reason guides the stubborn Choice,
Rules the bold Hand, or prompts the suppliant Voice,
How Nations sink, by darling Schemes oppressed,
When Vengeance listens to the Fool's Request.
Fate wings with every Wish th' afflictive Dart,[1]   15
Each Gift of Nature, and each Grace of Art,
With fatal Heat impetuous Courage glows,
With fatal Sweetness Elocution flows,
Impeachment stops the Speaker's pow'rful Breath,
And restless Fire precipitates on Death.[2]   20
   But scarce observed the Knowing and the Bold,[†]
Fall in the gen'ral Massacre of Gold;
Wide-wasting Pest! that rages unconfined,
And crowds with Crimes the Records of Mankind,
For Gold his Sword the Hireling Ruffian draws,   25
For Gold the hireling Judge distorts the Laws;
Wealth heaped on wealth, nor Truth nor Safety buys,[3]
The Dangers gather as the Treasures rise.

THE VANITY OF HUMAN WISHES

* Ver[ses in Juvenal's *Satire* 10]. 1–11 [Johnson's note; p. 479, lines 1–15 below].

1 *wing* "To furnish with wings; to enable to fly" (Johnson's *Dictionary*).

2 *precipitates on* "To hasten without just preparation" (Johnson's *Dictionary*).

† Ver. 12–22 [Johnson's note; pp. 479–80, lines 16–34 below].

3 *nor . . . nor* neither . . . nor.

Let Hist'ry tell where rival Kings command,
And dubious Title shakes the madded Land,[4]   30
When Statutes glean the Refuse of the Sword,[5]
How much more safe the Vassal than the Lord,
Low skulks the Hind beneath the Rage of Pow'r,
And leaves the *bonny Traitor* in the *Tow'r*,[6]
Untouched his Cottage, and his Slumbers sound,   35
Though Confiscation's Vultures clang around.
    The needy Traveler, serene and gay,
Walks the wild Heath, and sings his Toil away.
Does Envy seize thee? crush th' upbraiding Joy,
Increase his Riches and his Peace destroy;   40
Now Fears in dire Vicissitude invade,
The rustling Brake alarms, and quiv'ring Shade,
Nor Light nor Darkness bring his Pain Relief,
One shows the Plunder, and one hides the Thief.
    Yet still one gen'ral Cry the Skies assails,*   45
And Gain and Grandeur load the tainted Gales;[7]
Few know the toiling Statesman's Fear or Care,
Th' insidious Rival and the gaping Heir.
    Once more, Democritus, arise on Earth,[†8]
With cheerful Wisdom and instructive Mirth,   50
See motley Life in modern Trappings dressed,[9]
And feed with varied Fools th' eternal Jest:
Thou who couldst laugh where Want enchained Caprice,
Toil crushed Conceit, and Man was of a Piece;
Where Wealth unloved without a Mourner died,   55
And scarce a Sycophant was fed by pride;
Where ne'er was known the Form of mock Debate,
Or seen a new-made Mayor's unwieldy State;
Where change of Fav'rites made no Change of Laws,[10]

4 *madded* driven mad.
5 *When Statutes glean the Refuse of the Sword* when taxes take what direct assault leaves behind.
6 *bonny Traitor* refers to four Scottish lords imprisoned and executed after the Jacobite rebellion of 1745; Johnson dropped the allusion when he revised the poem in 1755.
* Ver. 23–7 [Johnson's note; p. 480, lines 35–40 below].
7 *Gale* "A wind not tempestuous, yet stronger than a breeze" (Johnson's *Dictionary*).
† Ver. 28–55 [Johnson's note; pp. 480–1, lines 41–84 below].

8 *Democritus* (fl. fifth century BCE), known as the "laughing philosopher" because of his ideal of cheerfulness, despite his recognition of severe human limitation; Robert Burton styled himself Democritus Junior in his *Anatomy of Melancholy* (1628), one of Johnson's favorite books.
9 *motley* the dress of court jesters or fools.
10 *Change of Laws* in 1746 the Act of 19 George II, c. 8, changed the administrative structure of London, giving more power to the Common Council and less to the Aldermen as a separate group.

And Senates heard before they judged a Cause;   60
How wouldst thou shake at *Britain*'s modish Tribe,
Dart the quick Taunt, and edge the piercing Gibe?
Attentive Truth and Nature to descry,
And pierce each Scene with Philosophic Eye.
To thee were solemn Toys or empty Show,   65
The Robes of Pleasure and the Veils of Woe:
All aid the Farce, and all thy Mirth maintain,
Whose Joys are causeless, or whose Griefs are vain.
   Such was the Scorn that filled the Sage's Mind,
Renewed at every Glance on Humankind;   70
How just that Scorn ere yet thy Voice declare,
Search every State, and canvass every Prayer.
   Unnumbered Suppliants crowd Preferment's Gate,*
Athirst for Wealth, and burning to be great;
Delusive Fortune hears th' incessant Call,   75
They mount, they shine, evaporate, and fall.[11]
On every Stage the Foes of Peace attend,[12]
Hate dogs their Flight, and Insult mocks their End.
Love ends with Hope, the sinking Statesman's Door
Pours in the Morning Worshiper no more;   80
For growing Names the weekly Scribbler lies,[13]
To growing Wealth the Dedicator flies,[14]
From every Room descends the painted Face,
That hung the bright *Palladium* of the Place,[15]
And smoked in Kitchens, or in Auctions sold,   85
To better Features yields the Frame of Gold;
For now no more we trace in every Line
Heroic Worth, Benevolence Divine:
The Form distorted justifies the Fall,
And Detestation rids th' indignant Wall.   90
   But will not *Britain* hear the last Appeal,
Sign her Foes' Doom, or guard her Favourites' Zeal?
Through Freedom's Sons no more Remonstrance rings,[16]
Degrading Nobles and controlling Kings;

---

* Ver. 56–107 [Johnson's note; pp. 481–4, lines 85–171 below].

11 *evaporate* "To fly away in vapours or fumes; to waste insensibly as a volatile spirit" (Johnson's *Dictionary*); the image is of a meteor.

12 *Stage* "Any place where any thing public is transacted or performed" (Johnson's *Dictionary*).

13 *weekly Scribbler* journalist.

14 *Dedicator* an author writing a dedication of his book or poem to someone important.

15 *Palladium* the sacred image of Pallas Athena sent by Zeus as symbol of protection to the city of Troy.

16 *Remonstrance* recalling the Grand Remonstrance, a catalogue of grievances against the king narrowly passed by the House of Commons in 1641.

Our supple Tribes repress their Patriot Throats,   95
And ask no Questions but the Price of Votes;
With Weekly Libels and Septennial Ale,[17]
Their Wish is full to riot and to rail.
   In full-blown dignity, see *Wolsey* stand,[18]
Law in his Voice, and Fortune in his Hand: 100
To him the Church, the Realm, their Pow'rs consign,
Through him the Rays of regal Bounty shine,
Turned by his Nod the Stream of Honour flows,
His Smile alone Security bestows:
Still to new Heights his restless Wishes tow'r,   105
Claim leads to Claim, and Pow'r advances Pow'r;
Till Conquest unresisted ceased to please,
And Rights submitted, left him none to seize.
At length his Sovereign frowns – the Train of State
Mark the keen Glance, and watch the Sign to hate.   110
Where'er he turns he meets a Stranger's Eye,
His Suppliants scorn him, and his Followers fly;
Now drops at once the Pride of awful State,
The golden Canopy, the glitt'ring Plate,
The regal Palace, the luxurious Board,   115
The liv'ried Army, and the menial Lord.[19]
With Age, with Cares, with Maladies oppressed,
He seeks the Refuge of Monastic Rest.
Grief aids Disease, remembered Folly stings,
And his last Sighs reproach the Faith of Kings.   120
   Speak thou, whose Thoughts at humble Peace repine,
Shall *Wolsey*'s Wealth, with *Wolsey*'s End be thine?
Or liv'st thou now, with safer Pride content,
The richest Landlord on the Banks of *Trent*?[20]
For why did *Wolsey* by the Steps of Fate,   125
On weak Foundations raise th' enormous Weight?
Why but to sink beneath Misfortune's Blow,
With louder Ruin to the Gulfs below?

17 *Libels* pamphlets for railing (Latin, *libellus*); *Septennial Ale* free booze for rioting on election day; parliaments were made seven years long under George I.
18 *Wolsey* Thomas (1475?–1530), cardinal and lord chancellor under Henry VIII, until he lost favor, was indicted in the King's Bench (1529), forfeited his estate, was falsely accused of treason, and soon died. Wolsey corresponds to Sejanus in Juvenal's poem (see p. 481 below).

19 *menial* "Belonging to the retinue or train of servants" (Johnson's *Dictionary*).
20 *Trent* the river goes no further south than the environs of Lichfield, Johnson's home town, about 85 miles north of London, the center of wealth and fame; in 1755 Johnson changed "richest Landlord" to "wisest justice."

What gave great *Villiers* to th' Assassin's Knife,*[21]
And fixed Disease on *Harley*'s closing Life?[22]   130
What murdered *Wentworth*, and what exiled *Hyde*,[23]
By Kings protected and to Kings allied?
What but their Wish indulged in Courts to shine,
And Pow'r too great to keep or to resign?
    When first the College Rolls receive his Name,†   135
The young Enthusiast quits his Ease for Fame;[24]
Through all his Veins the Fever of Renown,
Burns from the strong Contagion of the Gown;[25]
O'er *Bodley*'s Dome his future Labours spread,[26]
And *Bacon*'s Mansion trembles o'er his Head;[27]   140
Are these thy Views? proceed, illustrious Youth,
And virtue guard thee to the Throne of Truth!
Yet should thy Soul indulge the gen'rous Heat,
Till captive Science yields her last Retreat;[28]
Should Reason guide thee with her brightest Ray,   145
And pour on misty Doubt resistless Day;
Should no false Kindness lure to loose Delight,
Nor Praise relax, nor Difficulty fright;
Should tempting Novelty thy Cell refrain,
And Sloth effuse her Opiate Fumes in vain;   150
Should Beauty blunt on Fops her fatal Dart,
Nor claim the Triumph of a lettered Heart;

---

* Ver. 108–13 [Johnson's note; p. 484, lines 172–79 below].

21 *Villiers* George, first duke of Buckingham (1592–1628), court favorite whom the Commons tried to force Charles I to remove; his assassin, a naval lieutenant, believed he was acting on the will of the people. Villiers and the others mentioned here correspond to the late republican statesmen (e.g., Pompey) to whom Juvenal alludes (p. 484 below).

22 *Harley* Robert (1661–1724), first earl of Oxford, leader of the Tory ministry in 1710, dismissed in 1714, imprisoned in 1715, and impeached after the fact in 1717.

23 *Wentworth* Thomas, first earl of Strafford (1593–1641), Charles I's chief advisor, impeached by the House of Commons and executed in a flurry of rumors and fears of mob violence; *Hyde* Edward, earl of Clarendon (1609–1674), lord chancellor in 1660, impeached by the Commons and banished in 1668, died in exile.

† Ver. 114–32 [Johnson's note; pp. 484–5, lines 180–205 below].

24 *Enthusiast* "One of a hot imagination, or violent passions" (Johnson's *Dictionary*). Johnson's eager youth corresponds in Juvenal to the boy who aspires to the eloquence of Cicero and Demosthenes (p. 484 below).

25 *Gown* "The long habit of a man dedicated to acts of peace, as divinity, medicine, law" (Johnson's *Dictionary*).

26 *Dome* building; Sir Thomas Bodley (1545–1613) formed, endowed, and gave his name to the Oxford University library.

27 *Bacon's Mansion* the study used by the philosopher Roger Bacon (1214?–1294), a gatehouse on Folly Bridge in Oxford; an Oxford tradition said that the study would fall if someone more learned than Bacon walked under the bridge.

28 *Science* knowledge.

Should no Disease thy torpid Veins invade,
Nor Melancholy's Phantoms haunt thy Shade;
Yet hope not Life from Grief or Danger free,   155
Nor think the Doom of Man reversed for thee:
Deign on the passing World to turn thine Eyes,
And pause awhile from Learning, to be wise;
There mark what Ills the Scholar's Life assail,
Toil, Envy, Want, the Patron, and the Jail.[29]   160
See Nations slowly wise, and meanly just,
To buried Merit raise the tardy Bust.[30]
If Dreams yet flatter, once again attend,
Hear *Lydiat*'s life, and *Galileo*'s end.[31]
  Nor deem, when Learning her last Prize bestows   165
The glitt'ring Eminence exempt from Foes;
See when the Vulgar 'scape, despised or awed,[32]
Rebellion's vengeful Talons seize on *Laud*.[33]
From meaner Minds, though smaller Fines content
The plundered Palace or sequestered Rent;   170
Marked out by dangerous Parts he meets the Shock,
And fatal Learning leads him to the Block:
Around his Tomb let Art and Genius weep,
But hear his Death, ye Blockheads, hear and sleep.
  The festal Blazes, the triumphal Show,*   175
The ravished Standard, and the captive Foe,
The Senate's Thanks, the Gázette's pompous Tale,[34]
With Force resistless o'er the Brave prevail.
Such Bribes the rapid *Greek* o'er *Asia* whirled[35]
For such the steady *Romans* shook the World;   180
For such in distant Lands the *Britons* shine,[36]
And stain with Blood the *Danube* or the *Rhine*;
This Pow'r has Praise, that Virtue scarce can warm,

29 *Patron* "Commonly a wretch who supports with insolence, and is paid with flattery" (Johnson's *Dictionary*); it was "Garret" in the first edition; the change is connected with Johnson's formal repudiation of Chesterfield's tardy patronage of the *Dictionary,* which he effected with a famous letter written about the same time that he revised his poem in 1755.
30 *tardy Bust* the burial monument; compare Alexander Pope: "Patrons, who sneak from living worth to dead, /With-hold the pension, and set up the head" (*Dunciad* 4.95–6).
31 *Lydiat* Thomas (1572–1646), a famous astronomer in his time, died in poverty and was forgotten; *Galileo* (1564–1642), the great astron-omer, forced by the church to deny his Copernican views, lived the last eight years of his life under house arrest.
32 *Vulgar* common, unlearned persons.
33 *Laud* William (1573–1645), archbishop of Canterbury under Charles I, accused of high treason by Parliament and executed in 1645.
* Ver. 133–46 [Johnson's note; p. 485, lines 206–33 below].
34 *Gázette* the government-run newspaper.
35 *the rapid Greek* Alexander the Great.
36 *the Britons* an allusion to the surprising military victory over the French at Blenheim by the brilliant and ambitious John Churchill (1650–1722), first duke of Marlborough.

Till Fame supplies the universal Charm.
Yet Reason frowns on War's unequal Game,   185
Where wasted Nations raise a single Name,
And mortgaged States their Grandsires' Wreaths regret,[37]
From Age to Age in everlasting Debt;
Wreaths which at last the dear-bought Right convey
To rust on Medals, or on Stones decay.   190
    On what Foundation stands the Warrior's Pride?*
How just his Hopes let *Swedish Charles* decide;[38]
A Frame of Adamant, a Soul of Fire,
No Dangers fright him, and no Labours tire;
O'er Love, o'er Force, extends his wide Domain,   195
Unconquered Lord of Pleasure and of Pain;
No Joys to him pacific Scepters yield,
War sounds the Trump, he rushes to the Field;
Behold surrounding Kings their Pow'r combine,
And One capitulate, and One resign;   200
Peace courts his Hand, but spreads her Charms in vain;
"Think Nothing gained," he cries, "till nought remain,
On *Moscow*'s Walls till *Gothic* Standards fly,
And all is Mine beneath the Polar Sky."
The March begins in Military State,   205
And Nations on his Eye suspended wait;
Stern Famine guards the solitary Coast,
And Winter barricades the Realms of Frost;
He comes, nor Want nor Cold his Course delay; –
Hide, blushing Glory, hide *Pultowa*'s Day: 210
The vanquished Hero leaves his broken Bands,
And shows his Miseries in distant Lands;
Condemned a needy Supplicant to wait,
While Ladies interpose, and Slaves debate.
But did not Chance at length her Error mend?   215
Did no subverted Empire mark his End?
Did rival Monarchs give the fatal Wound?
Or hostile Millions press him to the Ground?
His Fall was destined to a barren Strand,
A petty Fortress, and a dubious Hand;[39]   220

---

37 *Wreaths* victory garlands.
* Ver. 147–67 [Johnson's note; pp. 486–7, lines 234–72 below].
38 *Swedish Charles* Charles XII of Sweden (1682–1718), a very active general and statesman; pursued the Russian army toward Moscow in 1707; defeated at Pultowa (Ukraine) in 1709; sought allies in Turkey, where he was involved in intrigues; sympathized with English Jacobites as a threat to George I and Hanover; began a new military campaign in 1718 but was killed in battle before it was well under way. Charles corresponds to Hannibal in Juvenal (p. 486 below).
39 *a dubious hand* some say Charles was killed by one of his own soldiers at the siege of Frederik-shald (Halden, Norway).

He left the Name, at which the World grew pale,
To point a Moral, or adorn a Tale.[40]
    All Times their Scenes of pompous Woes afford,*
From *Persia*'s Tyrant to *Bavaria*'s Lord.[41]
In gay Hostility, and barb'rous Pride,   225
With half Mankind embattled at his Side,
Great *Xerxes* comes to seize the certain Prey,
And starves exhausted Regions in his Way;
Attendant Flatt'ry counts his Myriads o'er,
Till counted Myriads soothe his Pride no more;   230
Fresh Praise is tried till Madness fires his Mind,
The Waves he lashes, and enchains the Wind;[42]
New Pow'rs are claimed, new Pow'rs are still bestowed,
Till rude Resistance lops the spreading God;
The daring *Greeks* deride the Martial Show,   235
And heap their Valleys with the gaudy Foe;[43]
Th' insulted Sea with humbler Thoughts he gains,
A single Skiff to speed his Flight remains;
Th' encumber'd Oar scarce leaves the dreaded Coast
Through purple Billows and a floating Host.   240
    The bold *Bavarian*, in a luckless Hour,
Tries the dread Summits of *Caesarean* Pow'r,
With unexpected Legions bursts away,
And sees defenseless Realms receive his Sway;
Short Sway! fair *Austria* spreads her mournful Charms,[44]   245
The Queen, the Beauty, sets the World in Arms;
From Hill to Hill the Beacons rousing Blaze
Spreads wide the Hope of Plunder and of Praise;
The fierce *Croatian*, and the wild *Hussar*,[45]
And all the Sons of Ravage crowd the War;   250
The baffled Prince in Honour's flatt'ring Bloom
Of hasty Greatness finds the fatal Doom,

40 *He . . . Tale* an excellent rendition of Juvenal's apostrophe to Hannibal (p. 487 below): literally, "Go, madman, hurry over the Alps, to please boys and become a subject for their speeches."
* Ver. 168–87 [Johnson's note; pp. 487–8, lines 273–300 below].
41 *Persia's Tyrant* Xerxes the Great (519–465 BCE), whose massive invasions of Greece failed. In this instance Johnson borrows the example of Juvenal, who, after Hannibal, cites Alexander and Xerxes; *Bavaria's Lord* Charles Albert (1697–1745), elector of Bavaria, became Holy Roman Emperor in 1742.

42 *Waves . . . Wind* when bad weather hindered his assault, he ordered his men to punish the sea (Herodotus 7.35, 54).
43 *Valleys* especially Thermopylae, where Xerxes won a costly victory, before he was defeated at sea near Salamis and had to retreat.
44 *fair Austria* Maria Theresa of Austria, ruler of the Hapsburg dominions; led the attack on Bavaria even as Charles was being crowned emperor.
45 *Hussar* Hungarian cavalryman.

His Foes' Derision, and his Subjects' Blame,
And steals to Death from Anguish and from Shame.
   Enlarge my Life with Multitude of Days,*   255
In Health, in Sickness, thus the Suppliant prays;
Hides from himself his State, and shuns to know,
That Life protracted is protracted Woe.
Time hovers o'er, impatient to destroy,
And shuts up all the Passages of Joy: 260
In vain their Gifts the bounteous Seasons pour,
The Fruit Autumnal, and the Vernal Flow'r,
With listless Eyes the Dotard views the Store,
He views, and wonders that they please no more;
Now pall the tasteless Meats, and joyless Wines,   265
And Luxury with Sighs her Slave resigns.
Approach, ye Minstrels, try the soothing Strain,
And yield the tuneful Lenitives of Pain:
No Sounds alas would touch th' impervious Ear,
Though dancing Mountains witnessed *Orpheus* near;[46]   270
Nor Lute nor Lyre his feeble Pow'rs attend,
Nor sweeter Music of a virtuous Friend,
But everlasting Dictates crowd his Tongue,
Perversely grave, or positively wrong.
The still returning Tale, and ling'ring Jest,   275
Perplex the fawning Niece and pampered Guest,
While growing Hopes scarce awe the gath'ring Sneer,
And scarce a Legacy can bribe to hear;
The watchful Guests still hint the last Offence,
The Daughter's Petulance, the Son's Expense,   280
Improve his heady Rage with treach'rous Skill,
And mould his Passions till they make his Will.
   Unnumbered Maladies each Joint invade,
Lay Siege to Life and press the dire Blockade;
But unextinguished Av'rice still remains,   285
And dreaded Losses aggravate his Pains;
He turns, with anxious Heart and crippled Hands,
His Bonds of Debt, and Mortgages of Lands;
Or views his Coffers with suspicious Eyes,
Unlocks his Gold, and counts it till he dies.   290
   But grant, the Virtues of a temp'rate Prime
Bless with an Age exempt from Scorn or Crime;
An Age that melts in unperceived Decay,
And glides in modest Innocence away;
Whose peaceful Day Benevolence endears,   295

---

* Ver. 188–288 [Johnson's note; pp. 488–92,   46 *Orpheus* legendary pre-Homeric poet whose
lines 301–443 below].   music could charm beasts and animate rocks.

Whose Night congratulating Conscience cheers;
The gen'ral Fav'rite as the gen'ral Friend:
Such Age there is, and who could wish its End?
   Yet ev'n on this her Load Misfortune flings,
To press the weary Minutes' flagging Wings: 300
New Sorrow rises as the Day returns,
A Sister sickens, or a Daughter mourns.
Now Kindred Merit fills the sable Bier,
Now lacerated Friendship claims a Tear.
Year chases Year, Decay pursues Decay,   305
Still drops some Joy from with'ring Life away;
New Forms arise, and diff'rent Views engage,
Superfluous lags the Vet'ran on the Stage
Till pitying Nature signs the last Release,
And bids afflicted Worth retire to Peace.   310
   But few there are whom Hours like these await,
Who set unclouded in the Gulfs of Fate.
From *Lydia*'s Monarch should the Search descend,[47]
By *Solon* cautioned to regard his End,[48]
In Life's last Scene what Prodigies surprise,   315
Fears of the Brave, and Follies of the Wise?
From *Marlborough*'s Eyes the Streams of Dotage flow,
And *Swift* expires a Driv'ler and a Show.[49]
   The teeming Mother, anxious for her Race,*[50]
Begs for each Birth the Fortune of a Face: 320
Yet *Vane* could tell what Ills from Beauty spring;[51]
And *Sedley* cursed the Form that pleased a King.[52]
Ye Nymphs of rosy Lips and radiant Eyes,
Whom Pleasure keeps too busy to be wise,
Whom Joys with soft Varieties invite,   325
By Day the Frolic, and the Dance by Night,
Who frown with Vanity, who smile with Art,
And ask the latest Fashion of the Heart,
What Care, what Rules your heedless Charms shall save,
Each Nymph your Rival, and each Youth your Slave?   330

47 *Lydia's Monarch* Croesus, the wealthy sixth-century BCE king defeated by Cyrus of Persia. The example is taken from Juvenal, who adds Mithridates, Marius, and Pompey.

48 *Solon* the Athenian lawgiver was said to have advised Croesus to "look to the end" in all things, since fortune, not wealth, determined happiness; the saying was later enshrined in the Latin motto, *respice finem*.

49 *Swift* at the age of 73, four years before his death, Swift was declared legally incompetent; it is said that his servants showed him to visitors for a fee.

* Ver. 289–345 [Johnson's note; pp. 492–4, lines 444–532 below].

50 *teeming* pregnant.

51 *Vane* Anne (1705–1736), mistress of Frederick, prince of Wales. Vane and Sedley correspond structurally to Juvenal's Lucretia and Virginia (p. 492 below), but, as mistresses of great men, they bear more resemblance to Juvenal's Silius, the lover of the empress Messalina (p. 494 below).

52 *Sedley* Catherine (1657–1717), mistress of the duke of York (later James II).

Against your Fame with Fondness Hate combines,
The Rival batters, and the Lover mines.
With distant Voice neglected Virtue calls,
Less heard, and less the faint Remonstrance falls;
Tired with Contempt, she quits the slipp'ry Reign,   335
And Pride and Prudence take her Seat in vain.
In crowd at once, where none the Pass defend,
The harmless Freedom, and the private Friend.
The Guardians yield, by Force superior plied;
By Interest, Prudence; and by Flatt'ry, Pride.   340
Here Beauty falls betrayed, despised, distressed,
And hissing Infamy proclaims the rest.
    Where then shall Hope and Fear their Objects find?*
Must dull Suspense corrupt the stagnant Mind?
Must helpless Man, in Ignorance sedate,   345
Swim darkling down the Current of his Fate?
Must no Dislike alarm, no Wishes rise,
No Cries attempt the Mercies of the Skies?
Enquirer, cease, Petitions yet remain,
Which Heav'n may hear, nor deem Religion vain.   350
Still raise for Good the supplicating Voice,
But leave to Heav'n the Measure and the Choice.
Safe in his Pow'r, whose Eyes discern afar
The secret Ambush of a specious Prayer.
Implore his Aid, in his Decisions rest,   355
Secure whate'er he gives, he gives the best.
Yet when the Sense of sacred Presence fires,
And strong Devotion to the skies aspires,
Pour forth thy Fervours for a healthful Mind,
Obedient Passions, and a Will resigned;   360
For Love, which scarce collective Man can fill;
For Patience sovereign o'er transmuted Ill;
For Faith, that panting for a happier Seat,
Counts Death kind Nature's Signal of Retreat:
These Goods for Man the Laws of Heav'n ordain,   365
These Goods he grants, who grants the Pow'r to gain;
With these celestial Wisdom calms the Mind,
And makes the Happiness she does not find.

---

* Ver. 346–66 [Johnson's note; pp. 494–5,
lines 533–62 below].

Thomas Gray (1716–1771)

At the age of nine Gray went to Eton College, where he was a brilliant student of the classics who liked to read Virgil for pleasure. He continued his studies at Cambridge on a special scholarship that required him to write Latin verses weekly. After a grand tour of the continent in the company of Horace Walpole, he returned to Cambridge, where he spent most of his life in continued study. Much of Gray's poetry, particularly his odes, displays the strong influence of the classics, and through the 1740s his main interests were classical poetry and history, especially Greek history. However, in mid-life Gray became interested in medieval history, medieval architecture, and the northern or "gothic" sources of British culture. Later his interests shifted again, this time to natural history and the classificatory work of Linnaeus. These later interests are anti-classical, at least in the way that most of Gray's teachers and contemporaries understood classicism. Furthermore, Gray's later anti-classical tendencies may be seen to mix with his classical training in his earlier poetry, and especially the poetry written during the transitional periods of his intellectual life. Gray uses classical modes and classical allusions, but his tone is often more modern: he mixes sentiment and sensibility into the classical situation and produces poems that are acutely aware of the classics but of a different temper.

Ode on the Death of a Favourite Cat

The classical tradition of animal poems, which we discuss at greater length in introducing William Cowper (p. 163 below), includes many epigrams from the *Greek Anthology*, Catullus 3 (p. 331 below), on the death of a sparrow, and Ovid *Amores* 2.6 (p. 423 below), on the death of a parrot. Gray's elevated tone and mock heroism recall Catullus and Ovid, whose poems also comment on the vanity of women, but he is less sharp and more broadly allegorical than his predecessors. As Roger Lonsdale notes in his edition (Longman, 1969, p. 80), Gray may get his moral not from love poetry but from Virgil's epic description of the death of the warrior woman Camilla in *Aeneid* 11 (p. 383 below). She cuts a splendid Amazonian figure in battle and is victorious until, distracted by an adversary's glittering armor and purple robe, she is struck down by an enemy arrow. Joseph Addison discussed the episode in *Spectator* 15 (March 17, 1711) and drew the same moral Gray does about women's love of "everything that is showy and superficial." Virgil pointed them in this direction at line 782, *femineo praedae et spoliorum ardebat amore*, "she burned with a woman's passion for booty and spoils." Gray was probably thinking of this line when he wrote, "What female heart can gold despise?" He composed the poem partly for his old friend Horace Walpole, with whom he had recently reconciled after a long period of estrangement.

The text is based on that in *A Collection of Poems in Several Hands*, ed. Robert Dodsley, 3 vols (1748), with a few widely accepted changes from later editions.

1

'Twas on a lofty vase's side,
Where China's gayest art had dyed
   The azure flowers, that blow;
Demurest of the Tabby kind,
The pensive Selima reclined,   5
   Gazed on the lake below.

2

Her conscious tail her joy declared;
The fair round face, the snowy beard,
   The velvet of her paws,
The coat that with the tortoise vies,   10
Her ears of jet, and emerald eyes,
   She saw; and purred applause.

3

Still had she gazed: but 'midst the tide
Two angel forms were seen to glide,
   The Genii of the stream:[1]   15
Their scaly armour's Tyrian hue[2]
Through richest purple to the view
   Betrayed a golden gleam.

ODE ON THE DEATH OF A FAVOURITE CAT

1 *Genii* plural of *genius*, "The protecting or ruling power of men, places, or things" (Johnson's *Dictionary*); lines 1–12 recall the myth of Narcissus (Ovid, *Metamorphoses* 3.339–510; p. 446 below).

2 *Tyrian* purple, a color produced from shellfish near the eastern Mediterranean city of Tyre. Dryden, in his translation of *Aeneid* 11.772 (p. 383 below), applies the epithet to the robe worn by Camilla's adversary.

4

The hapless nymph with wonder saw:
A whisker first and then a claw,   20
   With many an ardent wish,
She stretched in vain to reach the prize.
What female heart can gold despise?[3]
   What cat's averse to fish?

5

Presumptuous maid! with looks intent   25
Again she stretched, again she bent,
   Nor knew the gulf between;
(Malignant fate sat by and smiled)
The slipp'ry verge her feet beguiled.
   She tumbled headlong in.   30

6

Eight times emerging from the flood
She mewed to every watry God,
   Some speedy aid to send.[4]
No Dolphin came, no Nereid stirred:[5]
Nor cruel Tom, nor Harry heard.[6]   35
A favourite has no friend![7]

7

From hence, ye beauties, undeceived,
Know, one false step is ne'er retrieved,
   And be with caution bold.
Not all that tempts your wand'ring eyes   40
And heedless hearts, is lawful prize;
   Nor all, that glisters, gold.

---

3   *What . . . despise* compare Virgil's description of Camilla at *Aeneid* 11.782; see our introduction to this poem, above.

4   *She . . . send* just as Daphne prays (successfully) to her father, the river god Peneus, when she is pursued by Apollo (Ovid, *Metamorphoses* 1.543–6; p. 442 below).

5   *Dolphin* an allusion to the legendary rescue of Arion by a dolphin (Herodotus, *Histories* 1.23–4);

Nereid daughter of Nereus; sea nymph. Odysseus is rescued from drowning by the sea goddess Ino (Homer, *Odyssey* 5), though she is not a Nereid.

6   *Harry* other editions read "Susan"; both are, like "Tom," stereotypical servants' names.

7   *favourite* the meaning includes "One chosen as a companion by his superior; a mean wretch whose whole business is by any means to please" (Johnson's *Dictionary*, sense 2).

An Elegy Wrote in a Country Church Yard

The great example of Gray's use of classical material to write a sentimental poem is his famous *Elegy*. He completed the poem in the spring of 1750 and published it only when it was under threat of piracy in 1751. The most important classical precedents are the praises of country life at the end of *Georgics* 2 (p. 357 below) and in Horace, *Epodes* 2 (p. 393 below). Virgil hails "fortunate farmers" for their life of abundance, ease, natural beauty, and sturdy morality as contrasted with the unnaturalness, anxiety, and crime of the lives of the rich and powerful. Horace praises the country in similar terms but adds a surprise ending. It turns out that the encomium has been made by a usurer who has aspirations to be a countryman, but who says one thing and does another. This gives an ironic twist to the whole poem and points up the unreality of such musings. Moreover, at crucial points, both Virgil and Horace are recalling Lucretius (3.894–911; p. 327 below), whose description of domestic pleasures is part of his criticism of our thoughtless susceptibility to sentiment and self-pity. In effect, when Gray writes with real feeling about the lost joys of children running "to lisp their Sire's Return" (line 23), he is rewriting a classical topos handed down from Lucretius to Virgil and Horace. He is closer to Virgil than to Lucretius or Horace, but he knows all the relevant passages and he is both choosing one sensibility over another and creating something of his own. Some similar kinds of rewriting occur in other places, which we point out in our notes. But, in general, respect and sympathy for the lives of the poor and humble are not classical sentiments. There is also no classical precedent for the idea that, but for lack of education and opportunity, the obscure might have been great. This is not to say that the classics were never before Gray available to a non-classical sensibility. An account of such availability, beginning with the very late classical poet Ausonius, is the basis of the brilliant critical romance *The Wandering Scholars* by Helen Waddell (1927). However, what Gray did with the classics was a departure for his age, particularly in the context of his Etonian and Cambridgean training. Moreover, it is a departure that enabled him to write one of the best-loved and most durable poems in the English language.

The text presented here is based on the first edition (1751).

The *Curfew*[1] tolls the Knell of parting Day,
The lowing Herd wind slowly o'er the Lea,

1 *Curfew* "An evening peal, by which [William] the conqueror willed that every man should rake up his fire, and put out his light; so that in many places at this day, where a bell is customarily rung towards bed time, it is said to ring curfew" (Johnson's *Dictionary*, citing John Cowell, *The Interpreter*, who cites John Stowe).

The Plow-man homeward plods his weary Way,
And leaves the World to Darkness, and to me.[2]
    Now fades the glimmering Landscape on the Sight,   5
And all the Air a solemn Stillness holds;
Save where the Beetle wheels his droning Flight,
And drowsy Tinklings lull the distant Folds.[3]
    Save that from yonder Ivy-mantled Tow'r
The moping Owl does to the Moon complain   10
Of such, as wand'ring near her sacred Bower,
Molest her ancient solitary Reign.
    Beneath those rugged Elms, that Yew-Tree's Shade,
Where heaves the Turf in many a mould'ring Heap,
Each in his narrow Cell for ever laid,   15
The rude Forefathers of the Hamlet sleep.
    The breezy Call of Incense-breathing Morn,
The Swallow twitt'ring from the Straw-built Shed,
The Cock's shrill Clarion, or the echoing Horn,
No more shall rouse them from their lowly Bed.   20
    For them no more the blazing Hearth shall burn,
Or busy Housewife ply her Evening Care:
No Children run to lisp their Sire's Return,
Or climb his Knees the envied Kiss to share.[4]
    Oft did the Harvest to their Sickle yield,   25
Their Furrow oft the stubborn Glebe has broke;[5]
How jocund did they drive their Team afield!
How bowed the Woods beneath their sturdy Stroke!
    Let not Ambition mock their useful Toil,
Their homely Joys and Destiny obscure;   30

2   The first four lines recall Horace's description of Sabine farmers returning home "when the sun shifted the mountains' shadows and lifted the yoke from the weary cattle, bringing the welcome time with its departing chariot" (*Odes* 3.6.41–4).

3   *Fold* "The ground in which sheep are confined" (Johnson).

4   The ultimate source for lines 21–4 is Lucretius 3.894–6 (p. 327 below): "Now no longer will your joyful house receive you, nor your most virtuous wife, nor will your sweet children run to snatch your kisses first and touch your heart with quiet pleasure." In Lucretius, this touching scene is a sarcastic example of pointless anxiety about death, since the departed have no such feelings of loss. Gray's sentimentalism is influenced by Virgil's encomium of country life in the *Georgics* at 2.523–4 (p. 360 below), where he imitates the Lucretian passage: "Moreover his sweet children hang upon his kisses. . . ." Another relevant passage is Horace, *Epodes* 2.39–44 (p. 395 below): "what if a chaste wife tends the house and sweet children, like a Sabine or the sunburnt wife of an agile Apulian, and builds up the hearth with old logs for the return of her weary husband." This is the inspiration for Gray's "hearth," but the Horatian passage is ironic because it is spoken by a despicable Roman money lender.

5   *Glebe* soil.

Nor Grandeur hear with a disdainful Smile,
The short and simple Annals of the Poor.
    The boast of Heraldry, the Pomp of Power,
And all that Beauty, all that Wealth e'er gave,
Awaits alike th' inevitable Hour.   35
The Paths of Glory lead but to the Grave.[6]
    Nor you, ye Proud, impute to these the Fault,
If Mem'ry o'er their Tomb no Trophies raise,
Where through the long-drawn Aisle and fretted Vault[7]
The pealing Anthem swells the Note of Praise.[8]   40
    Can storied Urn or animated Bust
Back to its Mansion call the fleeting Breath?
Can Honour's Voice provoke the silent Dust,
Or Flatt'ry soothe the dull cold Ear of Death!
    Perhaps in this neglected Spot is laid   45
Some Heart once pregnant with celestial Fire,
Hands that the Rod of Empire might have swayed,
Or waked to Ecstasy the living Lyre.
    But Knowledge to their Eyes her ample Page
Rich with the Spoils of Time did ne'er unroll;   50
Chill Penury repressed their noble Rage,
And froze the genial Current of the Soul.
    Full many a Gem of purest Ray serene,[9]
The dark unfathomed Caves of Ocean bear:
Full many a Flower is born to blush unseen,[10]   55
And waste its Sweetness on the desert Air.
    Some village-*Hampden* that with dauntless Breast[11]
The little Tyrant of his Fields withstood;
Some mute inglorious *Milton* here may rest,
Some *Cromwell* guiltless of his Country's Blood.   60
    Th' Applause of list'ning Senates to command,
The Threats of Pain and Ruin to despise,
To scatter Plenty o'er a smiling Land,

---

6 *Paths . . . Grave* The impartiality of death is a
commonplace, of course, but one that Horace
made his own. Gray may have thought of Horace,
Odes 1.4.13, "pale death kicks with impartial foot
the huts of the poor and the turrets of kings";
2.14.9–12, "[the river Styx] which must be sailed
by all who feed on the earth's bounty, whether
we'll be kings or poor farmers"; 2.18.32–4 (pp.
399–400 below), "the impartial earth is opened
up for the poor and the sons of kings"; 3.1.14–
16, "with impartial law Necessity picks by lottery
the distinguished and the lowly"; or 1.28.15–16,

"but one night awaits all and the road of death
must be trodden once and for all."
7 *fretted* ornamented.
8 *Anthem* "A holy song" (Johnson).
9 *serene* clear, bright.
10 *Full many a Flower* two verse feet only.
11 *Hampden* John (1594–1643): like Milton
and Cromwell, he opposed the "Tyrant" Charles
I and urged civil war, in which he died fighting;
in one manuscript version of the poem, Gray had
Cato, Cicero, and Caesar in place of these English
figures.

And read their Hist'ry in a Nation's Eyes
    Their Lot forbade: nor circumscribed alone   65
Their growing Virtues, but their Crimes confined;
Forbade to wade through Slaughter to a Throne,
And Shut the Gates of Mercy on Mankind,
    The struggling Pangs of conscious Truth to hide,
To quench the Blushes of ingenuous Shame,   70
Or heap the Shrine of Luxury and Pride
With Incense, kindled at the Muse's Flame.[12]
    Far from the madding Crowd's ignoble Strife,[13]
Their sober Wishes never learned to stray;
Along the cool sequestered Vale of Life   75
They kept the noiseless Tenor of their Way.[14]
    Yet ev'n these Bones from Insult to protect
Some frail Memorial still erected nigh,
With uncouth Rhymes and shapeless Sculpture decked,[15]
Implores the passing Tribute of a Sigh.   80
    Their Name, their Years, spelt by th' unlettered Muse,[16]
The Place of Fame and Elegy supply:
And many a holy Text around she strews,
That teach the rustic Moralist to die.

12   At one stage in its composition the poem may have concluded after line 72 with the following four stanzas in the Eton College manuscript:

The thoughtless World to Majesty may bow
Exalt the brave, & idolize Success
But more to Innocence their Safety owe
Than Power & Genius e'er conspired to bless

And thou, who mindful of th' unhonoured Dead
Dost in these Notes their artless Tale relate
By Night & lonely Contemplation led
To linger in the gloomy Walks of Fate

Hark how the sacred Calm, that broods around
Bids every fierce tumultuous Passion cease
In still small Accents whispering from the Ground

A grateful Earnest of eternal Peace
No more with Reason & thyself at Strife;
Give anxious Cares & endless Wishes room

But through the cool sequestered Vale of Life
Pursue the silent Tenor of thy Doom.

13   *Far from . . . Strife* an imitation, perhaps, of *Georgics* 2.458–60 (p. 357 below): "O too fortunate farmers, if only they knew their blessings, for whom, far from discordant arms [*procul discordibus armis*], the most equitable earth pours out an easy living from the ground. . . ."
14   *Tenor* "Continuity of state" (Johnson). Overall, lines 65–76 are reminiscent of Virgil's contrast between the countryman's blessed, innocent life and the anxieties and crimes of the powerful. Compare *Georgics* 2.503–10 (p. 359 below): "Others stir up with oars unknown seas, dash upon the sword, or penetrate courts and the thresholds of kings. This one seeks out a city and its wretched homes for destruction, so that he may drink from a jeweled goblet and sleep on Tyrian purple; another piles up wealth and watches over buried gold. . . . They rejoice to be drenched in their brothers' blood."
15   *uncouth* "Odd; strange; unusual" (Johnson).
16   *unlettered* "Unlearned; untaught" (Johnson).

For who to dumb Forgetfulness a Prey,   85
This pleasing anxious Being e'er resigned,
Left the warm Precincts of the cheerful Day,
Nor cast one longing ling'ring Look behind![17]
   On some fond Breast the parting Soul relies,
Some pious Drops the closing Eye requires;   90
Ev'n from the Tomb the Voice of Nature cries
Awake, and faithful to her wonted Fires.[18]
   For thee, who mindful of th' unhonoured Dead
Dost in these Lines their artless Tale relate;
If chance, by lonely Contemplation led,   95
Some kindred Spirit shall inquire thy Fate,[19]
   Haply some hoary-headed Swain may say,
"Oft have we seen him at the Peep of Dawn
Brushing with hasty Steps the Dews away
To meet the Sun upon the upland Lawn.[20]   100
   "There at the Foot of yonder nodding Beech
That wreathes its old fantastic Roots so high,
His listless Length at Noontide would he stretch,
And pore upon the Brook that babbles by.
   "Hard by yon Wood, now frowning as in Scorn,   105
Mutt'ring his wayward Fancies he would rove,
Now drooping, woeful wan, like one forlorn,
Or crazed with Care, or crossed in hopeless Love.
   "One Morn I missed him on the customed Hill,
Along the Heath, and near his favourite Tree;   110
Another came; nor yet beside the Rill,
Nor up the Lawn, nor at the Wood was he.
   "The next with Dirges due in sad Array
Slow through the Church-way Path we saw him borne.
Approach and read (for thou can'st read) the Lay,   115
Graved on the Stone beneath yon agèd Thorn."

---

17 *For who . . . Look behind* compare *Paradise Lost* 2.146–51.

18 *wonted* customary.

19 In the Eton College manuscript this stanza is replaced by the following:

   If chance that e'er some pensive Spirit more
   By sympathetic Musings here delayed,
   With vain, though kind, Inquiry shall explore
   Thy once-loved Haunt, this long-deserted Shade.

20 After this line the Eton manuscript has,

   Him have we seen the Green-wood Side along,
   While o'er the Heath we hied, our Labours done,
   Oft as the Woodlark piped her farewell Song
   With wistful eyes pursue the setting Sun.

The Epitaph[21]

Here rests his Head upon the Lap of Earth
A Youth to Fortune and to Fame unknown:
Fair Science frowned not on his humble Birth,[22]
And Melancholy marked him for her own.[23]   120
   Large was his Bounty, and his Soul sincere,
Heav'n did a Recompense as largely send:
He gave to Misery all he had, a Tear:
He gained from Heav'n ('twas all he wished) a Friend.
   No farther seek his Merits to disclose,   125
Or draw his Frailties from their dread Abode,
(There they alike in trembling Hope repose)
The Bosom of his Father and his God.

---

21   Propertius, whose *Elegies* 2.1, which Gray translated, ends similarly:

  When then my fates that breath they gave
      shall claim,
  When the short marble but preserves a
      name,
  A little verse, my all that shall remain,
  Thy passing courser's slackened speed
      retain
  (Thou envied honor of thy poet's days,
  Of all our youth the ambition and the
      praise!);

Then to my quiet urn awhile draw near,
And say, while o'er the place you drop a
    tear,
Love and the fair were of his life the
    pride;
He lived while she was kind, and, when
    she frowned, he died.

22   *Science* knowledge.
23   *Melancholy* one of the characteristics of those favored by "Science"; a positive attribute, like sensibility, Roger Lonsdale suggests in his edition of Gray's poems.

Mary Leapor (1722–1746)

As the daughter of a gardener in rural Northamptonshire, Leapor had few oppor-
tunities for education. Nevertheless, she learned to read by age 10 or 11 and began
scribbling verse whenever she could, although her parents discouraged this unprof-
itable use of her time. She evidently owned only a handful of books, but when
she became a kitchen maid at Weston Hall she gained access to a library of about
500 volumes, including many classical works in translation as well as in the original
languages. How much classical poetry she read is impossible to know, but the
influence of Juvenal on her satires is manifest and has been noted before.[1] It seems
most likely that she encountered Juvenal, like most readers of her generation, in
the translations of Dryden.

  "An Essay on Woman" belongs formally to the Horatian tradition of the verse
epistle, and it is partly a response to Alexander Pope's work in the same genre,
"Of the Characters of Women: An Epistle to a Lady." Like Pope's "Epistle,"
however, Leapor's "Essay" includes many features of Juvenal's poetry, particularly
Satire 6 (p. 472 below). Among the stylistic features associated with Juvenal and
present in Leapor are the pointed antithesis ("too soft for Business, too weak for
Pow'r"), the rhetorical question ("who would be Wise . . . ?"), hyperbole ("snow
turns a Negro . . ."), bathos ("till mighty Hymen . . ."), cynicism about the wealthy
and sympathy for the poor (Cordia's sty), the aside ("though overlooked by . . ."),
and the angry generalization ("Unhappy Woman's but a Slave at large"). Leapor
draws on classical charges against women marshaled by Juvenal (and Pope), but
she looks at these charges from a new perspective – that of a working-class woman.
She focuses the tradition of satirizing women on a certain wealthy class of women,
and, at the same time, she exposes the destructive effect of classical generalizations

Mary Leapor

1   *The Works of Mary Leapor*, ed. Richard Greene
and Ann Messenger (Oxford University Press,
2003), p. xxxi. We are indebted to this book
throughout our treatment of Leapor.

about women. Also in the background of Leapor's epistle, and contributing to its complex of satirical elements, is Hesiod's story about the creation of Pandora (*Works and Days* 53–201; p. 279 below).

In addition to its Juvenalian misanthropy, Leapor's "Essay" also expresses a Horatian love of life's humble pleasures, such as, for example, "A Fire to warm me and a Friend to please." This desire for simplicity, material sufficiency, and friendship – a mean between the troubles of wealth and power on the one hand and poverty on the other – is the driving force behind much of Horace's moralistic poetry. He finds the fulfillment of this desire in his life on the Sabine farm given by Maecenas (see *Satires* 2.6; p. 388 below): "this was what I wished for – a modest plot of land, a garden, a spring. . . ."

The text of "An Essay on Woman" is based on the second volume of Leapor's *Poems on Several Occasions* (1751).

An Essay on Woman

Woman, a pleasing but a short-lived Flow'r,
Too soft for Business and too weak for Pow'r:[1]
A Wife in Bondage, or neglected Maid;
Despised, if ugly; if she's fair, Betrayed.
'Tis Wealth alone inspires every Grace,   5
And calls the Raptures to her plenteous Face.
What Numbers for those charming Features pine,
If blooming Acres round her Temples twine!
Her Lip the Strawberry, and her Eyes more bright
Than sparkling *Venus* in a frosty Night;   10
Pale Lilies fade and, when the Fair appears,
Snow turns a Negro and dissolves in Tears,
And, where the Charmer treads her magic Toe,
On *English* ground *Arabian* odours grow;[2]
Till mighty Hymen lifts his sceptred Rod,[3]   15
And sinks her Glories with a fatal Nod,
Dissolves her Triumphs, sweeps her Charms away,
And turns the Goddess to her native Clay.
    But, *Artemisia*, let your Servant sing[4]
What small Advantage Wealth and Beauties bring.   20

AN ESSAY ON WOMAN

1 *soft* recalls, through Pope's "Epistle" (lines 1–4), the Aristotelian notion that women are softer than men (Greene and Messenger, p. 341).

2 *Arabian odours* Arabia was an old source of aromatic spices and perfume.
3 *Hymen* god of marriage.
4 *Artemisia* a classical name for Leapor's patron, Bridget Fremantle.

Who would be Wise, that knew *Pamphilia*'s fate?[5]
Or who be Fair, and joined to *Sylvia*'s mate?
Sylvia, whose Cheeks are fresh as early Day,
As Evening mild, and sweet as spicy *May*:
And yet that Face her partial Husband tires,   25
And those bright Eyes, that all the World admires.
Pamphilia's Wit who does not strive to shun,
Like Death's Infection or a Dog-day's Sun?[6]
The Damsels view her with malignant Eyes,
The Men are vexed to find a Nymph so Wise: 30
And Wisdom only serves to make her know
The keen Sensation of superior Woe.
The secret Whisper and the list'ning Ear,
The scornful Eyebrow and the hated Sneer,
The giddy Censures of her babbling Kind,   35
With thousand Ills that grate a gentle Mind,
By her are tasted in the first Degree,
Though overlooked by *Simplicius* and me.
Does thirst of Gold a Virgin's Heart inspire,
Instilled by Nature, or a careful Sire?   40
Then let her quit Extravagance and Play,
The brisk Companion, and expensive Tea,
To feast with *Cordia* in her filthy Sty
On stewed Potatoes, or on a moldy Pie;
Whose eager Eyes stare ghastly at the Poor,   45
And fright the Beggars from her hated Door;
In greasy Clouts she wraps her smoky Chin,[7]
And holds that Pride's a never-pardoned Sin.
    If this be Wealth, no matter where it falls;
But save, ye Muses, save your *Mira*'s walls:[8]   50
Still give me pleasing Indolence and Ease,
A Fire to warm me and a Friend to please.
    Since, whether sunk in Avarice, or Pride,
A wanton Virgin, or a starving Bride,
Or, wond'ring Crowds attend her charming Tongue,   55
Or deemed an Idiot, ever speaks the Wrong;
Though Nature armed us for the growing Ill
With fraudful Cunning, and a headstrong Will;
Yet, with ten thousand Follies to her Charge,
Unhappy Woman's but a Slave at large.   60

5   *Pamphilia* possibly recalling the name of Pam-
phila, a female Greek historian in the reign of
Nero (Greene and Messenger); compare Juvenal's
obnoxiously learned woman (*Satires* 6.434 ff.;
p. 476 below).

6   *Dog-day* late summer, when Sirius, the Dog
Star, is prominent in the sky.
7   *Clouts* rags.
8   *Mira* Leapor's poetical name for herself.

William Cowper (1731–1800)

Like so many eighteenth-century British poets, William Cowper learned his classics at Westminster School. There he first read Homer, a life-long passion culminating in his translation of the *Iliad* and the *Odyssey* (1791). Instead of being allowed to follow his natural inclination for literary studies, however, Cowper was sent to study law after graduating from Westminster. He did enough work to qualify for the bar, though he took time out for literary endeavors like rereading Homer and translating two of Horace's satires for publication (1759). However, Cowper was phobic about public performance and suffered a nervous collapse when he was obliged to stand for an examination of his credentials to become clerk of the journals of the House of Lords. After several unconvincing attempts to commit suicide he found comfort and renewal in an evangelical form of Christianity. He kept to the country where his religion sustained him for 10 years, but he collapsed again in 1773 under the pressure of difficulties in his personal life. He recovered again and became more devoted to gardening and a retired life, a subject about which he wrote a 6,000-line poem entitled *The Task* (1785). Later in life, Cowper toyed with translating Virgil and revised his translation of Homer between bouts of depression and religious fervor.

Cowper admired John Gay's allegorical animal fables and translated some into Latin, but, unlike earlier performances in this genre, his animal poems look forward to an age concerned with cruelty to real animals and a sensitivity to animal rights.[1] Like Gay, Cowper was aware of the classical tradition of writing about animals. Book 7 of the *Greek Anthology* contains many epitaphs on working or pet animals and insects: hounds, horses, a cock, an ant, a cicada, locust, bird, etc. Few probably were meant to be inscribed on tombs (though there is evidence for this being done). As in many epitaphs, the persona of the deceased is frequently the speaker.

WILLIAM COWPER

1 On this subject, see David Perkins, *Romanti-cism and Animal Rights* (Cambridge University Press, 2003).

One of them, attributed to Meleager, is written in the imagined voice of a hare and begins, "I was a swift-footed long-eared leveret" (the complete poem is on p. 316 below). Like its Hellenistic models, Cowper's poem purports to be an epitaph (beginning "Here lies"), but its wit is indebted to Roman models of animal verse: Catullus 3 (p. 331 below), a mock-solemn lament for Lesbia's dead sparrow disguising what is really a witty love poem; Ovid, *Amores* 2.6 (p. 423 below), on Corinna's parrot, a bombastic parody of an epicedion or formal dirge; and Statius, *Silvae* 2.4, another poem about a favorite parrot's death. Cowper's poem takes from these works the self-conscious manner of enlarging a modest domestic event into something approaching tragedy, as if the death of a person were being mourned. Touches of the grand style add to the apparent incongruity, but there is a stream of real feeling for the animal in Cowper's poem that is absent in its classical antecedents. In addition, Cowper's poem is chaste, whereas the Roman poems on which it draws were written to female pet owners and include erotic suggestions.

The text is based on the first printing (*Gentleman's Magazine*, December 1784).

Epitaph on a Hare

Here lies, whom hound did ne'er pursue,
　　Nor swifter greyhound follow,
Whose foot ne'er tainted morning dew,[1]
　　Nor ear heard huntsman's halloo,

Tiney, the surliest of his kind,[2]　　　　　　　　　　　　　　　　　　5
　　Who, nursed with tender care,
And to domestic bounds confined,
　　Was still a wild Jack-hare.

Though duly from my hand he took
　　His pittance every night,　　　　　　　　　　　　　　　　　　　　10
He did it with a jealous look,
　　And, when he could, would bite.

His diet was of wheaten bread,
　　And milk, and oats, and straw;
Thistles, or lettuces instead;　　　　　　　　　　　　　　　　　　　15
　　And sand to cleanse his maw.

EPITAPH ON A HARE

1　*tainted* gave a scent to.

2　*surliest of his kind* with similar hyperbole Ovid praises Corinna's parrot as the best of mimics (*Amores* 2.6.23–4; p. 424 below).

On twigs of hawthorn he regaled,
   On pippins' russet peel;[3]
And, when his juicier salads failed,
   Sliced carrot pleased him well.[4]   20

A Turkey carpet was his lawn,
   Whereon he loved to bound,
To skip and gambol like a fawn,
   And swing himself around.[5]

His frisking was at evening hours,   25
   For then he lost his fear;
But most before approaching showers,
   Or when a storm drew near.

Eight years and five round rolling moons
   He thus saw steal away,   30
Dozing out all his idle noons,
   And every night at play.

I kept him for old service sake,[6]
   For he would oft beguile
My heart of thoughts that made it ache,   35
   And force me to a smile.[7]

But now, beneath this walnut-shade
   He finds his long, last home,
And waits in snug concealment laid,
   Till gentler Puss shall come.[8]   40

He, in his turn, must feel the shocks[9]
   From which no care can save,
And, partner once of Tiney's box,
   Be partner of his grave.[10]

---

3 *pippins* a kind of apple.

4 *his ... well* compare the diet of Corinna's parrot (Ovid, *Amores* 2.6.29–32; p. 424 below).

5 *himself* the ms and later editions read "his rump."

6 *old service* later editions have "his humour's."

7 *For ... smile* Lesbia's sparrow too consoled its mistress (Catullus, *Carmen* 2; p. 330 below).

8 The theme of the friend who survives (like Puss) is also prominent in Ovid, *Amores* 2.6.11–16 (p. 424 below).

9 *in his turn* later editions have "still more aged."

10 *Be partner of* the ms and later editions read "Must soon partake"; the idea of Tiney sharing Puss's grave may come from Patroclus' desire to have his and his friend Achilles' bones buried together in one urn (Homer, *Iliad* 23).

William Wordsworth (1770–1850)

By definition, the romantic revolution in poetry with which Wordsworth is so closely associated was anti-classical, but that does not mean that it ignored classical tradition or was unreceptive to classical poetry. Wordsworth's critique of poetic diction in the Preface to the *Lyrical Ballads* (1798) and his insistence that the poet keep his eye on the object are points of his opposition to neo-classical aesthetics. He did not, like Pope, believe that "Nature and Homer were . . . the same." He loved Homer nonetheless, however, and he loved many classical writers whose appeal to the romantic imagination is less obvious than Homer's. Early in life he worked on a Juvenalian satire, and his translation of the *Aeneid* (Books 1–3 and some other fragments) is the longest poetic effort of his last twenty years.

Alluding to the last eight lines of "Laodamia," Wordsworth said, "The incident of the trees growing and withering put the subject into my thoughts, and I wrote with the hope of giving it a loftier tone than, so far as I know, has been given to it by any of the Ancients who have treated of it. It cost me more trouble than almost anything of equal length I have ever written." His notes to the poem indicate that he read the "incident of the trees" in Pliny's *Natural History* (p. 458 below), but the classical background of the work is extensive and complicated. The myth is that soon after their marriage, Protesilaus leaves Laodamia to join the Trojan expedition. At Troy he is the first to leap ashore and gets killed by Hector, fulfilling an oracle. Laodamia's grief is so extreme that Zeus allows Protesilaus to return to his wife for a few hours, after which she ends her life ignobly. The story is most fully retold in Ovid's *Heroides* 13 (p. 429 below), an epistle from Laodamia to Protesilaus.

Ovid was probably Wordsworth's source for Laodamia's prayers and sacrifices, the appearance of Protesilaus' ghost, and, in general, for the characterization of Laodamia as a frenzied, sexually obsessed woman. For the details of line 112, however, and the general picture of the Greeks becalmed at Aulis on their way to Troy, Wordsworth draws on Euripides' play *Iphigenia at Aulis* (especially lines 194–9). Homer (*Iliad* 2.701) and Catullus (68) both supplied him with images of Protesilaus' half-built house (line 132), but Catullus also supplied much more. Catullus weaves the story of Laodamia and Protesilaus into his love affair with Lesbia and his brother's death in Asia Minor, near Troy. Wordsworth certainly knew this highly complex and influential poem (arguably the first love elegy), as his similar reference to the Parcae (line 65) suggests (cf. Catullus 68.85).

Like Catullus and Ovid, Virgil incorporated the story of Laodamia into his poetry. In his descent into Hades in *Aeneid* 6, Virgil's hero encounters on the Plains of Mourning those "whom harsh love consumed with cruel wasting." Dido is there and so is Laodamia. Wordsworth quotes the four bare words Virgil gives Laodamia, and in doing so he points the reader to the broader themes of *Aeneid* 6. The severity of Virgil's judgment on Laodamia becomes clear as Aeneas proceeds through the underworld and arrives in Elysium, where everyone is happy, and where Anchises gives the hero metaphysical instruction in the Lucretian mode (724–51; p. 378 below). He explains that the universe is nourished by a rational divine spirit from which life comes. However, our bodies encumber the pure spirit and cause our passions of fear and desire. After death the souls of the virtuous are purged of this taint and sent into Elysium to await reincarnation. The passionate Laodamia is not virtuous enough to be saved. Protesilaus, on the other hand, whom Wordsworth (without Virgilian precedent) locates in Elysium, is a model of virtue. Knowing the oracle that the first Greek to touch the beach of Troy would be the first killed, he purposely sacrifices himself for the greater good. Like Anchises in the *Aeneid*, Protesilaus tells Laodamia about Elysium, and he counsels her to emulate his dispassionate virtue so they can be reunited there. But Laodamia is incapable of following his advice, and Wordsworth too judges her harshly in the end. Yet, in earlier versions of the poem, he pleaded for leniency in her case. The description of her placement in Hades that we print below (lines 158–63) dates from 1845; in 1815 Wordsworth said more softly:

> Ah, judge her gently who so deeply loved!
> Her, who, in reason's spite, yet without crime,
> Was in a trance of passion thus removed;
> Delivered from the galling yoke of time,
> And these frail elements – to gather flowers
> Of blissful quiet mid unfading bowers.

In successive versions (1827, 1832, 1843) the judgment grew more strict. Perhaps Wordsworth's purgation of his judgment, gradually arriving where he did in 1845, is part of the reason that the aptly named Mr. Heard of Fettes College, Edinburgh, told William Knight, Wordsworth's late nineteenth-century editor, "This poem illustrates more completely than any other the sympathy of the poet with the spirit of antiquity in its purest and most exalted forms. The idea that underlies the poem is the same conception of 'pietas' which Virgil has embodied in the *Aeneid*. . . ."

As a basis for the text we use the version printed in the *Poetical Works* (1884). We have benefited, however, from textual information and commentary in *Shorter Poems 1807–1820*, ed. Carl H. Ketcham (Cornell University Press, 1989).

Laodamia (composed, 1814)

"With sacrifice before the rising morn
Vows have I made by fruitless hope inspired;
And from the infernal Gods, 'mid shades forlorn[1]
Of night, my slaughtered Lord have I required:[2]
Celestial pity I again implore; –   5
Restore him to my sight – great Jove, restore!"

So speaking, and by fervent love endowed
With faith, the Suppliant heavenward lifts her hands;
While, like the sun emerging from a cloud,
Her countenance brightens – and her eye expands;   10
Her bosom heaves and spreads, her stature grows;
And she expects the issue in repose.[3]

O terror! what hath she perceived? – O joy!
What doth she look on? – whom doth she behold?
Her Hero slain upon the beach of Troy?   15
His vital presence? his corporeal mould?
It is – if sense deceive her not – 'tis He!
And a God leads him, wingèd Mercury! [4]

Mild Hermes spake – and touched her with his wand[5]
That calms all fear; "Such grace hath crowned thy prayer,   20
Laodamía! that at Jove's command
Thy Husband walks the paths of upper air:
He comes to tarry with thee three hours' space;
Accept the gift, behold him face to face!"

Forth sprang the impassioned Queen her Lord to clasp;   25
Again that consummation she essayed;

LAODAMIA

1 *infernal* of the underworld.
2 *Lord* Protesilaus, the first Greek to be killed at Troy; *required* requested (a Latinism based on *quaerere*, to ask).
3 *expects* awaits (a Latinism based on *exspectare*).

4 *Mercury* the Latin name of Hermes; one of his functions was to conduct souls to and from the underworld.
5 *wand* Hermes carried a caduceus or herald's staff.

But unsubstantial Form eludes her grasp
As often as that eager grasp was made.[6]
The Phantom parts – but parts to re-unite,
And re-assume his place before her sight.   30

"Protesiláus, lo! thy guide is gone!
Confirm, I pray, the vision with thy voice:
This is our palace, – yonder is thy throne;
Speak, and the floor thou tread'st on will rejoice.
Not to appall me have the gods bestowed   35
This precious boon; and blest a sad abode."

"Great Jove, Laodamía! doth not leave
His gifts imperfect: – Spectre though I be,
I am not sent to scare thee or deceive;
But in reward of thy fidelity.   40
And something also did my worth obtain;
For fearless virtue bringeth boundless gain.

"Thou knowest, the Delphic oracle foretold[7]
That the first Greek who touched the Trojan strand
Should die; but me the threat could not withhold: 45
A generous cause a victim did demand;
And forth I leapt upon the sandy plain;
A self-devoted chief – by Hector slain."[8]

"Supreme of Heroes – bravest, noblest, best!
Thy matchless courage I bewail no more,   50
Which then, when tens of thousands were depressed
By doubt, propelled thee to the fatal shore;
Thou found'st – and I forgive thee – here thou art –
A nobler counselor than my poor heart.

"But thou, though capable of sternest deed,   55
Wert kind as resolute, and good as brave;
And he, whose power restores thee, hath decreed
Thou should'st elude the malice of the grave:
Redundant are thy locks, thy lips as fair[9]
As when their breath enriched Thessalian air.[10]   60

6 *But . . . made* compare Aeneas's futile embrace   9 *Redundant* flowing (a Latinate sense based
of Anchises in *Aeneid* 6.700–2 (p. 379 below).   on *unda*, wave).
7 *Delphic oracle* the oracle of Apollo at Delphi.   10 *Thessalian* Protesilaus was prince of Phylace
8 *self-devoted* self-sacrificial (a Latinate sense);   in Thessaly.
Hector son of Priam; the best Trojan warrior.

"No Spectre greets me, – no vain Shadow this;
Come, blooming Hero, place thee by my side!
Give, on this well known couch, one nuptial kiss[11]
To me, this day, a second time thy bride!"
Jove frowned in heaven: the conscious Parcae threw[12]   65
Upon those roseate lips a Stygian hue.[13]

"This visage tells thee that my doom is past:
Nor should the change be mourned, even if the joys
Of sense were able to return as fast
And surely as they vanish. Earth destroys   70
Those raptures duly – Erebus disdains:[14]
Calm pleasures there abide – majestic pains.

"Be taught, O faithful Consort, to control
Rebellious passion: for the Gods approve
The depth, and not the tumult, of the soul;   75
A fervent, not ungovernable, love.
Thy transports moderate; and meekly mourn
When I depart, for brief is my sojourn – "

"Ah, wherefore? – Did not Hercules by force[15]
Wrest from the guardian Monster of the tomb   80
Alcestis, a reanimated corse,[16]
Given back to dwell on earth in vernal bloom?
Medea's spells dispersed the weight of years,[17]
And Aeson stood a youth 'mid youthful peers.

"The Gods to us are merciful – and they   85
Yet further may relent: for mightier far
Than strength of nerve and sinew, or the sway
Of magic potent over sun and star,
Is love, though oft to agony distressed,
And though his favorite seat be feeble woman's breast.   90

"But if thou goest, I follow –" "Peace!" he said, –
She looked upon him and was calmed and cheered;
The ghastly color from his lips had fled;
In his deportment, shape, and mien, appeared

---

11 *couch* bed.
12 *conscious* aware; *Parcae* the Fates, who determine length of life.
13 *Stygian* deathly; the Styx was a river of Hades.
14 *Erebus* another name for the underworld.

15 *Hercules* hero who rescued Alcestis from Death after she sacrificed her life for her husband.
16 *corse* corpse.
17 *Medea* witch who rejuvenated Jason's old father Aeson.

Elysian beauty, melancholy grace,[18]   95
Brought from a pensive though a happy place.

He spake of love, such love as Spirits feel
In worlds whose course is equable and pure;
No fears to beat away – no strife to heal –
The past unsighed for, and the future sure;   100
Spake of heroic arts in graver mood
Revived, with finer harmony pursued;

Of all that is most beauteous – imaged there
In happier beauty; more pellucid streams,
An ampler ether, a diviner air,   105
And fields invested with purpureal gleams;[19]
Climes which the sun, who sheds the brightest day
Earth knows, is all unworthy to survey.

Yet there the Soul shall enter which hath earned
That privilege by virtue. – "Ill," said he,   110
"The end of man's existence I discerned,
Who from ignoble games and revelry[20]
Could draw, when we had parted, vain delight,
While tears were thy best pastime, day and night;

"And while my youthful peers before my eyes   115
(Each hero following his peculiar bent)
Prepared themselves for glorious enterprise
By martial sports, – or, seated in the tent,
Chieftains and kings in council were detained;
What time the fleet at Aulis lay enchained. [21]   120
The wished-for wind was given: – I then revolved
The oracle, upon the silent sea;
And, if no worthier led the way, resolved
That, of a thousand vessels, mine should be
The foremost prow in pressing to the strand, –   125
Mine the first blood that tinged the Trojan sand.

"Yet bitter, oft-times bitter, was the pang
When of thy loss I thought, belovèd Wife!

---

18 *Elysian* Elysium is the abode of the virtuous dead.
19 *purpureal* purple and therefore regal.
20 *Who . . . revelry* "For this feature in the character of Protesilaus, see the *Iphigenia in Aulis* of Euripides" [Wordsworth's note. The reference is to lines 194–9: "I saw Protesilaus and Palamedes, who was fathered by the son of Poseidon, sitting and enjoying the intricate shapes of checkers."]
21 *What time* a Latinism (*quo tempore*); *Aulis* harbor from which the Trojan expedition set sail after a long delay.

On thee too fondly did my memory hang,
And on the joys we shared in mortal life, –   130
The paths which we had trod – these fountains, flowers;
My new-planned cities, and unfinished towers.

"But should suspense permit the Foe to cry,[22]
'Behold they tremble! – haughty their array,
Yet of their number no one dares to die'?   135
In soul I swept the indignity away:
Old frailties then recurred: – but lofty thought,
In act embodied, my deliverance wrought.

"And Thou, though strong in love, art all too weak
In reason, in self-government too slow;   140
I counsel thee by fortitude to seek
Our blest re-union in the shades below.
The invisible world with thee hath sympathized;
Be thy affections raised and solemnized.

"Learn, by a mortal yearning, to ascend –   145
Seeking a higher object. Love was given,
Encouraged, sanctioned, chiefly for that end;
For this the passion to excess was driven –
That self might be annulled: her bondage prove
The fetters of a dream, opposed to love." –   150

Aloud she shrieked! for Hermes re-appears!
Round the dear Shade she would have clung – 'tis vain:
The hours are past – too brief had they been years;
And him no mortal effort can detain:
Swift, toward the realms that know not earthly day,   155
He through the portal takes his silent way,
And on the palace-floor a lifeless corse She lay.

Thus, all in vain exhorted and reproved,
She perished; and, as for a wilful crime,
By the just Gods whom no weak pity moved,   160
Was doomed to wear out her appointed time,
Apart from happy Ghosts, that gather flowers
Of blissful quiet mid unfading bowers.
– Yet tears to human suffering are due; [23]

---

22 *suspense* delay.
23 *Yet . . . due* an allusion to Virgil, *Aeneid*

1.462: "There are tears for things and mortal
matters touch the mind."

And mortal hopes defeated and o'erthrown   165
Are mourned by man, and not by man alone,
As fondly he believes. – Upon the side
Of Hellespont (such faith was entertained)[24]
A knot of spiry trees for ages grew[25]
From out the tomb of him for whom she died;   170
And ever, when such stature they had gained
That Ilium's walls were subject to their view,[26]
The trees' tall summits withered at the sight;
A constant interchange of growth and blight![27]

---

24 *Hellespont* sea channel between the Aegean and Propontis (Sea of Marmora); *such faith was entertained* i.e. so the story goes. Wordsworth amplifies Pliny's description of the withering trees and makes some changes; his trees, for example, grow *out* of the tomb and not *over* it (see n. 27 below).

25 *spiry* tall and slender without much branching.

26 *Ilium* Troy.

27 *A . . . blight* For the account of these long-lived trees, see Pliny's Natural History, lib. xvi. cap. 44 [16.238; p. 458 below]; and for the features in the character of Protesilaus, see the Iphigenia in Aulis of Euripides. Virgil places the Shade of Laodamia in a mournful region, among unhappy lovers [*Aeneid* 6.447–8],

———— His Laodamia
It Comes ———— [Wordsworth's note].

Samuel Taylor Coleridge (1772–1834)

In his intellectual autobiography, *Biographia Literaria*, Coleridge describes his precocious youth as an inspired charity-school student "deep in his Iamblichus" and other obscure classical authors. Even in his early years, his inquisitiveness and his irritable longing for profundity drew him from the well-worn paths of Virgil and Horace to the more remote recesses of Greek lyric poetry and philosophy.[1] Coleridge's relationship to the classics is complicated by his omnivorous reading habits and by the way he assimilated classical notions and made them part of his own somewhat discontinuous vision. It may be said, however, that his most characteristic interests were in Greek writers who played with the notion that ideas enjoy a reality preliminary or superior to experience: certain pre-Socratic philosophers, Plato, neo-Platonic writers such as Plotinus, and several Greek lyric poets. For Coleridge the imagination employed by true poets (and anyone employing the imagination was a poet in Coleridge's view) was closely related to the act of imagination by which we make the undifferentiated stream of sensation take on the ineluctable modality of the world as we know it; and that in turn was merely a "repetition in the finite mind" of the divine act of creation itself.

One of the works on which Coleridge drew in putting together his vision of the imagination was Plato's dialogue *Ion* (p. 297 below). He makes a specific reference to this work in "Kubla Khan," one of his many poems about the poetic imagination. In the *Ion* Plato wants to establish that poets operate not by art (which might give them a claim to knowledge) but by divine inspiration.[2] Plato compares poets with dancing worshippers of Cybele and with Bacchantes, who, when they are possessed by Dionysus, draw milk and honey

SAMUEL TAYLOR COLERIDGE

1 In *The Road to Xanadu* (Houghton Mifflin, 1927), John Livingstone Lowe describes Coleridge's amazing life of reading.

2 Similarly, in the *Phaedrus* (section 245) Plato refers to poetic inspiration as a form of madness.

from rivers.[3] He expands the association between poetic powers and honey by pointing out that poets, comparing themselves to bees, talk of bringing songs from honeyed fountains. When he assimilates Plato into his work, however, Coleridge (i) omits Plato's comparison of poets to Bacchantes and bees; (ii) transfers the feeding on milk and honey from the Bacchantes to the poet; (iii) changes honey to the more exotic notion of honey-dew – the sweet substance exuded by the leaves of some plants; (iv) and qualifies "milk" with the idea of Paradise. Preferring, as usual, symbols and metaphors to similes, Coleridge expresses the poet's state of supernatural possession more directly than Plato. But that is not the most dramatic change that Coleridge works in his source; Plato's description was meant to discredit the poets, whereas Coleridge gives them vatic, if not divine, status.

Other suggestions of classical poetry come into the poem in various ways. Coleridge specifically mentions Theocritus in his introduction and allies himself with him as a fellow poet, singer, and dreamer. More obscurely, the Abyssinian maid, the equivalent of Plato's Muse, also recalls Hesiod's vision of the Muses on Helicon, when they breathe the power of song into him (pp. 278–9 below). Coleridge's emphasis on song and music is very much in the spirit of Hesiod's Muses, whom he describes as dancers and singers. Coleridge strives to revive within himself the power of his Muse and imagines the sublime heights of poetry to which he could soar. He would be in a state of divine possession, his eyes glittering and his hair "floating," agitated by movement like the hair of dancing Bacchantes, like Plato's Corybantic revelers, and other possessed figures in classical literature, such as Virgil's Sibyl in *Aeneid* 6. Coleridge has the power to compress all these sources into images for his poetry and for his theory of poetry.

Although written sometime around 1798, "Kubla Khan" was first published in 1816. The text presented here is based on the one in *Poetical Works*, ed. E. H. Coleridge (1912), and we have benefited from the variorum edition by J. C. C. Mays in *Poetical Works* (Princeton University Press, 2001).

Kubla Khan

Or, A Vision in a Dream. A Fragment

In the summer of the year 1797, the Author, then in ill health, had retired to a lonely farm-house between Porlock and Linton, on the Exmoor confines of Somerset and

---

3 Plato may well be alluding to Euripides' *Bacchae*: "And one took her thyrsus and struck it against a rock, from which there leapt a fresh spring of water; and another drove her fennel wand into the earth, and there the god sent up a spring of wine; and those who wished for *milk* merely scratched the soil with their finger-tips, and jets of milk sprang forth; and from their ivy-wreathed wands there trickled sweet streams of *honey*" (lines 704–11; emphasis added).

Devonshire. In the consequence of a slight indisposition, an anodyne[1] had been prescribed, from the effects of which he fell asleep in his chair at the moment that he was reading the following sentence, or words of the same substance, in "Purchas's Pilgrimage:"[2] "Here the Khan Kubla commanded a palace to be built, and a stately garden thereunto. And thus ten miles of fertile ground were inclosed with a wall." The author continued for about three hours in a profound sleep, at least of the external senses, during which time he has the most vivid confidence, that he could not have composed less than from two to three hundred lines; if that indeed can be called composition in which all the images rose up before him as *things*, with a parallel production of the correspondent expressions, without any sensation or consciousness of effort. On awaking he appeared to himself to have a distinct recollection of the whole, and taking his pen, ink, and paper instantly and eagerly wrote down the lines that are here preserved. At this moment he was unfortunately called out by a person on business from Porlock,[3] and detained by him above an hour, and on his return to his room, found to his no small surprise and mortification, that though he still retained some vague and dim recollection of the general purpose of the vision, yet, with the exception of some eight or ten scattered lines and images, all the rest had passed away like the images on the surface of a stream into which a stone has been cast, but alas! without the after restoration of the latter:

> Then all the charm
> Is broken – all that phantom-world so fair
> Vanishes, and a thousand circlets spread,
> And each mis-shape the other. Stay awhile,
> Poor Youth! Who scarcely dar'st lift up thine eyes –   5
> The stream will soon renew its smoothness, soon
> The visions will return! And lo, he stays,
> And soon the fragments dim of lovely forms
> Come trembling back, unite, and now once more
> The pool becomes a mirror.[4]   10

Yet from the still surviving recollections in his mind, the Author has frequently purposed to finish for himself what had been originally, as it were, given to him. Αὔριον ἄδιον ἄσω:[5] but the to-morrow is yet to come.

As a contrast to this vision, I have annexed a fragment of a very different character, describing with equal fidelity the dream of pain and disease.[6]

Kubla Khan

1   *anodyne* a pain-killer; presumably opium.
2   *Purchas's Pilgrimage* a survey of peoples and religious customs (1613) that evolved in succeeding editions into a large compilation of travel literature.
3   *a person on business from Porlock* almost certainly a fiction invented by Coleridge to explain his inveterate failure to complete work he had begun.
4   These are lines 91–100 of Coleridge's poem "The Picture, or the Lover's Resolution."
5   Αὔριον ἄδιον ἄσω "Tomorrow I will sing more sweetly" (Theocritus, *Idyll* 1.145, adapted; see p. 306 below).
6   *dream of pain and disease* Coleridge refers to his poem "The Pains of Sleep."

In Xanadu did Kubla Khan
A stately pleasure-dome decree:
Where Alph, the sacred river, ran[7]
Through caverns measureless to man
Down to a sunless sea.   15
So twice five miles of fertile ground
With walls and towers were girdled round:
And there were gardens bright with sinuous rills,
Where blossomed many an incense-bearing tree;
And here were forests ancient as the hills,   20
Enfolding sunny spots of greenery.

But oh! that deep romantic chasm which slanted
Down the green hill athwart a cedarn cover!
A savage place! as holy and enchanted
As e'er beneath a waning moon was haunted   25
By woman wailing for her demon-lover!
And from this chasm, with ceaseless turmoil seething,
As if this earth in fast thick pants were breathing,
A mighty fountain momently was forced:
Amid whose swift half-intermitted burst   30
Huge fragments vaulted like rebounding hail,
Or chaffy grain beneath the thresher's flail:
And 'mid these dancing rocks at once and ever
It flung up momently the sacred river.

Five miles meandering with a mazy motion   35
Through wood and dale the sacred river ran,
Then reached the caverns measureless to man,
And sank in tumult to a lifeless ocean:
And 'mid this tumult Kubla heard from far
Ancestral voices prophesying war!   40

    The shadow of the dome of pleasure
    Floated midway on the waves;
    Where was heard the mingled measure
    From the fountain and the caves.
It was a miracle of rare device,   45
A sunny pleasure-dome with caves of ice!

---

7 *Alph* an imaginary river for which various
sources have been postulated; these include the
river Alpheus, which in Greek mythology flowed
underground from Arcadia to Sicily in pursuit of
Arethusa; and the Greek letter alpha.

A damsel with a dulcimer
In a vision once I saw:
It was an Abyssinian maid,
And on her dulcimer she played,   50
Singing of Mount Abora.
Could I revive within me
Her symphony and song,
To such a deep delight 'twould win me,
That with music loud and long,   55
I would build that dome in air,
That sunny dome! those caves of ice!
And all who heard should see them there,
And all should cry, Beware! Beware!
His flashing eyes, his floating hair!   60
Weave a circle round him thrice,
And close your eyes with holy dread,
For he on honey-dew hath fed,
And drunk the milk of Paradise.[8]

---

8 *For . . . Paradise* compare Plato, *Ion* 533e–534a (p. 297 below): "And as the Corybantian revellers when they dance are not in their right mind, so the lyric poets are not in their right mind when they are composing their beautiful strains: but when falling under the power of music and metre they are inspired and possessed; like Bacchic maidens who draw milk and honey from the rivers when they are under the influence of Dionysus but not when they are in their right mind" (translated by Jowett).

Percy Bysshe Shelley (1792–1822)

Shelley began learning Latin and Greek at the age of six. By the time he went to Eton he was already a strong classicist, and he continued his studies at University College, Oxford. His classical interests as an adult ran to Greek rather than Latin, and his poetic career is deeply intertwined with his Greek literature. His plays *Prometheus Unbound* and *Hellas* are based on Aeschylus; *Swellfoot the Tyrant* is mock-Aristophanes and mock-Sophocles. The title of *Epipsychidion* speaks for itself as do those of his many "Odes" and "Hymns." Shelley also made direct translations of many Greek works, including Plato's *Symposium*, Euripides' late drama *Cyclops*, several of the Homeric hymns, part of Bion's *Lament for Adonis* (p. 312 below), and part of the *Lament for Bion* attributed to Moschus (p. 319 below). Shelley draws heavily on these two elegies in *Adonais*, although he is certainly also aware of other classical works in the same genre, including Theocritus' *Idyll* 1 (p. 302 below) and Virgil's *Eclogue* 10 (p. 349 below). These are all important sources for Milton's *Lycidas*, and Shelley also followed Milton (just as the supposed Moschus followed Bion). Many of the close connections between *Adonais* and its classical sources are registered in our footnotes below. But, broadly speaking, Shelley takes from Bion his version of the myth of Adonis, a beloved youth violently killed and extravagantly mourned by Venus or Urania, and applies it to the death of his fellow poet John Keats, which he imagines hastened on if not caused by the "savage criticism on his *Endymion*, which appeared in the *Quarterly Review*." Like its predecessors, the poem is a thoroughgoing expression of grief in which all nature is transformed to its purposes; even the name of the poem resembles a cry of sorrow (Greek αἴ αἴ).

Despite its heavy reliance on Greek pastoral elegy, there are elements of Shelley's poem that are not classical. Shelley departs from the Adonis myth by making Aphrodite/Venus the mother rather than lover of Adonais. Her name, Urania, also suggests that she is Keats's Muse, as she was Milton's at times. (Urania as the Muse of astronomy inspires writers on the heavens.) The optimistic ending of *Adonais* contrasts with both of the classical *Laments* on which it is based but may owe something to Virgil's *Eclogue* 5 (p. 345 below), which mourns the death of Daphnis and then celebrates his apotheosis. Although he uses Plato to support them, Shelley's philosophical and aesthetic ideas are alien to his Greek pastoral models, though similarly large themes are found in some Virgilian *Eclogue*s, particularly the fourth, and in some Platonic dialogues. Also alien to the Greek pastoral tradition are Shelley's allusions to contemporary literary feuds (though Virgil, again, provides some precedent) and, in general, the way he makes his personal circumstances and reflections a part of his poetic material. However, the connections Shelley draws between Keats and earlier poets dying young are part of the tradition in which he worked, and his addition of himself to the poetic line is not generically improbable; Milton preceded Shelley in making it and did so even more explicitly.

The text is based on a facsimile reprint (1886) of the first edition (1821). For textual commentary and for help with many allusions in the poem we are indebted to Anthony D. Knerr, *Shelley's Adonais: A Critical Edition* (Columbia University Press, 1984).

Adonais

An Elegy on the Death of John Keats, Author of Endymion, Hyperion, etc.

ἀστὴρ πρὶν μὲν ἔλαμπες ἐνὶ ζωοῖσιν ἑῷος,
νῦν δὲ θανὼν λάμπεις ἕσπερος ἐν φθιμένοις – Plato[1]

I

I weep for Adonais – he is dead![2]
O, weep for Adonais! though our tears
Thaw not the frost which binds so dear a head!
And thou, sad Hour, selected from all years[3]
To mourn our loss, rouse thy obscure compeers,   5

ADONAIS

1 THOU WERT THE MORNING STAR AMONG THE
   LIVING,
     Ere thy fair light had fled;
     Now, having died, thou art as Hesperus,
       giving
     New splendour to the dead. (translated by
       Shelley)

The *morning star* is the planet Venus, which is

also the evening star, Hesperus. Plato was probably not the author of this epigram from the *Greek Anthology* (7.670).

2 *I . . . dead* the refrain is based on Bion's *Lament for Adonis* 1–2 (p. 312 below): "I wail for Adonis, 'Fair Adonis is dead!'/'Fair Adonis is dead!' the Loves wail in reply"; compare the *Lament for Bion* 1–2, 7 (p. 319 below).

3 *Hour* a classical personification.

And teach them thine own sorrow, say: "with me
Died Adonais; till the Future dares
Forget the Past, his fate and fame shall be
An echo and a light unto eternity!"

II

Where wert thou, mighty Mother, when he lay,[4]   10
When thy Son lay, pierced by the shaft which flies[5]
In darkness? where was lorn Urania[6]
When Adonais died? With veilèd eyes,
'Mid listening Echoes, in her Paradise
She sate, while one, with soft enamoured breath,   15
Rekindled all the fading melodies,
With which, like flowers that mock the corse beneath,[7]
He had adorned and hid the coming bulk of death.

III

O, weep for Adonais – he is dead!
Wake, melancholy Mother, wake and weep!   20
Yet wherefore? Quench within their burning bed
Thy fiery tears, and let thy loud heart keep
Like his, a mute and uncomplaining sleep;
For he is gone, where all things wise and fair
Descend; – oh, dream not that the amorous Deep[8]   25
Will yet restore him to the vital air;
Death feeds on his mute voice, and laughs at our despair.

IV

Most musical of mourners, weep again![9]
Lament anew, Urania! – He died,[10]
Who was the Sire of an immortal strain,   30
Blind, old, and lonely, when his country's pride,

4 *Where wert thou* the appeal to nymphs or
Muses is a convention of pastoral elegy; compare
Theocritus, *Idylls* 1.66 ff. (p. 304 below), Virgil,
Eclogues 10.9 ff. (pp. 349–50 below), and Milton,
Lycidas 50 ff. (p. 70 above); *Mother* Urania.
5 *pierced* like Adonis by a boar's tusk, but the
"shaft" sent "In darkness" represents the anony-
mous, murderous review of Keats's *Endymion*.
6 *lorn* forlorn; *Urania* literally, "the heavenly
one"; an epithet of Aphrodite (Venus), who
mourned for Adonis.

7 *corse* corpse.
8 *For . . . Descend* compare the *Lament for
Adonis* 55 (p. 313 below): "every fair thing flows
down to you [Persephone]."
9 *Most . . . again* compare the *Lament for
Bion* 70–1 (p. 321 below): "Meles, most sweet-
sounding of rivers, this is a second grief for you,
a new grief."
10 *He* Milton, who is cited as a precedent for the
death of Adonais, as is Homer for that of Bion in
the *Lament for Bion*, 70 ff. (pp. 321–2 below).

The priest, the slave, and the liberticide,[11]
Trampled and mocked with many a loathèd rite
Of lust and blood; he went, unterrified,
Into the gulf of death; but his clear Sprite[12]   35
Yet reigns o'er earth; the third among the sons of light.[13]

V

Most musical of mourners, weep anew!
Not all to that bright station dared to climb;
And happier they their happiness who knew,
Whose tapers yet burn through that night of time   40
In which suns perished; others more sublime,
Struck by the envious wrath of man or God,
Have sunk, extinct in their refulgent prime;
And some yet live, treading the thorny road,
Which leads, through toil and hate, to Fame's serene abode.   45

VI

But now, thy youngest, dearest one, has perished,[14]
The nursling of thy widowhood, who grew,
Like a pale flower by some sad maiden cherished,
And fed with true love tears, instead of dew;
Most musical of mourners, weep anew!   50
Thy extreme hope, the loveliest and the last,
The bloom, whose petals nipped before they blew[15]
Died on the promise of the fruit, is waste;
The broken lily lies – the storm is overpast.

VII

To that high Capital, where kingly Death[16]   55
Keeps his pale court in beauty and decay,
He came; and bought, with price of purest breath,
A grave among the eternal. – Come away!
Haste, while the vault of blue Italian day[17]
Is yet his fitting charnel-roof! while still[18]   60

---

11 *liberticide* killer of freedom; applied by the poet Southey to Julius Caesar, the dictator who served for many writers as the type of all imperial rulers; here, in particular, is meant Charles II.
12 *Sprite* spirit; soul.
13 *third* after Homer and Dante – the first and second greatest epic poets; Shelley perhaps skips Virgil because of his fealty to the undemocratic ruler Augustus.

14 *But . . . perished* compare the *Lament for Bion* 74–5 (p. 322 below): "now, again, you weep for another son. . . ."
15 *blew* blossomed.
16 *high Capital* Rome.
17 *vault* sky.
18 *charnel-roof* sepulcher; enclosure for a corpse.

He lies, as if in dewy sleep he lay;[19]
    Awake him not! surely he takes his fill
Of deep and liquid rest, forgetful of all ill.

VIII

He will awake no more, oh, never more! –
    Within the twilight chamber spreads apace,   65
    The shadow of white Death, and at the door
    Invisible Corruption waits to trace
    His extreme way to her dim dwelling-place;
    The eternal Hunger sits, but pity and awe
    Soothe her pale rage, nor dares she to deface   70
    So fair a prey, till darkness, and the law
Of mortal change, shall fill the grave which is her maw.[20]

IX[21]

O, weep for Adonais! – The quick Dreams,[22]
    The passion-wingèd Ministers of thought,
    Who were his flocks, whom near the living streams   75
    Of his young spirit he fed, and whom he taught
    The love which was its music, wander not, –
    Wander no more, from kindling brain to brain,
    But droop there, whence they sprung; and mourn their lot
    Round the cold heart, where, after their sweet pain,   80
They ne'er will gather strength, or find a home again.

X

And one with trembling hands clasps his cold head,
    And fans him with her moonlight wings, and cries;
    "Our love, our hope, our sorrow, is not dead;
    See, on the silken fringe of his faint eyes,   85
    Like dew upon a sleeping flower, there lies
    A tear some Dream has loosened from his brain."
    Lost Angel of a ruined Paradise!

---

19 *He . . . lay* compare Bion's *Lament for Adonis*
71 (p. 314 below): "although he is a corpse, he
is fair, a fair corpse, as if sleeping."
20 *Of mortal . . . maw* later editions of the poem
read "Of change, shall o'er his sleep the mortal
curtain draw."
21 Stanzas IX–XI imitate Bion's *Lament for
Adonis* 79 ff. (p. 314 below): "Graceful Adonis
lies in purple covers, and the weeping Loves groan
around him, cutting their hair for Adonis. This

one threw on arrows, this one a bow, this one a
feathered quiver. One loosened the sandal of
Adonis, others bring water in a golden basin,
another washes his thighs, and another cools
Adonis from behind with his wings"; compare the
Lament for Bion 20 ff. (pp. 319–20 below).
22 *Dreams* Keats's poems, which mourn him
just as the Loves mourn Adonis and the herds
Bion.

She knew not 'twas her own; as with no stain
She faded, like a cloud which had outwept its rain.   90

XI

One from a lucid urn of starry dew
Washed his light limbs as if embalming them;
Another clipped her profuse locks, and threw
The wreath upon him, like an anadem,[23]
Which frozen tears instead of pearls begem[24];   95
Another in her wilful grief would break
Her bow and wingèd reeds, as if to stem
A greater loss with one which was more weak;
And dull the barbèd fire against his frozen cheek.

XII

Another Splendour on his mouth alit,   100
That mouth, whence it was wont to draw the breath
Which gave it strength to pierce the guarded wit,[25]
And pass into the panting heart beneath
With lightning and with music: the damp death
Quenched its caress upon his icy lips;   105
And, as a dying meteor stains a wreath
Of moonlight vapour, which the cold night clips,[26]
It flushed through his pale limbs, and passed to its eclipse.

XIII

And others came . . . Desires and Adorations,
Wingèd Persuasions and veiled Destinies,   110
Splendours, and Glooms, and glimmering Incarnations
Of hopes and fears, and twilight Phantasies;
And Sorrow, with her family of Sighs,
And Pleasure, blind with tears, led by the gleam
Of her own dying smile instead of eyes,   115
Came in slow pomp; – the moving pomp might seem[27]
Like pageantry of mist on an autumnal stream.

XIV[28]

All he had loved, and moulded into thought,
From shape, and hue, and odour, and sweet sound,

---

23   *anadem* a wreath for the head; a garland.
24   *begem* decorate with precious stones.
25   *wit* intelligence, mind (of the reader).
26   *clips* holds; embraces.
27   *pomp* procession.
28   Stanzas XIV–XVII exploit the convention of

ascribing human emotions to nature or places
(the "pathetic fallacy"); the chief models are
Bion's *Lament for Adonis* 31 ff. (p. 313 below)
and the *Lament for Bion* 37 ff., 86 ff. (pp. 320,
322 below).

Lamented Adonais. Morning sought   120
Her eastern watchtower, and her hair unbound,
Wet with the tears which should adorn the ground,
Dimmed the aerial eyes that kindle day;
Afar the melancholy thunder moaned,
Pale Ocean in unquiet slumber lay,   125
And the wild winds flew round, sobbing in their dismay.

        XV

Lost Echo sits amid the voiceless mountains,[29]
And feeds her grief with his remembered lay,
And will no more reply to winds or fountains,
Or amorous birds perched on the young green spray,   130
Or herdsman's horn, or bell at closing day;
Since she can mimic not his lips, more dear
Than those for whose disdain she pined away
Into a shadow of all sounds: – a drear
Murmur, between their songs, is all the woodmen hear.   135

        XVI

Grief made the young Spring wild, and she threw down
Her kindling buds, as if she Autumn were,
Or they dead leaves; since her delight is flown,
For whom should she have waked the sullen year?
To Phoebus was not Hyacinth so dear[30]   140
Nor to himself Narcissus, as to both[31]
Thou Adonais: wan they stand and sere[32]
Amid the drooping comrades of their youth,[33]
With dew all turned to tears; odour, to sighing ruth.[34]

        XVII

Thy spirit's sister, the lorn nightingale   145
Mourns not her mate with such melodious pain;
Not so the eagle, who like thee could scale[35]
Heaven, and could nourish in the sun's domain

29   *Echo* a nymph who wasted away to a mere voice from unhappy love (Ovid, *Metamorphoses* 3; p. 449 below); she appears in the laments for Adonis (38) and Bion (30–1).
30   *Phoebus* Apollo; *Hyacinth* a youth loved by Apollo, who accidentally killed him and changed him into a flower (mentioned in the *Lament for Bion* 6–7; p. 319 below).
31   *Narcissus* a proud youth who pined away from love of his own reflection and turned into a flower (Ovid, *Metamorphoses* 3; p. 452 below).
32   *sere* dry; withered.
33   *drooping comrades* later editions read "faint companions."
34   *ruth* compassion; pity.
35   *eagle* who in legend could fly toward the sun and renew his youth by burning off the effects of age before plunging thrice in the water to be reborn.

Her mighty youth with morning, doth complain,
Soaring and screaming round her empty nest,   150
As Albion wails for thee: the curse of Cain[36]
Light on his head who pierced thy innocent breast,[37]
And scared the angel soul that was its earthy guest!

XVIII[38]

Ah woe is me! Winter is come and gone,
But grief returns with the revolving year;   155
The airs and streams renew their joyous tone;
The ants, the bees, the swallows reappear;
Fresh leaves and flowers deck the dead Seasons' bier;
The amorous birds now pair in every brake,
And build their mossy homes in field and brere;[39]   160
And the green lizard, and the golden snake,
Like unimprisoned flames, out of their trance awake.

XIX

Through wood and stream and field and hill and Ocean
A quickening life from the Earth's heart has burst
As it has ever done, with change and motion,   165
From the great morning of the world when first
God dawned on Chaos; in its steam immersed
The lamps of Heaven flash with a softer light;
All baser things pant with life's sacred thirst;
Diffuse themselves; and spend in love's delight,   170
The beauty and the joy of their renewèd might.

XX

The leprous corpse touched by this spirit tender
Exhales itself in flowers of gentle breath;[40]
Like incarnations of the stars, when splendour
Is changed to fragrance, they illumine death   175
And mock the merry worm that wakes beneath;
Nought we know, dies. Shall that alone which knows
Be as a sword consumed before the sheath
By sightless lightning? – th' intense atom glows
A moment, then is quenched in a most cold repose.   180

---

36 *Albion* Great Britain; *Cain* murderer of his brother Abel; cursed by God for his sin (Genesis 5.4).

37 *his head* the reviewer's.

38 The implicit contrast in stanzas XVIII–XX between the regenerative power of nature and the finality of human life recalls the *Lament for Bion* 99 ff. (pp. 322–3 below).

39 *brere* briar.

40 *flowers* similarly, the blood of Adonis gives birth to roses, the tears of Venus to anemones (*Lament for Adonis* 66; p. 314 below).

XXI

Alas! that all we loved of him should be,
But for our grief, as if it had not been,
And grief itself be mortal! Woe is me!
Whence are we, and why are we? of what scene
The actors or spectators? Great and mean   185
Meet massed in death, who lends what life must borrow.
As long as skies are blue, and fields are green,
Evening must usher night, night urge the morrow,
Month follow month with woe, and year wake year to sorrow.

XXII

He will awake no more, oh, never more!   190
"Wake thou," cried Misery, "childless Mother, rise[41]
Out of thy sleep, and slake, in thy heart's core,
A wound more fierce than his with tears and sighs."
And all the Dreams that watched Urania's eyes,
And all the Echoes whom their sister's song   195
Had held in holy silence, cried: "Arise!"
Swift as a Thought by the snake Memory stung,
From her ambrosial rest the fading Splendour sprung.

XXIII[42]

She rose like an autumnal Night, that springs
Out of the East, and follows wild and drear   200
The golden Day, which, on eternal wings,
Even as a ghost abandoning a bier,
Had left the Earth a corpse. Sorrow and fear
So struck, so roused, so rapt Urania;
So saddened round her like an atmosphere   205
Of stormy mist; so swept her on her way
Even to the mournful place where Adonais lay.

XXIV[43]

Out of her secret Paradise she sped,
Through camps and cities rough with stone, and steel,

---

41 *Wake thou* compare the *Lament for Adonis*
3–5 (p. 312 below): "Sleep no longer in purple
sheets, Cypris; wake, wretched one, and robed in
black beat your breast and tell to all, 'Fair Adonis
is dead!'"
42 In stanzas XXIII–XXIV Urania rushes to the
side of Adonais as Venus to Adonis in the *Lament
for Adonis* 19 ff. (p. 312 below).
43 Urania injures her feet upon rough ground

as Venus upon thorns in the *Lament for Adonis*
21–2 (p. 312 below); Shelley buttresses the idea
by extrapolating from Agathon's description of
Love in Plato's *Symposium*: "For Love walks not
upon the earth, nor over the heads of men, which
are not indeed very soft; but he dwells within, and
treads on the softest of existing things, etc."
(Shelley's translation).

And human hearts, which to her aery tread   210
Yielding not, wounded the invisible
Palms of her tender feet where'er they fell:
And barbèd tongues, and thoughts more sharp than they
Rent the soft Form they never could repel,
Whose sacred blood, like the young tears of May,   215
Paved with eternal flowers that undeserving way.

                                    XXV
In the death chamber for a moment Death
Shamed by the presence of that living Might
Blushed to annihilation, and the breath
Revisited those lips, and life's pale light   220
Flashed through those limbs, so late her dear delight.
"Leave me not wild and drear and comfortless,
As silent lightning leaves the starless night!
Leave me not!" cried Urania: her distress
Roused Death: Death rose and smiled, and met her vain caress.   225

                                    XXVI[44]
"Stay yet awhile! speak to me once again;
Kiss me, so long but as a kiss may live;
And in my heartless breast and burning brain
That word, that kiss shall all thoughts else survive,
With food of saddest memory kept alive,   230
Now thou art dead, as if it were a part
Of thee, my Adonais! I would give
All that I am to be as thou now art!
But I am chained to Time, and cannot thence depart!

                                    XXVII
"Oh gentle child, beautiful as thou wert,   235
Why didst thou leave the trodden paths of men
Too soon, and with weak hands though mighty heart
Dare the unpastured dragon in his den?
Defenceless as thou wert, oh where was then
Wisdom the mirrored shield, or scorn the spear?[45]   240
Or hadst thou waited the full cycle, when

44   The stanza is modeled upon the *Lament for Adonis* 42 ff. (p. 313 below): "wait, Adonis, ill-fated Adonis, wait. . . ."
45   *mirrored shield* an allusion to the stratagem of Perseus, who used his shield as a mirror in beheading Medusa in order to avoid being turned to stone by her gaze.

Thy spirit should have filled its crescent sphere,
The monsters of life's waste had fled from thee like deer.

XXVIII

"The herded wolves, bold only to pursue;
The obscene ravens, clamorous o'er the dead;   245
The vultures to the conqueror's banner true
Who feed where Desolation first has fed,
And whose wings rain contagion; – how they fled,
When like Apollo, from his golden bow,
The Pythian of the age one arrow sped[46]   250
And smiled! – The spoilers tempt no second blow,[47]
They fawn on the proud feet that spurn them as they go.

XXIX

"The sun comes forth, and many reptiles spawn;
He sets, and each ephemeral insect then
Is gathered into death without a dawn,   255
And the immortal stars awake again;
So is it in the world of living men:
A godlike mind soars forth, in its delight
Making earth bare and veiling heaven, and when
It sinks, the swarms that dimmed or shared its light   260
Leave to its kindred lamps the spirit's awful night."

XXX[48]

Thus ceased she: and the mountain shepherds came
Their garlands sere, their magic mantles rent;
The Pilgrim of Eternity, whose fame[49]
Over his living head like Heaven is bent,   265
An early but enduring monument,
Came, veiling all the lightnings of his song
In sorrow; from her wilds Ierne sent[50]
The sweetest lyrist of her saddest wrong,
And love taught grief to fall like music from his tongue.   270

---

46 *Pythian* Apollo, the Python-slayer; a disguised reference to Byron, who had satirized his critics.

47 *tempt* attempt.

48 The procession of poets in stanzas XXX–XXXIII observes the convention of gods and rural characters visiting the dying shepherd: compare,

e.g., Theocritus, *Idylls* 1.77 ff. (p. 305 below), Virgil, *Eclogue* 10.19 ff. (p. 350 below), Milton, *Lycidas* 88 ff. (pp. 71–2 above).

49 *Pilgrim of Eternity* the poet Lord Byron.

50 *Ierne* Ireland, meaning Thomas Moore (1779–1852).

XXXI

Midst others of less note, came one frail Form,[51]
A phantom among men; companionless
As the last cloud of an expiring storm
Whose thunder is its knell; he, as I guess,
Had gazed on Nature's naked loveliness,   275
Actaeon-like, and now he fled astray,[52]
With feeble steps o'er the world's wilderness,
And his own thoughts, along that rugged way,
Pursued, like raging hounds, their father and their prey.

XXXII

A pardlike Spirit beautiful and swift –[53]   280
A Love in desolation masked; – a Power
Girt round with weakness; – it can scarce uplift
The weight of the superincumbent hour;[54]
It is a dying lamp, a falling shower,
A breaking billow; – even whilst we speak[55]   285
Is it not broken? On the withering flower
The killing sun smiles brightly: on a cheek
The life can burn in blood, even while the heart may break.

XXXIII

His head was bound with pansies overblown,
And faded violets, white, and pied, and blue;   290
And a light spear topped with a cypress cone;[56]
Round whose rude shaft dark ivy tresses grew
Yet dripping with the forest's noonday dew,
Vibrated, as the ever-beating heart
Shook the weak hand that grasped it; of that crew   295
He came the last, neglected and apart;
A herd-abandoned deer struck by the hunter's dart.

XXXIV

All stood aloof, and at his partial moan
Smiled through their tears; well knew that gentle band

51 *one frail Form* Shelley himself.
52 *Actaeon* a youth who stumbled upon Artemis
(Diana) bathing naked; he was punished by being
turned into a stag and hunted down by his own
hounds.
53 *pardlike* like a panther or leopard.
54 *superincumbent* situated above; lying upon;
a Miltonic-sounding Latinism.

55 *billow* wave; swell of the sea.
56 *light spear . . . cone* the thyrsus – a wand
tipped with a pine cone and wreathed in ivy; it
was brandished by worshippers of Dionysus in
their ecstatic dances.

Who in another's fate now wept his own;   300
As in the accents of an unknown land,
He sung new sorrow; sad Urania scanned
The Stranger's mien, and murmured: "Who art thou?"
He answered not, but with a sudden hand
Made bare his branded and ensanguined brow,[57]   305
Which was like Cain's or Christ's – Oh! that it should be so!

XXXV

What softer voice is hushed over the dead?
Athwart what brow is that dark mantle thrown?
What form leans sadly o'er the white death-bed,
In mockery of monumental stone,   310
The heavy heart heaving without a moan?
If it be He, who, gentlest of the wise,[58]
Taught, soothed, loved, honoured the departed one;
Let me not vex, with inharmonious sighs,
The silence of that heart's accepted sacrifice.   315

XXXVI

Our Adonais has drunk poison – oh![59]
What deaf and viperous murderer could crown
Life's early cup with such a draught of woe?
The nameless worm would now itself disown:[60]
It felt, yet could escape the magic tone   320
Whose prelude held all envy, hate, and wrong,
But what was howling in one breast alone,
Silent with expectation of the song,
Whose master's hand is cold, whose silver lyre unstrung.

XXXVII

Live thou, whose infamy is not thy fame!   325
Live! fear no heavier chastisement from me,
Thou noteless blot on a remembered name![61]
But be thyself, and know thyself to be!
And ever at thy season be thou free
To spill the venom when thy fangs o'erflow: 330
Remorse and Self-contempt shall cling to thee;
Hot Shame shall burn upon thy secret brow,
And like a beaten hound tremble thou shalt – as now.

---

57 *ensanguined* bloodied.
58 *He* Leigh Hunt, a close friend of Shelley and Keats.
59 *Our . . . poison* modeled on the *Lament for*

Bion 109–12 (p. 323 below), which Shelley quotes in his preface to *Adonais.*
60 *worm* snake or dragon; the reviewer.
61 *noteless* unnoted; obscure.

XXXVIII

Nor let us weep that our delight is fled
Far from these carrion kites that scream below;[62]   335
He wakes or sleeps with the enduring dead;
Thou canst not soar where he is sitting now. –
Dust to the dust! but the pure spirit shall flow[63]
Back to the burning fountain whence it came,
A portion of the Eternal, which must glow[64]   340
Through time and change, unquenchably the same,
Whilst thy cold embers choke the sordid hearth of shame.

XXXIX

Peace, peace! he is not dead, he doth not sleep –
He hath awakened from the dream of life –
'Tis we, who lost in stormy visions, keep   345
With phantoms an unprofitable strife,
And in mad trance, strike with our spirit's knife
Invulnerable nothings. – *We* decay
Like corpses in a charnel; fear and grief
Convulse us and consume us day by day,   350
And cold hopes swarm like worms within our living clay.

XL

He has outsoared the shadow of our night;
Envy and calumny and hate and pain,
And that unrest which men miscall delight,
Can touch him not and torture not again;   355
From the contagion of the world's slow stain
He is secure, and now can never mourn
A heart grown cold, a head grown grey in vain;
Nor, when the spirit's self has ceased to burn,
With sparkless ashes load an unlamented urn.   360

XLI

He lives, he wakes – 'tis Death is dead, not he;
Mourn not for Adonais. – Thou young Dawn
Turn all thy dew to splendour, for from thee
The spirit thou lamentest is not gone;
Ye caverns and ye forests, cease to moan!   365

---

62 *carrion kites* birds of prey; vultures.
63 *Dust to the dust* Genesis 3.19; a statement of
man's mortality after expulsion from the Garden

of Eden; also a reference to the burial rite in the
Book of Common Prayer.
64 *the Eternal* a Platonic notion.

Cease, ye faint flowers and fountains, and thou Air
Which like a mourning veil thy scarf hadst thrown
O'er the abandoned Earth, now leave it bare
Even to the joyous stars which smile on its despair!

XLII

He is made one with Nature: there is heard   370
His voice in all her music, from the moan
Of thunder, to the song of night's sweet bird;
He is a presence to be felt and known
In darkness and in light, from herb and stone,
Spreading itself where'er that Power may move   375
Which has withdrawn his being to its own;
Which wields the world with never wearied love,
Sustains it from beneath, and kindles it above.

XLIII

He is a portion of the loveliness
Which once he made more lovely: he doth bear   380
His part, while the one Spirit's plastic stress
Sweeps through the dull dense world, compelling there,
All new successions to the forms they wear;
Torturing th'unwilling dross that checks its flight
To its own likeness, as each mass may bear;   385
And bursting in its beauty and its might
From trees and beasts and men into the Heaven's light.

XLIV

The splendours of the firmament of time
May be eclipsed, but are extinguished not;
Like stars to their appointed height they climb.   390
And death is a low mist which cannot blot
The brightness it may veil. When lofty thought
Lifts a young heart above its mortal lair,
And love and life contend in it, for what
Shall be its earthly doom, the dead live there   395
And move like winds of light on dark and stormy air.

XLV

The inheritors of unfulfilled renown
Rose from their thrones, built beyond mortal thought,
Far in the Unapparent. Chatterton[65]

---

65 *Chatterton* Thomas (1752–1770), a very   mitted suicide partly in despair over the attacks
precocious poet who was thought to have com-   on his character by Horace Walpole and others.

Rose pale, his solemn agony had not   400
Yet faded from him; Sidney, as he fought[66]
And as he fell and as he lived and loved
Sublimely mild, a Spirit without spot,
Arose; and Lucan, by his death approved:[67]
Oblivion as they rose shrank like a thing reproved.   405

XLVI

And many more, whose names on Earth are dark
But whose transmitted effluence cannot die
So long as fire outlives the parent spark,
Rose, robed in dazzling immortality.
"Thou art become as one of us," they cry,   410
"It was for thee yon kingless sphere has long
Swung blind in unascended majesty,
Silent alone amid an Heaven of song.
Assume thy wingèd throne, thou Vesper of our throng!"[68]

XLVII

Who mourns for Adonais? oh come forth   415
Fond wretch! and know thyself and him aright.
Clasp with thy panting soul the pendulous Earth;
As from a centre, dart thy spirit's light
Beyond all worlds, until its spacious might
Satiate the void circumference: then shrink   420
Even to a point within our day and night;
And keep thy heart light lest it make thee sink
When hope has kindled hope, and lured thee to the brink.

XLVIII

Or go to Rome, which is the sepulchre
O, not of him, but of our joy: 'tis nought   425
That ages, empires, and religions there
Lie buried in the ravage they have wrought;
For such as he can lend, – they borrow not
Glory from those who made the world their prey;
And he is gathered to the kings of thought   430

---

66 *Sidney* Sir Philip (1554–1586), Elizabethan courtier and poet who died of wounds received in battle.
67 *Lucan* Roman epic poet (39–65 ce), who committed suicide at 26 when implicated in a conspiracy against Nero.

68 *Vesper* the evening star (Greek Hesperus); a reference to the epigram ascribed to Plato which Shelley uses as the epigraph to *Adonais* (see n. 1 above).

Who waged contention with their time's decay,
And of the past are all that cannot pass away.

XLIX

Go thou to Rome, – at once the Paradise,
The grave, the city, and the wilderness;
And where its wrecks like shattered mountains rise,   435
And flowering weeds, and fragrant copses dress
The bones of Desolation's nakedness[69]
Pass, till the Spirit of the spot shall lead
Thy footsteps to a slope of green access
Where, like an infant's smile, over the dead,   440
A light of laughing flowers along the grass is spread.

L

And grey walls moulder round, on which dull Time
Feeds, like slow fire upon a hoary brand;[70]
And one keen pyramid with wedge sublime,[71]
Pavilioning the dust of him who planned   445
This refuge for his memory, doth stand
Like flame transformed to marble; and beneath,
A field is spread, on which a newer band
Have pitched in Heaven's smile their camp of death,
Welcoming him we lose with scarce extinguished breath.   450

LI

Here pause: these graves are all too young as yet
To have outgrown the sorrow which consigned
Its charge to each; and if the seal is set,
Here, on one fountain of a mourning mind,
Break it not thou! too surely shalt thou find   455
Thine own well full, if thou returnest home,
Of tears and gall. From the world's bitter wind
Seek shelter in the shadow of the tomb.
What Adonais is, why fear we to become?

LII

The One remains, the many change and pass;[72]   460
Heaven's light forever shines, Earth's shadows fly;

---

69 *And where . . . nakedness* the Protestant cemetery in Rome where Keats was buried.
70 *hoary brand* a grayish or musty torch.
71 *pyramid* a monument to Gaius Cestius, a Roman tribune.

72 *The One* a notion of Parmenides' developed by Plato and Plotinus.

Life, like a dome of many-coloured glass,
Stains the white radiance of Eternity,
Until Death tramples it to fragments. – Die,
If thou wouldst be with that which thou dost seek!   465
Follow where all is fled! – Rome's azure sky,
Flowers, ruins, statues, music, words, are weak
The glory they transfuse with fitting truth to speak.

LIII

Why linger, why turn back, why shrink, my Heart?
Thy hopes are gone before: from all things here   470
They have departed; thou shouldst now depart!
A light is past from the revolving year,
And man, and woman; and what still is dear
Attracts to crush, repels to make thee wither.
The soft sky smiles, – the low wind whispers near: 475
'Tis Adonais calls! oh, hasten thither,
No more let Life divide what Death can join together.

LIV

That Light whose smile kindles the Universe,
That Beauty in which all things work and move,
That Benediction which the eclipsing Curse   480
Of birth can quench not, that sustaining Love
Which through the web of being blindly wove
By man and beast and earth and air and sea,
Burns bright or dim, as each are mirrors of
The fire for which all thirst; now beams on me,   485
Consuming the last clouds of cold mortality.

LV

The breath whose might I have invoked in song
Descends on me; my spirit's bark is driven,[73]
Far from the shore, far from the trembling throng
Whose sails were never to the tempest given;   490
The massy earth and spherèd skies are riven!
I am borne darkly, fearfully, afar;
Whilst burning through the inmost veil of Heaven,
The soul of Adonais, like a star,
Beacons from the abode where the Eternal are.   500

---

73 *bark* boat.

John Keats (1795–1821)

In 1815 Keats abandoned his medical studies and devoted himself to poetry. From 1816 to 1819, when sickness and death cut him short, Keats produced a remarkable number of immortal poems. One of the first of these and one of the most important to Keats's development as a poet was "On First Looking into Chapman's Homer." A number of his other poems connect him to the classical poetic tradition, also through the medium of English writers, particularly Spenser, Shakespeare, and Milton. He describes himself in "To Homer" as "Standing aloof in giant ignorance" because he did not read Greek, but Keats got close to the classical tradition in his way. Among his best poems are the six famous odes: "To Psyche," "On Melancholy," "To a Nightingale," "To Autumn," "On Indolence," and "On a Grecian Urn." These works, freighted with difficult philosophical questions, are in the tradition of Horace's grand or ecstatic *Odes*, 1.12, for example, and 3.25. Keats's odes are more introspective than Horace's, but they belong to the Horatian tradition as it continued to develop after the classical period. Like other English poets, Keats thought of Pindar, as well as Horace, when composing an ode. "Pindaric" became synonymous in the seventeenth century with metrical irregularity or exuberance and with loosely organized, somewhat rhapsodic poetry in general. Keats's odes have some hints of that tradition, but their philosophical questioning marks them as more in the manner of Horace.

Another classical genre to which the "Ode on a Grecian Urn" is related is the ekphrasis, or description of a work of art. The description of the shield of Achilles in *Iliad* 18 (p. 250 below) is the greatest and earliest example, and the one Keats is most likely to have known. Like Keats's description of the urn, ancient ekphrases are not just digressional or ornamental but serve as a focus for an exploration of important ideas about life and the relation of art to life. Homer's shield, for example, presents a view of the world that puts war into perspective (see Auden's *Shield of Achilles*; p. 225 below). The ekphrasis on the carved wooden goblet in Theocritus' *Idyll* 1 (pp. 303–4 below) shares with Keats's ode the themes of love and of the conduct of ordinary life; it also contains an image of the poet. Conventions of ancient ekphrases include the expression of wonder at the realism of the art and, through the shading of description into narrative, a presumption that an action described is a present occurrence rather than a static picture.[1] Both features are present in Keats. By calling the urn a "historian" and praising its ability to tell a tale he salutes its realism. On the other hand, Keats balances his perception of the dynamism of the image with an apprehension of its stasis and timelessness. In a sense, he reconciles the two in his final formulation, if beauty may be taken as a thing of this changing world and truth an unalterable and timeless quality.

Truth and beauty are important ideas in Plato, and one may wish to compare Keats's reflections to, say, Socrates' speech on the form of beauty, or true beauty, in the *Symposium* (sections 209e–212a.; pp. 295–6 below). The climactic sentence makes a strong connection between beauty and truth. In fact, the adjective *alethes* (true) appears thrice in that sentence (Jowett translates the first two as "realities" and "reality"), and perhaps this lodged in Keats's memory. Plato here refers to the absolute of beauty as "that which is true" and says that the knowledge of beauty allows a person to produce "true things" and "true virtue." So, although he does not limit the idea of truth to beauty, Plato would say that the contemplation of beauty may lead us toward truth if we progress beyond sensual beauty to beauty in its abstract forms. Keats is Platonic in the sense that contemplation of the urn's beauty takes us out of the physical world into a permanent, unchanging world of truth that speaks to the spirit.

There are also many differences between Plato's thinking and Keats's. Plato, for example, would not see a work of art, like the urn, as a fit medium for the contemplation of truth or even true beauty. This is because he saw art as an imitation of an imitation, as it were, and two steps removed from the reality of the stable forms that constitute the highest truths. Moreover, comparing Keats and Plato or talking about Keats's "philosophy" is probably inappropriate; he was a poet, not a philosopher. But, as a poet, Keats is invoking Platonic ideas, and his poetry, which is of the highest order, would not be the same if those ideas were unknown.

The text comes from *The Poetical Works of Coleridge, Shelley, and Keats* (1829). We have benefited from the notes in many modern editions, including *The Poems of John Keats* ed. Jack Stillinger (Harvard University Press, 1978).

JOHN KEATS

1   Among other ancient ekphrases are Europa's basket in Moschus' *Europa*; the coverlet of Peleus and Thetis' marriage bed in Catullus 64; the paintings on the walls of Juno's temple in *Aeneid* 1; the shield of Aeneas in *Aeneid* 8; and the carved gates of the Sun's palace in Ovid, *Metamorphoses* 2.

Ode on a Grecian Urn[1]

Thou still unravished bride of quietness,
   Thou foster-child of silence and slow time,
Sylvan historian, who canst thus express
   A flowery tale more sweetly than our rhyme:
What leaf-fringed legend haunts about thy shape   5
   Of deities or mortals, or of both,
      In Tempe or the dales of Arcady?[2]
   What men or gods are these? What maidens loth?
What mad pursuit? What struggle to escape?
      What pipes and timbrels? What wild ecstasy?   10

2

Heard melodies are sweet, but those unheard
   Are sweeter; therefore, ye soft pipes, play on;
Not to the sensual ear, but, more endeared,
   Pipe to the spirit ditties of no tone:
Fair youth, beneath the trees, thou canst not leave   15
   Thy song, nor ever can those trees be bare;
      Bold Lover, never, never canst thou kiss,
Though winning near the goal – yet, do not grieve;
      She cannot fade, though thou hast not thy bliss,
   For ever wilt thou love, and she be fair!   20

3

Ah, happy, happy boughs! that cannot shed
   Your leaves, nor ever bid the Spring adieu;
And, happy melodist, unwearied,
   For ever piping songs forever new;
More happy love! more happy, happy love!   25
   For ever warm and still to be enjoyed,
      For ever panting, and for ever young;
All breathing human passion far above,
   That leaves a heart high-sorrowful and cloyed,
      A burning forehead, and a parching tongue.   30

ODE ON A GRECIAN URN

1 *Grecian Urn* a painted earthenware vessel.
The Keats–Shelley Memorial House in Rome
includes in its collection a tracing said to have
been made by Keats himself of the Sosibios Vase,
an amphora located in the Louvre. The Ode is an
artifact of Keats's imagination, not a description
of a particular vase. However, the shape and deco-
rative scheme of the Sosibios Vase provide a sense
of what Keats had in mind. Another source of
inspiration may have been the religious procession
depicted on the Parthenon frieze. See Ian Jack,
Keats and the Mirror of Art (Oxford University
Press, 1967), pp. 214–24.
2 *Tempe* a beautiful valley; *Arcady* Arcadia, a
region of southern Greece associated with Pan
and pastoral poetry.

4

Who are these coming to the sacrifice?
    To what green altar, O mysterious priest,
Lead'st thou that heifer lowing at the skies,
    And all her silken flanks with garlands dressed?
What little town by river or sea shore,   35
        Or mountain-built with peaceful citadel,
            Is emptied of this folk, this pious morn?
And, little town, thy streets for evermore
        Will silent be; and not a soul to tell
            Why thou art desolate, can e'er return.   40

5

O Attic shape! Fair attitude! with brede[3]
    Of marble men and maidens overwrought,
With forest branches and the trodden weed;
    Thou, silent form, dost tease us out of thought
As doth eternity: Cold Pastoral!   45
        When old age shall this generation waste,
            Thou shalt remain, in midst of other woe
        Than ours, a friend to man, to whom thou say'st,
Beauty is truth, truth beauty, – that is all
            Ye know on earth, and all ye need to know.   50

3   *Attic* Attica was the part of Greece containing
Athens; *brede* embroidery, interweaving of
colors.

Alfred, Lord Tennyson (1809–1892)

In 1833 Tennyson's great friend from his Cambridge days, Arthur Hallam, died very suddenly. Within a month of the shock Tennyson drafted three great poems, "all finding," writes the critic Christopher Ricks, "extraordinarily compelling correlatives, in ancient worlds, for his feelings personal and universal, ancient and modern."[1] The poems to which Ricks refers are "Ulysses," "Morte d'Arthur," and "Tithonus" – two of them obviously related to classical works. Many of Tennyson's other poems use classical tradition in a similar way as a "correlative" for the expression of feelings and thoughts engendered by experience. As he proved most conclusively in his great work *In Memoriam* (1850), Tennyson assumed the burden of correlating his experience and the greater cultural life not only of his time but of all times. Although he reached out to the past and present of other cultures – especially England's (as in *Idylls of the King*), but also sometimes Islam's or other traditions – the classical tradition remained central to his work throughout his life. The names of some of his last collections of verse attest to this fact: *Tiresias and Other Poems* (1885), *Demeter and Poems* (1889), and the posthumously published *The Death of Oenone, Akbar's Dream, and Other Poems* (1892).

"The Lotos-Eaters" (1832) uses both *Odyssey* 9.82–104 (p. 266 below) and a portion of Spenser's *Faerie Queene* 2 (see p. 12 above) as sources or correlatives in an exploration of the feelings of suicidal despair that often haunted Tennyson. In the Homeric story, a number of Odysseus' crewmen go ashore to explore an unknown isle, partake of the opiates consumed by the natives, and decide to abandon their quest for home (their *nostos*, to use a Homeric word that has been adopted into English) and live instead a life of pleasure. In fact, Homer's sailors, under the narcotic influence, just stop caring about home, but Tennyson's think about their choice and justify themselves: home will not be the same; it will just

ALFRED, LORD TENNYSON
1   *Oxford Dictionary of National Biography.*

cause confusion if we return after all these years; and so on. Tennyson explores personal feelings of despair rather than mere external dangers to one's resolve.

The practice of allegorizing Homeric stories began in ancient times; Spenser was merely extending that tradition when he interpreted the stories as a Protestant search for salvation. Tennyson goes further still, exploring the psychology of surrender, giving it a pleasing and plausible voice. Moreover, he does nothing to indicate that surrender is unacceptable. Odysseus orders his men back on the ship and keeps others from eating the narcotic. Spenser smashes the Bower of Bliss, but Tennyson leaves the chorus of lost souls ringing in our ears.

In Tennyson's poem not even the gods care what happens to the sailors or to mankind in general. There is classical precedent for this. Lines 150–73, where the men aspire to the life of the gods, imbues the Homeric scene with a Lucretian view of the gods. In Homer the gods imbibe nectar at ease on Olympus and enjoy watching the affairs of mortals as a spectacle, but they are emotionally involved in mortal doings and regularly intervene. Tennyson's gods are detached and indifferent. They "smile" indiscriminately at everything that happens on earth. At most, they find a "music" in the tale of human tribulations that wafts up to them, but it is "a tale of little meaning" chanted by a Lilliputian race whose concerns are too small to warrant much attention. These indifferent gods are closer to the Epicurean gods than to Homer's. Tennyson probably remembered passages of Lucretius' *De Rerum Natura* that define the untroubled, peaceful, self-sufficient, uncaring life of the gods (e.g., 2.646–60 and 3.1–30; pp. 325–7 below). However, for Lucretius, it is reassuring that the gods have nothing to do with mortals because therefore they need not be feared. For Tennyson, on the other hand, the uncaring gods represent cosmic fears of insignificance and despair – an impenetrable obstacle to the integration of individual life with something greater that might give it meaning, despite its brevity and fragility.

The text presented here is based on the one-volume edition of the *Works* by Hallam, Lord Tennyson (1913). We are indebted to the editorial work of Christopher Ricks in *The Poems of Tennyson* (University of California Press, 1987).

The Lotos-Eaters

"Courage!" he said, and pointed toward the land,[1]
"This mounting wave will roll us shoreward soon."
In the afternoon they came unto a land
In which it seemèd always afternoon.

THE LOTOS-EATERS

1 *he* Odysseus; the opening stanzas are Spense-   rian (see p. 12 above) and recall *Faerie Queene* 2.6.

All round the coast the languid air did swoon,   5
Breathing like one that hath a weary dream.
Full-faced above the valley stood the moon;
And like a downward smoke, the slender stream
Along the cliff to fall and pause and fall did seem.

A land of streams! some, like a downward smoke,   10
Slow-dropping veils of thinnest lawn, did go;[2]
And some through wavering lights and shadows broke,
Rolling a slumbrous sheet of foam below.
They saw the gleaming river seaward flow
From the inner land: far off, three mountain-tops,   15
Three silent pinnacles of agèd snow,
Stood sunset-flushed: and, dewed with showery drops,
Up-clomb the shadowy pine above the woven copse.

The charmèd sunset lingered low adown
In the red West: through mountain clefts the dale   20
Was seen far inland, and the yellow down[3]
Bordered with palm, and many a winding vale
And meadow, set with slender galingale;[4]
A land where all things always seemed the same!
And round about the keel with faces pale,   25
Dark faces pale against that rosy flame,
The mild-eyed melancholy Lotos-eaters came.

Branches they bore of that enchanted stem,
Laden with flower and fruit, whereof they gave
To each, but whoso did receive of them,   30
And taste, to him the gushing of the wave
Far far away did seem to mourn and rave
On alien shores; and if his fellow spake,
His voice was thin, as voices from the grave;
And deep-asleep he seemed, yet all awake,   35
And music in his ears his beating heart did make.

They sat them down upon the yellow sand,
Between the sun and moon upon the shore;
And sweet it was to dream of Fatherland,
Of child, and wife, and slave; but evermore   40
Most weary seemed the sea, weary the oar,
Weary the wandering fields of barren foam.

2 *lawn* a very fine fabric.   4 *galingale* a kind of sedge, or grasslike plant,
3 *down* elevated open land often used for   with an aromatic root.
grazing.

Then some one said, "We will return no more";
And all at once they sang, "Our island home[5]
Is far beyond the wave; we will no longer roam."   45

Choric Song[6]

I

There is sweet music here that softer falls
Than petals from blown roses on the grass,
Or night-dews on still waters between walls
Of shadowy granite, in a gleaming pass;
Music that gentlier on the spirit lies,   50
Than tired eyelids upon tired eyes;
Music that brings sweet sleep down from the blissful skies.
Here are cool mosses deep,
And through the moss the ivies creep,
And in the stream the long-leaved flowers weep,   55
And from the craggy ledge the poppy hangs in sleep.[7]

II

Why are we weighed upon with heaviness,
And utterly consumed with sharp distress,
While all things else have rest from weariness?
All things have rest: why should we toil alone,   60
We only toil, who are the first of things,
And make perpetual moan,
Still from one sorrow to another thrown:
Nor ever fold our wings,
And cease from wanderings,   65
Nor steep our brows in slumber's holy balm;
Nor harken what the inner spirit sings,
"There is no joy but calm!"
Why should we only toil, the roof and crown of things?[8]

---

5 *island home* Ithaca.
6 The "Choric Song" imitates the choruses of Greek tragedy and may recall Sophocles' *Philoctetes*, where Odysseus is a character and there is a chorus of sailors. The meter is more appropriate for song than the narrative Spenserian stanzas, and the content resembles Greek choral songs in being non-narrative, reflective, and concerned with universal issues.

7 *poppy* the flower from which sleep-inducing opium is produced.
8 *crown of things* in the great chain of being man is at the top of earthly things; the concept has a long history in Western thought. See A. O. Lovejoy, *The Great Chain of Being* (Harvard University Press, 1936).

III

Lo! in the middle of the wood,   70
The folded leaf is wooed from out the bud
With winds upon the branch, and there
Grows green and broad, and takes no care,
Sun-steeped at noon, and in the moon
Nightly dew-fed; and turning yellow   75
Falls, and floats adown the air.
Lo! sweetened with the summer light,
The full-juiced apple, waxing over-mellow,
Drops in a silent autumn night.
All its allotted length of days,   80
The flower ripens in its place,
Ripens and fades, and falls, and hath no toil,
Fast-rooted in the fruitful soil.

IV[9]

Hateful is the dark-blue sky,
Vaulted o'er the dark-blue sea.   85
Death is the end of life; ah, why
Should life all labour be?
Let us alone. Time driveth onward fast,
And in a little while our lips are dumb.
Let us alone. What is it that will last?   90
All things are taken from us, and become
Portions and parcels of the dreadful Past.
Let us alone. What pleasure can we have
To war with evil? Is there any peace
In ever climbing up the climbing wave?   95
All things have rest, and ripen toward the grave
In silence; ripen, fall and cease:
Give us long rest or death, dark death, or dreamful ease.

V

How sweet it were, hearing the downward stream,
With half-shut eyes ever to seem   100
Falling asleep in a half-dream!
To dream and dream, like yonder amber light,
Which will not leave the myrrh-bush on the height;
To hear each other's whispered speech;
Eating the Lotos day by day,   105
To watch the crisping ripples on the beach,
And tender curving lines of creamy spray;

9 This stanza resembles a Horatian ode about death (e.g., 1.11, p. 396 below; 2.14), but the message is not, as in Horace, "Carpe diem!" but some simple form of surrender.

To lend our hearts and spirits wholly
To the influence of mild-minded melancholy;
To muse and brood and live again in memory,   110
With those old faces of our infancy
Heaped over with a mound of grass,
Two handfuls of white dust, shut in an urn of brass!

VI

Dear is the memory of our wedded lives,
And dear the last embraces of our wives   115
And their warm tears: but all hath suffered change;
For surely now our household hearths are cold:
Our sons inherit us: our looks are strange:
And we should come like ghosts to trouble joy.
Or else the island princes over-bold[10]   120
Have eat our substance, and the minstrel sings[11]
Before them of the ten years' war in Troy,
And our great deeds, as half-forgotten things.
Is there confusion in the little isle?
Let what is broken so remain.   125
The Gods are hard to reconcile:
'Tis hard to settle order once again.
There is confusion worse than death,
Trouble on trouble, pain on pain,
Long labour unto agèd breath,   130
Sore task to hearts worn out by many wars
And eyes grown dim with gazing on the pilot-stars.

VII

But, propped on beds of amaranth and moly,[12]
How sweet (while warm airs lull us, blowing lowly)
With half-dropped eyelid still,   135
Beneath a heaven dark and holy,
To watch the long bright river drawing slowly
His waters from the purple hill –
To hear the dewy echoes calling
From cave to cave through the thick-twinèd vine –   140
To watch the emerald-coloured water falling
Through many a wov'n acanthus-wreath divine!

---

10 *island princes* Penelope's suitors in the *Odyssey.*
11 *eat* an old form of the past participle; *minstrel* an allusion to the Ithacan bard Phemius, who sings of the return of heroes from Troy (*Odyssey* 1).

12 *amaranth* "the never-fading flower"; *moly* the magic herb that Hermes gives to Odysseus to protect him from Circe's spells (*Odyssey* 10; p. 270 below).

Only to hear and see the far-off sparkling brine,
Only to hear were sweet, stretched out beneath the pine.

VIII

The Lotos blooms below the barren peak: 145
The Lotos blows by every winding creek:
All day the wind breathes low with mellower tone:
Through every hollow cave and alley lone
Round and round the spicy downs the yellow Lotos-dust is blown.
We have had enough of action, and of motion we,   150
Rolled to starboard, rolled to larboard, when the surge was seething free,
Where the wallowing monster spouted his foam-fountains in the sea.
Let us swear an oath, and keep it with an equal mind,
In the hollow Lotos-land to live and lie reclined
On the hills like Gods together, careless of mankind.[13]   155
For they lie beside their nectar, and the bolts are hurled
Far below them in the valleys, and the clouds are lightly curled
Round their golden houses, girdled with the gleaming world:
Where they smile in secret, looking over wasted lands,
Blight and famine, plague and earthquake, roaring deeps and fiery sands,   160
Clanging fights, and flaming towns, and sinking ships, and praying hands.
But they smile, they find a music centred in a doleful song
Steaming up, a lamentation and an ancient tale of wrong,
Like a tale of little meaning though the words are strong;
Chanted from an ill-used race of men that cleave the soil,   165
Sow the seed, and reap the harvest with enduring toil,
Storing yearly little dues of wheat, and wine and oil;
Till they perish and they suffer – some, 'tis whispered – down in hell
Suffer endless anguish, others in Elysian valleys dwell,[14]
Resting weary limbs at last on beds of asphodel.   170
Surely, surely, slumber is more sweet than toil, the shore
Than labour in the deep mid-ocean, wind and wave and oar;
Oh rest ye, brother mariners, we will not wander more.

13 *careless of mankind* like the Epicurean gods described by Lucretius (2.646–60; 3.1–30; pp. 325–7 below).

14 *Elysian* Elysium is the sweetest part of the classical underworld; the blessed dead live there.

Robert Browning (1812–1889)

Although he was enrolled for a time in the newly founded London University and scheduled to study Latin, Greek, and German, Browning was mainly and very thoroughly self-educated. Among his many other achievements as a student, Browning read Johnson's *Dictionary*, as he said, "to qualify myself for literature." His historical and literary studies extended across most of Europe and often provided the groundwork for his grand poetic projects. One of his earliest extended poems was called *Paracelsus*, after the sixteenth-century physician, and soon thereafter he wrote a work called *Sordello* based on thirteenth-century Italian history. Throughout his career Browning continued to display a penchant for medieval and early modern backgrounds – particularly in his vast poem *The Ring and the Book* – but he also made frequent direct use of the classics. He translated the *Agamemnon* of Aeschylus; he wrote poems on Pheidippides, the runner at the battle of Marathon, on Apollo, on Cleon (a fictional poet); and long poems with such names as *Aristophanes' Apology* and *Balustion's Adventure, including a Transcript from Euripides.*

"Pan and Luna" is one of what Browning called his "Dramatic Idylls." As in much of his poetry, he takes a hint from his reading and turns it into a scene with characters more fully imagined than their originals. The poem is entirely based on Virgil's *Georgics* 3.384–93 (p. 361 below). Virgil here gives advice on breeding sheep with the whitest wool; as an exemplum of the attractiveness of pure white wool, he mentions a curious and obscure myth about Luna and Pan. Virgil probably gathered a dry rendition of the story from the Hellenistic poet Nicander, but within a mere three lines he creates something beautiful and mysterious (see n. 1 below). Browning goes much further and imagines a detailed scene so rich in imagery that it recalls the ornate Sanskrit love poetry of Kalidasa in the *Meghaduta* rather than the sparser world of Greek myth.

The story itself is one of the many rape myths associated with the virile, goat-like demi-god Pan. Luna is Selene, the Greek moon goddess. When Virgil says, literally, "the god Pan captured and deceived you," he means that Pan lured Luna into the woods (with a snowy white fleece or by turning himself into a beautiful ram), captured and raped her. Since there is no extant extended version of the myth, Browning was free to embellish the story in any way he could imagine. However, he did slightly rewrite the myth too, either out of error or by design. Luna/Selene is not a virginal goddess; she is well known in myth for her love of Endymion, and she mates with Zeus. In treating her as a "maid" Browning either chose to ignore the myths about her love life; decided to locate this event in her virginal girlhood; or, more likely, conflated her with the virgin Diana/Artemis, who is associated with the moon but is not the moon goddess.

Like many poems, "Pan and Luna" is partly about the process of poetic creation. After giving free reign to his poetic imagination for about 100 lines, Browning pulls himself up short and reminds himself and us of the slender foundation of five nouns on which he has built his fantasy. This gesture returns us to the epigraph of the poem, *si credere dignum est*, the conditional clause from which the whole poem has sprung. If the story and Browning's elaboration are not worthy of belief, however, they do certainly give pleasure.

The text presented here is taken from the edition of Browning's *Poetical Works* edited by Augustine Birrell (Macmillan, 1900).

Pan and Luna

Si credere dignum est.[1]
– *Georgic*. iii. [391].

O worthy of belief I hold it was,
Virgil, your legend in those strange three lines!
No question, that adventure came to pass
One black night in Arcadia: yes, the pines,[2]
Mountains and valleys mingling made one mass   5
Of black with void black heaven: the earth's confines,
The sky's embrace, – below, above, around,
All hardened into black without a bound.

PAN AND LUNA

1 "If it is worthy of belief," part of the three lines (*Georgics* 3.391–3) to which Browning refers in line 2:

> munere sic niveo lanae, si credere dignum est,
> Pan deus Arcadiae captam te, Luna, fefellit

in nemora alta vocans; nec tu aspernata vocantem.

For the translation of the whole passage, see p. 361 below.

2 *Arcadia* mountainous region of Greece haunted by Pan.

Fill up a swart stone chalice to the brim
With fresh-squeezed yet fast-thickening poppy-juice: 10
See how the sluggish jelly, late a-swim,
Turns marble to the touch of who would loose
The solid smooth, grown jet from rim to rim,
By turning round the bowl! So night can fuse
Earth with her all-comprising sky. No less,   15
Light, the least spark, shows air and emptiness.

And thus it proved when – diving into space,
Stript of all vapour, from each web of mist
Utterly film-free – entered on her race
The naked Moon, full-orbed antagonist[3]   20
Of night and dark, night's dowry: peak to base,
Upstarted mountains, and each valley, kissed
To sudden life, lay silver-bright: in air
Flew she revealed, Maid-Moon with limbs all bare.

Still as she fled, each depth – where refuge seemed –   25
Opening a lone pale chamber, left distinct
Those limbs: mid still-retreating blue, she teemed
Herself with whiteness, – virginal, uncinct[4]
By any halo save what finely gleamed
To outline not disguise her: heaven was linked   30
In one accord with earth to quaff the joy,
Drain beauty to the dregs without alloy.

Whereof she grew aware. What help? When, lo,
A succourable cloud with sleep lay dense:[5]
Some pine-tree-top had caught it sailing slow,   35
And tethered for a prize: in evidence
Captive lay fleece on fleece of piled-up snow
Drowsily patient: flake-heaped how or whence,
The structure of that succourable cloud,
What matter? Shamed she plunged into its shroud.   40

Orbed – so the woman-figure poets call
Because of rounds on rounds – that apple-shaped
Head which its hair binds close into a ball
Each side the curving ears – that pure undraped
Pout of the sister paps – that . . . Once for all,   45

3 *Moon* Virgil's Luna is actually Selene, the   4 *uncinct* not encircled.
moon goddess; Browning (perhaps misled by a   5 *succourable* helpful.
reference to Cynthia in Dryden's translation)
takes her to be the virgin goddess Diana (Greek
Artemis), who was associated with the moon.

Say – her consummate circle thus escaped
With its innumerous circlets, sank absorbed,
Safe in the cloud – O naked Moon full-orbed!

But what means this? The downy swathes combine,
Conglobe. The smothery coy-caressing stuff   50
Curdles about her! Vain each twist and twine
Those lithe limbs try, encroached on by a fluff
Fitting as close as fits the dented spine[6]
Its flexile ivory outside-flesh: enough!
The plumy drifts contract, condense, constringe,[7]   55
Till she is swallowed by the feathery springe.[8]

As when a pearl slips lost in the thin foam
Churned on a sea-shore, and, o'er-frothed, conceits[9]
Herself safe-housed in Amphitrite's dome, – [10]
If, through the bladdery wave-worked yeast, she meets   60
What most she loathes and leaps from, – elf from gnome
No gladlier, – finds that safest of retreats
Bubble about a treacherous hand wide ope
To grasp her – (divers who pick pearls so grope) –

So lay this Maid-Moon clasped around and caught   65
By rough red Pan, the god of all that tract:[11]
He it was schemed the snare thus subtly wrought
With simulated earth-breath, – wool-tufts packed
Into a billowy wrappage. Sheep far-sought
For spotless shearings yield such: take the fact   70
As learnèd Virgil gives it, – how the breed
Whitens itself for ever: yes, indeed!

If one forefather ram, though pure as chalk
From tinge on fleece, should still display a tongue
Black 'neath the beast's moist palate, prompt men baulk   75
The propagating plague: he gets no young:[12]
They rather slay him, – sell his hide to caulk
Ships with, first steeped in pitch, – nor hands are wrung
In sorrow for his fate: protected thus,
The purity we love is gained for us.   80

---

6 *dented* indented or toothed (Latin *dens*, tooth).

7 *constringe* contract or become dense.

8 *springe* a snare or trap.

9 *conceits* fancies; imagines.

10 *Amphitrite* a sea nymph; wife of Poseidon.

11 *Pan* goat-featured god of shepherds.

12 *If one forefather . . . gets no young* a paraphrase of Virgil, *Georgics* 3.387–90 (p. 361 below).

So did Girl-moon, by just her attribute
Of unmatched modesty betrayed, lie trapped,
Bruised to the breast of Pan, half-god half-brute,
Raked by his bristly boar-sward while he lapped[13]
– Never say, kissed her! that were to pollute   85
Love's language – which moreover proves unapt
To tell how she recoiled – as who finds thorns
Where she sought flowers – when, feeling, she touched – horns!

Then – does the legend say? – first moon-eclipse
Happened, first swooning-fit which puzzled sore   90
The early sages? Is that why she dips
Into the dark, a minute and no more,
Only so long as serves her while she rips
The cloud's womb through and, faultless as before,
Pursues her way? No lesson for a maid   95
Left she, a maid herself thus trapped, betrayed?

Ha, Virgil? Tell the rest, you! "To the deep
Of his domain the wildwood, Pan forthwith
Called her, and so she followed" – in her sleep,
Surely? – "by no means spurning him." The myth[14]   100
Explain who may! Let all else go, I keep
– As of a ruin just a monolith –
Thus much, one verse of five words, each a boon:
Arcadia, night, a cloud, Pan, and the moon.

---

13 *boar-sward* boar-like, rough skin.   14 *To ... him* a paraphrase of Virgil *Georgics*
                                                3.392–3 (p. 361 below).

Matthew Arnold (1822–1888)

Although he was the first professor of poetry at Oxford to lecture in English rather than Latin, Arnold's engagement with classical literature was deep and long lasting. In a series of three lectures, published as *On Translating Homer* (1861), for example, he argued for the enduring importance of Greek poetry. He expressed the preference of his age for Greek over Latin poetry – a preference rare in the eighteenth century – but mainly he argued for the impersonal ethos of the Greeks as opposed to the self-absorption of the moderns. Later, he drew a distinction between Hellenism and Hebraism that divided for him the two great cultural tendencies that needed to be reconciled in successful individuals and societies. Classical poetry was not an antiquarian interest for Arnold but a permanent presence in culture, as he tried to describe it in his important work as a social and literary critic. The most famous essay in that work is *Culture and Anarchy* (1869), but it is a small part of Arnold's immense contribution to the varied field of cultural criticism.

Although he wrote about poetry all of his life, Arnold composed almost all of his own poetry before the age of 30. Written in the early 1850s, *Dover Beach* is, in a sense, a late poem and hints in some ways at the long career as a cultural critic on which Arnold was about to embark. In lines 15–18 he associates his feelings when listening to the sound of waves beating on the shore with the feelings they express for the Athenian playwright Sophocles. For Sophocles, the relentless sound of waves figures forth the "ebb and flow of human misery." Arnold adds a thought to the feeling and suggests that the waves represent the ebb of religious faith.

It is uncertain whether Arnold had a specific Sophoclean passage in mind or a composite idea formed from the many examples of sea imagery in Sophocles' extant plays. The two main contenders are *Antigone* 582 ff. and *Trachiniae* 112 ff., between which the reader may make his or her own choice (see pp. 288–90 below). In both passages the succession of waves is compared to the piling up of suffering, for Heracles in *Trachiniae*, for the house of Labdacus in *Antigone*. Both Sophoclean passages dwell on the constant succession of waves, but Arnold also uses the waves' ebbing to express a tragic view of modern life. An early modern or an eighteenth-century reader might have been inclined to abstract the image from Sophoclean thought and to use it as an epigram or an aphorism embodying a more general tragic vision of life: the ceaselessness of the waves, for example, might make an emblem of merely natural life, life without faith.[1] In an important way, Arnold is discovering a closer kinship with Sophocles than earlier readers, who saw him (and, to an even greater extent, Euripides) as a treasury of timeless truths.

The last three lines of *Dover Beach* are thought to be inspired by Thucydides' description of a night battle during the Athenian siege of Syracuse (p. 291 below). Line 36 may reflect a reading of Thucydides' account of how troops moving up to the front were thrown into confusion by the flight of those who had already been routed. Arnold's "darkling plain" may allude to Thucydides' "level ground" or "plain" (τὸ ὁμαλόν) below Epipolae, whither the Athenians fled. Thucydides would certainly have vouched for the historical accuracy of his report and valued that over its poetry, but Arnold sees in it an image of modern life that revivifies the fifth-century BCE sensibility in his own.

The text comes from *The Poetical Works of Matthew Arnold* (Macmillan, 1896). We also consulted *The Poems of Matthew Arnold*, eds Kenneth Allott and Miriam Allott (2nd edn; Longman, 1979).

Dover Beach

The sea is calm tonight.
The tide is full, the moon lies fair
Upon the straits; – on the French coast the light
Gleams and is gone; the cliffs of England stand,
Glimmering and vast, out in the tranquil bay.   5
Come to the window, sweet is the night-air!
Only, from the long line of spray
Where the sea meets the moon-blanched land,
Listen! you hear the grating roar
Of pebbles which the waves draw back, and fling,[1]   10
At their return, up the high strand,
Begin, and cease, and then again begin,
With tremulous cadence slow, and bring
The eternal note of sadness in.

MATTHEW ARNOLD

1 Shakespeare, for example, may be using the image this way in Sonnet 60 (p. 47 above and n. 1 below).

DOVER BEACH

1 Cf. Shakespeare, Sonnet 60, lines 1–2 (p. 47 above): "Like as the waves make towards the pebbled shore, / So do our minutes hasten to their end."

Sophocles long ago[2]   15
Heard it on the Aegean, and it brought[3]
Into his mind the turbid ebb and flow
Of human misery; we
Find also in the sound a thought,
Hearing it by this distant northern sea.   20

The Sea of Faith
Was once, too, at the full, and round earth's shore
Lay like the folds of a bright girdle furled.
But now I only hear
Its melancholy, long, withdrawing roar,   25
Retreating, to the breath
Of the night-wind, down the vast edges drear
And naked shingles of the world.[4]

Ah, love, let us be true
To one another! for the world, which seems   30
To lie before us like a land of dreams,
So various, so beautiful, so new,
Hath really neither joy, nor love, nor light,
Nor certitude, nor peace, nor help for pain;
And we are here as on a darkling plain   35
Swept with confused alarms of struggle and flight,
Where ignorant armies clash by night.

2 *Sophocles* Athenian tragedian (c. 496–406   4 *shingles* "small roundish stones; loose water-
BCE).   worn pebbles" (*OED*).
3 *Aegean* the Aegean Sea between Greece and
Asia Minor.

Alfred Edward Housman (1859–1936)

Housman was a classical scholar of the first rank who held important professorships at University College, London, and later at Cambridge University. He edited several Latin poets and produced, over a long period, a monumental edition of the astrological poet Manilius, superseding those of his scholarly heroes, Joseph Scaliger and Richard Bentley. Housman was exceedingly reticent about his poetry, however, and never discussed the influence of his classical studies. He published only two volumes of poetry – *A Shropshire Lad* (1889) and *Final Poems* (1922) – though his literary executor saw to it that these were supplemented after the poet's death.

A Shropshire Lad 15 is based on the Narcissus myth as it appears in Ovid, *Metamorphoses* 3 (pp. 447–52 below). Housman suggests his reliance on Ovid when, in recounting the tale, he says, "as I hear tell." The story is that Narcissus proudly rejects all lovers, male and female, including Echo. One of the lovers curses him, and he is punished by falling in love with his reflection. The story is one of the most frequently retold in British literature,[1] but Housman's version is original. He writes from the point of view of a lovelorn Echo who addresses Narcissus and warns him not to look into the pool of her eyes lest he see himself, become transfixed, and die.

The text is based on the first edition (1889), but we have also had reference to *Collected Poems and Selected Prose*, ed. Christopher Ricks (Allen Lane, 1988).

ALFRED EDWARD HOUSMAN

1 See, for example, Milton's version in *Paradise Lost* (p. 80 above).

A Shropshire Lad

15

Look not in my eyes, for fear
  They mirror true the sight I see,
And there you find your face too clear
  And love it and be lost like me.
One the long nights through must lie   5
  Spent in star-defeated sighs,[1]
But why should you as well as I
  Perish? gaze not in my eyes.

A Grecian lad, as I hear tell,[2]
  One that many loved in vain,[3]   10
Looked into a forest well
  And never looked away again.
There, when the turf in springtime flowers,
  With downward eye and gazes sad,
Stands amid the glancing showers   15
  A jonquil, not a Grecian lad.[4]

A Shropshire Lad

1 *One . . . sighs* compare Ovid, *Metamorphoses* 3.396 (p. 449 below): "sleepless cares wear out her [Echo's] wretched body."

2 *Grecian lad* Narcissus; *as I hear tell* an allusion to Ovid's narrative.

3 *One . . . in vain* compare Ovid, *Metamorphoses* 3.353–5 (p. 447 below): "Many young men, many girls desired him; but so hard was the pride in his tender form that no young men, no girls touched him."

4 *jonquil* the narcissus flower; the line recalls Ovid, *Metamorphoses* 3.509–10 (p. 452 below): "instead of his body they find a yellow flower, its center encircled by white petals."

William Butler Yeats (1865–1939)

Yeats's relationship to classical poetry is complicated by his immersion in mystical intellectual schemes and by his strange inability to learn a foreign language. The former, perhaps in combination with the latter, led him to learn and contemplate classical mythology as an expression of the *spiritus mundi* (the world's soul) that provided him with metaphors for his poetry as well as the inspiration for his own systems of thought. Yeats described his relationship to that permanent world of ideas in his *Autobiographies* and carved out his own systematic understanding of it in *A Vision* (1926). His use of these ideas and mythologies in his poetry grew later in his career, culminating for many readers in the brilliant volume *The Tower* (1928). The opening poem of the volume, "Sailing to Byzantium," uses a post-classical city to express thoughts about the old age of men and civilizations. Another famous poem in the volume, "Leda and the Swan," uses the story of Zeus, who, in the form of a swan, fathered upon Leda the twins Castor and Pollux. These heroic twins rescue their sister Helen from Theseus and provide a pattern for the Trojan War, a fact which Yeats exploits to charge the tale of Leda's rape with disturbing questions about personal and political history.

"A Thought from Propertius," published in *The Wild Swans at Coole* (1919), a volume leading up to *The Tower*, may also allude indirectly to the Trojan War. In *Elegies* 2.2 (p. 411 below) Propertius' speaker laments that his vow of chastity has been undone by his observation of an Amazonian beauty. His infatuation drives him to declare she is more beautiful than Minerva, Venus, or Juno, the three goddesses among whom Paris had to choose when bestowing the apple of discord that started the Trojan War. Yeats surely was drawn to the connection Propertius suggests between personal passion and historical events, and he must have seen an efflorescence of significance in Propertius' line, *cur haec in terris facies humana moratur?* (literally, "why does this human beauty dwell on earth?"). In effect, Yeats asks a similar question by offering two opposing lives for the Amazonian beauty: in the first part of the poem, as a chaste priestess of Athena, and, in the last two lines of the poem, as a rape victim of orgiastic centaurs.

The text is from *The Wild Swans at Coole* (1919).

A Thought from Propertius

She might, so noble from head
To great shapely knees
The long flowing line,
Have walked to the altar
Through the holy images   5
At Pallas Athena's side,[1]
Or been fit spoil for a centaur[2]
Drunk with the unmixed wine.

Two Songs from a Play

"Two Songs from a Play" was published in *The Tower*. In the first song Yeats
develops a parallel between Dionysus and Jesus. There is more than one myth of
Dionysus, the god of wine and intoxication. According to the usual story, he was
the son of Zeus and Semele, snatched from his dying mother's womb and brought
to term in Zeus' thigh. Yeats, however, alludes to an Orphic myth (found in lit-
erature ascribed to Orpheus) that Dionysus was a son of Zeus and Persephone
who was torn apart and eaten by the Titans at Hera's urging. Athena rescued his
heart and took it to Zeus, who recreated Dionysus in the womb of Semele. A
similar myth is told of the Egyptian god Osiris. The story of Jesus, Yeats suggests,
is a similar tale of murder, resurrection, and virgin birth, though not necessarily
in that order. As he explains in *A Vision*, Yeats was aware of cyclical patterns that
informed the history of the world, and he describes one such cycle in the first
song. He may call it a song from a play to indicate that it is a kind of recapitula-
tion of the action that occurs in a play or in part of a play "cycle," such as the
famous "Wakefield Cycle," in which biblical history is represented.

The second song hints at a large historical cycle in which Christianity both is
foreseen by and replaces Greco-Roman paganism. As R. J. Finneran's notes on
the text in *The Poems* (2nd edn; Scribner, 1997) explain, Yeats paraphrases the
Greek sophist Eunapius on the way Christianity eclipsed the "Doric" world of
Plato (lines 21–4) while embodying some of its thoughts. He then attempts to
express a universal kind of instability in which embodiment exhausts idea. In both
songs, Yeats may also be thinking of Virgil's fourth *Eclogue* (p. 342 below) which
was long interpreted as a prediction of Christ's coming and the success of
Christianity.

A THOUGHT FROM PROPERTIUS

1   *Pallas Athena* warrior goddess and patron of
the arts and crafts.

2   *centaur* a mythical being, half-man half-horse;
at the wedding of Pirithous, king of the Lapiths,
the centaurs, being unaccustomed to wine, got
drunk and attempted to abduct the bride and
other women.

The text is from *The Tower* (1928), and we have consulted the edition by R. J. Finneran cited above.

I

I saw a staring virgin stand[1]
Where holy Dionysus died,[2]
And tear the heart out of his side,
And lay the heart upon her hand
And bear that beating heart away;   5
And then did all the Muses sing
Of Magnus Annus at the spring,[3]
As though God's death were but a play.

Another Troy must rise and set,
Another lineage feed the crow,   10
Another Argo's painted prow[4]
Drive to a flashier bauble yet.[5]
The Roman Empire stood appalled:
It dropped the reins of peace and war
When that fierce virgin and her Star[6]   15
Out of the fabulous darkness called.

II

In pity for man's darkening thought
He walked that room and issued thence[7]
In Galilean turbulence;[8]
The Babylonian starlight brought[9]   20
A fabulous, formless darkness in;[10]
Odour of blood when Christ was slain
Made all Platonic tolerance vain
And vain all Doric discipline.[11]

TWO SONGS FROM A PLAY

1   *virgin* Athena.

2   *Dionysus* the god of wine and intoxication. For the myth see the head note to these songs, above.

3   *Magnus Annus* Latin for "Great Year"; a celestial cycle of thousands of years postulated by some Greek philosophers. Some have seen a reference to it in Virgil, *Eclogues* 4.5 (p. 343 below), "the great succession of generations is born anew."

4   *Argo* the ship in which Jason sailed in quest of the golden fleece.

5   *Another Troy . . . yet* compare Virgil, *Eclogue* 4.34–6 (p. 344 below), "there will be another

Tiphys then and another Argo to carry chosen heroes; there will be a repetition of wars too and great Achilles will be sent again to Troy."

6   *Star* the star Spica in the constellation Virgo, which biblical scholars identified as the Star of Bethlehem (Finneran, p. 663).

7   *that room* "in *The Resurrection*, 'that room' is the site of Christ's Last Supper" (Finneran, p. 663).

8   *Galilean* Galilee was the region of Palestine where Jesus preached.

9   *Babylonian starlight* the Babylonians were famous for their contributions to astronomy and astrology.

Everything that man esteems   25
Endures a moment or a day.
Love's pleasure drives his love away,
The painter's brush consumes his dreams;
The herald's cry, the soldier's tread
Exhaust his glory and his might: 30
Whatever flames upon the night
Man's own resinous heart has fed.

10 *A fabulous ... in* echoing the scholar E. R. Dodds, who wrote that "it is in Plato's city that Greek thought made its last stand against the Church which it envisaged as 'a fabulous and formless darkness mastering the loveliness of the world,'" where the last phrase is a paraphrase of the Greek sophist Eunapius (fourth century CE) (Finneran, p. 663).
11 *Doric* the plainest of the classical orders of architecture.

Wilfred Owen (1893–1918)

Owen was killed near the French town of Ors in some of the last fighting of World War I; the armistice was signed only one week later. He left a small but powerful body of poetry that was first collected for publication in 1920. He never attended university, but received classical training in school and took an interest in Roman archaeology. One of his early poems, "Uriconium, An Ode," imagines the fall of that Roman city near Shrewsbury, the county town of Owen's native Shropshire, England. Owen's war poetry, much of it written while he was with his regiment or behind the lines recovering from shock, tries to come to grips with the horrors of war. In "Dulce et Decorum Est," Owen takes a line from Horace, *Odes* 3.2.13, and makes it stand for the kind of slogan that the experience of war belies. Placing the line first and last, Owen also indicates that the experience of his poem discredits the Horatian tag.

By quoting the line out of context Owen makes Horace sound more propagandistic than he appears if one reads the whole poem (pp. 400–1 below). Horace's ode is much more a paean to *virtus* – manliness, steadiness, and courage – than it is specifically a call to arms. In addition, the sort of sweetness (*dulce*) that Horace applies to a manly death is more ethical and less sensuous than the English word allows us to imagine. Owen undoubtedly understood all this, but he nevertheless found striking the contrast between Horace's philosophical sentence and the reality of war. Particularly by leaving Horace's Latin untranslated, Owen strongly suggests that such sentences in the classics are not applicable in the modern world.

Only four of Owen's poems were published in his lifetime. The rest were rescued from manuscripts by a succession of editors, beginning with Siegfried Sassoon in 1920. The standard edition, to which we are indebted, is *Wilfred Owen, the Complete Poems and Fragments*, ed. Jon Stallworthy (Norton, 1983). The Wilfred Owen Multimedia Digital Archive makes standard texts and facsimiles of the manuscripts available to all at www.hcu.ox.ac.uk/jtap/.

Dulce et Decorum Est

Bent double, like old beggars under sacks,
Knock-kneed, coughing like hags, we cursed through sludge,
Till on the haunting flares we turned our backs
And towards our distant rest began to trudge.
Men marched asleep. Many had lost their boots   5
But limped on, blood-shod. All went lame; all blind;
Drunk with fatigue; deaf even to the hoots
Of tired, outstripped Five-Nines[1] that dropped behind.

Gas! GAS! Quick, boys! – An ecstasy of fumbling,
Fitting the clumsy helmets just in time;   10
But someone still was yelling out and stumbling
And floundering like a man in fire or lime . . .
Dim, through the misty panes and thick green light
As under a green sea, I saw him drowning.

In all my dreams, before my helpless sight,   15
He plunges at me, guttering, choking, drowning.

If in some smothering dreams you too could pace
Behind the wagon that we flung him in,
And watch the white eyes writhing in his face,
His hanging face, like a devil's sick of sin;   20
If you could hear, at every jolt, the blood
Come gargling from the froth-corrupted lungs,
Obscene as cancer, bitter as the cud
Of vile, incurable sores on innocent tongues, –
My friend, you would not tell with such high zest   25
To children ardent for some desperate glory,
The old Lie: *Dulce et decorum est*
Pro patria mori.[2]

Dulce et Decorum Est

1 *Five-Nines* Gas shells.
2 *Dulce . . . mori* "It is sweet and meet to die for

one's country. Sweet! and decorous!" [Owen's
translation from his letters of Horace, *Odes* 3.2.13;
p. 401 below].

Wystan Hugh Auden
(1907–1973)

The Icelandic sagas interested Auden from childhood and influenced his early poems. He told tales of family feuds and used half-lines reminiscent of Germanic medieval epic. Reykjavik, it must be said, not Rome, was the capital of Auden's heroic past. Moreover, much of his poetry is about modern figures. He wrote poetry for friends and for many other writers: A. E. Housman, Marianne Moore, E. M. Forster, and T. S. Eliot, to name but a few. Auden knew his classics, however, and invokes them in several poems. When he does so, his relationship to them is different from that of most earlier poets. To put it bluntly, the classics for Auden seem somehow to have missed the point. This is clear in "Secondary Epic," which begins "No, Virgil, no" and works its way through an indictment of Virgil's *ex post facto* prognostications to a final verse paragraph that begins,

> No, Virgil, no:
> Behind your verse so masterfully made
> We hear the weeping of a Muse betrayed.

In "The Horatians" Auden imagines a class of people who escape the grand questions and hide out in "obscure nooks in which Authority / never pokes a suspicious nose." In "Musée des Beaux Arts" Auden prefers the painting in which the fall of Icarus is barely noticed to the stirring tale in Ovid. "The Shield of Achilles" similarly focuses on what is not there in the classical model.

Homer's description of the shield of Achilles (*Iliad* 18.478–617; p. 250 below) is long and detailed, including sky, sea, earth, scenes of civic life, warfare, and the arts. Thetis, the divine mother of Achilles, asked Hephaestus, the armorer of the gods, to make the shield for her son Achilles, the greatest of all the Greek heroes at Troy. The splendor of the shield befits the divine maker and heroic bearer; it also epitomizes a vision of all human life that is fundamentally optimistic because of its comprehensiveness and its integration with the natural world. Auden's Thetis looks over the shoulder of his Hephaestus, however, and sees a very different scene

– an atomic-age nightmare of desolation, homelessness, injustice, tyranny, torture, and rape. Thetis is appalled, but Auden hints that a scene of such horror befits the ethos of her "Iron-hearted man-slaying" son or that of any warrior at all.

The poem is reprinted with permission from the volume of the same name (1955).

The Shield of Achilles

    She looked over his shoulder
       For vines and olive trees,
    Marble well-governed cities,
       And ships upon untamed seas,
    But there on the shining metal   5
       His hands had put instead
    An artificial wilderness
       And a sky like lead.

A plain without a feature, bare and brown,
  No blade of grass, no sign of neighborhood,   10
Nothing to eat and nowhere to sit down,
  Yet, congregated on its blankness, stood
  An unintelligible multitude,
A million eyes, a million boots in line,
Without expression, waiting for a sign.   15

Out of the air a voice without a face
  Proved by statistics that some cause was just
In tones as dry and level as the place:
  No one was cheered and nothing was discussed;
  Column by column in a cloud of dust   20
They marched away enduring a belief
Whose logic brought them, somewhere else, to grief.

    She looked over his shoulder
       For ritual pieties,
    White flower-garlanded heifers,   25
       Libation and sacrifice,
    But there on the shining metal
       Where the altar should have been,
    She saw by his flickering forge-light
       Quite another scene.   30

Barbed wire enclosed an arbitrary spot
  Where bored officials lounged (one cracked a joke)

And sentries sweated for the day was hot:
    A crowd of ordinary decent folk
    Watched from without and neither moved nor spoke   35
As three pale figures were led forth and bound
To three posts driven upright in the ground.

The mass and majesty of this world, all
    That carries weight and always weighs the same
Lay in the hands of others; they were small   40
    And could not hope for help and no help came:
    What their foes liked to do was done, their shame
Was all the worst could wish; they lost their pride
And died as men before their bodies died.

    She looked over his shoulder   45
        For athletes at their games,
    Men and women in a dance
        Moving their sweet limbs
    Quick, quick, to music,
        But there on the shining shield   50
    His hands had set no dancing-floor
        But a weed-choked field.

A ragged urchin, aimless and alone,
    Loitered about that vacancy; a bird
Flew up to safety from his well-aimed stone: 55
    That girls are raped, that two boys knife a third,
    Were axioms to him, who'd never heard
Of any world where promises were kept,
Or one could weep because another wept.

    The thin-lipped armorer,[1]   60
        Hephaestos, hobbled away;[2]
    Thetis of the shining breasts[3]
        Cried out in dismay
    At what the god had wrought
        To please her son, the strong   65
    Iron-hearted man-slaying Achilles[4]
    Who would not live long.[5]

THE SHIELD OF ACHILLES

1 *The thin-lipped armorer* this and other phrases in the stanza mimic the Homeric use of epithets such as "swift-footed," "grey-eyed," "sacker of cities."

2 *hobbled* Hephaestus has a limp in Greek mythology.

3 *shining breasts* Thetis was a sea goddess.

4 *man-slaying* a Homeric epithet, recalling the scene in which Priam kisses the "terrible, man-slaying hands" of Achilles (*Iliad* 24.478–9).

5 *Who . . . long* Achilles was fated to die at the hand of Paris soon after killing Hector in revenge for Hector's slaying of Patroclus.

Derek Walcott (1930–)

Walcott's birthplace, St. Lucia, is an island in the eastern Caribbean. During the seventeenth and early eighteenth centuries ownership of the island alternated between England and France, depending on the fortunes of war. (It was ceded finally to English rule at the end of the Napoleonic Wars in 1814 and did not gain independence as a nation until 1977.) As a result English is the dominant language on the island, but a French patois is also spoken. Walcott's poetry reflects the linguistic history of St. Lucia: his English is basically British, but it includes many West Indian colloquialisms and incorporates the French patois and the French place names with which he was familiar from childhood. Into the mix, however, Walcott also adds the language of European literature, including the Homeric tales. In his most ambitious work, he uses not only the names of Homeric heroes but also the kind of compound words (sometimes epithets) common to heroic poetry: "garden-cutlass," "red-kneed," "rope-bound," "flat-bed," and many others that are heroic linguistically but do not signify objects proper to a heroic world. This is altogether fitting, however, since throughout the poem, which won Walcott the Nobel Prize, he tells a modern story about poor people in a poor country, using the names of mighty princes from the heroic past.

"Omeros" is the modern Greek name for Homer. "Achille" and "Hector" are modern versions of Homeric names and the names of two characters in Walcott's poem; they fight over a woman named Helen who is pregnant, though she doesn't "know who for." Homer's heroes are only fighting over Helen in the secondary sense that they are agents of their countrymen – Menelaus and Paris – but Walcott is not bound to the letter of Homer's tale. Walcott's characters and themes have a history in Homeric epic, but they act in a modern world. The epic world resonates in the eastern Caribbean with its sea-girt isles and cutlass-bearing antagonists, but largely it recedes before the new reality of life, even as it provides the tone of the tale.

At the beginning of the poem another St. Lucian with a classical name, Philoctete, shows tourists where the gommier trees were cut down to make canoes, and he describes the making of the canoes in epic terms. The plunge *in medias res* (into the middle of things) is characteristic of ancient epic, and the use of the inner narrator recalls Odysseus in the *Odyssey* relating his adventures at the court of Alcinous on Phaeacia (and Aeneas at Carthage in the *Aeneid*). But, uncharacteristically, there is no invocation of any sort of Muse until 1.2.2, where Omeros is the name invoked, and there is little epic machinery. Some natural objects, such as the sun and moon, are described as gods, but they do not form a separate anthropomorphic world like that in classical epic. Structurally and thematically the canoe-making recalls Book 5 of the *Odyssey*, where Odysseus makes a raft to leave the island of Calypso (pp. 259–60 below). This is the first depiction of Odysseus in the *Odyssey* (Books 1–4 are mostly set on Ithaca and concern Telemachus), and perhaps it prompted Walcott to begin *Omeros* with the canoe-making scene. The tree-felling may also suggest a Judeo-Christian myth of the fall and expulsion from a biblical Paradise.

The passage from Walcott is reprinted with permission from *Omeros* (1990).

from *Omeros*

Book 1, Chapter 1

I

"This is how, one sunrise, we cut down them canoes."
Philoctete smiles for the tourists, who try taking[1]
his soul with their cameras. "Once wind bring the news[2]

to the *laurier-cannelles*, their leaves start shaking[3]
the minute the axe of sunlight hit the cedars,   5
because they could see the axes in our own eyes.

Wind lift the ferns. They sound like the sea that feed us
fishermen all our life, and the ferns nodded 'Yes,
the trees have to die.' So, fists jam in our jacket,

BOOK 1, CHAPTER 1

1 *Philoctete* the name recalls the hero Philoctetes, who was abandoned by the Troy-bound Greeks on the island of Lemnos when his leg became putridly infected from a snakebite. They returned for him near the end of the Trojan War when a prophet foretold that Troy could only be taken with the help of Heracles' bow and arrows, which were in the possession of Philoctetes. His wound was healed, and he contributed to the fall of Troy by shooting Paris.

2 *his soul with their cameras* Some West Indians believe that photographs steal the soul.

3 *laurier-cannelles* cinnamon trees or cinnamon laurels.

cause the heights was cold and our breath making feathers   10
like the mist, we pass the rum. When it came back, it
give us the spirit to turn into murderers.

I lift up the axe and pray for strength in my hands
to wound the first cedar. Dew was filling my eyes,
but I fire one more white rum. Then we advance."   15

For some extra silver, under a sea-almond,
he shows them a scar made by a rusted anchor,
rolling one trouser-leg up with the rising moan

of a conch. It has puckered like the corolla[4]
of a sea-urchin. He does not explain its cure.   20
"It have some things" – he smiles – "worth more than a dollar."

He has left it to a garrulous waterfall
to pour out his secret down La Sorcière, since[5]
the tall laurels fell, for the ground-dove's mating call

to pass on its note to the blue, tacit mountains   25
whose talkative brooks, carrying it to the sea,
turn into idle pools where the clear minnows shoot

and an egret stalks the reeds with one rusted cry
as it stabs and stabs the mud with one lifting foot.
Then silence is sawn in half by a dragonfly   30

as eels sign their names along the clear bottom-sand,
when the sunrise brightens the river's memory
and waves of huge ferns are nodding to the sea's sound.

Although smoke forgets the earth from which it ascends,
and nettles guard the holes where the laurels were killed,   35
an iguana hears the axes, clouding each lens

over its lost name, when the hunched island was called
"Iounalao," "Where the iguana is found."
But, taking its own time, the iguana will scale

the rigging of vines in a year, its dewlap fanned,   40
its elbows akimbo, its deliberate tail
moving with the island. The slit pods of its eyes

4   *corolla* the colorful, petal-like underside of the   5   *La Sorcière* a steep drop to the sea on the
sea-urchin.   island of Dominica in the eastern Caribbbean,
                                                             also known as L'Abym (the Abyss).

ripened in a pause that lasted for centuries,
that rose with the Aruacs' smoke till a new race[6]
unknown to the lizard stood measuring the trees.   45

These were their pillars that fell, leaving a blue space
for a single God where the old gods stood before.
The first god was a gommier. The generator[7]

began with a whine, and a shark, with sidewise jaw,
sent the chips flying like mackerel over water   50
into trembling weeds. Now they cut off the saw,

still hot and shaking, to examine the wound it
had made. They scraped off its gangrenous moss, then ripped
the wound clear of the net of vines that still bound it

to this earth, and nodded. The generator whipped   55
back to its work, and the chips flew much faster as
the shark's teeth gnawed evenly. They covered their eyes

from the splintering nest. Now, over the pastures
of bananas, the island lifted its horns. Sunrise
trickled down its valleys, blood splashed on the cedars,   60

and the grove flooded with the light of sacrifice.
A gommier was cracking. Its leaves an enormous
tarpaulin with the ridgepole gone. The creaking sound

made the fishermen leap back as the angling mast
leant slowly towards the troughs of ferns; then the ground   65
shuddered under the feet in waves, then the waves passed.

II
Achille looked up at the hole the laurel had left.[8]
He saw the hole silently healing with the foam
of a cloud like a breaker. Then he saw the swift

---

6 *Aruacs* the native people of the Caribbean.
7 *gommier* a tall, straight tree of the Caribbean
sometimes known as the candle tree; also the
name of a boat made from such a tree.
8 *Achille* recalling the pre-eminent Greek hero

Achilles, son of Peleus and Thetis; after killing the
Trojan captain Hector, Achilles was slain by Paris.
Achilles is the central character of the *Iliad*, as is
Odysseus of the *Odyssey* (see Homer, *Iliad* 1.1–
305; p. 240 below).

crossing the cloud-surf, a small thing, far from its home,   70
confused by the waves of blue hills. A thorn vine gripped
his heel. He tugged it free. Around him, other ships[9]

were shaping from the saw. With his cutlass he made
a swift sign of the cross, his thumb touching his lips
while the height rang with axes. He swayed back the blade,   75

and hacked the limbs from the dead god, knot after knot,
wrenching the severed veins from the trunk as he prayed:
"Tree! You can be a canoe! Or else you cannot!"

The bearded elders endured the decimation
of their tribe without uttering a syllable   80
of that language they had uttered as one nation,

the speech taught their saplings: from the towering babble
of the cedar to green vowels of *bois-campêche*.[10]
The *bois-flot* held its tongue with the *laurier-cannelle,*[11]

the red-skinned logwood endured the thorns in its flesh,   85
while the Aruacs' patois crackled in the smell
of a resinous bonfire that turned the leaves brown

with curling tongues, then ash, and their language was lost.
Like barbarians striding columns they have brought down,
the fishermen shouted. The gods were down at last.   90

Like pygmies they hacked the trunks of wrinkled giants
for paddles and oars. They were working with the same
concentration as an army of fire-ants.

But vexed by the smoke for defaming their forest,
blow-darts of mosquitoes kept needling Achille's trunk.   95
He frotted white rum on both forearms that, at least,[12]

those that he flattened to asterisks would die drunk.
They went for his eyes. They circled them with attacks
that made him weep blindly. Then the host retreated

---

9 *heel* presumably an allusion to the (non-Homeric) myth that Achilles was invulnerable except for his heel.

10 *bois-campêche* a tropical tree also known as bloodwood or logwood.

11 *bois-flot* Caribbean balsam tree.

12 *frotted* rubbed.

to high bamboo like the archers of Aruacs   100
running from the muskets of cracking logs, routed
by the fire's banner and the remorseless axe

hacking the branches. The men bound the big logs first
with new hemp and, like ants, trundled them to a cliff
to plunge through tall nettles. The logs gathered that thirst   105

for the sea which their own vined bodies were born with.
Now the trunks in eagerness to become canoes
ploughed into breakers of bushes, making raw holes

of boulders, feeling not death inside them, but use —
to roof the sea, to be hulls. Then, on the beach, coals   110
were set in their hollows that were chipped with an adze.

A flat-bed truck had carried their rope-bound bodies.
The charcoals, smouldering, cored the dugouts for days
till heat widened the wood enough for ribbed gunwales.

Under his tapping chisel Achille felt their hollows   115
exhaling to touch the sea, lunging towards the haze
of bird-printed islets, the beaks of their parted bows.

Then everything fit. The pirogues crouched on the sand[13]
like hounds with sprigs in their teeth. The priest
sprinkled them with a bell, then he made the swift's sign.   120

When he smiled at Achille's canoe, *In God We Troust,*
Achille said: "Leave it! Is God' spelling and mine."
After Mass one sunrise the canoes entered the troughs

of the surpliced shallows, and their nodding prows
agreed with the waves to forget their lives as trees;   125
one would serve Hector and another, Achilles.[14]

III

Achille peed in the dark, then bolted the half-door shut.
It was rusted from sea-blast. He hoisted the fishpot
with the crab of one hand; in the hole under the hut

13   *pirogues* canoes.
14   *Hector . . . Achilles* Hector is another charac-
ter in *Omeros*; the pairing of these names invokes
the *Iliad* and its heroic values. Note the deflation-
ary juxtaposition of the Latin form "Achilles"
with "Achille" (line 127).

he hid the cinder-block step. As he neared the depot,   130
the dawn breeze salted him coming up the grey street
past sleep-tight houses, under the sodium bars

of street-lamps, to the dry asphalt scraped by his feet;
he counted the small blue sparks of separate stars.
Banana fronds nodded to the undulating   135

anger of roosters, their cries screeching like red chalk
drawing hills on a board. Like his teacher, waiting,
the surf kept chafing at his deliberate walk.

By the time they met at the wall of the concrete shed
the morning star had stepped back, hating the odour   140
of nets and fish-guts, the light was hard overhead

and there was a horizon. He put the net by the door
of the depot, then washed his hands in its basin.
The surf did not raise its voice, even the ribbed hounds

around the canoes were quiet; a flask of l'absinthe   145
was passed by the fishermen, who made smacking sounds
and shook at the bitter bark from which it was brewed.

This was the light that Achille was happiest in.
When, before their hands gripped the gunwales, they stood
for the sea-width to enter them, feeling their day begin.   150

Seamus Heaney (1939–)

Born in Northern Ireland, Seamus Heaney studied Latin and Irish at St. Columb's College; he added Anglo-Saxon when he took his undergraduate degree at Queen's University Belfast in 1961. The study of ancient languages was an important part of his education, and it became an important part of his poetry in numerous ways. Heaney translated part of *Aeneid* 6 in his volume *Seeing Things* (1991), and his translation of *Beowulf* has become the standard throughout the English-speaking world. However, subtler, more pervasive influences of classical and medieval languages are also visible in Heaney's work as a poet, despite his attention to matters rooted in his own personal experience and in the political life of contemporary Ireland. The combination of translation, personal experience, and political awareness was, in fact, common in classical poetry, and there is no conflict between writing in response to the classics and in response to politics and personal life. Virgil triangulated the same elements in constructing his greatest works.

Heaney's "Bann Valley Eclogue" is in dialogue with Virgil literally and poetically.[1] The poem translates the theme, follows the order, and repeats much of the imagery of *Eclogue* 4 (p. 342 below), the famous poem in which Virgil envisions a return to the Golden Age through the birth of a child (probably a hoped-for son from the recent marriage of Antony and Octavia, Octavian's sister, but associated by Christian commentators with Jesus Christ). As a speaker in Heaney's poem, Virgil is the public, somewhat superior, voice of prophecy, history, and empire. His interlocutor, the Poet, is a more modest figure who feels incapable of producing a literary masterpiece. He is the personal, private voice of nostalgia, of memory and feeling, of the personal and the individual – of Heaney, one might say, as he thinks of himself at this moment. Heaney's Virgil delivers a sermon on the "stains" of history, while the Poet dwells in loving detail on the trefoil flowers

Seamus Heaney

1   Our selection and interpretation of this poem are indebted to Lorna Hardwick, *Reception*

Studies, Greece & Rome New Surveys in the Classics No. 33 (Oxford University Press, 2003), pp. 91–2.

he picked as a child. The thought of the new child and the hope of better times draw him back into his own childhood, so that he seems poised between past and future. But, like Virgil, Heaney is marking the beginning of the new millennium which he hopes will wash away the past and be free from "gunfires or explosions." Like Virgil, he associates the new era with a birth – not a child of powerful parents who will unite the known world, but a country girl who will bring to a smaller, greener world a peace no less magnificent.

The text is reprinted with permission from Heaney's collection *Electric Light* (2001).

Bann Valley Eclogue

Sicelides Musae, paulo maiora canamus[1]
– *VIRGIL, Eclogue IV*

POET: Bann Valley Muses, give us a song worth singing,[2]
Something that rises like the curtain in
Those words *And it came to pass* or *In the beginning.*
Help me to please my hedge-schoolmaster Virgil[3]
And the child that's due. Maybe, heavens, sing[4]   5
Better times for her and her generation.

VIRGIL: Here are my words you'll have to find a place for:
Carmen, ordo, nascitur, saeculum, gens.[5]
Their gist in your tongue and province should be clear
Even at this stage. Poetry, order, the times,   10
The nation, wrong and renewal, then an infant birth
And a flooding away of all the old miasma.

Whatever stains you, you rubbed it into yourselves:
Earth mark, birth mark, mould like the bloodied mould

BANN VALLEY ECLOGUE

1 *Sicelides . . . canamus* "Sicilian Muses, let us sing of greater things," *Eclogue* 4.1. "Sicilian," for Virgil, suggests Theocritus, the master of pastoral poetry.

2 *Bann Valley* separating Londonderry from Antrim in the northern part of Northern Ireland.

3 *hedge-schoolmaster* master of a hedge school – "a school held by a hedge-side or in the open air, as was once common in Ireland; hence, a poor, mean, low-class school" (*OED*).

4 *the child that's due* recalling the child whose birth is predicted in Virgil's fourth *Eclogue*.

5 *Carmen . . . gens* Latin words extracted from the fourth *Eclogue* (lines 4–5, 9): "song, order, he, she, or it is born, generation, race."

On Romulus's ditch-back. But when the waters break[6]   15
Bann's stream will overflow, the old markings
Will avail no more to keep east bank from west.
The valley will be washed like the new baby.

POET: *Pacatum orbem*: your words are too much nearly.[7]
Even "orb" by itself. What on earth could match it?   20
And then, last month, at noon-eclipse, wind dropped.
A millennial chill, birdless and dark, prepared.
A firstness steadied, a lastness, a born awareness
As name dawned into knowledge: I saw the orb.

VIRGIL: Eclipses won't be for this child. The cool she'll know   25
Will be the pram hood over her vestal head.
Big dog daisies will get fanked up in the spokes.
She'll lie on summer evenings listening to
A chug and slug going on in the milking parlour.
Let her never hear close gunfire or explosions.   30

POET: Why do I remember St. Patrick's mornings,
Being sent by my mother to the railway line
For the little trefoil, untouchable almost, the shamrock[8]
With its twining, binding, creepery, tough, thin roots
All over the place, in the stones between the sleepers.   35
Dew-scales shook off the leaves. Tear-ducts asperging.[9]

Child on the way, it won't be long until[10]
You land among us. Your mother's showing signs,
Out for her sunset walk among big round bales.
Planet earth like a teething ring suspended   40
Hangs by its world-chain. Your pram waits in the corner.
Cows are let out. They're sluicing the milk-house floor.

---

6   *Romulus* founder of Rome; he killed his twin
brother Remus when Remus leapt over the rising
walls of Rome in a dispute over who should rule
the new city. *ditch-back* (or *ditch-bank*) an earthen
mound or fence.
7   *Pacatum orbem* "the world pacified"; a phrase
from the fourth *Eclogue* (line 17).

8   *trefoil* a clover; an Irish version of the "wan-
dering ivy and cyclamen and lotus flowers mixed
with laughing acanthus" that appear in *Eclogue*
4.18–20.
9   *asperging* sprinkling, as with holy water in a
church.
10   *Child on the way* compare *Eclogue* 4.48–9
(p. 344 below).

Classical Writers

Homer (eighth century BCE?)

It is difficult to exaggerate the influence of the *Iliad* and *Odyssey*. For the Greeks, they defined the norms of Hellenic culture and were a perennial source of pride and imitation. From a broader perspective they inaugurate the history of western literature, setting a standard of quality that has rarely been equaled and never surpassed. The *Iliad* and *Odyssey* depict a heroic age when gods mingled on earth with human beings and a pan-Hellenic expedition sailed to Troy to restore Helen to her rightful husband. The *Iliad* recounts the wrath of Achilles, the best Greek hero, and its tragic consequences. It is a martial poem, much occupied with scenes of battle but infused with humanity and a keen awareness of the mortality that distinguishes human beings from the gods. The *Odyssey* describes the arduous return of Odysseus to Ithaca and his faithful wife Penelope. Its tale of wandering and adventure, reunion and vengeance, has a lighter and more varied character than the *Iliad*, and it deeply influenced the genre of the medieval romance.

The Greeks believed both epics to have been written by a single poet called Homer, of whom they knew virtually nothing – though linguistic evidence corroborates their supposition that the epics originated in Ionia, on the western coast of Asia Minor. Modern scholarship has labored on the "Homeric Question" for the past two hundred years and has done much to reveal traditional elements of the poems – their artificial dialect, formulaic language, typical scenes, and common stock of myths – that evolved over hundreds of years of oral composition and performance by non-literate bards. This is not to deny the possibility that a composer of unusual skill and imagination, perhaps named Homer, was responsible for their present form, for it is hard to accept that poems so unified and carefully structured resulted from mere accretion over time. Whether or not this was the case; whether or not the new technique of writing played a role in their composition and what that role might have been; and whether "Homer" was responsible for both epics or, as even some Greeks believed, the *Iliad* and *Odyssey* are by different authors, are matters that are still debated.

The works of Homer unified and inspired the scattered city-states of Greece with a common vision of heroic character and achievement. The poems have served a similar national purpose ever since, even though Plato complained that they encourage thoughtless acceptance of notions that an inquiring mind should question. There are parallels in the Anglo-Saxon epic tales told by scops; in the songs of the Slavic guslars; in the praise poetry of the southern African imbongi; and in many other forms in other cultures. But the *Iliad* and the *Odyssey* have transcended their local origins as no other oral poems and become part of what defines and unifies not only the Greek world but all of western culture.

Alexander the Great is reported to have kept a copy of the *Iliad* under his pillow, and Greek scholars of his period and beyond enshrined the text in numerous editions and commentaries. When Virgil designed a national epic for Augustan Rome, he took Homer as his model and consciously imitated the Greek poet. Although all Romans with any pretensions to learning read Homer in Greek, the Greek myths of Troy were of course translated into Latin and first penetrated medieval Western Europe in that form or, more often, in the form of Virgil's imitative *Aeneid*. Petrarch, although he was among the most learned men of thirteenth-century Europe, could not read Homer in Greek. Dante drew more on Virgil than on Homer, and for most other early modern poets, Virgil was the more influential author. In England, Milton, although he knew Greek well, modeled his epic more closely on the *Aeneid* than the *Iliad* (and he used biblical sources as much as classical ones). In fact, it was only in the nineteenth century that the balance of classical influence shifted among ambitious British poets from Latin to Greek. When Keats wrote "On First Looking into Chapman's Homer," he lamented his want of Greek and pointed the way toward a poetic idiom that would be more reflective of Homer than of Virgil. In the twentieth century the preference for Homer largely continued. To give just two examples, James Joyce called his modern epic *Ulysses* (1921) after the Latin name for the Greek hero, and Derek Walcott called his epic of modern West Indian life *Omeros* (p. 227 above), after the modern Greek name for Homer.

from the *Iliad*

Book 1, lines 1–305

The first line of the *Iliad* announces its subject – the wrath of Achilles, which decisively affected the course of the Trojan War. The first book relates the cause of Achilles' wrath. It arose over women who had been given as war-prizes to Achilles and Agamemnon. Agamemnon's concubine, Chryseis, was the daughter of a priest of Apollo called Chryses. When Agamemnon rejects Chryses' reasonable request to ransom his daughter, Apollo avenges the insult to his priest by raining destruction on the Greek host. At the prompting of Achilles, the Greek seer

Calchas identifies the cause of Apollo's anger, whereupon Achilles demands that Agamemnon return Chryseis to her father. A quarrel erupts, which ends in Agamemnon's agreeing to return Chryseis but only on condition of replacing her with Achilles' concubine, Briseis. The insult to his honor causes Achilles to withdraw from battle, which sets in motion the tragic events of the poem.

The scenes of Book 1 are among the most memorable in the epic. They introduce us to the key players on the Greek side with masterly economy. The opening scenes also introduce us to the most important gods, who split between supporters of the Greeks and Trojans. They introduce us too to the values of the Homeric hero, and in particular, his obsession with honor – his demand for recognition in the form of respect and prizes. Achilles is fond of Briseis, but his anger stems less from the loss of her company than from his loss of face before his comrades. The honor he receives is his sole compensation for bearing the brunt of battle, and his need for recognition is heightened by the knowledge that he is doomed to die before long.

The translation is by Edward George Geoffrey Smith Stanley, fourteenth earl of Derby (1799–1869). A serious student of the classics at Eton and at Christ Church, Oxford, Stanley returned to his studies in retirement after a busy political career in which he served in both Whig and Conservative cabinets, as opposition leader more than once, and briefly as prime minister. His *Iliad of Homer Rendered into English Blank Verse* (1864) was acclaimed and ran to six editions in the first three years of publication. Stanley uses alliteration, Miltonic blank verse, and inverted word order to represent the epic grandeur of Homer's dactylic hexameter. He employs many compound words, some of which, like his alliteration, seem to suggest the high style of Old English epic, to give the English poem the flavor of Homer's poetic diction – his epithets and his use of dialect. Late twentieth-century translators have tended to use more common words and fewer syntactical inversions, making a Homer who sounds less archaic and more normative. Derby's translation is still very readable, however, and his sense of the Homeric idiom is very plausible.

Of Peleus' son, Achilles, sing, O Muse,[1]
The vengeance, deep and deadly; whence to Greece[2]
Unnumbered ills arose; which many a soul
Of mighty warriors to the viewless shades
Untimely sent; they on the battle plain   5
Unburied lay, a prey to rav'ning dogs,
And carrion birds; but so had Jove decreed,[3]

BOOK 1, LINES 1–305

1 *Peleus* king of Phthia in Thessaly; *Achilles* the best Greek warrior at Troy.

2 *vengeance* literally, "wrath"; the first word of the *Iliad* in the original Greek (μῆνιν).

3 *Jove* Latin name for Zeus.

From that sad day when first in wordy war,
The mighty Agamemnon, King of men,[4]
Confronted stood by Peleus' godlike son.   10
    Say then, what God the fatal strife provoked?
Jove's and Latona's son; he, filled with wrath[5]
Against the King, with deadly pestilence
The camp afflicted – and the people died –
For Chryses' sake, his priest, whom Atreus' son[6]   15
With scorn dismissed, when to the Grecian ships
He came, his captive daughter to redeem,[7]
With costly ransom charged; and in his hand
The sacred fillet of his God he bore,[8]
And golden staff; to all he sued, but chief   20
To Atreus' sons, twin captains of the host:[9]
"Ye sons of Atreus, and ye well-greaved Greeks,[10]
May the great Gods, who on Olympus dwell,[11]
Grant you yon hostile city to destroy,
And home return in safety; but my child   25
Restore, I pray; her proffered ransom take,
And in his priest, the Lord of Light revere."
    Then through the ranks assenting murmurs ran,
The priest to rev'rence, and the ransom take:
Not so Atrides; he, with haughty mien,[12]   30
And bitter speech, the trembling sire addressed:
"Old man, I warn thee, that beside our ships
I find thee not, or ling'ring now, or back[13]
Returning; lest thou prove of small avail
Thy golden staff, and fillet of thy God.   35
Her I release not, till her youth be fled;
Within my walls, in Argos, far from home,[14]
Her lot is cast, domestic cares to ply,
And share a master's bed. For thee, begone!
Incense me not, lest ill betide thee now."   40
    He said: the old man trembled, and obeyed;
Beside the many-dashing Ocean's shore[15]

---

4 *Agamemnon* king of Mycenae; commander of the Greek expedition.
5 *Jove's and Latona's son* Apollo.
6 *Chryses* a priest of Apollo; *Atreus' son* Agamemnon.
7 *daughter* Chryseis.
8 *fillet* a ribbon worn in religious rituals.
9 *Atreus' sons* Agamemnon and Menelaus; Menelaus was the husband of Helen.
10 *well-greaved* a Homeric epithet; greaves were metal shin protectors.

11 *Olympus* a mountain in northern Greece believed to be the home of the gods.
12 *Atrides* the son of Atreus; Agamemnon.
13 *or . . . or* either . . . or.
14 *Argos* the part of Greece containing Mycenae.
15 *many-dashing* a Homeric epithet for the sea (πολύφλοισβος), variously translated; the Loeb Classical Library edition has "loud-resounding."

Silent he passed; and all apart, he prayed
To great Apollo, fair Latona's son:
"Hear me, God of the silver bow! whose care   45
Chrysa surrounds, and Cilla's lovely vale;[16]
Whose sov'reign sway o'er Tenedos extends;[17]
O Smintheus, hear! if e'er my offered gifts[18]
Found favour in thy sight; if e'er to thee
I burned the fat of bulls and choicest goats,   50
Grant me this boon – upon the Grecian host
Let thine unerring darts avenge my tears."
   Thus as he prayed, his prayer Apollo heard:
Along Olympus' heights he passed, his heart
Burning with wrath; behind his shoulders hung   55
His bow, and ample quiver; at his back
Rattled the fateful arrows as he moved;
Like the night-cloud he passed, and from afar
He bent against the ships, and sped the bolt;
And fierce and deadly twanged the silver bow.   60
First on the mules and dogs, on man the last,
Was poured the arrowy storm; and through the camp,
Constant and num'rous, blazed the fun'ral fires.
   Nine days the heav'nly Archer on the troops
Hurled his dread shafts; the tenth, th' assembled Greeks   65
Achilles called to council; so inspired
By Juno, white-armed Goddess, who beheld[19]
With pitying eyes the wasting hosts of Greece.
When all were met, and closely thronged around,
Rose the swift-footed chief, and thus began: 70
   "Great son of Atreus, to my mind there seems,
If we would 'scape from death, one only course,
Home to retrace our steps: since here at once
By war and pestilence our forces waste.
But seek we first some prophet, or some priest,   75
Or some wise vision-seer (since visions too[20]
From Jove proceed), who may the cause explain,
Which with such deadly wrath Apollo fires:
If for neglected hecatombs or prayers[21]
He blame us; or if fat of lambs and goats   80
May soothe his anger and the plague assuage."

---

16 *Chrysa . . . Cilla* towns in the region of Troy.
17 *Tenedos* island near Troy.
18 *Smintheus* an obscure epithet of Apollo.
19 *Juno* Latin name for Hera, wife of Zeus; a supporter of the Greeks; "white-armed" (λευκώλενος) is one of her regular epithets.

20 *vision-seer* ὀνειροπόλος, an interpreter of dreams.
21 *hecatombs* sacrifices of one hundred oxen.

This said, he sat; and Thestor's son arose,
Calchas, the chief of seers, to whom were known[22]
The present, and the future, and the past;
Who, by his mystic art, Apollo's gift,   85
Guided to Ilium's shore the Grecian fleet.[23]
Who thus with cautious speech replied, and said:
"Achilles, loved of Heav'n, thou bidd'st me say
Why thus incensed the far-destroying King;
Therefore I speak; but promise thou, and swear,   90
By word and hand, to bear me harmless through.
For well I know my speech must one offend,
The Argive chief, o'er all the Greeks supreme;
And terrible to men of low estate
The anger of a King; for though awhile   95
He veil his wrath, yet in his bosom pent
It still is nursed, until the time arrive;
Say, then, wilt thou protect me, if I speak?"
    Him answered thus Achilles, swift of foot:
"Speak boldly out whate'er thine art can tell;   100
For by Apollo's self I swear, whom thou,
O Calchas, serv'st, and who thy words inspires,
That, while I live, and see the light of Heav'n,
Not one of all the Greeks shall dare on thee,
Beside our ships, injurious hands to lay: 105
No, not if Agamemnon's self were he,
Who 'mid our warriors boasts the foremost place."
    Emboldened thus, th' unerring prophet spoke:
"Not for neglected hecatombs or prayers,
But for his priest, whom Agamemnon scorned,   110
Nor took his ransom, nor his child restored;
On his account the Far-destroyer sends[24]
This scourge of pestilence, and yet will send;
Nor shall we cease his heavy hand to feel,
Till to her sire we give the bright-eyed girl,   115
Unbought, unransomed, and to Chrysa's shore
A solemn hecatomb despatch; this done,
The God, appeased, his anger may remit."
    This said, he sat; and Atreus' godlike son,
The mighty monarch, Agamemnon, rose,   120
His dark soul filled with fury, and his eyes
Flashing like flames of fire; on Calchas first
A with'ring glance he cast, and thus he spoke:

22 *Calchas* a famous prophet.   24 *Far-destroyer* Apollo; ἐκηβόλος (far-shooter)
23 *Ilium* Troy.   is one of Apollo's epithets.

"Prophet of ill! thou never speak'st to me
But words of evil omen; for thy soul   125
Delights to augur ill, but aught of good
Thou never yet hast promised, nor performed.
And now among the Greeks thou spread'st abroad
Thy lying prophecies, that all these ills
Come from the Far-destroyer, for that I   130
Refused the ransom of my lovely prize,
And that I rather chose herself to keep,
To me not less than Clytemnestra dear,[25]
My virgin-wedded wife; nor less adorned
In gifts of form, of feature, or of mind.   135
Yet, if it must be so, I give her back;
I wish my people's safety, not their death.
But seek me out forthwith some other spoil,
Lest empty-handed I alone appear
Of all the Greeks; for this would ill beseem;   140
And how I lose my present share, ye see."
    To whom Achilles, swift of foot, replied:
"Haughtiest of men, and greediest of the prey!
How shall our valiant Greeks for thee seek out
Some other spoil? no common fund have we   145
Of hoarded treasures; what our arms have won
From captured towns, has been already shared,
Nor can we now resume th' apportioned spoil.
Restore the maid, obedient to the God!
And if Heav'n will that we the strong-built walls   150
Of Troy should raze, our warriors will to thee
A threefold, fourfold recompense assign."
    To whom the monarch Agamemnon thus:
"Think not, Achilles, valiant though thou art
In fight, and godlike, to defraud me thus;   155
Thou shalt not so persuade me, nor o'erreach.
Think'st thou to keep thy portion of the spoil,
While I with empty hands sit humbly down?
The bright-eyed girl thou bidd'st me to restore;
If then the valiant Greeks for me seek out   160
Some other spoil, some compensation just,
'Tis well: if not, I with my own right hand
Will from some other chief, from thee perchance,
Or Ajax, or Ulysses, wrest his prey;[26]
And woe to him, on whomsoe'er I call!   165

---

25 *Clytemnestra* wife of Agamemnon.   26 *Ajax* leader of the men of Salamis; *Ulysses*
                                               Latin name for Odysseus, king of Ithaca.

But this for future counsel we remit:
Haste we then now our dark-ribbed bark to launch,
Muster a fitting crew, and place on board
The sacred hecatomb; then last embark
The fair Chryseis; and in chief command   170
Let some one of our councillors be placed,
Ajax, Ulysses, or Idomeneus,[27]
Or thou, the most ambitious of them all,
That so our rites may soothe the angry God."
   To whom Achilles thus with scornful glance;   175
"Oh, clothed in shamelessness! oh, sordid soul!
How canst thou hope that any Greek for thee
Will brave the toils of travel or of war?
Well dost thou know that 't was no feud of mine
With Troy's brave sons that brought me here in arms;   180
They never did me wrong; they never drove
My cattle, or my horses; never sought
In Phthia's fertile, life-sustaining fields[28]
To waste the crops; for wide between us lay
The shadowy mountains and the roaring sea.   185
With thee, O void of shame! with thee we sailed,
For Menelaus and for thee, ingrate,
Glory and fame on Trojan crests to win.
All this hast thou forgotten, or despised;
And threat'nest now to wrest from me the prize   190
I laboured hard to win, and Greeks bestowed.
Nor does my portion ever equal thine,
When on some populous town our troops have made
Successful war; in the contentious fight
The larger portion of the toil is mine;   195
But when the day of distribution comes,
Thine is the richest spoil; while I, forsooth,
Must be too well content to bear on board
Some paltry prize for all my warlike toil.
To Phthia now I go; so better far,   200
To steer my homeward course, and leave thee here
But little like, I deem, dishonouring me,
To fill thy coffers with the spoils of war."
   Whom answered Agamemnon, King of men:
"Fly then, if such thy mind! I ask thee not   205
On mine account to stay; others there are
Will guard my honour and avenge my cause:
And chief of all, the Lord of counsel, Jove!
Of all the Heav'n-born Kings, thou art the man

---

27 *Idomeneus* leader of the Cretans.   28 *Phthia* Achilles' home in Thessaly.

I hate the most; for thou delight'st in nought   210
But war and strife: thy prowess I allow;
Yet this, remember, is the gift of Heav'n.
Return then, with thy vessels, if thou wilt,
And with thy followers, home; and lord it there
Over thy Myrmidons! I heed thee not![29]   215
I care not for thy fury! Hear my threat:
Since Phoebus wrests Chryseis from my arms,[30]
In mine own ship, and with mine own good crew,
Her I send forth; and, in her stead, I mean,
Ev'n from thy tent, myself, to bear thy prize,   220
The fair Briseis; that henceforth thou know[31]
How far I am thy master; and that, taught
By thine example, others too may fear
To rival me, and brave me to my face."
   Thus while he spake, Achilles chafed with rage;   225
And in his manly breast his heart was torn
With thoughts conflicting – whether from his side
To draw his mighty sword, and thrusting by
Th' assembled throng, to kill th' insulting King;
Or school his soul, and keep his anger down.   230
But while in mind and spirit thus he mused,
And half unsheathed his sword, from Heav'n came down
Minerva, sent by Juno, white-armed Queen,[32]
Whose love and care both chiefs alike enjoyed.
She stood behind, and by the yellow hair   235
She held the son of Peleus, visible
To him alone, by all the rest unseen.
Achilles, wond'ring, turned, and straight he knew
The blue-eyed Pallas; awful was her glance;[33]
Whom thus the chief with wingèd words addressed: 240
   "Why com'st thou, child of aegis-bearing Jove?[34]
To see the arrogance of Atreus' son?
But this I say, and will make good my words,
This insolence may cost him soon his life."
   To whom the blue-eyed Goddess thus replied: 245
"From Heav'n I came, to curb, if thou wilt hear,
Thy fury; sent by Juno, white-armed Queen,
Whose love and care ye both alike enjoy.

29 *Myrmidons* the contingent led by Achilles.   33 *Pallas* Athena.
30 *Phoebus* Apollo.
31 *Briseis* the concubine and war-prize of   34 *aegis-bearing* the aegis was a skin worn over
Achilles.   the breast, with snaky tassels and a picture of a
32 *Minerva* Latin name for Athena, a supporter   Gorgon's head; this is a common epithet of Jove,
of the Greeks.   from whose head Pallas Athena sprang
full-born.

Cease, then, these broils, and draw not thus thy sword;[35]
In words, indeed, assail him as thou wilt.   250
But this I promise, and will make it good,
The time shall come, when for this insolence
A threefold compensation shall be thine;
Only be swayed by me, and curb thy wrath."
    Whom answered thus Achilles, swift of foot: 255
"Goddess, I needs must yield to your commands,
Indignant though I be – for so 'tis best;
Who hears the Gods, of them his prayers are heard."
    He said: and on the silver hilt he stayed
His pow'rful hand, and flung his mighty sword   260
Back to its scabbard, to Minerva's word
Obedient: she her heav'nward course pursued
To join th' Immortals in th' abode of Jove.
But Peleus' son, with undiminished wrath,
Atrides thus with bitter words addressed: 265
    "Thou sot, with eye of dog, and heart of deer!
Who never dar'st to lead in armèd fight
Th' assembled host, nor with a chosen few
To man the secret ambush – for thou fear'st
To look on death – no doubt 'tis easier far,   270
Girt with thy troops, to plunder of his right
Whoe'er may venture to oppose thy will!
A tyrant King, because thou rul'st o'er slaves!
Were it not so, this insult were thy last.
But this I say, and with an oath confirm,   275
By this my royal staff, which never more
Shall put forth leaf nor spray, since first it left
Upon the mountain-side its parent stem,
Nor blossom more; since all around the axe
Hath lopped both leaf and bark, and now 'tis borne   280
Emblem of justice, by the sons of Greece,
Who guard the sacred ministry of law
Before the face of Jove! a mighty oath!
The time shall come, when all the sons of Greece
Shall mourn Achilles' loss; and thou the while,   285
Heart-rent, shalt be all-impotent to aid,
When by the warrior-slayer Hector's hand[36]
Many shall fall; and then thy soul shall mourn
The slight on Grecia's bravest warrior cast."
    Thus spoke Pelides; and upon the ground[37]   290
He cast his staff, with golden studs embossed,

35 *broils* arguments.   37 *Pelides* the son of Peleus; Achilles.
36 *Hector* son of Priam; the best Trojan warrior.

And took his seat; on th' other side, in wrath,
Atrides burned; but Nestor interposed;[38]
Nestor, the leader of the Pylian host,
The smooth-tongued chief, from whose persuasive lips   295
Sweeter than honey flowed the stream of speech.
Two generations of the sons of men
For him were past and gone, who with himself
Were born and bred on Pylos' lovely shore,
And o'er the third he now held royal sway.   300
He thus with prudent words the chiefs addressed:
  "Alas, alas! what grief is this for Greece!
What joy for Priam, and for Priam's sons![39]
What exultation for the men of Troy,
To hear of feuds 'tween you, of all the Greeks   305
The first in council, and the first in fight!
Yet, hear my words, I pray; in years, at least,
Ye both must yield to me; and in times past
I lived with men, and they despised me not,
Abler in counsel, greater than yourselves.   310
Such men I never saw, and ne'er shall see,
As Pirithous and Dryas, wise and brave,[40]
Coeneus, Exadius, godlike Polypheme,
And Theseus, Aegeus' more than mortal son.
The mightiest they among the sons of men;   315
The mightiest they, and of the forest beasts
Strove with the mightiest, and their rage subdued.
With them from distant lands, from Pylos' shore
I joined my forces, and their call obeyed;
With them I played my part; with them, not one   320
Would dare to fight of mortals now on earth.
Yet they my counsels heard, my voice obeyed;
And hear ye also, for my words are wise.
Nor thou, though great thou be, attempt to rob
Achilles of his prize, but let him keep   325
The spoil assigned him by the sons of Greece;
Nor thou, Pelides, with the monarch strive
In rivalry; for ne'er to sceptred King
Hath Jove such pow'rs, as to Atrides, giv'n;
And valiant though thou art, and Goddess-born,[41]   330
Yet mightier he, for wider is his sway.
Atrides, curb thy wrath! while I beseech

---

38 *Nestor* king of Pylos; the oldest and wisest
Greek hero.
39 *Priam* king of Troy.

40 *Pirithous* king of the Lapiths; he heads a list
of heroes of Nestor's generation.
41 *Goddess-born* Achilles' mother was the sea
goddess Thetis.

Achilles to forbear; in whom the Greeks
From adverse war their great defender see."
  To whom the monarch, Agamemnon, thus: 335
"O father, full of wisdom are thy words;
But this proud chief o'er all would domineer;
O'er all he seeks to rule, o'er all to reign,
To all to dictate; which I will not bear.
Grant that the Gods have giv'n him warlike might,   340
Gave they unbridled license to his tongue?"
  To whom Achilles, interrupting, thus:
"Coward and slave indeed I might be deemed,
Could I submit to make thy word my law;
To others thy commands; seek not to me   345
To dictate, for I follow thee no more.
But hear me speak, and ponder what I say:
For the fair girl I fight not (since you choose
To take away the prize yourselves bestowed)
With thee or any one; but of the rest   350
My dark swift ship contains, against my will
On nought shalt thou, unpunished, lay thy hand.
Make trial if thou wilt, that these may know;
Thy life-blood soon should reek upon my spear."
  After this conflict keen of angry speech,   355
The chiefs arose, the assembly was dispersed.

Book 18, lines 478–617

While Achilles remained with the ships and refused to fight, his best friend Patroclus borrowed his armor and took the field against the Trojans in the guise of the great Greek warrior. Hector brought him down, however, and stripped the armor from his corpse. Thetis, the divine mother of Achilles, then persuaded Hephaestus to forge new equipment for her son. The centerpiece of Hephaestus' handiwork is a magnificently decorated shield which Homer describes in minute detail. The decorations encompass the whole cosmos of the Homeric world. They include the sun, moon, and stars; a city at peace and a city at war; agricultural scenes and a dance. Such splendor is worthy of its divine craftsman and heroic recipient. In addition, the shield throws into broad perspective the claustrophobic world of battle that occupies the foreground of the *Iliad*. Homer's description of the shield of Achilles is the ultimate model for the literary feature known as ekphrasis – the description of a work of art. Among many later examples of ekphrasis are the cup description in Theocritus' *Idyll* 1 (pp. 303–4 below) and the paintings on Juno's temple in Virgil, *Aeneid* 1. A modern, though idiosyncratic, representative of this tradition is Keats's "Ode on a Grecian Urn" (p. 199 above).

  The translation is by Edward, earl of Derby (1864; see p. 241 above).

And first a shield he fashioned, vast and strong,[1]
With rich adornment; circled with a rim,
Threefold, bright-gleaming, whence a silver belt
Depended; of five folds the shield was formed;[2]
And on its surface many a rare design   5
Of curious art his practised skill had wrought.
   Thereon were figured earth, and sky, and sea,
The ever-circling sun, and full-orbed moon,
And all the signs that crown the vault of Heav'n;
Pleiads and Hyads, and Orion's might,[3]   10
And Arctos, called the Wain, who wheels on high
His circling course, and on Orion waits;
Sole star that never bathes in th' ocean wave.
   And two fair populous towns were sculptured there;
In one were marriage pomp and revelry.   15
And brides, in gay procession, through the streets
With blazing torches from their chambers borne,
While frequent rose the hymeneal song.[4]
Youths whirled around in joyous dance, with sound
Of flute and harp; and, standing at their doors,   20
Admiring women on the pageant gazed.
   Meanwhile a busy throng the forum filled:
There between two a fierce contention rose,
About a death-fine; to the public one[5]
Appealed, asserting to have paid the whole;   25
While one denied that he had aught received.
Both were desirous that before the Judge
The issue should be tried; with noisy shouts
Their several partisans encouraged each.
The heralds stilled the tumult of the crowd: 30
On polished chairs, in solemn circle, sat
The rev'rend Elders; in their hands they held
The loud-voiced heralds' sceptres; waving these,
They heard th' alternate pleadings; in the midst
Two talents lay of gold, which he should take   35
Who should before them prove his righteous cause.
   Before the second town two armies lay,
In arms refulgent; to destroy the town
Th' assailants threatened, or among themselves

BOOK 18, LINES 478–617

1 *he* Hephaestus.
2 *Depended* hung down.
3 *Pleiads* the Pleiades; the list of constellations continues with the Hyades, Orion, and Ursa

Major, also known as the Wain, the Big Dipper, and the Plough.
4 *hymeneal* nuptial; wedding.
5 *death-fine* (Greek ποινή) a sum exacted by survivors in a kind of civil suit involving wrongful death or manslaughter.

Of all the wealth within the city stored   40
An equal half, as ransom, to divide.
The terms rejecting, the defenders manned
A secret ambush; on the walls they placed
Women and children mustered for defence,
And men by age enfeebled; forth they went,   45
By Mars and Pallas led; these, wrought in gold,[6]
In golden arms arrayed, above the crowd
For beauty and stature, as befitting Gods,
Conspicuous shone; of lesser height the rest.
But when the destined ambuscade was reached,   50
Beside the river, where the shepherds drove
Their flocks and herds to water, down they lay,
In glitt'ring arms accoutred; and apart
They placed two spies, to notify betimes[7]
Th' approach of flocks of sheep and lowing herds.   55
These, in two shepherds' charge, ere long appeared,
Who, unsuspecting as they moved along,
Enjoyed the music of their past'ral pipes.
They on the booty, from afar discerned,
Sprang from their ambuscade; and cutting off   60
The herds, and fleecy flocks, their guardians slew.
Their comrades heard the tumult, where they sat
Before their sacred altars, and forthwith
Sprang on their cars, and with fast-stepping steeds
Pursued the plund'rers, and o'ertook them soon.   65
There on the river's bank they met in arms,
And each at other hurled their brazen spears.
And there were figured Strife, and Tumult wild,
And deadly Fate, who in her iron grasp
One newly-wounded, one unwounded bore,   70
While by the feet from out the press she dragged
Another slain: about her shoulders hung
A garment crimsoned with the blood of men.
Like living men they seemed to move, to fight,
To drag away the bodies of the slain.   75
    And there was grav'n a wide-extended plain
Of fallow land, rich, fertile, mellow soil,
Thrice ploughed; where many ploughmen up and down
Their teams were driving; and as each attained
The limit of the field, would one advance,   80
And tender him a cup of gen'rous wine:
Then would he turn, and to the end again

6 *Mars* Latin name for Ares, the war god; *Pallas*   7 *betimes* early.
Athena.

Along the furrow cheerly drive his plough.
And still behind them darker showed the soil,
The true presentment of a new-ploughed field, 85
Though wrought in gold; a miracle of art.
　　There too was grav'n a corn-field, rich in grain,[8]
Where with sharp sickles reapers plied their task,
And thick, in even swathe, the trusses fell;[9]
The binders, following close, the bundles tied: 90
Three were the binders; and behind them boys
In close attendance waiting, in their arms
Gathered the bundles, and in order piled.
Amid them, staff in hand, in silence stood
The King, rejoicing in the plenteous swathe. 95
A little way removed, the heralds slew
A sturdy ox, and now beneath an oak
Prepared the feast; while women mixed, hard by,
White barley porridge for the lab'rers' meal.
　　And, with rich clusters laden, there was grav'n 100
A vineyard fair, all gold; of glossy black
The bunches were, on silver poles sustained;
Around, a darksome trench; beyond, a fence
Was wrought, of shining tin; and through it led
One only path, by which the bearers passed, 105
Who gathered in the vineyard's bounteous store.
There maids and youths, in joyous spirits bright,
In woven baskets bore the luscious fruit.
A boy, amid them, from a clear-toned harp
Drew lovely music; well his liquid voice 110
The strings accompanied; they all with dance
And song harmonious joined, and joyous shouts,
As the gay bevy lightly tripped along.
　　Of straight-horned cattle too a herd was grav'n;
Of gold and tin the heifers all were wrought: 115
They to the pasture, from the cattle-yard,
With gentle lowings, by a babbling stream,
Where quiv'ring reed-beds rustled, slowly moved.
Four golden shepherds walked beside the herd,
By nine swift dogs attended; then amid 120
The foremost heifers sprang two lions fierce
Upon the lordly bull: he, bellowing loud,
Was dragged along, by dogs and youths pursued.
The tough bull's-hide they tore, and gorging lapped
Th' intestines and dark blood; with vain attempt 125

8　*corn-field* a field of any kind of grain.　　9　*trusses* bundles.

The herdsmen following closely, to the attack
Cheered their swift dogs; these shunned the lions' jaws,
And close around them baying, held aloof.
   And there the skilful artist's hand had traced
A pasture broad, with fleecy flocks o'erspread,   130
In a fair glade, with fold, and tents, and pens.
   There, too, the skilful artist's hand had wrought
With curious workmanship, a mazy dance,
Like that which Daedalus in Cnossus erst[10]
At fair-haired Ariadne's bidding framed.[11]   135
There, laying each on other's wrists their hand,
Bright youths and many-suitored maidens danced:
In fair white linen these; in tunics those,
Well woven, shining soft with fragrant oils;
These with fair coronets were crowned, while those   140
With golden swords from silver belts were girt.
Now whirled they round with nimble practised feet,
Easy, as when a potter, seated, turns
A wheel, new fashioned by his skilful hand,
And spins it round, to prove if true it run;   145
Now featly moved in well-beseeming ranks.[12]
A num'rous crowd, around, the lovely dance
Surveyed, delighted; while an honoured Bard
Sang, as he struck the lyre, and to the strain
Two tumblers, in the midst, were whirling round.   150
   About the margin of the massive shield
Was wrought the mighty strength of th' ocean stream.[13]
   The shield completed, vast and strong, he forged
A breastplate, dazzling bright as flame of fire;
And next, a weighty helmet for his head,   155
Fair, richly wrought, with crest of gold above;
Then last, well-fitting greaves of pliant tin.
   The skilled artificer his works complete
Before Achilles' Goddess-mother laid:[14]
She, like a falcon, from the snow-clad heights   160
Of huge Olympus, darted swiftly down,
Charged with the glitt'ring arms by Vulcan wrought.[15]

---

10   *Daedalus* legendary craftsman famous for the
labyrinth he built to house the Minotaur; *Cnossus*
city of Crete; *erst* formerly; some time ago.
11   *Ariadne* daughter of king Minos and
Pasiphae.
12   *featly* elegantly.

13   *ocean stream* a legendary river encircling the
world.
14   *Goddess-mother* Thetis.
15   *Charged* burdened; entrusted; *Vulcan* Latin
name for Hephaestus.

from the *Odyssey*

Book 1, lines 1–10

Homer invokes the Muse to tell the tale of Odysseus' homecoming from Troy to Ithaca. The first line means literally: "Tell me Muse of the man of many turns," where the pregnant epithet "of many turns" (*polutropos*) refers to both the range of his adventures and his mental versatility. Odysseus' wisdom – Greek *metis* – is of a practical rather than a philosophic kind. It helps him to return home safely while his men destroy themselves through folly.

The translation is by Alexander Pope (1688–1744), who wrote his mock epic *The Rape of the Lock* (p. 113 above) during the same period in which he began his translation of the *Iliad*. The first part of the *Iliad* came out in 1715 and was completed in 1720. The *Odyssey*, on which Pope received help from the less illustrious Fenton and Broome, was published in 1725–1726. As a Catholic, Pope was not eligible to attend Oxford or Cambridge, and his classical training was not of the highest order. Like other translators, and to a greater extent than some, he made use of earlier translations; Pope admitted that he made particularly widespread use of French translations of Homer. What he lacked in Hellenic learning, however, Pope certainly made up for in poetic ability. He was, as everyone acknowledged, the greatest versifier, if not the greatest poet, of his age. Many readers feel that Pope's heroic couplets and his purified poetic diction make the *Iliad* and *Odyssey* too decorous, artificial, or overly refined. For some, Pope gives us a Homer reduced to the style of a lady's dressing room. Certainly, late twentieth-century versions of Homer give greater scope to the violence and the occasional rawness of the epics, but Pope's translation is more attuned to Homer's power than many modern readers appreciate. Within the confines of his poetic givens, Pope expresses much of Homer's dynamic range. Every translator, after all, follows the poetic conventions of his time and his language; Pope is in the unusual position of having been the model of his age's poetic achievements; hence, his Homer is quintessentially the Homer of his age, but it is not, therefore, further from the original or "real" Homer than any other age's translation.

The Man for Wisdom's various arts renowned,
Long exercised in woes, O Muse! resound.
Who, when his arms had wrought the destined fall
Of sacred *Troy*, and razed her heaven-built wall,
Wand'ring from clime to clime, observant strayed,   5
Their Manners noted, and their states surveyed.
On stormy seas unnumbered toils he bore,
Safe with his friends to gain his natal shore:
Vain toils! their impious folly dared to prey

On Herds devoted to the God of Day;[1]   10
The God vindictive doomed them never more
(Ah, men unblessed!) to touch that natal shore.
Oh snatch some portion of these acts from fate,
Celestial Muse! and to our world relate.

Book 5, lines 145–281

Following the destruction of his men for eating the cattle of Helios, Odysseus – or
Ulysses (his Latin name) – was shipwrecked on the island of Ogygia, the habitation
of the goddess Calypso. Calypso kept him there as her lover for seven years, but
Odysseus longed to return to his wife Penelope; even Calypso's promise of immor-
tality could not dissuade him. Zeus sent Hermes (Mercury) to order Calypso to
release Odysseus. Regretfully, Calypso obeys Zeus' command and helps Odysseus
build a raft for his departure. This episode may have influenced the canoe-building
scene at the beginning of Derek Walcott's *Omeros* (p. 228 above).

The translation is, again, Pope's (see p. 255 above).

To her, the Power who bears the charming rod:[1]
"Dismiss the man, nor irritate the God;[2]
Prevent the rage of him who reigns above,
For what so dreadful as the wrath of *Jove?*"
Thus having said, he cut the cleaving sky,   5
And in a moment vanished from her eye.
The Nymph, obedient to divine command,
To seek *Ulysses*, paced along the sand.
Him pensive on the lonely beach she found,
With streaming eyes in briny torrents drowned,   10
And inly pining for his native shore;[3]
For now the soft Enchantress pleased no more:
For now, reluctant, and constrained by charms,
Absent he lay in her desiring arms,
In slumber wore the heavy night away,   15
On rocks and shores consumed the tedious day;
There sate all desolate, and sighed alone,
With echoing sorrows made the mountains groan,

BOOK 1, LINES 1–10

1 *God of Day* Helios, the sun god; for eating his
sacred cows Odysseus' men were killed by Zeus.

BOOK 5, LINES 145–281

1 *To her . . . rod* addressing Calypso, Hermes or

Mercury (*the Power* who carries a herald's staff)
speaks.
2 *man* Odysseus (Ulysses); *the God* Zeus
(Jove).
3 *inly* inwardly.

And rolled his eyes o'er all the restless main,[4]
Till, dimmed with rising grief, they streamed again.   20
    Here, on his musing mood the Goddess pressed,
Approaching soft, and thus the chief addressed:[5]
"Unhappy man! to wasting woes a prey,
No more in sorrows languish life away:
Free as the winds I give thee now to rove –   25
Go, fell the timber of yon lofty grove,
And form a Raft, and build the rising ship,
Sublime to bear thee o'er the gloomy deep.[6]
To store the vessel let the care be mine,
With water from the rock and rosy wine,   30
And life-sustaining bread, and fair array,
And prosperous gales to waft thee on the way.[7]
These, if the Gods with my desires comply
(The Gods, alas, more mighty far than I,
And better skilled in dark events to come),   35
In peace shall land thee at thy native home."
    With sighs *Ulysses* heard the words she spoke,
Then thus his melancholy silence broke:
"Some other motive, Goddess! sways thy mind
(Some close design, or turn of womankind),   40
Nor my return the end, nor this the way,
On a slight raft to pass the swelling sea,
Huge, horrid, vast! where scarce in safety sails
The best-built ship, though *Jove* inspire the gales.
The bold proposal how shall I fulfill,   45
Dark as I am, unconscious of thy will?[8]
Swear, then, thou mean'st not what my soul forebodes;
Swear by the solemn oath that binds the Gods."
    Him, while he spoke, with smiles *Calypso* eyed,
And gently grasped his hand, and thus replied: 50
"This shows thee, friend, by old experience taught,
And learned in all the wiles of human thought,
How prone to doubt, how cautious, are the wise!
But hear, O earth, and hear, ye sacred skies!
And thou, O *Styx*! whose formidable floods[9]   55
Glide through the shades, and bind the attesting gods!
No formed design, no meditated end,

---

4 *main* ocean.
5 *chief* the leader of any group or organization, particularly a military group.
6 *Sublime* high, lofty, rising over the waves.
7 *gales* gentle breezes.
8 *Dark* ignorant.
9 *Styx* a river of the underworld; the gods were bound by oaths taken in its name.

Lurks in the counsel of thy faithful friend;
Kind the persuasion, and sincere my aim;
The same my practice, were my fate the same.   60
Heaven has not cursed me with a heart of steel,
But given the sense, to pity, and to feel."
    Thus having said, the Goddess marched before:
He trod her footsteps in the sandy shore.
At the cool cave arrived, they took their state;[10]   65
He filled the throne where *Mercury* had sate.
For him the Nymph a rich repast ordains,
Such as the mortal life of man sustains:
Before herself were placed the cates divine,[11]
Ambrosial banquet and celestial wine.[12]   70
Their hunger satiate, and their thirst repressed,
Thus spoke *Calypso* to her godlike guest:
    "*Ulysses*! (with a sigh she thus began)
O sprung from Gods! in wisdom more than man!
Is then thy home the passion of thy heart?   75
Thus wilt thou leave me, are we thus to part?
Farewell! and ever joyful may'st thou be,
Nor break the transport with one thought of me.[13]
But ah, *Ulysses*! wert thou giv'n to know
What fate yet dooms thee, yet, to undergo,   80
Thy heart might settle in this scene of ease,
And e'en these slighted charms might learn to please.
A willing Goddess, and Immortal life,
Might banish from thy mind an absent wife.
Am I inferior to a mortal dame?   85
Less soft my feature, less august my frame?
Or shall the daughters of mankind compare
Their earth-born beauties with the heavenly fair?"
    "Alas! for this (the prudent man replies)
Against *Ulysses* shall thy anger rise?   90
Loved and adored, O Goddess, as thou art,
Forgive the weakness of a human heart.
Though well I see thy graces far above
The dear, though mortal, object of my love,
Of youth eternal well the difference know,   95
And the short date of fading charms below;
Yet every day, while absent thus I roam,
I languish to return and die at home.

10 *took their state* established, as it were, a tem-
porary court.
11 *cates* delicacies.

12 *Ambrosial* ambrosia ("immortality") is the
food of the gods and nectar their drink.
13 *transport* joy.

Whate'er the Gods shall destine me to bear
In the black ocean, or the wat'ry war,   100
'Tis mine to master with a constant mind;
Inured to perils, to the worst resigned.
By seas, by wars, so many dangers run,
Still I can suffer; Their high will be done!"
   Thus while he spoke, the beamy Sun descends,   105
And rising night her friendly shade extends.
To the close grot the lonely pair remove,[14]
And slept delighted with the gifts of love.
When rosy morning called them from their rest,
Ulysses robed him in the cloak and vest.   110
The nymph's fair head a veil transparent graced,
Her swelling loins a radiant Zone embraced[15]
With flowers of gold; an under robe, unbound,
In snowy waves flowed glittering on the ground.
Forth issuing thus, she gave him first to wield   115
A weighty axe with truest temper steeled,
And double-edged; the handle smooth and plain,
Wrought of the clouded olive's easy grain;[16]
And next, a wedge to drive with sweepy sway:[17]
Then to the neighboring forest led the way.   120
On the lone Island's utmost verge there stood
Of poplars, pines, and firs, a lofty wood,
Whose leafless summits to the skies aspire,
Scorched by the sun, or seared by heav'nly fire
(Already dried): These pointing out to view,   125
The Nymph just showed him, and with tears withdrew.
   Now toils the Hero; trees on trees o'erthrown
Fall crackling round him, and the forests groan:
Sudden, full twenty on the plain are strowed,
And lopped and lightened of their branchy load.   130
At equal angles these disposed to join,
He smoothed and squared them by the rule and line.
(The wimbles for the work *Calypso* found)[18]
With those he pierced them and with clinchers bound.
Long and capacious as a shipwright forms   135
Some bark's broad bottom to out-ride the storms,[19]
So large he built the Raft; then ribbed it strong

14 *grot* grotto; a picturesque cave or under-   17 *sweepy sway* sweeping force.
ground room.   18 *wimbles* augurs or drill bits.
15 *Zone* belt.   19 *bark* ship.
16 *Wrought . . . grain* made of smooth-grained
olive wood.

From space to space, and nailed the planks along;
These formed the sides: the deck he fashioned last;
Then o'er the vessel raised the taper mast,   140
With crossing sail-yards dancing in the wind;
And to the helm the guiding rudder joined
(With yielding osiers fenced, to break the force[20]
Of surging waves, and steer the steady course).
Thy loom, *Calypso*! for the future sails   145
Supplied the cloth, capacious of the gales.
With stays and cordage last he rigged the ship,[21]
And, rolled on levers, launched her in the deep.
   Four days were passed, and now the work complete,
Shone the fifth morn, when from her sacred seat   150
The nymph dismissed him (od'rous garments giv'n,
And bathed in fragrant oils that breathed of heaven),
Then filled two goatskins with her hands divine,
With water one, and one with sable wine;
Of every kind, provisions heaved aboard,   155
And the full decks with copious viands stored.
The Goddess, last, a gentle breeze supplies,
To curl old Ocean, and to warm the skies.[22]
   And now, rejoicing in the prosperous gales,
With beating heart *Ulysses* spreads his sails;   160
Placed at the helm he sate, and marked the skies,
Nor closed in sleep his ever-watchful eyes.
There viewed the *Pleiads*, and the northern Team,[23]
And great *Orion*'s more refulgent beam.[24]
To which, around the axle of the sky,   165
The Bear, revolving, points his golden eye;[25]
Who shines exalted on th' ethereal plain,
Nor bathes his blazing forehead in the main.
Far on the left those radiant fires to keep
The Nymph directed, as he sailed the deep.   170
Full sev'nteen nights he cut the foamy way;
The distant land appeared the following day:
Then swelled to sight *Phaeacia*'s dusky coast,[26]

20 *osiers* willow branches.
21 *stays* large ropes.
22 *curl* to make ripples upon the water, as signs of a gentle breeze.
23 *Pleiads* a constellation of seven stars; *northern Team* Boötes or the Wagoner.
24 *Orion* a giant hunter who was turned into a constellation.

25 *Bear* the Great Bear, a constellation that never dips below the horizon.
26 *Phaeacia* the land of King Alcinous, who entertains Odysseus and provides him with an escort to Ithaca.

And woody mountains, half in vapours lost;
That lay before him indistinct and vast,   175
Like a broad shield amid the wat'ry waste.

Book 8, lines 266–369

The bard Demodocus entertains Odysseus and the court of King Alcinous on
Phaeacia with the bawdy tale of Ares (Mars) and Aphrodite (Venus), the ill-
assorted wife of the lame smith god Hephaestus (Vulcan). The netting of Ares
and Aphrodite was Spenser's model for Guyon's capture of Acrasia in *The Faerie
Queene* (p. 35 above).

The translation is, again, Pope's (see p. 255 above).

Meantime the Bard, alternate to the strings,[1]
The loves of *Mars* and *Cytherea* sings;[2]
How the stern God, enamoured with her charms
Clasped the gay panting Goddess in his arms,
By bribes seduced; and how the Sun, whose eye   5
Views the broad heavens, disclosed the lawless joy.
Stung to the soul, indignant through the skies
To his black forge vindictive *Vulcan* flies:
Arrived, his sinewy arms incessant place
The eternal anvil on the massy base.   10
A wondrous Net he labours, to betray
The wanton lovers, as entwined they lay,
Indissolubly strong! then instant bears
To his immortal dome the finished snares:[3]
Above, below, around, with art dispread,   15
The sure enclosure folds the genial bed:
Whose texture ev'n the search of Gods deceives,[4]
Thin as the filmy threads the spider weaves.
Then, as withdrawing from the starry bowers,
He feigns a journey to the *Lemnian* shores,[5]   20
His favourite Isle! Observant *Mars* descries
His wished recess, and to the Goddess flies;
He glows, he burns: The fair-haired Queen of love
Descends, smooth-gliding from the Courts of *Jove*,

BOOK 8, LINES 266–369

1 *alternate to* performing alternately with; accompanied by.
2 *Cytherea* Aphrodite (Venus), who had a temple on the island of Cythera.
3 *dome* house.
4 *texture* woven construction.
5 *Lemnian* Lemnos was a volcanic island associated with Hephaestus.

Gay blooming in full charms: her hand he pressed   25
With eager joy, and with a sigh addressed:
   "Come, my beloved! and taste the soft delights;
Come, to repose the genial bed invites:
Thy absent spouse, neglectful of thy charms,
Prefers his barbarous *Sintians* to thy arms!"[6]   30
   Then, nothing loth, th' enamoured fair he led,
And sunk transported on the conscious bed.
Down rushed the toils, enwrapping as they lay[7]
The careless lovers in their wanton play:
In vain they strive; the entangling snares deny   35
(Inextricably firm) the power to fly:
Warned by the God who sheds the golden day,
Stern *Vulcan* homeward treads the starry way:
Arrived, he sees, he grieves, with rage he burns;
Full horribly he roars, his voice all heaven returns.   40
   "O *Jove*," he cried, "O all ye powers above,
See the lewd dalliance of the Queen of Love!
Me, awkward me, she scorns, and yields her charms
To that fair Lecher, the strong God of arms.
If I am lame, that stain my natal hour   45
By fate imposed; such me my parent bore:
Why was I born? See how the wanton lies,[8]
O sight tormenting to a husband's eyes!
But yet, I trust, this once e'en *Mars* would fly
His fair one's arms – he thinks her, once, too nigh.   50
But there remain, ye guilty, in my power,
Till *Jove* refunds his shameless daughter's dower.
Too dear I prized a fair enchanting face:
Beauty unchaste is beauty in disgrace."
   Meanwhile the Gods the dome of *Vulcan* throng;   55
Apollo comes, and Neptune comes along;
With these gay *Hermes* trod the starry plain;
But modesty withheld the Goddess-train.
All heaven beholds, imprisoned as they lie,
And unextinguished laughter shakes the sky.   60
   Then mutual, thus they spoke: "Behold on wrong
Swift vengeance waits; and Art subdues the strong!
Dwells there a God on all the *Olympian* brow
More swift than *Mars*, and more than *Vulcan* slow?
Yet *Vulcan* conquers, and the God of arms   65
Must pay the penalty for lawless charms."

6   *Sintians* early inhabitants of Lemnos.   8   *the wanton* the unfaithful woman.
7   *toils* snare; net.

Thus serious they; but he who gilds the skies,
The gay *Apollo*, thus to *Hermes* cries:
"Wouldst thou enchained like *Mars*, O *Hermes*, lie,   70
And bear the shame, like *Mars*, to share the joy?"
    "O envied shame! (the smiling Youth rejoined)
Add thrice the chains, and thrice more firmly bind;
Gaze all ye Gods, and every Goddess gaze,
Yet eager would I bless the sweet disgrace."   75
    Loud laugh the rest, e'en *Neptune* laughs aloud,
Yet sues importunate to loose the God:
"And free," he cries, "O *Vulcan*! free from shame
Thy captives; I ensure the penal claim."
    "Will *Neptune*" (*Vulcan* then) "the faithless trust?   80
He suffers who gives surety for the unjust:
But say, if that lewd scandal of the sky,
To liberty restored, perfidious fly,
Say, wilt thou bear the Mulct?" He instant cries,[9]
"The mulct I bear, if *Mars* perfidious flies."   85
    To whom appeased: "No more I urge delay;
When *Neptune* sues, my part is to obey."
    Then to the snares his force the God applies;
They burst; and *Mars* to *Thrace* indignant flies:
To the soft *Cyprian* shores the Goddess moves,   90
To visit *Paphos* and her blooming groves,[10]
Where to the power a hundred altars rise,[11]
And breathing odours scent the balmy skies.
Concealed she bathes in consecrated bowers,
The Graces unguents shed, ambrosial showers,[12]   95
Unguents that charm the Gods! she last assumes
Her wondrous robes; and full the Goddess blooms.
    Thus sung the Bard: *Ulysses* hears with joy,
And loud applauses rend the vaulted sky.

Book 9, lines 16–105

During his sojourn on the island of Phaeacia Odysseus (Ulysses) recounts his adventures among the many strange peoples he encountered in his travels after leaving Troy. He found the first two tribes he met to be antithetical in character: the hostile Ciconians and the hospitable Lotus-eaters. The Lotus-eaters live on a psycho-active plant that makes those who eat it content to do nothing else. Those of Odysseus' men who eat the lotus abandon all thoughts of home. The episode

---

9 *Mulct* fine.
10 *Paphos* a center of Aphrodite's cult.
11 *power* the goddess.

12 *Graces* goddesses of youth and beauty; *ambrosial* fragrant.

highlights Odysseus' love for his homeland of Ithaca, which, as shown by his opening remarks, is central to his sense of identity. It inspired Tennyson's poem "The Lotos-Eaters" (p. 202 above).

The translation is, again, Pope's (see p. 255 above).

"Know first the man (though now a wretch distressed)
Who hopes thee, Monarch, for his future guest.
Behold *Ulysses*! no ignoble name,
Earth sounds my wisdom and high heaven my fame.
　"My native soil is *Ithaca* the fair,[1]　　　　　　　　　　5
Where high *Neritus* waves his woods in air:
Dulichium, *Samè* and *Zacynthus* crowned
With shady mountains spread their isles around.
(These to the north and night's dark regions run,
Those to *Aurora* and the rising sun).[2]　　　　　　　　　　10
Low lies our Isle, yet blessed in fruitful stores;
Strong are her sons, though rocky are her shores;
And none, ah none so lovely to my sight,
Of all the lands that heaven o'erspreads with light!
In vain *Calypso* long constrained my stay,[3]　　　　　　　　15
With sweet, reluctant, amorous delay;
With all her charms as vainly *Circe* strove,[4]
And added magic to secure my love.
In pomps or joys, the palace or the grot,
My country's image never was forgot;　　　　　　　　　　20
My absent parents rose before my sight,
And distant lay contentment and delight.
　"Hear, then, the woes which mighty *Jove* ordained
To wait my passage from the *Trojan* land.
The winds from *Ilion* to the *Cicons*' shore,[5]　　　　　　　25
Beneath cold *Ismarus* our vessels bore.
We boldly landed on the hostile place,
And sacked the city, and destroyed the race,
Their wives made captive, their possessions shared,
And every soldier found a like reward.　　　　　　　　　　30
I then advised to fly; not so the rest,
Who stayed to revel, and prolong the feast:
The fatted sheep and sable bulls they slay,

BOOK 9, LINES 16–105

1　*Ithaca* an island west of mainland Greece.
2　*Aurora* the dawn goddess (Greek Eos).
3　*Calypso* a sea goddess (p. 256 above).

4　*Circe* a divine sorceress (p. 266 below).
5　*Ilion* Troy; *Cicons* the Cicones, a mythical people.

And bowls flow round, and riot wastes the day.
Meantime the *Cicons*, to their holds retired,   35
Call on the *Cicons*, with new fury fired;
With early morn the gathered country swarms,
And all the Continent is bright with arms:
Thick, as the budding leaves or rising flowers
O'erspread the land, when spring descends in showers: 40
All expert soldiers, skilled on foot to dare,
Or from the bounding courser urge the war.
Now Fortune changes (so the fates ordain),
Our hour was come to taste our share of pain.
Close at the ships the bloody fight began,   45
Wounded they wound, and man expires on man.
Long as the morning sun increasing bright
O'er heaven's pure azure spread the growing light,
Promiscuous death the form of war confounds,
Each adverse battle gored with equal wounds: 50
But when his evening wheels o'erhung the main,
Then conquest crowned the fierce *Ciconian* train.
Six brave companions from each ship we lost,
The rest escape in haste, and quit the coast.
With sails outspread we fly the unequal strife,   55
Sad for their loss, but joyful of our life.
Yet as we fled, our fellows' rites we paid,
And thrice we called on each unhappy Shade.
    "Meanwhile the God, whose hand the thunder forms,[6]
Drives clouds on clouds, and blackens heaven with storms: 60
Wide o'er the waste the rage of *Boreas* sweeps,[7]
And Night rushed headlong on the shaded deeps.
Now here, now there, the giddy ships are borne,
And all the rattling shrouds in fragments torn.[8]
We furled the sail, we plied the labouring oar,   65
Took down our masts, and rowed our ships to shore.
Two tedious days and two long nights we lay,
O'erwatched and battered in the naked bay.[9]
But the third morning when *Aurora* brings,
We rear the masts, we spread the canvas wings;   70
Refreshed and careless on the deck reclined,
We sit, and trust the pilot and the wind.
Then to my native country had I sailed:
But, the cape doubled, adverse winds prevailed.[10]

---

6 *God* Zeus.
7 *Boreas* the north wind.
8 *shrouds* ropes supporting the mast of a ship.

9 *O'erwatched* tired from being awake too long
(*OED*).
10 *the cape doubled* having passed around to the
other side of it.

Strong was the tide, which by the northern blast   75
Impelled, our vessels on *Cythera* cast,[11]
Nine days our fleet the uncertain tempest bore
Far in wide ocean, and from sight of shore:
The tenth we touched, by various errors tossed,
The land of *Lotos* and the flowery coast.   80
We climbed the beach, and springs of water found,
Then spread our hasty banquet on the ground.
Three men were sent, deputed from the crew
(A herald one) the dubious coast to view,
And learn what habitants possessed the place.   85
They went, and found a hospitable race:
Not prone to ill, nor strange to foreign guest,
They eat, they drink, and nature gives the feast;
The trees around them all their food produce:
Lotos the name, divine, nectareous juice!   90
(Thence called *Lotophagi*) which whoso tastes,[12]
Insatiate riots in the sweet repasts,[13]
Nor other home, nor other care intends,
But quits his house, his country, and his friends:
The three we sent, from off th' enchanting ground   95
We dragged reluctant, and by force we bound:
The rest in haste forsook the pleasing shore,
Or, the charm tasted, had returned no more.
Now placed in order, on their banks they sweep
The sea's smooth face, and cleave the hoary deep;   100
With heavy hearts we labour through the tide,
To coasts unknown, and oceans yet untried."

Book 10, lines 198–347

Odysseus (Ulysses) continues the tale of his wanderings with his encounter with
the divine sorceress Circe, a daughter of the sun god Helios. Circe lives on the
island of Aeaea, where she sings at her loom surrounded by the forms of men
transformed into animals by her magic. She turns Odysseus' men into swine, but
with the aid of Hermes he evades her spells, makes her restore his men, and spends
a year with her as her lover. Circe was one of Spenser's models for Acrasia in *The
Faerie Queene* (pp. 32–6 above).

The translation is, again, Pope's (see p. 255 above).

---

11 *Cythera* an island south of mainland   13 *Insatiate riots* revels insatiably.
Greece.
12 *Lotophagi* Greek for "Lotus-eaters"; *whoso*
whosoever.

"With broken hearts my sad companions stood,
Mindful of *Cyclops* and his human food,[1]
And horrid *Laestrygons*, the men of blood.[2]
Presaging tears apace began to rain;
But tears in mortal miseries are vain. 5
In equal parts I straight divide my band,
And name a chief each party to command;
I led the one, and of the other side
Appointed brave *Eurylochus* the guide.
Then in the brazen helm the lots we throw, 10
And fortune casts *Eurylochus* to go:
He marched with twice eleven in his train:
Pensive they march, and pensive we remain.
   "The Palace in a woody vale they found,
High raised of stone; a shaded space around: 15
Where mountain wolves and brindled lions roam,
(By magic tamed) familiar to the dome.[3]
With gentle blandishment our men they meet,
And wag their tails, and fawning lick their feet.
As from some feast a man returning late, 20
His faithful dogs all meet him at the gate,
Rejoicing round, some morsel to receive,
(Such as the good man ever used to give,)
Domestic thus the grisly beasts drew near;
They gaze with wonder not unmixed with fear. 25
Now on the threshold of the dome they stood,
And heard a voice resounding through the wood:
Placed at her loom within, the Goddess sung;[4]
The vaulted roofs and solid pavement rung.
O'er the fair web the rising figures shine, 30
Immortal labour! worthy hands divine.
Polites to the rest the question moved
(A gallant leader, and a man I loved):
   "'What voice celestial, chanting to the loom
(Or Nymph, or Goddess), echoes from the room? 35
Say, shall we seek access?' With that they call;
And wide unfold the portals of the hall.
   "The Goddess, rising, asks her guests to stay,
Who blindly follow where she leads the way.
Eurylochus alone of all the band, 40

BOOK 10, LINES 198–347

1 *Cyclops* the one-eyed Polyphemus from whom Odysseus escapes in Book 9.
2 *Laestrygons* a race of cannibal giants (*Odyssey* 10.80–132).
3 *dome* house.
4 *Goddess* Circe.

Suspecting fraud, more prudently remained.
On thrones around with downy coverings graced,
With semblance fair, the unhappy men she placed.
Milk newly pressed, the sacred flour of wheat,
And honey fresh, and *Pramnian* wines the treat:[5]   45
But venomed was the bread, and mixed the bowl,
With drugs of force to darken all the soul:
Soon in the luscious feast themselves they lost,
And drank oblivion of their native coast.
Instant her circling wand the Goddess waves,   50
To hogs transforms them, and the Sty receives.
No more was seen the human form divine,
Head, face, and members, bristle into swine:
Still cursed with sense, their mind remains alone,
And their own voice affrights them when they groan.   55
Meanwhile the Goddess in disdain bestows
The mast and acorn, brutal food! and strows
The fruits of cornel, as their feast, around;[6]
Now prone and groveling on unsavoury ground.
    "*Eurylochus*, with pensive steps and slow,   60
Aghast returns; the messenger of woe,
And bitter fate. To speak he made essay,[7]
In vain essayed, nor would his tongue obey.
His swelling heart denied the words their way:
But speaking tears the want of words supply,   65
And the full soul bursts copious from his eye.
Affrighted, anxious for our fellows' fates,
We press to hear what sadly he relates:
    "'We went, *Ulysses*! (such was thy command)
Through the lone thicket, and the desert land.   70
A Palace in a woody vale we found
Brown with dark forests, and with shades around.
A voice celestial echoed from the dome,
Or Nymph or Goddess, chanting to the loom.
Access we sought, nor was access denied: 75
Radiant she came; the portals opened wide:
The Goddess mild invites the guests to stay:
They blindly follow where she leads the way.
I only wait behind, of all the train;
I waited long, and eyed the doors in vain: 80
The rest are vanished, none repassed the gate;
And not a man appears to tell their fate.'

5 *Pramnian* variously interpreted; perhaps related to a dry, very strong wine of the same name produced later near Smyrna.

6 *cornel* the cornel-tree or cornelian cherry.

7 *essay* attempt.

"I heard, and instant o'er my shoulders flung
The belt in which my weighty falchion hung[8]
(A beamy blade); then seized the bended bow,[9]   85
And bade him guide the way, resolved to go.
He, prostrate falling, with both hands embraced
My knees, and weeping thus his suit addressed:
"'O King, beloved of *Jove*, thy servant spare,
And ah, thyself the rash attempt forbear!   90
Never, alas! thou never shalt return,
Or see the wretched for whose loss we mourn.
With what remains from certain ruin fly,[10]
And save the few not fated yet to die.'
"I answered stern: 'Inglorious then remain,   95
Here feast and loiter, and desert thy train.
Alone, unfriended, will I tempt my way;[11]
The laws of Fate compel, and I obey.'
"This said, and scornful turning from the shore
My haughty step, I stalked the valley o'er.   100
Till now approaching nigh the magic bower,
Where dwelt the enchantress skilled in herbs of power;
A form divine forth issued from the wood
(Immortal *Hermes* with the golden rod)[12]
In human semblance. On his bloomy face[13]   105
Youth smiled celestial, with each opening grace.
He seized my hand, and gracious thus began:
'Ah whither roam'st thou? much-enduring man!
O blind to fate! what led thy steps to rove
The horrid mazes of this magic grove?   110
Each friend you seek in yon enclosure lies,
All lost their form, and habitants of sties.
Think'st thou by wit to model their escape?[14]
Sooner shalt thou, a stranger to thy shape,
Fall prone their equal: First thy danger know,   115
Then take the antidote the Gods bestow.
The plant I give through all the direful bower
Shall guard thee, and avert the evil hour.
Now hear her wicked arts: Before thy eyes
The bowl shall sparkle, and the banquet rise;   120
Take this, nor from the faithless feast abstain,
For tempered drugs and poison shall be vain.
Soon as she strikes her wand, and gives the word,

8   *falchion* broad sword.
9   *beamy* massive.
10 *what remains* the remainder of his crew.
11 *tempt* attempt; pursue.
12 *Hermes* the messenger god, who carries a herald's staff.
13 *bloomy* youthful.
14 *model* to frame or fashion.

Draw forth and brandish thy refulgent sword,
And menace death: those menaces shall move   125
Her altered mind to blandishment and love.
Nor shun the blessing proffered to thy arms,
Ascend her bed, and taste celestial charms:
So shall thy tedious toils a respite find,
And thy lost friends return to humankind.   130
But swear her first by those dread oaths that tie
The powers below, the blessed in the sky;
Lest to thee naked secret fraud be meant,
Or magic bind thee, cold and impotent.'
      "Thus while he spoke, the sovereign plant he drew,   135
Where on the all-bearing earth unmarked it grew,
And showed its nature and its wondrous power:
Black was the root, but milky white the flower;
Moly the name, to mortals hard to find,[15]
But all is easy to the ethereal kind.   140
This *Hermes* gave, then, gliding off the glade,
Shot to *Olympus* from the woodland shade.
      "While, full of thought, revolving fates to come,
I speed my passage to the enchanted dome:
Arrived, before the lofty gates I stayed;   145
The lofty gates the Goddess wide displayed:
She leads before, and to the feast invites;
I follow sadly to the magic rites.
Radiant with starry studs, a silver seat
Received my limbs; a footstool eased my feet.   150
She mixed the potion, fraudulent of soul;
The poison mantled in the golden bowl.
I took, and quaffed it, confident in heaven:
Then waved the wand, and then the word was given.
'Hence, to thy fellows! (dreadful she began)   155
Go, be a beast!' – I heard, and yet was man.
      "Then, sudden whirling, like a waving flame,
My beamy falchion, I assault the dame.
Struck with unusual fear, she trembling cries,
She faints, she falls; she lifts her weeping eyes.   160
      "'What art thou? say! from whence, from whom you came?
O more than human! tell thy race, thy name.
Amazing strength, these poisons to sustain!
Not mortal thou, nor mortal is thy brain.
Or art thou he? the man to come (foretold   165
By *Hermes*, powerful with the wand of gold),
The man from *Troy*, who wandered Ocean round;

15   *Moly* a mythical plant.

The man for Wisdom's various arts renowned,
Ulysses? oh! thy threatening fury cease,
Sheathe thy bright sword, and join our hands in peace;   170
Let mutual joys our mutual trust combine,
And Love and love-born confidence be thine.'
    " 'And how, dread *Circe*! (furious I rejoin)
Can Love and love-born confidence be mine,
Beneath thy charms when my companions groan,   175
Transformed to beasts, with accents not their own?
O thou of fraudful heart! shall I be led
To share thy feast-rites, or ascend thy bed;
That, all unarmed, thy vengeance may have vent,
And magic bind me, cold and impotent?   180
Celestial as thou art, yet stand denied:
Or swear that oath by which the Gods are tied,
Swear, in thy soul no latent frauds remain,
Swear, by the Vow which never can be vain.'
    "The Goddess swore: then seized my hand, and led   185
To the sweet transports of the genial bed."

Book 12, lines 142–259

Leaving Circe's island, Odysseus uses characteristic guile to pass safely by the Sirens
while satisfying his desire to hear their fatally alluring song: he orders his men to
block their ears with wax, to lash him to the mast, and to ignore his orders to
stop as the ship sails by the Sirens' island. Next, Odysseus and his men sail between
the monster Scylla and the whirlpool of Charybdis through what the ancients
identified as the Straits of Messina. The ship survives, but Scylla seizes six of Odys-
seus' men. These adventures influenced Spenser's description of Guyon's voyage
in *The Faerie Queene* (pp. 13–15 above).

The translation is, again, Pope's (see p. 255 above).

"She ceased: And now arose the morning ray;[1]
Swift to her dome the Goddess held her way.[2]
Then to my mates I measured back the plain,[3]
Climbed the tall bark, and rushed into the main;[4]
Then, bending to the stroke, their oars they drew   5
To their broad breasts, and swift the galley flew.
Up sprung a brisker breeze; with freshening gales[5]

BOOK 12, LINES 142–259

1 *She* Circe, who has warned Odysseus of the
perils awaiting him.

2 *dome* house.

3 *measured* walked.

4 *bark* ship; *main* sea.

5 *gales* gentle breezes.

The friendly Goddess stretched the swelling sails;
We drop our oars: at ease the pilot guides;
The vessel light along the level glides.   10
When, rising sad and slow, with pensive look,
Thus to the melancholy train I spoke:[6]
   "'O friends, oh ever partners of my woes,
Attend while I what Heaven foredooms disclose.
Hear all! Fate hangs o'er all! on you it lies   15
To live, or perish! to be safe, be wise!
   "'In flowery meads the sportive *Sirens* play,[7]
Touch the soft lyre, and tune the vocal lay;[8]
Me, me alone, with fetters firmly bound,
The Gods allow to hear the dangerous sound.   20
Hear and obey: If freedom I demand,
Be every fetter strained, be added band to band.'
   "While yet I speak the wingèd galley flies,
And lo! the *Siren* shores like mists arise.
Sunk were at once the winds; the air above,   25
And waves below, at once forgot to move!
Some Demon calmed the Air, and smoothed the deep,
Hushed the loud winds, and charmed the waves to sleep.
Now every sail we furl, each oar we ply;
Lashed by the stroke, the frothy waters fly.   30
The ductile wax with busy hands I mould,
And cleft in fragments, and the fragments rolled;
The aerial region now grew warm with day,
The wax dissolved beneath the burning ray;
Then every ear I barred against the strain,   35
And from access of frenzy locked the brain.
Now round the mast my mates the fetters rolled,
And bound me limb by limb, with fold on fold.
Then bending to the stroke, the active train
Plunge all at once their oars, and cleave the main.   40
   "While to the shore the rapid vessel flies,
Our swift approach the *Siren* choir descries;
Celestial music warbles from their tongue,
And thus the sweet deluders tune the song:
   "'O stay, O pride of *Greece*! *Ulysses*, stay!   45
O cease thy course, and listen to our lay!
Blest is the man ordained our voice to hear,
The song instructs the soul, and charms the ear.
Approach! thy soul shall into raptures rise!
Approach! and learn new wisdom from the wise!   50

6 *train* crew.   8 *lay* song.
7 *Sirens* bird-women who lure sailors to their
death with seductive song.

We know whate'er the Kings of mighty name
Achieved at *Ilion* in the field of fame;[9]
Whate'er beneath the sun's bright journey lies.
O stay, and learn new wisdom from the wise!'
   "Thus the sweet charmers warbled o'er the main;   55
My soul takes wing to meet the heavenly strain;
I give the sign, and struggle to be free:
Swift row my mates, and shoot along the sea;
New chains they add, and rapid urge the way,
Till, dying off, the distant sounds decay: 60
Then scudding swiftly from the dangerous ground,
The deafened ear unlocked, the chains unbound.
   "Now all at once tremendous scenes unfold;
Thundered the deeps, the smoking billows rolled!
Tumultuous waves embroiled the bellowing flood,   65
All trembling, deafened, and aghast we stood!
No more the vessel ploughed the dreadful wave,
Fear seized the mighty, and unnerved the brave;
Each dropped his oar: But swift from man to man
With look serene I turned, and thus began: 70
'O friends! O often tried in adverse storms!
With ills familiar in more dreadful forms!
Deep in the dire *Cyclopean* den you lay,[10]
Yet safe returned – *Ulysses* led the way.
Learn courage hence! and in my care confide: 75
Lo! still the same *Ulysses* is your guide!
Attend my words! your oars incessant ply;
Strain every nerve, and bid the vessel fly.
If from yon jostling rocks and wavy war
Jove safety grants, he grants it to your care.   80
And thou, whose guiding hand directs our way,
Pilot, attentive listen and obey!
Bear wide thy course, nor plough those angry waves
Where rolls yon smoke, yon tumbling ocean raves;
Steer by the higher rock; lest whirled around   85
We sink, beneath the circling eddy drowned.'
   "While yet I speak, at once their oars they seize,
Stretch to the stroke, and brush the working seas.
Cautious the name of *Scylla* I suppressed;[11]
That dreadful sound had chilled the boldest breast.   90
   "Meantime, forgetful of the voice divine,
All dreadful bright my limbs in armour shine;

---

9 *Ilion* Troy.
10 *Cyclopean den* the cave of the Cyclops Poly-
phemus (*Odyssey* 9).

11 *Scylla* a many-headed monster who snatches
sailors as they pass her cave.

High on the deck I take my dangerous stand,
Two glittering javelins lighten in my hand;[12]
Prepared to whirl the whizzing spear I stay,   95
Till the fell fiend arise to seize her prey.[13]
Around the dungeon, studious to behold
The hideous pest, my labouring eyes I rolled;
In vain! the dismal dungeon, dark as night,
Veils the dire monster, and confounds the sight.   100
   "Now through the rocks, appalled with deep dismay,
We bend our course, and stem the desperate way;
Dire *Scylla* there a scene of horror forms,
And here *Charybdis* fills the deep with storms.[14]
When the tide rushes from her rumbling caves,   105
The rough rock roars, tumultuous boil the waves;
They toss, they foam, a wild confusion raise,
Like waters bubbling o'er the fiery blaze;
Eternal mists obscure the aerial plain,
And high above the rock she spouts the main: 110
When in her gulfs the rushing sea subsides,
She drains the ocean with the refluent tides:[15]
The rock rebellows with a thundering sound;
Deep, wondrous deep, below appears the ground.
   "Struck with despair, with trembling hearts we viewed   115
The yawning dungeon, and the tumbling flood;
When lo! fierce *Scylla* stooped to seize her prey,
Stretched her dire jaws, and swept six men away;
Chiefs of renown! loud echoing shrieks arise;
I turn, and view them quivering in the skies;   120
They call, and aid with outstretched arms implore:
In vain they call! those arms are stretched no more.
As from some rock that overhangs the flood,
The silent fisher casts the insidious food,
With fraudful care he waits the finny prize,   125
And sudden lifts it quivering to the skies:
So the foul monster lifts her prey on high,
So pant the wretches, struggling in the sky;
In the wide dungeon she devours her food,
And the flesh trembles while she churns the blood.   130
Worn as I am with griefs, with care decayed,
Never, I never, scene so dire surveyed!
My shivering blood, congealed, forgot to flow;
Aghast I stood, a monument of woe!"

12 *lighten* shine.   14 *Charybdis* a monster who sucks in and expels
13 *fell* deadly.   the sea three times a day.
                                        15 *refluent* flowing back.

Hesiod (fl. c. 700 BCE)

According to his self-portrait, Hesiod was born on a farm in Boeotia, a rural region of central Greece; he was inspired by a vision of the Muses on Mount Helicon to compose poetry and celebrate the gods; and he won a great poetry contest at the funeral games of Amphidamas at Chalcis on the island of Euboea. Whether or not these, and the few other stories about Hesiod, are true, his name has been given to a group of poems written around the time of Homer and a few hundred years before the fifth-century BCE flowering of culture in Athens. The Hesiodic poems belong by meter and dialect to the genre of epic, but they are didactic or genealogical rather than heroic in the mode of Homer. *Works and Days* is a didactic poem on farming, full of exhortations to industry. Through the telling of myths and moral fables, it strives, at a more general level, to place the human condition in the context of divine justice. The *Theogony* is largely genealogical. Its theme is the generations of the gods, from the primordial forms of Chaos, Gaia, Eros, and Tartarus to the birth, victory, and sexual unions of Zeus and the Olympians. As an important source of Greek mythology, Hesiod finds his way into a great deal of British literature. His poetry was continuously available in manuscripts and early printed books and truly widespread as a source for fables of all kinds and for works, like James Thomson's *Seasons* (p. 125 above), that meditate on the natural world.

from *Theogony*

lines 1–80

The *Theogony* opens with a hymn to the Muses describing their activities and birth. Hesiod may have given the Muses their names; he certainly shaped later conceptions of them and their relationship to poets. According to the poem, the Muses appeared to Hesiod in an epiphany as he tended his flocks on Mount Helicon. They presented him with a staff of laurel and breathed into him the gift of song.

Scenes of poetic initiation, modeled on Hesiod, later became a literary convention, and they may have belonged to the poet's stock in trade even in Hesiod's time. However, this does not exclude the possibility that Hesiod experienced an epiphany that convinced him of his divine poetic calling. A complex example of the hymn's influence is found in the proem to Milton's *Paradise Lost* (pp. 76–7 above).

The translation by Thomas Cooke (1703–1756) comes from *The Works of Hesiod* (2nd edn; 1740).

Begin, my song, with the melodious nine
Of *Helicon* the spacious and divine;[1]
The *Muses* there, a lovely choir, advance,[2]
With tender feet to form the skilful dance,
Now round the sable font in order move, 5
Now round the altar of *Saturnian Jove*;[3]
Or, if the cooling streams to bathe invite,
In thee, *Permessus*, they awhile delight;[4]
Or now to *Hippocrene* resort the fair,
Or, *Olmius*, to thy sacred spring repair. 10
Veiled in thick air, they all the night prolong,
In praise of *Aegis*-bearing *Jove* the song;[5]
And thou, O *Argive Juno*, golden shod,[6]
Art joined in praises with thy consort god;
Thee, goddess, with the azure eyes, they sing, 15
Minerva, daughter of the heav'nly king;[7]
The sisters to *Apollo* tune their voice,[8]
And, *Artemis*, to thee whom darts rejoice;[9]
And *Neptune* in the pious hymn they sound,[10]
Who girts the earth, and shakes the solid ground; 20
A tribute they to *Themis* chaste allow,[11]
And *Venus* charming with the bending brow,[12]
Nor *Hebe*, crowned with gold, forget to praise,[13]

LINES 1–80

1 *Helicon* mountain in Boeotia sacred to the Muses.

2 *Muses* daughters of Zeus and Mnemosyne (Memory).

3 *Saturnian* Saturn (the Latin name for Cronus) was Zeus' father.

4 *Permessus*, like *Hippocrene* and *Olmius*, a stream on Helicon.

5 *Aegis* an attribute of Zeus and Athena; a snake-fringed skin ornamented with a Gorgon's head.

6 *Juno* Latin name for Hera, who had a cult center in Argos.

7 *Minerva* Latin name for Athena, daughter of Zeus.

8 *Apollo* god of poetry.

9 *Artemis* goddess of the wild and the hunt; *darts* arrows.

10 *Neptune* Latin name for Poseidon, god of the sea.

11 *Themis* a Titan goddess; the second wife of Zeus.

12 *Venus* Latin name for Aphrodite.

13 *Hebe* goddess of youth.

Nor fair *Dione* in their holy lays;[14]
Nor thou, *Aurora*, nor the *Day's great light*,[15]   25
Remain unsung, nor the fair *lamp of Night*;[16]
To thee, *Latona*, next the numbers range;[17]
Iäpetus, and *Saturn* wont to change,[18]
They chant; thee, *Ocean*, with an ample breast,[19]
They sing, and *Earth*, and *Night* in sable dressed;   30
Nor cease the virgins here the strain divine;
They celebrate the whole immortal line.
Erewhile as they the shepherd swain behold
Feeding, beneath the sacred mount, his fold,
With love of charming song his breast they fired;   35
There me the heav'nly *Muses* first inspired;
There, when the maids of *Jove* the silence broke,
To *Hesiod* thus, the shepherd swain, they spoke.
     "Shepherds attend, your happiness who place
In gluttony alone, the swain's disgrace;   40
Strict to your duty in the field you keep,
There vigilant by night to watch your sheep;
Attend ye swains on whom the *Muses* call,
Regard the honour not bestowed on all;[20]
'Tis ours to speak the truth in language plain,   45
Or give the face of truth to what we feign."
     So spoke the maids of *Jove*, the sacred nine,
And plucked a sceptre from the tree divine,
To me the branch they gave, with look serene,
The laurel ensign, never fading green: 50
I took the gift with holy raptures fired,
My words flow sweeter, and my soul's inspired;
Before my eyes appears the various scene
Of all that is to come, and what has been.
Me have the *Muses* chose, their bard to grace,   55
To celebrate the blessed immortal race;
To them the honours of my verse belong;
To them I first and last devote the song:
But where, O where, enchanted do I rove,
Or o'er the rocks, or through the vocal grove![21]   60

14   *Dione* a goddess; one of Zeus' consorts.
15   *Aurora* Latin name for Eos, goddess of
dawn; *Day's great light* literally, "great Helios,"
the sun god.
16   *lamp of Night* literally, "bright Selene," the
moon goddess.
17   *Latona* mother of Apollo and Artemis.
18   *Iäpetus* one of the Titans.

19   *Ocean* the god Oceanus, whose freshwater
river surrounds the world.
20   *Strict . . . all* these three lines are interpo-
lated by the translator and do not appear at all in
Hesiod.
21   *But . . . grove* literally, "But what is this
about oak and stone?" – an obscure phrase possi-
bly meaning "But I digress."

Now with th' harmonious nine begin, whose voice
Makes their great sire, Olympian *Jove*, rejoice;
The present, future, and the past, they sing,
Joined in sweet concert to delight their king;
Melodious and untired their voices flow;   65
Olympus echoes, ever crowned with snow.
The heav'nly songsters fill th' ethereal round;
Jove's palace laughs, and all the courts resound:
Soft warbling endless with their voice divine,
They celebrate the whole immortal line: 70
From *Earth*, and *Heav'n*, great parents, first they trace[22]
The progeny of gods, a bounteous race;
And then to *Jove* again returns the song,
Of all in empire, and command, most strong;
Whose praises first and last their bosom fire,   75
Of mortals, and immortal gods, the sire:
Nor to the sons of men deny they praise,
To such as merit of their heav'nly lays;
They sing the giants of puïssant arm,[23]
And with the wond'rous tale their father charm.   80
      Mnemosyne, in the *Pierian* grove,[24]
The scene of her intrigue with mighty *Jove*,
The empress of *Eleuther*, fertile earth,[25]
Brought to Olympian *Jove* the *Muses* forth;
Blessed offsprings, happy maids, whose pow'rful art   85
Can banish cares, and ease the painful heart.
Absent from heav'n, to quench his am'rous flame,
Nine nights the god of gods compressed the dame.[26]
Now thrice three times the moon concludes her race,
And shows the produce of the god's embrace,   90
Fair daughters, pledges of immortal *Jove*,
In number equal to the nights of love;
Blessed maids, by harmony of temper joined;
And verse, their only care, employs their mind.
The virgin songsters first beheld the light   95
Near where *Olympus* rears his snowy height;
Where to the maids fair stately domes ascend,[27]
Whose steps a constant beauteous choir attend.[28]

---

22 *Earth*, and *Heav'n* Gaia and Ouranos; pri-
mordial parents of the gods.

23 *giants* the mythical Giants, who fought with
the Olympian gods.

24 *Mnemosyne* goddess of memory; *Pierian
grove* a haunt of the Muses near Mt. Olympus.

25 *Eleuther* Eleutherae on Mt. Cithaeron; its
empress is Mnemosyne.

26 *compressed* embraced.

27 *domes* houses.

28 *choir* translating *choroi*, which means
"dancing bands."

Not far from hence the *Graces* keep their court,[29]
And with the god of love in banquets sport;   100
Meanwhile the nine their heav'nly voices raise
To the immortal pow'rs, the song of praise;
They tune their voices in a sacred cause,
Their theme the manners of the gods, and laws:
When to *Olympus* they pursue their way,   105
Sweet warbling, as they go, the deathless lay,
Meas'ring to *Jove*, with gentle steps, the ground,
The sable earth returns the joyful sound.
Great *Jove*, their sire, who rules th' ethereal plains,
Confirmed in pow'r, of gods the monarch reigns;   110
His father *Saturn* hurled from his command,
He grasps the thunder with his conqu'ring hand;
He gives the bolts their vigour as they fly,
And bids the red-hot lightning pierce the sky;
His subject deities obey his nod,   115
All honours flow from him of gods the god;
From him the *Muses* sprung, no less their sire,
Whose attributes the heav'nly maids inspire:
Clio begins the lovely tuneful race,[30]
Melpomene which, and *Euterpe*, grace,   120
Terpsichore all joyful in the choir,
And *Erato* to love whose lays inspire;
To these *Thalia* and *Polymnia* join,
Urania, and *Calliope* divine,
The first, in honour, of the tuneful nine;   125
She the great acts of virtuous monarchs sings,
Companion only for the best of kings.

from *Works and Days*

lines 53–201

In the *Theogony* Hesiod relates how Prometheus tricked Zeus into accepting the bones and fat of sacrificial victims instead of the meat, which was reserved for men. In response Zeus deprived men of fire. Prometheus then stole fire from the gods and restored it to men, thereby incurring the wrath of Zeus. He was punished by being chained to a rock where an eagle daily plucked out his nightly regenerative liver. Zeus allowed men to keep fire but he offset this blessing with Pandora – the

29 *Graces* goddesses of beauty and charm.
30 *Clio* from the Greek verb "to celebrate"; the names of the Muses all convey their role as heav-enly singers. The assignment of particular arts to individual Muses was a later refinement.

Greek Eve – who released evils into the world from her jar. The myth of Pandora implies a deterioration of the human condition. The myth of the five races (later converted into four ages) treats systematically of this decline. The golden race was blessed with youth, happiness, and plenty. The silver enjoyed a long childhood but was foolish and neglectful of the gods. The bronze, a violent race, was consumed with war. The iron race, among whom Hesiod locates himself, is marked by work and sorrow.

The scheme of four deteriorating metallic races found its way to Greece from the Near East, where it appears in several mythological forms. Hesiod breaks the regularity of the scheme by inserting a fifth race between the bronze and the iron – the race of heroes whom the Greeks believed to have lived before their own historical era. This race was sometimes omitted in later versions of the myth, all of which derive ultimately from Hesiod. Hesiod's misogyny and pessimism contribute to his gloomy picture of the human condition. Within the larger context of the *Works and Days* they function, however, more as a warning than as a final judgment. Hesiod's pessimism, like Adam's sadness after the Fall in *Paradise Lost*, is tempered with trust in the justice of God and the capacity of humans to support a tolerable existence through hard work.

This passage is the earliest classical source for two major themes in English literature – those of misogyny and the Golden Age. The first is represented in this anthology by Chaucer's *Wife of Bath's Prologue* (p. 4 above) and (in reaction to male attitudes) Leapor's "Essay on Woman" (p. 161 above). The second is represented by Lovelace's "Love Made in the First Age: To Chloris" (p. 83 above) and Behn's "The Golden Age" (p. 100 above), among others.

The translation is again by Thomas Cooke (see p. 276 above).

Again defrauded of celestial fire,
Thus spoke the cloud-compelling god in ire:[1]
"Son of *Iäpetus*, o'er-subtle, go,[2]
And glory in thy artful theft below;
Now of the fire you boast by stealth retrieved,   5
And triumph in almighty *Jove* deceived;
But thou too late shall find the triumph vain,
And read thy folly in succeeding pain;
Posterity the sad effect shall know,
When, in pursuit of joy, they grasp their woe."   10
He spoke, and told to *Mulciber* his will,[3]
And, smiling, bade him his commands fulfil,

LINES 53–201

1 *cloud-compelling god* Zeus.

2 *Iäpetus* a Titan and the father of Prometheus.

3 *Mulciber* Hephaestus, the smith god.

To use his greatest art, his nicest care,
To frame a creature exquisitely fair,
To temper well the clay with water, then   15
To add the vigour, and the voice, of men,
To let her first in virgin lustre shine,
In form a goddess, with a bloom divine:
And next the sire demands *Minerva*'s aid,[4]
In all her various skill to train the maid,   20
Bids her the secrets of the loom impart,
To cast a curious thread with happy art:
And golden *Venus* was to teach the fair[5]
The wiles of love, and to improve her air,
And then, in awful majesty, to shed[6]   25
A thousand graceful charms around her head:
Next *Hermes*, artful god, must form her mind,[7]
One day to torture, and the next be kind,
With manners all deceitful, and her tongue
Fraught with abuse, and with detraction hung.   30
Jove gave the mandate; and the gods obeyed.
First *Vulcan* formed of earth the blushing maid;[8]
Minerva next performed the task assigned,
With ev'ry female art adorned her mind.
To dress her *Suada*, and the *Graces*, join;[9]   35
Around her person, lo! the diamonds shine.[10]
To deck her brows the fair-tressed *Seasons* bring[11]
A garland breathing all the sweets of spring.
Each present *Pallas* gives its proper place,[12]
And adds to ev'ry ornament a grace.   40
Next *Hermes* taught the fair the heart to move,
With all the false alluring arts of love,
Her manners all deceitful, and her tongue
With falsehoods fruitful, and detraction hung.
The finished maid the gods *Pandora* call,[13]   45
Because a tribute she received from all:
And thus, 'twas *Jove*'s command, the sex began,
A lovely mischief to the soul of man.
When the great sire of gods beheld the fair,
The fatal guile, th' inevitable snare,   50

---

4   *Minerva* Latin name for Athena, goddess of crafts.
5   *Venus* Latin name for Aphrodite.
6   *awful* producing awe in the beholder.
7   *Hermes* the messenger god; a famous trickster.
8   *Vulcan* Latin name for Hephaestus.

9   *Suada* Latin for Peitho, the goddess of persuasion; *Graces* goddesses of beauty and charm.
10   *diamonds* literally, "golden chains."
11   *Seasons* the Horae, goddesses of the seasons.
12   *Pallas* Athena.
13   *Pandora* "All-gift."

Hermes he bids to *Epimetheus* bear.[14]
Prometheus, mindful of his theft above,
Had warned his brother to beware of *Jove*,
To take no present that the god should send,
Lest the fair bribe should ill to man portend;   55
But he, forgetful, takes his evil fate,
Accepts the mischief, and repents too late.
Mortals at first a blissful earth enjoyed,
With ills untainted, nor with cares anoyed;
To them the world was no laborious stage,   60
Nor feared they then the miseries of age;
But soon the sad reversion they behold,
Alas! they grow in their afflictions old;
For in her hand the nymph a casket bears,[15]
Full of diseases, and corroding cares,   65
Which opened, they to taint the world begin,
And *Hope* alone remains entire within.
Such was the fatal present from above,
And such the will of cloud-compelling *Jove*:
And now unnumbered woes o'er mortals reign,   70
Alike infected is the land, and main,[16]
O'er human race distempers silent stray,
And multiply their strength by night and day;
'Twas *Jove*'s decree they should in silence rove;
For who is able to contend with *Jove*!   75
And now the subject of my verse I change;
To tales of profit and delight I range;
Whence you may pleasure and advantage gain,
If in your mind you lay the useful strain.
  Soon as the deathless gods were born, and man,   80
A mortal race, with voice endowed, began,
The heav'nly pow'rs from high their work behold,
And the first age they style an age of gold.[17]
Men spent a life like gods in *Saturn*'s reign,[18]
Nor felt their mind a care, nor body pain;   85
From labour free they ev'ry sense enjoy;
Nor could the ills of time their peace destroy;
In banquets they delight, removed from care;
Nor troublesome old age intruded there:
They die, or rather seem to die, they seem   90
From hence transported in a pleasing dream.

---

14   *Epimetheus* "Afterthought"; the brother of
Prometheus (Forethought).
15   *casket* a jar in Hesiod; the idea of "Pandora's
box" originates from an error of Erasmus'.

16   *main* sea.
17   *age* a race, not an age, in Hesiod.
18   *Saturn* Latin name for Cronus.

The fields, as yet untilled, their fruits afford,
And fill a sumptuous, and unenvied board:
Thus, crowned with happiness their ev'ry day,
Serene, and joyful, passed their lives away.   95
    When in the grave this race of men was laid,
Soon was a world of holy daemons made,
Aërial spirits, by great *Jove* designed,
To be on earth the guardians of mankind;
Invisible to mortal eyes they go,   100
And mark our actions, good, or bad, below;
Th' immortal spies with watchful care preside,
And thrice ten thousand round their charges glide:
They can reward with glory, or with gold;[19]
A pow'r they by divine permission hold.   105
    Worse than the first, a second age appears,
Which the celestials call the silver years.
The golden age's virtues are no more;
Nature grows weaker than she was before;
In strength of body mortals much decay;   110
And human wisdom seems to fade away.
A hundred years the careful dames employ,
Before they formed to man th' unpolished boy;
Who when he reached his bloom, his age's prime,
Found, measured by his joys, but short his time.   115
Men, prone to ill, denied the gods their due,
And, by their follies, made their days but few.
The altars of the blessed neglected stand,
Without the off'rings which the laws demand;
But angry *Jove* in dust this people laid,   120
Because no honours to the gods they paid.
This second race, when closed their life's short span,
Was happy deemed beyond the state of man;
Their names were grateful to their children made;
Each paid a rev'rence to his father's shade.   125
    And now a third, a brazen, people rise,
Unlike the former, men of monstrous size:
Strong arms extensive from their shoulders grow,
Their limbs of equal magnitude below;
Potent in arms, and dreadful at the spear,   130
They live injurious, and devoid of fear:
On the crude flesh of beasts, they feed, alone,
Savage their nature, and their hearts of stone;
Their houses brass, of brass the warlike blade,
Iron was yet unknown, in brass they trade: 135

19 *They . . . gold* Hesiod calls them "givers of
wealth," probably in the sense of good crops.

Furious, robust, impatient for the fight,
War is their only care, and sole delight.
To the dark shades of death this race descend,
By civil discords, an ignoble end!
Strong though they were, death quelled their boasted might,   140
And forced their stubborn souls to leave the light.
    To these a fourth, a better, race succeeds,
Of godlike heroes, famed for martial deeds;
Them demigods, at first, their matchless worth
Proclaim aloud, all through the boundless earth.   145
These, horrid wars, their love of arms, destroy,
Some at the gates of *Thebes*, and some at *Troy*.[20]
These for the brothers fell, detested strife!
For beauty those, the lovely *Grecian* wife![21]
To these does *Jove* a second life ordain,   150
Some happy soil far in the distant main,
Where live the hero-shades in rich repast,
Remote from mortals of a vulgar cast:
There in the islands of the blessed they find,
Where *Saturn* reigns, an endless calm of mind;   155
And there the choicest fruits adorn the fields,
And thrice the fertile year a harvest yields.
    O! would I had my hours of life began
Before this fifth, this sinful, race of man;
Or had I not been called to breathe the day,   160
Till the rough iron age had passed away!
For now, the times are such, the gods ordain,
That ev'ry moment shall be winged with pain;
Condemned to sorrows, and to toil, we live;
Rest to our labour death alone can give;   165
And yet, amid the cares our lives annoy,
The gods will grant some intervals of joy:
But how degen'rate is the human state!
Virtue no more distinguishes the great;[22]
No safe reception shall the stranger find;   170
Nor shall the ties of blood, or friendship, bind;
Nor shall the parent, when his sons are nigh,
Look with the fondness of a parent's eye,
Nor to the sire the son obedience pay,
Nor look with rev'rence on the locks of grey,   175
But, o! regardless of the pow'rs divine,

20 *Thebes* an allusion to the struggle between Eteocles and Polyneices, the sons of Oedipus, for the kingship of Thebes.
21 *Grecian wife* Helen.
22 *But . . . great* not in Hesiod, who says: "But Zeus will destroy this race of mortal men when babies are born with white hair."

With bitter taunts shall load his life's decline.
Revenge and rapine shall respect command,
The pious, just, and good, neglected stand.
The wicked shall the better man distress,   180
The righteous suffer, and without redress;
Strict honesty, and naked truth, shall fail,
The perjured villain, in his arts, prevail.
Hoarse envy shall, unseen, exert her voice,
Attend the wretched, and in ill rejoice.   185
At last fair *Modesty* and *Justice* fly,[23]
Robed their pure limbs in white, and gain the sky;
From the wide earth they reach the blessed abodes,
And join the grand assembly of the gods,
While mortal men, abandoned to their grief,   190
Sink in their sorrows, hopeless of relief.

lines 504–35

In this selection Hesiod gives a lively description of winter, prompted by the
thought that farmers should prepare themselves for its rigors. This and similar
descriptions of the seasons in ancient poetry were among the sources of inspiration
for Thomson's *Winter* (p. 126 above).

The translation is again by Thomas Cooke (see p. 276 above).

The month all hurtful to the lab'ring kine,[1]
In part devoted to the god of wine,
Demands your utmost care; when raging forth,
O'er the wide seas, the tyrant of the north,
Bellowing through *Thrace*, tears up the lofty woods,[2]   5
Hardens the earth, and binds the rapid floods.
The mountain oak, high tow'ring to the skies,
Torn from his root across the valley lies;
Wide spreading ruin threatens all the shore,
Loud groans the earth, and all the forests roar: 10
And now the beast amazed, from him that reigns[3]
Lord of the woods to those which graze the plains,[4]

---

23 *Justice* Nemesis, goddess of retribution.

LINES 504–535

1 *The month* a winter month called Lenaeon, in
which the feast of the Lenaea was held in honor
of Dionysus, the god of wine.

2 *Thrace* a country north of the Aegean Sea.
3 *beast* a singular form with plural or collective
meaning.
4 *And now . . . plains* an expansion of Hesiod's
simple "beasts."

Shiv'ring the piercing blast, affrighted, flies,
And guards his tender tail betwixt his thighs.
Now nought avails the roughness of the bear,   15
The ox's hide, nor the goat's length of hair,
Rich in their fleece, alone the well-clothed fold[5]
Dread not the blust'ring wind, nor fear the cold.
The man, who could erect support his age,
Now bends reluctant to the north-wind's rage: 20
From accidents like these the tender maid,
Free and secure, of storms nor winds afraid,
Lives, nurtured chaste beneath her mother's Eye,
Unhurt, unsullied, by the winter's sky;
Or now to bathe her lovely limbs she goes,   25
Now round the fair the fragrant ointment flows;
Beneath the virtuous roof she spends the nights,
Stranger to golden *Venus*, and her rites.
Now does the boneless *Polypus*, in rage,[6]
Feed on his feet, his hunger to assuage;   30
The sun no more, bright shining in the day,
Directs him in the flood to find his prey;
O'er swarthy nations while he fiercely gleams,
Greece feels the pow'r but of his fainter beams.
Now all things have a different face below;   35
The beasts now shiver at the falling snow;
Through woods, and through the shady vale, they run
To various haunts, the pinching cold to shun;
Some to the thicket of the forest flock,
And some, for shelter, seek the hollow rock.[7]   40

---

5 *fold* flock of sheep.
6 *Polypus* the octopus, which was reputed to eat its own "feet."
7 *The beasts . . . rock* Cooke omits Hesiod's callous yet vivid simile: "Then like the three-footed one [an old man holding a stick] whose back is bent and head turned to the ground they wander in search of shelter from the white snow."

Sophocles
(c. 496–406 BCE)

Aeschylus, Sophocles, and Euripides are the three giants of Athenian tragic drama. Of these Sophocles lived the longest, probably produced the most work, and was most valued in his lifetime. Only seven of his more than 120 plays survive, but his three Theban plays (*Oedipus Tyrannus*, *Oedipus at Colonus*, and *Antigone*), composed at different times but often combined as a trilogy in modern translations, are among the most famous and influential works of Greek tragedy. When Aristotle delivered his lectures on poetry (the *Poetics*), he used *Oedipus Tyrannus* as his model for his seminal description of successful tragic drama. Its clear plot, complete with the dramatic discovery (or anagnorisis) of Oedipus' crime, and the emotional release or cleansing (catharsis) that it effects make *Oedipus Tyrannus* the archetypal tragedy in the western tradition. The play ends with Oedipus' self-inflicted blinding and the suicide of Jocasta, his wife and mother. *Oedipus at Colonus* follows the blind king to his last days in rustic isolation in Attica with his daughter Antigone. After her father's death, Antigone returns to Thebes and defies the new ruler, her uncle Creon, by honoring the body of her brother Polyneices. Polyneices had attacked Thebes to wrest the kingship from his brother Eteocles, but both brothers had died in battle leaving the city to Creon.

The supreme importance of Aristotle in the formation of neo-classical dramatic theory kept Sophocles in the forefront of thinking about classical drama from the late Renaissance through the eighteenth century. His name is most often linked with that of Euripides. Some neo-classical writers valued Euripides more because of the perceived epigrammatic and gnomic features of his verse, but Sophocles is present in every discussion of dramatic form, and he too is consistently valued as a poet. In the nineteenth century, Shelley went to his watery grave with copies of Sophocles and Keats in his pockets, and Matthew Arnold famously described him as one "who saw life steadily, and saw it whole." In the twentieth century E. M. Forster transmitted the Arnoldian dictum in *Howards End*; Yeats translated the two Oedipus plays; and Ezra Pound composed a version of Sophocles' *Trachiniae*. Sophoclean tragedies are perpetually in performance on the contemporary stage;

new translations (such as that of *Oedipus at Colonus* by Rachel Kitzinger and Eamon Grennan [2004]) continue to appear, and the influence of Sophocles goes on and on.

from *Antigone*

lines 582–603

In the passage below, the chorus – a singing and dancing band of actors tradition-ally featuring in Greek drama – responds to Creon's imprisonment of Antigone and reflects upon the curse of the house of Labdacus (Oedipus' ancestor). Matthew Arnold may have been thinking of the first stanza when he composed *Dover Beach* (p. 214 above).

The translation is by Edward Plumptre (1821–1891), a professor at King's College, London, and later dean of Wells Cathedral. His translations of Sophocles were first published in 1865.

Blessed are those whose life no woe doth taste!	
For unto those whose house	
The Gods have shaken, nothing fails of curse	
Or woe, that creeps to generations far.	
E'en thus a wave (when spreads,	5
With blasts from Thracian coasts,	
The darkness of the deep)	
Up from the sea's abyss	
Hither and thither rolls the black sand on,	
And every jutting peak,	10
Swept by the storm-wind's strength,	
Lashed by the fierce wild waves,	
Re-echoes with the far-resounding roar.	
I see the woes that smote, in ancient days,	15
The seed of Labdacus,[1]	
Who perished long ago, with grief on grief	
Still falling, nor does this age rescue that;	
Some God still smites it down,	
Nor have they any end:	20
For now there rose a gleam,	
Over the last weak shoots,	
That sprang from out the race of Oedipus;[2]	
Yet this the blood-stained scythe	

LINES 582–603

1 *Labdacus* king of Thebes and ancestor of Oedipus.

Of those that reign below 25
  Cuts off relentlessly,
And maddened speech, and frenzied rage of heart.

from *Trachiniae*

lines 112–40

The name of the play comes from Trachis, a place in Thessaly, some of whose inhabitants make up the chorus. The play opens with a scene depicting the anxiety of Deianira about her husband Heracles, who has been long absent. The chorus of Trachinian women acknowledges his many trials but offers the consolation that troubles do not last forever. The consolation is tinged with irony, however, because the play turns out to be about Heracles' death. The simile of the billows in the first stanza is one of the possible sources for Arnold's allusion to Sophocles in *Dover Beach* (p. 215 above).

The translation is by Lewis Campbell (1830–1908), a professor of Greek at St. Andrews University who was much influenced by his Oxford teacher Benjamin Jowett. Campbell's translations of Sophocles were first published in 1883.

For many as are billows of the South
Blowing unweariedly, or Northern gale,
One going and another coming on
Incessantly, baffling the gazer's eye,
Such Cretan ocean of unending toil 5
Cradles our Cadmus-born, and swells his fame.[1]
  But still some power doth his foot recall
  From stumbling down to Hades' darkling hall.

Wherefore, in censure of thy mood, I bring[2]
Glad, though opposing, counsel. Let not hope 10
Grow weary. Never hath a painless life
Been cast on mortals by the power supreme
Of the All-disposer, Cronos' son. But joy[3]
And sorrow visit in perpetual round
  All mortals, even as circleth still on high 15
  The constellation of the Northern sky.[4]

---

2 *Oedipus* king of Thebes who fulfilled an oracle that he would kill his father and marry his mother.

LINES 112–140

1 *Cadmus-born* Heracles was born in Thebes, a city founded by Cadmus.

2 *thy* Deianira's.

3 *Cronos' son* Zeus.

4 *constellation of the Northern sky* Ursa Major or the Big Dipper, which appears to revolve around the pole.

What lasteth in the world? Not starry night,
Nor wealth, nor tribulation; but is gone
All suddenly, while to another soul
The joy or the privation passeth on.　　　　　　　　　　20
These hopes I bid thee also, O my Queen!
Hold fast continually, for who hath seen
Zeus so forgetful of his own?
How can his providence forsake his son?[5]

5　*son* Heracles.

Thucydides
(c. 455–400 BCE)

As *strategos* – an elected commander – in 424 BCE, Thucydides commanded an Athenian fleet in the struggle against Sparta until an accident of war led to his arraignment and banishment for failure to save the colony of Amphipolis from capture. In exile he put together his thoughts on the Peloponnesian War (431–404 BCE), which he perceived from its beginning would be the most important war fought up to that time in the western world. He returned to Athens when the war was over but died before completing his history, which breaks off in the winter of 411/410. Unlike most early historians, Thucydides strove for accuracy above all in his historical account. This would make it "a possession for all time," he averred, since human events tend to repeat themselves. His style is energetic but rough and compressed rather than fluid or smooth. He seems to be representing reality in all its asperity. Some of the speeches he created for his principals are among the most famous and most difficult in Greek literature. The most famous of these is Pericles' funeral oration for the fallen Athenian soldiers. Equally great are some of Thucydides' accounts of military action. High among these are his accounts of the Sicilian Expedition in Books 6–7, which occurred after he had gone into exile. Matthew Arnold probably thought of one of these accounts when he composed *Dover Beach* (p. 214 above).

In 415 BCE, during a latter phase of the Peloponnesian War, the Athenians sent a large expedition to besiege the Sicilian city of Syracuse. Two years later, the expedition ended in disaster. In this passage Thucydides describes the Athenians' failure to capture a Syracusan fortress by nocturnal assault.

The translation is by Richard Crawley (1840–1893), a fellow of Worcester College, Oxford, and author of plays and poems. His translation of Thucydides, considered his most important work, was published in 1866 but thoroughly revised in 1874.

from *The Peloponnesian War*

Book 7, section 44

The Athenians now fell into great disorder and perplexity, so that it was not easy to get from one side or the other any detailed account of the affair. By day certainly the combatants have a clearer notion, though even then by no means of all that takes place, no one knowing much of anything that does not go on in his own immediate neighbourhood; but in a night engagement (and this was the only one that occurred between great armies during the war) how could any one know anything for certain? Although there was a bright moon they saw each other only as men do by moonlight, that is to say, they could distinguish the form of the body, but could not tell for certain whether it was a friend or an enemy. Both had great numbers of heavy infantry moving about in a small space. Some of the Athenians were already defeated, while others were coming up yet unconquered for their first attack. A large part also of the rest of their forces either had only just got up, or were still ascending, so that they did not know which way to march. Owing to the rout that had taken place all in front was now in confusion, and the noise made it difficult to distinguish anything. The victorious Syracusans and allies were cheering each other on with loud cries, by night the only possible means of communication, and meanwhile receiving all who came against them; while the Athenians were seeking for one another, taking all in front of them for enemies, even although they might be some of their now flying friends; and by constantly asking for the watchword,[1] which was their only means of recognition, not only caused great confusion among themselves by asking all at once, but also made it known to the enemy, whose own they did not so readily discover, as the Syracusans were victorious and not scattered, and thus less easily mistaken. The result was that if the Athenians fell in with a party of the enemy that was weaker than they, it escaped them through knowing their watchword; while if they themselves failed to answer they were put to the sword. But what hurt them as much, or indeed more than anything else, was the singing of the Paean,[2] from the perplexity which it caused by being nearly the same on either side: the Argives[3] and Corcyraeans[4] and any other Dorian peoples[5] in the army, struck terror into the Athenians whenever they raised their Paean, no less than did the enemy. Thus, after being once thrown into disorder, they ended by coming into collision with each other in many parts of the field, friends with friends, and citizens with citizens, and not only terrified one another, but even came to blows and could only be parted with difficulty. In the

BOOK 7, SECTION 44

1   *watchword* a code word established to serve as an identification badge for soldiers of the same army.

2   *Paean* war chant.

3   *Argives* Athenian allies from Argos in southern Greece.

4   *Corcyraeans* Athenian allies from the island of Corcyra, modern Corfu.

5   *Dorian peoples* Greeks of common ancestry who used the Doric dialect; confusion resulted from the presence of Dorians on both sides.

pursuit many perished by throwing themselves down the cliffs, the way down from Epipolae[6] being narrow; and of those who got down safely into the plain, although many, especially those who belonged to the first armament, escaped through their better acquaintance with the locality, some of the newcomers lost their way and wandered over the country, and were cut off in the morning by the Syracusan cavalry and killed.

6   *Epipolae* a fortified plateau overlooking Syracuse.

Plato (c. 429–347 BCE)

Plato was born into a wealthy family at the height of Athens' power and glory, three years into the Peloponnesian War that ended in 404 BCE with its humiliating defeat. As he grew to manhood, he came under the spell of Socrates, one of the most familiar figures on the streets of Athens – a snub-nosed, satyr-like philosopher who delighted in impromptu discussion and puncturing the pretensions of his interlocutors. The execution of Socrates in 399 BCE on trumped-up charges made him, for some, a martyr to truth. Plato used the trial and death of Socrates as the basis for works such as the *Apology* and *Phaedo* and retained him as his central literary character throughout most of his life. His surviving writings, including the famous *Republic*, an investigation of justice, are mainly dialogues in which Socrates debates important philosophical questions with other historical figures of the time. Using the method named after him, Socrates leads his interlocutors to greater heights of understanding than they have achieved on their own. In general, the thrust of Plato's work is to stimulate thinking and reduce the thoughtless acceptance of traditional values and practices. He taught the European world to believe that the unexamined life is not worth living. Plato's work is also the source of most thinking about the realm of ideas, and of the notion that such a realm may be permanent and immutable while the world of experience is constantly changing. Plato lived and taught at the Academy, a gymnasium sacred to the hero Academus, which became the first school of philosophy in antiquity and the forerunner of the modern university.

The great twentieth-century thinker Alfred North Whitehead observed that the entire "European philosophical tradition" could safely be described as "a series of footnotes to Plato." Amongst his most influential ideas have been the theory of Forms or Ideas, the educative notion of love known as Platonic Love, the criticism of poetry and art as a corrupting influence, and the call for philosopher-kings. His influence on literary tradition is not as clear, but it is certainly deep. Plato's ideas have penetrated so deeply into western thinking that it is almost impossible for writers to avoid their influence, even if they have not read Plato's works.

from *Symposium*

sections 209e–212a

The *Symposium* is a dialogue in which the guests at a dinner party take turns prais-
ing *eros* or love. The following extract is from the speech of Socrates, which
expounds some of Plato's profoundest views on love under the guise of instruction
that Socrates claims to have received from a wise woman called Diotima. Although
he most often dwelt on the power of reason to reveal the eternal truths hidden
by the shifting shadow of experience, in this dialogue Plato examines the educa-
tional potential of love. From the love of a physical form, Socrates argues, a person
may be guided toward the love of spiritual beauty and thence to the beauty of
institutions, laws, and sciences, and finally to Beauty itself – the form or idea of
beauty. Knowledge of true beauty will in turn inspire thoughts and actions that
are truly beautiful. When Keats ended his "Ode on a Grecian Urn" with the
famous teaching "Beauty is truth, truth beauty," he was echoing, in a distant but
unmistakable way, the lessons of Plato's *Symposium*.

The translation is by Benjamin Jowett (1817–1893), the master of Balliol
College, Oxford, and first appeared in 1871. Although Jowett's translation was
criticized by later scholars and critics, it was for many years the most read and
continues to be one of the most influential versions of Plato in English.

"These are the lesser mysteries[1] of love, into which even you, Socrates, may enter;
to the greater and more hidden ones which are the crown of these, and to which, if
you pursue them in a right spirit, they will lead, I know not whether you will be able
to attain. But I will do my utmost to inform you, and do you follow if you can. For
he who would proceed aright in this matter should begin in youth to visit beautiful
forms; and first, if he be guided by his instructor aright, to love one such form only
– out of that he should create fair thoughts; and soon he will of himself perceive that
the beauty of one form is akin to the beauty of another; and then if beauty of form
in general is his pursuit, how foolish would he be not to recognize that the beauty
in every form is one and the same! And when he perceives this he will abate his violent
love of the one, which he will despise and deem a small thing, and will become a
lover of all beautiful forms; in the next stage he will consider that the beauty of the
mind is more honourable than the beauty of the outward form. So that if a virtuous
soul have but a little comeliness, he will be content to love and tend him, and will
search out and bring to the birth thoughts which may improve the young, until he
is compelled to contemplate and see the beauty of institutions and laws, and to
understand that the beauty of them all is of one family, and that personal beauty is

SECTIONS 209E–212A

1   *mysteries* a metaphor referring to mystery-cults
that required initiation.

a trifle; and after laws and institutions he will go on to the sciences, that he may see their beauty, being not like a servant in love with the beauty of one youth or man or institution, himself a slave mean and narrow-minded, but drawing towards and contemplating the vast sea of beauty, he will create many fair and noble thoughts and notions in boundless love of wisdom; until on that shore he grows and waxes strong, and at last the vision is revealed to him of a single science, which is the science of beauty everywhere. To this I will proceed; please to give me your very best attention:

"He who has been instructed thus far in the things of love, and who has learned to see the beautiful in due order and succession, when he comes toward the end will suddenly perceive a nature of wondrous beauty (and this, Socrates, is the final cause of all our former toils) – a nature which in the first place is everlasting, not growing and decaying, or waxing and waning; secondly, not fair in one point of view and foul in another, or at one time or in one relation or at one place fair, at another time or in another relation or at another place foul, as if fair to some and foul to others, or in the likeness of a face or hands or any other part of the bodily frame, or in any form of speech or knowledge, or existing in any other being, as for example, in an animal, or in heaven, or in earth, or in any other place; but beauty absolute, separate, simple, and everlasting, which without diminution and without increase, or any change, is imparted to the ever-growing and perishing beauties of all other things. He who from these ascending under the influence of true love, begins to perceive that beauty, is not far from the end. And the true order of going, or being led by another, to the things of love, is to begin from the beauties of earth and mount upwards for the sake of that other beauty, using these as steps only, and from one going on to two, and from two to all fair forms, and from fair forms to fair practices, and from fair practices to fair notions, until from fair notions he arrives at the notion of absolute beauty, and at last knows what the essence of beauty is. This, my dear Socrates," said the stranger of Mantineia,[2] "is that life above all others which man should live, in the contemplation of beauty absolute; a beauty which if you once beheld, you would see not to be after the measure of gold, and garments, and fair boys and youths, whose presence now entrances you; and you and many a one would be content to live seeing them only and conversing with them without meat or drink, if that were possible – you only want to look at them and to be with them. But what if man had eyes to see the true beauty – the divine beauty, I mean, pure and clear and unalloyed, not clogged with the pollutions of mortality and all the colours and vanities of human life – thither looking, and holding converse with the true beauty simple and divine? Remember how in that communion only, beholding beauty with the eye of the mind, he will be enabled to bring forth, not images of beauty, but realities (for he has hold not of an image but of a reality), and bringing forth and nourishing true virtue to become the friend of God[3] and be immortal, if mortal man may. Would that be an ignoble life?"

2 *stranger of Mantineia* Diotima.

3 *friend of God* an anachronistic translation of Plato's adjective "dear to the gods" (θεοφιλής).

from *Ion*

sections 533c–535a

The *Ion* is a dialogue between Socrates and the rhapsode Ion, a professional reciter of poetry. Ion is a brilliant performer and explicator of Homer but not of other poets. Socrates deduces from this that he owes his ability not to art but to divine inspiration – a kind of possession – transmitted from the Muse to Homer and thence to Ion like the power of a magnet through a chain of iron rings. Plato's attitude to poetry is ambivalent. He recognizes its power to move the soul but questions its claim to teach knowledge or wisdom, the goal of philosophy. Plato pulls together his central thesis in a passage that is itself poetic in its richness of imagery and its linguistic beauty. The deep impression left by this passage on the mind of Samuel Taylor Coleridge is visible in the final lines of "Kubla Khan" (p. 178 above).

The translation is again by Benjamin Jowett (see p. 295 above).

SOCRATES: I perceive, Ion; and I will proceed to explain to you what I imagine to be the reason of this. The gift which you possess of speaking excellently about Homer is not an art, but, as I was just saying, an inspiration; there is a divinity moving you, like that contained in the stone which Euripides[1] calls a magnet, but which is commonly known as the stone of Heraclea.[2] This stone not only attracts iron rings, but also imparts to them a similar power of attracting other rings; and sometimes you may see a number of pieces of iron and rings suspended from one another so as to form quite a long chain: and all of them derive their power of suspension from the original stone. In like manner the Muse first of all inspires men herself; and from these inspired persons a chain of other persons is suspended, who take the inspiration. For all good poets, epic as well as lyric, compose their beautiful poems not by art, but because they are inspired and possessed. And as the Corybantian revellers[3] when they dance are not in their right mind, so the lyric poets are not in their right mind when they are composing their beautiful strains: but when falling under the power of music and metre they are inspired and possessed; like Bacchic maidens[4] who draw milk and honey from the rivers when they are under the influence of Dionysus[5] but not when they are in their right mind. And the soul of the lyric poet does the same, as they themselves say; for they tell us that they bring songs from honeyed fountains, culling them out of the gardens and dells of the Muses; they, like the bees, winging their way from flower to flower. And this is true. For the poet is a light and winged and holy thing, and there is no invention in him until he has been inspired and is

SECTIONS 533C–535A

1 *Euripides* Athenian tragedian (c. 485–406 BCE).

2 *Heraclea* city of Asia Minor.

3 *Corybantian revellers* worshippers of the goddess Cybele and Dionysus.

4 *Bacchic maidens* worshippers of Dionysus who in myth could perform miracles.

5 *Dionysus* god of wine and the release of inhibition.

out of his senses, and the mind is no longer in him: when he has not attained to this
state, he is powerless and is unable to utter his oracles. Many are the noble words in
which poets speak concerning the actions of men; but like yourself when speaking
about Homer, they do not speak of them by any rules of art: they are simply inspired
to utter that to which the Muse impels them, and that only; and when inspired, one
of them will make dithyrambs,[6] another hymns of praise, another choral strains,
another epic or iambic verses – and he who is good at one is not good at any other
kind of verse: for not by art does the poet sing, but by power divine. Had he learned
by rules of art, he would have known how to speak not of one theme only, but of
all; and therefore God[7] takes away the minds of poets, and uses them as his ministers,
as he also uses diviners and holy prophets, in order that we who hear them may know
them to be speaking not of themselves who utter these priceless words in a state of
unconsciousness, but that God himself is the speaker, and that through them he is
conversing with us. And Tynnichus[8] the Chalcidian affords a striking instance of what
I am saying: he wrote nothing that any one would care to remember but the famous
paean[9] which is in everyone's mouth, one of the finest poems ever written, simply an
invention of the Muses, as he himself says. For in this way the God would seem to
indicate to us and not allow us to doubt that these beautiful poems are not human,
or the work of man, but divine and the work of God; and that the poets are only
the interpreters of the Gods by whom they are severally possessed. Was not this the
lesson which the God intended to teach when by the mouth of the worst of poets
he sang the best of songs? Am I not right, Ion?

ION: Yes, indeed, Socrates, I feel that you are; for your words touch my soul, and
I am persuaded that good poets by a divine inspiration interpret the things of the
Gods to us.

---

6   *dithyrambs* choral songs to Dionysus.
7   *God* literally in Greek, "the god," a way of
describing divine agency without specifying a par-
ticular god.

8   *Tynnichus* poet of Chalcis (fifth century
BCE).
9   *paean* cult hymn of Apollo.

Asclepiades (fl. early third century BCE)

Asclepiades of Samos, also known as Sicelidas, was born around 320 BCE at the beginning of the Hellenistic age (conventionally dated from the death of Alexander the Great in 323 to the death of Cleopatra in 30 BCE). Many of his epigrams survive in the so-called *Greek Anthology*, a Byzantine compilation in 16 books of short poems dating from the seventh century BCE to the tenth century CE. The epigram (Greek for "inscription") originated as a short metrical composition to be inscribed on tombstones, votive tablets, and other material objects. Asclepiades was one of the pioneers of non-inscriptional, literary epigram, which became hugely popular in the Hellenistic age and later. The main characteristics of literary epigram are concision, elegance, and wit; its meter is the elegiac couplet. Erotic epigrams, a type invented or at least defined by Asclepiades, run the gamut of the pangs and pleasures attending love affairs with women and boys. A bowdlerized form of the anthology edited by a monk named Planudes in 1301 was the best-known form of the book until the original collection, known as the *Palatine Anthology*, was rediscovered in 1606. In one form or another, however, the *Anthology* has had a continuous effect on poetry since the tenth century. No less a poet and a moralist than Samuel Johnson is known to have beguiled sleepless hours in translating these long-lived poems.

from the *Greek Anthology*

Book 5, number 85

This poem delivers a *carpe diem* message sharpened by a graphic image of death that may have influenced Andrew Marvell's "To His Coy Mistress" (p. 90 above). The translation is by Dudley Fitts (1903–1968) and comes from *Poems from the Greek Anthology* (New Directions, 1956), where it is entitled "To His Mistress."

You deny me: and to what end?
There are no lovers, dear, in the under world,
No love but here: only the living know
The sweetness of Aphrodite –[1]
                                              but below,
But in Acheron, careful virgin, dust and ashes[2]
Will be our only lying down together.

Theocritus (fl. early third century BCE)

Theocritus was born in Syracuse in Sicily around 300 BCE but lived most of his life in the eastern Mediterranean, first on the island of Cos and then in the cosmopolitan city of Alexandria in northern Egypt. Founded by Alexander the Great in 331 BCE, this city quickly became a cultural magnet for poets and scholars, who were drawn to the famous library of Alexandria and the patronage of the ruling Ptolemies. Theocritus produced a small but highly original collection of what came to be called *Idylls* or "vignettes" (probably not his own title) together with a number of epigrams. The *Idylls* are for the most part hexameter poems of short length – the longest is 223 lines – written in an artificial, literary form of the Doric dialect that was spoken in the Peloponnese and places like Sicily which had been colonized by Doric speakers. They contain a variety of forms and subjects, including mythological narrative, encomia, and urban "mimes" comprising realistic conversation and monologue. (A famous one describes a girl's attempt to win her lover back by magic.) But the largest group of *Idylls* consists of the songs of rural herdsmen. To these charming poems Theocritus owes his renown as the inventor of bucolic or pastoral poetry (the former name deriving from Greek *boukolos*, an oxherd, the latter from Latin *pastor*, a shepherd). Though not devoid of realistic touches, the world of the bucolic poems is an idealized and sophisticated poetic invention, designed to awaken the nostalgia of an urban audience. It is populated by a cast of pseudo-naïve rustic characters who pause from their labors to banter and sing of their rivalries and loves amidst the beauty of the Sicilian countryside. Several poems take the form of a contest, in which the songs of rival singers alternate in the so-called amoebean form. *Idyll* 7 contains a thin disguise of Theocritus himself and his poetic friends, which opened the door to the fanciful allegories of Virgil in the *Eclogues* and his English imitators.

Theocritus was popular in the Hellenistic and Roman eras. As the model of ancient pastoral poets such as Bion, Moschus, and Virgil he rates among the most influential figures in western literature. The ancient pastoral poems provide the model for a vast amount of modern poetry. From the sixteenth to the nineteenth centuries, working in the pastoral form was virtually a requirement for aspiring poets. Marlowe, Spenser, Shakespeare, Milton, Marvell, Pope, and Shelley – to name only some of the greatest English poets who wrote in the pastoral form – would have been very different poets without the presence of Theocritus in their poetic backgrounds.

Idyll 1

The poem begins with a conversation between two herdsmen who compliment one another on their singing. The unnamed goatherd begs Thyrsis to sing his song about the passion of Daphnis and promises to reward him with a goat and an intricately carved wooden cup. Thyrsis obliges with an elaborate lament on the death of Daphnis. Daphnis was a legendary Sicilian herdsman and the inventor of pastoral song. According to one story he was blinded for infidelity by a nymph who loved him. In the version of Theocritus he dies of a passion inflicted on him by Aphrodite, who is angry at him for rejecting love. After invoking the Nymphs and the Muses, Thyrsis describes the reaction of nature, his fellow herdsmen, and the gods to Daphnis' suffering. Daphnis responds proudly to the taunts of Aphrodite, whom he taunts in turn with allusions to her misadventures in love and war. The poem ends with Thyrsis claiming his prize from the satisfied goatherd. As the first of the *Idylls*, the poem is programmatic and defines many of the elements that became standard in the pastoral genre: e.g., the *locus amoenus* or beautiful setting; the shepherd-singer; song competition; unhappy love; the "pathetic fallacy"; and the figure of the adynaton. The ekphrasis on the wooden cup – an exquisitely carved rustic object – defines the subject matter and aesthetics of bucolic poetry as opposed to traditional genres such as epic. In fact, it consciously invites comparison with the grand Homeric ekphrasis on the shield of Achilles (p. 250 above). The lament for Daphnis was much imitated by later exponents of pastoral elegy. Features such as the interrogation of the Nymphs ("Where were you . . . ?"), the refrain, the response of nature to human suffering, and the visitation of the gods recur in later examples such as Bion's *Lament for Adonis*, the *Lament for Bion* attributed to Moschus, and Virgil's *Eclogue* 10, as well as modern descendants such as Milton's *Lycidas* and Shelley's *Adonais*.

The translation is by the contemporary poet Robert Wells (1947–), reproduced with permission from *The Idylls: Theocritus* (Penguin Books, 1989).

THYRSIS

That pine tree by the spring and your touch on the pipe:
Both whisper a music to draw the listener in
With its sweetness, goatherd. Only Pan plays sweeter.[1]

IDYLL 1

1 *Pan* the Arcadian god of shepherds, in form half-man, half-goat; Pan plays the panpipes, which he invented by combining seven reeds of unequal length.

If he chooses the horned goat, you shall take the she-goat
For your prize. If he takes the she-goat, the kid shall be yours.   5
It tastes delicious, the flesh of an unmilked kid.

GOATHERD

Your song is sweeter, shepherd, than the waternoise
Made by the stream tumbling from its rocky spout.
If the Muses claim the ewe as a gift, you shall have[2]
The plump pet lamb. If they want the plump pet lamb   10
You shall take the sheep, and be second only to them.

THYRSIS

Sit down now, goatherd, (think the Nymphs had asked you)
And play your pipe, here where the hillside steepens
And tamarisks grow on the slope. I will watch your goats.

GOATHERD

There must be no piping at midday, shepherd, none: 15
We are scared of Pan. Now is the time when he rests
Tired out from the morning's hunting. He can turn nasty,
Tilting his nose at us, quick to take offence.
But, Thyrsis, you have composed 'The Passion of Daphnis'
And have made yourself a master of herdsmen's song.   20
Let's sit underneath this elm, with the glade before us:
There Priapus stands, there water spreads and gushes[3]
By the oaks and the shepherds' bench set into the hill.
If you sing as you did in the match with Libyan Chromis
I will let you have a goat that can suckle twins   25
And fill two pails besides, to be milked three times;
And will give you a deep, two-handled cup, new-made,
Washed in fresh wax, still fragrant from the knife.
About the lip of the cup an ivy pattern
Is carved, with golden points among the leaves: 30
A fluent tendril flaunting its yellow bloom.
Beneath is a woman's figure, delicately worked:
She is robed and wears a circlet to keep her hair.
On either side of her stand two bearded suitors
Arguing their claim. But she takes no notice,   35
Looks smilingly at one man, or so it appears,
Then at the other; while, hollow-eyed with love,
They struggle against her kindly indifference.

2 *Muses* the nine daughters of Zeus and   3 *Priapus* i.e. a statue of Priapus, a fertility
Mnemosyne, who preside over poetry and other   god.
arts (see Hesiod, *Theogony* 1–80; p. 275 above).

Beside these is carved an aged fisherman
On a jutting rock. He strains at the very edge   40
Of his strength to draw in a net with its heavy catch.
You can see the effort bunching in each tense limb
And in his neck as he gives himself to the task.
He has white hair, but his strength is supple and fresh.
A little distance from the old man's sea-labour   45
There is a vineyard hung with darkening clusters.
A small boy perches on a dry stone wall to guard them.
Two foxes shadow him. One sneaks along the rows
For plunder; another has fixed her tricky eye
On the quarter-loaf the boy keeps for his breakfast   50
And will not let him alone till she has snatched it.
Blithely intent, he shapes a cage for a cricket
From asphodel stalks and rushes. The bag with his food[4]
Is forgotten; so are the vines. The toy absorbs him.
The base of the cup is overspread with acanthus.   55[5]
A goatherd's treasure! It is too fine a thing.
I paid the Calydna ferryman a good price for it,[6]
A goat, a large cheese made of the best milk.
It felt too precious to drink from; I put it away
Unused. But how cheerfully I would part with it   60
For that beautiful elegy. Do you think I mock you?
No holding back! You cannot take your song with you
In the end. Hades and forgetfulness are the same.[7]

*

THYRSIS

Muses, sing for a herdsman, sing me your song.
   Thyrsis from Etna asks you. Listen to his voice.   65
Where were you, Nymphs, when Daphnis came to grief?
What distant valley or mountain gave you delight?
You could not be found beside Anapus, the great river,[8]
Nor by the water of Acis, nor on Etna's height.[9]
   Muses, sing for a herdsman, sing me your song.   70
Jackals and wolves howled their lament for Daphnis.
The lion wept in its forest-bound retreat.
Many the cattle that watched about him dying,
The bulls and cows and calves couched at his feet.

---

4 *asphodel* a lily which in poetry became an
immortal flower flourishing in Hades.
5 *acanthus* a thorny plant with elegant leaves,
sometimes pictured on classical columns.
6 *Calydna* an island off the coast of Cos.

7 *Hades* the god of the underworld or the
underworld itself.
8 *Anapus* river that find its outlet to the sea at
Syracuse.
9 *Acis* a Sicilian river; *Etna* the great volcanic
mountain on Sicily.

Muses, sing for a herdsman, sing me your song.   75
Hermes came from the mountain, said to him, "Daphnis,
Tell me what passion hurts you. Who is to blame?"
The cowherds, shepherds and goatherds gathered round him,
"Tell us your trouble," they asked. Old Priapus came.
    Muses, sing for a herdsman, sing me your song.   80
"Daphnis," he said, "an unhappy girl goes searching
Each glade and spring for the one on whom she dotes.
Are you her lover, incompetent, feeble-hearted?
You should change your cattle and take a flock of goats;
You are no better than a goatherd, watching and pining   85
While the billy does his work and the nanny bleats.
    Muses, sing for a herdsman, sing me your song.
"In tears you watch the girls, you hear their laughter;
Poor hobbledehoy, you long to join their dance."[10]
But the cowherd drew near the limit of his passion,   90
Deaf to taunts, absorbed in a bitter trance.
    Muses, sing for a herdsman, repeat your song.
Next came Cypris, her smile sweet and empty;[11]
Her heart was heavy, her cheerfulness a pretence.
"You boasted you were a match for Love in wrestling;   95
You lie there overthrown for your offence."
    Muses, sing for a herdsman, repeat your song.
Daphnis answered her, "Tormenting Cypris,
Hateful to all men, goddess of jealous pride,
Do you think my last sun is sinking? Even in Hades   100
Daphnis will be the thorn in Love's sleek side.
    Muses, sing for a herdsman, repeat your song.
"They say that a certain cowherd.... Hurry to Ida,[12]
Anchises lies there on a bed of galingale;[13]
The oaks will screen you, the humming bees tell no tale.   105
    Muses, sing for a herdsman, repeat your song.
"Adonis the shepherd-boy needs to take a lover.[14]
He hunts the hare and chases all kinds of prey.
Go set yourself before Diomede, and tell him[15]
'Daphnis paid for his boldness. You too must pay.'   110
    Muses, sing for a herdsman, repeat your song.
"Goodbye, you wolves and jackals, you skulking bears.
The forest-glades and thickets where you hide

10 *hobbledehoy* an awkward youth.

11 *Cypris* Aphrodite; she had a cult center on Cyprus.

12 *Ida* mountain overlooking Troy.

13 *Anchises* Trojan prince; Aphrodite was made to fall in love with him by Zeus, who resented her power; *galingale* a sedge with an aromatic root.

14 *Adonis* a youth loved by Aphrodite who was killed by a wild boar.

15 *Diomede* Greek hero at Troy who wounds and mocks Aphrodite (Homer, *Iliad* 5.334–51).

Shall never see me again. Goodbye, Arethusa,[16]
Goodbye, you streams that pour down Etna's side.　　　　　　115
Here Daphnis fed his cattle, here he watered them:
Remember him in the place where he lived and died.
　　Muses, sing for a herdsman, repeat your song.
"O Pan, are you ranging the long hills of Lycaeus[17]
Or the heights of Maenalus? Leave your ground and come[18]　　120
To Sicily. Leave Helice's peak and the mountain,[19]
Cherished by the gods, where Arcas has his tomb.[20]
　　Goodbye to the herdsman, Muses, goodbye to the song.
"Come, master, and take this pipe of mine, sweet-smelling,
Fastened with wax, the lip-piece delicately bound.　　　　　125
Love drags me into the darkness where no songs sound.
　　Goodbye to the herdsman, Muses, goodbye to the song.
"Bear violets now, you bramble-bushes and thorntrees,
Let the world turn cross-natured, since Daphnis dies.
Let the prickly juniper bloom with soft narcissus,　　　　　130
The pine be weighed with pears. Let the stag hunt the hounds,
Let the nightingale attend to the screech-owl's cries."[21]
　　Goodbye to the herdsman, Muses, goodbye to the song.
He said nothing more. Aphrodite struggled to raise him,
But the thread allowed by the Fates had run to its end.[22]　　135
Daphnis drew near the water and the current took him,
Unhappy child of the Muses, the Nymphs' lost friend.
　　Goodbye to the herdsman, Muses, goodbye to the song.

*

Now give me the goat and the carved cup. Let me milk her
And drink to the Muses.　　　　　　　　　　　　　140
　　　　　　　　Muses, goodbye, but only
For the moment! In time I shall sing you a sweeter song.

GOATHERD
Then, Thyrsis, you must stop your mouth with sweetness,
Eat only honeycomb and the best dried figs,

16　*Arethusa* famous spring of Syracuse; in myth, Arethusa was a nymph who was changed to water when pursued by the river god Alpheus; she flowed under the sea and emerged on the island of Ortygia off Syracuse.

17　*Lycaeus* Arcadian mountain sacred to Pan.

18　*Maenalus* another mountain associated with Pan.

19　*Helice* a nymph also known as Callisto.

20　*Arcas* son of Zeus and Callisto, whom the jealous Hera turned into a bear; when Arcas was about to kill her in a hunt, Zeus changed them into the constellations of the Great Bear and Little Bear.

21　*Bear violets . . . cries* a list of natural impossibilities – a figure known as the adynaton (Greek for "impossible").

22　*Fates* three goddesses whose function is to spin, draw out, and cut the thread of human life.

Since, even as it is, you out-sing the cicada.   145
Here is the cup. Smell the scented wood, so fresh
You would think it had been dipped at the well of the Hours.[23]
Cissaetha!
   Yours for milking!
       Gently, my goats,   150
Down! or you'll have the billy force you down.

Idyll 11

In this poem Theocritus extends the bucolic genre by casting the Cyclops Poly-
phemus as a lovesick shepherd-singer. His unsuccessful wooing of Galatea is
introduced, humorously, as proof that poetry is the best cure for love. The bum-
bling and innocent Polyphemus of Theocritus contrasts delightfully with the can-
nibal of *Odyssey* 9. Theocritus' sly allusions to the Homeric story add to the fun.
This poem is essential to an understanding of our selections from Marlowe (p. 44)
and Ralegh (p. 42). Those selections are only two of the most famous versions of
Theocritus' poem, which is the model for hundreds of *carpe diem* songs and poems
in which the speaker is a rustic man (or sometimes a woman) begging a more
sophisticated beauty to "come hither."

 The translation is by Elizabeth Barrett Browning (1806–1861) (see p. 311
below).

And so an easier life our Cyclops drew,[1]
 The ancient Polyphemus, who in youth[2]
Loved Galatea, while the manhood grew[3]
 Adown his cheeks and darkened round his mouth.
No jot he cared for apples, olives, roses;   5
 Love made him mad: the whole world was neglected,
The very sheep went backward to their closes
 From out the fair green pastures, self-directed.
  And singing Galatea, thus, he wore
  The sunrise down along the weedy shore,   10

---

23 *Hours* goddesses of the seasons.

IDYLL 11

1 *Cyclops* one of a race of one-eyed giants sup-
posed to inhabit Sicily. Browning has omitted the
first six lines in which Theocritus addresses his
friend Nicias – a doctor and a poet: "It seems to
me, Nicias, that there's no other medicine for

love, whether smeared or sprinkled, than the
Pierian maidens. This is a light and sweet thing
for men but not easy to find. I think you know
this well, being a doctor and exceptionally loved
by the nine Muses."
2 *Polyphemus* the Cyclops encountered by
Odysseus.
3 *Galatea* a sea nymph.

And pined alone, and felt the cruel wound
   Beneath his heart, which Cypris' arrow bore,[4]
With a deep pang; but, so, the cure was found;
    And sitting on a lofty rock he cast
    His eyes upon the sea, and sang at last: –   15
"O whitest Galatea, can it be
   That thou shouldst spurn me off who love thee so?
More white than curds, my girl, thou art to see,
More meek than lambs, more full of leaping glee
   Than kids, and brighter than the early glow   20
On grapes that swell to ripen, – sour like thee!
Thou comest to me with the fragrant sleep,
   And with the fragrant sleep thou goest from me;
Thou fliest . . . fliest, as a frightened sheep
   Flies the grey wolf! – yet Love did overcome me,   25
So long; – I loved thee, maiden, first of all
   When down the hills (my mother fast beside thee)[5]
I saw thee stray to pluck the summer-fall
   Of hyacinth bells, and went myself to guide thee:
And since my eyes have seen thee, they can leave thee   30
    No more, from that day's light! But thou . . . by Zeus,
Thou wilt not care for *that*, to let it grieve thee!
   I know thee, fair one, why thou springest loose
From my arm round thee. Why? I tell thee, Dear!
   One shaggy eyebrow draws its smudging road   35
Straight through my ample front, from ear to ear, –
   One eye rolls underneath; and yawning, broad
Flat nostrils feel the bulging lips too near.
Yet . . . ho, ho! – *I*, – whatever I appear, –
   Do feed a thousand oxen! When I have done,   40
I milk the cows, and drink the milk that's best!
   I lack no cheese, while summer keeps the sun;
And after, in the cold, it's ready pressed!
   And then, I know to sing, as there is none
Of all the Cyclops can, . . . a song of thee,   45
Sweet apple of my soul, on love's fair tree,
And of myself who love thee . . . till the West
Forgets the light, and all but I have rest.
I feed for thee, besides, eleven fair does,
   And all in fawn; and four tame whelps of bears.   50
Come to me, Sweet! thou shalt have all of those
   In change for love! I will not halve the shares.

---

4 *Cypris* Aphrodite.
5 *mother* the sea nymph Thoösa; his father was Poseidon.

Leave the blue sea, with pure white arms extended
   To the dry shore; and, in my cave's recess,
Thou shalt be gladder for the noonlight ended, –   55
   For here be laurels, spiral cypresses,
Dark ivy, and a vine whose leaves enfold
Most luscious grapes; and here is water cold,
   The wooded Etna pours down through the trees
From the white snows, – which gods were scarce too bold   60
   To drink in turn with nectar. Who with these
   Would choose the salt wave of the lukewarm seas?
Nay, look on me! If I am hairy and rough,
   I have an oak's heart in me; there's a fire
In these grey ashes which burns hot enough;   65
   And when I burn for *thee*, I grudge the pyre
No fuel . . . not my soul, nor this one eye, –
Most precious thing I have, because thereby
I see thee, Fairest! Out, alas! I wish
My mother had borne me finnèd like a fish,   70
That I might plunge down in the ocean near thee,
   And kiss thy glittering hand between the weeds,
If still thy face were turned; and I would bear thee
   Each lily white, and poppy fair that bleeds
Its red heart down its leaves! – one gift, for hours   75
   Of summer, . . . one, for winter; since, to cheer thee,
I could not bring at once all kinds of flowers.
Even now, girl, now, I fain would learn to swim,
   If stranger in a ship sailed nigh, I wis, –[6]
   That I may know how sweet a thing it is   80
To live down with you, in the Deep and Dim!
Come up, O Galatea, from the ocean,
   And having come, forget again to go!
As I, who sing out here my heart's emotion,
   Could sit for ever. Come up from below!   85
Come, keep my flocks beside me, milk my kine, –[7]
   Come, press my cheese, distrain my whey and curd![8]
Ah, mother! she alone . . . that mother of mine . . .
   Did wrong me sore! I blame her! – Not a word
Of kindly intercession did she address   90
Thine ear with for my sake; and ne'ertheless
   She saw me wasting, wasting, day by day!
   Both head and feet were aching, I will say,
All sick for grief, as I myself was sick!
   O Cyclops, Cyclops, whither hast thou sent   95

6 *I wis* literally "I know"; an archaism that   7 *kine* cattle; a poetic archaism.
mainly adds emphasis, "indeed!"   8 *distrain* strain out; consciously archaic.

Thy soul on fluttering wings? If thou wert bent
On turning bowls, or pulling green and thick[9]
  The sprouts to give thy lambkins, – thou wouldst make thee
  A wiser Cyclops than for what we take thee.
Milk dry the present! Why pursue too quick   100
That future which is fugitive aright?
  Thy Galatea thou shalt haply find, –
  Or else a maiden fairer and more kind;
For many girls do call me through the night,
  And, as they call, do laugh out silverly.   105
I, too, am something in the world, I see!"

  While thus the Cyclops love and lambs did fold,
  Ease came with song, he could not buy with gold.

---

9 *turning* carving or shaping.

Bion (fl. late second century BCE?)

Bion of Smyrna was a pastoral poet in the tradition of Theocritus and Moschus. Some fragments of his pastoral poetry survive and he is credited with the composition of the *Lament for Adonis*, a 98-line poem in hexameters. In mythology Adonis is a Cyprian youth with whom Aphrodite falls in love; she mourns grievously when he is gored to death by a boar in a hunting accident. By decree of Zeus he spends four months of the year in the underworld, four with Aphrodite, and four on his own. This suggests that he was an agricultural god of some kind. At the midsummer religious festival of the Adonia in Athens, women planted seeds in shallow soil on rooftops; the sprouts quickly wilted after springing up. The celebrations included a ritual cry of lamentation for the dead Adonis in imitation of Aphrodite's mourning. Bion's description of her grief draws upon the lament for Daphnis in Theocritus' *Idyll* 1 (p. 302 above) but takes the theme to new heights of sentimentality in its exploitation of the "pathetic fallacy" – the poetic idea that nature responds to human (or here, divine) emotions.

Along with Theocritus, Virgil, and the author of the *Lament for Bion*, Bion influenced the European pastoral tradition. His *Lament for Adonis* is clearly present in Milton's *Lycidas* (p. 67 above) and Shelley's *Adonais* (p. 180 above), two of the greatest English pastoral poems. The influence of Bion is also evident in Shakespeare's *Venus and Adonis* and Keats's *Hyperion*.

The translation is by Elizabeth Barrett Browning (1806–1861). Browning began her study of Greek at 10, and at 11 she wrote her own Homeric epic. Later in life she translated Aeschylus' *Prometheus Bound*, and then, dissatisfied with her first effort, translated it again. She was steeped in modern as well as classical authors, particularly Byron, Shelley, and Keats. She also, of course, produced a large body of her own poetry, including *Aurora Leigh* (1856), a lengthy "novel-poem" which one important contemporary critic called the greatest poem of the century.

Lament for Adonis

I

I mourn for Adonis – Adonis is dead,
    Fair Adonis is dead and the Loves are lamenting.[1]
Sleep, Cypris, no more on thy purple-strewed bed:[2]
    Arise, wretch stoled in black; beat thy breast unrelenting,
And shriek to the worlds, "Fair Adonis is dead!"   5

II

I mourn for Adonis – the Loves are lamenting,
    He lies on the hills in his beauty and death;
The white tusk of a boar has transpierced his white thigh.
    Cytherea grows mad at his thin gasping breath,[3]
While the black blood drips down on the pale ivory,   10
    And his eyeballs lie quenched with the weight of his brows,
The rose fades from his lips, and upon them just parted
    The kiss dies the goddess consents not to lose,
Though the kiss of the Dead cannot make her glad-hearted:
    He knows not who kisses him dead in the dews.   15

III

I mourn for Adonis – the Loves are lamenting.
    Deep, deep in the thigh is Adonis's wound,
But a deeper, is Cypris's bosom presenting.
    The youth lieth dead while his dogs howl around,
And the nymphs weep aloud from the mists of the hill,   20
    And the poor Aphrodité, with tresses unbound,
All dishevelled, unsandaled, shrieks mournful and shrill
    Through the dusk of the groves. The thorns, tearing her feet,
Gather up the red flower of her blood which is holy,
    Each footstep she takes; and the valleys repeat   25
The sharp cry she utters and draw it out slowly.
    She calls on her spouse, her Assyrian, on him[4]
Her own youth, while the dark blood spreads over his body,
    The chest taking hue from the gash in the limb,
And the bosom, once ivory, turning to ruddy.   30

LAMENT FOR ADONIS

1 *Loves* a pluralization of the god Eros.
2 *Cypris* Aphrodite, who came ashore at Paphos in Cyprus after springing from the severed genitals of Ouranos.

3 *Cytherea* Aphrodite; another version of her birth myth says that she landed on the island of Cythera.
4 *Assyrian* i.e. eastern; his father, Cinyras, came from Syria (see n. 14 below).

IV

Ah, ah, Cytherea! the Loves are lamenting.
    She lost her fair spouse and so lost her fair smile:
When he lived she was fair, by the whole world's consenting,
    Whose fairness is dead with him: woe worth the while!
All the mountains above and the oaklands below   35
    Murmur, "ah, ah, Adonis!" the streams overflow
Aphrodité's deep wail; river-fountains in pity
    Weep soft in the hills, and the flowers as they blow
Redden outward with sorrow, while all hear her go
    With the song of her sadness through mountain and city.   40

V

Ah, ah, Cytherea! Adonis is dead,
    Fair Adonis is dead – Echo answers, Adonis!
Who weeps not for Cypris, when bowing her head
    She stares at the wound where it gapes and astonies?[5]
– When, ah, ah! – she saw how the blood ran away   45
    And empurpled the thigh, and, with wild hands flung out,
Said with sobs: "Stay, Adonis! unhappy one, stay,
    Let me feel thee once more, let me ring thee about
With the clasp of my arms, and press kiss into kiss!
    Wait a little, Adonis, and kiss me again,   50
For the last time, beloved, – and but so much of this
    That the kiss may learn life from the warmth of the strain!
– Till thy breath shall exude from thy soul to my mouth,
    To my heart, and, the love-charm I once more receiving
May drink thy love in it and keep of a truth   55
    That one kiss in the place of Adonis the living.
Thou fliest me, mournful one, fliest me far,
    My Adonis, and seekest the Acheron portal, –[6]
To Hell's cruel King goest down with a scar,[7]
    While I weep and live on like a wretched immortal,   60
And follow no step! O Persephoné, take him,[8]
    My husband! – thou'rt better and brighter than I,
So all beauty flows down to thee: *I* cannot make him
    Look up at my grief; there's despair in my cry,
Since I wail for Adonis who died to me – died to me –   65
    Then, I fear *thee*! – Art thou dead, my Adored?

5 *astonies* makes astonished.
6 *Acheron* a river of the underworld or the underworld itself.
7 *Hell's cruel King* Hades.

8 *Persephoné* wife of Hades who spent half the year above ground with her mother Demeter and half in the underworld; her myth has something in common with that of Adonis.

Passion ends like a dream in the sleep that's denied to me,
   Cypris is widowed, the Loves seek their lord
All the house through in vain. Charm of cestus has ceased[9]
   With thy clasp! O too bold in the hunt past preventing,   70
Ay, mad, thou so fair, to have strife with a beast!"
   Thus the goddess wailed on – and the Loves are lamenting.

VI

Ah, ah, Cytherea! Adonis is dead.
She wept tear after tear with the blood which was shed,
And both turned into flowers for the earth's garden-close,   75
Her tears, to the windflower; his blood, to the rose.

VII

I mourn for Adonis – Adonis is dead.
   Weep no more in the woods, Cytherea, thy lover!
So, well: make a place for his corse in thy bed,[10]
   With the purples thou sleepest in, under and over.   80
He's fair though a corse – a fair corse, like a sleeper.
   Lay him soft in the silks he had pleasure to fold
When, beside thee at night, holy dreams deep and deeper
   Enclosed his young life on the couch made of gold.
Love him still, poor Adonis; cast on him together   85
   The crowns and the flowers: since he died from the place,
Why, let all die with him; let the blossoms go wither,
   Rain myrtles and olive-buds down on his face.
Rain the myrrh down, let all that is best fall a-pining,[11]
   Since the myrrh of his life from thy keeping is swept.   90
Pale he lay, thine Adonis, in purples reclining;
   The Loves raised their voices around him and wept.
They have shorn their bright curls off to cast on Adonis;
One treads on his bow, – on his arrows, another, –
One breaks up a well-feathered quiver, and one is   95
   Bent low at a sandal, untying the strings,
   And one carries the vases of gold from the springs,
While one washes the wound, – and behind them a brother
   Fans down on the body sweet air with his wings.

VIII

Cytherea herself now the Loves are lamenting.   100
   Each torch at the door Hymenaeus blew out;[12]

---

9 *cestus* Aphrodite's bewitching girdle.
10 *corse* corpse.

11 *myrrh* an aromatic gum resin used from ancient times in perfume and incense.
12 *Hymenaeus* god of marriage.

And, the marriage-wreath dropping its leaves as repenting,
    No more "Hymen, Hymen," is chanted about,
But the *ai ai* instead – "Ai alas!" is begun[13]
    For Adonis, and then follows "Ai Hymenaeus!"   105
The Graces are weeping for Cinyras' son,[14]
    Sobbing low each to each, "His fair eyes cannot see us!"
Their wail strikes more shrill than the sadder Dioné's.[15]
The Fates mourn aloud for Adonis, Adonis,[16]
Deep chanting; he hears not a word that they say: 110
    He *would* hear, but Persephoné has him in keeping.
– Cease moan, Cytherea! leave pomps for today,[17]
    And weep new when a new year refits thee for weeping.

13   *ai ai* the Greek way of stylizing the sound of lamentation.

14   *Graces* three goddesses of charm and beauty; *Cinyras* king of Cyprus; Adonis was the product of his incestuous union with his daughter Zmyrna or Myrrha.

15   *Dioné* mother of Aphrodite.

16   *Fates* three goddesses who apportion life and death.

17   *pomps* ostentatious displays.

Meleager (fl. 100 BCE)

Meleager was a Greek poet from Gadara in Syria about whom little is known. Many of his epigrams, mostly erotic in nature, survive in the *Greek Anthology* (for which see our introduction to Asclepiades; p. 299 above). Meleager himself compiled a famous anthology of epigrams entitled the *Garland*, which was one of the sources for the *Greek Anthology*.

from the *Greek Anthology*

Book 7, number 207

Book 7 of the *Greek Anthology* contains many epitaphs for animals and insects including hounds, horses, birds, and cicadas – even an ant! It is unlikely that many were actually inscribed on tombs. Some may be farewell pieces to beloved companions; others are outright fictions. It was conventional to represent the dead person or animal as speaking to the reader, who is imagined standing before a grave marker on which the epigram is inscribed. This epitaph for a hare surely came to William Cowper's mind when he memorialized Tiney (p. 164 above).

The translation is by Dudley Fitts (1903–1968) and comes from *Poems from the Greek Anthology* (New Directions, 1956).

Light-footed, floppy eared,
The baby hare:
Snatched away from my mother to be the pet

Of sweet-skinned Phanion:[1]
                          Spring blossoms   5
Were all my food,
                my mother was soon forgotten:
But I died at last of surfeit of dewy petals!
Now beside her bed my mistress has made my grave,
Even in dreams to keep me close to her breast.   10

1 *Phanion* a girl's name.

Moschus, so-called (first century BCE?)

Once attributed to Moschus (fl. 150 BCE), the *Lament for Bion* was probably composed a generation later by an unknown author, perhaps a disciple of Bion. Bion, whose *Lament for Adonis* is included in this volume (p. 312 above), flourished probably at the end of the second century BCE. The *Lament for Bion* alludes to Bion's *Lament for Adonis* (see n. 24 below) and makes the sensational claim that he died by poison. The poem became the model for other pastoral elegies honoring poets such as Virgil's *Eclogue* 10 (where Gallus dies, metaphorically, of love), Milton's *Lycidas*, and especially Shelley's *Adonais*, a tribute to Keats. Shelley translated the first seven lines of the poem in the following "Fragment of the Elegy on the Death of Bion":

> Ye Dorian woods and waves, lament aloud, –
> Augment your tide, O streams, with fruitless tears,
> For the belovèd Bion is no more.
> Let every tender herb and plant and flower,
> From each dejected bud and drooping bloom,
> Shed dews of liquid sorrow, and with breath
> Of melancholy sweetness on the wind
> Diffuse its languid love; let roses blush,
> Anemones grow paler for the loss
> Their dells have known; and thou, O hyacinth,
> Utter thy legend now – yet more, dumb flower,
> Than "Ah! alas!" – thine is no common grief –
> Bion the [sweetest singer] is no more.

Along with Theocritus, Virgil, and Bion, the unknown author of the *Lament for Bion* was influential throughout the European pastoral tradition. Clearly present in Milton's *Lycidas* (p. 67 above) and Shelley's *Adonais* (p. 180 above), he also influenced Milton's *Epitaphium Damonis* and Matthew Arnold's *Thyrsis*.

The translation offered here is by Thomas Warton junior (1728–1790), a scholar and poet laureate who edited Theocritus and wrote on Greek bucolic poetry. The translation was originally published in *Poems on Several Occasions* (1748), ostensibly a posthumous collection of Thomas Warton senior's poetry, but actually a combined effort of Thomas junior, his brother Joseph, and their father.

Lament for Bion

Ye Vales, and *Doric* Floods, or Fount, or Rill,[1]
Lament with me the much loved *Bion* dead;
Ye Forests pour your Plaints, ye Flow'rets mourn;
Utter, ye Hyacinths, the baleful Words[2]
That on your velvet Bells inscribed are seen;   5
Be clad, ye Roses, in sad Purple's Robe;
Dead is the Pride of Swains, and rural Song.
   Begin, *Sicilian* Muse, the plaintive Lay.[3]
Ye Poplar-shrouded Nightingales that oft
In midnight Hour complain, the dreary Tale   10
To listening *Arethusa*'s Waves prolong,[4]
And that with him each *Doric* Muse is fled.
   Begin, &c.
Ye Swans that warble sweet on *Strymon*'s Bank[5]
Come, steep in bitter Tears your sorrowing Song,   15
And tell in Notes like his th' Oeagrian Maids,[6]
And *Bacchus'* Nymphs that haunt *Bistonian* Hills,[7]
That *Doria*'s Vales their *Orpheus* dear have lost![8]
   Begin, &c.
No more the lovely Shepherd soothes his Herd   20
With soft-voiced Flute, beneath some ample Oak
At Ease reclined: But in black *Pluto*'s Bow'r[9]

LAMENT FOR BION

1 *Doric* an allusion to the Doric dialect established by Theocritus as the norm for pastoral poetry.

2 *baleful Words* the Greek exclamation *ai ai* (alas!), which the markings on hyacinth petals were supposed to resemble; the hyacinth was said to have sprung from the blood of Hyacinthus, a youth loved by Apollo who was killed by a discus throw.

3 *Sicilian Muse* the Muse of pastoral poetry, since Theocritus, its inventor, came from Sicily.

4 *Arethusa* a famous spring on the island of Ortygia off Syracuse.

5 *Strymon* a river of Thrace, where Orpheus (see n. 8 below) lived.

6 *Oeagrian* after Oeagrus, father of Orpheus; hence Thracian.

7 *Bacchus* god of wine and intoxication; *Bistonian* Thracian.

8 *That Doria's vales . . . lost* literally, "the Dorian Orpheus [i.e. Bion] is dead" – another allusion to the Doric dialect; *Orpheus* a mythical poet-singer of Thrace whose songs had the power to move nature.

9 *Pluto* god of the underworld.

Pours forth to grisly Ghosts *Lethëan* Lays,[10]
While here above each Mountain silent stands,
And his deserted Herds in Mutt'rings hoarse,   25
And sullen Lowings moan, nor deign to feed.
    Begin, &c.
Thy cruel Fate, dear Swain, *Apollo* wept,[11]
Thee too *Priapus* Sable-mantled mourned;[12]
And *Pan* surrounded with his Satyr-train[13]   30
Sighed sore, nor joyed to lead the merry Dance;
Wept the mild *Naiads* in their coral Caves;[14]
Nor Echo more from her far-winding Grot[15]
Is heard to sing, since now no more thy Verse,
And wonted tuneful Notes she can prolong.   35
    Begin, &c.
At thy sad Death the sympathizing Trees,
Dropt their half-ripened Fruits, and fading Flowers,
Hung down their blasted Blooms; the pining Flocks
Refused the milky Stream, nor more the Bee   40
With Thyme enriched his Nectar-streaming Cell.
    Begin, &c.
The Dolphin ne'er upon the sunny Shore
Made such deep Plaints, or in the rocky Wilds
Did *Philomel* e'er tune so sad a Dirge,[16]   45
Nor Mountain-loving Swallow such sad Notes
Was heard to pour, or with such heart-felt Woe
Cëyx deplored her dead *Halcyone*,[17]
Nor *Cerylus* in the *Caerulean* Deep[18]
Sorrowed so deep, or in th' *Eöan* Vale[19]   50
The Bird of *Memnon*, fair *Aurora*'s Son,[20]
As when they wept their best-loved *Bion*'s Fate.

10 *Lethëan Lays* songs able to cause forgetfulness like the waters of the infernal river Lethe.
11 *Apollo* god of poetry.
12 *Priapus* a fertility god.
13 *Pan* Arcadian god of shepherds and inventor of the panpipes.
14 *Naiads* water nymphs.
15 *Echo* a nymph condemned to repeat the words of others; her story provided a mythical origin for the existence of echoes (Ovid, *Metamorphoses* 3; pp. 447–9 below).
16 *Philomel* the ill-fated sisters Philomela and Procne were changed into a nightingale and swallow, whose songs were considered expressive of grief.

17 *Cëyx . . . Halcyone* Warton reverses the characters in this myth; according to the story, Alcyone grieves for her drowned husband Ceyx. Like other characters in this list, they were turned into birds.
18 *Cerylus* the human prototype of a mythical sea bird with the same name; *Caerulean* deep blue.
19 *Eöan* Eastern; from *eos*, the Greek word for dawn.
20 *Memnon* mythical king of Ethiopia who was killed at Troy; Zeus caused flocks of birds to rise from his funeral pyre; *Aurora* the dawn goddess, who was Memnon's mother.

Begin, &c.
Ye Nightingales, and Swallows swift, that oft
Have heard delighted his heart-thrilling Lays,   55
Whom seated in your leafy Groves he wont
To teach sweet Notes, responsive now repeat
The Voice of Woe, re-echoing through the Vale,
Join too ye Doves your sadly-pleasing Lays.
    Begin, &c.   60
Who now, forever dear, will tune thy Pipe?
Who to their Lip apply thy sacred Reed
Advent'rous? But to *Pan* the precious Gift
I'll bear, nor haply will he dare inspire
Thy Reed, lest thee superior he should prove.   65
    Begin, &c.
Thy Loss the green-haired *Galatëa* mourns,[21]
Who loved with thee upon the sea-beat Shore,
To sit enraptured with thy magic Verse.
For sweeter far than *Polypheme*'s thy Lay[22]   70
Flowed through her Ear; she fled the Cyclop-swain;
But ever to thy Song she hastened swift,
With dimply Cheek, and Looks of fond Desire.
No more she now regards old *Nereus'* Bow'r,[23]
But on the bare Sand sits, and tends thy Flock.   75
    Begin, &c.
With thee the Muse's choicest Joys are fled,
No more the Virgin's luscious Kiss delights;
Quenched is the Lamp of Love, and at thy Tomb
The weeping *Cupids* sprinkle freshest Flow'rs;   80
To *Venus* wert thou sweeter, gentlest Swain,
Than the last Kiss which on the clay-cold Lip
Of her *Adonis* dead the Goddess pressed.[24]
Come, *Meles*, hither turn thy sedge-crowned Head,[25]
Renew thy wonted Voice of baleful Woe;   85
That erst around thy saddened Banks was heard,[26]
And echoing filled blue *Neptune*'s distant Shores;
When cruel Fate thy first-born *Homer* snatched,
Whose Mouth *Calliope* with Nectar dewed.[27]

---

21 *Galatëa* a sea nymph.
22 *Polypheme* the Cyclops Polyphemus, whose unsuccessful wooing of Galatea was often mentioned in bucolic poetry (see Theocritus, *Idyll* 11; p. 307 above).
23 *Nereus* sea god; father of Galatea.
24 *Adonis* youth beloved of Aphrodite who was killed by a boar while hunting; an allusion to Bion's *Lament for Adonis* (p. 312 above).
25 *Meles* river of Smyrna, home of Bion. Smyrna was one of several cities that claimed to be the birthplace of Homer.
26 *erst* formerly.
27 *Calliope* one of the Muses.

But now thy second Son demands thy Grief;   90
Each loved two fav'rite Founts. To *Homer* dear
Was *Pindus'* springing Well, while *Bion* drank[28]
The Waves of *Arethuse*. This sung the Charms[29]
Of beauteous *Helen*, strife-exciting Fair,
And the dire Wrath of *Thetis'* sea-born Son;[30]   95
While This neglected War's resounding Trump;[31]
Well could he sing the woodland Wanderer *Pan*;
Skilled was his Hand to form the rustic Flute;
Nor seldom would he milk the shaggy Goat,
Or Heifer breathing Sweets. Meantime he sung   100
How soft the Kiss of tender-blooming Boys;
While in his Bosom *Cupid* wont to sleep,
And *Venus* joyed to hear his Lays divine.
   Begin, &c.
Each towered City, *Bion*, thee deplores,   105
More heart-felt Plaints o'er *Ascra*'s Hills resound[32]
Than when Her *Hesiod* died. *Boeotia*'s Shades[33]
Forget their *Pindar*, and the *Lesbian* Streets[34]
Alcaeus dead, and all thy Death lament
In sympathizing Grief; while *Paros* deigns[35]   110
With louder Woe to greet thy cypressed Hearse,
Than when *Archilochus'* sweet Tongue was stopped
By cruel Fate; and *Mytilene* forgets[36]
Her beauteous *Sappho*'s wonted Lays for thine.[37]
In *Teos* soft *Anacreon* bears the Palm,[38]   115
Theocritus in *Syracuse* is famed,
My mournful Muse delights *Ausonian* Swains,[39]
Nor to the *Sylvan* Lay disdains to stoop;
Which eager from thy tuneful Mouth she caught,
Oft raptured with the Sound. The shining Stores   120
Let others, narrow-souled possess, while I
Thy Lays inherit, and thy *Doric* Art.
   Begin, &c.
Though nipped by Winter's Blast the Mallow fades,
And twining Parsley, Pride of Gardens, feels   125

---

28 *Pindus' . . . Well* literally, "Pegasus' spring"; i.e. Hippocrene on Mt. Helicon; Pindus was another mountain sacred to the Muses.

29 *Arethuse* a fit source of inspiration for pastoral poets like Bion (see n. 4 above); *This* Homer.

30 *Thetis* mother of Achilles.

31 *This* Bion.

32 *Ascra* home of Hesiod, author of the *Theogony* and *Works and Days* (p. 275 above).

33 *Boeotia* home of the poet Pindar.

34 *Lesbian* the island of Lesbos was home to the poets Alcaeus and Sappho.

35 *Paros* home of the poet Archilochus.

36 *Mytilene* main city of Lesbos.

37 There is a short lacuna in the Greek text following this line.

38 *Teos* home of the poet Anacreon.

39 *Ausonian* Italian.

Th' untimely Frost; yet each with Verdure fresh
Renew their Bloom, and with the Spring return.
But Man, though Strength and Wisdom stamp him Great,
When once the beaming Lamp of Life is spent,
To Caves of Darkness, subterranean Glooms,   130
Immersed, in Sleep's eternal Shackles lies
Fast bound, no more to tread the Walks of Men.
Thou too to Realms of silent Night art gone,
While here above mean Bards usurp thy Reign,
Whose Brows the Muse's Laurel never bound.   135
    Begin, &c.
O ruthless Hand that to thy Lips applied
The poisonous Cup, and baleful Draught of Death!
How could the baleful Drugs approach thy Lips,
Nor still preserve its native noxious Gall[40]   140
Unblended with the Nectar of thy Mouth?
How could the Felon drear that mixed the Bowl
Escape the Magic of thy tuneful Strains?
    Begin, &c.
On each the Fates adjust the Share of Pain,   145
And each receives his portioned Lot of Grief.
O that like *Orpheus* I could tread the Shades,
Or great *Ulysses*, or brave *Hercules*,[41]
Then would these Eyes behold th' infernal Pow'rs
Melt at thy Song, and *Pluto*, grisly King,   150
To Softness soothed, and murm'ring hoarse Applause.
But chief to *Hecate* thy sweet Song address,[42]
And let her hear thy wonted *Doric* Songs,
For she of Yore the Vales of Aetna loved.
Haply deceived by the mellifluous Sound,   155
She may return thee to thy desert Seats:
I too, my Friend, if this rude Lip was skilled
In Music's Charms, or knew to sing like thee,
Would to the Ways of darksome *Dis* descend,[43]
And from dun Night redeem thy sacred Shade.   160

40 *Gall* poison; bitterness (of bile secreted by the liver).

41 *Orpheus . . . Ulysses . . . Hercules* heroes who visited the underworld.

42 *Hecate* literally, "the Maiden," i.e. Persephone, who was sometimes identified with Hecate as a dweller of the underworld.

43 *Dis* Pluto.

Lucretius (c. 94–55 BCE)

A late and unreliable source – St. Jerome – reports that Titus Lucretius committed suicide after being driven mad by a love potion. The lurid claim reflects hostility to Lucretius' unreligious philosophical doctrine. His masterpiece, *De Rerum Natura* (On the Nature of Things), is a poem of epic grandeur devoted to the exposition of Epicurean philosophy and dedicated to the aristocrat Gaius Memmius. Epicurus (341–270 BCE) taught that the end of life is pleasure – not so much the pleasure of physical sensations but freedom from pain in body and mind. The chief impediment to mental peace, he thought, is the fear of the gods and of death. Borrowing and elaborating upon the atomistic theory of Democritus, Epicurus explained the universe in materialistic and mechanistic terms. The Epicurean universe is the result of the chance aggregation of atoms – imperfect, purposeless, harsh. Gods exist, but they played no part in the creation of the world and do not interact with us. We must make the best of our situation, guided by enlightened self-interest and relying upon knowledge and the mutual support of like-minded friends. Lucretius expands the bleak Epicurean view of nature to encompass its vitality and beauty, the contemplation of which is a source of pleasure and consolation to the anxious soul. His missionary zeal and energetic verse made a deep impression on the Roman poets, including Virgil, but the hedonistic and apolitical doctrines of Epicureanism repelled many Romans, who found the ethics of Stoicism more compatible with their traditional values. Moreover, Lucretius' Epicurean theology, which granted the existence of gods but made them irrelevant, inevitably attracted the ire of the pious, both pagan and Christian.

Lucretius was barely known in the Middle Ages. The surviving manuscripts derive from two extant ninth-century Carolingian efforts that in turn derive from a single archetype of the fourth or fifth century CE. Lucretius was rediscovered by Poggio in the early fifteenth century and first printed in 1473. *De Rerum Natura* influenced many English poets: Spenser's "Hymn to Venus" is virtually a translation; Donne, Milton, Dryden, Swift, and many others reflect both the imagery and the thinking of Lucretius' philosophical poem. Gray's *Elegy* in this anthology (p. 154 above) and Tennyson's *Lotos Eaters* (p. 202 above) both respond to Lucretius.

from *De Rerum Natura*

Book 2, lines 646–60

In this short passage, which contributed to Lucretius' reputation for atheism in the Christian era, the poet describes the true nature of the gods. In the atomic system of Lucretius' philosophical master Epicurus, the gods, if they exist at all, are filmy atomic beings in the cosmic interstices between worlds. There they live in perfect self-sufficiency and peace. Having nothing to do with human affairs, they nevertheless serve as models of felicity in their freedom from pain, desire, and fear. The Epicurean gods bear no relation to the traditional Olympian gods, whom Lucretius reduces to mere metaphors.

Our translator is William Ellery Leonard (1876–1944). He was a professor, poet, author, and a translator of *Beowulf* as well as Lucretius.

For all the gods must of themselves enjoy
Immortal aeons and supreme repose,
Withdrawn from our affairs, detached, afar:
Immune from peril and immune from pain,
Themselves abounding in riches of their own,   5
Needing not us, they are not touched by wrath,
They are not taken by service or by gift.
Truly is earth insensate for all time;
But, by obtaining germs of many things,[1]
In many a way she brings the many forth   10
Into the light of sun. And here, whoso
Decides to call the ocean Neptune, or
The grain-crop Ceres, and prefers to abuse
The name of Bacchus rather than pronounce
The liquor's proper designation, him   15
Let us permit to go on calling earth
Mother of Gods, if only he will spare[2]
To taint his soul with foul religion.

BOOK 2, LINES 646–660   2 *Mother of Gods* one of the titles of Cybele.

1 *germs* elementary particles.

Book 3, lines 1–30

These lines at the beginning of Book 3 are Lucretius' hymn to Epicurus. His teachings penetrate the barriers of nature to reveal the peaceful abode of the gods and the non-existence of the underworld. (Book 3 concerns the mortality of the soul and ends with a diatribe against the fear of death.) The beautiful lines on the abode of the gods are adapted from Homer's description of Olympus (*Odyssey* 6.42–6) to Epicurean specifications.

The translation is again Leonard's (see p. 325 above).

O thou who first uplifted in such dark[1]
So clear a torch aloft, who first shed light
Upon the profitable ends of man,
O thee I follow, glory of the Greeks,
And set my footsteps squarely planted now   5
Even in the impress and the marks of thine –
Less like one eager to dispute the palm,
More as one craving out of very love
That I may copy thee! – for how should swallow
Contend with swans or what compare could be   10
In a race between young kids with tumbling legs
And the strong might of the horse? Our father thou,
And finder-out of truth, and thou to us
Suppliest a father's precepts; and from out
Those scriven leaves of thine, renownèd soul,   15
(Like bees that sip of all in flowery wolds),[2]
We feed upon thy golden sayings all –
Golden, and ever worthiest endless life.
For soon as ever thy planning thought that sprang
From god-like mind begins its loud proclaim   20
Of nature's courses, terrors of the brain
Asunder flee, the ramparts of the world
Dispart away, and through the void entire
I see the movements of the universe.
Rises to vision the majesty of gods,   25
And their abodes of everlasting calm
Which neither wind may shake nor rain-cloud splash,
Nor snow, congealèd by sharp frosts, may harm
With its white downfall: ever, unclouded sky
O'er roofs, and laughs with far-diffusèd light.   30
And nature gives to them their all, nor aught

BOOK 3, LINES 1–30   2   *wolds* forests.

1   *thou* Epicurus.

May ever pluck their peace of mind away.
But nowhere to my vision rise no more
The vaults of Acheron, though the broad earth[3]
Bars me no more from gazing down o'er all   35
Which under our feet is going on below
Along the void. O, here in these affairs
Some new divine delight and trembling awe
Takes hold through me, that thus by power of thine
Nature, so plain and manifest at last,   40
Hath been on every side laid bare to man!

Book 3, lines 894–911

This selection is taken from Lucretius' diatribe against the fear of death, which
follows his proof that the soul is material and mortal. He imagines the words of
mourners lamenting the dead man's loss of joys and their own everlasting grief.
Lucretius undercuts their mawkishness with the tart observation that the dead man
lacks any desire for the things he has lost. Death is like sleep, so what is the point
of endless weeping? Echoes of his argument can be heard, famously, in Donne's
sonnet "Death be not proud," and Thomas Gray borrowed some of the imagery
in his *Elegy Wrote in a Country Church Yard*.

The translation is again Leonard's (see p. 325 above).

                    "Thee now no more
The joyful house and best of wives shall welcome,
Nor little sons run up to snatch their kisses
And touch with silent happiness thy heart.
Thou shalt not speed in undertakings more,   5
Nor be the warder of thine own no more.
Poor wretch," they say, "one hostile hour hath ta'en
Wretchedly from thee all life's many guerdons,"
But add not, "yet no longer unto thee
Remains a remnant of desire for them."   10
If this they only well perceived with mind
And followed up with maxims, they would free
Their state of man from anguish and from fear.
"O even as here thou art, aslumber in death,
So shalt thou slumber down the rest of time,   15
Released from every harrying pang. But we,
We have bewept thee with insatiate woe,

---

3 *Acheron* river of the underworld or the under-
world itself.

Standing beside whilst on the awful pyre
Thou wert made ashes; and no day shall take
For us the eternal sorrow from the breast."   20
But ask the mourner what's the bitterness
That man should waste in an eternal grief,
If, after all, the thing's but sleep and rest?

Catullus (c. 84–54 BCE)

Gaius Valerius Catullus came from a well-to-do family of Verona. Although in 57–56 BCE he served on the staff of the governor of Bithynia (an experience he jokes about in his poetry), he eschewed a public career. Instead, he devoted himself to literature. Catullus was the leading light in a circle of Roman modernists whom his contemporary, the orator Cicero, mockingly called "neoterics" in reference to their striving for novelty. Catullus and his fellow poets revolutionized Roman poetry. Modeling themselves on Greek poets of the Hellenistic era, such as Callimachus, they rejected traditional Roman genres like epic and drama in favor of highly crafted short poems on personal and occasional themes. The slim Catullan corpus of 113 poems or *Carmina* (Songs), as they are often known, contains an astonishing variety of styles and meters. It includes passionate love poems, invectives, epithalamia (wedding songs), expressions of friendship, consolations, obscene jokes, mythological narratives, and translations from the Greek. No other Roman poet exploits a wider range of sentiment and language, from tenderness to sarcasm, grandeur to vulgarity. These extremes are all to be found in his love poems, for which he is best known. Catullus was the first writer in antiquity to develop a cycle of poems around a single love affair. The object of his love is a woman he names Lesbia, a pseudonym which probably masks the historical person of Clodia, an aristocratic woman of beauty, culture, and – if Cicero (who attacks her in one of his speeches) is to be believed – a taste for younger men. Catullus' Lesbia poems cover the spectrum from joyous infatuation, such as we see in the famous "sparrow" poems, to bitter disillusionment. They were an essential impetus to the development of Latin love elegy by Gallus, Propertius, Tibullus, and Ovid, and, directly or indirectly, influenced the entire history of western love poetry.

Catullus was popular and influential in antiquity but virtually unknown in the Middle Ages. Undoubtedly, the erotic character of his work made him less welcome in the scriptoria of medieval monasteries than many other classical writers. The personal nature of his work probably contributed to his exclusion, however, as it may have made converting his work into some kind of Christian allegory (a common fate of classical texts in the medieval period) difficult. Catullus barely survived into the Renaissance: all the extant manuscripts are derived from a single manuscript made in Verona (now lost) that survived into the early fourteenth century.

Catullus did not appear on the British scene until the sixteenth century. Like so many classical authors, Catullus came to England via Italy. Petrarch read the Veronese manuscript and reflected his reading in his *Canzoniere*. Wyatt and Surrey picked up the influence in their mid-sixteenth-century love poetry and passed it on to later poets such as Thomas Campion, Ben Jonson, Sir Philip Sidney, Edmund Spenser, and William Shakespeare. In the next generation Catullus was admired and imitated by cavalier poets, such as Robert Herrick and Richard Lovelace, as well as by urbane Protestant writers like Andrew Marvell. Moreover, his poems were by that time so entwined with the tradition of English personal poetry that they were unavoidable. Only in the eighteenth century when personal poetry itself diminished in importance did Catullus recede on the poetical landscape. When personal poetry came back in the nineteenth century, Catullus came with it. In fact, despite a lull in interest when public and political poetry held the stage, Catullus has never fallen out of fashion or lost his freshness. In the English part of this anthology we track him in the selections from Sidney, Marlowe, Campion, Jonson, Herrick, Marvell, Dryden, Behn, Gray, and Cowper.

Carmen 2

The poem conventionally numbered 2 in Catullus' canon is an address to his beloved's pet sparrow. Thinking of his beloved's play with her pet leads Catullus to surmise that the bird offers a distraction from the pain of love, and he wishes that he could assuage his pangs in the same way. Although its ostensible subject is the sparrow, the poem is really aimed at the girl and amounts to a declaration of passion. Together with *Carmen* 5, this is the most famous and most often imitated poem of Catullus. For all its seeming simplicity it poses two difficult questions of interpretation. First, it is disputed whether the reference to the myth of Atalanta (the last four lines of our translation) belongs to this poem or is a fragment of another poem. The poem is satisfying without it and the juncture is awkward. Some critics, however, perceive an ironic parallel between the sparrow and the golden apples which Hippomenes dropped in front of Atalanta, both being causes of distraction. The second controversy runs deeper. The epigrammatist Martial, in an allusion to this poem and poem 5 (p. 332 below), asks a slave boy for "Catullan kisses" (*Epigrams* 11.6.14) – "which," he goes on, "if they are as many as he [Catullus] said, I will give you Catullus' sparrow." This can be read on several levels, almost certainly including an obscene equation between sparrow and penis: in other words, "I will have intercourse with you after kissing you." From the Renaissance on, and partly on the strength of Martial's allusion, many readers have sensed a double entendre in Catullus 2. A fierce debate still rages, but innuendo is likely in view of the frequency – and ingenuity – of Catullus' obscenity elsewhere. Yet the double meaning is not indisputably clear, and many readers find it unnecessary to choose between an absolutely innocent or obscene meaning. The two coexist as a conundrum for the experienced reader – a piquant embodiment of Catullus' contradictory attitudes to love and sex. Among the poem's many imitators is Sir Philip Sidney in *Astrophel and Stella* 83 (p. 41 above).

The translation is by Charles Elton (1778–1853), a theologian and translator of the classics, including Hesiod and Propertius. His most important literary work is his three-volume collection of translations, *Specimens of the Classic Poets* (1814).

Sparrow! my nymph's delicious pleasure![1]
Who with thee, her pretty treasure,
Fanciful in frolic, plays
Thousand, thousand wanton ways;
And, flutt'ring, lays to panting rest   5
On the soft orbings of her breast;
Thy beak with finger-tip incites,
And dallies with thy becks and bites;[2]
When my beauty, my desire,
Feels her darling whim inspire,   10
With nameless triflings, such as these,
To snatch, I trow, a tiny ease[3]
For some keen fever of the breast,
While passion toys itself to rest;
I would that happy lady be,   15
And so in pastime sport with thee,
And lighten love's soft agony.
The sweet resource were bliss untold,
Dear as that apple of ripe gold,[4]
Which, by the nimble virgin found,   20
Unloosed the zone that had so fast been bound.[5]

Carmen 3

This poem on the death of his girlfriend's sparrow is a companion piece to *Carmen* 2 and an innovative representative of the minor genre of pet epigrams found in

CARMEN 2

1 *nymph* literally, "girl."

2 *becks* mute signals (*OED*).

3 *trow* believe; think.

4 *apple* one of the mythical golden apples that Hippomenes dropped in the path of Atalanta during a footrace to determine whether she would marry him.

5 *zone* girdle (a Grecism); its loosening connotes the loss of virginity.

the *Greek Anthology* (compare Meleager, p. 316 above). Like *Carmen* 2, it is less about the bird than about Catullus' relationship with Lesbia. The description of the sparrow's play with Lesbia is sweet, but the lament for its death is rendered ironic by hyperbole. If there is an obscene interpretation of *Carmen* 2, in which the sparrow stands for the poet's penis, the sparrow's death in *Carmen* 3 inevitably hints at impotence. As with *Carmen* 2, it is unnecessary to read the poem entirely one way or the other; its wit lies in the delicate balance of possible yet contradictory readings. The poem decisively shaped the later tradition of animal poems, represented in this volume by Gray's "Ode on the Death of a Favourite Cat" (p. 151 above) and Cowper's "Epitaph on a Hare" (p. 164 above).

The translator is Walter Savage Landor (1775–1864), a prolific poet in both Latin and English but most famous for his *Imaginary Conversations*, dialogues between famous characters of the past, including many classical figures. Landor's characteristic outspokenness is audible in his translation.

> Venus! Cupid! Beaux! deplore –
> Lesbia's sparrow is no more!
> That which she was wont to prize
> Dearer than her lovely eyes.
> Like a child, her voice it knew, 5
> 'Twittering here and there it flew:
> Cunningly her breast it loved,
> Whence it very seldom moved.
> Now, alas! 'tis in the bourn[1]
> Whence it never may return. 10
> Cruel shades! that round it lour!
> All that's pretty ye devour.
> Lesbia's sparrow ye have ta'en! –
> Cause of unabating pain!
> Little bird! now thou art fled, 15
> Lesbia's weeping eyes are red.

Carmen 5

Like poem 2, this poem is very widely celebrated and vastly influential; it is the source of countless translations and *carpe diem* imitations in Latin and English, including works in this anthology by Marlowe, Campion, Herrick, Marvell, and Behn. The exuberant opening and conclusion surround a serious center in which Catullus contrasts the cyclical rising and setting of the sun with the linear finitude

---

CARMEN 3

1 *bourn* country; an allusion to the famous "To be or not to be" speech in Shakespeare's *Hamlet*.

of death. Awareness of this contrasts adds urgency to his injunction "let us live and love" and calls forth an extravaganza of kissing. (The theme of kisses is picked up in *Carmen* 7, a companion piece.) The impression of freshness and simplicity results from artistry rather than spontaneous expression. Every word in the Latin is carefully selected and placed for best effect. A marvel of succinctness and originality, the poem captures an entire philosophy of life within its 13 Latin lines. The translation, which occupies 20 lines, is by Richard Crashaw (1612/1613–1648), a metaphysical poet who wrote religious as well as amorous verse. The text is based on its publication in *Steps to the Temple. Sacred Poems, with other Delights of the Muses* (London, 1646).

Come and let us live my Dear,
Let us love and never fear,
What the sourest Fathers say:
Brightest *Sol* that dies today[1]
Lives again as blithe tomorrow,   5
But if we dark sons of sorrow
Set; oh then, how long a Night
Shuts the Eyes of our short light!
Then let amorous kisses dwell
On our lips, begin and tell   10
A Thousand, and a Hundred score,
An Hundred, and a Thousand more,
Till another Thousand smother
That, and that wipe off another.
Thus at last when we have numbered   15
Many a Thousand, many a Hundred;
We'll confound the reckoning quite,
And lose ourselves in wild delight:
While our joys so multiply,
As shall mock the envious eye.[2]   20

Carmen 8

Poem 8 is an internal dialogue in which Catullus struggles to reconcile himself to the loss of his beloved. The poem is notable for its self-address and the psychological realism with which it fluctuates between resolve and weakness, dismissal and nostalgia. The string of questions at the end is a futile attempt to transfer his feeling of loss from himself to Lesbia. Tantalized by the memory of her love-bites,

CARMEN 5
1 *Sol* the sun.

2 *envious eye* the "evil eye"; according to magical lore, to know the number of their kisses would enable an enemy to put a spell on the lovers.

he pulls himself together with a final adjuration – but not, we are led to suspect, for long. Many later love poets repeated versions of Catullus' adjuration, arming them with equal amorous hostility. Perhaps the most famous is John Donne, who began his poem "The Apparition," with the line, "When by thy scorn, O Murderess, I am dead." Sir Philip Sidney imitates the poem in *Astrophel and Stella* 47 (p. 40 above).

The translation is by Arthur Symons (1865–1945), a literary scholar, poet, and playwright, closely associated with the "art for art's sake" movement in the early twentieth century. It comes from his collection *From Catullus: Chiefly Concerning Lesbia* (Martin Secker, 1924).

Miserable Catullus, put an end of this folly:
Let all things dead be over and ended wholly.
Once the sun was bright and the light was fair,
And there was a woman to love, and she waited there,
And never a woman was better loved than she.   5
Surely the sun was bright and fair to see,
And merrily then the hours of love went by
When nothing that you desired would she deny.
Now the woman, desiring no more, denies:
You too, deny, nor follow her as she flies.   10
Be miserable no more, for all is vain:
Set your soul steadfast and harden your heart again.
Farewell: Catullus has hardened his heart again,
He will not follow nor cry to you now in vain.
No, it is you that shall weep, as you lie alone,   15
And no man cries at your gate, and the night goes on.
What shall remain to you then? who shall come to your call?
Who shall call you fair? nay, whom shall you love at all?
Who shall have you for his? whose lips shall you bite and kiss?
But you, Catullus, harden your heart at this.   20

Carmen 13

Poem 13 in the Catullan collection is a humorous invitation to dinner in which the guest is asked to bring the food, a girl, wine, and wit. In return Catullus will supply pure love or, even better, a choice unguent – the Greeks and Romans anointed themselves with fragrant oils at banquets – presented by "the Venuses and Cupids" to his girlfriend; she, presumably, will be present too. There was some Greek precedent for invitation poetry, but the brilliant example of Catullus created a minor genre of Latin literature – best represented by Horace and Martial – and is the ultimate source of modern invitation poems such as Ben Jonson's "Inviting a Friend to Supper" (p. 61 above).

The translation is by James Cranstoun (1837–1901), a poet and an editor of early modern Scottish verse.

> If the gods will, Fabullus mine,
> With me right heartily you'll dine,
> Bring but good cheer – that chance is thine
>   Some days hereafter;
> Mind a fair girl, too, wit, and wine,   5
>   And merry laughter.
>
> Bring these – you'll feast on kingly fare –
> But bring them – for my purse – I swear
> The spiders have been weaving there;
>   But thee I'll favour   10
> With a pure love, or, what's more rare,
>   More sweet of savour,
>
> An unguent I'll before you lay
> The Loves and Graces t'other day[1]
> Gave to my girl – smell it – you'll pray   15
>   The gods, Fabullus,
> To make you turn all nose straightway.
>   Yours aye, Catullus.

Carmen 101

This poem is Catullus' moving tribute to his dead brother, whose grave he visited in Asia Minor near the site of Troy. Catullus fully addresses the propinquity of his brother's grave to Troy in poem 68. Here, however, he merely touches upon the coincidence with an allusion to the *Odyssey* in line 1 that makes Catullus an Odysseus in reverse, a wanderer who sails from home to seek his kinsman in the foreign land of Troy. Despite Catullus' awareness that he is writing premeditated verse, his sorrow and sense of futility break through the performance of the traditional rituals. The poem ends with the famous salutation *ave atque vale*! *Lycidas* (p. 67 above) is only the most famous of the innumerable elegiac poems in English that are aware of Catullus' performance in this genre. Dryden alludes to it in "To the Memory of Mr. *Oldham*" (p. 93 above).

Like *Carmen* 8 (p. 333 above), 101 is translated by Arthur Symons.

> Wandering many waters and many lands,
> I come, my brother, to do sad rites as of old;
> See, I bring you the death-gift in my hands,[1]

CARMEN 13

1 *Loves and Graces* literally, "Venuses and Cupids."

CARMEN 101

1 *death-gift* sacrificial offerings.

Hear, I speak to you, speak to the ashes cold.
All that fortune has left me in place of you,   5
Alas, poor brother, bereft of innocent breath!
Yet, as our sires before us have done, I do,
I bring the same sad gifts, an offering for death.
Take them, that they of a brother's tears may tell;
And now for all time, brother, hail and farewell.   10

Virgil (70–19 BCE)

Virgil – some prefer Vergil on the strength of his Latin name, Publius Vergilius Maro – came from Mantua in north Italy but spent most of his life in Rome and Campania. The years of his youth were fraught with political unrest. When he was in his twenties, Julius Caesar and Pompey plunged into a ruinous civil war from which Caesar emerged victorious. His assassination on the Ides of March in 44 BCE ignited a new spate of civil wars which ended in the triumph of Octavian – better known as Augustus, the first emperor of Rome. The events of the Roman Revolution, as the eminent historian Sir Ronald Syme described it, deeply marked the life and works of Virgil. His father is said to have lost his estate after the battle of Philippi, when the victorious Antony and Octavian instituted a program of land confiscation for the benefit of demobilized veterans. Virgil portrayed with sympathy the plight of the evicted farmers in *Eclogues* 1 and 9. The *Eclogues* is a collection of 10 beautiful and complex poems, in which Virgil reworked the conventional world of Theocritean pastoral. While in some ways detaching the genre even further from reality, Virgil employed allegory to introduce contemporary politics and literary history into the idealized bucolic landscape. His experiments in this direction, which went far beyond Theocritus, decisively affected later development of the genre.

To make one's way as a Roman poet required help, unless one was independently wealthy. In writing the *Eclogues* Virgil enjoyed the patronage of Gaius Asinius Pollio, an important politician, author, and founder of the first public library at Rome. Subsequently he entered the circle of Maecenas, a wealthy associate of Octavian and an enthusiastic man of letters who provided assistance to other important poets of this era, including Horace. Because of his connection with Maecenas Virgil found himself on the winning side when Octavian defeated Antony and Cleopatra at the battle of Actium in 31 BCE. Both Maecenas and Octavian were dedicatees of Virgil's next work, the *Georgics* – Greek for "agricultural matters." A didactic poem inspired by Hesiod's *Works and Days* (p. 279 above), the *Georgics* divides into four books, each devoted to a major topic: crops

(Book 1), vines and trees (Book 2), livestock (Book 3), and bees (Book 4). But Virgil ranges beyond practical advice into the realms of metaphysics, morality, and politics. His artistry is exquisite. For Dryden it was "the best poem by the best poet" and for Addison "the most complete, elaborate, and finished piece of all antiquity."

The proem to Book 3 of the *Georgics* predicts an epic on the wars of Octavian. What transpired, of course, was the *Aeneid*, the most celebrated of all Roman poems. The *Aeneid* occupied Virgil for the last decade of his life (29–19 BCE) and was still under revision when he died. He is said to have told his executors to burn the manuscript, but Augustus intervened. Even before Virgil's death the work had been hailed as "something greater than the *Iliad*" (Propertius), and it quickly entered the literary pantheon. Epic ranked highest in the ancient hierarchy of literary genres, owing largely to the supremacy of Homer. In the *Aeneid* Virgil set himself the monumental task of reworking the *Iliad* and *Odyssey* into an epic of equivalent cultural significance for his fellow Romans. The poem relates the myth of Aeneas, a Trojan hero revered by the Romans as the founder of their race. After surviving the fall of Troy, Aeneas wandered through the Mediterranean in search of his promised destination in Italy (Books 1–6) only to become embroiled on his arrival in a war with the native inhabitants (Books 7–12). The *Aeneid* ends with the military victory of Aeneas, but through the devices of prophecy and foreshadowing it draws into its orbit the entire span of Roman history, culminating in the reign of Augustus. Aeneas thus transcends his mythical circumstances to become a representative of Roman character and achievement – a national symbol. His defining characteristic of unselfish regard for gods, family, and fellow countrymen (his famous *pietas*) embodies a new conception of the epic hero. Book 12 ends with Aeneas' slaughter of Turnus, his Italian enemy, in a fit of vengeance. To assuage the injury inflicted by this ending on the sensibilities of early modern readers, Maffeo Vegio (1407–1458) composed an optimistic thirteenth book that was included in several fifteenth- and sixteenth-century editions of Virgil. In truth, the ending is a fitting climax to a poem that courageously acknowledges the corporal and moral destruction wrought by empire builders, however glorious their legacy may be.

In 19 BCE Virgil sailed to Greece to visit some of the places described in the *Aeneid*. Reportedly, he planned to spend three years on revision and then devote his life to philosophy. He took ill before reaching Greece and returned to Brundisium, where he died. Before long Virgil became a national icon, as Homer had been to the Greeks. On top of his poetic renown he also acquired a reputation as a proto-Christian because his fourth or "Messianic" *Eclogue* came to be read as a prediction of the birth of Jesus. So revered was Virgil's book that it was long used as a form of prognostication called the *sortes Virgilianae* (Virgilian lots). To read the future one had only to open the text of Virgil at a random line and interpret it properly, as though the poem were a bundle of fortunes in a fortune cookie. When he visited the Bodleian Library in Oxford during the English Civil

War, Charles I (captured and executed in 1649) is said to have tried the *sortes Virgilianae* and hit upon the line, "But harassed by the warfare and weaponry of a bold nation" (*Aeneid* 4.615). Virgil can, and has been, read in numerous ways: as imperial panegyrist and critic, optimist and pessimist, mystic and skeptic. He is enigmatic and elusive, and none the worse for that. Among his best qualities, however, most critics would include his supreme control of language, melody, and meter, his close observation of nature, and his sensitivity to human suffering and loss. Delight and glorification are not lacking in Virgil's poetry, but he is drawn more to the sadder aspects of life.

Virgil and Ovid have always been the most famous and influential Roman poets, with Horace a close third. Since the beginning of the Renaissance in Europe they have inspired countless poetic imitations, paintings, sculptures, and operas. For most of western literary history it has been Virgil rather than his Greek models who epitomized the three genres in which he worked: pastoral, didactic, and epic. "Our classic, the classic of all Europe, is Virgil," as T. S. Eliot famously observed. The three extant ancient manuscripts of Virgil's works engendered a huge number of later manuscripts, so the survival of Virgil, unlike that of most classical authors, was never in doubt. The first printed edition of the complete works was in 1459, and there were 100 printed editions in the next 40 years. The first complete English translation was by the Scot Gavin Douglas (1553), but there was an influential partial translation by Henry Howard, earl of Surrey, not long afterward. Through the eighteenth century Virgil remained the pre-eminent epic poet, and therefore in many ways the pre-eminent poet, of Europe. The nineteenth century saw a shift toward Hellenic models that affected the popularity of both Virgil and Ovid, but they have recovered from that, especially Ovid. One of Virgil's noblest panegyrists was Dante, for whom he was the "glory and light of other poets" (*de li altri poeti onore e lume*), and his guide through Hell and Purgatory. Another was Tennyson, who in his poem, "To Virgil," addresses him as "lord of language" and "wielder of the stateliest measure ever moulded by the lips of man."

Eclogue 2

By having the shepherd Corydon sing of his unrequited passion for the boy Alexis Virgil has turned his Theocritean model (p. 307 above) into a poem of homosexual longing. The theme appears elsewhere in Theocritus and many other Greek and Latin love poets and it is often combined with heterosexual longing. Even in this poem, at one point Corydon weighs indifferently the choice between Amaryllis and Menalcas as alternative partners to Alexis. The ancients were less categorical about sexual attraction than we are; significantly, they had no words for "homosexuality" and "heterosexuality." There was an ancient tradition that Corydon's passion for Alexis masks Virgil's love for a slave-boy called Alexander. The story is not implausible but must be viewed with skepticism, for the details of ancient biographies are commonly based upon unwarranted textual inference. Quoting the first three words of the poem, Byron jests: "But Virgil's songs are pure, except that horrid one / Beginning with *Formosum Pastor Corydon*" (*Don Juan* 1.42.7–8).

The translator is Cecil Day-Lewis (1904–1972), a poet laureate of England whose translation of Virgil's *Aeneid* (1951) was commissioned by the BBC and broadcast as part of the Festival of Britain. The text is reprinted, with permission, from *The Eclogues, Georgics, and Aeneid of Virgil* (Oxford University Press, 1966).

> A shepherd, Corydon, burned with love for his master's favourite,[1]
> Handsome Alexis. Little reason had he for hope;[2]
> But he was always going into the beech plantation
> Under whose spires and shades, alone with his futile passion,
> He poured forth words like these, piecemeal, to wood and hill: –   5
> "Cruel Alexis, can my sad airs mean nothing to you?
> No pity for me? One day you'll drive me to my death.
> Even the cattle now are making for cool shade,
> Even the green lizards are hiding in thorn thickets,
> And Thestylis prepares a pottage of savoury herbs,   10
> Garlic and thyme, for harvesters whom the fierce heat has wearied.
> But I trail in your footsteps under the blazing sun
> While copses thrum with my hoarse voice and the cicada's.
> I'd have done better to bear the sulks and rages, the insolent
> Disdain of Amaryllis, or to make do with Menalcas,   15
> Swarthy though he is, compared with your dazzling fairness.
> Don't bank too much on your complexion, lovely boy –
> Pale privet-blossom falls, no less than the dark-toned hyacinth.
> "Alexis, you look down on me; you never think
> What I am – how rich in livestock, in wealth of snowy milk.   20
> A thousand lambs of mine roam the Sicilian hills;[3]
> I never have run short of fresh milk, summer or winter.
> I sing as, on a time, Amphion used to sing,[4]
> Calling his cattle home down the slopes of Aracynthus.
> I'm not so ill-favoured, either: the other day on the shore,   25
> When the sea's face was unfretted, I saw myself; if that mirror
> Tells true, I could compete with Daphnis and win your verdict.[5]
> "How wonderful it would be to live together in these
> Rough fields, in a homely cottage, hunting the deer with our bows,

---

ECLOGUE 2

1 *Corydon* a character drawn from Theocritus, like most pastoral personae in the *Eclogues* (cf. *Thestylis, Menalcas, Damoetas, Daphnis*, and *Amyntas* below).

2 *Alexis* "the traditional name of a catamite" (Wendell Clausen, *Virgil: Eclogues* [Oxford University Press, 1994], p. 64).

3 *mine* not literally, for Corydon is a slave (line 1); *Sicilian hills* the homeland of Theocritus (and Polyphemus, Corydon's literary model).

4 *Amphion* mythical musician reputed to have built the walls of Thebes by charming the stones into place with his lyre.

5 *Daphnis* "the ideal shepherd" (Clausen).

Herding a flock of kids with green marsh-mallow switches!   30
Here with me in the woodlands, you'd rival Pan for music.[6]
Pan invented the shepherd's pipes, waxing a handful
Of reeds together: Pan looks after sheep and shepherd.
You'd never regret chafing your lip upon the pipes –
Think what Amyntas gladly suffered to learn the art.   35
I have an instrument – seven hemlock stalks of graded[7]
Lengths went to its making: Damoetas gave it me
Long ago on his death-bed, saying, 'You'll be its second
And lucky slave.' That boor, Amyntas, envied me.
What's more, I have two roes which I found in a dangerous combe – [8]   40
Their hides have not yet lost the white markings: twice a day now
They're milking a ewe dry. I'm keeping them for you.
Thestylis has been begging for ages, to take them off me;
And she can have them, as you turn up your nose at my presents.
    "Handsome boy, come here! Look how the nymphs are bringing[9]   45
Great basketfuls of lilies for you; for you the shining
Naiad picks a bunch of pale iris and poppy-heads,[10]
Blends them with narcissus and the sweet-smelling anise,
Twines cassia in, and other fragrant herbs, and sets off
Unassuming blueberries with flamboyant marigold.   50
Myself will gather you quinces of pale and velvety bloom
And the chestnuts Amaryllis loved when she was mine;
Waxy-looking plums too – that fruit shall have its due;
And I'll cut branches of laurel, and of myrtle that grows near it –
Sweet is their mingled fragrance when they are put together.   55
    "Bumpkin! as if Alexis cared twopence for your offerings!
And anyway, Iollas could beat you at present-giving.[11]
Poor fool that I was, to have such daydreams. Now in my folly
I've let the wind get at my flowers, the boars muddy my spring.
Who are you running from, you crazy man? Why, Trojan   60
Paris, and even gods, have lived in the woods like me.[12]
Let Athene dwell in the cities she's founded. For me, the woodlands.[13]
Fierce lioness goes after wolf, wolf after goat,
The wanton goat goes after the flowering clover, and I
Go after you, Alexis – each towed by his own fancy.[14]   65

---

6 *Pan* the shepherds' god and inventor of the syrinx or panpipes.

7 *hemlock* a hollow-stemmed plant.

8 *roes* a species of deer; *combe* "a deep hollow or valley" (*OED*).

9 *nymphs* spirits of nature, personified as beautiful girls.

10 *Naiad* water nymph.

11 *Iollas* the "master" (line 1) who is Corydon's rival.

12 *Paris* son of Priam and Hecuba; exposed at birth on Mt. Ida and raised by shepherds.

13 *Athene* patroness of Athens.

14 *Fierce lioness . . . Alexis* an example of the rhetorical device called a priamel – an ascending series of analogies used to highlight a specific preference or point of interest.

"Look, ploughs feather the ground as the ox-teams draw them home,
And a declining sun enlarges the lengthening shadows:
Yet love still scorches me – love has no lull , no limit.
    "Ah Corydon, Corydon, what is this lunacy you're possessed by?
You've left your vines half-pruned, and the leafy elms they grow on.   70
Why not, instead of moping, get down to something useful,
Weaving from reeds and withies some article that you need?[15]
If you're brushed off by this Alexis, you'll find another."

Eclogue 4

The fourth *Eclogue*, nicknamed the "Messianic" *Eclogue*, is the grandest and most famous of the collection. Contrary to its mystical misinterpretation, it is rooted in a mundane historical event. This was the Pact of Brundisium in 40 BCE – a settlement between Antony and Octavian that was negotiated with the help of Pollio (Virgil's patron and one of the consuls for that year) and sealed by the marriage of Antony to Octavia, the sister of Octavian. To a nation sick of unrest, the Pact held out the hope of stability. In tune with the spirit of optimism, Virgil declares the advent of the "last age" of Sibylline prophecy, which he identifies as a new Golden Age. (For the myth of the ages, see Hesiod, *Works and Days*, pp. 282–5 above.) To usher in the new era, a glorious child will be born in Pollio's consulship, for whom the earth will spontaneously pour forth its blessings and shed its vestiges of sinful warfare, agriculture, sailing – and the dying of clothes! For Christians reading the poem in succeeding ages it was clear that the child in Virgil's lines was Jesus Christ. For Virgil's original audience, however, the child could only be an anticipated son of Antony and Octavia. When the hopes raised by this marriage had been dashed, the poem lent itself to other interpretations and may even have been revised by Virgil to remove specific details when he collected the *Eclogues* for publication some years later. In any case, its lack of specificity allows it to be read as a timeless expression of yearning for a peaceful and virtuous world. Among the countless poems it has influenced are Yeats's "Two Songs from a Play" (p. 219 above) and Seamus Heaney's "Bann Valley Eclogue" (p. 235 above).
    The translation is by John Dryden (1631–1700; pp. 92 above, 362 below); the text is based on that included in his *Works of Virgil* (1697).

Sicilian Muse, begin a loftier strain![1]
Though lowly Shrubs, and Trees that shade the Plain,
Delight not all; *Sicilian* Muse, prepare

---

15 *withies* young, flexible willow branches.

ECLOGUE 4

1 *Sicilian Muse* the Muse of bucolic poetry (after Theocritus' birthplace).

To make the vocal Woods deserve a Consul's care.[2]
The last great Age, foretold by sacred Rhymes,[3]   5
Renews its finished Course: *Saturnian* times[4]
Roll round again; and mighty years, begun
From their first Orb, in radiant Circles run.
The base degenerate Iron offspring ends;[5]
A golden Progeny from Heaven descends.   10
O chaste *Lucina* speed the Mother's pains;[6]
And haste the glorious Birth! thy own *Apollo* reigns![7]
The lovely Boy, with his auspicious Face,
Shall *Pollio*'s Consulship and Triumph grace;
Majestic Months set out with him to their appointed Race.   15
The Father banished Virtue shall restore,[8]
And Crimes shall threat the guilty world no more.[9]
The Son shall lead the life of Gods, and be
By Gods and Heroes seen, and Gods and Heroes see.[10]
The jarring Nations he in peace shall bind,   20
And with paternal Virtues rule Mankind.
Unbidden Earth shall wreathing Ivy bring,
And fragrant Herbs (the promises of Spring),
As her first Off'rings to her Infant King.[11]
The Goats with strutting Dugs shall homeward speed,   25
And lowing Herds secure from Lions feed.
His Cradle shall with rising Flow'rs be crowned:
The Serpent's Brood shall die: the sacred ground[12]
Shall Weeds and poisonous Plants refuse to bear;
Each common Bush shall *Syrian* Roses wear.[13]   30
But when Heroic Verse his Youth shall raise,
And form it to Hereditary Praise,[14]
Unlaboured Harvests shall the Fields adorn,

2 *Consul* one of two annually elected chief magistrates.

3 *sacred Rhymes* literally, "Cumaean song," i.e. the Sibylline books – a collection of prophetic utterances in verse kept in the Capitoline temple of Jupiter.

4 *Saturnian times* the Golden Age, often associated with the reign of Saturn (Greek Cronus).

5 *Iron offspring* people of the (present) "iron" age – the nadir of human history, awash with immorality and injustice (see Hesiod, pp. 284–5 above).

6 *Lucina* an epithet of Diana in her role as goddess of childbirth.

7 *Apollo* Diana's brother and god of prophecy; hailed as patron of the new era.

8 *Father* added to Virgil, who probably envisages a son of Antony (see head note to this selection).

9 *Crimes* literally, "our crime," a reference to the Roman civil wars.

10 *The Son . . . see* i.e. he will be made a god.

11 *King* added to Virgil; literally, "to you" (apostrophizing the boy).

12 *sacred* added to Virgil.

13 *Syrian Roses* literally, "Assyrian amomum" (a spice-plant).

14 Literally, "when you [the boy] can now read the praises of heroes and your father's deeds, and recognize what courage is . . . ."

And clustered Grapes shall blush on every Thorn;
The knotted Oaks shall showers of Honey weep;   35
And through the Matted Grass the liquid Gold shall creep.
Yet, of old Fraud some footsteps shall remain;
The Merchant still shall plough the deep for gain,
Great Cities shall with Walls be compassed round,
And sharpened Shares shall vex the fruitful ground;   40
Another *Tiphys* shall new Seas explore;[15]
Another *Argos* land the Chiefs upon th' *Iberian* shore;[16]
Another *Helen* other Wars create,[17]
And great *Achilles* urge the *Trojan* Fate.[18]
But when to ripened Manhood he shall grow,   45
The greedy Sailor shall the Seas forego;
No Keel shall cut the Waves for foreign Ware,
For every Soil shall every Product bear.
The labouring Hind his Oxen shall disjoin;
No Plow shall hurt the Glebe, no Pruning-hook the Vine;   50
Nor Wool shall in dissembled Colours shine;
But the luxurious Father of the Fold,
With native Purple, or unborrowed Gold,[19]
Beneath his pompous Fleece shall proudly sweat;
And under *Tyrian* Robes the Lamb shall bleat.[20]   55
The Fates, when they this happy Web have spun,[21]
Shall bless the sacred Clue, and bid it smoothly run.[22]
Mature in years, to ready Honours move,
O of Celestial Seed! O foster Son of *Jove*!
See, labouring Nature calls thee to sustain   60
The nodding Frame of Heaven, and Earth, and Main!
See to their Base restored, Earth, Seas, and Air;
And joyful Ages, from behind, in crowding Ranks appear.
To sing thy Praise, would Heav'n my breath prolong,
Infusing Spirits worthy such a Song;   65
Not *Thracian Orpheus* should transcend my Lays,[23]

15 *Tiphys* the helmsman of the Argo, the ship that carried the Argonauts to Colchis in quest of the Golden Fleece. Before the Golden Age reaches perfection, there will be a new round of heroic feats – a hint of further Roman imperialism in the east.

16 *Argos* properly Argo; *Iberian* added to Virgil; Dryden must be thinking not of Spain but the Hiberes, a tribe living south of the Caucasus mentioned by the epicist Valerius Flaccus in his *Argonautica*.

17 *Helen* Greek beauty whose abduction by Paris caused the Trojan War.

18 *Achilles* the best Greek warrior.

19 *Gold* literally, "saffron yellow."

20 *Tyrian* purple (Tyre being the source of a famous dye). The fleeces of sheep will miraculously turn purple, yellow, and – in Virgil – scarlet, thus rendering obsolete the unnatural practice of dying wool.

21 *Fates* three old goddesses who spun, twisted, and cut the thread of one's life.

22 *Clue* thread (of life).

23 *Orpheus* son of the Muse Calliope; his songs mesmerized the underworld and drew trees down from the mountains.

Nor *Linus* crowned with never-fading Bays: [24]
Though each his Heav'nly Parent should inspire;
The Muse instruct the Voice, and *Phoebus* tune the Lyre.[25]
Should *Pan* contend in Verse, and thou my Theme,[26]   70
Arcadian judges should their God condemn.
Begin, auspicious Boy! to cast about
Thy Infant Eyes, and, with a smile, thy Mother single out.
Thy Mother well deserves that short delight,
The nauseous Qualms of ten long Months and Travail to requite.[27]   75
Then smile! the frowning Infant's Doom is read;
No God shall crown the Board, nor Goddess bless the Bed.[28]

Eclogue 5

In this poem a chance meeting of two shepherds leads to conversation and a
friendly exchange of songs that balance one another in length and content. Mopsus
sings a dirge for the pastoral hero Daphnis, Menalcas a panegyric proclaiming his
deification. Virgil associates himself with Menalcas by citing the opening lines of
two of his *Eclogues,* and this has encouraged interpreters to search for other con-
temporary allusions in the poem. For example, some readers, even in antiquity,
identified Daphnis with Julius Caesar, who was officially deified by the senate after
his assassination. Such an association may be found, but the poem is less a political
allegory than a meditation on the composition of pastoral poetry. The poem holds
an important place in the history of pastoral elegy, as represented in the English-
language part of this anthology by Milton's *Lycidas* (p. 67 above) and Shelley's
Adonais (p. 180 above).

The translator is, again, Cecil Day-Lewis (see p. 340 above).

MENALCAS
Good-day to you, Mopsus. Now we have met here, both of us experts
– You at playing the light reed-pipe, and I at singing –
Let us sit down together in this grove of elm and hazel.

24 *Linus* son of Apollo (*Phoebus*); another mythical composer; *Bays* the laurel wreath awarded to victors in poetry contests.
25 *Voice . . . Lyre* Dryden's antithesis.
26 *Pan* shepherds' god from the wild region of Arcadia in southern Greece; a skilled player of the syrinx or panpipes; *and thou my Theme* if you were the subject of my verse.
27 *ten* "sidereal" months of roughly 27 days, measured by the moon's revolution about the earth.

28 *Then . . . Bed* unless the baby smiles at his mother (a miraculous feat for a newborn [Clausen]), no god will invite him to dinner, no goddess to bed – as they had done for Hercules and other heroes. Dryden brilliantly anticipated modern scholarship in doubting the Virgilian manuscript tradition that makes the parents smile upon the child rather than vice versa (see his note).

MOPSUS

You are the elder, Menalcas: it's for me to fall in with your wishes.
Shall we go under the trees, where light airs stir the shadows,   5
Or would you prefer a cave? – look, there is one, its opening
Festooned with hanging swags of wild vine, over there.

MENALCAS

No singer in these hills but Amyntas dares to challenge you.

MOPSUS

Yes, but Amyntas fancies himself to beat Apollo.[1]

MENALCAS

Lead off with a song then, Mopsus – "The Loves of Phyllis", or   10
"In Alcon's Praise", or "Quarrelsome Codrus" – any you know.[2]
Lead off, and Tityrus here will look after our grazing kids.

MOPSUS

I'd rather try a song which I wrote the other day
On a green beech trunk, and set to music for voice and pipe[3]
Antiphonally: let Amyntas improve on this, if he can.   15

MENALCAS

Well, in my view Amyntas compares with you no more
Than a dejected willow with the olive's silvery sheen,
Or the unassuming flower of valerian with red roses.[4]
But here we are in the cave, my lad, so sing away.

Song (tune: "The Lark in the Clear Air")[5]

MOPSUS

Daphnis died. The nymphs bewailed his death – [6]   20
   rivers and hazels heard them weeping:

"Cruel stars and gods!" his mother cried,
   clasping the poor corpse close in her arms.

Eclogue 5

1 *Apollo* god of music and poetry.
2 "*The Loves of Phyllis*" etc. made-up titles (contrast the titles mentioned by Menalcas at the end of the poem; see n. 17 below).
3 *On a green beech trunk* Mopsus' song is 25 lines long – a heroic feat of carving!
4 *valerian* general name of several species of wild flowers often used for medicinal purposes, especially as a sedative.

5 *Song* this is Day-Lewis's direction; "*The Lark in the Clear Air*" is a traditional Irish air. Virgil keeps to the same meter throughout the poem but elevates the style of the Daphnis songs above the conversations that frame them.
6 *Daphnis* the son of Mercury (Greek Hermes) and a nymph; an idealized shepherd and singer. Virgil evokes the first *Idyll* of Theocritus (p. 302 above), in which Daphnis dies mysteriously of love.

No one drove his oxen to the stream,
    no beast ate or drank at all from sadness: 25
Even Afric lions roared their grief,
    forest and hill keened Daphnis dead.[7]

Daphnis first enwreathed our wands with leaves,
    Daphnis was first to harness tigers,
Daphnis led the revellers through a dance –   30
    all for the Wine-god's festival day.[8]
Vines grace elms, and grapes the vine,
    bulls grace herds and corn the joyous tillage:
Daphnis graced all nature – when he died,
    Corn-god and Song-god left us too.[9]   35

Where we sowed our champion barley seed,
    darnel and wild oats choke the furrow:[10]
Where sweet violets with narcissus grew,
    thistle and thorn are growing today.
Scatter leaves and shade the springs,   40
    raise a tomb (he asks) and write this upon it –
I lived in woods, my fame lives in the stars:
    lovely my flock was, lovelier I.

MENALCAS

What an inspired poet you are! To me, your singing
Is good as a sleep on the grass to a tired man, or a draught of   45
Fresh water from a dancing brook when the noonday parches
One's throat. My lucky lad, you are your master's equal
At piping and singing now; you'll be his worthy successor.
Still, I'll do what I can to make you some return
By way of this song, extolling your Daphnis to the stars –   50
Yes, I'll enstar Daphnis, for Daphnis loved me too.

MOPSUS

Nothing you could give me would please me more than that;
For Daphnis, if any, deserved elegies; and besides,
Stimichon often has praised to me this song of yours.

Song (tune: the same)[11]

---

7 *keen* to intone the keen, an Irish lamentation for the dead. The mourning of lions, forest, and hill exemplifies the "pathetic fallacy" – the attribution of human feelings to nature.

8 *Wine-god* Bacchus (Dionysus); Virgil means that Daphnis was the first to introduce Bacchic rites to the countryside, including the thyrsus – a fennel wand entwined with ivy or vines that was brandished by ecstatic worshippers; his tiger-taming imitates the feats of Bacchus.

9 *Corn-god* literally, "Pales," a rustic Italian deity; *Song-god* literally, "Apollo."

10 *darnel* a grass that grows as a weed often considered harmful to crops.

11 *Song* see n. 5 above.

MENALCAS

Daphnis shines at heaven's dazzling gate,   55
    under his feet sees clouds and planets.
Shepherds, nymphs and Pan are glad for this,
    forest and champaign quickened with joy.[12]
Sheep nor deer have anything to dread –
    wolf or snare – for Daphnis loves the gentle: 60
Wooded hills, crags, orchards cry to heaven
    jocund hymns – "A god is he!"[13]

Bring us luck, good Daphnis! Here are two
    altars for you, and two for Phoebus,[14]
Where I'll set two bowls of olive oil,   65
    two cups of creaming milk every year.
Ah, what feasts, what junketings there'll be
    here in summer shade or winter firelight!
Wine shall flow, and friends shall sing for me,
    Alphesiboeus dance like a faun.[15]   70

These shall be your rites, whenever we
    honour the nymphs or bless our acres.
Long as boars love heights and fish love streams,
    long as cicadas sip at the dew,
Long as bees suck thyme – will you remain   75
    praised and famed, our yearly vows receiving,
Binding us to make them good, the way
    Corn-god and Wine-god also do.[16]

MOPSUS

What, oh what can I do to reward you for such singing?
Sweeter it was to me than a south wind's rising murmur   80
Or the rhythmic drumming of waves on a beach; more sweet than the music
Rivulets make as they scamper down through rocky glens.

MENALCAS

But I will give you a present first – this delicate reed-pipe,
The one on which I learnt to play "Handsome Alexis,
Corydon's Flame", and "Tell me, is this Meliboeus' Flock?"[17]   85

---

12 *champaign* plain.
13 *jocund* merry, cheerful.
14 *Phoebus* Apollo.
15 *faun* literally, "satyrs," the goat-like, rowdy companions of Bacchus.
16 *Corn-god* literally, "Ceres"; *Wine-god* literally, "Bacchus"; Day-Lewis creates an echo of

Mopsus' song (line 35: "Corn-god and Song-god left us too") which is not present in Virgil but which faithfully conveys the balance of the songs.
17 Quoting (partially) the first lines of *Eclogues* 2 (p. 340 above) and 3.

MOPSUS

And you shall have this beautiful crook, evenly studded
With bronze. Antigenes often asked me for it (and he was
Lovable then), but I would not part with it. Now it's yours.

Eclogue 10

This is the last poem of the collection – a playfully allusive and complex one. It is dedicated to Gallus, a friend and influential love elegist. No doubt many details of *Eclogue* 10 would be clearer if we had the poems of Gallus to which they allude (alas, only fragments survive). Like Daphnis in Theocritus' first *Idyll* (p. 302 above), Gallus is dying of love. Pastoral deities and sundry countrymen comfort him as he languishes somewhere in Arcadia, a wild and beautiful region of southern Greece and the home of the god Pan, which, in this very poem, Virgil transformed into the pastoral fantasy-land of European literature. Gallus contemplates taking up a pastoral existence as a remedy for passion, but he gives up in resignation – for "love conquers all, and I too must yield to love." This sets the stage for Virgil's allegorical farewell to the pastoral genre. Like *Eclogue* 5, the poem deeply influenced the later development of pastoral elegy.

Joseph Trapp's *Works of Virgil* (1731) is the source of the text we present below. It was accounted dull in its time, but its accuracy was never in doubt. Trapp (1679–1747) was a Church of England clergyman and a political writer who was particularly active during the Tory administration of 1710–1714.

Indulge me, *Arethusa*, This my Last[1]
Of Labours: To my *Gallus* must be paid
Some Verse, which ev'n *Lycoris* may peruse:[2]
What *Bard* to *Gallus* can a Verse deny?
So while Thou glid'st beneath *Sicanian* Waves,[3]   5
May brackish *Doris* never mix with Thine.[4]
Begin; and while the Goats the Thickets browse,
Let us relate how *Gallus* pined with Love.
Nor sing we to the Deaf; the Woods reply.
  What Groves, ye Nymphs, detained you hence? What Lawns?[5]   10

ECLOGUE 10

1 *Arethusa* an Arcadian nymph who, when pursued by the river god Alpheus, was turned into a stream and flowed under the sea from Greece to Sicily, where she emerged as a spring in the harbor of Syracuse; here invoked by Virgil both as a pastoral muse and as a native of Arcadia.

2 *Lycoris* the name of Gallus' mistress in his poetry.
3 *Sicanian* Sicilian.
4 *Doris* a sea goddess; here, metonymy for "the sea"; Virgil prays that the sea not pollute the freshwater stream of Arethusa.
5 *detained you hence* kept you from getting here.

When *Gallus* died of Love's tormenting Wound?
For 'twas not *Cynthus'* nor *Parnassus'* Top,
Nor yet *Aonian Aganippe*'s Stream.[6]
Him lonely, stretched beneath a desert Rock,
Ev'n the low Shrubs, and ev'n the Laurels mourned;　　　　　　15
Him piney *Maenalus*, and the tall Cliffs[7]
Of bleak *Lycaeus*. Round him stood the Sheep;
For they too sympathize with human Woe:
Them, Heav'nly Poet, blush not Thou to own:
Ev'n fair *Adonis*, did not scorn to tend[8]　　　　　　　　20
Along the River's side, his fleecy Charge.
To Him the slow-paced Herdsmen, and the Swains,
And wet with Winter-Mast *Menalcas* came;[9]
All ask, "Whence This thy Love?" *Apollo* came;
"*Gallus*, What Frenzy This? Thy Care *Lycoris*　　　　　　25
Follows Another, through rough Camps, and Snows."[10]
Sylvanus came, with rural Honours crowned,[11]
Boughs, and big Lilies nodding round his Head.
Pan came, th'*Arcadian* God, whom We ourselves
Have seen, with red Vermilion, and the Blood　　　　　　　30
Of Elder-berries stained: "Where will This end?"
He said; "Love heeds it not: Nor Meads with Streams[12]
Are satisfied, nor Goats with Browse, nor Bees[13]
With Trefoil-Flow'rs, nor cruel Love with Tears."[14]
　　But pensive He: "Yet You these Tears shall sing,[15]　　35
Arcadians, on your Hills; ye only skilled
In Song: O! softly then my Bones shall rest,
If You in future times shall sing my Loves.
O! had kind Fortune made me one of You,
Keeper of Flocks, or Pruner of the Vine:　　　　　　　　40
Were *Phyllis*, or *Amyntas* my Desire,[16]

6　*Cynthus* a mountain on Delos (birthplace of
Apollo), a substitute for Virgil's Mt. Pindus in
Thessaly; *Parnassus* a ridge above Delphi and site
of the Castalian spring (sacred to the Muses);
Aganippe a spring on Mt. Helicon in Boeotia also
sacred to the Muses. All these places are here
imagined as haunts of the nymphs.

7　*Maenalus* like *Lycaeus*, a mountain in Arcadia.

8　*Adonis* a young lover of Venus who met a
tragic end.

9　*Winter-Mast* acorns soaked in water; food for
animals in winter; *Menalcas* a pastoral figure
(compare pp. 340 and 345 above).

10　*Camps* military encampments; Gallus' rival is
a soldier – and so is he, it transpires (lines
49–50).

11　*Sylvanus* Italian god of the woods.

12　*He* Pan.

13　*Browse* young shoots and twigs.

14　*Trefoil-Flow'rs* clover leaves.

15　*He* Gallus.

16　*Phyllis . . . Amyntas* female and male pastoral
figures (for the bisexual implication, see p. 339
above). Gallus is attracted to the idyllic nature of
pastoral romance, as opposed to the turbulent
passion of love elegy.

Or any Other (and what Fault, though black[17]
Amyntas be? Violets, and Hyacinths
Are black). Sure either would with Me repose,
Amidst the Willows, under the soft Vine,   45
Phyllis weave Garlands, and *Amyntas* sing.
See, here, cool Springs, *Lycoris*, Meads, and Groves;
Here I could melt all Life away with Thee.
Now frantic Love amidst thick Darts and Foes
Detains me in the rigid Toil of Arms.[18]   50
While Thou (but can I yet believe 'tis so?)
Far from thy native Soil art wand'ring o'er
The *Alpine* Snows, or near the frozen *Rhine*,
Ah! cruel! Not with me. Ah! how I fear
Lest the sharp Cold should pierce thee, or the Ice   55
On the rough Mountains cut thy tender Feet.[19]
I'll go, and sing my *Chalcis*' Strains, composed[20]
To the *Sicilian* Shepherd's tuneful Reed:
It is resolved; To Wilds, and Dens of Beasts
I'll fly, and any Pain, but This, endure;   60
On the Trees' tender Bark inscribe my Love,
And with the growing Bark my Love shall grow.
Meanwhile among the Woodland Nymphs I'll rove
O'er *Maenalus*, or hunt the foaming Boar;
In spite of Frosts *Parthenian* Thickets round[21]   65
I'll pitch my Toils; Now, now, methinks I go[22]
O'er Rocks, through sounding Woods, shoot *Cretian* Shafts,[23]
And twang the *Parthian* Horn: As if Those Sports[24]
Could prove a Med'cine to my frantic Pain,
Or Love could learn to pity human Woes.   70
And now again the Nymphs can please no more;

---

17 *black* literally, "swarthy"; a dark complexion was considered inferior to a light, owing to its association with menial outdoors labor (cf. *Eclogues* 2.15–18; p. 340 above); not an ethnic reference.
18 *Toil of Arms* literally, "arms of Mars." The lines are difficult. It seems that Gallus is serving on a military campaign (perhaps under Antony in the east) and temporarily forgets his Arcadian location. But how does love "detain" him? A good case can be made for interpreting the Latin to mean, "mad love of Mars detains me." Having been drawn into the army by the allure of war, Gallus suffers now the pain of separation from Lycoris, who has run away to the north with another soldier.

19 The ancient commentator Servius says that these lines are borrowed from Gallus' poetry.
20 *Chalcis' Strains* poems written in the highly wrought style of the learned Greek poet Euphorion of Chalcis (third century BCE); Gallus proposes to set his own "Chalcidic verse" to the shepherd's pipe – i.e. transform it into pastoral.
21 *Parthenian* Parthenius is another mountain of Arcadia.
22 *Toils* hunting nets.
23 *Cretian Shafts* the Cretans, like the Parthians of the east, were famed for their archery.
24 *Horn* a bow made of horn.

Nor ev'n my Verse; Ev'n You, ye Groves, farewell.
No Toils of Ours the cruel God can change;[25]
Whether we drink of *Hebrus'* frozen Stream,[26]
And rainy Winter, and *Sithonian* Snows[27]   75
Endure; or, when the dying Bark is scorched
Round the tall Elm, we tend our Flocks beneath
The Tropic of the *Ethiopian* Crab:[28]
Love conquers All, and We must yield to Love."
   Thus much, Ye Muses, has your Poet sung,[29]   80
(Let This suffice) while underneath a Shade
He sat, and Baskets with smooth Osiers wove.
You shall for *Gallus* dignify This Verse;
Gallus, for whom my Friendship grows each Hour,
As the green Alder, when the Spring returns.   85
Rise we; The Shade is noxious, while we sing:[30]
Noxious, if we delay, is ev'n the Shade
Of Juniper: The Shade too hurts the Fruit:
Go, my fed Goats; The Ev'ning comes; Go home.

from the *Georgics*

The practice of providing scientific or practical knowledge in verse was much more common in the classical world than in modern or even early modern Europe. There were some such works on agriculture, such as Thomas Tusser's *Hundreth Good Points of Husbandry* (1557), and there are georgic moments in much great English poetry, including *Paradise Lost*. In the seventeenth and eighteenth centuries, however, agricultural knowledge more often appeared in prose manuals, dictionaries, encyclopedias, and journals. Verse about the country was more often pastoral than georgic in nature at this time, but the georgic influence never disappeared completely. In fact, it became stronger as later eighteenth-century verse scorned pastoral modes and focused on details of country life. The re-emergence of the georgic is visible in James Thomson's *Seasons*, in George Crabbe's *The Borough*, and in William Cowper's *The Task*, where we get instructions, among other things, on planting cucumbers by building up a "stercoraceous heap" – i.e. a pile of dung. There is a georgic impulse in some Romantic poetry attending to rural life and in some post-Romantic poets such as Robert Frost, who often positions georgic truths to defeat pastoral ideas. In our time, we see elements of the

25 *Toils* labors.
26 *Hebrus* a river of Thrace.
27 *Sithonian* Thracian.
28 *Ethiopian Crab* the constellation of Cancer, associated with summer heat.

29 *your Poet* Virgil, speaking of himself in the third person.
30 *Shade* the locus of pastoral composition.

georgic in some of the many works that focus on personal experience. Seamus Heaney jocularly describes himself as starting a fashion for the "poem de terre" in his early verse by writing about dibbling in the earth.

Book 1, lines 299–423

A brief account of the farmer's winter work (lines 1–15) is followed by a description of a great storm in epic style and a charming list of weather-signs that shows off Virgil's sensitivity toward nature at its best. Jonathan Swift burlesques the catalogue of weather-signs in "A Description of a City Shower" (p. 109 above).

Our translator, Thomas May (1596–1650), graduated from Cambridge and pursued a career as a dramatist. He produced a couple of comedies and earned praise in a poem by Ben Jonson. After translating Virgil's *Georgics* (1628) and Lucan's *Civil War* (or *Pharsalia*), he wrote three tragedies based on classical themes. Later he translated the Roman historian Tacitus and himself became the historian of the Long Parliament, which governed England from 1640 to 1653. May's *Georgics* are an early example of heroic couplets in English, the form of poetry that became dominant in the eighteenth century. His translation is largely unembellished, even plain. For example, May often translates metonyms in Virgil into plain sense: he writes "wine" for Virgil's "Bacchus"; "sea" for Virgil's "wave"; and "olive" for Virgil's "Sicyonian berry." Dryden, who also translated the *Georgics* (1697), creates a more "answerable" style (to use Milton's phrase), but May's simplicity is refreshing and seems appropriate to the topic.

> Cold Winter rest on plowmen doth bestow.
> Then they enjoy what they before did gain,
> And with glad feasts each other entertain.
> The genial Winter to free joy invites
> From care. Such are the Mariners' delights,   5
> When laden ships long absent from their home
> Now decked with garlands to the haven come.
> Besides the Winter is a season fit
> To gather acorns, and ripe berries get
> Of bays, of olive trees, and myrtles red.   10
> To catch wild cranes in springes, and to spread,[1]
> Toils for red Deer; the long-eared Hare to start,[2]
> And fallow Deer with a looped Spanish dart[3]
> Well thrown to kill, when with deep snow the ground

BOOK 1, LINES 299–423

1 *springes* "snare[s] for catching small game, esp. birds" (*OED*).

2 *Toils* nets used for trapping large animals.

3 *fallow Deer* like *red Deer*, a variant species of the well-known quadruped; *looped Spanish dart* a weapon with a strap attached for throwing.

Is hid, and rivers with strong ice are bound.   15
The storms of Autumn why should I relate?
When days grow shorter, and more moderate
The heat? what care good husbands entertain?[4]
Or when the showery spring doth promise rain?
When all the fields with green eared corn are proud[5]   20
And tender blades the swelling grain do shroud?
I oft have seen, when corn was ripe to mow,
And now in dry, and brittle straw did grow,
Winds from all quarters oppositely blow.
By whose dire force the full-eared blades were torn   25
Up by the roots, and into th' air were borne:
No otherwise than when black whirlwinds rise,
And toss dry straw and stubble to the skies.
Oft fall huge gusts of water from the sky,
And all the full-swelled clouds whirl from on high   30
Black showers & storms about: the thunder's noise
Even rends high heaven, & falling rain destroys
All crops, and all that th' Oxen's toil has done.
Dikes fill: with sound the swellèd rivers run;
The seas with troubled agitations move.   35
In midst of that tempestuous night, great *Jove*
From a bright hand his wingèd thunder throws:
Which shakes the earth; beasts fly; sad terror goes
Through mortal breasts. His burning dart doth awe
Rhodope, Athos, th' high Ceraunia.[6]   40
The showery South winds double now, and round
The woods do murmur, and beat shores resound.
For fear of this observe the months and signs:
Mark to what house *Saturn*'s cold star inclines:[7]
And with what planet *Mercury* doth join.   45
But first give worship to the powers divine:
Offer to *Ceres* yearly sacrifice[8]
With feasts upon the grass, when winter is
Quite spent, and now the spring doth fresh appear.
Then lambs are fat, then wines are purged & clear: 50
The shady mountains then sweet sleeps afford.
Let her by all thy plowmen be adored:
Let honey, milk, and wine be offerèd

---

4 *husbands* husbandmen; farmers.
5 *corn* any kind of grain, such as wheat, rye, or
barley.
6 *Rhodope, Athos . . . Ceraunia* mountains in
Thrace and Greece.

7 *Saturn* the coldest planet, as *Mercury* was the
hottest (a contrast lost in May's translation).
8 *Ceres* the grain goddess, worshipped at rustic
festivals such as the Cerealia.

To her, and th' happy sacrifice be led[9]
About the new corn thrice, whilst everyone   55
Follows with joyful acclamation,
Imploring *Ceres'* favour; and let none
Presume to thrust a sickle into corn,
Unless with oaken wreaths he first adorn
His head, and dance unartificially[10]   60
With hymns of praise to *Ceres'* Deity.
And that by certain tokens we might know
When heat will come, when rain, when winds shall blow,
Great *Jove* ordainèd monthly what the Moon
Should teach, what signs foretell, when winds go down,   65
That husbandmen, marking what oft befalls,
Know when to keep their cattle in the stalls.
Just ere the winds arise, the Sea swells high,
Great noise is heard from all the mountains nigh,
Then hollow murmurs through the woods you hear,   70
And all the shores resounding far and near.
Then Seas are ill to Sailors evermore,
When Cormorants fly crying to the shore
From the mid-sea, when Sea fowl pastime make
Upon dry land, when Herns the ponds forsake,[11]   75
And mounted on their wings do fly aloft.
You may discern, when winds are rising, oft
The stars in heaven do seem to fall, and make
Through night's dark air a long and fiery track.
Oft straw and withered leaves in th' air fly up,   80
And feathers swim upon the water's top.
But when it lightens from the boisterous North,
And th' East, and Western houses thunder forth,
The Lands o'erflowed, the Dikes filled everywhere,
And Mariners wet sails on th' Ocean bear,   85
The storm can ne'er thee unawares surprise,
For from the Valleys, ere it thence arise,
The Cranes do fly, the Bullock upward throws[12]
His head, and snuffs the air into his nose;
The subtle Swallow flies about the brook,   90
And querulous Frogs in muddy pools do croak.
Th' industrious Ant through narrow paths doth roll
Her eggs along from out her little hole.
The Rainbow seems to drink the waves, & home[13]

---

9 *led* walked in procession, in a ritual of
purification.
10 *unartificially* without artifice, naturally; cap-
tures the effect of Virgil's multi-syllabic adjective
incompositos meaning unaffected or clumsy.

11 *Herns* herons.
12 *Bullock* for Virgil's "heifer"!
13 *seems to drink* according to an ancient belief
that rainbows suck up moisture.

The Crows in mighty shoals from feeding come,   95
And clap their wings aloud; Sea-fowls, and those
That feed along where fair *Caÿster* flows[14]
Through th' Asian meadows, you may often see
Bathing themselves in water greedily.
They oft dive down, and swimming to and fro   100
A glad, though vain, desire of washing show.
Then with full throats the wicked Rooks call on
The rain, and wander on the shores alone,
Off'ring their heads to the approaching show'rs,[15]
As maids in spinning spend the night's late hours,   105
Their burning lamps the storm ensuing show,
Th' oil sparkles, thieves about the snuff do grow.[16]
By no less true, and certain signs may we
Fair days and sunshine in a storm foresee.
For then the stars' aspects are clear to us,   110
Nor does the moon arise obnoxious[17]
Unto her brother's rays, nor o'er the sky[18]
Do little clouds like woolly fleeces fly:
The Thetis-loved Kingfishers spread not then[19]
Their wings against the sun; nor Hogs unclean   115
Prepare them heaps of straw to lie upon.
But to the lowest vales the clouds fall down.
The fatal owl high mounted at sunset[20]
Does not the baleful evening song repeat.
Nisus his wings in th' air aloft displays,   120
And for his purple lock false Scylla pays.
Wherever Scylla through the air doth fly,
Nisus, her fierce and cruel enemy,[21]
With eager flight pursues; from thence where he
Appears, with fearful wing doth Scylla flee.[22]   125

14   *Caÿster* a river in Asia Minor.
15   *Off'ring . . . show'rs* added by May for the
sake of his metrical scheme.
16   *thieves* "excrescence[s] in the snuff [or useless
stump] of a candle" (Johnson's *Dictionary*).
17   *obnoxious* a Latinism for Virgil's *obnoxia*,
"indebted to"; the moon shines so brightly that
it seems to possess its own light, not merely to
reflect the sun.
18   *brother's* Apollo's, the moon being identified
with his sister Diana.
19   *Thetis* a sea goddess; *Kingfishers* literally,

"halcyons," a mythical bird believed to nest in the
ocean.
20   *fatal owl* a bird foreboding evil; May alters
Virgil's picture of an owl singing "vainly" for bad
weather into an owl that refrains from singing at
all.
21   *Nisus* a legendary king who changed into a
sea-eagle when his daughter Scylla cut off the
purple lock of hair on which his life depended (cf.
Pope's *Rape of the Lock*).
22   *Scylla* in her altered form as the *ciris* (a myth-
ical bird).

The Ravens with a loud, and strainèd throat
From their high nest do oft repeat their note,
And 'mongst the leaves they croak together all
As taken with a joy unusual;
It does them good, the storm now spent, to see   130
Their nests of young ones, and dear progeny.
I do not think that all these creatures have
More wisdom than the fates to mankind gave;[23]
But thus; as tempests, as th' unconstant skies
Do change their course, as several winds arise   135
In th' air, and do condense, or rarify,
Just so their natures alter instantly.
Their breasts receive impressions different;
As some by calms, so some by storms are sent.
Hence that consent of joy or woe doth flow   140
Which croaking ravens, fowl, and cattle show.

Book 2, lines 458–542

Book 2 concludes with a famous encomium of the farmer's life. His blissful environment, simplicity, and moral uprightness – each evocative of the Golden Age – are contrasted with the corruption of urban Rome. In a programmatic digression, the author, in allusive and symbolic terms, questions his ability to offer a scientific explanation of Nature and defines himself as the poet of the countryside – its beauty, gods, and moral ambience. Virgil's poetic persona conveys both admiration for and rivalry with his great predecessor, Lucretius, who had attempted in his didactic poem, *De Rerum Natura* (p. 324 above), to dispel fears of death and the gods through a rational explanation of the universe. The passage inspired much idealization of country life in English poetry, including Jonson's "To Penshurst" (p. 58 above), Thomson's *Winter* (p. 126 above), and Gray's *An Elegy Wrote in a Country Church Yard* (p. 154 above).

Our translator is, again, Thomas May (see p. 353 above).

Oh too too happy, if their bliss they knew,
Plain Husbandmen; to whom the earth with true
And bounteous justice, free from bloody war
Returns an easy food; who, though they are[1]
Not early waked in high-roofed Palaces   5

---

23 *I do not think ... gave* Virgil, in Lucretian fashion, prefers a scientific explanation to a supernatural one.

BOOK 2, LINES 458–542

1 *easy* easily obtained; the bounty of the earth is a Golden Age motif, like peace and justice.

When waiting Clients come; though they possess[2]
No Posts, which Indian shells adorn in state,[3]
No gold embroidered clothes, Corinthian plate,[4]
Nor rich Assyrian scarlet; nor abuse[5]
With sweetest Casia the plain simple use[6]   10
Of oil; yet rest secure, a harmless life[7]
Enriched with several blessings, free from strife,
Cool caves, dark shady groves, & fountains clear,[8]
Untroubled sleeps, and cattle's lowing there,
And pleasant huntings want not; there they live   15
By labour and small wealth; honour they give
Unto their gods and parents; justice took[9]
Her last step there, when she the earth forsook.
But let the sacred Muse, whose priest I am,[10]
Me above all with her sweet love inflame;   20
Teach me each star, each heavenly motion.
The oft eclipses of the Sun and Moon,
The cause of Earthquakes: why the swelling main
Rises, and falls into itself again:
Why winter suns so soon haste to the sea: 25
What makes the Summer nights so short to be.
But if dull blood, which 'bout my heart doth flow,[11]
These parts of nature will not let me know;
Then let me (fameless) love the fields and woods,[12]
The fruitful watered vales, and running floods.   30
Those plains, where clear Sperchius runs, that mount[13]
Where Spartan Virgins to great *Bacchus* wont[14]
To sacrifice, or shady vales that lie
Under high Haemus, let my dwelling be.[15]

2   *Clients* social dependents; it was the custom
in Rome for clients to greet their patrons at dawn
as a mark of respect.

3   *Posts . . . state* doorposts decorated with
tortoise-shell.

4   *Corinthian plate* imported bronze-ware of
exceptional quality.

5   *Assyrian scarlet* purple dye from Tyre on the
coast of Syria; condemned by moralists as an
unnatural luxury.

6   *Casia* a sweet-smelling eastern substance.

7   *oil* olive oil.

8   *caves . . . groves . . . fountains* staple features of
the *locus amoenus*, the ideal place of happiness and
pleasure.

9   *justice* according to Aratus (*Phaenomena*
96–136), Justice was the last deity to abandon the
earth after the Golden Age.

10   *priest* Virgil figures his poem as a sacrifice to
the Muses, the divine patrons of the arts.

11   *But . . . flow* according to the Greek philoso-
pher Empedocles, the blood surrounding the
heart is the seat of intelligence.

12   *love* i.e. not just feel affection for but write
about.

13   *Sperchius* a river in Sparta; *mount* Mt. Tay-
getus in Sparta.

14   *Bacchus* Dionysus, whose rituals included
dancing on mountains; *wont* are accustomed.

15   *Haemus* a mountain in Thrace.

Happy is he that knows the cause of things![16]   35
That all his fears to due subjection brings,
Yea fate itself, and greedy Acheron![17]
Yea happy sure is he, who ere has known[18]
The rural gods, *Sylvanus*, and great *Pan*,[19]
And all the sister Nymphs! that happy man[20]   40
Nor people's voices, nor kings' purple move:[21]
Nor dire ambition sund'ring brothers' love:[22]
Nor th' Istrian Dacians' fierce conspiracies:[23]
Nor Rome's estate, nor falling monarchies.
He sees no poor, whose miserable state   45
He suffers for; he envies no man's fate;
He eats such fruits as of their own accord
The willing grounds, and laden trees afford;
He sees no wrangling courts, no laws undone
By sword, nor people's forced election.   50
Some search the Sea's hid paths, some rush to war,
In Courts of Kings others attendants are.
One would his country, and dear gods destroy,[24]
That he himself might drink in gems, and lie[25]
On purple beds; another hoards up gold,   55
And ever wakes his hidden wealth to hold.
The pleading bars another doth admire,[26]
And high applause from every seat desire
Plebeians, and Patricians; some for goods[27]
Their guilty hands imbrue in brothers' bloods.[28]   60
Some from their houses and dear countries roam
In banishment, to seek a foreign home:
Whilst the industrious husband plows the soil,[29]

---

16 *Happy is he* i.e. the philosopher; *cause of things* Virgil evokes the title of Lucretius' *De Rerum Natura* (On the Nature of Things).

17 *Acheron* a river of the underworld; here a metonymy for death.

18 *happy sure is he* literally, "happy too is he," *he* being the countryman and, by extension, the countryman's poet (Virgil).

19 *Sylvanus* god of the woods; *Pan* god of shepherds.

20 *Nymphs* divine spirits inhabiting springs, trees, and mountains.

21 *Nor ... nor* neither ... nor; *people's voices* literally, "the people's rods" (*fasces*), i.e. the bundles of rods and axes symbolizing the authority of the highest magistrates; shorthand for "political office conferred by popular vote."

22 *brothers* an allusion either to the Roman civil wars or to dynastic dissension in the eastern kingdom of Parthia.

23 *Istrian Dacians* a warlike people north of the river Danube (Ister), which marked the northern frontier of the Roman empire.

24 *dear gods* the Penates or household gods.

25 *in gems* from a gem-encrusted goblet.

26 *pleading bars* literally, "the rostra," the speakers' platform in the forum.

27 *Plebeians* the common people; *Patricians* aristocrats; senators occupied separate seats in the theater.

28 *imbrue* steep; *brothers' bloods* a certain reference to the Roman civil wars.

29 *husband* husbandman, farmer.

And takes the profit of his yearly toil.
With which his house and country too he serves   65
And feeds his Herds, & th' Ox that well deserves.
No fruitless time; young Cattle still are bred,
Or Corn is reaped, or fruits are gatherèd,
Corn that the furrows lades, and barns doth fill.[30]
When Winter comes, Oil in the Olive mill   70
They make; and Porkers fat with Acorns grow;
The woods yield Crabs, but Autumn does bestow[31]
All kinds of pleasant fruit; the grapes hang by
Hot sunny walls, and ripen perfectly.
Meanwhile his pretty children kissing cull[32]   75
His neck: his house is chaste; with Udders full
His Kine come home; and in the flowery Meads[33]
His frisking Kids do butt with tender heads.
He feasts himself upon the grassy ground,
Whilst 'bout the fire carousing cups are crowned;[34]   80
And *Bacchus* is invoked in sacrifice;
Then 'mongst his herdsmen makes a darting prize,[35]
And sets the mark upon an Elm; or they
Prepared for wrestling, their hard limbs display.
Such lives as this the ancient Sabines led,[36]   85
And so were *Romulus* and *Remus* bred;[37]
So grew renownèd Tuscany to fame,[38]
So Rome the greatest of all lands became,
And in one wall did seven great hills contain.
And thus before Dictaean *Jove* did reign,[39]   90
And impious nations on slain cattle fed,
His life on earth the golden Saturn led.
No classics sounded then, nor mortal blade[40]
Of swords, the Smith's laborious anvil made.
But we enough have now produced our course,[41]   95
And time it is to ease our wearied horse.[42]

30 *the furrows lades* loads the furrows with produce.

31 *Crabs* crab-apples; literally, "fruits of the arbutus tree."

32 *cull* hug.

33 *Kine* cows.

34 *crowned* garlanded.

35 *darting prize* a prize for marksmanship.

36 *Sabines* an Italian people of proverbial austerity and high morals.

37 *Romulus . . . Remus* mythical founders of Rome, who were raised by a herdsman.

38 *Tuscany* Etruria, whose civilization flourished before Rome's.

39 *Dictaean Jove* Jupiter was born on Mt. Dicte in Crete; his usurpation of *Saturn*'s throne is equated with the end of the Golden Age.

40 *classics* a Latinism for Virgil's *classica*, "military trumpets."

41 *produced our course* advanced the poem.

42 *wearied horse* i.e. chariot-team – a traditional metaphor for the poet's effort, here punctuating the end of Book 2.

Book 3, lines 384–93

Book 3 of the *Georgics* deals with animal husbandry. In this selection Virgil rounds off a brief piece of advice about wool production with an allusion to the obscure myth of Pan and Luna, goddess of the moon. (Macrobius ascribes the story to the Greek poet Nicander.) Pan lured Luna into the woods, either by proffering a beautiful fleece or by turning himself into a ram, and there he had his way with her. These lines are the basis for Browning's *Pan and Luna* (p. 209 above).

Our translator is, again, Thomas May (see p. 353 above).

> If thou regard their Wool, let them not go
> Where bushes are, where burs and thistles grow,
> Nor in a grass too rich. Be sure to choose
> Thy flocks with white soft fleeces, but refuse
> That Ram (although the fleece upon his back   5
> Be ne'er so white) whose only tongue is black,
> Lest he do stain the fleeces of his Lambs
> With spots, but choose another 'mongst the Rams.
> So with a Snowy fleecèd Ram (if we
> Trust fame) did *Pan* the god of Arcady[1]   10
> Deceive thee *Luna*, nor didst thou disdain[2]
> Within the Woods to ease a Lover's pain.[3]

from the *Aeneid*

Book 1, lines 1–215

The proem of the *Aeneid* announces its central theme: the foundation of the Roman race by Aeneas. When the epic begins, Aeneas has been journeying for several years from Troy toward his fated destination in Italy. (The tale of the fall of Troy and his earlier wanderings is related by Aeneas as a flashback in Books 2–3.) However, as he sets sail from Sicily on the last leg of his journey, the goddess Juno, a relentless enemy of Troy, persuades Aeolus, the lord of the winds, to raise a great storm which wrecks the Trojans on the coast of Africa near Carthage. This sets the scene for Aeneas' greatest trial, his love affair with Dido, queen of Carthage.

BOOK 3, LINES 384–393

1 *Pan* goat-footed god of shepherds; *Arcady* Arcadia, a region of southern Greece.
2 *Luna* the moon goddess.

3 *Pan . . . pain* literally, "Pan the god of Arcadia snared and deceived you, Luna, when he called you into the deep woods and you did not reject his calling." It is not clear that Luna consented to his sexual advances.

Many traditional features of epic appear in Book 1: for example, the use of "divine machinery"; set-piece descriptions and typical scenes; extended similes; elaborate speeches; and prophecy. Book 1 also introduces many of the *Aeneid*'s salient themes: the rivalry of Juno and Venus; the role of fate (as embodied in Jupiter); the *pietas* and suffering of Aeneas; the destructive effect of passion; and the supreme effort it took to create Rome.

John Dryden (1631–1700), our translator, was the pre-eminent poet of his time. After the Glorious Revolution brought William and Mary to the throne in 1689, he lost his government positions and largely gave up writing political verse and plays. He turned instead to translation, which had always been important to him, and produced wonderful versions of Virgil, Ovid, Homer, and many other classical poets, as well as the first translation of Chaucer. Dryden's translation of the *Aeneid* (1697) was the crowning achievement of this period of his life. Earlier, in his preface to *Ovid's Epistles* (1680), he had articulated his conception of translation. He favored a middle way between slavishly literal "metaphrase" and very loose "imitation." He called his middle way "Paraphrase, or Translation with Latitude, where the Authour is kept in view by the Translator, so as never to be lost, but his words are not so strictly followed as his sense, and that too is admitted to be amplified, but not altered."[1] Dryden's *Aeneid* is an English poem which is coherent and beautiful in its own right, as well as a translation of another poem. It is significantly longer than its original, partly because Latin, as a relatively synthetic language (that is, one which expresses syntactical relations by means of grammatical inflection), is more compressed than English, which is relatively analytic. Dryden's poem is also longer than Virgil's, however, because Dryden's unit of expression is the heroic couplet, and sometimes the triplet, whereas Virgil wrote in hexameters. Furthermore, Dryden is not inclined to compression in his poetry, relatively speaking, but prefers to express his thoughts and images more fully. The eight lines of the second verse paragraph below, for example, translate four lines of Virgil, and there is nothing in the Virgilian lines quite as direct and explanatory as "the Queen of Heav'n began / To persecute so brave, so just a Man." It may also be remarked that Dryden's adjectives for Aeneas – "brave" and "just" – make him a somewhat simpler, and perhaps more universal, hero than the figure Virgil suggests with the words *insignem pietate* – eminent for dutifulness to family, gods, and country.

Our text is based on the first edition of *The Works of Virgil* (1697), but we have benefited from the textual notes and commentary in the California Edition of Dryden, Vols. V–VI (1987).

Arms, and the Man I sing, who, forced by Fate,
And haughty *Juno*'s unrelenting Hate,[2]

BOOK 1, LINES 1–215

1 *Works of John Dryden*, Vol. I (University of California Press, 1956), p. 114.

2 *Juno* wife and sister of Jupiter; a fierce enemy of Troy.

Expelled and exiled, left the *Trojan* Shore:
Long Labours, both by Sea and Land, he bore,
And in the doubtful War, before he won   5
The *Latian* Realm, and built the destined Town;[3]
His banished Gods restored to Rites Divine,[4]
And settled sure Succession in his Line:
From whence the Race of *Alban* Fathers come,[5]
And the long Glories of Majestic *Rome*.[6]   10
   O Muse! the Causes and the Crimes relate,
What Goddess was provoked, and whence her hate;
For what Offence the Queen of Heav'n began
To persecute so brave, so just a Man![7]
Involved his anxious Life in endless Cares,   15
Exposed to Wants, and hurried into Wars!
Can Heav'nly Minds such high resentment show,
Or exercise their Spite in Human Woe?[8]
   Against the *Tiber*'s Mouth, but far away,[9]
An ancient Town was seated on the Sea;   20
A *Tyrian* Colony; the People made[10]
Stout for the War, and studious of their Trade:
Carthage the Name, beloved by *Juno* more[11]
Than her own *Argos*, or the *Samian* Shore.[12]
Here stood her Chariot; here, if Heav'n were kind,   25
The Seat of awful Empire she designed.
Yet she had heard an ancient Rumour fly,
(Long cited by the People of the Sky),[13]
That times to come should see the *Trojan* Race
Her *Carthage* ruin, and her Tow'rs deface;   30
Nor thus confined, the Yoke of Sov'reign Sway
Should on the Necks of all the Nations lay.
She pondered this, and feared it was in Fate;
Nor could forget the War she waged of late

3   *Latian Realm* Latium, the region of Italy containing Rome; *Town* Lavinium; the town founded by Aeneas in Latium.
4   *Gods* the household gods of Troy, whose images Aeneas brought to Italy.
5   *Alban Fathers* kings of Alba Longa, a city founded by Aeneas' son.
6   *Rome* traditionally founded in 753 BCE by Romulus and Remus.
7   *so just a Man* literally, "a man outstanding in *pietas*"; Aeneas' defining quality as a hero, *pietas* signifies devotion to gods, family, and country (a broader idea than "piety").

8   One of many lines added to Virgil; we note only a few.
9   *Against the Tiber's Mouth* facing Ostia, where Rome's river empties into the sea.
10   *Tyrian* Phoenician (from the city of Tyre).
11   *Carthage* harbor city on the coast of Tunisia; Rome's chief rival for supremacy in the western Mediterranean; defeated in the three Punic Wars (third to second centuries BCE), through which Rome acquired its first overseas provinces.
12   *Argos . . . Samian Shore* cult centers of Juno in Greece; Virgil mentions only Samos.
13   *People of the Sky* ethereal beings, gods; the line is not in Virgil.

For conq'ring *Greece* against the *Trojan* State.   35
Besides, long Causes working in her Mind,[14]
And secret Seeds of Envy, lay behind;
Deep graven in her Heart the Doom remained[15]
Of partial *Paris*, and her Form disdained;[16]
The Grace bestowed on ravished *Ganymed*,[17]   40
Electra's Glories, and her injured Bed.[18]
Each was a Cause alone, and all combined
To kindle Vengeance in her haughty Mind.
For this, far distant from the *Latian* Coast
She drove the Remnants of the *Trojan* Host;[19]   45
And sev'n long Years th' unhappy wand'ring Train
Were tossed by Storms, and scattered through the Main.
Such Time, such Toil, required the *Roman* Name,
Such length of Labour for so vast a Frame.[20]
  Now scarce the *Trojan* Fleet, with Sails and Oars,   50
Had left behind the Fair *Sicilian* Shores,[21]
Ent'ring with cheerful Shouts the wat'ry Reign,
And plowing frothy Furrows in the Main;
When, lab'ring still with endless discontent,
The Queen of Heav'n did thus her Fury vent: 55
  "Then am I vanquished? must I yield?" said she,
"And must the *Trojans* Reign in *Italy*?
So Fate will have it, and *Jove* adds his Force;
Nor can my Pow'r divert their happy Course.
Could angry *Pallas*, with revengeful Spleen,[22]   60
The *Grecian* navy burn, and drown the Men?
She, for the Fault of one offending Foe,
The Bolts of *Jove* himself presumed to throw:
With Whirlwinds from beneath she tossed the Ship,
And bare exposed the Bosom of the deep;   65
Then, as an Eagle grips the trembling Game,[23]

14   *long Causes* old reasons for anger; the word *cause* was inseparable in Dryden's day from *The Cause* or *The Old Cause* of the Parliamentary side in the British Civil War.

15   *Doom* judgment (Old English *dom*).

16   *Paris* Trojan hero who awarded the prize to Venus in a beauty contest between Juno, Minerva, and Venus – the "Judgment of Paris"; *Form* beauty (Virgil's *forma*).

17   *Ganymed* young Trojan prince abducted by Jupiter to be his cup-bearer.

18   *Electra* mother, by Jupiter, of Dardanus, the founder of the Trojan race; not mentioned by Virgil.

19   *Host* army.

20   *Frame* anything constructed of various parts; an order of government; an empire.

21   *Sicilian Shores* the last stop before Italy (until Juno intervened).

22   *Pallas* Minerva (Greek Athena); during the Greeks' voyage home, she killed the "lesser" Ajax (son of Oileus), who had violated the prophetess Cassandra in her temple; *Spleen* capricious hot temper (a word for a variety of emotions frequently used in the sixteenth to eighteenth centuries; not in Virgil).

23   The simile is not in Virgil.

The Wretch, yet hissing with her Father's Flame,
She strongly seized, and with a burning Wound
Transfixed and naked, on a Rock she bound.
But I, who walk in awful State above,   70
The Majesty of Heav'n, the Sister-wife of *Jove*,
For length of Years my fruitless Force employ
Against the thin remains of ruined *Troy*!
What Nations now to *Juno*'s Pow'r will pray,
Or off'rings on my slighted Altars lay?"   75
    Thus raged the Goddess; and, with Fury fraught,
The restless Regions of the Storms she sought:
Where, in a spacious Cave of living Stone,
The Tyrant *Aeolus*, from his Airy Throne,[24]
With Pow'r Imperial curbs the struggling Winds,   80
And sounding Tempests in dark Prisons binds.
This Way, and that, th' impatient Captives tend,
And, pressing for Release, the Mountains rend;
High in his Hall th' undaunted Monarch stands,
And shakes his Scepter, and their Rage commands: 85
Which did he not, their unresisted Sway
Would sweep the World before them, in their Way:
Earth, Air, and Seas through empty Space would roll,
And Heav'n would fly before the driving Soul.[25]
In fear of this, the Father of the Gods   90
Confined their Fury to those dark Abodes,
And locked 'em safe within, oppressed with Mountain loads:
Imposed a King, with arbitrary Sway,[26]
To loose their Fetters, or their Force allay.
To whom the suppliant Queen her Prayers addressed,   95
And thus the tenor of her Suit expressed:[27]
    "O *Aeolus*! for to thee the King of Heav'n
The Pow'r of Tempests and of Winds has giv'n;
Thy Force alone their Fury can restrain,
And smooth the Waves, or swell the troubled Main.   100
A race of wand'ring Slaves, abhorred by me,
With prosp'rous Passage cut the *Tuscan* Sea;[28]
To fruitful *Italy* their Course they steer,
And for their vanquished Gods design new Temples there.
Raise all thy Winds, with Night involve the Skies;   105

24 *Aeolus* god of the winds.
25 *Soul* Dryden plays on the Latin word for soul, *anima*, which means breath or air, as earlier editors point out.
26 *Imposed a King, with arbitrary Sway* a line more reflective of Dryden's belief in British, specifically Stuart, monarchy than of Virgil's sense.
27 *tenor* meaning, import.
28 *Tuscan Sea* the waters between Sicily and the west coast of Italy.

Sink or disperse my fatal Enemies.[29]
Twice sev'n, the charming Daughters of the Main,[30]
Around my Person wait, and bear my Train:
Succeed my Wish, and second my Design,[31]
The fairest, *Deiopeia*, shall be thine,   110
And make thee Father of a happy Line."
   To this the God – "'Tis yours, O Queen ! to will
The Work, which Duty binds me to fulfil.
These airy Kingdoms, and this wide Command,
Are all the Presents of your bounteous Hand: 115
Yours is my Sov'reign's Grace; and, as your Guest,[32]
I sit with Gods at their Celestial Feast;
Raise Tempests at your Pleasure, or subdue;
Dispose of Empire, which I hold from you."
He said, and hurled against the Mountain side   120
His quiv'ring Spear; and all, the God applied.
The raging Winds rush through the hollow Wound,
And dance aloft in Air, and skim along the Ground;
Then, settling on the Sea, the Surges sweep,
Raise liquid Mountains, and disclose the deep.   125
South, East, and West with mixed Confusion roar,
And roll the foaming Billows to the Shore.
The Cables crack; the Sailors' fearful Cries
Ascend; and sable Night involves the Skies;
And Heav'n itself is ravished from their Eyes.   130
Loud Peals of Thunder from the Poles ensue;[33]
Then flashing Fires the transient Light renew;
The Face of things a frightful Image bears,
And present Death in various Forms appears.
Struck with unusual Fright, the *Trojan* Chief,   135
With lifted Hands and Eyes, invokes Relief;[34]
And, "Thrice and four times happy those," he cried,
"That under *Ilian* Walls before their Parents died![35]
Tydides, bravest of the *Grecian* Train![36]
Why could not I by that strong Arm be slain,   140

---

29 *fatal* meaning both ordained by Fate and deadly; not in Virgil.

30 *Daughters of the Main* sea nymphs.

31 *Succeed* further; bring to fruition; or a Latinism meaning "yield to" (California ed.).

32 *Yours is my Sov'reign's Grace* i.e. "to you I owe Jupiter's favor."

33 *Poles* i.e. it thundered "from pole to pole" (Conington; see p. 375 below).

34 Literally, "At once the limbs of Aeneas grew slack with cold fear; he groaned and stretching his palms to the stars, he spoke as follows. . . ." Dryden plays down Aeneas' weakness to protect his Stoic vision of the hero.

35 *Ilian* Trojan (from "Ilium").

36 *Tydides* Diomedes, son of Tydeus.

And lie by noble *Hector* on the Plain,[37]
Or great *Sarpedon*, in those bloody Fields,[38]
Where *Simois* rolls the Bodies and the Shields[39]
Of Heroes, whose dismembered Hands yet bear
The Dart aloft, and clench the pointed Spear!"[40]   145
Thus while the Pious Prince his Fate bewails,
Fierce *Boreas* drove against his flying Sails,[41]
And rent the Sheets; the raging Billows rise,
And mount the tossing Vessels to the Skies:
Nor can the shiv'ring Oars sustain the Blow;   150
The Galley gives her side, and turns her Prow;
While those astern, descending down the Steep,
Through gaping Waves behold the boiling deep.
Three Ships were hurried by the Southern Blast,
And on the secret Shelves with Fury cast.   155
Those hidden Rocks th' *Ausonian* Sailors knew:[42]
They called them Altars, when they rose in view,
And showed their spacious Backs above the Flood.
Three more fierce *Eurus*, in his angry Mood,[43]
Dashed on the Shallows of the moving Sand,   160
And in mid Ocean left them moored a-land.
Orontes' Bark, that bore the Lycian Crew,[44]
(A horrid Sight!) ev'n in the Hero's view,
From Stem to Stern by Waves was overborne:
The trembling Pilot, from his Rudder torn,   165
Was headlong hurled; thrice round the Ship was tossed,
Then bulged at once, and in the deep was lost;[45]
And here and there above the Waves were seen
Arms, Pictures, precious Goods, and floating Men.
The stoutest Vessel to the Storm gave way,   170
And sucked through loosened Planks the rushing Sea.
Ilioneus was her Chief: *Alethes* old,
Achates faithful, *Abas* young and bold,[46]
Endured not less; their Ships, with gaping Seams,
Admit the Deluge of the briny Streams.   175

37   *noble Hector* son of Priam and Hecuba and
the foremost Trojan hero; killed by Achilles in a
duel (*Iliad* 22).
38   *Sarpedon* mortal son of Zeus; a Trojan ally
killed by Patroclus (*Iliad* 16).
39   *Simois* river of Troy and scene of slaughter
in the *Iliad*.
40   *Of Heroes . . . Spear* literally, "the shields and
helmets of heroes and their great bodies"; Dryden
imports a flight of fancy.

41   *Boreas* the north wind.
42   *Ausonian* Italian.
43   *Eurus* the east wind.
44   *Bark* ship; *Lycian Crew* the Lycians were
allies of Troy.
45   *bulged* bilged; of a ship, smashed in the
bottom and taking on water.
46   *Ilioneus . . . Alethes . . . Achates . . . Abas*
Trojan captains.

Meantime Imperial *Neptune* heard the Sound[47]
Of raging Billows breaking on the Ground.
Displeased, and fearing for his Wat'ry Reign,
He reared his awful Head above the Main,
Serene in Majesty; then rolled his Eyes   180
Around the space of Earth, and Seas, and Skies.
He saw the *Trojan* Fleet dispersed, distressed,
By Stormy Winds and wintry Heav'n oppressed.
Full well the God his Sister's envy knew,
And what her Aims and what her Arts pursue.   185
He summoned *Eurus* and the western Blast,
And first an angry glance on both he cast;
Then thus rebuked: "Audacious Winds! from whence
This bold Attempt, this Rebel Insolence?
Is it for you to ravage Seas and Land,   190
Unauthorized by my supreme Command?
To raise such Mountains on the troubled Main?
Whom I – but first 'tis fit the Billows to restrain,[48]
And then you shall be taught obedience to my Reign.
Hence! to your Lord my Royal Mandate bear,[49]   195
The Realms of Ocean and the Fields of Air
Are mine, not his; by fatal Lot to me
The liquid Empire fell, and Trident of the Sea.
His Pow'r to hollow Caverns is confined:
There let him reign, the Jailor of the Wind: 200
With hoarse Commands his breathing Subjects call,
And boast and bluster in his empty Hall."
He spoke: and, while he spoke, he smoothed the Sea,
Dispelled the Darkness, and restored the Day.
Cymothoe, *Triton*, and the Sea-green Train[50]   205
Of beauteous Nymphs, the Daughters of the Main,
Clear from the Rocks the Vessels with their hands:
The God himself with ready Trident stands,
And ope's the Deep, and spreads the moving sands;
Then heaves them off the shoals: where'er he guides   210
His finny Coursers and in Triumph rides,
The Waves unruffle and the Sea subsides.
As when in Tumults rise th' ignoble crowd,[51]

---

47 *Neptune* sea god and brother of Jupiter and
Juno.
48 *Whom I* – the rhetorical figure called apo-
siopesis (breaking off in silence); Neptune is
choking with anger.
49 *your Lord* Aeolus.
50 *Cymothoe* a sea nymph (Wave-Runner);
Triton a sea god.

51 This famous simile, the first of the poem,
depicts a revered Roman statesman silencing an
unruly crowd; it enacts an antithesis between
furor and *pietas* that is fundamental to the
meaning of the *Aeneid*.

Mad are their Motions, and their Tongues are loud;
And Stones and Brands in rattling Volleys fly, 215
And all the Rustic Arms that Fury can supply:
If then some grave and Pious Man appear,
They hush their Noise, and lend a list'ning Ear;
He soothes with sober Words their angry Mood,
And quenches their innate Desire of Blood: 220
So, when the Father of the Flood appears,
And o'er the Seas his Sov'reign Trident rears,
Their Fury falls: he skims the liquid Plains,
High on his Chariot, and, with loosened Reins,
Majestic moves along, and awful Peace maintains. 225
The weary *Trojans* ply their shattered Oars
To nearest Land, and make the *Libyan* Shores.
   Within a long Recess there lies a Bay:
An Island shades it from the rolling Sea,
And forms a Port secure for Ships to ride; 230
Broke by the jutting Land, on either side,
In double Streams the briny Waters glide.
Betwixt two rows of Rocks, a Sylvan Scene
Appears above, and Groves for ever green:[52]
A Grot is formed beneath, with Mossy Seats,[53] 235
To rest the *Nereids*, and exclude the Heats.[54]
Down through the Crannies of the living Walls
The Crystal Streams descend in murm'ring Falls:
No Haulsers need to bind the Vessels here,[55]
Nor bearded Anchors, for no Storms they fear.[56] 240
Sev'n Ships within this happy Harbour meet,
The thin Remainders of the scattered Fleet.
The *Trojans*, worn with Toils, and spent with Woes,
Leap on the welcome Land, and seek their wished Repose.
First, good *Achates*, with repeated strokes[57] 245
Of clashing Flints, their hidden Fire provokes:
Short Flame succeeds; a Bed of withered Leaves
The dying Sparkles in their Fall receives:
Caught into Life, in fiery Fumes they rise,
And, fed with stronger Food, invade the Skies. 250
The *Trojans*, dropping wet, or stand around

52 *Groves for ever green* literally, "a dark glade looms with trembling shade." Dryden removes the sinister element from Virgil's description of the harbor.

53 *Grot* grotto, "a cave; a cavern for coolness and pleasure" (Johnson); *Mossy Seats* comfier than Virgil's "seats of living rock!"

54 *Nereids* sea nymphs; daughters of the sea god Nereus.

55 *Haulsers* obs. form of *hawser*, "a large rope or small cable" (*OED*).

56 *bearded* "barbed or jagged like an arrow or fish-hook" (*OED*).

57 *Achates* Aeneas' right-hand man.

The cheerful blaze, or lie along the Ground:[58]
Some dry their Corn, infected with the Brine,[59]
Then grind with Marbles, and prepare to dine.[60]
Aeneas climbs the Mountain's airy Brow,   255
And takes a Prospect of the Seas below,
If *Capys* thence, or *Antheus* he could spy,
Or see the Streamers of *Caïcus* fly.[61]
No Vessels were in view: but, on the Plain,
Three beamy Stags command a Lordly Train[62]   260
Of branching Heads: the more ignoble Throng
Attend their stately Steps, and slowly graze along.
He stood; and, while secure they fed below,
He took the Quiver and the trusty Bow
Achates used to bear: the Leaders first   265
He laid along, and then the Vulgar pierced;
Nor ceased his Arrows, till the shady Plain
Sev'n mighty Bodies with their Blood distain.[63]
For the sev'n Ships he made an equal Share,
And to the Port returned, Triumphant from the War.   270
The Jars of gen'rous Wine (*Acestes'* gift,[64]
When his *Trinacrian* Shores the Navy left)[65]
He set abroach, and for the Feast prepared,
In equal Portions with the Ven'son shared.
Thus while he dealt it round, the pious Chief   275
With cheerful Words allayed the common Grief:
"Endure, and conquer! *Jove* will soon dispose
To future Good our past and present Woes.
With me, the Rocks of *Scylla* you have tried;
Th' inhuman *Cyclops* and his Den defied.[66]   280
What greater Ills hereafter can you bear?
Resume your Courage and dismiss your Care,
An Hour will come, with Pleasure to relate
Your Sorrows past, as Benefits of Fate.
Through various Hazards and Events, we move   285
To *Latium* and the Realms foredoomed by *Jove*.
Called to the Seat (the Promise of the Skies)
Where *Trojan* Kingdoms once again may rise,

---

58 *or . . . or* either . . . or.
59 *Corn* any grain.
60 *Marbles* pieces of any hard stone.
61 *Capys . . . Antheus . . . Caïcus* other missing Trojans.
62 *beamy* "possessing full grown horns" (*OED*).
63 *distain* stain.

64 *Acestes* Sicilian king who had recently hosted Aeneas.
65 *Trinacrian* Sicilian.
66 *Scylla . . . Cyclops* a sea monster and a one-eyed cannibalistic giant, best known for their predations upon Odysseus and his men (*Odyssey* 9 and 12); Aeneas avoided them both (*Aeneid* 3).

Endure the Hardships of your present State;
Live, and reserve yourselves for better Fate."   290
    These Words he spoke, but spoke not from his Heart;
His outward Smiles concealed his inward Smart.
The jolly Crew, unmindful of the past,
The Quarry share, their plenteous Dinner haste.
Some strip the Skin, some portion out the Spoil;   295
The Limbs, yet trembling, in the Cauldrons boil;
Some on the Fire the reeking Entrails broil.
Stretched on the grassy Turf, at ease they dine,
Restore their Strength with Meat, and cheer their Souls with Wine.

Book 2, lines 1–56

Aeneas begins his narration of the fall of Troy with an account of the Greeks' construction of the Trojan Horse and their pretended withdrawal. Fearful of "Greeks bearing gifts," the Trojan noble Laocoön hurls his spear at the horse, causing it to reverberate ominously. (For this attempt to resist fate, Laocoön and his sons later suffer the grisly death of strangulation by sea serpents, as represented by the famous statue in the Vatican.) Swift makes humorous use of the passage in his "Description of a City Shower" (p. 109 above).

The translation was first published by Christopher Pitt (1699–1748) in 1740 and was included in 1753 in Joseph Warton's edition of the *Works of Virgil*. Almost all of Pitt's literary production was in the realm of translation. His couplets may not compare with Pope's or Dryden's for literary excellence, but his translation is faithful to Virgil's sense.

All gazed in silence, with an eager look,
Then from the golden couch the hero spoke.
"Ah mighty queen! you urge me to disclose,
And feel, once more, unutterable woes;
How vengeful Greece with victory was crowned,   5
And Troy's fair empire humbled to the ground;
Those direful scenes I saw on Phrygia's shore,[1]
Those wars in which so large a part I bore,
The fiercest Argive would with tears bewail,[2]
And stern Ulysses tremble at the tale:[3]   10
And lo! the night precipitates away;[4]

BOOK 2, LINES 1–56

1   *Phrygia* western Asia Minor.

2   *Argive* Greek.

3   *Ulysses* literally, "soldier of hard Ulysses." Virgil depicts Ulysses (Odysseus) as a deceitful bully.

4   *precipitates* a Latinism for Virgil's *praecipitat* (rushes headlong); compare *The Vanity of Human Wishes*, l. 20 (p. 140 above).

The stars, grown dim before the dawning day,
Call to repose; but since you long to know,
And curious listen to the storied woe;
Though my shocked soul recoils, my tongue shall tell,   15
But with a bleeding heart, how Ilion fell.[5]
   The Grecian kings (for many a rolling year,
Repelled by fate, and harassed by the war),
By Pallas' aid, of seasoned fir compose[6]
A steed, that tow'ring like a mountain rose;   20
This they pretend their common vow, to gain[7]
A safe return, and measure back the main:[8]
Such the report; but guileful Argos hides[9]
Her bravest heroes in the monster's sides;
Deep, deep within, they thronged the dreadful gloom,   25
And half a host lay ambushed in the womb.
   An isle, in ancient times renowned by fame,
Lies full in view, and Tenedos the name;
Once blest with wealth, while Priam held the sway,[10]
But now a broken, rough, and dang'rous bay: 30
Thither their unsuspected course they bore,
And hid their hosts within the winding shore.
We deemed them sailed for Greece; transported Troy
Forgot her woes, and gave a loose to joy;
Threw wide her gates, and poured forth all her train,   35
To view th' abandoned camp, and empty plain.
Here the Dolopian troops their station held;[11]
There proud Achilles' tent o'erlooked the field;[12]
Here ranged the thousand vessels stood, and there[13]
In conflict joined the furious sons of war.   40
Some view the gift of Pallas with surprise,
The fatal monster, and its wondrous size.
And first Thymoetes moved the crowd to lead
And lodge within the tower the lofty steed;
Or, with design, his country to destroy,   45
Or fate determined now the fall of Troy.[14]
But hoary Capys, and the wise, require

---

5 *Ilion* Troy.
6 *Pallas* Minerva (Greek Athena).
7 *vow* votive offering, an obsolete usage even at the time.
8 *measure back the main* go back across the sea.
9 *Argos* Greece.
10 *Priam* last king of Troy.

11 *Dolopian* Thessalian.
12 *proud Achilles* literally, "harsh Achilles" – the merciless killer of Hector and many other Trojan heroes. Achilles, by now, had himself been killed.
13 *thousand* added to Virgil.
14 *Or . . . Or* either . . . or.

To plunge the treacherous gift of Greece in fire,
Or whelm the mighty monster in the tides,
Or bore the ribs, and search the caverned sides.   50
Their own wild will the noisy crowds obey,
And vote, as partial fancy points the way;
Till bold Laocoön, with a mighty train,[15]
From the high tower rushed furious to the plain;
And sent his voice from far, with rage inspired –   55
'What madness, Trojans, has your bosoms fired?
Think you the Greeks are sailed before the wind?
Think you these presents safe, they leave behind?
And is Ulysses banished from your mind?
Or this prodigious fabric must enclose,   60
Deep in its darksome womb, our ambushed foes;
Or 'tis some engine, raised to batter down
The tow'rs of Ilion, or command the town;
Ah! trust not Greece, nor touch her gifts abhorred;[16]
Her gifts are more destructive than her sword.'   65
     Swift as the word, his pond'rous lance he threw;
Against the sides the furious javelin flew,
Through the wide womb a spacious passage found,
And shook with long vibrations in the wound.
The monster groans, and shakes the distant shore;   70
And, round his caverns rolled, the deep'ning thunders roar.
Then, had not partial fate conspired to blind,
With more than madness, every Trojan mind,
The crowd the treach'rous ambush had explored,
And not a Greek had 'scaped the vengeful sword;   75
Old Priam still his empire would enjoy,
And still thy tow'rs had stood, majestic Troy!"

Book 4, lines 1–30

Having been deeply affected by Aeneas' tale of the fall of Troy and of his wanderings (Books 2–3), Dido confesses her passion for Aeneas to her sister. Her anguish is due to a vow which she had made to remain faithful to her dead husband Sychaeus, whose murder by her brother Pygmalion had caused her to flee from her homeland with a band of followers and found the city of Carthage. Pope brazenly parodies the scene at the beginning of Canto 4 of *The Rape of the Lock* (pp. 119–20 above).

John Dryden is again the translator (see p. 362 above).

---

15 *Laocoön* a Trojan prince.   16 Literally, "whatever it is, I fear Greeks even
                                                  when bearing gifts."

But anxious Cares already seized the Queen:[1]
She fed within her Veins a Flame unseen;
The Hero's Valour, Acts, and Birth inspire
Her Soul with Love, and fan the secret Fire.
His Words, his Looks, imprinted in her Heart,   5
Improve the Passion, and increase the Smart.
Now, when the Purple Morn had chased away
The dewy Shadows, and restored the Day,
Her Sister first with early Care she sought,
And thus in mournful Accents eased her Thought: 10
"My dearest *Anna*, what new Dreams affright
My lab'ring Soul! what Visions of the Night
Disturb my Quiet, and distract my Breast
With strange Ideas of our *Trojan* Guest!
His Worth, his Actions, and Majestic Air,   15
A Man descended from the Gods declare.
Fear ever argues a degenerate kind;
His Birth is well asserted by his Mind.
Then, what he suffered, when by Fate betrayed,
What brave Attempts for falling *Troy* he made!   20
Such were his Looks, so gracefully he spoke,
That, were I not resolved against the Yoke
Of hapless Marriage, never to be cursed
With second Love, so fatal was my first,
To this one Error I might yield again;   25
For, since *Sychaeus* was untimely slain,
This only Man is able to subvert
The fixed Foundations of my stubborn Heart.
And, to confess my Frailty, to my shame,
Somewhat I find within, if not the same,   30
Too like the Sparkles of my former Flame.
    "But first let yawning Earth a Passage rend,
And let me through the dark Abyss descend;
First let avenging *Jove*, with Flames from high,
Drive down this Body to the nether Sky,   35
Condemned with Ghosts in endless Night to lie,
Before I break the plighted Faith I gave!
No! he who had my Vows, shall ever have;
For, whom I loved on Earth, I worship in the Grave."
    She said: the Tears ran gushing from her Eyes,   40
And stopped her Speech.

BOOK 4, LINES 1–30
1 *Queen* Dido.

Book 5, lines 315–39

These lines describe the running match that took place during the funeral games that Aeneas held in Sicily for his father, Anchises, after leaving Carthage. The passage features the homoerotic friendship of the Trojan heroes Nisus and Euryalus, whom Virgil has previously introduced as "Euryalus remarkable for his beauty and green youth, Nisus for his devoted love of the boy" (lines 295–6). The pair meet a tragic end later in the *Aeneid* (Book 9). Dryden refers to the passage in "To the Memory of Mr. *Oldham*" (p. 93 above).

The translation is by John Conington (1825–1869), a classical scholar, first holder of the Corpus chair in Latin at Oxford and principal author of the most comprehensive English commentary on the *Aeneid*. His translation of the *Aeneid* in ballad form (1866) is the basis of the text presented herewith.

He said: at once they take their place,[1]
And at the sign begin the race,
Pour from their base like rain-cloud dark,
And strain their eyes the goal to mark.
First, far before each flying form,   5
Comes Nisus rushing like the storm;
Then, nearest him where none are near,
Young Salius strains in full career;
Then with brief interval of space
Euryalus, the third in place;   10
Then Helymus: behind him, lo!
Diores, touching heel with toe,
    Close hangs upon his rear,
And, had they run but few roods more,[2]
Had passed him shooting on before,   15
    And made the vantage clear.[3]

  And now the race was all but o'er,
    And panting to the goal they drew,
When Nisus trips in slippery gore
Chance-sprinkled on the grassy floor   20
    From beasts the sacrificers slew;
So late the conqueror, blithe and bold,[4]
He fails to keep his foot's sure hold,
And falls in prone confusion flung
'Mid victim blood and loathly dung.[5]   25

BOOK 5, LINES 315–339

1 *He* Aeneas, who has just listed the prizes for this event.

2 *roods* a rood is a "linear measure . . . varying from 6 to 8 yards" (*OED*).

3 *vantage* advantage.

4 *so late* just now.

5 *loathly* loathsome.

E'en then affection claims its part:
Euryalus is in his heart:
Uprising from the sodden clay,
He casts himself in Salius' way,
And Salius tripped and sprawling lay.   30
Euryalus like lightning flies
'Mid plaudits and assenting cries,
And through his friend attains the prize:
Next Helymus, and next comes in
Diores, thus the third to win.   35

Book 6, lines 268–316

Guided by the Sibyl, Aeneas descends into the underworld to find his father. At
the threshold he encounters images of suffering and monstrosity. Further on,
Charon ferries the souls of the dead to their final destination. From the very first
phrase, *ibant obscuri* (they went in darkness), Virgil builds an atmosphere of
mystery, dread, and suffering that set the standard for later descriptions of Hell,
most notably Dante's *Inferno*. Among the features that contribute most to the
overall effect are two expressive similes (of the moon and migratory birds), the
personifications of suffering, and the striking description of the unkempt but
vigorous and spooky Charon. Alexander Pope parodies this and similar classical
descents to the underworld in Canto 4 of *The Rape of the Lock* (pp. 119–24
above).

The translation is by Robert Seymour Bridges (1844–1930) from a book enti-
tled *Ibant Obscuri, an Experiment in the Classical Hexameter* (1916). Because
Bridges's spelling may indicate syllable length, in order to imitate classical meter,
we provide a literatim version of his lines.

They wer' amid the shadows by night in loneliness obscure[1]
Walking forth i' the void and vasty dominyon of Ades;[2]
As by an uncertain moonray secretly illumin'd
One goeth in the forest, when heav'n is gloomily clouded,
And black night hath robb'd the colours and beauty from all things.   5
Here in Hell's very jaws, the threshold of darkening Orcus,[3]
Have the avenging Cares laid their sleepless habitation,
Wailing Grief, pallid Infections, & heart-stricken Old-age,
Dismal Fear, unholy Famine, with low-groveling Want,
Forms of spectral horror, gaunt Toil and Death the devourer,   10

BOOK 6, LINES 268–316
1 *They* Aeneas and the Sibyl.

2 *Ades* Hades (Latin Dis), god of the
underworld.
3 *Orcus* the underworld.

And Death's drowsy brother, Torpor; with whom, an inane rout,
All the Pleasures of Sin; there also the Furies in ambusht[4]
Chamber of iron, afore whose bars wild War bloodyhanded
Raged, and mad Discord high brandisht her venomous locks.
Midway of all this tract, with secular arms an immense elm[5]   15
Reareth a crowd of branches, aneath whose leafy protection
Vain dreams thickly nestle, clinging unto the foliage on high:
And many strange creatures of monstrous form and features
Stable about th' entrance, Centaur and Scylla's abortion,[6]
And hundred-handed Briareus, and Lerna's wildbeast[7]   20
Roaring amain, and clothed in frightful flame the Chimaera,[8]
Gorgons and Harpies, and Pluto's three-bodied ogre.[9]
In terror Aeneas upheld his sword to defend him,
With ready naked point confronting their dreaded onset:
And had not the Sibyl warn'd how these lively spirits were[10]   25
All incorporeal, flitting in thin maskery of form,
He had assail'd their host, and wounded vainly the void air.
Hence is a road that led them a-down to the Tartarean streams,[11]
Where Acheron's whirlpool impetuous, into the reeky[12]
Deep of Cokytos disgorgeth, with muddy burden.[13]   30
These floods one ferryman serveth, most awful of aspect,
Of squalor infernal, Chāron: all filthily unkempt[14]
That woolly white cheek-fleece, and fiery the blood-shotten eyeballs:
On one shoulder a cloak knotted-up his nudity vaunteth.
He himself plieth oar or pole, manageth tiller and sheet,   35
And the relics of mén in his ash-grey barge ferries over;
Already old, but green to a god and hearty will age be.
Now hitherward to the bank much folk were crowding, a medley
Of men and matrons; nor did death's injury conceal
Bravespirited heroes, young maidens beauteous unwed,   40
And boys borne to the grave in sight of their sorrowing sires.
Countless as in the forest, at a first white frosting of autumn
Sere leaves fall to the ground; or like whenas over the ocean

4   *Furies* demons of vengeance.
5   *secular* centuries old ("after F. *séculaire*"
[*OED*]).
6   *Centaur* a monster with human head and
horse's body; *Scylla's abortion* i.e. the misbegot-
ten Scylla; she was a sea monster with a woman's
upper body and dogs below her waist; *abortion*
"any dwarfed and misshapen product of genera-
tion " (*OED*).
7   *Briareus* a giant; *Lerna's wildbeast* the Hydra,
a many-headed snake.

8   *Chimaera* a fire-breathing monster composed
of lion, goat, and snake.
9   *Gorgons* snaky-haired female monsters;
Harpies bird-like female monsters; *Pluto* another
name for Hades or Dis; *ogre* the giant Geryon.
10   *Sibyl* priestess of Apollo who guides Virgil
through the underworld.
11   *Tartarean* of Tartarus, the lowest region of
the underworld.
12   *Acheron* a river of the underworld.
13   *Cokytos* another river.
14   *Chāron* ferryman of the dead.

Myriâd birds come thickly flocking, when wintry December
Drives them afar southward for shelter upon sunnier shores,   45
So throng'd they; and each his watery journey demanded,
All to the further bank stretching-oút their arms impatient:
But the sullen boatman took now one now other at will,
While some from the river forbade he', an' drave to a distance.

Book 6, lines 679–751

In this passage Aeneas is reunited with his father in Elysium, the abode of virtuous souls. Anchises explains that the souls thronging the river Lethe are undergoing purification before they can be reborn in new bodies. Anchises' speech conflates Pythagorean, Platonic, and Stoic views on the divine spirit of the universe, the dichotomy of soul and body, and the transmigration of souls into other bodies after death. Following his philosophical speech, Anchises identifies great figures in Roman history who will one day be born from the souls awaiting rebirth. Anchises' majestic vision has inspired many imitations, including Pope's description of sylphs in Canto 1 of *The Rape of the Lock* (pp. 116–18 above) and the speech of Protesilaus in Wordsworth's *Laodamia* (pp. 171–2 above).

The translation is again by John Dryden (see p. 362 above).

But old *Anchises*, in a flow'ry Vale,[1]
Reviewed his mustered Race, and took the Tale:[2]
Those Happy Spirits, which, ordained by Fate,
For future Beings and new Bodies wait:
With studious Thought observed th' illustrious Throng,   5
In Nature's Order as they passed along:
Their Names, their Fates, their Conduct, and their Care,
In peaceful Senates and successful War.
He, when *Aeneas* on the Plain appears,
Meets him with open Arms, and falling Tears.   10
"Welcome," he said, "the Gods' undoubted Race!
O long expected to my dear Embrace!
Once more 'tis giv'n me to behold your Face!
The Love and Pious Duty which you pay
Have passed the Perils of so hard a way.   15
'Tis true, computing times, I now believed
The happy Day approached; nor are my Hopes deceived.
What length of Lands, what Oceans have you passed;
What Storms sustained, and on what Shores been cast?
How have I feared your Fate! but feared it most,   20

BOOK 6, LINES 679–751   2   *Tale* tally; total.

1   *Anchises* father of Aeneas.

When Love assailed you, on the *Libyan* Coast."[3]
To this, the Filial Duty thus replies:
"Your sacred Ghost before my sleeping Eyes
Appeared, and often urged this painful Enterprise.
After long tossing on the *Tyrrhene* Sea,[4]   25
My Navy rides at Anchor in the Bay.
But reach your Hand, O Parent Shade, nor shun
The dear Embraces of your longing Son!"
He said; and falling Tears his Face bedew:
Then thrice, around his Neck, his Arms he threw;   30
And thrice the flitting Shadow slipped away,
Like Winds, or empty Dreams that fly the Day.
Now, in a secret Vale, the *Trojan* sees
A separate Grove, through which a gentle Breeze
Plays with a passing Breath, and whispers through the Trees;   35
And, just before the Confines of the Wood,
The gliding *Lethe* leads her silent Flood.[5]
About the Boughs an Airy Nation flew,
Thick as the humming Bees, that hunt the Golden Dew;
In Summer's heat on tops of Lilies feed,   40
And creep within their Bells, to suck the balmy Seed.
The wingèd Army roams the Fields around;
The Rivers and the Rocks remurmur to the sound.
Aeneas wond'ring stood, then asked the Cause,
Which to the Stream the Crowding People draws.   45
Then thus the Sire: "The Souls that throng the Flood
Are those, to Whom, by Fate, are other Bodies owed:
In *Lethe*'s Lake they long Oblivion taste,
Of future Life secure, forgetful of the Past.
Long has my Soul desired this time and place,   50
To set before your sight your glorious Race,
That this presaging Joy may fire your Mind
To seek the Shores by Destiny designed."
"O Father, can it be, that Souls sublime
Return to visit our Terrestrial Clime,   55
And that the gen'rous Mind, released by Death,
Can Covet lazy Limbs and Mortal Breath?"
Anchises then, in order, thus begun
To clear those Wonders to his Godlike Son:
"Know, first, that Heav'n, and Earth's compacted Frame,   60
And flowing Waters, and the starry Flame,

---

3 *Libyan Coast* at Carthage, where Aeneas fell   4 *Tyrrhene Sea* between Italy and Sardinia.
in love with Dido.   5 *Lethe* the river of forgetfulness.

And both the Radiant Lights, one common Soul[6]
Inspires and feeds, and animates the whole.
This Active Mind, infused through all the Space,
Unites and mingles with the mighty Mass.   65
Hence Men and Beasts the Breath of Life obtain,
And Birds of Air, and Monsters of the Main.
Th' Ethereal Vigour is in all the same,
And every Soul is filled with equal Flame;
As much as Earthy Limbs, and gross allay[7]   70
Of Mortal Members, subject to decay,
Blunt not the Beams of Heav'n and edge of Day.
From this coarse Mixture of Terrestrial parts,
Desire, and Fear, by turns possess their Hearts:
And Grief, and Joy; nor can the groveling Mind,   75
In the dark Dungeon of the Limbs confined,
Assert the Native Skies; or own its heav'nly Kind.[8]
Nor Death itself can wholly wash their Stains;
But long-contracted Filth ev'n in the Soul remains.
The Relics of inveterate Vice they wear,   80
And Spots of Sin obscene in ev'ry Face appear.
For this are various Penances enjoined;
And some are hung to bleach, upon the Wind,
Some plunged in Waters, others purged in Fires,
Till all the Dregs are drained, and all the Rust expires. 85
All have their *Manes*, and those *Manes* bear:[9]
The few, so cleansed, to these Abodes repair,
And breathe, in ample Fields, the soft *Elysian* Air.
Then are they happy, when by length of time
The Scurf is worn away of each committed Crime;[10]   90
No Speck is left of their habitual Stains,
But the pure Ether of the Soul remains.
But, when a Thousand rolling Years are past,
(So long their Punishments and Penance last),
Whole Droves of Minds are, by the driving God,   95
Compelled to drink the deep *Lethean* Flood,
In large forgetful draughts to steep the Cares
Of their past Labours, and their irksome Years,
That, unrememb'ring of its former Pain,
The Soul may suffer mortal Flesh again."   100

6 *And both the Radiant Lights* the sun and the
moon.
7 *allay* mixture.
8 *own* acknowledge.
9 *All . . . bear* literally, "we each endure our
own *manes*"; Virgil extends the basic sense of
Manes, "spirits of the dead," to mean the soul's
fate after death.
10 *Scurf* dross; impurity.

Book 6, lines 854–92

In Elysium, Anchises inspires Aeneas with a vision of future glory by showing him the souls of great Romans awaiting birth. Among them is the military hero M. Claudius Marcellus (d. 208 BCE), and alongside Marcellus is a sad young man who turns out to be a descendant of the same name. This Marcellus (42–23 BCE) was nephew and son-in-law of Augustus, and hence a potential heir to Augustus. His early death was a stunning blow to his mother Octavia and to Augustus, who gave him a magnificent funeral, which Virgil probably attended. Ancient sources relate that Octavia was overcome with tears when the poet recited these lines to her and Augustus in private. Dryden draws on the passage in "To the Memory of Mr. *Oldham*" (p. 93 above).

The translation is, again, from Dryden's *Aeneis* (1697) (see p. 362 above).

He paused: And, while with wond'ring Eyes they viewed
The passing Spirits, thus his Speech renewed:
"See great *Marcellus*! how, untired in Toils,[1]
He moves with Manly grace, how rich with Regal Spoils!
He, when his Country (threatened with Alarms)   5
Requires his Courage, and his Conqu'ring Arms,
Shall more than once the *Punic* Bands affright;[2]
Shall kill the *Gaulish* King in single Fight;
Then to the Capitol in Triumph move,
And the third Spoils shall grace *Feretrian Jove*."[3]   10
Aeneas, here, beheld, of Form Divine,
A Godlike Youth in glitt'ring Armour shine,
With great *Marcellus* keeping equal pace;
But gloomy were his Eyes, dejected was his Face.
He saw, and, wond'ring, asked his airy Guide,   15
What, and of whence was he, who pressed the Hero's side?
"His Son, or one of his Illustrious Name?
How like the former, and almost the same!
Observe the Crowds that compass him around;
All gaze, and all admire, and raise a shouting sound: 20

BOOK 6, LINES 854–892

1 *Marcellus* great general of the third century BCE, nicknamed "the sword of Rome"; five times consul, he played a leading role in wars against the Gauls and the Carthaginians.
2 *Punic* Carthaginian, with reference to the Second Punic War (218–201 BCE).

3 *Feretrian Jove* the temple of Jupiter Feretrius, where Marcellus deposited the *spolia opima* (rich spoils) he won for killing the king of the Insubrian Gauls of northern Italy in 222 BCE; Marcellus was only the third Roman to win the *spolia opima*, which were awarded to a Roman general who killed the enemy's commander in personal combat.

But hov'ring Mists around his Brows are spread,
And Night, with sable Shades, involves his Head."
"Seek not to know (the Ghost replied with Tears)
The Sorrows of thy Sons in future Years.
This Youth (the blissful Vision of a Day)   25
Shall just be shown on Earth, and snatched away.
The Gods too high had raised the *Roman* State;
Were but their Gifts as permanent as great.
What Groans of Men shall fill the *Martian* field!⁴
How fierce a blaze his flaming pile shall yield!   30
What Fun'ral Pomp shall floating *Tiber* see,
When, rising from his Bed, he views the sad Solemnity!
No Youth shall equal hopes of Glory give,
No Youth afford so great a Cause to grieve;
The *Trojan* Honour, and the *Roman* Boast,   35
Admired when living, and Adored when lost!
Mirror of ancient Faith in early Youth!
Undaunted Worth, Inviolable Truth!
No foe, unpunished, in the fighting Field
Shall dare thee, Foot to Foot, with Sword and Shield;   40
Much less in Arms oppose thy matchless Force,
When thy sharp Spurs shall urge thy foaming Horse.
Ah! couldst thou break through Fate's severe Decree,
A new *Marcellus* shall arise in thee!⁵
Full Canisters of fragrant Lilies bring,   45
Mixed with the Purple Roses of the Spring;
Let me with Fun'ral Flow'rs his Body strow;
This Gift which Parents to their Children owe,
This unavailing Gift, at least, I may bestow!"
Thus having said, He led the Hero round   50
The confines of the blest *Elysian* Ground;⁶
Which when *Anchises* to his Son had shown,
And fired his Mind to mount the promised Throne,
He tells the future Wars, ordained by Fate;
The Strength and Customs of the *Latian* State;⁷   55
The Prince, and People; and forearms his Care
With Rules, to push his Fortune, or to bear.

---

4 *Martian field* the Campus Martius, or "Field
of Mars," on the east bank of the Tiber.

5 *new Marcellus* i.e. the equal of his great
forebear.

6 *Elysian Ground* Elysium, the abode of blessed
souls.

7 *Latian State* the future Rome.

Book 11, lines 759–831

One of Virgil's most brilliant inventions, Camilla is an Amazon-like warrior maiden who fights alongside the Italians to resist Aeneas and the Trojans. In Book 11 Virgil honors her with an *aristeia* – an account of her valorous feats in battle – such as normally is reserved in epic poetry for the leading male heroes. Like many a hero in Greek tragedy, Camilla brings her downfall upon herself – in her case not through male arrogance but what Virgil, herein reflecting the prejudices of his culture, identifies as a female greed for spoil. Distracted by her desire to obtain the glittering armor of Chloreus, Camilla is ambushed by Arruns and dies a tragic death. Thomas Gray casts his cat in the role of a modern Camilla in his mock-heroic "Ode on the Death of a Favourite Cat" (p. 151 above), and Alexander Pope borrowed features of Camilla's exploits to describe the contest between the Baron and Belinda in *The Rape of the Lock*.

The text is, again, based on Dryden's *Aeneis* (1697) (see p. 362 above).

Then, *Arruns*, doomed to Death, his Arts assayed,[1]
To murther, unespied, the *Volscian* Maid:[2]
This way, and that his winding Course he bends,
And, wheresoe'er she turns, her Steps attends.
When she retires victorious from the Chase,   5
He wheels about with Care, and shifts his place;
When, rushing on, she seeks her Foes in Fight,
He keeps aloof, but keeps her still in sight:
He threats, and trembles, trying ev'ry Way
Unseen to kill, and safely to betray.   10
   Chloreus, the priest of *Cybele*, from far,[3]
Glitt'ring in *Phrygian* Arms amidst the War,
Was by the Virgin viewed. The steed he pressed[4]
Was proud with Trappings, and his brawny Chest
With scales of gilded Brass was covered o'er;   15
A Robe of *Tyrian* Dye the Rider wore.[5]
With deadly Wounds he galled the distant Foe;
Gnossian his Shafts, and *Lycian* was his Bow:[6]
A Golden Helm his Front and head surrounds;[7]
A gilded Quiver from his Shoulder sounds.   20
Gold, weaved with Linen, on his Thighs he wore,
With Flowers of Needlework distinguished o'er,

BOOK 11, LINES 759–831

1 *Arruns* an Etruscan warrior.

2 *Volscian maid* Camilla; the Volsci were a people of ancient Italy.

3 *Cybele* a mother goddess of Phrygia in Asia Minor.

4 *Virgin* Camilla.

5 *Tyrian* purple.

6 *Gnossian* Cretan; *Lycian* from Lycia in Asia Minor.

7 *Front* forehead.

With Golden Buckles bound, and gathered up before.
Him the fierce Maid beheld with ardent Eyes,
Fond and Ambitious of so Rich a Prize: 25
Or that the Temple might his Trophies hold,
Or else to shine herself in *Trojan* Gold.[8]
Blind in her haste, she chases him alone.
And seeks his Life, regardless of her own.[9]
This lucky Moment the sly Traitor chose: 30
Then, starting from his Ambush, up he rose,
And threw, but first to Heav'n addressed his Vows:
"O Patron of *Soracte's* high Abodes,[10]
Phoebus, the Ruling Pow'r among the Gods,[11]
Whom first we serve, whole Woods of unctuous Pine   35
Are felled for thee, and to thy Glory shine;
By thee protected, with our naked Soles,
Through Flames unsinged we march, and tread the kindled Coals:
Give me, propitious Pow'r, to wash away
The Stains of this dishonourable Day: 40
Nor Spoils, nor Triumph, from the Fact I claim;
But with my future Actions trust my Fame.
Let me, by stealth, this Female Plague o'ercome,
And from the Field return inglorious home."
    Apollo heard, and granting half his Prayer,   45
Shuffled in Winds the rest, and tossed in empty Air.
He gives the Death desired; his safe return
By Southern Tempests to the Seas is borne.
    Now, when the Javelin whizzed along the Skies,
Both armies on *Camilla* turned their Eyes,   50
Directed by the Sound. Of either Host,
Th' unhappy Virgin, though concerned the most,
Was only deaf; so greedy was she bent
On Golden Spoils, and on her Prey intent;
Till in her Pap the wingèd Weapon stood   55
Infixed, and deeply drunk the purple Blood.
Her sad Attendants hasten to sustain
Their dying Lady, drooping on the Plain.
Far from their sight the trembling *Arruns* flies,
With beating Heart, and Fear confused with Joys;   60
Nor dares he farther to pursue his Blow,
Or ev'n to bear the sight of his expiring Foe.

---

8 *Or . . . Or* either . . . or.
9 *Blind . . . own* literally, "Blindly and incau-
tiously she followed him throughout all the ranks
and burned with a woman's love of spoil."

10 *Soracte* mountain near Rome; the site of a
cult of Apollo which involved walking over hot
coals.
11 *Phoebus* Apollo.

   As when the Wolf has torn a Bullock's Hide
At unawares, or ranched a Shepherd's Side,[12]
Conscious of his audacious deed, he flies,   65
And claps his quiv'ring Tail between his Thighs:
So, speeding once, the Wretch no more attends;
But, spurring forward, herds among his Friends.
She wrenched the Javelin with her dying Hands,
But wedged within her Breast the Weapon stands;   70
The Wood she draws, the steely Point remains;
She staggers in her Seat, with agonizing Pains:
A gath'ring Mist o'erclouds her cheerful Eyes;
And from her Cheeks the rosy Colour flies:
Then, turns to her, whom of her Female Train   75
She trusted most, and thus she speaks with Pain:
"*Acca*, 'tis past! He swims before my sight,
Inexorable Death; and claims his right.
Bear my last Words to *Turnus*, fly with speed,[13]
And bid him timely to my Charge succeed,   80
Repel the *Trojans*, and the Town relieve:
Farewell! and in this Kiss my parting Breath receive."
She said, and, sliding, sunk upon the Plain:
Dying, her opened Hand forsakes the Rein;
Short, and more short, she pants; by slow degrees   85
Her Mind the Passage from her Body frees.
She drops her Sword; she nods her plumy Crest,
Her drooping Head declining on her Breast:
In the last Sigh her struggling Soul expires;
And, murm'ring with Disdain, to *Stygian* Sounds retires.[14]   90

12 *ranched* cut.   14 *Stygian* the Styx was a river of Hades; *Sounds*
13 *Turnus* captain of the Italian forces opposing   straits; channels.
Aeneas.

Horace (65–8 BCE)

Quintus Horatius Flaccus, known simply as Horace, ranks with Catullus, Virgil, and Ovid as one of the most versatile and influential Roman authors. Because of the autobiographical slant of much of his work, more is known about Horace than about most Roman poets. He projects a most likeable persona – easy-going, sophisticated, witty, and appreciative of life's pleasures, from the carnal joys of wine and sex to conversation and friendship. Horace came from a humble background; his father was a freedman – an ex-slave – who scraped together enough to give his son an education far above his social station. This included a period of study in Athens, where Horace entered the service of Brutus, one of Julius Caesar's assassins, as an officer in his army. Brutus and Cassius were defeated by Antony and Octavian at the battle of Philippi (42 BCE), where Horace says that he fled the field. Deprived of his ancestral property, he found a job in Rome as a scribe in the treasury. Here he began to write poetry, which brought him to the attention of the poets Virgil and Varius. In 38 BCE they introduced him to Maecenas, a wealthy and influential patron of literature and friend of the triumvir Octavian. They developed a friendship that went beyond their patron–client relationship, and in 33 BCE Maecenas presented Horace with a small estate in the Sabine hills that gave him financial security and leisure. Like Virgil, Horace hailed the emergence of Augustus, who restored peace and prosperity to an empire stricken with civil war. His friendship with Maecenas brought him into personal contact with the emperor, who admired his work and offered him the post of his personal secretary. Horace tactfully refused. The change from republic to autocracy brought new pressures to bear on intellectuals and artists, who might be suspected of disloyalty if they did not praise the emperor and his policies. In his poetry Horace steers adroitly between flattery and independence and between political and personal themes. The formal and thematic variety of his work is astonishing, but common to it all is a wry sense of humor, an ironic detachment, and a humanity that is uniquely Horatian.

His first works, composed in the 30s BCE, were the *Epodes* and the two books of *Satires*. The former is a miscellany of acerbic poems inspired by Greek iambic poetry. Satire, on the other hand, was a homegrown Roman genre – the only one, according to Quintilian. Horace's satire is of a more genial kind than that of his model Lucilius or his great successor Juvenal. Its staple is autobiography, moral reflection, dramatic sketches, and literary criticism rather than the scathing denunciation of vice. Horace resumed the moralistic and didactic mode of the *Satires* in his later years, composing verse *Epistles*, which take the form of letters addressed to friends and acquaintances on a variety of philosophical, social, and literary themes, and a vastly influential poem on literary criticism known as the *Ars Poetica*. In between, during the decade of the 20s, came the *Odes* – his crowning achievement. The first three books (88 poems in all) were published together in 23 BCE; a fourth book appeared later in his life. Horace's achievement in the *Odes* (Greek for "songs") was to assimilate and extend the tradition of the Greek lyric poets, especially Alcaeus, Sappho, and Pindar. Catullus had paved the way, but Horace showed enormous originality and skill in adapting the meters and subject matter of archaic Greek poetry to Augustan Rome. Lyric poetry takes its name from the accompaniment of poetry with the lyre, which had been the practice in ancient Greece. Horace upholds the fiction of performing to the lyre, but his lyric is a purely literary form, influenced by the sophisticated taste of the scholarly Greek poets of the Hellenistic era. His themes, however, are universal – love, wine, death, friendship, politics, the seasons, and the countryside. Above all Horace calls upon us to enjoy life in the best possible way – in moderation but with gusto. It is not an original message, but few have ever expressed it so engagingly or so quotably. Many writers have urged their readers to make the most of the time allotted them in this world, but, characteristically, it was Horace who found the immortal phrase that epitomizes the idea – *carpe diem*!

In his verse Horace knew that he was creating, as he put it and as Shakespeare would later repeat, " a monument more lasting than bronze." He became a classic in his own lifetime and remained popular throughout antiquity. Like Shakespeare's sonnets, however, Horace's greatest poems – his *Odes* – defied imitation and virtually terminated the genre. Horace's *Satires*, though also inimitable in some ways, were a major influence on Juvenal.

Although not as assiduously preserved as Virgil's, the texts of Horace made it from antiquity to the early modern period in pretty good shape. About 250 manuscripts exist and the first printed edition appeared around 1470. Like Virgil and Ovid, Horace was recommended by many medieval moralists, with the caveat that the reader must take care to interpret the poems properly (often allegorically) and to avoid the spots of unredeemable immorality. Later in the Renaissance and especially in the seventeenth and eighteenth centuries in England, Horace rose in importance. He became in many ways the poet's poet, the writer in antiquity with whom a modern poet could most easily identify. He wrote about poetry, patronage, the city and the country, and himself – all subjects that engrossed the learned and sophisticated poets of seventeenth- and eighteenth-century London. He was Samuel Johnson's favorite poet; Johnson read Horace all his life, and both his first

and his last translations from the classics are of Horatian poems. Alexander Pope
– the poet's poet of the eighteenth century – was another devotee. Horace is less
visible in the works of Romantic poets; he is in some respects an anti-Romantic.
The tradition he heads is urbane, witty, worldly, tolerant, satirical, and reasonable.
He is the father of Ben Jonson more often than of Shakespeare (though he is in
Shakespeare too); of Andrew Marvell more than of Milton; of Pope more than of
Thomson; of Wordsworth more than Keats; of Eliot more than Wallace Stevens;
of Heaney more than Walcott. All of these comparisons, however, only serve from
a distance. Up close, there are few British poets whose work is not improved and
illuminated by a knowledge of the Horatian background. Byron's ambivalent
tribute in *Childe Harold's Pilgrimage* suggests the way in which even poets who
reject Horace do so with a lingering sense that he sets a standard for poetry that
can only be ignored at one's peril:

> Then farewell Horace, whom I hated so, –
> Not for thy faults, but mine.

from the *Satires*

Book 2, number 6

The poem revolves around the Sabine farm which Horace received as a gift from
Maecenas. In addition to its practical benefits, the farm came to embody for
Horace his most cherished ideals of friendship, contentment, and independence.
The poem falls roughly into three parts. In the first, Horace describes how his
prayers have been answered by his acquisition of the farm. The second is an impres-
sionistic sketch of the harried life he leads in Rome – such a contrast to the peace
of the countryside, for which he yearns. In the third, he recalls the delightful eve-
nings he has spent with his rustic neighbors and retells the story of the town mouse
and the country mouse, which gathers up the poem's thematic threads with a
charming informality.

Satires 2.6, along with *Epode* 2 and Virgil's *Georgics*, did much to shape the
English literary conception of the happy man – he who, "far from the madding
crowd's ignoble strife," leads a simple life in the countryside, content with little
and yet rich in all that matters most. Its influence is felt in poems as diverse as
Jonson's "To Penshurst" (p. 58 above) and "Inviting a Friend to Supper" (p. 61
above), Thomson's *The Seasons* (for *Winter*, see p. 126 above), and Gray's *Elegy*
(p. 154 above).

The following translation is the work of Sir John Beaumont (1583–1627), an
aristocratic court poet under James I. His most famous poem, "Bosworth Field,"
celebrates James I and Prince Charles as descendants of the victorious Tudors.
Beaumont's translations of poetry extolling country virtues and decrying urban
vices foreshadow the poetry of Royalists, like Herrick, who had to leave the city

after the execution of Charles I in 1649. The following translation comes from the posthumously published volume *Bosworth-Field: with a Taste of the Variety of other Poems* (1629).

This was my wish: no ample space of ground,
T' include my Garden with a mod'rate bound,
And near my house a Fountain never dry,
A little Wood, which might my wants supply;
The gods have made me blest with larger store: 5
It is sufficient, I desire no more,
O son of *Maia*, but this grant alone,[1]
That quiet use may make these gifts mine own.
If I increase them by no lawless way,
Nor through my fault will cause them to decay.   10
If not to these fond hopes my thoughts decline,
O that this joining corner could be mine,[2]
Which with disgrace deforms, and maims my field,
Or *Fortune* would a pot of silver yield,
(As unto him who being hired to work,   15
Discovered treasure, which in mold did lurk,[3]
And bought the Land, which he before had tilled,
Since friendly *Hercules* his bosom filled).[4]
If I with thankful mind these blessings take,
Disdain not this petition which I make.   20
Let fat in all things, but my wit, be seen,
And be my safest guard as thou hast been.
When from the City I myself remove[5]
Up to the hills, as to a tower above,
I find no fitter labours, nor delights   25
Than *Satires*, which my lowly *Muse* indites.[6]
No foul ambition can me there expose
To danger, nor the leaden wind that blows
From *Southern* parts, nor *Autumn's* grievous rain,
Whence bitter *Libitina* reaps her gain.[7]   30
O father of the morning's purple light!
Or if thou rather would'st be *Janus* hight,[8]
From whose divine beginning, mortals draw

BOOK 2, NUMBER 6

1 *son of Maia* Mercury, god of trade and good fortune.
2 *joining* adjoining.
3 *mold* soil.
4 *Hercules* Greek hero and god; Horace alludes to a story in which he rewarded a man with a treasure trove.

5 *City* Rome.
6 *indites* composes.
7 *Libitina* goddess of funeral rites.
8 *Janus* god of entrances and beginnings; *hight* called; Horace gives his muse a choice of names by which to be addressed.

The pains of life, according to the law,
Which is appointed by the Gods' decree,   35
Thou shalt the entrance of my verses be.
At *Rome* thou driv'st me, as a pledge to go,[9]
That none himself may more officious show.
Although the fury of the *Northern* blast
Shall sweep the earth; or *Winter*'s force hath cast   40
The snowy day into a narrow Sphere,
I must proceed, and having spoken clear
And certain truth, must wrestle in the throng,
Where by my haste, the slower suffer wrong,
And cry, "What ails the mad man? whither tend   45
His speedy steps?" while mine imperious friend
Entreats, and chafes, admitting no delay,
And I must beat all those, that stop my way.
The glad remembrance of *Maecenas* lends[10]
A sweet content: but when my journey bends,   50
To black *Esquiliae*, there a hundred tides[11]
Of strangers' causes press my head and sides.
"You must, before the second hour, appear[12]
In Court tomorrow, and for *Roscius* swear."[13]
"The Scribes desire you would to them repair,[14]   55
About a public, great, and new affair."
"Procure such favour, from *Maecenas*' hand,
As that his seal may on this paper stand."
I answer, "I will try": he urgeth still,
"I know you can perform it if you will."   60
Sev'n years are fled, the eighth is almost gone,
Since first *Maecenas* took me for his own,
That I with him might in his chariot sit,
And only then would to my trust commit
Such toys as these: "What is the time of day?"[15]   65
"The Thracian is the Syrian's match in play."[16]
"Now careless men are nipped with morning cold":
And words which open ears may safely hold.
In all this space for every day and hour
I grew more subject to pale envy's power   70

9   *pledge* guarantor; surety.
10   *Maecenas* wealthy confidant of Augustus and patron of Horace.
11   *Esquiliae* the Esquiline, one of the hills of Rome; before Maecenas built a mansion there it had been used as a cemetery.
12   *second hour* between one and two hours after sunrise, according to the Roman system.
13   *Roscius* unknown friend of Horace.
14   *Scribes* treasury officials, of which Horace himself was one.
15   *toys* trifles.
16   *Thracian . . . Syrian* gladiators.

"This son of Fortune to the Stage resorts,
And with the favourite in the field disports."
Fame from the pulpits runs through every street,[17]
And I am strictly asked by all I meet:
"Good Sir (you needs must know, for you are near   75
Unto the Gods) do you no tidings hear
Concerning Dacian troubles?" "Nothing I."[18]
"You always love your friends with scoffs to try."
"If I can tell, the Gods my life confound."
"But where will *Caesar* give his soldiers ground,[19]   80
In Italy, or the Trinacrian Isle?"[20]
I swear I know not; they admire the while,
And think me full of silence, grave and deep,
The only man that should high secrets keep.
For these respects (poor wretch) I lose the light,   85
And longing thus repine: when shall my sight
Again be happy in beholding thee
My country farm? or when shall I be free
To read in books what ancient writers speak,
To rest in sleep, which others may not break,   90
To taste (in hours secure from courtly strife)
The soft oblivion of a careful life?
O when shall beans upon my board appear,
Which wise *Pythagoras* esteemed so dear?[21]
Or when shall fatness of the Lard anoint   95
The herbs, which for my table I appoint?[22]
O suppers of the Gods! O nights divine!
When I before our Lar might feast with mine,[23]
And feed my prating slaves with tasted meat,
As every one should have desire to eat.   100
The frolic guest not bound with heavy laws,[24]
The liquor from unequal measures draws:
Some being strong delight in larger draughts,
Some call for lesser cups to clear their thoughts.
Of others' house and lands no speeches grow,   105

17   *pulpits* an adaptive translation of Latin *rostra*, a public platform in the Forum.
18   *Dacian* the Dacians lived across the River Danube; they had caused alarm by siding with Antony in the civil war.
19   *Caesar* the emperor Augustus; *give . . . ground* grant land as a reward for service.
20   *Trinacrian Isle* Sicily.
21   *Pythagoras* Greek sage who for obscure reasons prohibited the eating of beans; Horace refers to the beans as his "kinsmen," with a joking allusion to Pythagoras' belief that the souls of the dead pass into other bodies.
22   *herbs* leafy vegetables.
23   *Lar* household god, or the sacred hearth where such gods – the Lares – were placed; *mine* his household.
24   *laws* drinking rules that were customary at a formal dinner party.

Nor whether *Lepos* danceth well or no.[25]
We talk of things which to ourselves pertain,
Which not to know would be a sinful stain.
Are men by riches or by virtue blest?
Of friendship's ends is use or right the best?   110
Of good what is the nature, what excels?
My neighbour *Cervius* old wives' fables tells,
When any one *Arellius'* wealth admires,
And little knows what troubles it requires.
He thus begins: "Long since a country Mouse   115
Received into his low and homely house
A City Mouse, his friend and guest before;
The host was sharp and sparing of his store,
Yet much to hospitality inclined:
For such occasions could dilate his mind.   120
He Chiches gives for winter laid aside,[26]
Nor are the long and slender Oats denied:
Dry Grapes he in his liberal mouth doth bear,
And bits of Bacon which half-eaten were:
With various meats to please the stranger's pride,   125
Whose dainty teeth through all the dishes slide.
The Father of the family in straw
Lies stretched along, disdaining not to gnaw
Base corn or darnel, and reserves the best,[27]
To make a perfect banquet for his guest.   130
To him at last the Citizen thus spake,
'My friend, I muse what pleasure thou canst take,
Or how thou canst endure to spend thy time
In shady Groves, and up steep hills to climb.
In savage Forests build no more thy den: 135
Go to the City, there to dwell with men.
Begin this happy journey, trust to me;
I will thee guide, thou shalt my fellow be.
Since earthly things are tied to mortal lives,
And every great, and little creature strives,   140
In vain the certain stroke of death to fly,
Stay not till moments past thy joys deny.
Live in rich plenty, and perpetual sport:
Live ever mindful, that thine age is short.'
The ravished field-mouse holds these words so sweet,   145
That from his home he leaps with nimble feet.
They to the City travel with delight,
And underneath the walls they creep at night.

---

25 *Lepos* "Grace," the name of a famous male   26 *Chiches* chick-peas.
dancer.   27 *darnel* a weed that grows in cornfields.

Now darkness had possessed heav'n's middle space,
When these two friends their weary steps did place   150
Within a wealthy Palace, where was spread
A scarlet cov'ring on an Ivory bed:
The baskets (set far off aside) contained
The meats, which after plenteous meals remained.
The City Mouse with courtly phrase entreats   155
His Country friend to rest in purple seats;
With ready care the Master of the feast
Runs up and down to see the store increased:
He all the duties of a servant shows,
And tastes of every dish, that he bestows.   160
The poor plain Mouse, exalted thus in state,
Glad of the change, his former life doth hate,
And strives in looks and gesture to declare
With what contentment he receives this fare.
But straight the sudden creaking of a door   165
Shakes both these Mice from beds into the floor.
They run about the room half dead with fear,
Through all the house the noise of dogs they hear.
The stranger now counts not the place so good,
He bids farewell, and saith, 'The silent Wood   170
Shall me hereafter from these dangers save,
Well pleased with simple *Vetches* in my *Cave.*' "[28]

Epode 2

Epode 2 is an encomium of country life with a sting in its tail. The bulk of the poem lays out the blessings of a farmer's life as compared to the life of the soldier, merchant, and politician. The encomium is too good to be true and strikes some discordant notes – the references to debt (line 4), love (lines 37–8), and gourmet oysters (line 49), for instance – so it may not come as a complete surprise to the reader, especially one sensitive to the acerbic tradition of iambic poetry, that its author is the usurer Alfius, who called in his debts, presumably to buy a farm, but changed his mind and let it out on interest again two weeks later. The ending throws cold water on the escapist fantasies of urban dwellers and forces a reassessment of the picture of rustic bliss. It is possible that Horace's poem was a response to Virgil's idealization of the farmer's life in *Georgics* 2 (p. 357 above). *Epode* 2 deeply influenced English visions of country life and "the happy man" in the poetry of the sixteenth through the eighteenth centuries, but its irony largely escaped notice.

---

28 *Vetches* a genus of plants (*vicia*) sometimes
called mouse peas.

The translation is by Ben Jonson (1572–1637; p. 56 above), and the text is based on that in the second folio edition of his *Works* (1640). The original Latin poem is in iambic couplets composed of lines of unequal length – a trimeter followed by a dimeter; Jonson's metrical form mimics Horace's.

> *"Happy* is he, that from all Business clear,
>   As the old race of Mankind were,
> With his own Oxen tills his Sire's left lands,
>   And is not in the Usurer's bands:
> Nor Soldier-like started with rough alarms,   5
>   Nor dreads the Seas' enragèd harms:
> But flees the Bar and Courts, with the proud boards,
>   And waiting Chambers of great Lords.
> The Poplar tall, he then doth marrying twine[1]
>   With the grown issue of the Vine;   10
> And with his hook lops off the fruitless race,
>   And sets more happy in the place:
> Or in the bending Vale beholds afar
>   The lowing herds there grazing are:
> Or the pressed honey in pure pots doth keep   15
>   Of Earth, and shears the tender Sheep:[2]
> Or when that Autumn, through the fields lifts round
>   His head, with mellow Apples crowned,
> How plucking Pears, his own hand grafted had,
>   And purple-matching Grapes, he's glad!   20
> With which, *Priapus*, he may thank thy hands,[3]
>   And, *Sylvan*, thine that kept'st his Lands![4]
> Then now beneath some ancient Oak he may,
>   Now in the rooted Grass, him lay,
> Whilst from the higher Banks do slide the floods;   25
>   The soft birds quarrel in the Woods,
> The Fountains murmur as the streams do creep,
>   And all invite to easy sleep.
> Then when the thund'ring *Jove*, his Snow and showers
>   Are gathering by the Wintry hours;   30
> Or hence, or thence, he drives with many a Hound[5]
>   Wild Boars into his toils pitched round:[6]
> Or strains on his small fork his subtle nets
>   For th' eating Thrush, or Pit-falls sets:
> And snares the fearful Hare, and new-come Crane,   35
>   And 'counts them sweet rewards so ta'en.

EPODE 2

1 *Poplar* a tree used for training vines.
2 *Earth* i.e. clay.
3 *Priapus* a fertility god.

4 *Sylvan* Silvanus, a woodland deity.
5 *Or . . . or* either . . . or.
6 *toils* traps.

Who (amongst these delights) would not forget
    Love's cares so evil, and so great?
But if, to boot with these, a chaste Wife meet[7]
    For household aid, and Children sweet;   40
Such as the *Sabines*, or a Sunburnt blowze,[8]
    Some lusty quick *Apulian's* spouse,[9]
To deck the hallowed Hearth with old wood fired
    Against the Husband comes home tired;
That penning the glad flock in hurdles by   45
    Their swelling udders doth draw dry:
And from the sweet Tub Wine of this year takes,
    And unbought viands ready makes:
Not Lucrine Oysters I could then more prize,[10]
    Nor Turbot, nor bright Golden eyes: 50
If with bright floods, the Winter troubled much,
    Into our Seas send any such:
Th' Ionian God-wit, nor the Ginny hen[11]
    Could not go down my belly then
More sweet than Olives, that new gathered be   55
    From fattest branches of the Tree:
Or the herb Sorrel, that loves Meadows still,
    Or Mallows loosing body's ill:
Or at the Feast of Bounds, the Lamb then slain,[12]
    Or Kid forced from the Wolf again.   60
Among these Cates how glad the sight doth come[13]
    Of the fed flocks approaching home!
To view the weary Oxen draw, with bare
    And fainting necks, the turnèd Share![14]
The wealthy household swarm of bondmen met,[15]   65
    And 'bout the steaming Chimney set!"
These thoughts when Usurer *Alfius*, now about[16]
    To turn mere farmer, had spoke out,
'Gainst th' Ides, his moneys he gets in with pain,[17]
    At th' Kalends, puts all out again.[18]   70

---

7   *to boot* in addition.

8   *Sabines* an Italian people proverbial for their sturdiness and virtue; *blowze* wench.

9   *Apulian* Apulia was a region of southeastern Italy; it was Horace's birthplace.

10 *Lucrine* from the Lucrine Lake near Baiae.

11 *Ionian God-wit* a game bird from Asia Minor.

12 *Feast of Bounds* the Terminalia (February 23); a festival in honor of Terminus, god of boundaries.

13 *Cates* victuals.

14 *turnèd Share* upturned (disengaged) ploughshare.

15 *bondmen* literally, "homebred slaves."

16 *Alfius* a famous money lender.

17 *Ides* a fixed date within the month falling on either the thirteenth or fifteenth day; one of the dates by which the interest on loans was calculated.

18 *Kalends* the first day of the month. Alfius calls in his debts as if to use the money for a purchase but reinvests it two weeks later.

from the *Odes*

Book 1, number 11

In this subtle poem of seduction – the inspiration of countless *carpe diem* poems in English – Horace bids his female friend Leuconoe forget about the future and make the most of the fleeting moment. The imagery at the end of the original (see n. 3) hints at the setting of a classical symposium, where drinking wine will lead to making love.

The translation is by David Ferry (1924–), reprinted with his permission from his *Odes of Horace* (1997).

Don't be too eager to ask
  What the gods have in mind for us,
What will become of you,
  What will become of me,
What you can read in the cards,   5
  Or spell out on the Ouija board.[1]
It's better not to know.
  Either Jupiter says
This coming winter is not
  After all going to be   10
The last winter you have,
  Or else Jupiter says
This winter that's coming soon,
  Eating away the cliffs
Along the Tyrrhenian Sea,[2]   15
  Is going to be the final
Winter of all. Be mindful.
  Take good care of your household.[3]
The time we have is short.
  Cut short your hopes for longer.   20
Now as I say these words,
  Time has already fled
Backwards away –
  Leuconoë –
    Hold on to the day.[4]   25

BOOK 1, NUMBER 11

1 *cards . . . Ouija board* modern equivalents of Horace's "Babylonian numbers," i.e. astrological calculations.

2 *Tyrrhenian Sea* the waters off the west coast of Italy.

3 *Take . . . household* literally, "be wise, strain the wine" (in preparation for drinking).

4 *Hold on to the day* literally, "pluck the day" (*carpe diem*); the phrase has become hackneyed but, in this, its first use, it is an original metaphor of picking fruit.

Book 1, number 37

The occasion for this impressive poem was the news of the suicides of Antony and Cleopatra, which brought to an end the civil war. Octavian – the soon-to-be emperor Augustus – had pursued the lovers from Greece to Egypt after defeating them at the naval battle of Actium (31 BCE). The poem opens with a triumphal fanfare. This develops into a contrast between Cleopatra, who is unfairly portrayed as a decadent barbarian, and Octavian, her noble conqueror. Unexpectedly, the tone shifts in the final stanzas to one of grudging admiration for Cleopatra's courage. A skillful piece of propaganda on behalf of Octavian, the ode obscures the fact that he and Antony had been engaged in a civil war, not a foreign one. However, the ending evokes sympathy for Cleopatra, reinstates her as an individual, rather than a symbol, and complicates the glee of the opening stanzas. Horace's depiction of Cleopatra influenced Andrew Marvell's treatment of Charles I in "An *Horatian* Ode upon *Cromwell's* Return from *Ireland*" (p. 87 above).

    The translator is, again, David Ferry (see p. 396 above).

At last the day has come for celebration,
For dancing and for drinking, bringing out
The couches with their images of gods[1]
Adorned in preparation for the feast.

Before today it would have been wrong to call   5
For the festive Caecuban wine from the vintage bins,[2]
It would have been wrong while that besotted queen,[3]
With her vile gang of sick polluted creatures,[4]

Crazed with hope and drunk with her past successes,
Was planning the death and destruction of the empire.[5]   10
But, comrades, she came to and sobered up
When not one ship, almost, of all her fleet

Escaped unburned, and Caesar saw to it[6]
That she was restored from madness to a state
Of realistic terror. The way a hawk   15
Chases a frightened dove or as a hunter

Chases a hare across the snowy steppes,
His galleys chased this fleeing queen, intending

BOOK 1, NUMBER 37

1 *couches* refers to the ritual of the *lectisternium* (strewing of couches) in which images of the gods were laid upon couches and served with a feast.

2 *Caecuban* a choice Italian wine.

3 *queen* Cleopatra VII, the last queen of Egypt.

4 *vile gang* the eunuchs of Cleopatra's court.

5 *empire* the Roman empire.

6 *Caesar* Octavian (Julius Caesar's adopted son).

To put the monster prodigy into chains
And bring her back to Rome. But she desired   20

A nobler fate than that; she did not seek
To hide her remnant fleet in a secret harbor;
Nor did she, like a woman, quail with fear
At the thought of what it is the dagger does.

She grew more fierce as she beheld her death.   25
Bravely, as if unmoved, she looked upon
The ruins of her palace; bravely reached out,
And touched the poison snakes, and picked them up,[7]

And handled them, and held them to her so
Her heart might drink its fill of their black venom.   30
In truth – no abject woman she – she scorned
In triumph to be brought in galleys unqueened

Across the seas to Rome to be a show.[8]

Book 2, number 18

Horace contrasts his unpretentious house with the extravagant mansions of the
wealthy to point out that simplicity brings greater contentment and that greed is
futile in the face of death. Ben Jonson surely had this poem in mind when he
wrote "To Penshurst" (p. 58 above), and it is a source for many other poems
about modest abodes.

The translation is by Thomas Hawkins (1575–1640?), a translator of many
works both continental and classical. His *Odes of Horace, the Best of Lyric Poets*
(1625) was reprinted four times by 1638, and many of his versions were swept up
into later collections of translations of Horace. His couplets in modest iambic
tetrameter mimic the iambic meter used by Horace in this ode and seem self-
consciously suited to the expression of the poem's message. The text presented
here is based on the version in *The Poems of Horace consisting of Odes, Satyres, and
Epistles, Rendered in English Verse by Several Persons* (1666).

No gilded roof, nor Ivory Fret
For splendour in my house is set;

---

7 *snakes* asps, or Egyptian cobras.   8 *show* an exhibit in a triumphal procession.

Nor are beams from *Hymettia* sought,[1]
To lie athwart rich Columns, brought
From *Afric*; nor I, heir unknown,[2]   5
Make *Attalus* his wealth mine own.[3]
No honest Tenants' wives you see,
Laconian purples weave for me:[4]
A loyal heart and ready vein
Of wit I have, which doth constrain   10
Rome's richest men to seek the love
Of me, though poor: Nor *gods* above
Do I invoke for larger store;
Nor of *Maecenas* ask I more.[5]
To me my single *Sabine* field   15
Sufficient happiness doth yield.
One day thrusts on another fast,
And new Moons to the wane do haste.
When Death, perhaps, is near at hand,
Thou fairest Marbles dost command   20
Be cut for use, yet dost neglect
Thy grave, and houses still erect:
Nay, would'st abridge the vast Sea's shore,
Which loudly doth at *Baiae* roar:[6]
Enrichèd little, less content,   25
With limits of the Continent.
Why often pull'st thou up the bounds
T'enlarge the circuit of thy grounds,
Encroaching far from Confines known
To make the neighbouring field thine own?   30
The husband, wife, and sordid brood,
With ancient household *gods*, that stood
In quiet peace, must be expelled:
Yet is not any Mansion held
For the rich Landlord, so assured,   35
As deep in Hell to be immured.[7]
Then whither do you further tend?
Th' indifferent earth, an equal friend,

BOOK 2, NUMBER 18

1 *Hymettia* properly Hymettus, a Greek mountain quarried for fine marble.
2 *Afric* the Roman province of Africa.
3 *Attalus* a Hellenistic king who left his kingdom to Rome; proverbial for his wealth.
4 *Laconian* Spartan.
5 *Maecenas* Horace's patron and a close associate of Augustus. He had rewarded Horace with an estate in the Sabine hills that contained five tenant farms – hardly "a single field!"
6 *Baiae* a pleasure resort on the bay of Naples; Horace alludes to the practice of building luxurious villas that extended into the sea.
7 *Hell* literally, "rapacious Orcus" (another name for the king of the dead); all souls are destined for the underworld, not just sinners.

As willingly opens her womb
For Beggar's grave, as Prince's tomb.   40
Gold could of *Charon* not obtain,[8]
To bear *Prometheus* back again.[9]
Proud *Tantalus* and all his stock,[10]
Death, with the bands of *fate*, doth lock:
And, called or not called, ready stands   45
To free the poor from painful bands.

Book 3, number 2

This is the second of the six so-called "Roman Odes," which open Book 3 of the *Odes*. All are written in the Alcaic meter (short, four-line stanzas named after Alcaeus, a politically active archaic Greek poet) and deal with moral and political subjects important to Augustus. This poem is directed primarily at the teenage sons of senators and knights (*equites*) whom Augustus organized in fraternities (*collegia iuvenum*) for the purpose of military training. Horace's exhortation to the youth leads, via the theme of courage, to an encomium of virtue that is a thinly disguised compliment to Augustus. Wilfred Owen borrowed the title of his anti-war poem "Dulce et Decorum Est" (p. 223 above) from line 13 of the Latin. Only Horace calls it "sweet" to die for one's country, but others had called it "fortunate" and "beautiful" – the general sentiment was, and remains, widespread.

The translator selected here, as for *Odes* 2.18, is Thomas Hawkins (see p. 398 above). The text likewise is based on the version in *The Poems of Horace* (1666).

Let th' able youth, himself inure
By sharp wars taught, want to endure:[1]
And mounted on his horse, with spear,
Confront bold *Parthians*, free from fear:[2]
Let him exposed to open air,   5
Live, and attempt the hard'st affair:
Whom when some warlike *Tyrant*'s Queen,
Or Virgin marriage-ripe hath seen,
Afar from hostile walls, may cry
With sighs, which from sad passion fly: 10
"O, that my Royal Lord, untrained

---

8 *Charon* the ferryman of the river Styx, who carried the souls of the dead to their destination.
9 *Prometheus* a god who rebelled against the reign of Jupiter; his punishment is usually located in the Caucasus, but Horace places him in the underworld.

10 *Tantalus* a famous sinner whose punishment consisted of being "tantalized" by water and fruits that eluded his grasp.

BOOK 3, NUMBER 2
1 *want to endure* to endure want (poverty).
2 *Parthians* enemies who threatened Rome's eastern frontier.

In Martial feats, would be restrained,
Not by fierce Combat's fatal stroke,
That wrathful Lion to provoke,
Whom bloody Anger's direful rage,　　　　　　　　　　15
In thickest slaughters doth engage."
It is a sweet, and noble gain,
In Country's *quarrel* to be slain.[3]
Death the swift flying man pursues
With ready steps: Nor doth he use　　　　　　　　　　20
To spare from unavoided wrack,
Youth's supple hams, or fearful back.
Virtue, that ne'er repulse admits,[4]
In taintless honours, glorious sits,
Nor takes, or leaveth Dignities,　　　　　　　　　　25
Raised with the noise of vulgar cries.
Virtue (to worth Heav'n opening wide)
Dauntless, breaks through ways denied.
And (taught) the Rabble to despise,
Forsaking *earth* to *heaven* flies.　　　　　　　　　　30
Yea trusty *silence* is not barred,
From having a deserved reward.
He, who to blab the holy Rites
Of secret *Ceres'* fane delights,[5]
Under the same roof shall not be,　　　　　　　　　　35
Nor in frail Vessel sail with me.
Oft *Jove* neglected makes the just
To smart with those are stained with lust;
Seldom Revenge, though slow of pace,
Leaves ill fore-going men to trace.[6]　　　　　　　　　　40

Book 3, number 30

This poem seals the third book of *Odes*, which Horace published in 23 BCE together with Books 1–2. He forecasts that his fame will last as long as the Roman state – too modestly, as it turns out! The poem has been much imitated, most famously by Shakespeare in Sonnet 55 (p. 47 above).

The translation is by Ezra Pound (1885–1972), one of the great modernist poets who wrote, among much else, a series of loose translations entitled *Homage to Sextus Propertius* (1917). The translation of Horace, of whom Pound was often

---

3　*It . . . slain* translating the famous line *dulce et decorum est pro patria mori* (it is sweet and honorable to die for one's country).

4　*Virtue* Latin *virtus*, whose basic meaning is "manliness" or "courage"; by extension, ethical virtue.

5　*secret Ceres* the grain goddess; an allusion to the Eleusinian mysteries of her Greek counterpart Demeter; *fane* temple.

6　Revenge usually catches up with the guilty.

critical, was written in 1964 and is reprinted with permission from *Ezra Pound: Translations*, ed. Hugh Kenner (New Directions, 1963).

This monument will outlast metal and I made it
More durable than the king's seat, higher than pyramids.
Gnaw of the wind and rain?
             Impotent
The flow of the years to break it, however many.   5

Bits of me, many bits, will dodge all funeral,
O Libitina-Persephone and, after that,[1]
Sprout new praise. As long as
Pontifex and the quiet girl pace the Capitol[2]
I shall be spoken where the wild flood Aufidus[3]   10
Lashes, and Daunus ruled the parched farmland:[4]

Power from lowliness: "First brought Aeolic song to Italian[5]
   fashion" –
Wear pride, work's gain! O Muse Melpomene,[6]
By your will bind the laurel.   15
           My hair, Delphic laurel.[7]

Book 4, number 10

Odes 4.10 is a love poem addressed to the disdainful boy Ligurinus, warning him of the regret he will feel when he loses his good looks. Many Greek and Roman men openly found boys sexually attractive from the age of puberty until the growth of a beard. Apart from its general legacy as a *carpe diem* poem, the influence of the ode is discernible in Shakespeare's Sonnet 77 (p. 48 above.)

The translation is by Edward Sherburne (1618–1702), who did extensive work on Manilius, Theocritus, and Seneca.

Cruel and fair! when this soft down
   (Thy Youth's bloom) shall to bristles grow;
And these fair Curls thy shoulders crown,
   Shall shed, or covered be with snow:

BOOK 3, NUMBER 30

1 *Libitina-Persephone* goddesses of death – the first Italic, the second Greek; Horace mentions only Libitina.
2 *Pontifex* a Roman high priest; *quiet girl* a Vestal Virgin; *Capitol* site of the main Roman temple to Jupiter.
3 *Aufidus* a river in Horace's homeland of Apulia.

4 *Daunus* a legendary king of Apulia.
5 *Aeolic song* Greek lyric poetry, especially the work of Sappho and Alcaeus of Lesbos, who spoke the Aeolic dialect. Horace claims to be the first, in his *Odes*, to have adapted Aeolic meters to Latin.
6 *Melpomene* one of the nine Muses.
7 *Delphic* i.e. bestowed by Apollo, the god of poetry.

When those bright Roses that adorn   5
   Thy Cheeks shall wither quite away,
And in thy Glass (now made Time's scorn)
   Thou shalt thy changèd Face survey:

Then, ah then (sighing) thou'lt deplore
   Thy Ill-spent Youth; and wish, in vain,   10
Why had I not those thoughts before?
*   Or come not my first Looks again?*

from the *Epistles*

Book 1, number 5

Invitation poems were a minor genre of Greek and Latin poetry. Catullus' *Carmen*
13 (p. 334 above) is the first example in Latin. Other examples occur in Horace's
Odes (1.20, 3.29, 4.12), the epigrams of Martial (5.78, 10.48, 11.52; pp. 468–70
below), and Juvenal's *Satire* 11. Such invitations usually promise a simple but
nourishing meal, good wine, and good company. Horace adds to this a political
touch: the occasion is Augustus' birthday and this, he says, justifies a break from
his invitee's exertions. Horace manages to be deferential and complimentary to
Torquatus, his social superior, while at the same time celebrating his own relaxed
philosophy of life. This poem was one of the models for Jonson's "Inviting a
Friend to Supper" (p. 61 above).

   The translator is John Duncombe (1729–1786); the text comes from his *Works
of Horace* (1757–1759). Duncombe is best known for his poem *The Feminead*
(1754), a celebration of women poets active in the previous 125 years. He was
also an occasional writer for numerous journals and a parodist; he laughed at the
high tones of Gray's *Elegy* in *An Evening's Contemplation* and wrote a mock-heroic
poem about a cricket match. Duncombe's relatively plain and light manner seems
suitable for this epistle, which mixes quotidian details with timeless truths.

If you can loll on antique Beds, and eat[1]
Herbs for your Supper, on an earthen Plate,[2]
Tonight, *Torquatus*, I'll expect you here.[3]
My Wine was casked in *Taurus*' second Year:[4]
Minturna's marshy Valley yields the Vine;[5]   5

BOOK 1, NUMBER 5

1 *Beds* dining couches.
2 *Herbs* a vegetable salad.
3 *Torquatus* a barrister from a patrician family.

4 *Taurus* T. Statilius Taurus, consul for the
second time in 26 BCE.
5 *Minturna* a town in southern Latium; an
ancestor of Torquatus had won a victory near
there in 340 BCE.

Bring yours, if better; if not, drink of mine.
    Already shines my Sideboard, smokes my Fire:
From Hopes, and Fears, and Thirst of Gain retire,
And *Moschus'* Cause. Tomorrow's glorious Morn[6]
Indulges Rest; for then was *Caesar* born;[7]   10
So may we safely, till the rising Light,
In social Converse wear the shortened Night.
    Say, why are Riches giv'n, but to enjoy?
Who starves himself to glut some favourite Boy[8]
Is little less than mad. Flowers will I spread,   15
And deeply drink, and no Reproaches dread.
What Wonders Wine effects? By that, revealed
Are Secrets; Cowards hurried to the Field;
To the dejected, Courage it imparts,
Fires with fresh Hopes the bold, and teaches Arts.   20
Bumpers inspire with Eloquence divine,[9]
And ev'n the needy drown their Wants in Wine.
I, for my part, will strict Attention lend,
Lest a stained Bed, or dirty Cloth offend;
And every Plate and Dish shall, like a Glass,   25
Reflect your Face – 'Mongst Friends let nothing pass
The Door. That well-matched Tempers may be joined,
You here will *Brutus* and *Septimius* find;
Sabinus too, if by no better Feast
And a kind Girl detained, shall be my Guest: 30
And Room will still be left for other Friends;
But in the Dog-days' Heat a Crowd offends.[10]
Your Number fix; and, letting Business wait,[11]
Slip from your Client through the Garden Gate.

---

6 *Moschus' Cause* Torquatus defended Moschus against a charge of poisoning.
7 *Caesar* the emperor Augustus, who was born between September 21 and September 23, 63 BCE.
8 *Boy* an heir.

9 *Bumpers* wine-cups filled to the brim (*OED*).
10 *Dog-days* the hot dry months of late summer when Sirius, the Dog Star, is prominent in the sky; *offends* with body odor.
11 *Your Number fix* indicate how many should be invited to dinner.

Tibullus (c. 50–19 BCE)

Little is known about Albius Tibullus. He belonged to the literary circle of Messalla Corvinus, a general and statesman who also sponsored the young Ovid, and he flourished in the first decade of the reign of Augustus. Horace addressed two poems to Tibullus, teasing him about his love poetry and his comfortable existence in his country villa. Ovid laments his death. Together with Propertius, Tibullus brought the genre of Latin love elegy to fruition (for further details, see our introduction to Propertius; p. 410 below). He published two books of elegies, a kind of verse defined by its meter, the elegiac couplet. The first has a bisexual character and describes his love for Delia and a boy called Marathus; the second addresses itself to another mistress whom he calls Nemesis. Like Propertius, Tibullus places love at the center of his world, representing himself as a soldier in the warfare of love and a slave to his mistress.

Tibullus was admired by Ovid and Quintilian but left little mark on later Roman literature. Despite the frankly erotic nature of his verse, he survived the Middle Ages (in a single manuscript) and was printed with Catullus, Propertius, and Statius' *Silvae* in 1472. English poets unafraid of erotic themes, such as Lovelace, Behn, and Marlowe, seem responsive to Tibullus, but even the sober moralist could quote him, as Samuel Johnson did more than once, as a writer sensitive to the variability of truth, the occult passage of time, and the delusions of our interior lives.[1] Making Roman erotic literature available for the expression of various moral themes was part of the work of humanism in the Renaissance. Recovering the Roman authors' attention to various forms of sexuality has been the work of more recent times.

Our translator is John Dart, an antiquary and a curate in Hampshire who died in 1730. The text comes from *The Works of Tibullus* (1720).

from the *Elegies*

Book 2, number 3

This elegy paradoxically reverses attitudes about the country that Tibullus developed in Book 1. Instead of being a place of love, the countryside has become a scene of heartbreak. Nemesis has gone off to the country estate of a rich rival, leaving the poet alone in the city. Tibullus declares his willingness to labor in the fields, as Apollo did for Admetus, if only he might see Nemesis. He attacks the power of money (while wishing that he too could shower Nemesis with gifts) and curses the agricultural gods responsible for her absence. He dreams of a return to the pre-agricultural age of free love, an alfresco fantasy developed by Lovelace in "Love Made in the First Age: To Chloris" (p. 83 above) and Behn in "The Golden Age" (p. 100 above).

Dear Friend, my Mistress at her Country Seat[1]	
Enjoys the Hamlets, and the cool Retreat;	
Who that has common Tenderness can stay	
In the dull lonely Town when she's away?	
Venus, to taste the Joys the Country yields,	5
Sports in the smiling Meads, and laughing Fields:	
Ev'n Love himself about the Meadows plays,[2]	
Forgets his own, and learns the rustic Phrase.	
Ah me! How would I with a willing Hand	
Direct the Hoe, and turn the restive Land!	10
Urge on the crooked Plow, and lash the Teams,	
Nor fear the scorching Heat, and sultry Beams;	
Bear all the Hardships of the rural Trade,[3]	
So I might there enjoy the lovely Maid.	
Thus Great *Apollo* ever young and fair,[4]	15
Unbent himself to tend *Admetus'* Care:[5]	
Vain was his Vocal Shell to ease his Grief,[6]	

TIBULLUS

1 Bruce Redford identifies two quotations of Tibullus in Johnson's *Letters* (5 vols., Princeton University Press, 1992–1994); in his life of Addison, Johnson quotes Tibullus on the various forms in which Truth can appear (*Lives of the English Poets* [Oxford University Press, 2006] Vol. III, p. 38).

BOOK 2, NUMBER 3

1 *Friend* the poem is addressed to Cornutus.

2 *Love* Cupid.

3 *Nor . . . Trade* literally, "nor would I complain that the sun burned my slender limbs and a burst blister hurt my tender hands."

4 *Apollo* god of music, healing, and prophecy.

5 *Admetus* king of Pherae in Thessaly; Apollo was condemned by Jupiter to serve Admetus for a year in punishment for killing the Cyclopes.

6 *Vocal Shell* his lyre, made from a tortoise-shell.

Nor could his flowing Hair afford Relief,
Nor healing Herbs could soothe the smarting Pain,
When Love's the Cause, the med'c'nal Pow'rs are vain.   20
His Sister from her wheeling Orb of Light
Looked down, and often blushed to see the Sight;
When lonely through the dusky Fields he'd roam,
Wet with the Dew, to drive the Cattle Home.[7]
Oft in the lowly Vale and wat'ry Ground   25
He sung, the hanging Hills return the Sound;
While lowing Oxen interrupt the Song,
And drown the heav'nly Accents of his Tongue.
Oft Princes came, and all th' enquiring Train,
Trembling at future Fears to seek his Fame:[8]   30
In vain they ask, and offer Rites Divine,
A solitary Silence fills the Shrine.
With Grief *Latona* saw her Offspring's Head,[9]
With Hair ensnarled, and matted Tresses spread.
Those heav'nly Curls, which round his Shoulders flew,   35
And ev'n from *Juno* claimed their Praises due.[10]
His uncombed Head, and tangled Locks, who e'er
Had seen, no more would wish *Apollo*'s Hair.
Where, *Phoebus!* where are all thy Honours flown[11]
Of *Delos*, and of *Delphic Pytho*'s Town?[12]   40
For Love commands thee to a less Abode,
And in a lowly Hut confines the God.
   Blessed Times when Gods did *Venus'* Laws adore,
And owned in Public her superior Power.
'Tis now a Jest, a Jest let me too prove,   45
Rather than be a God, and not to love.
   But you whom Love surveys with angry Eye
Attend his Wars, and pitch your Tent with me.
This Iron Age for Spoil its Arts employs,[13]
Nor prizes *Venus* and her tender Joys.   50
Though many Dangers tend the Spoiler's Trade,
And num'rous Ills the daring Man invade;

---

7 *His . . . Home* literally, "O how often his sister [Diana] is said to have met him carrying a calf through the fields and blushed." The translation omits Tibullus' humorous reference to Apollo's cheese-making and basket-weaving.

8 *Oft . . . Fame* a reference to Delphi (see n. 12 below).

9 *Latona* mother of Apollo.

10 *Juno* Apollo's stepmother.

11 *Phoebus* another name for Apollo.

12 *Delos* birthplace of Apollo and a center of his cult; *Delphic Pytho* the oracle of Apollo at Delphi.

13 *Iron Age* last of the mythical ages of man; *Spoil* booty.

Spoil sheathes the Warrior Train in hostile Arms,
And hence arose a world of various Harms.
Hence Blood and Murder made their first Essay, 55
And Death discovered hence a shorter Way.
Spoil urges on to tempt th' uncertain Main,
And slight the Dangers of the Sea for Gain:
Nay, doubles all the Dangers and the Fear
When threat'ning Prows and Naval Fights appear. 60
The Spoiler covets the extended Plain,
Whose Herbage may his num'rous Flocks maintain:
He seeks the Stone in distant Quarries veined,
And the huge Column for his Seat ordained.
A thousand Yoke of Oxen draw the Freight, 65
And Crowds surprised, admire the pond'rous Weight:
His Moles stupenduous, curb th' unmanaged Sea,[14]
That Fish may winter in the quiet Bay.
But may neat Earthen Vessels serve too thee,[15]
Small cheerful Meals in humble Decency. 70
   But, Ah! I see! too plainly see! the Fair
Make Wealth and sordid Gain their chiefest Care;
Then Spoils your useful Aid will I employ,
Since Love requires Wealth, that Wealth he shall enjoy.
Then, *Nemesis*, by my Profuseness gay,[16] 75
May through the City and the crowded Way,
Conspicuous in my Gifts, the shining Spoils display.
She shall the Vestments' subtle Texture wear,
By Cöan Women wrought with artful Care;[17]
Shot through with Gold, and tissued richly o'er, 80
Slaves shall be sent for from the Eastern Shore:
The tawny Eunuch shall attend her State,
And Sun-burnt *Indians* shall around her wait.
The Dyes shall struggle on her Vestments spread,
And *Afric*'s Violet strive with *Tyrian* Red.[18] 85
'Tis Truth I spake, she should a Kingdom sway,
And Crowds of fettered Servants should obey.[19]

---

14 *Moles* piers, breakwaters.
15 *thee* Latin *tibi* – addressing Nemesis; however, some modern editors read *mihi* ("for me"), in which case Tibullus is addressing himself.
16 *Nemesis* "Retribution" – the fictitious name of Tibullus' girlfriend.
17 *Cöan* from the island of Cos, which was famous for its silks.

18 *Tyrian* from Tyre, a source of purple dye.
19 *'Tis . . . obey* a mistranslation; literally, "let him hold sway whom the foreign platform has often forced to display his chalked feet" – an allusion to the auction of slaves from abroad, whose feet were marked to distinguish them from domestic slaves. Tibullus makes the shocking revelation that his rival, Nemesis' present lover, is an ex-slave.

But you, O Harvest, which detains my Dear,
May the unfertile Earth for Plenty bear
The small Produce of an ungrateful Year.   90
And you kind Fost'rer of the Vineyard Store,
Soft *Bacchus* fill thy much-loved Vat no more.
'Tis wrong the Fair should lie in Fields obscure,
Joys less than them even thy own Wines procure.
Perish the Fruit, and fade the rural Field,   95
Rather than beauteous Maids be there concealed.
Let Mast, as once it did, supply the Board,[20]
And Springs, as once, a Native Drink afford.
Of Old our Fathers fed on Mast alone;
Then Love was common, nor was Envy known.   100
They always loved, they'd nothing else to do,
Nor Corn had they to reap, nor Fields to plough.
But *Venus* fav'ring those intent on Love,
Led to the shady Vale, and silent Grove.
No Dog was then to fright with op'ning Roar;   105
No fastened Portal, nor obstructing Door.
How happy would it be should Fates ordain
Those quiet Days, and pleasing Rules again!
    Oh! perish all the Forms of studied Dress
Of Woman's Pride, and polished Artfulness.[21]   110
Would that as in the former Times each Maid
Was meanly dressed, and carelessly arrayed;
Since *Nemesis* lies hid in Privacy,
Since very rarely I, the Maid can see.
Wretch! that I am, what serves it me to wear   115
A gay Attire, or show a courtly Air?
    Bring me where I may *Nemesis* obey,
Where I may see her, and allow her Sway:
I'll plough the Land, so I may view the Maid,
Nor scorn the Hardships of the rural Trade.[22]   120

---

20 *Mast* acorns; reputedly the food of primitive
humans.

21 *Oh!* . . . *Artfulness* a free invention to fill a
lacuna in the text of Tibullus.

22 *Nor* . . . *Trade* literally, "I won't withhold
myself from chains and blows."

Propertius (c. 50–16 BCE)

Sextus Propertius came from Assisi. Despite losing some of his ancestral property in confiscations that followed the victory of Octavian and Antony at Philippi, he belonged, like Tibullus, to the well-to-do equestrian class and seems to have been self-supporting. Propertius published four books of poetry between 28 and 16 BCE, one of the most fertile periods in Roman literary history. Together with Tibullus, Propertius perfected the form of Latin love elegy – a genre whose roots lay in the poetry of Catullus (and the lost writer Gallus) and whose final flowering would come in the works of Ovid. Composed in elegiac couplets, consisting of unequal lines of six and five feet, a Roman elegy is not a lament, as in the modern sense, but a personal love poem. Taking their cue from Catullus' passionate series of poems to Lesbia, the elegists each composed a cycle of poems around a beloved for whom they invented a fanciful literary name: Cynthia (Propertius), Delia and Nemesis (Tibullus), and Corinna (Ovid). Their elegies record the ups and downs of their affairs, the beauty of their mistresses, their devotion, and her infidelities. As followers of love, the speakers in these poems embrace a countercultural way of life, a life of love that is opposed to the political, commercial, and military lives that men of their class were expected to pursue. To express their dissent, Propertius and Tibullus developed the metaphors of *militia amoris* (the soldiery of love) and *servitium amoris* (the slavery of love), each of which implies a shocking reversal of traditional Roman values. Another important feature of Propertius' poetry, again indebted to Catullus, is his appropriation of the world of mythology – traditionally the province of epic and high drama – to embellish his love affair. Propertius is one of the most independent Roman poets, not only in his social but in his political attitudes. After publishing his first book he joined Virgil and Horace in the circle of Maecenas, a wealthy patron of the arts and minister of Augustus. However, Propertius maintained an ironic detachment from the regime of Augustus, even in his last two books of elegies, where he expanded his range beyond love to antiquarian and patriotic themes.

The genre of the love elegy died with Ovid, so neither Propertius nor Tibullus had much impact on Roman literature beyond the Augustan age. Propertius was predictably ignored in the Middle Ages, but, predictably again, was rediscovered by Petrarch and the Renaissance. His *Elegies* were printed in 1472, not long after the invention of the press. A copy of his works, often included with those of Catullus and Tibullus, was common on the shelves of English poets throughout the seventeenth and eighteenth centuries, including those of moralists like Samuel Johnson. In the modern era both Yeats and Pound (*Homage to Sextus Propertius*) draw explicitly on his work.

from the *Elegies*

Book 2, number 2

The poet's attempt to break free of love is nullified by the sight of a beautiful woman, whom he compares in a learned manner to a number of mythical females – the recherché allusions are typical of Propertius. This poem is the basis for Yeats's "A Thought from Propertius" (p. 219 above).

The translation offered here is by W. G. Shepherd (1935–) from his Penguin edition (1984).

> I was free, and would not share my bed again.
> A pact was made, Love played me false. Why
> Does human beauty subsist on earth? I condone
> Your prehistoric seductions, Jove.
>   Her hair is yellow, her hands slender, superlative   5
> All her person, her carriage worthy of Jupiter's sister;[1]
> Or Pallas approaching Dulichian altars,[2]
> Her breasts concealed by a Gorgon's snaky ringlets;[3]
> Or like the Lapiths' heroic child Ischomache,[4]
> Lovely plunder for Centaurs deep in wine;[5]   10
> Or Brimo, credibly reported to have laid her virginity[6]
> At Mercury's side, by the waves of Boebeis.[7]

BOOK 2, NUMBER 2

1 *Jupiter's sister* Juno.
2 *Pallas* Minerva (Greek Athena); *Dulichian* of Dulichium, an island adjoining Ithaca.
3 *Gorgon* female monster with snaky hair and staring eyes; an allusion to the decoration on Minerva's aegis – a special skin worn like a breastplate.
4 *Lapiths* a mythical tribe of Thessaly; *Ischomache* a Lapith woman.

5 *Centaurs* mythical beings with a human head and equine body; invited by the Lapiths to a wedding, they got drunk and tried to abduct the women.
6 *Brimo* a name for Hecate or Proserpina; she bore three children to Mercury.
7 *Mercury* the messenger god; *Boebeis* lake in Thessaly.

Then yield, goddesses whom the Shepherd once saw[8]
Strip off your tunics on Ida's heights.[9]
Let age refuse to alter that beauty even though　　　　　　　　15
She attain to the ages-long span of Cumae's Sibyl.[10]

Book 2, number 15

Inspired by a rapturous night of love-making, the poet praises the joys of nudity
and expresses his devotion to his mistress. He reflects that war would cease to exist
if all men lived the life of love, and, in the *carpe diem* spirit of Catullus, he exhorts
his mistress to make the most of love while she can. Propertius' contrast between
love and war lies behind the second stanza of Campion's *My Sweetest Lesbia*
(p. 51 above). The first part of the poem, which is comparable to Ovid's *Amores*
1.5 (p. 420 below), may, like Ovid's poem, have influenced Donne's *Elegy* 19,
"To His Mistress Going to Bed" (p. 53 above) – especially its celebration of
nakedness.

　　Again, the translation is by W. G. Shepherd (see p. 411 above).

How I prosper! O shining night! And O
You little bed made blest by my delights!
How much we told each other by lamplight,
How great our strife when the light was removed!
For now with bare nipples she wrestled me,　　　　　　　　5
And now procrastinated, tunic closed.
She opened my rolling eyes from sleep
With her lips and said, "Will you lie so sluggish?"
What varied embraces shifted our arms! And how
My kisses loitered on your lips!　　　　　　　　　　　10
　　Blind movements don't assist but mar desire –
You should know that eyes are guides in love:
Paris himself was undone when the Spartan[1]
Rose naked from Menelaus' marriage-bed;[2]
Endymion likewise naked captivated[3]　　　　　　　　15
Phoebus' sister and lay with a naked goddess.[4]

8　*goddesses* Minerva, Venus, and Juno; *Shep-
herd* Paris, who judged the famous beauty contest
among the three.
　9　*Ida* mountain overlooking Troy.
10　*Cumae* Italian city; *Sibyl* a prophet of Apollo
who was destined to live a thousand years.

BOOK 2, NUMBER 15

1　*Paris* Trojan prince who abducted Helen; *the
Spartan* Helen.
2　*Menelaus* king of Sparta.
3　*Endymion* youth loved by the moon
goddess.
4　*Phoebus' sister* Diana, who was associated with
the moon; however, it was Selene (or Luna), not
Diana, who loved Endymion.

If you persist in your whim, and lie down clothed,
Your ripped shift will have to cope with my hands:
What's more, if anger carries me further,
You'll display bruised arms to your mother.   20
Sagging breasts don't yet forbid you to play:
Let that fret her who's ashamed to have given birth.
While our fates allow, let's sate our eyes with love:
Long night comes on, and day will not return.
  Would that you were willing to bind us clinging thus,   25
With fetters no day would ever unloose!
May doves coupled in love be your example,
Male and female, utterly married.
He errs, who seeks the term of lunatic love:
True love does not recognize measure.   30
First will earth dupe farmers with mock springing,
Sooner the Sun whip on the horses of darkness,
And streams call back their flowings to the source,
The fish be parched in dried-up deeps,
Than I may transfer to another my ache: 35
Hers I will be in life, and hers in death.
But if she is willing to yield to me such nights
With her, a year of life will be an age:
If she will give many, in them I'll be immortal:
In one night any man might be a god.   40
  If all men longed to run through such a life,
And lie, their limbs relaxed by much neat wine,
There'd be no cruel swords, nor any warship,
And our bones not roll in Actium's sea,[5]
Nor would Rome, beset by internecine   45
Triumphs, be weary from tearing her own locks.
This at least posterity may justly praise:
Our wine-cups never outraged any gods.
  You then, while it's light, don't leave life's fruit!
Though you give them all, your kisses will be few: 50
And as petals trickle from parching garlands,
And you see them, strewn at random, float in the bowls,
So for us lovers, who momently expect great things,
Perhaps tomorrow will close our allotted span.

5 *Actium* site of naval battle between Antony
and Octavian in 31 BCE.

Ovid (43 BCE–17 CE)

The magnitude of Ovid's influence upon English literature is equaled only by
Virgil's. Virgil was Ovid's elder, his model, and also, at times, his target. For this
reason, it is impossible to speak of Ovid's influence as greater than Virgil's, but
English writers frequently were more attracted to Ovid's position in relation to
his great predecessor and the freedom he exercised as a versatile performer against
the backdrop of the Virgilian poetic monuments. Ovid's sensuousness and his
sensuality, his linguistic pyrotechnics, and his wit are probably more often visible
in English literature than the high political seriousness of his master. Ovid's privi-
leged background and his precociousness as a student of rhetoric fitted him for a
career in law or politics, but he chose instead the path of literature, which meant
for him, as for so many English writers, a path of criticism and subversiveness.

Ovid's earliest work was the *Amores* (Loves), love elegies that follow in the
footsteps of Propertius and Tibullus and burlesque the conventions that they had
established, such as the lovesick narrator and the haughty beauty whom he pursues.
Ovid's lover is a more urbane and slippery character than his predecessors, an ironic
hedonist whose love of wit rivals his love for his fictitious mistress Corinna. Ovid
was the last of the love elegists. Like Cervantes killing off his Quixote, Ovid seems
to have extinguished the form when he abandoned it. In subsequent works – the
Heroides (Heroines) and the *Ars Amatoria* (Art of Love) – Ovid renounced the
love elegy, but he found ways to continue writing about love in the elegiac meter.
The *Heroides* consist of "letters" sent mainly by mythical heroines to their absent
husbands and lovers. The exploration of love from the perspective of lonely and
anxiety-ridden women offers a novel and ironic perspective on myths of male
heroism. The *Ars Amatoria* claims to be a manual on seduction and adopts the
style of a didactic poem, like Virgil's *Georgics* for example, but only to parody the
form and poke fun at Roman society. Its irreverence and risqué subject matter
offended an emperor who around the time of the work's publication felt compelled
to banish his own daughter Julia for breaking his laws against adultery.

Ovid's most ambitious works were the *Fasti* (Calendar), an unfinished catalogue of Roman religious festivals and myths, and the *Metamorphoses* (Transformations), his masterpiece. In this unorthodox and humorous epic Ovid weaves together a massive collection of myths that include the motif of metamorphosis, a rubric which, generously interpreted, allows him to retell in his own way almost all the stories of Greece and Rome. He strings these together in ingenious ways to form a continuous fictive history of the world from its creation to the time of Augustus. Such is the power of Ovid's reinventions that they have in many cases supplanted their models and become canonical – the stories of Daphne, Phaethon, Europa, Narcissus, Arachne, Daedalus, and Pygmalion are now Ovid's and no longer belong to earlier tellers of the tales. In his successful appropriation of what Dryden called the *materia literaria* (the stuff of literary tradition), Ovid is a forerunner of Shakespeare and Milton, great poets who also asserted their dominance over oft-told tales and became, in the most important sense, their authors.

In 8 CE, while finishing the *Metamorphoses*, Ovid was banished by Augustus to the town of Tomis on the bleak shores of the Black Sea, where he lived until his death around 17 CE. His spirit subdued but unbroken, Ovid redirected his energies into several books of exilic poetry entitled the *Tristia* (Sorrows) and *Epistulae ex Ponto* (Letters from the Black Sea). The reason for Ovid's banishment is irrecoverable. He alludes to the double cause of a *carmen* (poem) and *error* (mistake). The *carmen* was the *Ars Amatoria*, which had blatantly contradicted the moral regeneration fostered by Augustus in his marital legislation. But Ovid had completed this poem several years earlier, so it was not the main cause. The *error* possibly involved knowledge of sexual impropriety within the imperial family that led to the banishment of the emperor's granddaughter in the same year.

His banishment did nothing to dim Ovid's popularity throughout later antiquity. Even when he was the object of official disapproval and warning at the hands of the church fathers, he never ceased to be read and copied. The Christian apologist Lactantius (c. 240–320 CE), for example, warned of the risks of reading Ovid but clearly read him himself. Later in the Middle Ages Ovid's love poetry influenced the troubadours and writers on courtly love such as Andreas Capellanus. One way of converting Ovid to moral uses was to interpret the tales of the *Metamorphoses* as moral allegories. This practice reached its height of popularity in the late thirteenth-century French work *Ovide moralisé*. Ovid may have been the favorite Latin poet of the Renaissance. His followers include Petrarch, Dante, Chaucer, Spenser, Marlowe, and Shakespeare. In the seventeenth and eighteenth centuries in England he had growing competition from Horace, as well as Virgil, but his influence is pre-eminent in the works of the greatest poets of that period, Dryden and Pope. Ovid suffered some decrease of fame from the late eighteenth to the early twentieth centuries, but in the late twentieth century he underwent a revival which still continues. Ted Hughes's translations of the *Metamorphoses* are evidence of Ovid's revival, as are the many recent scholarly books devoted to him. In the English part of this anthology we note the influence of Ovid on Chaucer,

Sidney, Shakespeare, Donne, Milton, Behn, Wilmot, Pope, Wordsworth, and
Housman among others.

from the *Amores*

Book 1, number 1

The opening poem of the *Amores* is programmatic, as is often the case in Roman
poetry books. It defines the genre (elegy), subject matter (love), and tone (light)
of the collection. Ovid's handling of this topic is strikingly original. In a famous
preface, the Greek poet Callimachus had defined his aesthetic ideals by means of
a parable. He says that when he attempted to write of "kings and heroes" in the
grand style, he was interrupted by Apollo, who instructed him "to feed the flock
fat but keep the muse thin" – in other words, to avoid bloated narrative in favor
of concise, finely crafted verse. The passage was much imitated by Roman poets
of the Augustan age (see for example Horace, *Satires* 2.6.14–15, p. 389 above;
Virgil, *Eclogues* 6.1–8), some of whom, feeling pressured to tackle patriotic themes
in epic style, adapted it to justify their choice of non-epic genres such as pastoral,
elegy, and lyric. Ovid spoofs this tradition by substituting Cupid for Apollo, the
god of poetry. He says that when he set out to write an epic in hexameters, Cupid
stole a foot from the second line, thereby creating a pentameter and, in combina-
tion with the hexameter, an elegiac couplet – the meter of love poetry. In annoy-
ance, Ovid castigates the god and objects that he lacks amatory material, whereupon
Cupid promptly shoots him with an arrow. Suitably inflamed with love, Ovid
buckles down to the composition of elegies. The opening poems of the *Amores*
deeply influenced later sonnet sequences, including Sidney's *Astrophel and Stella*
(p. 39 above).

The translation is by Christopher Marlowe (1564–1593; p. 44 above) and is
based on the printing in *All Ovid's Elegies* (1603).

> We which were *Ovid's* five books now are three,
> For these before the rest preferreth he.
> If reading five thou plain'st of tediousness,
> Two ta'en away, thy labour will be less.[1]
> With Muse upreared I meant to sing of Arms,   5
> Choosing a subject fit for fierce alarms.
> Both verses were alike till Love (men say)[2]

BOOK 1, NUMBER 1

1   *We . . . less* Marlowe incorporates into the first
poem an epigram that Ovid composed as a

heading to the second edition of the *Amores* after
reducing them from five to three books.
2   *Love* Cupid.

Began to smile and took one foot away.[3]
Rash boy, who gave thee power to change a line?
We are the Muses' Prophets, none of thine. 10
What if thy mother take *Diana's* bow?[4]
Shall *Dian* fan, when love begins to glow?
In woody groves is't meet that *Ceres* reign,[5]
And quiver-bearing *Dian* till the plain?
Who'll set the fair-tressed sun in battle ray,[6] 15
While *Mars* doth take the *Aonian* Harp to play?[7]
Great are thy kingdoms, over-strong and large,
Ambitious imp, why seek'st thou further charge?
Are all things thine? the Muses' *Tempe* thine?[8]
Then scarce can *Phoebus* say, this Harp is mine. 20
When in this work's first verse I trod aloft,
Love slacked my Muse, and made my numbers soft.
I have no mistress; nor no favourite,
Being fittest matter for a wanton wit.
Thus I complained, but Love unlocked his quiver, 25
Took out the shaft, ordained my heart to shiver:
And bent his sinewy bow upon his knee,
Saying, "Poet here's a work beseeming thee."
Oh woe is me, he never shoots but hits,
I burn, love in my idle bosom sits. 30
Let my first verse be six, my last five feet,
Farewell stern war, for blunter Poets meet.
Elegian Muse, that warblest amorous lays,[9]
Girt my shine brow with Sea-bank Myrtle praise.[10]

Book 1, number 2

The poem develops the subject of love introduced in the opening poem. With mock naïveté Ovid ponders the cause of his insomnia and realizes it to be love. He debates with himself whether to resist or yield and decides on the latter via a string of logical-seeming but comically inept analogies. In deference to the elegiac

3 *foot* one of the six metrical units forming a hexameter.

4 *mother* Venus; *Diana* virgin goddess of the wild.

5 *Ceres* goddess of grain.

6 *sun* literally, "Phoebus," i.e. Apollo, god of music; *ray* array.

7 *Aonian* Aonia was the part of Boeotia containing Mt. Helicon, which was sacred to the Muses.

8 *Tempe* beautiful valley in which the river Peneus flows.

9 *Elegian Muse* literally, "Muse that must be set to rhythm in eleven feet" (i.e. a hexameter plus a pentameter, comprising an elegiac couplet).

10 *shine* "shining; bright" (*OED*); *Myrtle* the myrtle was sacred to Venus.

convention of the lover's enslavement to his mistress, he subjects himself to Cupid.
The rest of the poem is a parody of Roman triumphal processions, in which a
conquering general rode by chariot to the temple of Jupiter on the Capitol fol-
lowed by his captives, booty, and soldiers. Ovid imagines himself as a captive in
the triumph of Cupid, an unlikely general, who rides in a chariot drawn by birds.
The last two lines contain a cheeky reference to the emperor Augustus.

The translation, like that of 1.1, is Christopher Marlowe's (see p. 416 above).

What makes my bed seem hard seeing it is soft?
Or why slips down the coverlet so oft?
Although the nights be long, I sleep not tho,[1]
My sides are sore with tumbling to and fro.
Were Love the cause, it's like I should descry him,[2]   5
Or lies he close, and shoots where none can spy him.
'Twas so, he struck me with a slender dart,
'Tis cruel Love turmoils my captive heart.
Yielding or struggling do we give him might,
Let's yield, a burthen easily borne is light.   10
I saw a brandished fire increase in strength,
Which being not flacked, I saw it die at length.[3]
Young Oxen newly yoked are beaten more,
Than Oxen which have drawn the plough before.
And rough Jades' mouths with stubborn bits are torn,[4]   15
But managed horses' heads are lightly borne.
Unwilling lovers, love doth more torment,
Than such as in their bondage feel content.
Lo, I confess, I am thy captive I,
And hold my conquered hands for thee to tie.   20
What need'st thou war, I sue to thee for grace,
With arms to conquer armless men is base.
Yoke *Venus'* Doves, put Myrtle on thy hair,
Vulcan will give thee chariots rich and fair.[5]
The people thee applauding, thou shalt stand,   25
Guiding the harmless Pigeons with thy hand.
Young men, and women shalt thou lead as thrall,
So will thy triumph seem magnifical.
I, lately caught, will have a new-made wound,
And captive-like be manacled and bound.   30
Good meaning, shame, and such as seek Love's wrack,
Shall follow thee their hands tied at their back.

BOOK 1, NUMBER 2

1 *tho* then.
2 *like* likely.
3 *flacked* flapped; shaken.

4 *Jade* a bad-tempered horse.
5 *Vulcan* literally, "[your] step-father"; he was
Venus' husband.

Thee all shall fear, and worship as a King,
Io, triumphing shall thy people sing.[6]
Smooth speeches, fear, and rage shall by thee ride,   35
Which troops have always been on *Cupid's* side:
Thou with these soldiers, conquer'st Gods and men,
Take these away, where is thine honour then?
Thy mother shall from heaven applaud this show,
And on their faces heaps of Roses strow.   40
With beauty of thy wings, thy fair hair gilded,
Ride, golden Love, in chariots richly builded.
Unless I err, full many shalt thou burn,
And give wounds infinite at every turn.
In spite of thee forth will thine arrows fly,   45
A scorching flame burns all the standers by.
So having conquered *Inde* was *Bacchus'* hue,[7]
Thee pompous Birds, and him two Tigers drew.
Then seeing I grace thy show in following thee,
Forbear to hurt thyself in spoiling me.   50
Behold thy kinsman *Caesar's* prosperous bands,[8]
Who guards the conquered with his conquering hands.

Book 1, number 3

The first two poems have introduced the subject of love and revealed its power over Ovid. The sequence unfolds with mention of the woman whom he loves, though she remains, as yet, anonymous. Ovid asks only that she allow herself to be loved by him and – what amounts to the same thing – to supply him with material for his poetry. He presses his case in rhetorical style through mythological precedents of women made famous by song – all three of whom happen to be victims of divine rape.

Marlowe again is the translator (see p. 416 above).

I ask but right: let her that caught me late,
Either love, or cause that I may never hate.
I ask too much; would she but let me love her!
Love knows with such like prayers I daily move her.[1]
Accept him that will serve thee all his youth,   5

---

6   *Io* a triumphal shout.
7   *Bacchus* the wine god, whose entry into Greece from the east was pictured as a triumphal procession.
8   *Caesar* Augustus, who could – riskily – be called a relative of Cupid through his alleged

descent from Venus' son Aeneas; *bands* literally, "arms."

BOOK 1, NUMBER 3
1   *Love* Venus.

Accept him that will love with spotless truth,
If lofty titles cannot make me thine,
That am descended but of Knightly line,[2]
(Soon may you plow the little land I have;
I gladly grant my parents given to save),[3]   10
Apollo, Bacchus and the Muses may,[4]
And *Cupid* who hath marked me for thy prey;
My spotless life, which but to God's gives place,
Naked simplicity, and modest grace.
I love but one, and her I love change never;   15
If men have faith, I'll live with thee forever.
The years that fatal destiny shall give,
I'll live with thee, and die, ere thou shalt grieve.
Be thou the happy subject of my books,
That I may write things worthy thy fair looks.   20
By verses hornèd *Io* got her name,[5]
And she to whom in shape of Swan *Jove* came.[6]
And she that on a feigned Bull swam to land,[7]
Gripping his false horns with her virgin hand.
So likewise we will through the world be rung,   25
And with my name shall thine be always sung.

Book 1, number 5

Having defined the world of the *Amores* in poems 1–3 and, in poem 4, given an indirect glimpse of his mistress, Ovid finally names her and narrates a direct encounter. Ovid's predecessors in the elegiac genre, Tibullus and Propertius, had been relatively coy about describing nudity and sex. The sensuality and frank detail of this poem were something new and still retain their freshness. The poem's intensity is heightened by the restraint – not normally one of his virtues – with which Ovid stops short of describing intercourse itself: *cetera quis nescit?* (who doesn't know the rest?). Among the many poems it has influenced is Donne's *Elegy* 19, "To His Mistress Going to Bed" (p. 53 above).

The translation is again by Marlowe (see p. 416 above).

2 *Knightly* of the equestrian class, second in rank to senators.
3 *Soon . . . save* i.e. "I don't own a big estate, and my family is impecunious." Ovid relies, instead, on his poetic talent and good character.
4 *Apollo, Bacchus . . . Muses* gods associated with poetic inspiration; *may* i.e. "may make me thine."

5 *hornèd Io* literally, "Io terrified by her horns"; Io was turned into a cow by Jupiter to conceal her from Juno (Ovid, *Metamorphoses* 1).
6 *she . . . came* Leda, the mother of Helen.
7 *she . . . land* Europa, who was carried to Crete by Jupiter disguised as a bull (Ovid, *Metamorphoses* 2).

In summer's heat and mid-time of the day,
To rest my limbs upon a bed I lay.
One window shut, the other open stood,
Which gave such light, as twinkles in a wood.
Like twilight glimpse at setting of the Sun,[1]   5
Or night being past, and yet not day begun.
Such light to shamefast maidens must be shown,[2]
Where they may sport, and seem to be unknown.
Then came *Corinna* in a long loose gown,[3]
Her white neck hid with tresses hanging down.   10
Resembling fair *Semiramis* going to bed,[4]
Or *Laïs* of a thousand wooers sped.[5]
I snatched her gown: being thin, the harm was small,
Yet strived she to be covered there withal.
And striving thus as one that would be cast,[6]   15
Betrayed herself, and yielded at the last.
Stark naked as she stood before mine eye,
Not one wen in her body could I spy.
What arms and shoulders did I touch and see,
How apt her breasts were to be pressed by me.   20
How smooth a belly under her waist saw I!
How large a leg, and what a lusty thigh!
To leave the rest, all liked me passing well;[7]
I clinged her naked body, down she fell.[8]
Judge you the rest: being tired she bade me kiss;[9]   25
Jove send me more such afternoons as this.

Book 1, number 13

Ovid begs the dawn goddess not to rise, so that he can stay in bed with his girlfriend. There are epigrammatic precursors of this idea in the *Greek Anthology*, but nothing so elaborate as Ovid's poem, which inspired many similar lover's complaints in the Middle Ages and Renaissance, notably Donne's *The Sun Rising* (p. 52 above). The poem mimics the form of a hymn appealing to a god for aid and gives it a comic twist. Instead of summoning the divinity in the normal fashion, Ovid begs her to go away. The poem is a good illustration of the persuasive skills

BOOK 1, NUMBER 5

1 *glimpse* a flash of light.
2 *shamefast* bashful.
3 *Corinna* Ovid's mistress in the *Amores*.
4 *Semiramis* a legendary Assyrian queen.
5 *Laïs* a famous courtesan; *sped* "so dealt with as to be satisfied or well situated" (*OED*).

6 *cast* thrown down; defeated.
7 *To . . . well* literally, "Why go into details? I saw nothing that wasn't praiseworthy."
8 *clinged* embraced.
9 *Judge . . . kiss* a loose translation; literally, "Who doesn't know the rest? Worn out [by love-making], we both rested."

that Ovid learned in the schools of rhetoric. Note in particular his virtuoso performance on the theme of dawn arousing men to work and the ingenuity with which he exploits Aurora's marriage to Tithonus. The arts of persuasion, however, cannot deter nature from its course, and therein lies much of the humor in the poem.

The translator is, again, Christopher Marlowe (p. 416 above).

Now o'er the sea from her old Love comes she[1]
That draws the day from heaven's cold axletree.[2]
"*Aurora* whither slidest thou? Down again,[3]
And birds from *Memnon* yearly shall be slain.[4]
Now in her tender arms I sweetly bide;   5
If ever, now well lies she by my side.
The air is cold, and sleep is sweetest now
And birds send forth shrill notes from every bough.
Whither run'st thou, that men and women love not?
Hold in thy rosy horses that they move not![5]   10
Ere thou rise, stars teach seamen where to sail
But when thou comest they of their courses fail.
Poor travelers though tired, rise at thy sight,
And soldiers make them ready to the fight.
The painful hind by thee to field is sent,   15
Slow Oxen early in the yoke are pent.
Thou cozen'st boys of sleep, and do'st betray them
To *Pedants* that with cruel lashes pay them.
Thou mak'st the surety to the Lawyer run,[6]
That with one word hath nigh himself undone.   20
The Lawyer and the client hate thy view,
Both whom thou raisest up to toil anew.
By thy means women of their rest are barred,
Thou setst their labouring hands to spin and card.[7]
All could I bear, but that the wench should rise,   25
Who can endure save him with whom none lies?
How oft wished I, night would not give thee place,
Nor morning stars shun thy uprising face.

BOOK 1, NUMBER 13

1   *old Love* her aged husband Tithonus; Aurora got Jupiter to make him immortal but forgot to ask for eternal youth.
2   *from . . . axletree* literally, "with her frosty axletree," i.e. her chariot.
3   *Aurora* the dawn goddess (Greek Eos).
4   *Memnon* son of Aurora and king of Ethiopia; when he was killed at Troy, birds arose from his

ashes and were said to revisit his grave annually, where they fought to the death.
5   *Hold . . . not* literally, "hold in the dewy reins with your rosy hand."
6   *surety* "one who makes himself liable for the default or miscarriage of another" (*OED*).
7   *spin and card* operations in the making of thread and cloth.

How oft that either wind would break thy coach,
Or steeds might fall forced with thick clouds' approach.   30
Whither goest thou hateful Nymph? *Memnon* the elf
Received his coal-black colour from thyself.
Say that thy love with *Cephalus* were not known,[8]
Then thinkest thou thy loose life is not shown?[9]
Would *Tithon* might but talk of thee a while,   35
Not one in heaven should be more base and vile;
Thou leavest his bed, because he's faint through age,
And early mountest thy hateful carriage,
But heldst thou in thine arms some *Cephalus*,
Then wouldst thou cry, 'Stay night and run not thus.'   40
Do'st punish me, because years make him wane?[10]
I did not bid thee wed an aged swain.
The Moon sleeps with *Endymion* every day,[11]
Thou art as fair as she, then kiss and play.
Jove that thou should'st not haste but wait his leisure,   45
Made two nights one to finish up his pleasure."[12]
I chid no more; she blusht and therefore heard me,
Yet lingered not the day, but morning scared me.

Book 2, number 6

Ovid drew the idea of writing a parodic lament for Corinna's dead parrot from
Catullus' elegy for Lesbia's sparrow (*Carmen* 3; p. 331 above). Catullus' poem is
a deft creation of 18 lines that mingles wit with sympathy – less, however, for the
bird than for its mistress. Ovid's is a full-scale parody of the epicedion or formal
dirge, 62 lines long and entirely lacking in seriousness. Its guiding principle is that
of incongruity. From beginning to end the parrot is treated as a human being – a
beloved, upright, peace-loving, and gifted citizen destined for a place amongst the
blessed in the afterlife. The connection of the bird to its mistress, which is central
to Catullus' poem, is swamped by the flood of bombastic lamentation. Ovid, of
course, was trying to do something different than Catullus: he was not trying to
express love but to evoke laughter. The later tradition of animal poems is repre-
sented in this volume by Gray's "Ode on the Death of a Favourite Cat" (p. 151
above) and Cowper's "Epitaph on a Hare" (p. 164 above).

The translator again is Christopher Marlowe (see p. 416 above). We have been
freer than usual in adjusting the punctuation and spelling to make the meaning
of the text clear.

---

8   *Cephalus* a youth loved by Aurora.
9   *Say . . . shown* modern editors of Ovid reject
this couplet as spurious.
10   *wane* dwindle.

11   *Endymion* a youth loved by Selene (or Luna),
the moon goddess.
12   *two nights* Jupiter doubled the length of
night to prolong his love-making with Alcmena.

The parrot from east *India* to me sent,
Is dead, all fowls her exequies frequent.
Go goodly birds, striking your breasts, bewail,
And with rough claws your tender cheeks assail.
For woeful hairs let piece-torn plumes abound,   5
For long-shrilled trumpets let your notes resound.
Why, *Philomele,* do'st *Tereus'* lewdness mourn?[1]
All wasting years have that complaint not worn?
Thy tunes let this rare bird's sad funeral borrow;
Itys is great, but ancient cause of sorrow.[2]   10
All you whose pinions in the clear air soar,
But most thou friendly turtle-dove, deplore.[3]
Full concord all your lives was you betwixt,
And to the end your constant faith stood fixed.
What *Pylades* did to *Orestes* prove,[4]   15
Such to the parrot was the turtle-dove.
But what availed this faith? her rarest hue?
Or voice that how to change the wild notes knew?
What helps it thou wert given to please my wench,
Birds' hapless glory, death thy life doth quench.   20
Thou with thy quills mightst make green *Emeralds* dark,
And pass our scarlet of red saffron's mark.[5]
No such voice-feigning bird was on the ground,[6]
Thou spokest thy words so well with stammering sound.
Envy hath rapt thee: no fierce wars thou movedst;   25
Vain babbling speech, and pleasant peace thou lovedst.
Behold how quails among their battles live,
Which do perchance old age unto them give.
A little filled thee, and for love of talk,
Thy mouth to taste of many meats did balk.   30
Nuts were thy food, and Poppy caused thee sleep,
Pure water's moisture thirst away did keep.
The ravenous vulture lives, the Puttock hovers[7]
Around the air, the Caddesse rain discovers.[8]

BOOK 2, NUMBER 6

1 *Philomele* the nightingale, which Philomela became after avenging Tereus' rape and mutilation of her by assisting her sister Procne to kill Itys (Ovid, *Metamorphoses* 6).

2 *Itys* son of Tereus and Procne.

3 *deplore* weep; grieve.

4 *Pylades* mythical friend of Orestes who assisted him in killing Clytemnestra to avenge her murder of Orestes' father Agamemnon.

5 In the original it is clear that this line refers to the bird's beak; *saffron* an orange-red substance made from the stigmas of the flower *crocus sativus.*

6 *on the ground* on earth.

7 *Puttock* "a bird of prey; usually applied to the kite" (*OED*).

8 *Caddesse* the jackdaw; a prognosticator of rain.

And Crows survive arms-bearing *Pallas'* hate,[9]   35
Whose life nine ages scarce bring out of date.
Dead is that speaking image of man's voice,
The Parrot given me, the far world's best choice.[10]
The greedy spirits take the best things first,
Supplying their void places with the worst.   40
Thersites did *Protesilaus* survive;[11]
And *Hector* died his brothers yet alive.[12]
My wench's vows for thee what should I show,[13]
Which stormy South winds into sea did blow?
The seventh day came; none following mightst thou see,   45
And the Fate's distaff empty stood to thee:[14]
Yet words in thy benumbèd palate rung:
"Farewell *Corinna*," cried thy dying tongue.[15]
Elysium hath a wood of holm trees black,[16]
Whose earth doth not perpetual green-grass lack;   50
There good birds rest (if we believe things hidden)
Whence unclean fouls are said to be forbidden.
There harmless Swans feed all abroad the river,
There lives the *Phoenix* one alone bird ever.[17]
There *Juno's* bird displays his gorgeous feather:[18]   55
And loving Doves kiss eagerly together.
The Parrot into wood received with these,
Turns all the goodly birds to what she please.
A grave her bones hides; on her corps' great grave,
The little stones these little verses have: 60
"This tomb approves, I pleased my mistress well,
My mouth in speaking did all birds excel."

Book 3, number 7

In this monologue the poet bemoans a recent occasion on which he was unable to perform sexually, despite the beauty and seductive wiles of his mistress. With

9 *Pallas* Minerva, who punished a crow for tattling by changing its white feathers to black.
10 *far world's best choice* literally, "a gift given from the ends of the earth."
11 *Thersites* an ugly rabble-rouser (Homer, *Iliad* 2); *Protesilaus* the first Greek to die at Troy (see Ovid, *Heroides* 13; p. 429 below).
12 *Hector* son of the Trojan king Priam; among the brothers who survived him was Paris, whose abduction of Helen had provoked the Greek invasion.

13 *what . . . show* literally, "why should I mention?"
14 *distaff* from which the Fates drew, spun, and cut the thread of life.
15 *Corinna* Ovid's mistress.
16 *Elysium* the region of the underworld inhabited by the blessed dead; *holm trees* evergreen oaks.
17 *Phoenix* a mythical bird which was perpetually reborn from its own remains.
18 *Juno's bird* the peacock.

comical indignation the poet blames his impotence on magic, to which his departing mistress adds the suggestive alternative that he has come to her bed after making love with another woman. Ovid's tone is self-mocking and unserious. He turns a mundane into a mock-tragic event through incongruous mythological allusions and inflationary devices such as hyperbole, rhetorical questions, and apostrophe. For the reader the pleasure of the poem lies less in its obscenity than in the twists and turns of the speaker's imagination as he desperately seeks for ways to reconcile himself to an embarrassing failure. Ovid's original generated a number of imitations in the Renaissance and later, including, in this volume, Lord Rochester's "The Imperfect Enjoyment" (p. 107 above) and Aphra Behn's "The Disappointment" (p. 96 above).

The translator is, again, Christopher Marlowe (see p. 416 above).

Either she was foul, or her attire was bad,
Or she was not the wench I wished t' have had.[1]
Idly I lay with her, as if I loved not,
And like a burthen grieved the bed that moved not.
Though both of us performed our true intent,   5
Yet could I not cast anchor where I meant.
She on my neck her Ivory arms did throw,
Her arms far whiter than the *Scythian* snow.
And eagerly she kissed me with her tongue,
And under mine her wanton thigh she flung.   10
Yea, and she soothed me up, and called me sire,
And used all speech that might provoke and stir.
Yet like as if cold Hemlock I had drunk,[2]
It mocked me, hung down the head, and sunk.
Like a dull Cipher, or rude block I lay,[3]   15
Or shade, or body was I, who can say?[4]
What will my age do? Age I cannot shun,
When in my prime my force is spent and done.
I blush that being youthful, hot and lusty,
I prove neither youth nor man, but old and rusty.   20
Pure rose she, like a Nun to sacrifice,[5]

BOOK 3, NUMBER 7

1 *Either . . . had* since the speaker goes on to present her as highly desirable, the opening couplet must be ironic; this is clearer in the Latin, where line 2 is qualified by the interjection *puto,* "I suppose."
2 *Hemlock* in Plato's *Phaedo* Socrates describes the effect of drinking hemlock as a numbness spreading upwards from the feet.
3 *Cipher* zero; meaningless number; blank; fool.
4 *Or . . . or* whether . . . or; *shade* shadow, as opposed to substance.
5 *Nun* "In religions of antiquity: a woman devoted to a religious life" (*OED*); a Vestal Virgin.

Or one that with her tender brother lies.
Yet boarded I the golden *Chie* twice,[6]
And *Libas*, and the white cheeked *Pitho* thrice.[7]
Corinna craved it in a summer's night,[8]　　　　　　　　25
And nine sweet bouts we had before daylight.
What! waste my limbs through some *Thessalian* charms?[9]
May spells, and drugs do silly souls such harms?[10]
With virgin wax hath some embaste my joints?[11]
And pierced my liver with sharp needles' points?[12]　　　　30
Charms change corn to grass and make it die.
By charms are running springs and fountains dry.
By charms mast drops from oaks, from vines grapes fall[13]
And fruit from trees when there's no wind at all.
Why might not then my sinews be enchanted?　　　　　　35
And I grow faint as with some spirit haunted?
To this add shame: shame to perform it quailed me[14]
And was the second cause why vigour failed me.
My idle thoughts delighted her no more,[15]
Than did the robe or garment which she wore.　　　　　　40
Yet might her touch make youthful *Pylius* fire[16]
And *Tithon* livelier than his years require.[17]
Even her I had, and she had me in vain,
What might I crave more, if I ask again?
I think the great gods grieved they had bestowed,　　　　45
The benefit which lewdly I forslowed.[18]
I wished to be received in; in I get me,
To kiss, I kiss: to lie with her she let me.
Why was I blessed? Why made King to refuse it?
Chuff-like had I not gold and could not use it?[19]　　　　50

6　*Chie* Ovid names her Chlide, Greek for "wantonness."

7　*Libas...Pitho* suggestive Greek names meaning "trickle" and "persuasion."

8　*Corinna* the usual name for Ovid's mistress in the *Amores.*

9　*waste my limbs* that is, "do my limbs waste?" *Thessalian* Thessaly was notorious for its witches, partly because Medea lived there with Jason for some time.

10　*silly* weak.

11　*virgin wax* pure, white wax; *embaste* in candle-making, to coat the wick in wax; an odd form of the past tense.

12　*liver* often regarded as the seat of lust.

13　*mast* acorns.

14　*quailed* impaired.

15　*delighted* took delight in.

16　*Pylius* Nestor, king of Pylos, who was proverbial for his long life.

17　*Tithon* Tithonus, beloved of Eos, the dawn goddess, who got Zeus to make him immortal but forgot to ask for eternal youth.

18　*lewdly* vilely; *forslowed* lost through laziness or neglect.

19　*Chuff-like* like a rustic fool or boor.

So in a spring thirsts he that told so much,[20]
And looks upon the fruits he cannot touch.[21]
Hath any rose so from a fresh young maid,
As she might straight have gone to church and prayed?
Well I believe, she kissed not as she should,   55
Nor used the sleight and cunning which she could.
Huge oaks, hard adamants might she have moved,[22]
And with sweet words cause deaf rocks to have moaned.
Worthy she was to move both gods and men,
But neither was I man nor livèd then.   60
Can deaf ear take delight when *Phemius* sings?[23]
Or *Thamyris* in curious painted things?[24]
What sweet thought is there but I had the same?
And one gave place still as another came.
Yet notwithstanding like one dead it lay,   65
Drooping more than a rose pulled yesterday.
Now when he should not jet, he bolts upright,[25]
And craves his task, and seeks to be at fight.
Lie down with shame, and see thou stir no more,
Seeing thou wouldst deceive me as before.   70
Thou cozenest me: by thee surprised am I,
And bide sore loss with endless infamy.
Nay more the wench did not disdain a whit,
To take it in her hand, and play with it.
But when she saw it would by no means stand,   75
But still drooped down, regarding not her hand.
"Why mock'st thou me?" she cried. "Or being ill
Who bade thee lie down here against thy will?
Either th' art witched with blood of frogs new dead,
Or jaded cam'st thou from some other's bed."   80
With that her loose gown on, from me she cast her,
In skipping out her naked feet much graced her.
And lest her maid should know of this disgrace,
To cover it, spilled water on the place.

---

20 *thirsts* our emendation; all early texts have "thrives" but the Latin is *aret* (he thirsts), and we note the sixteenth-century spelling *thrust* for *thirst*, which could have been corrupted to *thrives*, especially as *u* and *v* were written as the same letter; *told* counted up.

21 *So . . . touch* the allusion is to Tantalus, who for revealing secrets of the gods was punished in Hades by having to stand in a pool that receded when he tried to drink and beneath a tree whose fruits were whisked away when he reached for them.

22 *adamant* mythical immoveable or impenetrable rock.

23 *Phemius* a bard at Odysseus' court in Ithaca.

24 *Thamyris* a bard who was blinded for boasting that he would win a contest with the Muses.

25 *jet* "strut, swagger" (*OED*).

Heroides 13

There was an oracle that the first Greek hero to land at Troy would be the first to die. The prophecy was fulfilled by Protesilaus, a prince of Thessaly who had recently been married to Laodamia. *Heroides* 13 purports to be a letter from Laodamia to Protesilaus, whom she believes to be still at Aulis waiting for a fair wind to carry the Greek fleet to Troy. In fact, as we are probably meant to infer from his mournful appearance in her dreams, Laodamia's husband is already dead when she writes to him. The irony lends pathos to Laodamia's speech, almost every part of which is based on false information and false hopes. Her ignorance is magnified by an obsessive, histrionic personality that latches onto every idea with eager yet fearful speculation. It is the lament of a woman who will soon, according to the myth, meet her own untimely death, either from wasting away or from suicide. Ovid's poem was one of the sources for Wordsworth's "Laodamia" (p. 168 above).

The translation is the work of Thomas Flatman (1637–1688), a painter, political writer, and practitioner of the loose verse form called "Pindarick," which was largely invented by Abraham Cowley (1618–1667). Flatman made this translation for an edition of *Ovid's Epistles* (1680) organized by the publisher Jacob Tonson and introduced by John Dryden.

> Health to the gentle Man of War, and may
> What *Laodamia* sends, the Gods convey.
> The Wind that still in *Aulis* holds my Dear,
> Why was it not so cross to keep Him here?
> Let the Wind raise an *Hurricane* at Sea,   5
> Were he but safe and warm ashore with me.
> Ten thousand kisses I had more to give him,
> Ten thousand cautions, and soft words to leave him:
> In haste he left me, summoned by the Wind,
> (The Wind to barbarous Mariners only kind).   10
> The Seaman's pleasure is the Lover's pain,
> (*Protesilaus* from my bosom ta'en!).
> As from my falt'ring tongue half speeches fell,
> (Scarce could I speak that wounding word *Farewell*),
> A merry Gale (at Sea they call it so)[1]   15
> Filled every Sail with joy, my breast with woe,
> There went my dear *Protesilaus* –
> While I could see Thee, full of eager pain,
> My greedy eyes epicurized on Thine,[2]
> When Thee no more, but thy spread Sails I view,   20

---

2 *epicurized* feasted luxuriously.

1 *merry Gale* a favorable wind for sailing.

I looked, and looked, till I had lost them too;
But when nor Thee, nor them I could descry,
And all was Sea that came within my eye,
They say (for I have quite forgot), they say
I straight grew pale, and fainted quite away;   25
Compassionate *Iphiclus,* and the good old man,[3]
My Mother too to my assistance ran;
In haste cold water on my face they threw,
And brought me to myself with much ado,
They meant it well, to me it seemed not so,   30
Much kinder had they been to let me go;
My anguish with my Soul together came,
And in my heart burst out the former flame:
Since which, my uncombed locks unheeded flow
Undressed, forlorn, I care not how I go;   35
Inspired with wine, thus *Bacchus'* frolic rout[4]
Staggered of old, and straggled all about.
"Put on, Put on," the happy Ladies say,
"Thy Royal Robes, fair *Laodamia.*"
Alas! before *Troy*'s Walls my Dear does lie,   40
What pleasure can I take in *Tyrian* dye?[5]
Shall Curls adorn my head, an Helmet thine?
I in bright Tissues, thou in Armour shine?[6]
Rather with studied negligence I'll be
As ill, if not disguisèd worse than Thee.   45
        O *Paris!* raised by ruins! may'st thou prove[7]
As fatal in thy War, as in thy Love!
O that the *Grecian Dame* had been less fair,
Or thou less lovely hadst appeared to Her!
O *Menelaus!* timely cease to strive,   50
With how much blood wilt thou thy loss retrieve?
From me, ye Gods, avert your heavy doom,
And bring my Dear, laden with Laurels home:
But my heart fails me, when I think of War,
The sad reflection costs me many a tear: 55
I tremble when I hear the very name
Of every place where thou shalt fight for fame;
Besides th' adventurous *Ravisher* well knew
The safest Arts his Villainy to pursue;

3 *Iphiclus, and the good old man* her father-in-law and her father, as the original makes clear.
4 *Bacchus' frolic rout* the god of wine and his drunken crew.
5 *Tyrian* purple, royal (famously produced at Tyre).

6 *Tissues* rich fabric interwoven with gold.
7 *Paris* the Trojan ravisher of Helen, whom he stole from Greek Menelaus.

In noble dress he did her heart surprise,   60
With gold he dazzled her unguarded Eyes,
He backed his Rape with Ships and armèd Men,
Thus stormed, thus took the beauteous Fortress in.
Against the power of Love and force of Arms
There's no security in the brightest Charms.   65
    Hector I fear, much do I *Hector* fear,[8]
A man (they say) experienced in War,
My Dear, if thou hast any love for me,
Of that same *Hector* prithee mindful be,
Fly him be sure, and every other Foe,   70
Lest each of them should prove an *Hector* too.
Remember, when for fight thou shalt prepare,
Thy *Laodamia* charged thee, Have a care,
For what wounds thou receiv'st, are giv'n to her.
If by thy valour *Troy* must ruined be,   75
May not the ruin leave one scar on thee;
Sharer in th' honour from the danger free!
Let *Menelaus* fight, and force his way
Through the false *Ravisher*'s Troops to his *Helena*.
Great be his Victory, as his Cause is good,   80
May he swim to her in his Enemies' blood,
Thy Case is different, – may'st thou live to see
(Dearest) no other Combatant but me!
    Ye gen'rous *Trojans,* turn your Swords away
From his dear Breast, find out a nobler prey,   85
Why should you harmless *Laodamia* slay?
My poor good natured Man did never know
What 'tis to fight, or how to face a Foe;
Yet in Love's Field what wonders can he do?
Great is his Prowess and his Fortune too;   90
Let them go fight, who know not how to woo.
    Now I must own, I feared to let thee go,
My trembling lips had almost told thee so.
When from thy Father's House thou didst withdraw,
Thy fatal stumble at the door I saw,   95
I saw it, sighed, and prayed the sign might be
Of thy return a happy Prophecy!
I cannot but acquaint thee with my fear,
Be not too brave, – Remember, – Have a care,
And all my dreads will vanish into Air.   100
    Among the *Grecians* someone must be found
That first shall set his foot on *Trojan* ground;

8 *Hector* the greatest of the Trojan warriors,
who kills Protesilaus.

Unhappy she that shall his loss bewail,
Grant, O ye Gods, thy courage then may fail.
    Of all the Ships, be thine the very last,   105
Thou the last man that lands; there needs no haste
To meet a potent, and a treacherous foe;
Thou'lt land I fear too soon, though ne'er so slow.
At thy return ply every Sail and Oar,
And nimbly leap on thy deserted shore.   110
    All the day long, and all the lonely night
Black thoughts of thee my anxious Soul affright:
Darkness, to other women's pleasures kind,
Augments, like Hell, the torments of my mind.
I court e'en Dreams, on my forsaken Bed,   115
False Joys must serve, since all my true are fled.
What's that same airy *Phantom* so like thee!
What wailings do I hear, what paleness see?
I wake, and hug myself, 'tis but a Dream –
The *Grecian* Altars know I feed their flame,   120
The want of hallowed Wine my tears supply,
Which make the sacred fire burn bright and high.
    When shall I clasp thee in these Arms of mine,
These longing Arms, and lie dissolved in thine?
When shall I have thee by thyself alone,   125
To learn the wondrous Actions thou hast done?
Which when in rapturous words thou hast begun
With many, and many a kiss, prithee tell on;
Such interruptions graceful pauses are;
A Kiss in Story 's but an Halt in War.   130
    But, when I think of *Troy,* of winds and waves,
I fear the pleasant dream my hope deceives:
Contrary winds in *Port* detain thee too,
In spite of wind and tide why wouldst thou go?
Thus, to thy Country thou wouldst hardly come,   135
In spite of wind & tide thou went'st from home.
To his own City *Neptune* stops the way,[9]
Revere the *Omen,* and the Gods obey.
Return ye furious *Grecians,* homeward fly,
Your stay is not of Chance, but Destiny: 140
How can your Arms expect desired success,
That thus contend for an *Adulteress?*
But, let not me forespeak you, no, – set Sail,[10]
And Heav'n befriend you with a prosperous gale!

---

9 *Neptune* one of the founders of Troy.   10 *forespeak* speak ahead of time or
                                                      beforehand.

Ye *Trojans!* with regret methinks I see   145
Your first encounter with your Enemy;
I see fair *Helen* put on all her Charms,
To buckle on her lusty Bridegroom's Arms;
She gives him Arms, and kisses she receives,
(I hate the transports each to other gives).   150
She leads him forth, and she commands him come
Safely victorious, and triumphant home,
And he (no doubt) will make no nice delay,[11]
But diligently do whate'er she say;
Now he returns! – see with what amorous speed   155
She takes the pond'rous Helmet from his head,
And courts the weary Champion to her bed.
    We women, too too credulous alas!
    Think what we fear, will surely come to pass.
Yet, while before the Leagure thou dost lie,[12]   160
Thy *Picture* is some pleasure to my Eye,
That, I caress in words most kind and free,
And lodge it on my Breast, as I would Thee;
There must be something in It more than Art,
'Twere very Thee, could it thy mind impart;   165
I kiss the pretty *Idol,* and complain,
As if (like Thee) 'twould answer me again.
    By thy return, by thy dear Self, I swear,
By our Love's Vows, which most religious are,
By thy belovèd Head, and those gray Hairs   170
Which Time may on it Snow, in future years,
I come, where'er thy Fate shall bid Thee go,
Eternal Partner of thy weal and woe,
So Thou but live, though all the Gods say No.
    Farewell, – but prithee very careful be   175
    Of thy beloved Self (I mean) of me.

from the *Ars Amatoria*

Book 1, lines 269–344

To prove the point that any girl can be won, Ovid gives a list of mythical women who succumbed to unnatural love. The proof is specious because the mythical examples are irrelevant to Augustan Rome. The purpose of this catalogue of immoral women is to entertain the reader with a witty and allusive anthology of

---

11   *nice* fussy, fastidious.   12   *Leagure* military camp.

scandalous myths. A similar list, which may have been partly suggested by this passage, is found in Chaucer's *Wife of Bath's Prologue* (pp. 7–9 above).

The translation is John Dryden's (1631–1700); it was published posthumously in 1709.

First then believe, all Women may be won;
Attempt with Confidence, the Work is done.
The Grasshopper shall first forbear to sing
In Summer Season, or the Birds in Spring,
Than Women can resist your flattering Skill: 5
Ev'n She will yield, who swears she never will.
To Secret Pleasure both the Sexes move;
But Women most, who most dissemble Love.
'Twere best for us, if they would first declare,
Avow their Passion, and submit to Prayer.   10
The Cow, by lowing, tells the Bull her Flame;
The neighing Mare invites her Stallion to the Game.
Man is more temp'rate in his Lust than they,
And more than Women can his Passion sway.
Byblis, we know, did first her Love declare,[1]   15
And had Recourse to Death in her Despair.
Her Brother She, her Father *Myrrha* sought,[2]
And loved, but loved not as a Daughter ought.
Now from a Tree she stills her odorous Tears,[3]
Which yet the Name of her who shed them bears.   20
    In *Ida*'s shady Vale a Bull appeared,[4]
White as the Snow, the fairest of the Herd;
A Beauty Spot of black there only rose,
Betwixt his equal Horns and ample Brows:
The Love and Wish of all the *Cretan* cows.   25
The Queen beheld him as his Head he reared,
And envied every Leap he gave the Herd.
A Secret Fire she nourished in her Breast,
And hated ev'ry Heifer he caressed.
A Story known, and known for true, I tell;   30
Nor *Crete*, though lying, can the Truth conceal.
She cut him Grass (so much can Love command);
She stroked, she fed him with her Royal Hand;
Was pleased in Pastures with the Herd to roam;

BOOK 1, LINES 269–344

1   *Byblis* girl who fell in love with her brother.
2   *Myrrha* girl who fell in love with her father; she was changed into a myrrh tree.
3   *stills* discharges; weeps.
4   *Ida* mountain in Crete.

And *Minos* by the Bull was overcome.[5]   35
    Cease, Queen, with Gems t'adorn thy beauteous Brows;
The Monarch of thy Heart no Jewel knows.
Nor in thy Glass compose thy Looks and Eyes;
Secure from all thy Charms thy Lover lies;
Yet trust thy Mirror, when it tells thee true;   40
Thou art no Heifer to allure his View.
Soon wouldst thou quit thy Royal Diadem
To thy fair Rivals, to be horned like them.
If *Minos* please, no Lover seek to find;
If not, at least seek one of human Kind.   45
    The wretched Queen the *Cretan* Court forsakes;
In Woods and Wilds her Habitation makes:
She curses ev'ry beauteous Cow she sees;
"Ah, why dost thou my Lord and Master please!
And think'st, ungrateful Creature as thou art,   50
With frisking awkwardly, to gain his Heart!"
She said, and straight commands, with frowning Look,
To put her, undeserving, to the Yoke;
Or feigns some holy Rites of Sacrifice,
And sees her Rival's Death with joyful Eyes: 55
Then, when the Bloody Priest has done his Part,
Pleased, in her Hand she holds the beating Heart;
Nor from a scornful Taunt can scarce refrain:
"Go, Fool, and strive to please my Love again."
    Now she would be *Europa*, *Io* now;[6]   60
(One bore a Bull, and one was made a Cow).
Yet she at last her Brutal Bliss obtained,
And in a wooden Cow the Bull sustained:
Filled with his Seed, accomplished her Desire,
Till, by his Form, the Son betrayed the Sire.   65
    If *Atreus'* Wife to Incest had not run,[7]
(But, ah, how hard it is to love but one!)
His Coursers *Phoebus* had not driv'n away,[8]
To shun that Sight, and interrupt the Day.
Thy Daughter, *Nisus*, pulled thy purple Hair,[9]   70
And barking Sea-Dogs yet her Bowels tear.

---

5 *Minos* king of Crete, whom Neptune punished for disobedience by making his wife, Pasiphae, fall in love with a bull; she satisfied her desire by entering a wooden cow that Daedalus built for her.

6 *Europa* girl whom Jupiter abducted in the disguise of a bull; *Io* girl whom Jupiter changed into a cow after raping her.

7 *Atreus' wife* Aerope, who committed adultery with her brother-in-law Thyestes; in revenge, Atreus fed Thyestes with his own children – an act that made the sun recoil in horror.

8 *Phoebus* the sun god.

9 *Daughter* Scylla; she betrayed her city to Minos, whom she loved, by cutting off her father's magic lock of hair.

At Sea and Land *Atrides* saved his Life,[10]
Yet fell a Prey to his adult'rous Wife.
Who knows not what Revenge *Medea* sought,[11]
When the slain Offspring bore the Father's Fault?   75
Thus *Phoenix* did a Woman's Love bewail;[12]
And thus *Hippolytus* by *Phaedra* fell.[13]
These Crimes revengeful Matrons did commit;
Hotter their Lust, and sharper is their Wit.[14]
Doubt not from them an easy Victory: 80
Scarce of a thousand Dames will one deny.

from the *Metamorphoses*

Book 1, lines 89–112

Ovid's treatment of the traditional topic of the Golden Age (compare Hesiod, *Works and Days*, pp. 282–3 above) emphasizes the absence of anxious human institutions such as law, sailing, and war. The spontaneous bounty of nature made all of these unnecessary in better days. The myth is probably as old as poetry itself, and it may never cease to be retold.

The translator of this passage from the *Metamorphoses* is George Sandys (1578–1644). The text is based on the first complete edition (1626). Sandys was a world traveler who went as far east as Turkey and as far west as Virginia. Though ornate by modern standards, Sandys's Ovid is much clearer than Golding's, its greatest predecessor; it has a kind of easy urbanity that seems suitable to Ovidian narrative.

The *Golden Age* was first; which uncompelled,
And without rule, in Faith and Truth excelled.
As then, there was nor punishment nor fear;[1]
Nor threat'ning Laws in brass prescribèd were;[2]
Nor suppliant crouching pris'ners shook to see   5
Their angry Judge; but all was safe and free.

---

10 *Atrides* Agamemnon; he was murdered by Clytemnestra on his return from Troy.
11 *Medea* wife of Jason; she killed their children to avenge his abandonment of her.
12 *Phoenix* son of Amyntor; wrongly accused of seducing Amyntor's mistress, he was blinded by his father.
13 *Hippolytus* son of Theseus; when he resisted

the sexual advances of his stepmother *Phaedra*, she accused him of rape and Theseus laid a curse on him that brought about his death.
14 *Wit* cunning; intelligence.

BOOK 1, LINES 89–112

1 *nor . . . nor* neither . . . nor.
2 *brass* bronze tablets displayed in public.

To visit other Worlds, no wounded Pine
Did yet from Hills to faithless Seas decline.[3]
Then, unambitious Mortals knew no more,[4]
But their own Country's Nature-bounded shore.   10
Nor Swords, nor Arms were yet: no trenches round
Besiegèd Towns, nor strifeful Trumpets' sound:
The Soldier of no use. In firm content
And harmless ease, then happy days were spent.
The yet-free Earth did of her own accord   15
(Untorn with ploughs) all sorts of fruit afford.
Content with Nature's un-enforcèd food,
They gather Wildings, Strawberries of the Wood,[5]
Sour Cornels, what upon the Bramble grows,[6]
And Acorns, which *Jove*'s spreading Oak bestows.[7]   20
'Twas always Spring: warm *Zephyrus* sweetly blew[8]
On smiling Flow'rs, which without setting grew.[9]
Forthwith the Earth corn, unmanurèd, bears;[10]
And every year renews her golden Ears:
With Milk and Nectar were the Rivers filled;   25
And yellow Honey from green Elms distilled.[11]

Book 1, lines 253–312

One of the most widespread myths of the Mediterranean world was that of the great Flood. Its most famous exposition occurs in the biblical Book of Genesis. Ovid tells the story too, but in his version, of course, it is Jupiter who destroys the wicked human race, and he does so by activating more auxiliaries and making more interesting choices than the comparatively dull though equally terrifying biblical God. Jonathan Swift probably remembered this passage in composing "A Description of a City Shower" (p. 109 above).

The translator again is Sandys (see p. 436 above).

And now about to let his lightning fly,
He feared lest so much flame should catch the sky,[1]
And burn heaven's Axletree. Besides, by doom[2]

---

3   *decline* descend.
4   *unambitious* added to Ovid.
5   *Wildings* crab apples.
6   *Cornels* berries of the cornel tree, or cornelian cherry.
7   *Jove's . . . Oak* by association with the sacred oak at Dodona, a sanctuary of Jupiter.
8   *Zephyrus* the gentle west wind.

9   *setting* planting.
10   *unmanurèd* literally, "unploughed."
11   *Elms* literally, "holm-oak."

BOOK 1, LINES 253–312

1   *He* Jupiter.
2   *Axletree* the imaginary shaft around which the universe revolves.

Of certain Fate, he knew the time should come,
When Sea, Earth, ravished Heaven, the curious Frame   5
Of this World's mass, should shrink in purging flame.
He therefore those *Cyclopean* darts rejects;[3]
And different-natured punishments elects:
To open all the Floodgates of the sky,
And Man by inundation to destroy.   10
    Rough *Boreas* in *Aeolian* prison laid,[4]
And those dry blasts which gathered Clouds invade;
Out flies the South, with dropping wings; who shrouds
His terrible aspect in pitchy clouds.[5]
His white hair streams, his swol'n Beard big with show'rs;   15
Mists bind his brows, Rain from his bosom pours.
As with his hands the hanging clouds he crushed,
They roared, and down in show'rs together rushed.
All-coloured *Iris, Juno's* messenger,[6]
To weeping Clouds doth nourishment confer.[7]   20
The Corn is lodged, the Husbandmen despair;[8]
Their long year's labour lost, with all their care.
Jove, not content with his ethereal rages,
His brother's auxiliary floods engages.[9]
The Streams convented, "'Tis too late to use   25
Much speech," said *Neptune*; "all your pow'rs effuse; [10]
Your doors unbar, remove whate'er restrains
Your liberal Waves, and give them the full reins."[11]
Thus chargèd, they return; their Springs unfold;
And to the Sea with headlong fury rolled.   30
He with his Trident strikes the Earth: She shakes;
And way for Water by her motion makes.
Through open fields now rush the spreading Floods,
And hurry with them Cattle, People, Woods,
Houses, and Temples with their Gods enclosed.   35
What such a force unoverthrown, opposed,[12]
The higher-swelling Water quite devours;

---

3 *Cyclopean* forged by the Cyclopes, the giant smiths of Vulcan.

4 *Boreas* the north wind; *Aeolian prison* the cave of the winds on the island of Aeolia (compare Virgil, *Aeneid* 1.50-63; p. 365 above). Jupiter confines all winds except the stormy *South*.

5 *aspect* face or countenance; *pitchy* black.

6 *Iris* goddess of the rainbow and divine messenger.

7 *nourishment* i.e. moisture sucked up by the rainbow.

8 *Corn* any kind of grain for food or fodder; *lodged* beaten down; *Husbandmen* farmers.

9 *brother* Neptune, god of the sea.

10 *convented . . . Neptune* having assembled (the streams) in one place, Neptune said to them. . . .

11 *liberal* free, liberated.

12 *What . . . opposed* whatever (house) withstood the rush of waters; *unoverthrown* an exact rendition of Ovid's *indeiecta* (not thrown down).

Which hides th' aspiring tops of swallowed tow'rs.
Now Land and Sea no different visage bore:
For, all was Sea, nor had the Sea a shore.   40
He, takes a Hill: He, in a Boat deplores;[13]
And, where He lately plowed, now strikes his Oars,
O'er Corn, o'er drownèd Villages He sails:
He, from high Elms entangled Fishes hales.[14]
In Fields they anchor cast, as Chance did guide: 45
And Ships the underlying Vineyards hide.
Where Mountain-loving Goats did lately graze,
The Sea-calf now his ugly body lays.[15]
Groves, Cities, Temples, covered by the Deep,
The Nymphs admire; in woods the Dolphins keep,   50
And chase about the boughs: the Wolf doth swim[16]
Amongst the Sheep: the Lion (now not grim)
And Tigers tread the Waves. Swift feet no more
Avail the Hart; nor wounding tusks the Boar.[17]
The wand'ring Birds, hid Earth long sought in vain,   55
With weary wings descend into the Main.
Licentious Seas o'er drownèd Hills now fret;[18]
And unknown surges Eyrie Mountains beat.[19]
The Waves the greater part devour; the rest
Death, with long-wanted sustenance, oppressed.   60

Book 1, lines 452–567

This selection contains the myth of Apollo's attempted rape of Daphne. The myth of Daphne is etiological: it explains the origin of the use of the laurel as an emblem of victory. However, Ovid's main interest lies in depicting the effect of love on the arrogant Apollo, who boasts of his archery to Cupid only to find out that Cupid excels him. Striking a distinctly unheroic pose, Apollo woos Daphne like a lover in Roman elegy, and, when she will not listen, surrenders all his dignity in giving chase. Ovid's wonderful description of Daphne's metamorphosis was the inspiration for Bernini's statue of Apollo and Daphne, which similarly catches the transformation in mid-process. Among its literary echoes is the flight of Cloris in Behn's "The Disappointment" (p. 99 above).

The translator again is George Sandys (see p. 436 above).

---

13 *He . . . He* one man . . . another man; *deplores* weeps or laments.
14 *hales* literally, "catches."
15 *Sea-calf* seal.
16 *chase about* Ovid's dolphins blunder into oak trees.

17 *Hart* stag; a male deer with mature horns.
18 *fret* chew; consume; destroy.
19 *Eyrie Mountains* mountains that serve as nesting places for eagles and other birds of prey.

Peneian Daphne was his first beloved:[1]
Not Chance, but *Cupid*'s wrath, that fury moved.
Whom *Delius* (proud of his late Conquest) saw,[2]
As he his pliant Bow began to draw;
And said: "Lascivious Boy, how ill agree   5
Thou and these Arms! too Manly far for thee.
Such suit our shoulders, whose strong arm confounds[3]
Both Man and Beast, with never missing wounds;
That *Python*, bristled with thick Arrows, quelled,[4]
Who o'er so many poisoned Acres swelled.   10
Be thou content to kindle with thy Flame
Desires we know not; nor our praises claim."
Then, Venus' son: "Self-praisèd ever be:[5]
All may thy Bow transfix, as mine shall thee.
As much as Jove excelleth human pow'rs;   15
So much thy glory is excelled by ours."
With that, he breaks the Air with nimble wings,
And to *Parnassus*' shady summit Springs;[6]
Two different arrows from his Quiver draws:
One, hate of Love; the other Love doth cause.   20
What caused, was sharp, and had a golden Head:
But what repulsed, was blunt, and tipped with Lead.
The God this in *Peneia* fixed: that struck[7]
Apollo's bones and in his Marrow stuck.
Forthwith he loves; a Lover's name she flies: 25
And emulating unwed *Phoebe*, joys[8]
In spoils of savage Beasts, and sylvan Lairs;
A fillet binding her neglected hairs.[9]
Her, many sought: but she, averse to all,
Unknown to Man, nor brooking such a thrall,[10]   30
Frequents the pathless Woods, and hates to prove,
Nor cares to hear, what *Hymen* is, or Love.[11]
Oft said her Father: "Daughter, thou do'st owe
A Son-in-law, who Nephews may bestow."[12]

BOOK 1, LINES 452–567

1 *Peneian* Daphne's father was the river god Peneus; *his* Apollo's.

2 *Delius* Apollo, who was born on Delos; *Conquest* his defeat at Delphi of the Python, a huge snake.

3 *our* i.e. my; formal or "royal" form of the singular.

4 *that* who (an old form of the relative pronoun used of things and beings).

5 *Venus' son* Cupid.

6 *Parnassus* the mountain overlooking Delphi.

7 *this . . . that* the latter . . . the former (a Latinism); *Peneia* Daphne.

8 *Phoebe* Diana.

9 *fillet* a woolen band worn in religious rituals.

10 *Unknown to Man* a virgin; *thrall* bondage.

11 *Hymen* god of marriage; hence marriage itself.

12 *Nephews* grandsons.

But she, who Marriage as a Crime eschewed   35
(Her Face with blushing shamefac'dness imbued)
Hung on his neck with fawning arms, and said,
"Dear Father, give me leave to live a Maid:
This boon *Diana*'s did to her afford."[13]
He, too indulgent, gave thee his accord:[14]   40
But thee, thy excellency countermands;
And thy own beauty thy desire withstands.
Apollo loves, and fain would *Daphne* wed:
What he desires, he hopes; and is misled
By his own Oracles. As stubbles burn,   45
As hedges into sudden blazes turn,
Fire set too near, or left by chance behind
By passengers, and scattered with the wind:
So springs he into flames: a fire doth move
Through all his veins: hope feeds his barren love.   50
He on her shoulders sees her hair untressed:
"O what," said he, "if these were neatly dressed!"
He sees her Eyes, two Stars! her Lips which kiss
Their happy Selves, and longs to taste their bliss:
Admires her fingers, hands, her arms half bare;   55
And Parts unseen conceives to be more rare.
Swifter than following Winds, away she runs;
And him, for all this his entreaty, shuns.
   "Stay Nymph, I pray thee stay; I am no Foe:
So Lambs from Wolves, Harts fly from Lions so;   60
So from the Eagle springs the trembling Dove:
They, from their deaths: but my pursuit is Love.
Woe's me, if thou should't fall, or thorns should race[15]
Thy tender legs, whilst I enforce the chase!
These roughs are craggy: moderate thy haste,   65
And, trust me, I will not pursue so fast.
Yet know, who 'tis you please: No Mountaineer,
No homebred Clown; nor keep I Cattle here.[16]
From whom thou fly'st thou know'st not (silly fool!)
And therefore fly'st thou. I in *Delphos* rule.[17]   70
Ionian Claros, Lycian Patara,
And Sea-girt *Tenedos* do me obey.[18]
Jove is my Father. What shall be, hath been,
Or is, by my instructive rays is seen.

13 *Diana's* Jupiter.
14 *thee* Daphne, apostrophized by the poet.
15 *race* cut; etch.
16 *Clown* rustic; uneducated farmhand.

17 *Delphos* Delphi, site of the famous oracle of Apollo.
18 *Claros ... Patara ... Tenedos* cult sites of Apollo in Asia Minor.

Immortal Verse from our invention springs;[19]   75
And how to strike the well-concording strings.[20]
My shafts hit sure: yet He one surer found,[21]
Who in my empty bosom made this wound.
Of herbs I found the virtue; and through all[22]
The World they Me the great Physician call.   80
Ay me, that herbs can Love no cure afford!
That Arts, relieving all, should fail their Lord!"
   More had he said, when she, with nimble dread,
From him, and his unfinished courtship fled.
How graceful then! The Wind that obvious blew,[23]   85
Too much betrayed her to his amorous view;
And played the Wanton with her fluent hair:[24]
Her Beauty, by her flight, appeared more rare.[25]
No more the God will his entreaties lose;
But, urged by Love, with all his force pursues.   90
As when a Hare the speedy Greyhound spies,
His feet for prey, she hers for safety plies;
Now bears he up; now, now he hopes to fetch her;
And, with his snout extended, strains to catch her:
Not knowing whether caught or no, she slips   95
Out of his wide-stretched jaws, and touching lips.
The God and Virgin in such strife appear:
He, quickened by his hope; She, by her fear,
But, the Pursuer doth more nimble prove:
Enabled by th' industrious wings of love.   100
Nor gives he time to breathe: now at her heels,
His breath upon her dangling hair she feels.
Clean spent, and fainting, her affrighted blood
Forsakes her cheeks. She cries unto the Flood.[26]
"Help Father, if your streams contain a Power!   105
May Earth, for too well pleasing, me devour:
Or, by transforming, O destroy this shape,
That thus betrays me to undoing rape."
Forthwith, a numbness all her limbs possessed;
And slender films her softer sides invest.   110
Hair into leaves, her Arms to branches grow:
And late swift feet, now roots, are less than slow.
Her graceful head a leafy top sustains:

---

19 *our* i.e. my (see n. 3 above).
20 *Verse . . . strings* Apollo is the god of poetry
and music.
21 *He* Cupid; Venus' son.
22 *virtue* power.

23 *obvious* against; in the face (a Latinism, for
Ovid's *obvia*).
24 *Wanton* unruly boy; *fluent* flowing.
25 *rare* "splendid; excellent; fine" (*OED*).
26 *Flood* the river Peneus, home of her father.

One beauty throughout all her form remains.
Still *Phoebus* loves. He handles the new Plant;   115
And feels her Heart within the bark to pant:
Embraced the bole, as he would her have done;[27]
And kissed the boughs: the boughs his kisses shun.
To whom the God: "Although thou canst not be
The Wife I wished, yet shalt thou be my Tree,   120
Our Quiver, Harp, our Tresses never shorn,[28]
My Laurel, thou shalt evermore adorn;
And Brows triumphant, when they *Io* sing,[29]
And to the Capitol their Trophies bring.[30]
Thou shalt defend from Thunder's blasting stroke,   125
Augustus' doors, on either side the Oak.[31]
And, as our uncut hair no change receives,
So ever flourish with unfading leaves."
Here *Paean* ends. The Laurel all allows:[32]
In sign whereof her grateful head she bows.   130

Book 2, lines 760–832

When Mercury fell in love with Herse, daughter of the king of Athens, and tried to visit her, he was stopped by Herse's sister Aglauros, who demanded a bribe. The sight of this infuriated Minerva, who was already angry at Aglauros for peeking into a chest containing the infant Ericthonius that Minerva had left in her and her sisters' care with strict instructions not to open it. Minerva travels to the house of Envy, whom she persuades to infect Aglauros with envy of her sister Herse. While attempting to deny entry to Mercury, when he returns, Aglauros is turned to stone. Ovid's description of Envy is the first of several personification allegories in the *Metamorphoses*. In its fullness and ingenuity it far exceeds previous attempts at allegory of this kind, such as Virgil's description of Gossip in Book 4 of the *Aeneid*. Ovid's Envy, followed by a few other personifications (such as that of Sleep in *Metamorphoses* 11), established an allegorizing trend in epic poetry that expanded in the Middle Ages and Renaissance. Although much allegorical poetry intervened, ultimately, Ovid's house of Envy is the model for Alexander Pope's Cave of Spleen in Canto 4 of *The Rape of the Lock* (pp. 120–2 above).

27 *bole* trunk of the tree.
28 *our* i.e. my.
29 *Io* ceremonial cry in a Roman triumphal procession, where the victorious general wore a crown wreathed in laurel.
30 *Capitol* hill in Rome where triumphal processions terminated and sacrifice to Jupiter took place.

31 *Augustus* the first emperor; in 27 BCE the senate decreed that he be honored with a crown of oak leaves hanging on his door and laurel bushes growing each side of it.
32 *Paean* Apollo.

The translator is, again, George Sandys (see p. 436 above).

Forthwith to *Envy's* cave her course she bent,[1]
Furred with black filth, within a deep descent
Between two hills; where *Phoebus* never shows[2]
His cheerful face; where no wind ever blows:
Replete with sadness, and unactive cold;   5
Devoid of fire, yet still in smoke enrolled.
Whither whenas the feared in battle came,
She stayed before the house (that hateful frame
She might not enter) and the dark door struck
With her bright lance; which straight in sunder broke.   10
There saw she *Envy* lapping Viper's blood;
And feeding on their flesh, her vice's food:
And, having seen her, turned away her eyes.
The Caitiff slowly from the ground doth rise[3]
(Her half-devourèd Serpents laid aside)   15
And forward creepeth with a lazy stride.
Viewing her form so fair; her arms, so bright;
She groaned, and sighed at such a cheerful sight.
Her body more than meager; pale her hue;
Her teeth all rusty; still she looks askew;   20
Her breast with gall, her tongue with poison swelled:
She only laughed, when she sad sights beheld.
Her ever-waking cares exiled soft sleep:
Who looks on good success with eyes that weep;
Repining, pines: who, wounding others, bleeds: 25
And on her self revengeth her misdeeds.
Although *Tritonia* did the Hag detest;[4]
Yet briefly thus her pleasure she expressed:
"*Aglauros*, one of the *Cecropides*,[5]
Do thou infest with thy accursed disease."   30
This said; the hasty Goddess doth advance
Her body, with her earth-repelling lance.
Envy cast after her a wicked eye,
Mutters, and could for very sorrow die
That such her power: a snaggy staff then took   35
Wreathèd with thorns, and her dark Cave forsook.
Wrapped in black clouds, which way so e'er she turns,
The Corn she lodges, flow'ry pastures burns,[6]

BOOK 2, LINES 760–832   4   *Tritonia* Minerva.
1   *she* Minerva.   5   *Cecropides* daughters of Cecrops, king of
2   *Phoebus* the sun.   Athens.
3   *Caitiff* wretch.   6   *Corn* any grain; *lodges* flattens.

Crops what grows high; Towns, Nations, with her breath
Pollutes; and Virtue persecutes to death.   40
When she the fair *Athenian* tow'rs beheld,
Which so in wealth, in learned Arts excelled,
And feastful Peace; to cry she scarce forbears,
In that she saw no argument for tears.
When she *Aglauros'* lodging entered had,   45
She gladly executes what *Pallas* bade:[7]
Her cankered hand upon her breast she laid,
And crooked thorns into her heart conveyed,
And breathed in baneful poison; which she sheds
Into her bones, and through her spirits spreads.   50
And that her envy might not want a cause;
The God in his divinest form she draws:
And with it, sets before her wounded eyes
Her happy sister, and their nuptial joys:
Augmenting all. These secret woes excite,   55
And gnaw her soul. She sighs all day, all night;
And with a slow infection melts away,
Like Ice before the Sun's uncertain ray.
Fair *Herse's* happy state such heart-burn breeds[8]
In her black bosom, as when spiny weeds[9]   60
Are set on fire: which without flame consume,
And seem (so small their heat) to burn with fume.[10]
Oft she resolves to die, such sights to shun:
Oft, by disclosing, to have both undone.
Now sits she on the threshold, to prevent   65
The God's access; who with lost blandishment,
And his best Art, persuades. Quoth she, "Forbear;
I cannot be removed, if you stay here."
"I to this bargain," he replied, "will stand."
The figured door then forces with his wand.   70
Striving to rise, to second her debate,
Her hips could not remove, pressed with dull weight.
Again she struggled to have stood on end:
But, those unsupple sinews would not bend.
Encroaching cold now enters at her nails: 75
And lack of blood her veins' blue branches pales.
And as a Canker, slighting helpless Arts,
Creeps from th' infected to the sounder parts:
So by degrees the winter of wan Death
Congeals the path of life, and stops her breath: 80

---

7 *Pallas* Minerva.   9 *spiny* hard and dry.
8 *Herse* sister of Aglauros loved by Mercury.   10 *fume* smoke.

Nor strove she: had she strove to make her moan,
Voice had no way; her neck and face now stone.
There she a bloodless Statue sat, all freckt:[11]
Her spotted mind the Marble did infect.

Book 3, lines 316–510

The myths in Books 3–4 of the *Metamorphoses* revolve around the House of
Cadmus, founder of Thebes. In the section preceding the present selection, Ovid
tells the story of Semele, daughter of Cadmus and mother by Jupiter of the god
Dionysus (or Bacchus), who was tricked by jealous Juno into asking Jupiter to
appear to her in his full glory, thus ensuring her destruction. The present selection
falls into two parts – the short story of Tiresias, the famous prophet who appears
in many Theban plays of the Greek tragedians, and the lengthy tale of Narcissus,
which is interwoven with the tale of the nymph Echo. Both stories are etiological:
that is, they explain the origin of something – in the first case, the blindness and
prophetic ability of Tiresias, and in the second, the phenomenon of echoes and
the existence of the narcissus flower. Ovid, however, is less interested in etiology
than in the subjects of sexuality and knowledge: the Narcissus sequence is a bril-
liant exploration of both. Ovid's version has become canonical, but before his
treatment the story of Narcissus was neither well known, nor, as far as we can tell,
connected with that of Echo. Ovid makes of these characters a complementary yet
dysfunctional pair – the one paralyzed by his own reflection, the other dependent
on the words of others – whose deficiencies prevent a normal relationship and
doom them to waste away from frustration. Ovid's narrative has been vastly influ-
ential, not least upon the thought of Sigmund Freud. In this anthology we have
noted its influence on Milton's depiction of Eve in *Paradise Lost* 4 (pp. 80–1
above) and poem 15 of Housman's *A Shropshire Lad* (p. 217 above).

The translation, again, is by George Sandys (see p. 436 above).

While this on earth befell by Fates' decree
(The twice-born *Bacchus* now from danger free),[1]
Jove, weighty cares expelling from his breast
With flowing Nectar, and disposed to jest
With well-pleased *Juno*, said: "In *Venus'* deeds,   5
The Female's pleasure far the Male's exceeds."
This she denies; *Tiresias* must decide[2]

---

11 *freckt* freckled; spotted.

BOOK 3, LINES 316–510

1 *twice-born* having been rescued from Semele's

womb, Bacchus was born a second time from his
father Jupiter's thigh.

2 *Tiresias* mythical prophet of Thebes.

The difference, who both delights had tried.
For, two engend'ring Serpents once he found,[3]
And with a stroke their slimy twists unbound;   10
Who straight a Woman of a Man became:
Seven Autumns fast, he in the eighth the same
Refinding, said: "If such your power, so strange,
That they who strike you must their nature change;
Once more I'll try." Then, struck, away they ran: 15
And of a Woman he became a Man.
He, chosen Umpire of this sportful strife,
Jove's words confirmed. This vexed his froward wife[4]
More than the matter craved. To wreak her spite,[5]
His eyes she muffled in eternal night.   20
Th' omnipotent (since no God may undo
Another's deed) with Fates which should ensue
Informed his Intellect; and did supply
His body's eyesight, with his mind's clear eye.
    He giving sure replies to such as came,   25
Through all th' *Aonian* Cities stretched his fame.[6]
First, blue *Liriope* sad trial made[7]
How that was but too true which he had said:
Whom in times past *Cephisus*' flood embraced[8]
Within his winding streams, and forced the chaste.   30
The lovely Nymph (who not unfruitful proved)
Brought forth a Boy, even then to be beloved,
Narcissus named. Enquiring if old age
Should crown his Youth; He, in obscure presage,
Made this reply: "Except himself he know."[9]   35
Long, they no credit on his words bestow:
Yet did the event the prophecy approve,[10]
In his strange ruin, and new kind of love.
Now, he to twenty added had a year:[11]
Now in his looks both Boy and Man appear.   40
Many a love-sick Youth did him desire;
And many a Maid his beauty set on fire:
Yet, in his tender age his pride was such,
That neither Youth nor Maiden might him touch.
    The vocal Nymph, this lovely Boy did spy   45

---

3 *engend'ring* copulating.
4 *froward* oppositional; ungovernable.
5 *craved* required, warranted.
6 *Aonian* Boeotian (the region of Thebes).
7 *Liriope* a nymph.

8 *Cephisus* a Boeotian river.
9 *Except himself he know* unless he knows himself.
10 *event* outcome; happenings; *approve* vindicate.
11 *twenty* he is only 16 in Ovid.

(She could not proffer speech, nor not reply)
When busy in pursuit of salvage spoils,[12]
He drove the deer into his corded toils.[13]
Echo was then a Body, not a Voice:[14]
Yet then, as now, of words she wanted choice;   50
But only could reiterate the close
Of every speech. This *Juno* did impose.
For, often when she might have taken *Jove*,
Compressing there the Nymphs, who weakly strove;[15]
Her long discourses made the Goddess stay,   55
Until the Nymphs had time to run away.
Which when perceived, she said, "For this abuse
Thy tongue henceforth shall be of little use."
Those threats are deeds: She yet ingeminates[16]
The last of sounds, and what she hears relates.   60
    Narcissus seen, intending thus the chase;
She forthwith glows, and with a noiseless pace
His steps pursues; the more she did pursue,
More hot (as nearer to her fire) she grew:
And might be likened to a sulph'rous match;[17]   65
Which instantly th' approachèd flame doth catch.
How oft would she have wooed him with sweet words!
But, Nature no such liberty affords:
Begin she could not, yet full readily
To his expected speech she would reply.   70
The Boy, from his Companions parted, said;
"Is any nigh?" "I," *Echo* answer made.
He, round about him gazèd (much appalled)
And cried out, "Come." She him, who callèd, called.
Then looking back; and seeing none appeared,   75
"Why shun'st thou me?" The selfsame voice he heard,
Deceivèd by the Image of his words;
"Then let us join," said he: no sound accords
More to her wish: her faculties combine
In dear consent; who answered, "*Let us join!*"   80
Flatt'ring herself, out of the Woods she sprung;[18]
And would about his struggling neck have hung.
Thrust back; he said, "Life shall this breast forsake,
Ere thou, light Nymph, on me thy pleasure take."

---

12 *salvage spoils* rustic trophies; i.e. wild animals,
with their hides and horns.
13 *toils* nets.
14 *Echo* a nymph capable only of repeating, not
initiating, speech.

15 *Compressing* embracing sexually (*OED*).
16 *ingeminates* doubles; echoes (for Ovid's
ingeminat).
17 *match* in Ovid a pine torch.
18 *Flatt'ring* encouraging, inspiring hope in.

"On me thy pleasure take," the Nymph replies   85
To that disdainful boy, who from her flies.
Despised; the wood her sad retreat receives:
Who covers her ashamèd face with leaves;
And skulks in desert Caves. Love still possessed
Her soul; through grief of her repulse, increased.   90
Her wretched body pines with sleepless care;
Her skin contracts: her blood converts to air.
Nothing was left her now but voice and bones:
The voice remains; the other turn to stones.
Concealed in Woods, in Mountains never found,   95
She's heard of all: and all is but a Sound.[19]
   Thus her, thus other Nymphs, in mountains born,
And sedgy brooks, the Boy had killed with scorn.
Thus many a Youth he had afore deceived:
When one thus prayed, with hands to heav'n upheaved;   100
"So may he love himself, and so despair!"
Rhamnusia condescends to his just prayer.[20]
   A Spring there was, whose silver Waters were
As smooth as any mirror, nor less clear:
Which neither Herdsmen, tame, nor savage Beast,   105
Nor wand'ring Fowl, nor scattered leaves molest;
Girt round with grass, by neighb'ring moisture fed,
And Woods, against the Sun's invasion spread.
He, tired with heat and hunting, with the Place
And Spring delighted, lies upon his face.   110
Quenching his thirst, another thirst doth rise;
Raised by the form which in that glass he spies.[21]
The hope of nothing doth his powers invade:
And for a body he mistakes a shade.[22]
Himself, himself distracts: who pores thereon   115
So fixedly, as if of *Parian* stone.[23]
Beholds his eyes, two stars! his dangling hair
Which with unshorn *Apollo's* might compare!
His fingers worthy *Bacchus*! his smooth chin![24]
His Ivory neck! his heav'nly face! wherein   120
The linkèd Deities their Graces fix!

19 *heard of all* heard by all.
20 *Rhamnusia* Nemesis, goddess of vengeance,
who had a sanctuary at Rhamnus.
21 *Raised* roused, excited; *glass* mirror (the
smooth surface of the spring).
22 *shade* shadow.

23 *Parian stone* white marble from the island of
Paros, valued as a medium for sculpture.
24 *fingers* translates a manuscript variant rejected
in modern texts, which say, literally, "hair worthy
of Bacchus, worthy of Apollo too."

Where Roses with unsullied Lilies mix![25]
Admireth all; for which, to be admired:[26]
And unconsiderately himself desired.
The praises, which he gives, his beauty claimed.   125
Who seeks, is sought: th' Inflamer is inflamed.
How often would he kiss the flatt'ring spring!
How oft with down-thrust arms sought he to cling
About that lovèd neck! Those coz'ning lips
Delude his hopes; and from himself he slips.   130
Not knowing what, with what he sees he fries:[27]
And th' error that deceives, incites his eyes.
O Fool! that striv'st to catch a flying shade!
Thou seek'st what's nowhere: Turn aside, 'twill vade.[28]
Thy form's reflection doth thy sight delude: 135
Which is with nothing of its own endued.
With thee it comes; with thee it stays; and so
'Twould go away, hadst thou the power to go.
Nor sleep, nor hunger could the Lover raise:[29]
Who, laid along, on that false form doth gaze   140
With looks, which looking never could suffice;
And ruinates himself with his own eyes.
At length, a little lifting up his head:
   "You Woods, that round about your branches spread,
Was ever so unfortunate a Lover!   145
You know, to many you have been a cover;
From your first growth to this long distant day
Have you known any, thus to pine away!
I like, and see: but yet I cannot find
The liked, and seen. O Love, with error blind!   150
What grieves me more; no Sea, no Mountain steep,
No waves, no walls, our joys asunder keep:
Whom but a little water doth divide;
And he himself desires to be enjoyed.
As oft as I to kiss the flood decline,[30]   155
So oft his lips ascend, to close with mine.
You'd think we touched: so small a thing doth part
Our equal loves! Come forth, what e'er thou art.
Sweet Boy, a simple Boy beguile not so:

---

25 *Roses . . . Lilies* an ideal complexion – white
skin with ruddy highlights.
26 *Admireth . . . admired* he admires all for
which he is to be admired; one of many verbal
mirror effects that Ovid creates to convey the situ-
ation of Narcissus.

27 *fries* literally, "burns."
28 *vade* disappear; fade.
29 *Nor . . . nor* neither . . . nor.
30 *decline* lie down.

From him that seeks thee, whither would'st thou go?   160
My age nor beauty merit thy disdain:
And me the Nymphs have often loved in vain.
Yet in thy friendly shows my poor hopes live;
Still striving to receive the hand I give:
Thou smil'st my smiles: when I a tear let fall,   165
Thou shed'st another; and consent'st in all.
And, lo, thy sweetly-moving lips appear
To utter words, that come not to our ear.
Ah, He is I! now, now I plainly see:
Nor is't my shadow that bewitcheth me.   170
With love of me I burn (oh too too sure!);
And suffer in those flames which I procure.
Shall I be wooed, or woo? What shall I crave?
Since what I covet, I already have.
Too much hath made me poor! O, you divine   175
And favoring Powers, me from myself disjoin!
Of what I love, I would be dispossessed:
This, in a Lover, is a strange request!
Now, strength through grief decays: short is the time
I have to live; extinguished in my Prime.   180
Nor grieves it me to part with well-missed breath;
For grief will find a perfect cure in death:
Would he I love might longer life enjoy!
Now, two ill-fated Lovers, in one, die."
　　This said; again upon his Image gazed;   185
Tears on the troubled water circles raised:
The motion much obscured the fleeting shade.
With that, he cried (perceiving it to vade),
"O, whither wilt thou! stay: nor cruèl prove,
In leaving me, who infinitely love.   190
Yet let me see, what cannot be possessed;
And, with that empty food, my fury feast."
Complaining thus, himself he disarrays;[31]
And to remorseless hands his breast displays:
The blows that solid snow with crimson stripe;[32]   195
Like Apples parti-red, or Grapes scarce ripe.
But, in the water when the same appear,
He could no longer such a sorrow bear.
As Virgin wax dissolves with fervent heat;[33]
Or morning frost, whereon the Sunbeams beat: 200
So thaws he with the ardour of desire;

---

31 *disarrays* disrobes.   33 *Virgin wax* white wax.
32 *that solid snow* his snow-white breast.

And, by degrees, consumes in unseen fire.[34]
His meagre cheeks now lost their red and white;
That life, that favour lost, which did delight.
Nor those divine proportions now remain,   205
So much by *Echo* lately loved in vain.
Which when she saw; although she angry were,
And still in mind her late repulse did bear;
As often as the miserable cried,
"Alas!" "Alas," the woeful Nymph replied.   210
And ever when he struck his sounding breast,
Like sounds of mutual sufferance expressed.
His last words were, still hanging o'er his shade;
"Ah, Boy, belov'd in vain!" so *Echo* said.
"Farewell." "Farewell," sighed she. Then down he lies: 215
Death's cold hand shuts his self-admiring eyes:
Which now eternally their gazes fix
Upon the Waters of infernal *Styx*.[35]
The woeful *Naiades* lament the dead;[36]
And their clipped hair upon their brother spread.   220
The woeful *Dryades* partake their woes:[37]
With both, sad *Echo* joins at every close.
The funeral Pile prepared, a Hearse they brought
To fetch his body, which they vainly sought.
Instead whereof a yellow flower was found,[38]   225
With tufts of white about the button crowned.

Book 15, lines 143–260

A large part of *Metamorphoses* 15 is devoted to the speech of the Greek philosopher
Pythagoras. Pythagoras taught the doctrine of metempsychosis or the transmigra-
tion of souls – the belief that the soul enters another body upon death. As a corol-
lary of this, he and his followers practiced vegetarianism. Like nearly everyone else
in the poem, Ovid's Pythagoras is a humorous character; his obsession with the
sin of eating flesh is laughable in Ovid's view. His tirade against the practice pre-
cedes the selection below in which he explains the doctrine of transmigration and
launches into a grandiloquent speech on the theme of universal change. The topic
of change resonates with the whole *Metamorphoses*, whose very title refers to
transformation from one shape into another. Among the works which the passage
has inspired are Shakespeare's Sonnet 60 (p. 47 above) and Belinda's dream in
Pope's *Rape of the Lock* 1 (pp. 115–18 above).

34 *consumes* is consumed.
35 *Styx* the river of the underworld.
36 *Naiades* water nymphs.
37 *Dryades* wood nymphs.
38 *flower* the narcissus.

The translator is Arthur Golding (1535/1536–1606), whose work as a translator was mostly confined to works of religion and religious controversy. Completed in 1567, Golding's Ovid is the first translation into English of the full *Metamorphoses*. Shakespeare, Spenser, and Marlowe all read Golding and were deeply influenced by him. Ezra Pound called Golding's Ovid "the most beautiful book in our language." Golding's 14-syllable lines expand Ovid and lengthen the reading experience but they do not slow it down, and they are faithful to Ovid's sense.[1]

"And forasmuch as God this instant hour[2]
Doth move my tongue to speak, I will obey his heavenly power.
My God *Apollo*'s temple I will set you open, and[3]
Disclose the wondrous heavens themselves, and make you understand
The Oracles and secrets of the Godly majesty.   5
Great things, and such as wit of man could never yet espy,
And such as have been hidden long, I purpose to descry.
I mind to leave the earth, and up among the stars to sty.[4]
I mind to leave this grosser place, and in the clouds to fly,
And on stout *Atlas*' shoulders strong to rest myself on high,[5]   10
And looking down from heaven on men that wander here and there
In dreadful fear of death as though they void of reason were,
To give them exhortation thus: and plainly to unwind
The whole discourse of destiny as nature hath assigned.
O men amazed with dread of death, why fear ye *Limbo Styx*,[6]   15
And other names of vanity, which are but *Poets*' tricks?
And perils of another world all false surmisèd gear?[7]
For whether fire or length of time consume the bodies here,
Ye well may think that further harms they cannot suffer more.
For souls are free from death. Howbeit, they leaving evermore   20
Their former dwellings are received and live again in new.
For I myself (right well in mind I bear it to be true)
Was in the time of Trojan war *Euphorbus Panthus*' son,[8]
Quite through whose heart the deathful spear of *Menelay* did run.[9]
I late ago in *Juno*'s Church at *Argos* did behold[10]   25

BOOK 15, LINES 143–260

1 Our introductory notes are indebted to the *ODNB* article on Golding by John Considine.
2 Ovid's Pythagoras, a somewhat foolish philosopher, is speaking as the passage opens.
3 *Apollo* god of prophecy and poetry.
4 *sty* ascend.
5 *Atlas* a giant who holds up the sky.
6 *Limbo* in Christian thought a region on the border of Hell; hence analogous to the river Styx, which souls crossed over to enter the underworld.
7 *gear* stuff; discourse.
8 *Euphorbus* a Trojan; son of Panthus.
9 *Menelay* Menelaus; brother of Agamemnon and Helen's husband.
10 *Juno* wife to Jupiter, and an enemy to the Trojans; *Argos* Greek city.

And knew the target which I in my left hand there did hold.[11]
All things do change. But nothing sure doth perish. This same sprite
Doth fleet, and fisking here and there doth swiftly take his flight[12]
From one place to another place, and ent'reth every wight,[13]
Removing out of man to beast, and out of beast to man.   30
But yet it never perisheth nor never perish can.
And even as supple wax with ease receiveth figures strange,
And keeps not aye one shape, ne bides assurèd aye from change,[14]
And yet continueth always wax in substance: So I say
The soul is aye the selfsame thing it was, and yet astray   35
It fleeteth into sundry shapes. Therefore lest Godliness
Be vanquished by outrageous lust of belly beastliness,[15]
Forbear (I speak by prophecy) your kinsfolk's ghosts to chase[16]
By slaughter: neither nourish blood with blood in any case.
And sith on open sea the winds do blow my sails apace,[17]   40
In all the world there is not that that standeth at a stay.
Things ebb and flow: and every shape is made to pass away.
The time itself continually is fleeting like a brook.
For neither brook nor lightsome time can tarry still. But look
As every wave drives other forth, and that that comes behind   45
Both thrusteth and is thrust itself: Even so the times by kind[18]
Do fly and follow both at once, and evermore renew.
For that that was before is left, and straight there doth ensue
Another that was never erst. Each twinkling of an eye[19]
Doth change. We see that after day comes night and darks the sky,   50
And after night the lightsome Sun succeedeth orderly.
Like colour is not in the heaven when all things weary lie
At midnight sound asleep, as when the daystar clear and bright
Comes forth upon his milk-white steed. Again in other plight
The morning, *Pallant*'s daughter fair, the messenger of light[20]   55
Delivereth into *Phoebus*' hands the world of clearer hue.[21]
The circle also of the sun what time it riseth new
And when it setteth, looketh red, but when it mounts most high,
Then looks it white, because that there the nature of the sky
Is better, and from filthy dross of earth doth further fly   60
The image also of the Moon, that shineth aye by night,
Is never of one quantity. For that that giveth light

11 *target* shield.
12 *fleet* move swiftly; *fisking* flitting.
13 *wight* person.
14 *ne* nor; *aye* ever.
15 *belly* bodily.
16 *chase* persecute.
17 *And . . . apace* a metaphor for broaching a
grand subject; *sith* since.

18 *kind* nature.
19 *erst* formerly.
20 *Pallant's daughter* Aurora, the dawn goddess;
a descendant of the Titan Pallas.
21 *Phoebus* Apollo, the sun god.

Today, is better than the next that followeth, till the full.
And then contrariwise each day her light away doth pull.
What? seest thou not how that the year as representing plain   65
The age of man, departs itself in quarters four? first bain[22]
And tender in the spring it is, even like a sucking babe.
Then green, and void of strength, and lush, and foggy, is the blade,[23]
And cheers the husbandman with hope. Then all things flourish gay.
The earth with flow'rs of sundry hue then seemeth for to play,   70
And virtue small or none to herbs there doth as yet belong.
The year from springtide passing forth to summer, waxeth strong,
Becometh like a lusty youth. For in our life throughout
There is no time more plentiful, more lusty hot and stout.
Then followeth Harvest when the heat of youth grows somewhat cold,   75
Ripe, mild, disposèd mean betwixt a young man and an old,
And somewhat sprent with grayish hair. Then ugly winter last[24]
Like age steals on with trembling steps, all bald, or overcast
With shirl thin hair as white as snow. Our bodies also aye[25]
Do alter still from time too time, and never stand at stay.   80
We shall not be the same we were today or yesterday.
The day hath been we were but seed and only hope of men,
And in our mother's womb we had our dwelling place as then,
Dame Nature put to cunning hand and suffered not that we
Within our mother's strainèd womb should aye distressèd be,   85
But brought us out to air, and from our prison set us free.
The child newborn lies void of strength. Within a season tho[26]
He waxing four-footed learns like savage beasts to go.
Then somewhat falt'ring, and as yet not firm of foot, he stands
By getting somewhat for to help his sinews in his hands.   90
From that time growing strong and swift, he passeth forth the space
Of youth: and also wearing out his middle age apace,
Through drooping age's steepy path he runneth out his race.
This age doth undermine the strength of former years, and throws
It down: which thing old *Milo* by example plainly shows.[27]   95
For when he saw those arms of his (which heretofore had been
As strong as ever *Hercules'* in working deadly teen[28]
Of biggest beasts) hang flapping down, and naught but empty skin,
He wept. And *Helen* when she saw her agèd wrinkles in[29]
A glass, wept also: musing in herself what men had seen,   100

22 *bain* supple, limber (*OED*).
23 *foggy* flabby; spongy (*OED*).
24 *sprent* sprinkled.
25 *shirl* rough.
26 *tho* then.

27 *Milo* a famous wrestler.
28 *Hercules* a famously brawny hero; *teen* harm.
29 *Helen* renowned beauty who was abducted first by Theseus, king of Athens, and then by Paris, a prince of Troy.

That by two noble princes' sons she twice had ravished been.
Thou time, the eater up of things, and age of spiteful teen,
Destroy all things. And when that long continuance hath them bit,
You leisurely by ling'ring death consume them every whit.
And these that we call Elements do never stand at stay.   105
The interchanging course of them I will before ye lay.
Give heed thereto. This endless world contains therein I say
Four substances of which all things are gend'red. Of these four[30]
The Earth and Water for their mass and weight are sunken lower.
The other couple Air and Fire the purer of the twain,   110
Mount up, and naught can keep them down. And though there do remain
A space between each one of them: yet everything is made
Of them same four, and into them at length again do fade.
The earth resolving leisurely doth melt to water sheer,
The water finèd turns to air. The air eke purgèd clear [31]   115
From grossness, spireth up aloft, and there becometh fire.
From thence in order contrary they back again retire.
Fire thickening passeth into Air, and Air waxing gross,
Returns to water: Water eke congealing into dross,
Becometh earth. No kind of thing keeps aye his shape and hue.   120
For nature loving ever change repairs one shape anew
Upon another; neither doth there perish aught (trust me)
In all the world, but alt'ring takes new shape. For that which we
Do term by name of being born, is for to gin to be[32]
Another thing than that it was: And likewise for to die,   125
To cease to be the thing it was. And though that variably
Things pass perchance from place to place: yet all from whence they came
Returning, do unperishèd continue still the same.
But as for in one shape, be sure that nothing long can last."

Book 15, lines 871–9

Somewhat ironically, Ovid concludes his epic poem on change with a prediction of his own eternal fame. Shakespeare's sonnets (pp. 47–8 above) are perhaps the most famous English works that echo Ovid's bold claims.

We present these lines in the translation that Shakespeare knew, that of Arthur Golding (see p. 453 above).

Now have I brought a work to end which neither *Jove*'s fierce wrath,
Nor sword, nor fire, nor fretting age with all the force it hath[1]

---

30 *gend'red* engendered; created.
31 *finèd* refined.
32 *gin* begin.

BOOK 15, LINES 871–879
1 *fretting* devouring.

Are able to abolish quite. Let come that fatal hour
Which (saving of this brittle flesh) hath over me no power,
And at his pleasure make an end of mine uncertain time.   5
Yet shall the better part of me assurèd be to climb
Aloft above the starry sky. And all the world shall never
Be able for to quench my name. For look how far so ever
The Roman Empire by the right of conquest shall extend,
So far shall all folk read this work. And time without all end   10
(If Poets as by prophecy about the truth may aim)
My life shall everlastingly be lengthened still by fame.

Pliny the Elder
(c. 23–79 CE)

Born of an affluent family in Comum, in north Italy, Pliny enjoyed a successful public career as soldier, advocate, and administrator. He was among the counselors of the emperors Vespasian and Titus; he was commander of the fleet at Misenum in 79 CE when Vesuvius erupted and destroyed Pompeii. His nephew, Pliny the Younger, an eye-witness of the eruption, describes how his uncle sailed heroically to the rescue of inhabitants of the bay of Naples and suffocated in the fumes. Pliny was a prodigiously prolific author. His histories and scholarly treatises on cavalry tactics, grammar, and oratory are lost, but his monumental encyclopedia survives. The *Natural History*, in 37 books, is a compendium of contemporary lore on a vast range of topics – natural, artistic, medical, and scientific. Although it is the source of much valuable information, it also abounds in curiosities and superstitions – what the seventeenth-century Englishman Sir Thomas Browne would call "pseudodoxia" in his encyclopedia of error, *Pseudodoxia Epidemica*. Browne's contemporary, John Milton, knew Pliny, as did all other European writers with pretensions to epic or encyclopedic modes of writing.

The first English translation was by Philemon Holland (1601). Our translation is by John Bostock (1772–1846) and H. T. Riley (1816–1878); it comes from *The Natural History of Pliny* (H. G. Bohn, 1855).

from the *Natural History*

Book 16, section 238

Book 16 of the *Natural History* is devoted to trees. This excerpt is taken from Pliny's discourse on the age of trees. Wordsworth cited it as the original inspiration for his composition of "Laodamia" (p. 173 n. 27 above).

There are some authors, too, who state that a plane-tree at Delphi was planted by the hand of Agamemnon,[1] as also another at Caphyae, a sacred grove in Arcadia. At the present day, facing the city of Ilium,[2] and close to the Hellespont,[3] there are trees growing over the tomb of Protesilaus[4] there, which, in all ages since that period, as soon as they have grown of sufficient height to behold Ilium, have withered away, and then begun to flourish again. Near the city, at the tomb of Ilus,[5] there are some oaks which are said to have been planted there when the place was first known by the name of Ilium.

BOOK 16, SECTION 238

1 *Agamemnon* commander of the Greeks at Troy.
2 *Ilium* Troy.
3 *Hellespont* the channel connecting the Aegean and Propontis (Sea of Marmora).

4 *Protesilaus* the first Greek to be killed at Troy (see Ovid, *Heroides* 13; p. 429 above).
5 *Ilus* the legendary founder of Troy.

Lucan (39–65 CE)

Marcus Annaeus Lucanus was born in Cordoba, Spain, of an upper-class family with literary connections. His poetic prowess won the admiration of the emperor Nero (himself an aspiring poet), but Nero turned against him for unknown reasons, perhaps jealousy. At the age of 26 Lucan became involved in the same conspiracy against Nero as his uncle Seneca and like Seneca was forced to commit suicide, a martyr of intellectual resistance to tyranny. His only surviving work is the *Civil War* (also known as the *Pharsalia*), an unfinished epic in 10 books of dactylic hexameters on the struggle between Julius Caesar and Pompey that effectively destroyed the Roman republic and heralded the rise of imperial autocracy. The grandiose scale, meter, and military content of Lucan's epic stand in the tradition of Homer's *Iliad* and Virgil's *Aeneid*, but his bleak and often horrific vision of a Rome brought down by its own generals contrasts with the patriotic *Aeneid*. In many ways the epic reads as a critique of heroic values and conventions, which are nullified by partisan politics. Lucan is famous for eliminating the traditional role of anthropomorphic gods as an explanatory factor; he substitutes an emphasis on perverse human will, magic, and a sinister concept of fate.

In cultural eras when the gods – or their modern equivalents – seem absent, Lucan has risen in popularity. He had a marked influence on Civil War writing in England, and Robert Graves (1895–1985), the poet and novelist, saw the modernist movement of the twentieth century in terms of Lucan's poetic stance. Lucan has become popular again in the last twenty or so years. However, all eras have their wars and political machinations, so he has never been very distant. When Dante wrote about the Guelphs and Ghibellines, he thought of Lucan; Nicholas Rowe's translation in 1718 suited a world used to the maneuvers of the Whigs and Tories; Byron and Shelley admired Lucan too as they tried to understand the revolutionary movements of their time. Lucan is in all times the antidote to the nationalism and nation-building tendencies of Virgil. He is a spokesman for a more cynical view of politics that always has its followers.

The translation is by Thomas May (1596–1650). As we note in our introduction to Virgil's *Georgics* (p. 353 above), which May also translated, he uses a plain style in his translations and simple heroic couplets. His approach seems suitable to Lucan's stern Roman subjects and his rather blunt view of human motivations.

from the *Civil War*

Book 1, lines 119–57

When the term of Caesar's command lapsed, the senate insisted that he surrender his Gallic provinces, disband his army, and return to Rome as a private citizen. Caesar saw this correctly as an attempt to destroy him politically and invaded Italy by crossing the river Rubicon under arms. Here, at the outset of the war and the poem, Lucan captures the character of the two antagonists in a pair of contrasting sketches. The brilliant image of lightning that Lucan creates to describe Caesar was later taken up by Andrew Marvell in the construction of "An *Horatian* Ode upon *Cromwell*'s Return from *Ireland*" (p. 87 above).

Thy death, fair *Julia*, breaks off all accords,[1]
And gives them leave again to draw their swords:[2]
On both sides powerful emulation bears
On their ambitious spirits: great *Pompey* fears[3]
That his piratic Laurel should give place[4]   5
To conquered France, and *Caesar*'s deeds deface[5]
His ancient triumphs; fortune's constant grace
Makes him impatient of a second place;
Nor now can *Caesar* a superior brook,[6]
Nor *Pompey* brook a peer; who justlier took   10
Up arms, great Judges differ, heaven approves
The conquering cause; the conquered *Cato* loves.[7]
Nor were they equal: one in years was grown,[8]

BOOK 1, LINES 119–157

1 *Julia* daughter of Julius Caesar, whom he had given in marriage to Pompey to cement good relations; her death in 54 BCE removed an obstacle to open conflict.

2 *them* Pompey and Caesar.

3 *great Pompey* Gnaeus Pompeius Magnus (106–48 BCE), famous general and statesman of the late republic who led the Senate in opposing Caesar's bid for supremacy.

4 *piratic Laurel* political power conferred by his stunning conquest of pirates in the Mediterranean in 67 BCE.

5 *France* Roman Gaul, which Caesar conquered in the years 58–50 BCE.

6 *brook* bear; stand.

7 *Cato* M. Porcius Cato ("the Younger") (95–46 BCE); a senatorial leader of renowned integrity who committed suicide rather than surrender to Caesar.

8 *one* Pompey was 57 when the Civil War broke out in 49 BCE.; Caesar (100–44 BCE) was only six years younger.

And long accustomed to a peaceful gown[9]
Had now forgot the Soldier: Fame he bought   15
By bounty to the people: and much sought
For popular praise: his Theatre's loud shout[10]
Was his delight; new strength he sought not out,
Relying on his ancient fortune's fame,
And stood the shadow of a glorious name.   20
As an old lofty Oak, that heretofore
Great Conquerors' spoils, and sacred Trophies bore,[11]
Stands firm by his own weight, his root now dead,
And through the Air his naked boughs does spread,
And with his trunk, not leaves, a shadow makes: 25
He, though each blast of Eastern wind him shakes,
And round about well-rooted Trees do grow,
Is only honoured; but in *Caesar* now
Remains not only a great General's name,
But restless valour, and in war a shame   30
Not to be Conqueror; fierce, not curbed at all,
Ready to fight, where hope, or anger call
His forward Sword; confident of success,
And bold the favour of the gods to press:
O'erthrowing all that his ambition stay,[12]   35
And loves that ruin should enforce his way;
As lightning by the wind forced from a cloud
Breaks through the wounded air with thunder loud,
Disturbs the day, the people terrifies,
And by a light oblique dazzles our eyes,   40
Not *Jove's* own Temple spares it; when no force,
No bar can hinder his prevailing course,
Great waste, as forth it sallies and retires,
It makes, and gathers his dispersèd fires.

Book 1, lines 223–43

By crossing the River Rubicon, which divided the province of Cisalpine Gaul from
Italy, Julius Caesar committed an illegal act that precipitated the Civil War. The
first town he occupied was Ariminum.

The translator again is Thomas May (see p. 461 above).

9 *a peaceful gown* toga worn in times of   11 *Trophies* enemy armor hung on a stake or
peace.   tree to commemorate a victory.
10 *Theatre* Pompey built the first permanent   12 *stay* impede; oppose.
theater in Rome.

But now when *Caesar* had o'ercome the flood,[1]
And Italy's forbidden ground had trod,
"Here Peace, and broken Laws I leave," quoth he,
"Farewell all Leagues; Fortune I'll follow thee.
No more we'll trust: War shall determine all."   5
This said, by night the active General
Swifter than Parthian back-shot shaft, or stone[2]
From Balearic Slinger, marches on[3]
T'invade Ariminum; when every star[4]
Fled from th' approaching Sun but Lucifer,[5]   10
And that day dawned, that first these broils should see,[6]
Either the moist South winds, or Heaven's decree
With pitchy clouds darkened the fatal day;
When now the Soldiers by command made stay
I' th' Marketplace, shrill Trumpets flourished round,   15
And the hoarse Horns wicked alarums sound.
With this sad noise the people's rest was broke,
The Young men rose, and from the Temples took
Their Arms, now such as a long peace had marred,
And their old bucklers now of leathers bared: 20
Their blunted Piles not of a long time used,[7]
And Swords with th' eatings of black rust abused.

BOOK 1, LINES 223–43

1 *o'ercome the flood* crossed the Rubicon.

2 *Parthian* the Parthians occupied an empire extending roughly from the Euphrates to the Indus; they were famous for the skill of their mounted archers at shooting their arrows even as they retreated (the "Parthian shot").

3 *Balearic* the inhabitants of the Balearic islands, the largest being Mallorca, were known as experts in firing stone or lead bullets from hand-held slings.

4 *Ariminum* a north Italian harbor city on the Adriatic Sea.

5 *Lucifer* the morning star ("the light-bringer").

6 *broils* civic disturbances.

7 *Piles* lances (Latin *pila*).

Martial (c. 40–104 CE)

Marcus Valerius Martialis was born at Bilbilis in Spain. He came to Rome around 64 CE, during the reign of Nero, and lived there until a few years before his death, when he returned to his native Spain. Little is known about his life. Despite his literary success and fame, he lived modestly on the sometimes unreliable benefactions of patrons – a subject of complaint in his poetry. His earliest extant work is a set of poems written to celebrate the opening of the Flavian amphitheater – the Colosseum – in 80 CE. His fame rests on the 12 books of epigrams (some 1,175 poems in all) that he began publishing in 86 CE. The literary epigram was a Greek invention that flourished in the Hellenistic era (see our introduction to Asclepiades; p. 299 above). Like other Greek genres, it was imitated by the Romans, including lost predecessors of Martial. Of surviving models the most important is Catullus, a portion of whose poems can be described as epigrams – short, witty performances with a realistic veneer, many of them obscene or vitriolic, written in the elegiac meter on a variety of everyday themes including love, politics, and individual friends or enemies. Martial expanded the range of epigram to embrace all aspects of Roman life. His themes include mockery of individuals and social types such as the fortune-hunter, the glutton, and the adulterer; current events; gifts received; invitations to friends; patronage; literary taste; and flattery of the emperor Domitian, to name a few. His tone is generally light-hearted; he laughs at vice rather than attacking it in the manner of a more ambitious poetical satirist such as Juvenal. Through the variety of his subject matter, his keen eye, verbal dexterity, and caustic wit he brought the epigram to an unsurpassed level of sophistication and gave it what was to remain its definitive form.

Martial was very popular in the ancient world, and influenced Juvenal, as well as many lesser writers. His works were printed only 20 years after the invention of printing (c. 1470). Pithy and brief, Martial's poems are conspicuous in the commonplace books and vade mecums used by English poets from the sixteenth through the eighteenth centuries. Satirists with an inclination to be epigrammatic themselves knew him well; it is difficult to imagine Ben Jonson's poems or Pope's without the influence of Martial. Samuel Johnson often inserted quotations from Martial in his *Ramblers*, either as epigraphs or to sum up a favorite topic of human life. Coleridge and Goethe read Martial and wove him into their works, but, like other sharp-tongued satirists, he was neglected later in the nineteenth century. Even earlier, he had been a poet for daring readers; the young Elizabeth Carter's father suspected her friend Samuel Johnson's taste (in 1738) because it included Martial. Perhaps it is because there was always a taint associated with pursuing Martial's poetry that his widely influential works have only received detailed scholarly commentaries in the last thirty or so years.

from the *Epigrams*

Book 1, number 3

In this epigram Martial bids farewell to his book of poems, which is anxious to be published. To address one's book is a conceit that was developed by Catullus, Horace, and Ovid. Horace, *Epistles* 1.20, in which the poet speaks to his book as if it were a slave, is Martial's main model for *Epigram* 1.3. There are several other examples in Martial and many in later literature of this sort of address. This particular poem inspired Herrick's "To His Muse" (p. 65 above). To understand Martial's poem, one must remember that Martial thought of the addressee not as a bound volume but a papyrus roll. The translator, James Michie (1927–), tries to adjust things for the modern reader by replacing Martial's "cylinder," a place where rolls were stored, to "shelves," a place for storing books.

The text is taken with permission from Michie's *Martial: The Epigrams* (Penguin, 1978).

> Frail book, although there's room for you to stay
> Snug on my shelves, you'd rather fly away[1]
> To the bookshops and be published. How I pity
> Your ignorance of this supercilious city!
> Believe me, little one, our know-all crowd[2]   5
> Is hard to please. Nobody sneers as loud
> As a Roman: old or young, even newly-born,
> He turns his nose up like a rhino horn.
> As soon as one hears the deafening "bravos!"
> And begins blowing kisses, up one goes   10
> Skywards, tossed in a blanket. And yet you,
> Fed up with the interminable "few,"

BOOK 1, NUMBER 3

1 *shelves* for Martial's "cylinders," in which papyrus rolls were stored.

2 *know-all crowd* literally "the crowd of Mars" (father of Romulus).

"Final" revisions of your natural song
By my strict pen, being a wild thing, long
To try your wings and flutter about Rome.   15
Off you go, then! You're safer, though, at home.

Book 3, number 58

In this poem Martial compares the country house of Faustinus with that of the addressee Bassus. Faustinus has a villa at Baiae, a resort of the upper classes who built lavish villas there. Faustinus, however, puts his land to agricultural use. In the tradition of Virgil and Horace's praises of country life, Martial paints an ideal picture of plenitude, sound morals, and satisfaction with simple pleasures. In contrast, Bassus' elegant house outside Rome is unable to supply his most basic needs. The historical accuracy of the contrast is doubtful. The very idea of a farmhouse at Baiae is unlikely, and certain aspects of the encomium – the grandiose roll of poultry, for instance – are intentionally overdrawn. But this is what one expects from Martial's poetry, an aesthetic realm in which wit and ingenuity are far more important than fidelity to the mere historical facts of Roman life. Ben Jonson drew upon Martial's poem in the composition of "To Penshurst" (p. 58 above).

The translator again is James Michie (see p. 465 above).

Our friend Faustinus at his Baian place[1]
Doesn't go in, Bassus, for wasted space –
No useless squads of myrtle, no unmated
Planes, no clipped box; true, unsophisticated[2]
Country's his joy. His corners overflow   5
With tight-packed grain, and jars in a long row[3]
Exhale the breath of autumns long ago.
After November, when the frosts begin,
The rugged pruner brings the last grapes in.
Bulls roar in his coombs, and steers, the nap[4]   10
Still on their harmless brows, lust for a scrap.
The poultry from the mired yard all roam loose –
Jewelled peacock, speckled partridge, squawking goose,
Guinea-fowl, and the bird that gets the name
Flamingo from its feathering of flame,   15
And pheasant from unholy Colchis; proud[5]
Cocks tread their Rhodian hens; the cotes are loud[6]

BOOK 3, NUMBER 58

1 *Baian* Baiae was a fashionable resort on the bay of Naples.

2 *Planes* plane trees; ornamental trees; *box* an ornamental shrub.

3 *jars* wine jars.

4 *coombs* deep valleys.

5 *Colchis* home of the murderous witch Medea.

6 *Rhodian* from the Greek island of Rhodes.

With whirring wings; wood-pigeons coo, wax-pale
Turtle-doves answer; greedy piglets trail
After the aproned bailiff's wife, and lambs   20
Queue for the bulging udders of their dams.
Young slaves born on the farm, with skins as white
As milk, sit in a circle round the bright
Fireside, and logs, heaped liberally, blaze
For the domestic gods on holidays.   25
No butler lolls about indoors whey-faced[7]
With sloth, no wrestling-master's hired to waste
The household oil; there they make use of time[8]
To lure with artfully spread net and lime
The glutton thrush, or play the catch with taut   30
Rod, or bring home the doe their traps have caught.
The garden's such light sweat to hoe and weed,
The town slaves tend it happily; there's no need
For a nagging overseer – the long-haired,
Mischievous boys are cheerfully prepared,   35
When the bailiff gives his orders, to obey,
And even the pampered eunuch finds work play.
The country-folk who call never arrive
Without some gift – pale combs straight from the hive,
Somnolent dormice, a cheese pyramid   40
From Umbria's woods, or capons, or a kid:[9]
The big-boned daughters of the honest peasants
In wicker baskets bring their mothers' presents.
When work is done, the neighbour, a glad guest,
Is asked to dine; no hoarding of the best   45
Food for tomorrow's feast; all get their fill,
Servers as well; fed slaves feel no ill-will
Waiting on tipplers.
                    You, though, who reside
In the suburbs, Bassus, starve in genteel pride: 50
Your belvedere looks on mere laurel-leaves,[10]
Your garden god is smugly safe from thieves,[11]
You feed your workers city corn, your cheese,
Apples, eggs, wine, fowls, fruit and cabbages
Are carted for you to your frescoed home.   55
Is this "the countryside" – or outer Rome?

---

7   *whey-faced* pale-faced.
8   *oil* for smearing on the body of wrestlers.
9   *Umbria* a rural region of Italy.

10   *belvedere* a turret on the top of a house.
11   *garden god* Priapus.

Book 5, number 78

Operating in the mode of Horace's *Epistles* 1.5 (p. 403 above), Martial composes in this poem an invitation to a simple dinner; any culinary deficiencies, he writes, will be more than made up for by the pleasure of relaxed and sincere friendship. The question at the end of the poem also hints at romantic possibilities. This poem, along with the next two selections from Martial, was one of Jonson's models for "Inviting a Friend to Supper" (p. 61 above).

The translator is, again, James Michie (see p. 465 above).

Toranius, if the prospect of a cheerless, solitary dinner
Bores you, eat with me – and get thinner.
If you like appetite-whetters,
There'll be cheap Cappadocian lettuce,[1]
Pungent leeks, and tunny-fish   5
Nestling in sliced eggs. Next, a black earthenware dish
(Watch out – a finger-scorcher!) of broccoli just taken
From its cool bed, pale beans with pink bacon,
And a sausage sitting in the centre
Of a snow-white pudding of polenta.   10
If you want to try a dessert, I can offer you raisins (my own),
Pears (from Syria), and hot chestnuts (grown
In Naples, city of learning)[2]
Roasted in a slow-burning
Fire. As for the wine, by drinking it you'll commend it.   15
When this great feast has ended,
If, as he well might,
Bacchus stirs up a second appetite,
You'll be reinforced by choice Picenian olives fresh from the trees,[3]
Warm lupins and hot chick-peas.[4]   20
Let's face it,
It's a poor sort of dinner; yet, if you deign to grace it,
You'll neither say nor hear
One word that's not sincere,
You can lounge at ease in your place,   25
Wearing your own face,
You won't have to listen while your host reads aloud from some thick book
Or be forced to look
At girls from that sink, Cadiz, prancing
Through the interminable writhings of professional belly-dancing.   30

BOOK 5, NUMBER 78

1 *Cappadocian* from Cappadocia, a region of what is now central Turkey.

2 *city of learning* Naples was a center of Greek culture.

3 *Picenian* from Picenum, a region of central Italy east of the Apennines.

4 *lupins* a sort of beans eaten by common folk in Rome.

Instead, Condylus, my little slave,
Will pipe to us – something not too rustic, nor yet too grave.
Well, that's the "banquet." I shall invite
Claudia to sit on my left. Who would you like on my right?

Book 10, number 48

The dramatic setting of this invitation poem is the early afternoon, when it was customary to attend the baths. Martial varies the conventionally modest menu by stressing the medicinal properties of three of the foods he intends to offer his guests. First in mind and first on the list is a laxative. The end of the poem reflects anxiety about the dangers of loose talk under the rule of suspicious emperors like Domitian (81–96 CE).

The translator is Peter Whigham (1925–1987); the text comes, with permission, from *Epigrams of Martial Englished by Divers Hands* (University of California Press, 1987).

Two o'clock: the Egyptian priests have barred[1]
    the temple gates, the Palace troop changed guard.
The baths are cooler now, that still breathed steam
    at one, and noon seemed hot as Nero's stream.[2]
Cerialis, Stella, Canius, Flaccus, Nepos –   5
    with you we're six – my couch holds sev'n: add Lupus.
Okra (that purges) by my good dame got,
    expect, with riches from my garden plot.
Mint there'll be (for wind), leeks in slices,
    short-head lettuce, rocket (for what's nice is).[3]   10
Scad, dressed with devilled eggs & sprigs of rue,[4]
    sows' teats well sprinkled with a tunny stew.
These for tasters: the meal itself – one course,
    a kid made tender in some wild beast's jaws,[5]
With morselled meats so carving is left out,   15
    & builders' beans & tender cabbage sprouts.[6]
A chicken & a thrice-left-over ham
    as well. When filled, you've fruit & Nomentan –[7]
Decanted from the flagon with no dreg,
    (Frontinus consul) three years in the keg.[8]   20
And add to this, the jest that does not bite,

BOOK 10, NUMBER 48

1 *Egyptian priests* of the goddess Isis.
2 *Nero* an emperor notorious for his excess.
3 *rocket eruca*, an herb used as an aphrodisiac.
4 *Scad* mackerel.
5 *a kid . . . jaws* Plutarch records a belief that animals bitten by wolves became more tender (*Quaestiones conviviales* 2.9).

6 *builders' beans* Martial refers to beans as the food of artisans.
7 *Nomentan* wine from Nomentum, a town in Latium.
8 *Frontinus* consul for the second time in 98 CE (the year in which Martial issued a revised edition of Book 10).

a lack of fear of what you did last night,[9]
Or said. Talk Green & Blue – the Circus show . . .[10]
None from my Nomentan shall bad-mouthed go.[11]

Book 11, number 52

In this invitation Martial includes bathing as well as dining. In order to entice his invitee Martial abandons his usual protestations about the simplicity of his table and pretends that there will be gourmet dishes. The end of the poem suggests a twist on the evidently unpopular practice of reciting one's work to one's dinner guests, the classical equivalent of the home video show. Martial sugars his invitation by indicating that he will listen to his guest's verse rather than recite his own.

The translator is J. A. Pott, a classicist who died in 1920. The text is taken from *Martial, the Twelve Books of Epigrams* (Routledge, 1924).

Come, Julius, share a pleasant meal with me,[1]
    If you should have no better occupation,
(We'll bathe together – keep the eighth hour free,[2]
    You know the bath adjoins my habitation),
Sliced leeks and wholesome lettuce there will be,[3]   5
    And tunny fry in happy combination
With rue and sauce of egg – I like it well
When rather larger than a mackerel.

Eggs also, poached upon a slack-wood fire,[4]
    Picenian olives touched by frost but lightly,[5]   10
These first. Shall I tell more? – in my desire
    To bring you, pardon my romancing slightly;[6]
My fish, birds, game, a gourmet might inspire,
    A Stella's table does not see them nightly;[7]
No verse I'll read but you shall give me all   15
Your epic and Virgilian pastoral.[8]

9   *a lack . . . night* literally, "liberty that need not be feared in the morning."
10   *Green & Blue* factions of charioteers named after their racing colors; *Circus* the Circus Maximus.
11   *None . . . go* literally, "my cups make no man a defendant"; i.e. get him indicted for treason.

BOOK 11, NUMBER 52
1   *Julius* Julius Cerealis, a friend and amateur poet.
2   *eighth hour* mid-afternoon; the Romans counted twelve hours from sunrise to sunset.

3   *wholesome lettuce* literally, "lettuce for moving the bowels."
4   *slack-wood fire* a slow fire; one of moderate heat.
5   *Picenian* from Picenum a region of central Italy, east of the Apennines.
6   *To . . . slightly* literally, "I'll lie, so that you'll come."
7   *Stella* L. Arruntius Stella; a friend of Martial's and a man of high rank.
8   *Your epic* literally, " your Giants"; i.e. an epic on the war between gods and giants.

Juvenal (fl. early second century CE)

Juvenal (Decimus Iunius Iuvenalis) is famous for his 16 satires, composed in dactylic hexameters and arranged in five books. He came from Aquinum in Italy, but almost nothing else is known for certain of his life. Internal evidence indicates that he endured the reign of the tyrannical Domitian (81–96) and wrote his satires during the first three decades of the second century CE in the reigns of Trajan and Hadrian. Like the epigrams of Martial (three of which are addressed to Juvenal), Juvenal's satires offer an indictment of contemporary social evils as they might have appeared to an educated Italian male of conservative leanings: the corruption of the aristocracy, foreign upstarts, the humiliation of clients by their patrons, sexual deviance, greed, the excesses of women, and so forth. It is a highly distorted picture, however, and one may well suspect Juvenal of being less interested in social reform than entertainment. His criticisms rely less on logic than colorful descriptions of Roman life, seen with an unmatched eye for the telling detail. In contrast to the genial satire of Horace, Juvenal's satire is, by his own account, driven by "indignation," though his tone mellows in the later books. One hallmark of his style is the exploitation of the grand style from epic and tragedy for the treatment of low material, which, in combination with mundane and sometimes obscene language, is a frequent source of parody, irony, and bathos. He is notable too for his arsenal of rhetorical fireworks and epigrammatic wit, which make him one of the most quotable Roman authors; from *Satire* 10, below, for example, comes the famous tag *mens sana in corpore sano*, "a sound mind in a sound body."

Despite their interest in sex and violence, the satires of Juvenal have been read and carefully preserved throughout European history. Their contempt for immoral behavior has given the satires a privileged place, and early readers seem often not to have noticed, or admitted, how much Juvenal revels in the sins that he excoriates. The grandeur of the satires too, particularly that of numbers 10 and 14, has given them an elevated status among satirical works. They rose to new heights of popularity in the seventeenth and eighteenth centuries when urban satire became a popular genre of English literature. Dryden translated some of Juvenal (and oversaw the rest), and he wrote brilliantly on the satirical forms of Horace and Juvenal in his introduction. However, Samuel Johnson made the literary territory his own by writing his famous imitations of *Satires* 3 and 10 – respectively, *London* and *The Vanity of Human Wishes* (p. 140 above). Juvenal's reputation declined as the genre of satire weakened in the nineteenth century, and his extreme misogyny can be an obstacle for modern readers. On the other hand, his acuity and his satirical view of corruption in the political, commercial, and private spheres are appealing and prescient in light of twenty-first-century events and trends.

from *Satire* 6

lines 1–54

Satire 6 is nearly 700 lines long – Juvenal's longest. It is addressed to one Postumus, who is planning to marry, and sets out to dissuade him from this course. Soon it develops into a general tirade against women in which Juvenal draws on a stock of misogynistic commonplaces that goes back to archaic Greece. These he marshals into a catalogue of vices – lust, greed, superstition, and many others – which he develops by free association rather than logic. Dryden, in his preface to his translation, deems it Juvenal's wittiest satire but deplores its content, and many readers may agree. Defenders of Juvenal have pointed out that he attacks mostly men in his other satires, and with equal scorn. Some have also argued that Juvenal's persona is a literary pose, even a caricature. Stylistically, the poem displays Juvenal's mastery of rhetoric in its exaggeration, invention, and straining for point. It is nevertheless rife with irrational prejudices, not just against women but foreigners (especially Greeks), the ruling class, homosexuals, and others. Juvenal probably shared these prejudices with most Roman men of his class, and he probably exaggerates them wildly more for the sake of entertainment than to persuade his audience or to vent personal fury. The poem is therefore less concerned with discovering new truths than it is with amplifying old ones in a way that is rationally outrageous but poetically brilliant. It opens with an amusing travesty of the myth of the Golden Age.

   Satire 6 is one of the most extravagant productions in the long western tradition of poetry that is hostile to women and to marriage. The influence of this tradition is visible in Chaucer's *Wife of Bath's Prologue* (p. 4 above) and Leapor's "Essay on Woman" (p. 161 above), though it cannot be proved that they had read Juvenal's poem.

   John Dryden's (1631–1700) translations of Juvenal and Persius came out in 1692 (though dated 1693) in a volume that he organized for his publisher Jacob Tonson. Dryden translated five of Juvenal's satires, including numbers 6 and 10, and almost all of Persius'; the others he farmed out to others, including his two sons. As a preface to the volume Dryden wrote his "Discourse concerning the Original and Progress of Satire," a seminal essay on this complex genre which remains important to this day. Dryden balks occasionally at Juvenal's obscenities, substituting less direct or bawdy language, but he is, overall, remarkably faithful to the sense and the flippant, though harsh, tone of the Latin poet.

The text of Dryden's translation is based on the first edition of the poem (1692); we have benefited from the textual notes and commentary in the standard edition in *The Works of John Dryden*, Vol. IV (University of California Press, 1974).

In *Saturn*'s Reign, at Nature's Early Birth,[1]
There was that Thing called Chastity on Earth;
When in a narrow Cave, their common shade,
The Sheep, the Shepherds and their Gods were laid:
When Reeds and Leaves, and Hides of Beasts were spread   5
By Mountain Huswifes for their homely Bed,
And Mossy Pillows raised, for the rude Husband's head.
Unlike the Niceness of our Modern Dames
(Affected Nymphs with new Affected Names:)
The *Cynthia*s and the *Lesbia*s of our Years,[2]   10
Who for a Sparrow's Death dissolve in Tears.
Those first unpolished Matrons, Big and Bold,
Gave Suck to Infants of Gigantic Mold;
Rough as their Savage Lords who Ranged the Wood,
And Fat with Acorns Belched their windy Food.[3]   15
For when the World was Buxom, fresh, and young,[4]
Her Sons were undebauched, and therefore strong;
And whether Born in kindly Beds of Earth,
Or struggling from the Teeming Oaks to Birth,[5]
Or from what other Atoms they begun,[6]   20
No Sires they had, or if a Sire the Sun.[7]
Some thin Remains of Chastity appeared

LINES 1–54

1   *Saturn* king of the gods in the Golden Age.

2   *Cynthia . . . Lesbia* literary mistresses of the poets Propertius and Catullus; Catullus wrote a poem on the death of Lesbia's pet sparrow in which he describes her eyes as red and swollen with weeping (p. 332 above).

3   *Acorns* the food of primitive man, before corn was discovered.

4   *Buxom* healthy; good-tempered (*OED*).

5   *And . . . Birth* according to myth, the first men were born from earth and water or from oak trees.

6   *Or . . . begun* Dryden's addition; *Atoms* i.e. indivisible particles of matter; an allusion to the Democritean theory of creation.

7   *if a Sire the Sun* another addition by Dryden.

Ev'n under *Jove*, but *Jove* without a Beard:[8]
Before the servile *Greeks* had learnt to Swear[9]
By Heads of Kings; while yet the Bounteous Year   25
Her common Fruits in open Plains exposed,
Ere Thieves were feared, or Gardens were enclosed:
At length uneasy Justice upwards flew,[10]
And both the Sisters to the Stars withdrew;
From that Old *Era* Whoring did begin,   30
So Venerably Ancient is the Sin.
Adult'rers next invade the Nuptial State,
And Marriage-Beds creaked with a Foreign Weight;
All other Ills did Iron times adorn;[11]
But Whores and Silver in one Age were Born.[12]   35
     Yet thou, they say, for Marriage do'st provide:[13]
Is this an Age to Buckle with a Bride?[14]
They say thy Hair the Curling Art is taught,
The Wedding-Ring perhaps already bought:
A Sober Man like thee to change his Life!   40
What Fury would possess thee with a Wife?
Art thou of ev'ry other Death bereft,
No Knife, no Ratsbane, no kind Halter left?[15]
(For every Noose compared to Hers is cheap)
Is there no City Bridge from whence to leap?   45
Would'st thou become her Drudge who do'st enjoy,
A better sort of Bedfellow, thy Boy?[16]
He keeps thee not awake with nightly Brawls,
Nor with a begged Reward, thy Pleasure palls:
Nor with insatiate heavings calls for more,   50
When all thy Spirits were drained out before.[17]
But still *Ursidius* Courts the Marriage-Bait,[18]
Longs for a Son, to settle his Estate,

8 *Jove without a Beard* i.e. in the Silver Age, when Jove or Jupiter's reign began; by the time he grew up and had a beard, morals had deteriorated.

9 *Swear* i.e. perjure themselves – a vice of the Iron Age; Juvenal regarded the Greeks as a devious race.

10 *Justice* Astraea, the last deity to desert the earth for the skies, where she became the constellation Virgo; Juvenal wittily makes Chastity her sister.

11 *Iron times* the degenerate Iron Age in which we live.

12 *But . . . Born* i.e. adultery began in the Silver Age, long before the other vices.

13 *thou* Postumus, the addressee of the poem; *provide* prepare.

14 *Buckle* "to unite oneself in wedlock" (*OED*).

15 *Ratsbane* rat poison; *Halter* rope for hanging oneself.

16 *Boy* catamite.

17 *Spirits* "vital power or energy" (*OED*).

18 *But . . . Marriage-Bait* literally, "but the Julian Law pleases Ursidius." The law provided incentives to encourage marriage and parenthood.

And takes no Gifts, though every gaping Heir[19]
Would gladly Grease the Rich Old Bachelor.   55
What Revolution can appear so strange,
As such a Lecher, such a Life to change?
A rank, notorious Whoremaster, to choose
To thrust his Neck into the Marriage Noose!
He who so often in a dreadful fright   60
Had in a Coffer 'scaped the jealous Cuckold's sight,[20]
That he to Wedlock, dotingly betrayed,
Should hope, in this lewd Town, to find a Maid!
The Man's grown Mad: To ease his Frantic Pain,
Run for the Surgeon; breathe the middle Vein:[21]   65
But let a Heifer with Gilt Horns be led
To *Juno*, Regent of the Marriage-Bed,
And let him every Deity adore,
If his new Bride prove not an arrant Whore,
In Head and Tail, and every other Pore.   70
On *Ceres'* feast, restrained from their delight,[22]
Few Matrons, there, but Curse the tedious Night:
Few whom their Fathers dare Salute, such Lust[23]
Their Kisses have, and come with such a Gust.
With Ivy now Adorn thy Doors, and Wed;[24]   75
Such is thy Bride, and such thy Genial Bed.[25]
Think'st thou one Man, is for one Woman meant?
She, sooner, with one Eye would be content.

lines 434–511

In this selection Juvenal attacks two types of woman: the learned and the rich. Juvenal's contempt for the cultured woman contrasts with Mary Leapor's sympathy for Pamphilia in "An Essay on Woman" (p. 162 above). His account of the rich woman's hairdressing probably influenced Pope's description of Belinda's toilet in *The Rape of the Lock* 1 (pp. 118–19 above).

The translator is again Dryden (see p. 473 above).

19 *gaping Heir* legacy hunter.
20 *Had . . . sight* i.e. hidden in a chest to save himself from a jealous husband – a familiar scene in Roman farce.
21 *breathe the middle Vein* lance the median vein of the forearm in order to let blood; literally, "drill his over-swollen vein." "The commentaries [on Juvenal used by Dryden] note that lancing the middle vein eases madness, and Dryden incorporates the explanation into his translation"

(*Works of John Dryden* IV, p. 620).
22 *Ceres' feast* "when the Roman women were forbidden to bed with their husbands" (Dryden's note). However, the couplet is mostly an interpolation by Dryden.
23 *dare Salute* risk greeting with a kiss.
24 *Ivy* houses were garlanded for weddings and other festive occasions.
25 *Genial* nuptial.

     But of all Plagues, the greatest is untold;
The Book-Learn'd Wife, in *Greek* and *Latin* bold.
The Critic-Dame, who at her Table sits;
Homer and *Virgil* quotes, and weighs their Wits;
And pities *Dido's* Agonizing Fits.[1]   5
She has so far th' ascendant of the Board;[2]
The Prating Pedant puts not in one Word:
The Man of Law is Nonplused, in his Suit;
Nay every other Female Tongue is mute.
Hammers, and beating Anvils, you would Swear,   10
And *Vulcan* with his whole Militia there.[3]
Tabors and Trumpets cease; for she alone
Is able to Redeem the lab'ring Moon.[4]
Ev'n Wit's a burthen, when it talks too long:
But she, who has no Continence of Tongue,   15
Should walk in Breeches, and should wear a Beard;
And mix among the Philosophic Herd.
O what a midnight Curse has he, whose side
Is pestered with a Mood and Figure Bride![5]
Let mine, ye Gods (if such must be my Fate)   20
No Logic Learn, nor History Translate:
But rather be a quiet, humble Fool:
I hate a Wife, to whom I go to School.
Who climbs the Grammar-Tree; distinctly knows[6]
Where Noun, and Verb, and Participle grows;   25
Corrects her Country Neighbour; and, a Bed,
For breaking *Priscian's*, breaks her Husband's Head.[7]
     The Gaudy Gossip, when she's set agog,[8]
In Jewels dressed, and at each Ear a Bob,[9]
Goes flaunting out, and in her trim of Pride,   30
Thinks all she says or does, is justified.

LINES 434–511

1 *Dido* queen of Carthage who commits suicide when abandoned by Aeneas.

2 *th' ascendant of the Board* command of the conversation at table.

3 *Vulcan* the smith god; an interpolation of Dryden's.

4 *Tabors ... Moon* when eclipses (labors of the moon) were believed the effect of demons, men tried to frighten them off with loud noises and bring the moon back to life, or redeem it.

5 *Mood and Figure Bride* "a woman who had learned logic" (Dryden's note). *Mood* and *figure* are terms in grammar and rhetoric.

6 *Grammar-Tree* a table of grammatical forms found in textbooks, like Priscian's grammar.

7 *For ... Head* "a woman grammarian who corrects her husband for speaking false Latin, which is called 'breaking Priscian's head'" (Dryden's note). Priscian lived later than Juvenal, who cites the grammarian Palaemon and jests that "husbands should be excused for a solecism!"

8 *agog* eager, ready.

9 *Bob* pendant.

When Poor, she's scarce a tolerable Evil;
But Rich, and Fine, a Wife's a very Devil.
    She duly, once a Month, renews her Face;
Meantime, it lies in Daub, and hid in Grease;   35
Those are the Husband's Nights; she craves her due,
He takes fat Kisses, and is stuck in Glue.
But, to the Loved Adult'rer when she steers,
Fresh from the Bath, in brightness she appears:
For him the Rich *Arabia* sweats her Gum;[10]   40
And precious Oils from distant *Indies* come.
How Haggardly so e'er she looks at home.
Th' Eclipse then vanishes; and all her Face
Is opened, and restored to every Grace.
The Crust removed, her Cheeks as smooth as Silk;   45
Are polished with a wash of Ass's Milk;
And, should she to the farthest *North* be sent,
A Train of these attend her Banishment.
But, hadst thou seen her Plastered up before,
'Twas so unlike a Face, it seemed a Sore.   50
    'Tis worth our while, to know what all the day
They do; and how they pass their time away.
For, if o'er-night, the Husband has been slack,
Or counterfeited Sleep, and turned his Back,
Next day, be sure, the Servants go to wrack.   55
The Chamber-Maid and Dresser, are called Whores;
The Page is stripped, and beaten out of Doors.
The whole House suffers for the Master's Crime;
And he himself, is warned, to wake another time.
    She hires Tormentors, by the Year; she Treats   60
Her Visitors, and talks; but still she beats.
Beats while she Paints her Face, surveys her Gown,
Casts up the day's Account, and still beats on:[11]
Tired out, at length, with an outrageous Tone,
She bids 'em, in the Devil's Name, begone.   65
Compared with such a Proud, Insulting Dame,
Sicilian Tyrants may renounce their Name.[12]
    For, if she hastes abroad, to take the Air,
Or goes to *Isis'* Church (the Bawdy House of Prayer),[13]

---

10 *Arabia ... Gum* she uses perfume made from the juices of Arabian plants.

11 *Casts up* reckons up; *and still beats on* Dryden's echo of the preceding lines mimics Juvenal's use of a repetitive figure called epiphora, in which successive clauses end in the same word.

12 *Sicilian Tyrants* proverbial for their cruelty (e.g., Phalaris, a ruler of the sixth century BCE who was said to have roasted his victims alive in a brazen bull).

13 *Isis* the temple of Isis was a notorious rendezvous for lovers.

She hurries all her Handmaids to the Task; 70
Her Head, alone, will twenty Dressers ask.
Psecas, the chief, with Breast and Shoulders bare,
Trembling, considers every Sacred Hair;
If any Straggler from his Rank be found,
A pinch must, for the Mortal Sin, compound.[14] 75
Psecas is not in Fault: But, in the Glass,
The Dame's Offended at her own ill Face.
That Maid is Banished; and another Girl
More dextrous, manages the Comb, and Curl:
The rest are summoned, on a point so nice; 80
And first, the Grave Old Woman gives Advice;
The next is called, and so the turn goes round,
As each for Age, or Wisdom, is Renowned:
Such Counsel, such delib'rate care they take,
As if her Life and Honour lay at stake. 85
With Curls, on Curls, they build her Head before;
And mount it with a Formidable Tow'r.
A Giantess she seems; but, look behind,[15]
And then she dwindles to the Pigmy kind.
Duck-legg'd, short-waisted, such a Dwarf she is, 90
That she must rise on Tiptoes for a Kiss.
Meanwhile, her Husband's whole Estate is spent;
He may go bare while she receives his Rent.
She minds him not; she lives not as a Wife,
But like a Bawling Neighbour, full of Strife: 95
Near him, in this alone, that she extends
Her Hate, to all his Servants, and his Friends.

Satire 10

Second only to *Satire* 6 in length, the tenth is one of Juvenal's most popular satires. Juvenal runs through the wrong objects of human prayer – wealth, power, eloquence, military glory, long life, and beauty – but ends on the positive note of what men ought to pray for: good health and gifts of the mind that do not depend upon Fortune. One of the poem's finest features is its vivid parade of historical and mythological figures: Sejanus, Hannibal, Xerxes, Priam, Marius, and others. More than any other of Juvenal's satires, and as much as any classical poem, the tenth has been taken as a statement of rational ethics applicable to all times and

---

14   *compound* be paid by contract.

15   *Giantess* Juvenal wrote "Andromache," the tall wife of Hector.

thoroughly amenable to Christian assimilation. It was the model for Samuel Johnson's *The Vanity of Human Wishes* (p. 140 above).

The translator is again Dryden (see p. 473 above).

Look round the Habitable World, how few
Know their own Good; or knowing it, pursue.
How void of Reason are our Hopes and Fears!
What in the Conduct of our Life appears
So well designed, so luckily begun,   5
But, when we have our wish, we wish undone?
 Whole Houses, of their whole Desires possessed,[1]
Are often Ruined, at their own Request.
In Wars, and Peace, things hurtful we require,
When made Obnoxious to our own Desire.[2]   10
 With Laurels some have fatally been Crowned;
Some who the depths of Eloquence have found,
In that unnavigable Stream were Drowned.[3]
The Brawny Fool, who did his Vigour boast;[4]
In that Presuming Confidence was lost: 15
But more have been by Avarice oppressed,
And Heaps of Money crowded in the Chest:
Unwieldy Sums of Wealth, which higher mount
Than Files of Marshaled Figures can account.
To which the Stores of *Croesus*, in the Scale,[5] 20
Would look like little Dolphins, when they sail
In the vast Shadow of the *British* Whale.
 For this, in *Nero*'s Arbitrary time,[6]
When Virtue was a Guilt, and Wealth a Crime,
A Troop of Cut-Throat Guards were sent, to seize 25
The Rich Men's Goods, and gut their Palaces:[7]
The Mob, Commissioned by the Government,
Are seldom to an Empty Garret, sent.[8]
The Fearful Passenger, who Travels late,
Charged with the Carriage of a Paltry Plate,[9] 30
Shakes at the Moonshine shadow of a Rush;

SATIRE 10

1 *Houses* extended families.

2 *Obnoxious to* subservient or subject to.

3 *Stream* a pun, meaning a stream of eloquence and a stream of water.

4 *Brawny Fool* "Milo of Crotona, who for a trial of his strength going to rend an oak perished in the attempt, for his arms were caught in the trunk and he was devoured by wild beasts" (Dryden's note).

5 *Croesus* the proverbially rich king of Lydia, eventually overthrown by the Persians.

6 *Nero's Arbitrary time* during the reign of the Roman emperor Nero, 54–68 CE.

7 *Rich Men* e.g., Seneca, the writer and tutor of Nero.

8 *Garret* an apartment on the top floor of a house, where the poorest tenants lived.

9 *Plate* silver plate; silverware.

And sees a Red-Coat rise from every Bush:[10]
The Beggar Sings, ev'n when he sees the place
Beset with Thieves, and never mends his pace.
    Of all the Vows, the first and chief Request   35
Of each, is to be Richer than the rest:
And yet no doubts the Poor Man's Draught control;[11]
He dreads no Poison in his homely Bowl.
Then fear the deadly Drug, when Gems Divine
Enchase the Cup, and sparkle in the Wine.[12]   40
    Will you not now, the pair of Sages praise,[13]
Who the same End pursued, by several Ways?
One pitied, one contemned the Woeful Times:
One laughed at Follies, one lamented Crimes:
Laughter is easy; but the Wonder lies   45
What stores of Brine supplied the Weeper's Eyes.
Democritus, could feed his Spleen, and shake[14]
His sides and shoulders till he felt 'em ache;
Though in his Country Town, no Lictors were;[15]
Nor Rods nor Ax nor Tribune did appear:[16]   50
Nor all the Foppish Gravity of show
Which cunning Magistrates on Crowds bestow.
    What had he done, had he beheld, on high
Our Praetor seated, in Mock Majesty;[17]
His Chariot rolling o'er the Dusty place[18]   55
While, with dumb Pride, and a set formal Face,
He moves, in the dull Ceremonial track,
With Jove's Embroidered Coat upon his back:[19]
A Suit of Hangings had not more oppressed[20]
His Shoulders, than that long, Laborious Vest.   60
A heavy Gugaw (called a Crown) that spread[21]
About his Temples, drowned his narrow Head:
And would have crushed it, with the Massy Freight,

10 *Red-Coat* ruffian, bully.

11 *Draught control* hinder his drinking.

12 *Enchase* inlay.

13 *pair of Sages* the pre-Socratic philosophers Democritus and Heraclitus; the former was said to laugh, the latter weep, at the spectacle of human life.

14 *Spleen* the organ associated in earlier medical theories with anger.

15 *Lictors* magistrates' attendants who carried symbolic rods and axes.

16 *Tribune* speaker's platform.

17 *Praetor* a Roman magistrate, depicted here as president of the games riding in a ceremonial procession in the garb of a triumphing general; metaphorically any high elected office.

18 *Dusty place* the Circus Maximus where chariot races were held.

19 *Jove's Embroidered Coat* ceremonial dress borrowed from the temple of Jupiter.

20 *Suit of Hangings* dress made of heavy tapestries.

21 *Gugaw* or geegaw, "a gaudy trifle, plaything, or ornament" (*OED*).

But that a sweating Slave sustained the weight:[22]
A Slave in the same Chariot seen to ride,   65
To mortify the mighty Madman's Pride.
Add now th' Imperial Eagle, raised on high,[23]
With Golden Beak (the Mark of Majesty)
Trumpets before, and on the Left and Right,
A Cavalcade of Nobles, all in White: 70
In their own Natures false, and flatt'ring Tribes;
But made his Friends, by Places and by Bribes.[24]
    In his own Age *Democritus* could find
Sufficient cause to laugh at Human kind:
Learn from so great a Wit; a Land of Bogs[25]   75
With Ditches fenced, a Heav'n Fat with Fogs,
May form a Spirit fit to sway the State;
And make the Neighb'ring Monarchs fear their Fate.
    He laughs at all the Vulgar Cares and Fears;
At their vain Triumphs, and their vainer Tears: 80
An equal Temper in his Mind he found,
When Fortune flattered him, and when she frowned.
'Tis plain from hence that what our Vows request,
Are hurtful things, or Useless at the best.
    Some ask for Envied Pow'r; which public Hate   85
Pursues, and hurries headlong to their Fate:
Down go the Titles; and the Statue Crowned,
Is by base Hands in the next River Drowned.
The Guiltless Horses, and the Chariot Wheel
The same Effects of Vulgar Fury feel: 90
The Smith prepares his Hammer for the Stroke,
While the Lunged Bellows hissing Fire provoke;
Sejanus almost first of *Roman* Names,[26]
The great *Sejanus* crackles in the Flames:
Formed in the Forge, the Pliant Brass is laid   95
On Anvils; and of Head and Limbs are made,
Pans, Cans, and Pisspots, a whole Kitchen Trade.
    Adorn your Doors with Laurels; and a Bull[27]
Milk white and large, lead to the Capitol;[28]

22 *Slave* whose job was to remind the great man that he was mortal, in order to placate Nemesis.
23 *Eagle* figure topping the staff held by a triumphing general.
24 *Places* appointments; *Bribes* the dole distributed by the rich and powerful to their clients.
25 *Land of Bogs* the birthplace of Democritus, Abdera, in Thrace; proverbial for its dull inhabitants.

26 *Sejanus* rose to a great height as advisor to the emperor Tiberius, who had him executed for treachery in 31 CE; his statues were dismantled and his corpse dragged to the Tiber.
27 *Bull* a beast for high sacrifice to the gods.
28 *Capitol* the Capitoline Hill, site of the temple of Jupiter.

Sejanus with a Rope, is dragged along;   100
The Sport and Laughter of the giddy Throng!
"Good Lord," they Cry, "what *Ethiop* Lips he has,[29]
How foul a Snout, and what a hanging Face?[30]
By Heav'n I never could endure his sight;
But say, how came his Monstrous Crimes to Light?   105
What is the Charge, and who the Evidence,
(The Saviour of the Nation and the Prince?)"
"Nothing of this; but our Old *Caesar* sent[31]
A Noisy Letter to his Parliament."
"Nay Sirs, if Caesar writ, I ask no more;   110
He's Guilty; and the Question's out of Door."
How goes the Mob (for that's a Mighty thing)?
When the King's Trump, the Mob are for the King:[32]
They follow Fortune, and the Common Cry
Is still against the Rogue Condemned to Die.   115
    But the same very Mob; that Rascal crowd
Had cried *Sejanus*, with a Shout as loud;[33]
Had his Designs (by Fortune's favour Blessed)
Succeeded, and the Prince's Age oppressed.
But long, long since, the Times have changed their Face,   120
The People grown Degenerate and base:
Not suffered now the Freedom of their choice,
To make their Magistrates, and sell their Voice.[34]
    Our Wise Forefathers, Great by Sea and Land,
Had once the Pow'r, and absolute Command;   125
All Offices of Trust, themselves disposed;
Raised whom they pleased, and whom they pleased, Deposed.
But we who give our Native Rights away,
And our Enslaved Posterity betray,
Are now reduced to beg an Alms, and go   130
On Holidays to see a Puppet show.[35]
    "There was a Damned Design," cries one, "no doubt;
For Warrants are already Issued out:
I met Brutidius in a Mortal fright:[36]

---

29   *Ethiop* Dryden's addition.
30   *hanging* drooping.
31   *Caesar* Tiberius, now a recluse in his 70s living on the island of Capri, from where he sent the Senate a letter denouncing Sejanus.
32   *Trump* the supreme authority.
33   *Had* would have.
34   *sell their Voice* i.e. sell their votes – a sarcastic reference to the electoral bribery prevalent under the republic; in 14 CE Tiberius transferred the election of magistrates from the people to the Senate.
35   *Alms . . . Puppet show* literally, "the anxious populace now desires only two things: bread and circuses" (i.e. the grain dole and chariot races) – a famous line.
36   *Brutidius* a senator who played some part in the fall of Sejanus.

He's dipped for certain, and plays least in sight:[37]   135
I fear the Rage of our offended Prince,[38]
Who thinks the Senate slack in his defence!
Come let us haste, our Loyal Zeal to show,
And spurn the Wretched Corpse of Caesar's Foe:[39]
But let our Slaves be present there, lest they[40]   140
Accuse their Masters, and for Gain betray."
    Such were the Whispers of those jealous Times,
About *Sejanus*' Punishment, and Crimes.
    Now tell me truly, wouldst thou change thy Fate
To be, like him, first Minister of State?   145
To have thy Levees Crowded with resort,[41]
Of a depending, gaping, servile Court:
Dispose all Honours, of the Sword and Gown,
Grace with a Nod, and Ruin with a Frown;
To hold thy Prince in Pupilage and sway,   150
That Monarch, whom the Mastered World obey?
While he, intent on secret Lusts alone,[42]
Lives to himself, abandoning the Throne;
Cooped in a narrow Isle, observing Dreams
With flatt'ring Wizards, and erecting Schemes![43]   155
    I well believe, thou would'st be Great as he;
For every Man's a Fool to that Degree:
All wish the dire Prerogative to kill;
Ev'n they would have the Pow'r, who want the Will:
But wouldst thou have thy Wishes understood,   160
To take the Bad together with the Good?[44]
Wouldst thou not rather choose a small Renown,
To be the May'r of some poor Paltry Town,[45]
Bigly to Look, and Barb'rously to speak;[46]
To pound false Weights, and scanty Measures break?[47]   165
Then, grant we that *Sejanus* went astray,
In ev'ry Wish, and knew not how to pray:

---

37 *dipped* involved or implicated in something illegal or immoral.

38 *Prince* Tiberius.

39 *spurn* kick.

40 *Slaves* required as witnesses, to prevent them from informing on their masters for treason.

41 *Levees* early morning gatherings in the private rooms of a monarch or other great man; *resort* crowd, gathering.

42 *secret Lusts* an addition by Dryden, based on

allegations that Tiberius led a life of sexual depravity on Capri.

43 *Wizards* literally, "Chaldaean flock" – Tiberius' retinue of astrologers.

44 *But . . . Good* i.e. "are you willing to accept the bad that all success entails?"

45 *Paltry Town* Juvenal specifies Fidenae, Gabii, and Ulubrae.

46 *Bigly . . . speak* added by Dryden.

47 *pound* impound.

For he who grasped the World's exhausted Store
Yet never had enough, but wished for more,
Raised a Top-heavy Tow'r, of monst'rous height,   170
Which Mould'ring, crushed him underneath the Weight.
        What did the mighty *Pompey*'s Fall beget?[48]
And ruined him, who Greater than the Great,[49]
The stubborn Pride of *Roman* Nobles broke;
And bent their Haughty Necks beneath his Yoke?   175
What else, but his immoderate Lust of Pow'r,
Prayers made, and granted in a Luckless Hour:
For few Usurpers to the Shades descend[50]
By a dry Death, or with a quiet End.[51]
        The Boy, who scarce has paid his Entrance down[52]   180
To his proud Pedant, or declined a Noun
(So small an Elf, that when the days are foul,
He and his Satchel must be borne to School)
Yet prays and hopes and aims at nothing less,
To prove a *Tully*, or *Demosthenes*:[53]   185
But both those Orators, so much Renowned,
In their own Depths of Eloquence were Drowned:
The Hand and Head were never lost, of those
Who dealt in Doggerel, or who punned in Prose:
Fortune fore-tuned the Dying Notes of Rome: 190
Till I, thy Consul sole, consoled thy Doom.[54]
His Fate had crept below the lifted Swords,
Had all his Malice been to Murder words.
I rather would be *Maevius*, Thrash for Rhymes[55]
Like his, the scorn and scandal of the Times,   195
Than that *Philippic*, fatally Divine,[56]
Which is inscribed the Second, should be Mine.
        Nor he, the Wonder of the *Grecian* throng,
Who drove them with the Torrent of his Tongue,

---

48 *Pompey* general and statesman of the late
republic, who opposed Julius Caesar in the Civil
War; following his defeat at Pharsalus (48 BCE),
Pompey fled to Egypt, where he was
assassinated.

49 *Greater than the Great* Julius Caesar, dicta-
tor of Rome, who was assassinated by a band of
senators in 44 BCE; Dryden plays upon Pompey's
epithet Magnus, "the Great."

50 *Shades* ghosts; the underworld.

51 *dry* bloodless.

52 *Entrance* tuition fee.

53 *Tully* Marcus Tullius Cicero (106–43 BCE);
he and Demosthenes (384–322 BCE) were

regarded as the greatest orators of Rome and
Athens. Demosthenes poisoned himself after
being condemned to death; Cicero was murdered
and had his head and hands cut off by order of
Mark Antony.

54 *Fortune . . . Doom* Juvenal quotes a punning
verse from Cicero's poem *De Consulatu Suo* (On
his Consulship), to make the point that Cicero
would have avoided his fate had he stuck to
writing bad poetry.

55 *Maevius* a poor poet of whom Horace and
Virgil made fun; the name is added by Dryden.

56 *Philippic* Cicero's Second Philippic, a scath-
ing attack on Mark Antony.

Who shook the Theatres, and swayed the State 200
Of *Athens*, found a more Propitious Fate.
Whom, born beneath a boding Horoscope,
His Sire, the Blear-Eyed Vulcan of a Shop,[57]
From *Mars* his Forge, sent to *Minerva*'s Schools,[58]
To learn th' unlucky Art of wheedling Fools.[59] 205
   With Itch of Honour, and Opinion, Vain,
All things beyond their Native worth we strain:[60]
The Spoils of War, brought to *Feretrian Jove*,[61]
An empty Coat of Armour hung above
The Conqueror's Chariot, and in Triumph borne,[62] 210
A Streamer from a boarded Galley torn,
A Chap-fall'n Beaver loosely hanging by[63]
The cloven Helm, an Arch of Victory,
On whose high Convex sits a Captive Foe[64]
And sighing casts a Mournful Look below; 215
Of ev'ry Nation, each Illustrious Name,
Such Toys as these have cheated into Fame:
Exchanging solid Quiet, to obtain
The Windy satisfaction of the Brain.
   So much the Thirst of Honour Fires the Blood; 220
So many would be Great, so few be Good.
For who would Virtue for herself regard,
Or Wed, without the Portion of Reward?
Yet this Mad Chase of Fame, by few pursued,
Has drawn Destruction on the Multitude: 225
This Avarice of Praise in Times to come,
Those long Inscriptions, crowded on the Tomb,
Should some Wild Fig-Tree take her Native bent,
And heave below the gaudy Monument,
Would crack the Marble Titles, and disperse 230
The Characters of all the lying Verse.
For Sepulchres themselves must crumbling fall
In time's Abyss, the common Grave of all.

---

57 *Vulcan* god of fire; Demosthenes' father, who owned a sword factory, is caricatured as a common blacksmith.

58 *From . . . Schools* literally, "from the sword-making anvil to the rhetorician"; Dryden invents the antithesis between the gods of war and wisdom.

59 *th' unlucky Art of wheedling Fools* oratory, cynically defined.

60 *With . . . strain* a transition added by Dryden, who also expands Juvenal's preface on martial glory from 14 to 28 lines.

61 *Feretrian Jove* the temple of Jupiter Feretrius, to whom military trophies were dedicated.

62 *Triumph* triumphal procession.

63 *Beaver* the lower part of the face guard on a knight's helmet, or helm.

64 *Convex* vault, arch.

Great *Hannibal* within the Balance lay;[65]
And tell how many Pounds his Ashes weigh;   235
Whom *Afric* was not able to contain,
Whose length runs Level with th' Atlantic main,
And wearies fruitful *Nilus*, to convey
His Sun-beat Waters by so long a way;
Which *Ethiopia*'s double Clime divides,[66]   240
And Elephants in other Mountains hides.[67]
Spain first he won, the *Pyreneans* passed,[68]
And steepy *Alps*, the Mounds that Nature cast:
And with Corroding Juices, as he went,[69]
A passage through the living Rocks he rent.   245
Then, like a Torrent, rolling from on high,
He pours his headlong Rage on *Italy*;
In three Victorious Battles overrun;[70]
Yet still uneasy, Cries there's nothing done:
Till, level with the Ground, their Gates are laid;   250
And *Punic* Flags, on *Roman* Tow'rs displayed.[71]
   Ask what a Face belonged to this high Fame;
His Picture scarcely would deserve a Frame:
A Sign-Post Dauber would disdain to paint
The one-Eyed Hero on his Elephant.[72]   255
Now what's his End, O Charming Glory, say
What rare fifth Act, to Crown this huffing Play?[73]
In one deciding Battle overcome,[74]
He flies, is banished from his Native home:
Begs refuge in a Foreign Court, and there   260
Attends his mean Petition to prefer:
Repulsed by surly Grooms, who wait before
The sleeping Tyrant's interdicted Door.

65   *Hannibal* great general who extended the Carthaginian empire in Spain and invaded Italy during the Second Punic War (218–201 BCE).

66   *double Clime* above and below the equator; a detail added by Dryden.

67   *Which . . . hides* literally, "[Africa extending] southwards to the peoples of Ethiopia and other elephants," where Juvenal probably means "the second race of elephants," i.e. African as opposed to Indian.

68   *Pyreneans* the mountains separating Spain and France.

69   *Corroding Juices* literally, "vinegar"; Hannibal is said to have broken up rocks blocking his path by heating them and sluicing them with water and vinegar.

70   *three Victorious Battles* not in Juvenal; Dryden's source lists Ticinus, Trebia, and Cannae.

71   *Punic* Carthaginian; *on Roman Tow'rs* literally, "in the middle of the Subura" (a Roman slum); Dryden loses the bathos of Juvenal's phrase.

72   *The . . . Elephant* Hannibal lost the sight of one eye to infection while riding through the swamps of the Arno on the sole surviving elephant.

73   *huffing* blustering.

74   *Battle* Zama (202 BCE), where he was defeated by Scipio Africanus; having fled to Asia Minor, Hannibal eventually committed suicide by means of a poison hidden in his ring.

What wondrous sort of Death, has Heav'n designed,
Distinguished from the Herd of Human Kind,   265
For so untamed, so turbulent a Mind!
Nor Swords at hand, nor hissing Darts afar,
Are doomed t' Avenge the tedious bloody War,
But Poison, drawn through a Ring's hollow plate,
Must finish him; a sucking Infant's Fate.[75]   270
Go, climb the rugged *Alps*, Ambitious Fool,
To please the Boys, and be a Theme at School.[76]
   One World sufficed not *Alexander*'s Mind;[77]
Cooped up, he seemed in Earth and Seas confined:
And, struggling, stretched his restless Limbs about   275
The narrow Globe, to find a passage out.
Yet, entered in the Brick-built Town, he tried[78]
The Tomb, and found the strait dimensions wide:
'Death only this Mysterious Truth unfolds,
The mighty Soul, how small a Body holds.'[79]   280
   Old *Greece* a Tale of *Athos* would make out,[80]
Cut from the Continent, and Sailed about;
Seas hid with Navies, Chariots passing o'er
The Channel, on a Bridge from shore to shore:[81]
Rivers, whose depth no sharp beholder sees,   285
Drunk, at an Army's Dinner, to the Lees;
With a long Legend of Romantic things,
Which, in his Cups, the Bowsy Poet sings.[82]
But how did he return, this haughty Brave[83]
Who whipped the Winds, and made the Sea his Slave?   290
(Though *Neptune* took unkindly to be bound;
And *Eurus* never such hard usage found[84]

---

75 *a sucking Infant's Fate* an addition by Dryden in dubious taste.

76 *Theme* literally, "declamation" – a set speech on a fictitious theme, often consisting of advice to a historical figure such as Hannibal; declamation was the principal means of teaching oratory at Rome.

77 *Alexander* Alexander the Great (356–323 BCE), king of Macedon and conqueror of the Persian empire; told that there were many worlds, he purportedly lamented he had not yet conquered even one.

78 *Brick-built Town* Babylon, where Alexander died.

79 *Soul* added by Dryden: Juvenal refers only to the smallness of men's bodies.

80 *Athos* peninsula through which the Persian king Xerxes cut a canal in preparation for his massive invasion of Greece in 480 BCE; Juvenal alludes to the historical account of Herodotus.

81 *Channel* the Hellespont, which Xerxes bridged to carry his army.

82 *Bowsy* drunk, intoxicated.

83 *Brave* Xerxes, who is said to have had the sea lashed and fetters sunk in it when a storm broke the bridge across the Hellespont.

84 *Eurus* the east-southeast wind.

In his *Aeolian* Prisons under ground.)[85]
What God so mean ev'n he who points the way,
So Merciless a Tyrant to Obey!   295
But how returned he, let us ask again?
In a poor Skiff he passed the bloody Main,
Choked with the slaughtered Bodies of his Train.[86]
For Fame he prayed, but let th' Event declare
He had no mighty penn'worth of his Prayer.   300
    "*Jove* grant me length of Life, and Years' good store
Heap on my bending Back, I ask no more."
Both Sick and Healthful, Old and Young, conspire
In this one silly, mischievous desire.
Mistaken Blessing which Old Age they call,   305
'Tis a long, nasty, darksome Hospital.[87]
A ropy Chain of Rheums; a Visage rough,[88]
Deformed, Unfeatured, and a Skin of Buff.[89]
A stitch-fall'n Cheek, that hangs below the Jaw;
Such Wrinkles, as a skilful Hand would draw   310
For an old Grandam Ape, when, with a Grace,
She sits at squat, and scrubs her Leathern Face.
    In Youth, distinctions infinite abound;
No Shape, or Feature, just alike are found;
The Fair, the Black, the Feeble, and the Strong;   315
But the same foulness does to Age belong,
The self-same Palsy, both in Limbs, and Tongue.
The Skull and Forehead one Bald Barren plain;
And Gums unarmed to Mumble Meat in vain:
Besides th' Eternal Drivel, that supplies   320
The dropping Beard, from Nostrils, Mouth, and Eyes.
His Wife and Children loathe him, and, what's worse,
Himself does his offensive Carrion Curse!
Flatt'rers forsake him too; for who would kill
Himself, to be Remembered in a Will?   325
His taste, not only palled to Wine and Meat,
But to the Relish of a Nobler Treat.[90]
The limber Nerve, in vain provoked to rise,
Inglorious from the Field of Battle flies:
Poor Feeble Dotard, how could he advance   330

85 *Aeolian* belonging to Aeolus, god of the winds.

86 *In . . . Train* Xerxes returned to Persia after the total defeat of his fleet at the battle of Salamis (480 BCE).

87 *Hospital* an anachronistic addition by Dryden.

88 *Rheums* head colds or other illnesses accompanied by the discharge of mucus.

89 *Buff* buffalo hide, wrinkly and hard.

90 *Nobler Treat* sexual intercourse.

With his Blew head-piece, and his broken Lance?[91]
Add, that endeavouring still without effect,
A Lust more sordid justly we suspect.[92]
   Those Senses lost, behold a new defeat:
The Soul, dislodging from another seat.[93]   335
What Music, or Enchanting Voice, can cheer
A Stupid, Old, Impenetrable Ear?
No matter in what Place, or what Degree
Of the full Theatre he sits to see;
Cornets and Trumpets cannot reach his Ear: 340
Under an Actor's Nose, he's never near.
   His Boy must bawl, to make him understand[94]
The Hour o' th' Day, or such a Lord's at hand:
The little Blood that creeps within his Veins,
Is but just warmed in a hot Fever's pains.   345
In fine, he wears no Limb about him sound:[95]
With Sores and Sicknesses, beleaguered round:
Ask me their Names, I sooner could relate
How many Drudges on Salt *Hippia* wait;[96]
What Crowds of Patients the Town Doctor kills,   350
Or how, last fall, he raised the Weekly Bills.[97]
What Provinces by *Basilus* were spoiled,[98]
What Herds of Heirs by Guardians are beguiled:
How many bouts a Day that Bitch has tried;[99]
How many Boys that Pedagogue can ride!   355
What Lands and Lordships for their Owners know,
My Quondam Barber, but his Worship now.[100]
   This Dotard of his broken Back complains,
One his Legs fail, and one his Shoulder pains:
Another is of both his Eyes bereft;   360
And Envies who has one for Aiming left.
A Fifth with trembling Lips expecting stands;
As in his Childhood, crammed by others' hands;
One, who at sight of Supper opened wide
His Jaws before, and Whetted Grinders tried;   365
Now only Yawns, and waits to be supplied:
Like a young Swallow, when with weary Wings,

91 *Blew* blown: destroyed, or discredited.
92 *A Lust more sordid* a desire for oral stimulation.
93 *Soul* mind.
94 *Boy* slave.
95 *In fine* finally.
96 *Salt Hippia* an attractive female "in heat" (*salt*).

97 *Weekly Bills* bills of mortality or death counts.
98 *What . . . spoiled* literally, "how many partners Basilus has cheated"; Dryden follows an erroneous source.
99 *How . . . tried* literally, "how many men tall Maura sucks in one day."
100 *Quondam* former.

Expected Food, her fasting Mother brings.
   His loss of Members is a heavy Curse,
But all his Faculties decayed, a worse!   370
His Servants' Names he has forgotten quite:
Knows not his Friend who supped with him last Night:
Not ev'n the Children, he Begot and Bred;
Or his Will knows 'em not: For, in their stead,
In Form of Law, a common Hackney Jade,[101]   375
Sole Heir, for secret Services, is made:
So lewd, and such a battered Brothel Whore,
That she defies all Comers, at her Door.[102]
Well, yet suppose his Senses are his own,
He lives to be chief Mourner for his Son: 380
Before his Face his Wife and Brother burns;
He Numbers all his Kindred in their Urns.
These are the Fines he pays for living long;
And dragging tedious Age, in his own wrong:
Griefs always Green, a Household still in Tears,   385
Sad Pomps: A Threshold thronged with daily Biers;[103]
And Liveries of Black for Length of Years.
   Next to the Raven's Age, the *Pylian* King[104]
Was longest lived of any two-legg'd thing;
Blest, to Defraud the Grave so long, to Mount   390
His Numbered Years, and on his Right Hand Count;[105]
Three Hundred Seasons, guzzling Must of Wine:
But, hold a while, and hear himself Repine
At Fate's Unequal Laws; and at the Clue[106]
Which, Merciless in length, the midmost Sister drew.   395
When his Brave Son upon the Fun'ral Pyre,
He saw extended, and his Beard on Fire;
He turned, and Weeping, asked his Friends, what Crime
Had Cursed his Age to this unhappy Time?
   Thus Mourned Old *Peleus* for *Achilles* slain,[107]   400
And thus *Ulysses'* Father did complain.[108]
   How Fortunate an End had *Priam* made,[109]
Among his Ancestors a mighty shade,
While *Troy* yet stood: When *Hector* with the Race

---

101 *Hackney Jade* a worn out horse; a name for a whore.
102 *defies* takes on.
103 *Pomps* processions.
104 *Pylian King* Nestor, king of Pylos, who lived through three generations of men only to witness the death of his son, Antilochus.
105 *Right Hand* on which the ancients counted hundreds (units and tens on the left).

106 *Clue* thread; in this case the thread of life, drawn out to its destined length by *the midmost Sister* of the three Fates, Lachesis.
107 *Peleus* father of Achilles, who was killed by Paris.
108 *Ulysses' Father* Laertes, who grew old during Ulysses' 20-year absence.
109 *Priam* king of Troy who witnessed the death of his son Hector.

Of Royal Bastards might his Fun'ral Grace: 405
Amidst the Tears of *Trojan* Dames inurned,
And by his Loyal Daughters, truly mourned.[110]
Had Heaven so Blessed him, he had Died before
The fatal Fleet to *Sparta Paris* bore.[111]
But mark what Age produced; he lived to see   410
His Town in Flames, his falling Monarchy:
In fine, the feeble Sire, reduced by Fate,
To change his Sceptre for a Sword, too late,
His last Effort before *Jove*'s Altar tries;[112]
A Soldier half, and half a Sacrifice: 415
Falls like an Ox, that waits the coming blow;
Old and unprofitable to the Plough.
    At least, he Died a Man, his Queen survived;[113]
To Howl, and in a barking Body lived.
    I hasten to our own; Nor will relate   420
Great *Mithridates'*, and Rich *Croesus'* Fate;[114]
Whom *Solon* wisely Counseled to attend,[115]
The Name of Happy, till he knew his End.
    That *Marius* was an Exile, that he fled,[116]
Was ta'en, in Ruined Carthage begged his Bread,   425
All these were owing to a Life too long:
For whom had *Rome* beheld so Happy, Young!
High in his Chariot and with Laurel Crowned,
When he had led the *Cimbrian* Captives round[117]
The *Roman* Streets; descending from his State,   430
In that Blessed Hour he should have begged his Fate:
Then, then he might have died of all admired,
And his Triumphant Soul with Shouts expired.
    Campania, Fortune's Malice to prevent,[118]
To *Pompey* an indulgent Favour sent: 435

110 *Daughters* e.g., Cassandra and Polyxena.
111 *Paris* he sailed to Sparta to steal Helen from Menelaus, thus creating the immediate cause of the Trojan War.
112 *Jove's Altar* the altar in his palace where Priam tried feebly to fend off his Greek killer, Neoptolemus; the scene was described by Virgil and became a favorite for painters in the Renaissance.
113 *Queen* Hecuba, mother of Hector; according to myth she was transformed into a bitch while being transported to Greece after the fall of Troy.
114 *Mithridates* Mithridates VI of Pontus rose to vast power in the first century BCE, only to be defeated by Pompey and deposed by his own son's rebellion.
115 *Solon* statesman of Athens; according to the Greek historian Herodotus, Solon warned Croesus "to count no man happy until he is dead" and "to look to the end in everything," since fortune is unstable.
116 *Marius* illustrious general and statesman who fled to Carthage in 88 BCE to escape his enemy Sulla.
117 *Cimbrian Captives* Marius defeated the Cimbri at Vercellae in 101 BCE and brought captives to Rome for a triumphal procession.
118 *Campania* region of Italy where Pompey recovered from a dangerous fever in 50 BCE.

But public Prayers imposed on Heav'n, to give
Their much Loved Leader an unkind Reprieve.
The City's Fate and his, conspired to save
The Head, reserved for an *Egyptian* Slave.[119]
   Cethegus, though a Traitor to the State,[120]   440
And Tortured, 'scaped this Ignominious Fate:
And *Sergius*, who a bad Cause bravely tried,[121]
All of a Piece, and undiminished Died.
   To *Venus*, the fond Mother makes a Prayer,
That all her Sons and Daughters may be Fair: 445
True, for the Boys a Mumbling Vow she sends;
But, for the Girls, the Vaulted Temple rends:
They must be finished Pieces: 'Tis allowed
Diana's Beauty made *Latona* Proud;[122]
And pleased, to see the Wond'ring People Pray   450
To the New-rising Sister of the Day.[123]
   And yet *Lucretia*'s Fate would bar that Vow:[124]
And Fair *Virginia* would her Fate bestow[125]
On *Rutila*; and change her Faultless Make[126]
For the foul rumple of Her Camel back.   455
   But, for his Mother's Boy, the Beau, what frights
His Parents have by Day, what Anxious Nights!
Form joined with Virtue is a sight too rare:
Chaste is no Epithet to suit with Fair.
Suppose the same Traditionary strain   460
Of Rigid Manners, in the House remain;
Inveterate Truth, an Old plain *Sabine*'s Heart;[127]
Suppose that Nature, too, has done her part;
Infused into his Soul a sober Grace,
And blushed a Modest Blood into his Face;   465
(For Nature is a better Guardian far,
Than Saucy Pedants, or dull Tutors are:)
Yet still the Youth must ne'er arrive at Man;[128]
(So much Almighty Bribes, and Presents, can:)

---

119 *Head* cut off when he was assassinated in Egypt.
120 *Cethegus* executed for his part in the Catilinarian conspiracy of 63 BCE.
121 *Sergius* Catiline, who was killed in battle when his conspiracy failed.
122 *Latona* mother of Diana and Apollo.
123 *Sister . . . Day* Diana and Apollo, representing the moon and the sun – a conceit added by Dryden.
124 *Lucretia* legendary heroine who committed suicide when raped by Sextus Tarquinius.
125 *Virginia* a beautiful girl killed by her father to prevent her violation by Appius Claudius.
126 *Rutila* unknown.
127 *Sabine's Heart* the Sabines were an Italian people proverbial for their strict morals.
128 *Yet . . . Man* i.e. without being sexually corrupted.

Ev'n with a Parent, where Persuasions fail, 470
Money is impudent, and will prevail.
   We never Read of such a Tyrant King,
Who guelt a Boy deformed, to hear him Sing.[129]
Nor *Nero*, in his more Luxurious Rage,
E'er made a Mistress of an ugly Page: 475
Sporus, his Spouse, nor Crooked was, nor Lame[130]
With Mountain Back, and Belly, from the Game
Cross-barred: But both his Sexes well became.
Go, boast your Springal, by his Beauty Cursed[131]
To Ills; nor think I have declared the worst: 480
His Form procures him Journey-Work; a strife
Betwixt Town-Madams, and the Merchant's Wife:
Guess, when he undertakes this public War,
What furious Beasts offended Cuckolds are.
   Adult'rers are with Dangers round beset; 485
Born under *Mars*, they cannot 'scape the Net;[132]
And from Revengeful Husbands oft have tried
Worse handling, than severest Laws provide:
One stabs, one slashes, one, with Cruel Art,
Makes Colon suffer for the Peccant part.[133] 490
   But your *Endymion*, your smooth, Smock-faced Boy,[134]
Unrivalled, shall a Beauteous Dame enjoy:
Not so: One more Salacious, Rich, and Old,
Outbids, and buys her Pleasure for her Gold:
Now he must Moil, and Drudge, for one he loathes: 495
She keeps him High, in Equipage, and Clothes:
She Pawns her Jewels, and her Rich Attire,
And thinks the Workman worthy of his Hire:
In all things else immoral, stingy, mean;
But, in her Lusts, a Conscionable Quean.[135] 500
   "She may be handsome, yet be Chaste," you say:
Good Observator, not so fast away:

129 *guelt* gelded.
130 *Sporus* a youth beloved by Nero, who castrated and "married" him in a ceremony.
131 *Springal* "a young man" (*OED*).
132 *Mars* caught in adultery with Venus in a snare set by her husband Vulcan (Homer, *Odyssey* 8.266–369; p. 261 above).
133 *Colon* a punishment for adultery was to have a mullet stuffed up one's anus.

134 *Endymion* a beautiful youth beloved of the moon goddess; *Smock-faced* "having a pale smooth face; effeminate-looking" (*OED*).
135 *And ... Quean* Dryden bowdlerizes the Latin: literally, "for what would any woman deny to her wet groin? Whether she's Oppia or Catulla, it's from there that a degenerate woman gets her morals"; *Quean* whore.

Did it not cost the Modest Youth his Life,[136]
Who shunned th' Embraces of his Father's Wife?
And was not t'other Stripling forced to fly,[137]   505
Who, coldly, did his Patron's Queen deny;
And pleaded Laws of Hospitality?
The Ladies charged 'em home, and turned the Tale:[138]
With shame they reddened, and with spite grew Pale.
'Tis Dang'rous to deny the longing Dame;   510
She loses Pity, who has lost her Shame.
   Now *Silius* wants thy Counsel, give Advice;[139]
Wed *Caesar*'s Wife, or Die; the Choice is nice.
Her Comet-Eyes she darts on ev'ry Grace;
And takes a fatal liking to his Face.   515
Adorned with Bridal Pomp she sits in State;
The Public Notaries and *Auspex* wait:[140]
The Genial Bed is in the Garden dressed;[141]
The Portion paid, and ev'ry Rite expressed,
Which in a *Roman* Marriage is professed.   520
'Tis no stol'n Wedding, this; rejecting awe,
She scorns to Marry, but in Form of Law:
In this moot case, your Judgment: To refuse
Is present Death, besides the Night you lose.
If you consent, 'tis hardly worth your pain;   525
A Day or two of Anxious Life you gain:
Till loud Reports through all the Town have passed,
And reach the Prince: For Cuckolds hear the last.
Indulge thy Pleasure, Youth, and take thy swing:
For not to take, is but the selfsame thing: 530
Inevitable Death before thee lies;
But looks more kindly through a Lady's Eyes.
   What then remains? Are we deprived of Will?
Must we not Wish, for fear of wishing Ill?
Receive my Counsel, and securely move;   535
Entrust thy Fortune to the Pow'rs above.
Leave them to manage for thee, and to grant
What their unerring Wisdom sees thee want:

136 *Youth* Hippolytus, a chaste boy proposi-
tioned by his stepmother Phaedra and falsely
accused of rape; he died by the curse of his father
Theseus.
137 *t'other Stripling* the hero Bellerophon,
accused in similar circumstances by Stheneboea,
the wife of his host Proetus.
138 *turned the Tale* told a different story;
changed their tune (*OED*).

139 *Silius* the lover of Messalina, wife of the
emperor Claudius; they went through a wedding
ceremony, were found out, and destroyed.
140 *Auspex* augur who obtained divine sanction
for the marriage.
141 *Genial* nuptial.

In Goodness as in Greatness they excel;
Ah that we loved ourselves but half so well!   540
We, blindly by our headstrong Passions led,
Are hot for Action, and desire to Wed;
Then wish for Heirs: But to the Gods alone
Our future Offspring, and our Wives are known;
Th' audacious Strumpet, and ungracious Son.[142]   545
 Yet, not to rob the Priests of pious Gain,
That Altars be not wholly built in vain;
Forgive the Gods the rest, and stand confined
To Health of Body, and Content of Mind:[143]
A Soul, that can securely Death defy,   550
And count it Nature's Privilege, to Die;
Serene and Manly, hardened to sustain
The load of Life, and Exercised in Pain;
Guiltless of Hate, and Proof against Desire;
That all things weighs, and nothing can admire: 555
That dares prefer the Toils of *Hercules*[144]
To Dalliance, Banquets, and Ignoble ease.
 The Path to Peace is Virtue: What I show,
Thyself may freely, on Thyself bestow:
Fortune was never Worshipped by the Wise;   560
But, set aloft by Fools, Usurps the Skies.

---

142 *Th' audacious ... Son* added by Dryden.
143 *To ... Mind* literally, "a sound mind in a sound body" – a well-known motto.
144 *Hercules* a model of virtue to Stoic philosophers.

Cross-Reference Tables

English-language and classical authors are listed in alphabetical order (with first name given first for English-language authors). Readings are listed chronologically, in the same order that they appear in the text.

I English–Classical

Matthew Arnold

Dover Beach

Sophocles, *Antigone* 582–603;
Trachiniae 112–40
Thucydides, *Peloponnesian War* 7.44

Wystan Hugh Auden

The Shield of Achilles

Homer, *Iliad* 18.478–617

Aphra Behn

The Disappointment

Ovid, *Amores* 3.7; *Metamorphoses*
1.452–567

The Golden Age

Hesiod, *Works and Days* 53–201
Catullus, *Carmen* 5
Virgil, *Eclogue* 4
Tibullus, *Elegies* 2.3
Ovid, *Metamorphoses* 1.89–112

Robert Browning

Pan and Luna

Virgil, *Georgics* 3.384–93

Thomas Campion
  My Sweetest Lesbia   Catullus, *Carmen* 5
                                        Propertius, *Elegies* 2.15

Geoffrey Chaucer
  from *The Wife of Bath's Prologue*
    lines 627–822   Hesiod, *Works and Days* 53–201
                                        Ovid, *Ars Amatoria* 1.269–344
                                        Juvenal, *Satires* 6.1–54, 434–511

Samuel Taylor Coleridge
  Kubla Khan   Plato, *Ion* 533c–535a

William Cowper
  Epitaph on a Hare   Meleager, *Greek Anthology* 7.207
                                        Catullus, *Carmen* 3
                                        Ovid, *Amores* 2.6

John Donne
  The Sun Rising   Ovid, *Amores* 1.13

  Elegy 19: *To His Mistress*   Propertius, *Elegies* 2.15
    Going to Bed   Ovid, *Amores* 1.5

John Dryden
  To the Memory of Mr. Oldham   Catullus, *Carmen* 101
                                        Virgil, *Aeneid* 5.315–39; 6.854–92

Thomas Gray
  Ode on the Death of a Favourite   Meleager, *Greek Anthology* 7.207
    Cat   Catullus, *Carmen* 3
                                        Virgil, *Aeneid* 11.759–831
                                        Ovid, *Amores* 2.6

  An Elegy Wrote in a Country   Lucretius, *De Rerum Natura*
    Church Yard   3.894–911
                                        Virgil, *Georgics* 2.458–542
                                        Horace, *Epode* 2

Seamus Heaney
  Bann Valley Eclogue   Virgil, *Eclogue* 4

Robert Herrick
  To the Virgins, to Make Much   Asclepiades, *Greek Anthology* 5.85
    of Time   Catullus, *Carmen* 5
                                        Horace, *Odes* 1.11; 4.10

  To His Muse   Martial, *Epigrams* 1.3

Alfred Edward Housman
 A Shropshire Lad 15   Ovid, *Metamorphoses* 3.316–510

Samuel Johnson
 The Vanity of Human Wishes   Juvenal, *Satire* 10

Ben Jonson
 To Penshurst   Virgil, *Georgics* 2.458–542
                                         Horace, *Satires* 2.6; *Epode* 2; *Odes* 2.18
                                         Martial, *Epigrams* 3.58

 Inviting a Friend to Supper   Catullus, *Carmen* 13
                                         Horace, *Epistles* 1.5
                                         Martial, *Epigrams* 5.78; 10.48; 11.52

John Keats
 Ode on a Grecian Urn   Homer, *Iliad* 18.478–617
                                         Plato, *Symposium* 209e–212a
                                         Theocritus, *Idyll* 1

Mary Leapor
 An Essay on Woman   Hesiod, *Works and Days* 53–201
                                         Juvenal, *Satires* 6.1–54, 434–511

Richard Lovelace
 Love Made in the First Age: Hesiod, *Works and Days* 53–201
  To Chloris   Virgil, *Eclogue* 4
                                         Tibullus, *Elegies* 2.3
                                         Ovid, *Metamorphoses* 1.89–112

Christopher Marlowe
 The Passionate Shepherd to   Theocritus, *Idyll* 11
  His Love   Catullus, *Carmen* 5
                                         Virgil, *Eclogue* 2

Andrew Marvell
 An Horatian Ode upon   Horace, *Odes* 1.37
  Cromwell's Return from Ireland   Lucan, *Civil War* 1.119–57, 223–43

 To His Coy Mistress   Asclepiades, *Greek Anthology* 5.85
                                         Catullus, *Carmen* 5
                                         Horace, *Odes* 1.11

John Milton
   Lycidas

                    Theocritus, *Idyll* 1
                    Bion, *Lament for Adonis*
                    "Moschus," *Lament for Bion*
                    Virgil, *Eclogues* 5, 10

   from *Paradise Lost*
      Book 1, lines 1–74

                    Homer, *Iliad* 1.1–305; *Odyssey* 1.1–10
                    Hesiod, *Theogony* 1–80
                    Virgil, *Aeneid* 1.1–215

      Book 4, lines 411–91

                    Ovid, *Metamorphoses* 3.316–510

Wilfred Owen
   Dulce et Decorum Est

                    Horace, *Odes* 3.2

Alexander Pope
   from *The Rape of the Lock*
      Canto 1

                    Homer, *Iliad* 1.1–305; *Odyssey* 1.1–10
                    Virgil, *Aeneid* 1.1–215; 6.679–751
                    Ovid, *Metamorphoses* 15.143–260
                    Juvenal, *Satires* 6.434–511

      Canto 4

                    Homer, *Iliad* 1.1–305
                    Virgil, *Aeneid* 4.1–30; 6.268–316
                    Ovid, *Metamorphoses* 2.760–832

Sir Walter Ralegh
   The Nymph's Reply to the Shepherd   Theocritus, *Idyll* 11
                    Virgil, *Eclogue* 2

William Shakespeare
   Sonnet 55

                    Horace, *Odes* 3.30
                    Ovid, *Metamorphoses* 15.871–9

   Sonnet 60   Ovid, *Metamorphoses* 15.143–260

   Sonnet 74   Ovid, *Metamorphoses* 15.871–9

   Sonnet 77   Horace, *Odes* 4.10

Percy Bysshe Shelley
   Adonais

                    Theocritus, *Idyll* 1
                    Bion, *Lament for Adonis*
                    "Moschus," *Lament for Bion*
                    Virgil, *Eclogues* 5, 10

Sir Philip Sidney
   Astrophel and Stella 1–3   Ovid, *Amores* 1.1–3

   Astrophel and Stella 47   Catullus, *Carmen* 8

   Astrophel and Stella 83   Catullus, *Carmen* 2

Edmund Spenser
   from *The Faerie Queene*
      Book 2, Canto 12   Homer, *Odyssey* 8.266–369;
                                         10.198–347; 12.142–259

Jonathan Swift
   A Description of a City Shower   Virgil, *Georgics* 1.299–423;
                                         Aeneid 1.1–215; 2.1–56
                                   Ovid, *Metamorphoses* 1.253–312

Alfred, Lord Tennyson
   The Lotos-Eaters   Homer, *Odyssey* 9.16–105
                                   Lucretius, *De Rerum Natura*
                                   2.646–60; 3.1–30

James Thomson
   Winter: A Poem (1726)   Hesiod, *Works and Days* 504–35
                                   Virgil, *Georgics* 1.299–423; 2.458–542

Derek Walcott
   from *Omeros*
      Book 1, Chapter 1   Homer, *Iliad* 1.1–305;
                                       Odyssey 5.145–281

John Wilmot, second earl of Rochester
   The Imperfect Enjoyment   Ovid, *Amores* 3.7

William Wordsworth
   Laodamia   Virgil, *Aeneid* 6.679–751
                                   Ovid, *Heroides* 13
                                   Pliny, *Natural History* 16.238

William Butler Yeats
   A Thought from Propertius   Propertius, *Elegies* 2.2

   Two Songs from a Play   Virgil, *Eclogue* 4

II Classical–English

Asclepiades
Greek Anthology
Book 5, number 85

Herrick, *To the Virgins, to Make Much of Time*
Marvell, *To His Coy Mistress*

Bion
Lament for Adonis

Milton, *Lycidas*
Shelley, *Adonais*

Catullus
Carmen 2

Sidney, *Astrophel and Stella* 83

Carmen 3

Gray, *Ode on the Death of a Favourite Cat*
Cowper, *Epitaph on a Hare*

Carmen 5

Marlowe, *Passionate Shepherd to His Love*
Campion, *My Sweetest Lesbia*
Herrick, *To the Virgins, to Make Much of Time*
Marvell, *To His Coy Mistress*
Behn, *The Golden Age*

Carmen 8

Sidney, *Astrophel and Stella* 47

Carmen 13

Jonson, *Inviting a Friend to Supper*

Carmen 101

Dryden, *To the Memory of Mr. Oldham*

Hesiod
from *Theogony*
lines 1–80

Milton, *Paradise Lost* 1.1–74

from *Works and Days*
lines 53–201

Chaucer, *Wife of Bath's Prologue* 627–822
Lovelace, *Love Made in the First Age: To Chloris*
Behn, *Golden Age*
Leapor, *Essay on Woman*

lines 504–35

Thomson, *Winter: A Poem* (1726)

Homer
  from the *Iliad*
    Book 1, lines 1–305   Milton, *Paradise Lost* 1.1–74
                                     Pope, *Rape of the Lock* 1, 4
                                     Walcott, *Omeros* 1.1

    Book 18, lines 478–617   Keats, *Ode on a Grecian Urn*
                                     Auden, *Shield of Achilles*

  from the *Odyssey*
    Book 1, lines 1–10   Milton, *Paradise Lost* 1.1–74
                                     Pope, *Rape of the Lock* 1

    Book 5, lines 145–281   Walcott, *Omeros* 1.1

    Book 8, lines 266–369   Spenser, *Faerie Queene* 2.12

    Book 9, lines 16–105   Tennyson, *Lotos-Eaters*

    Book 10, lines 198–347   Spenser, *Faerie Queene* 2.12

    Book 12, lines 142–259   Spenser, *Faerie Queene* 2.12

Horace
  from the *Satires*
    Book 2, number 6   Jonson, *To Penshurst*

  Epode 2   Jonson, *To Penshurst*
                                     Gray, *Elegy Wrote in a Country
                                       Church Yard*

  from the *Odes*
    Book 1, number 11   Herrick, *To the Virgins, to Make Much
                                       of Time*
                                     Marvell, *To His Coy Mistress*

    Book 1, number 37   Marvell, *Horatian Ode upon
                                       Cromwell's Return from Ireland*

    Book 2, number 18   Jonson, *To Penshurst*

    Book 3, number 2   Owen, *Dulce et Decorum Est*

    Book 3, number 30   Shakespeare, *Sonnet* 55

    Book 4, number 10   Shakespeare, *Sonnet* 77
                                     Herrick, *To the Virgins, to Make Much
                                       of Time*

from the *Epistles*
    Book 1, number 5   Jonson, *Inviting a Friend to Supper*

Juvenal
from *Satire* 6
    lines 1–54   Chaucer, *Wife of Bath's Prologue*
          627–822
          Leapor, *Essay on Woman*

    lines 434–511   Chaucer, *Wife of Bath's Prologue*
          627–822
          Pope, *Rape of the Lock* 1
          Leapor, *Essay on Woman*

    Satire 10   Johnson, *Vanity of Human Wishes*

Lucan
from the *Civil War*
    Book 1, lines 119–57   Marvell, *Horatian Ode upon Cromwell's Return from Ireland*

    Book 1, lines 223–43   Marvell, *Horatian Ode upon Cromwell's Return from Ireland*

Lucretius
from *De Rerum Natura*
    Book 2, lines 646–60   Tennyson, *Lotos-Eaters*

    Book 3, lines 1–30   Tennyson, *Lotos-Eaters*

    Book 3, lines 894–911   Gray, *Elegy Wrote in a Country Church Yard*

Martial
from the *Epigrams*
    Book 1, number 3   Herrick, *To His Muse*

    Book 3, number 58   Jonson, *To Penshurst*

    Book 5, number 78   Jonson, *Inviting a Friend to Supper*

    Book 10, number 48   Jonson, *Inviting a Friend to Supper*

    Book 11, number 52   Jonson, *Inviting a Friend to Supper*

Meleager
  from the *Greek Anthology*
    Book 7, number 207   Gray, *Ode on the Death of a Favourite Cat*
                                  Cowper, *Epitaph on a Hare*

Moschus, so-called
    Lament for Bion   Milton, *Lycidas*
                                  Shelley, *Adonais*

Ovid
  from the *Amores*
    Book 1, numbers 1–3   Sidney, *Astrophel and Stella* 1–3

    Book 1, number 5   Donne, *Elegy* 19: *To His Mistress Going
                                    to Bed*

    Book 1, number 13   Donne, *Sun Rising*

    Book 2, number 6   Gray, *Ode on the Death of a
                                    Favourite Cat*
                                  Cowper, *Epitaph on a Hare*

    Book 3, number 7   Behn, *Disappointment*
                                  Wilmot, *Imperfect Enjoyment*

  Heroides 13   Wordsworth, *Laodamia*

  from *Ars Amatoria*
    Book 1, lines 269–344   Chaucer, *Wife of Bath's Prologue*
                                    627–822

  from the *Metamorphoses*
    Book 1, lines 89–112   Lovelace, *Love Made in the First Age:
                                    To Chloris*
                                  Behn, *Golden Age*

    Book 1, lines 253–312   Swift, *Description of a City
                                    Shower*

    Book 1, lines 452–567   Behn, *Disappointment*

    Book 2, lines 760–832   Pope, *Rape of the Lock* 4

    Book 3, lines 316–510   Milton, *Paradise Lost* 4.411–91
                                  Housman, *Shropshire Lad* 15

    Book 15, lines 143–260   Shakespeare, *Sonnet* 60
                                  Pope, *Rape of the Lock* 1

    Book 15, lines 871–9   Shakespeare, *Sonnets* 55, 74

Plato
from *Symposium*
    sections 209e–212a   Keats, *Ode on a Grecian Urn*

from *Ion*
    sections 533c–535a   Coleridge, *Kubla Khan*

Pliny the Elder
from the *Natural History*
    Book 16, section 238   Wordsworth, *Laodamia*

Propertius
from *Elegies*
    Book 2, number 2   Yeats, *Thought from Propertius*

    Book 2, number 15   Campion, *My Sweetest Lesbia*
                                  Donne, *Elegy* 19: *To His Mistress Going to Bed*

Sophocles
from *Antigone*
    lines 582–603   Arnold, *Dover Beach*

from *Trachiniae*
    lines 112–40   Arnold, *Dover Beach*

Theocritus
    Idyll 1   Milton, *Lycidas*
                                    Shelley, *Adonais*
                                    Keats, *Ode on a Grecian Urn*

    Idyll 11   Ralegh, *Nymph's Reply to the Shepherd*
                                    Marlowe, *Passionate Shepherd to His Love*

Thucydides
from *The Peloponnesian War*
    Book 7, section 44   Arnold, *Dover Beach*

Tibullus
from *Elegies*
    Book 2, number 3   Lovelace, *Love Made in the First Age: To Chloris*
                                    Behn, *Golden Age*

Virgil

Eclogue 2	Ralegh, *Nymph's Reply to the Shepherd*
	Marlowe, *Passionate Shepherd to His Love*
Eclogue 4	Lovelace, *Love Made in the First Age: To Chloris*
	Behn, *Golden Age*
	Yeats, *Two Songs from a Play*
	Heaney, *Bann Valley Eclogue*
Eclogue 5	Milton, *Lycidas*
	Shelley, *Adonais*
Eclogue 10	Milton, *Lycidas*
	Shelley, *Adonais*
from the *Georgics*	
Book 1, lines 299–423	Swift, *Description of a City Shower*
	Thomson, *Winter: A Poem* (1726)
Book 2, lines 458–542	Jonson, *To Penshurst*
	Thomson, *Winter: A Poem* (1726)
	Gray, *Elegy Wrote in a Country Church Yard*
Book 3, lines 384–93	Browning, *Pan and Luna*
from the *Aeneid*	
Book 1, lines 1–215	Milton, *Paradise Lost* 1.1–74
	Swift, *Description of a City Shower*
	Pope, *Rape of the Lock* 1
Book 2, lines 1–56	Swift, *Description of a City Shower*
Book 4, lines 1–30	Pope, *Rape of the Lock* 4
Book 5, lines 315–39	Dryden, *To the Memory of Mr. Oldham*
Book 6, lines 268–316	Pope, *Rape of the Lock* 4
Book 6, lines 679–751	Pope, *Rape of the Lock* 1
	Wordsworth, *Laodamia*
Book 6, lines 854–92	Dryden, *To the Memory of Mr. Oldham*
Book 11, lines 759–831	Gray, *Ode on the Death of a Favourite Cat*

List of Authors

Authors are listed in alphabetical order, with first name given first.

I British, Irish, and Caribbean

Matthew Arnold

Wystan Hugh Auden

Aphra Behn

Robert Browning

Thomas Campion

Geoffrey Chaucer

Samuel Taylor Coleridge

William Cowper

John Donne

John Dryden

Thomas Gray

Seamus Heaney

Robert Herrick

Alfred Edward Housman

Samuel Johnson

Ben Jonson

John Keats

Mary Leapor

Richard Lovelace

Christopher Marlowe

Andrew Marvell

John Milton

Wilfred Owen

Alexander Pope

Sir Walter Ralegh

William Shakespeare

Percy Bysshe Shelley

Sir Philip Sidney

Edmund Spenser

Jonathan Swift

Alfred, Lord Tennyson

James Thomson

Derek Walcott

John Wilmot, second earl of Rochester

William Wordsworth

William Butler Yeats

II Classical

Asclepiades

Bion

Catullus

Hesiod

Homer
Horace
Juvenal
Lucan
Lucretius
Martial
Meleager
"Moschus"
Ovid

Plato
Pliny the Elder
Propertius
Sophocles
Theocritus
Thucydides
Tibullus
Virgil

III Translators

John Beaumont (1583–1627)
John Bostock (1772–1846)
Robert Seymour Bridges (1844–1930)
Elizabeth Barrett Browning
  (1806–1861)
Lewis Campbell (1830–1908)
John Conington (1825–1869)
Thomas Cooke (1703–1756)
James Cranstoun (1837–1901)
Richard Crashaw (1612/1613–1648)
Richard Crawley (1840–1893)
John Dart (d. 1730)
Cecil Day-Lewis (1904–1972)
John Dryden (1631–1700)
John Duncombe (1729–1786)
Charles Elton (1778–1853)
David Ferry (1924–)
Dudley Fitts (1903–1968)
Thomas Flatman (1637–1688)
Arthur Golding (1535/1536–1606)
Thomas Hawkins (1575–1640?)
Ben Jonson (1572–1637)

Benjamin Jowett (1817–1893)
Walter Savage Landor (1775–1864)
William Leonard (1876–1944)
Christopher Marlowe (1564–1593)
Thomas May (1596–1650)
James Michie (1927–)
Christopher Pitt (1699–1748)
Edward Plumptre (1821–1891)
Alexander Pope (1688–1744)
John Pott (d. 1920)
Ezra Pound (1885–1972)
Henry Riley (1816–1878)
George Sandys (1578–1644)
W. G. Shepherd (1935–)
Edward Sherburne (1618–1702)
Edward Stanley, fourteenth earl of
  Derby (1799–1869)
Arthur Symons (1865–1945)
Joseph Trapp (1679–1747)
Thomas Warton (1728–1790)
Robert Wells (1947–)
Peter Whigham (1925–1987)

List of Titles

I English

II Classical

Index to the Introductions and Footnotes

The main page references for authors and works included in this anthology are printed in **bold type**.